The new edition of this widely popular, market-leading text gives pre- and in-service teachers valuable knowledge and practical guidance for using literacy-related instructional strategies to help students think and learn with content area print and digital texts.

Comprehensible and accessible, this new edition places an emphasis on the comprehensive content focus of the previous editions, including an ever-expanding knowledge base in the areas of literacy, cognition, and learning; educational policy; new literacies and technologies; and student diversity.

 Outstanding features of the new Eleventh Edition include:

- An emphasis on content literacy practices and instructional strategies.

- A perspective from school administrators and support staff.

- Additional strategies for working effectively with all learners.

- A look at current trends in urban education and the education of immigrants in all settings.

- An exploration of issues in assessment and multimodal learning.

- Incorporation of the Common Core State Standards.

Content Area Reading

Eleventh Edition

Content Area Reading

Literacy and Learning Across the Curriculum

Richard T. Vacca

Emeritus, Kent State University

Jo Anne L. Vacca

Emerita, Kent State University

Maryann Mraz

University of North Carolina at Charlotte

PEARSON

Boston   Columbus   Indianapolis   New York   San Francisco   Upper Saddle River
Amsterdam   Cape Town   Dubai   London   Madrid   Milan   Munich   Paris   Montréal   Toronto
Delhi   Mexico City   São Paulo   Sydney   Hong Kong   Seoul   Singapore   Taipei   Tokyo

Vice President, Editor in Chief: Aurora Martínez Ramos
Acquisitions Editor: Kathryn Boice
Development Editor: Max Effenson Chuck
Editorial Assistant: Michelle Hochberg
Executive Marketing Manager: Krista Clark
Production Editor: Cynthia DeRocco/Janet Domingo
Editorial Production Service: Electronic Publishing Services Inc.
Manufacturing Buyer: Megan Cochran
Electronic Composition: Jouve
Interior Design: Electronic Publishing Services Inc.
Photo Researcher: Jorgensen Fernandez
Cover Designer: Diane Lorenzo

Photo Credits: Vacca author photo, Denise Ritchie. Maryann Mraz author photo, Brian Kissel. Swirled hand, Cienpiesnf/Fotolia. Response Journal, Vege/Fotolia. Frame of Mind, Monkey Business/Fotolia. Voices from the Field, Ambrophoto/Shutterstock. Evidence-Based Best Practices, Monkey Business/Fotolia. Looking Back, Looking Forward, Jojje11/Fotolia. Minds On, Dmitryelagin/Fotolia. Hands On, Robert/Fotolia. eResources, Fenton/Fotolia.

Library of Congress Cataloging-in-Publication Data

Vacca, Richard T.
  Content area reading : literacy and learning across the curriculum / Richard T. Vacca, Jo Anne L. Vacca, Maryann E. Mraz.
    pages cm
  Includes bibliographical references and index.
  ISBN 978-0-13-306678-4
1. Content area reading. I. Title.
  LB1050.455.V33 2014
  428.4'3—dc23
                                                                                          2013000184

10 9 8 7 6 5 4 3 2 1 EBM 16 15 14 13

www.pearsonhighered.com

ISBN-10: 0-13-306678-9
ISBN-13: 978-0-13-306678-4

To Teachers,

Who do not choose their profession to make a world of money,

but instead, make a world of difference in the lives of their students.

Thank you!

—Rich and Jo Anne Vacca

To the Sisters of Notre Dame, Chardon, Ohio,

for your wisdom and guidance shared long ago,

for your encouragement through the years,

for your friendship today.

Thank you.

—Maryann Mraz

About the Authors

Richard and Jo Anne Vacca are professors emeriti in the School of Teaching, Learning and Curriculum Studies in the College of Education, Health and Human Services at Kent State University. They have published numerous books, chapters, and articles. They met as undergraduate English majors at SUNY Albany and have been partners ever since. Jo Anne taught language arts in middle schools in New York and Illinois, and received her doctorate from Boston University. Rich taught high school English, and earned his doctorate at Syracuse University. He is a past president of the International Reading Association.

The Vaccas live in Vero Beach, Florida, where they keep active professionally, golf, volunteer, and walk their toy poodles, Tiger, Gigi, and Joely. They especially enjoy visiting and traveling with their daughter, Courtney; son-in-law, Gary; and grandsons, Simon, Max, and Joe.

Maryann Mraz is a professor in the Reading and Elementary Education Department at the University of North Carolina at Charlotte (UNCC). She is the Doctoral Program Coordinator for Curriculum and Instruction. Maryann earned her Ph.D. from Kent State University under the guidance of Jo Anne and Rich Vacca, and her B.A. and M.Ed. from John Carroll University. She is a proud alumna of Notre Dame Academy in Chardon, Ohio (now Notre Dame Cathedral Latin). Maryann has served as a board member of the Association of Literacy Educators and Researchers (ALER) and is the author of over 50 books, articles, chapters, and instructional materials on literacy education. She teaches graduate courses in literacy and provides professional development programs to teachers and literacy coaches.

Brief Contents

Contents

**Chapter 3 Culturally Responsive Teaching in Diverse
Classrooms 58**

Chapter 4 **Assessing Students and Texts 94**

 Chapter 5 **Planning Instruction for Content Literacy 132**

Chapter 6   Activating Prior Knowledge and Interest   172

 Chapter 7   Guiding Reading Comprehension   198

Chapter 8   Developing Vocabulary and Concepts   238

Chapter 9   Writing Across the Curriculum   280

Chapter 10   Studying Text   310

Chapter 11   Learning with Trade Books   344

 Chapter 12   Supporting Effective Teaching with Professional Development   384

Preface

Here we go again! There is much in this edition of *Content Area Reading: Literacy and Learning Across the Curriculum* that is new and revitalized. Changes are interwoven throughout the book in the form of new and updated sections of content in many of the chapters, a new chapter on supporting teacher effectiveness with professional development, updated references, and new examples of instructional strategies. A wealth of practical activities and instructional strategies for content literacy remain at the core of this edition. These activities and strategies are sensible and powerful tools for helping students think and learn with text. How teachers adapt them to align with the peculiarities and conventions of their disciplines is the key to literacy and learning in content areas.

New to This Edition

This edition continues to reflect an ever-expanding knowledge base grounded in research and practice in the areas of content literacy, cognition and learning, educational policy, national and state standards, new literacies, instructional scaffolding, teacher effectiveness, differentiated instruction, writing to learn, and student diversity. Chapter content has been rigorously updated to reflect current theory, research, and practice related to literacy and learning across the curriculum. Expanded emphasis has been given throughout many of the chapters on what it means to be literate in the twenty-first century. New and updated content and features of this text include the following:

- **Chapter 1, Literacy Matters,** includes new sections on effective teaching, differentiated instruction, and the Common Core State Standards.

- **Chapter 2, Learning with New Literacies,** is updated to include expanded coverage of content standards related to digital learning and a new section on the use threaded discussions.

- **Chapter 3, Culturally Responsive Teaching in Diverse Classrooms,** contains several new sections on culturally responsive instruction, including five essential themes to consider when developing a framework for culturally relevant pedagogy; an expanded discussion of multicultural literature including how such literature can be used across content areas to meet diverse learner needs; and a major reworking of the ELL sub-sections which now includes a discussion of why content literacy can be particularly challenging for English learners.

- **Chapter 4, Assessing Students and Texts,** includes updated content on current issues related to high-stakes testing, legislation, standards, and accountability; an extended discussion of the evolution of NCLB as well as of current legislative initiatives, in particular the Common Core Standards; a revised section on portfolios to reflect electronic-portfolio use and strategies to adapt portfolios to various disciplines; and an updated section on Lexile levels and suggestions for their use in content area classrooms.

- **Chapter 6, Activating Prior Knowledge and Interest,** incorporates new content and examples throughout, including a detailed discussion of the importance of self-efficacy and a survey to assess teachers' self-efficacy as part of their pre-service training or in-service professional development.

• **Chapter 12, Supporting Effective Teaching with Professional Development,** is new to this edition and reflects the current emphasis placed on teacher effectiveness and the challenges and trends associated with ongoing professional development. The chapter also focuses on the leadership roles of teacher, principal, and literacy coach and features two programs for collaborative professional learning.

• **Voices from the Field** features in many of the chapters include interviews with teachers, administrators, and literacy coaches and specialists related to content literacy policies and practices. The interviews capture the particular challenges that various school personnel have encountered relative to chapter topics and the strategies used to address those challenges.

• **RTI for Struggling Adolescent Learners** features in several of the chapters have been updated and show how it may be adapted to various aspects of content literacy instruction.

• **New instructional examples** throughout many of the chapters replace some of the examples that have been in previous editions.

• **Updates of new research** and ways of thinking about literacy, learning, and instructional practice appear throughout the chapters.

Did you know this book is also available as an enhanced Pearson eText? The affordable, interactive version of this text includes 3–5 videos per chapter that exemplify, model, or expand upon chapter concepts.

To learn more about the enhanced Pearson eText, go to **www.pearsonhighered.com/etextbooks.**

Organization and Features of This Edition

As part of the revision process for this edition, we decided to keep the same structure as the previous edition by organizing chapters into two main parts. Part One, Learners, Literacies, and Texts, places the focus on the cultural, linguistic, and academic diversity of today's learners; their personal and academic literacies; and the kinds of texts that are integral to their lives in and out of school. Part Two, Instructional Practices and Strategies, contains a multitude of evidence-based instructional strategies waiting to be adapted to meet the conceptual demands inherent in disciplinary learning.

This edition of *Content Area Reading* retains many of the features of the previous edition while improving its overall coverage of content literacy topics. It continues to emphasize a contemporary, functional approach to content literacy instruction. In a functional approach, content area teachers learn how to integrate literacy-related strategies into instructional routines without sacrificing the teaching of content. Our intent is not to morph a content teacher into a reading specialist or writing instructor. Rather, our goal has always been, and shall continue to be, to improve the overall coverage of instructional strategies and practices that remain at the heart of this book. In every chapter, special pedagogical features are provided to aid in this effort.

Features at the beginning of each chapter include the following:

◀ **An organizing principle** provides readers with a "heads-up" by introducing the rationale for the chapter and highlighting its underlying theme.

A graphic organizer depicts the relationships among ideas presented in the chapter.

▼

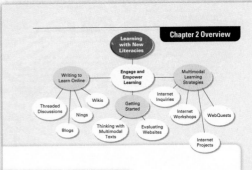

Frame of Mind ▶ questions help readers approach the text in a critical frame of mind as they analyze and interpret information presented.

In-text features include the following:

◀ **Voices from the Field** include interviews with teachers, administrators, and curriculum specialists related to instructional practices and policies.

RTI for Struggling Adolescent Learners occur in many of the chapters and show how Response to Intervention (RTI) may be adapted to various aspects of content literacy instruction.

▼

Evidence-Based Best Practices ▶ highlight the steps and procedures involved in using high-visibility strategies that are supported by theoretically sound rationales and/ or evidence-based, scientific research.

Special marginal notations and callouts provide opportunities to enhance the basic instruction within the chapters:

Response Journal ▶
marginal icons
signal readers to use
a "response journal"
while reading to
make personal and
professional
connections as they
react to ideas
presented in each
chapter.

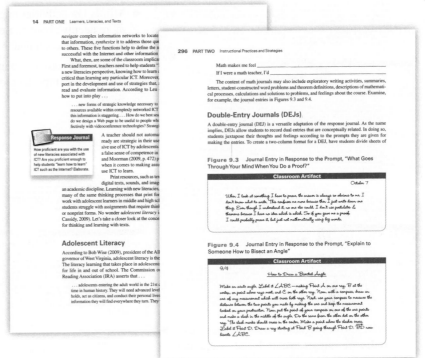

▲
Classroom Artifact figures throughout the book illustrate instructional procedures and materials developed by teachers for authentic teaching situations.

Chapters conclude with additional features that help readers review and practice the concepts introduced in the chapter:

◀ **Looking Back, Looking Forward** sections at the end of each chapter offer a summative review of the concepts introduced and a perspective on where the discussion will lead to next.

◄ **Minds On** activities engage students in thinking more deeply about some of the important ideas that they have studied.

Hands On activities engage students in applying some of the important ideas that they have studied.

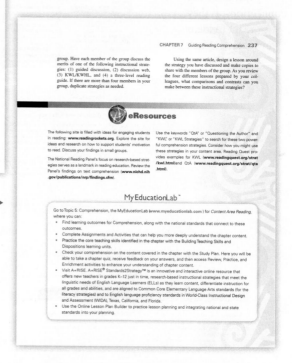

eResources signal readers to investigate online resources to enrich and extend the topics presented. ►

MyEducationLab™

MyEducationLab is an online homework, tutorial, and assessment product designed to improve results by helping students quickly master concepts, and by providing educators with a robust set of tools for easily gauging and addressing the performance of individuals and classrooms.

MyEducationLab engages students with high-quality multimedia learning experiences that help them build critical teaching skills and prepare them for real-world practice. In practice exercises, students receive immediate feedback so they see mistakes right away, learn precisely which concepts are holding them back, and master concepts through targeted practice.

For educators, MyEducationLab provides highly-visual data and performance analysis to help them quickly identify gaps in student learning and make a clear connection between coursework, concept mastery, and national teaching standards. And because MyEducationLab comes from Pearson, it's developed by an experienced partner committed to providing content, resources, and expertise for the best digital learning experiences.

In *Preparing Teachers for a Changing World,* Linda Darling-Hammond and her colleagues point out that grounding teacher education in real classrooms—among real teachers and students and among actual examples of students' and teachers' work—is an important, and perhaps even an essential, part of training teachers for the complexities of teaching in today's classrooms.

In the MyEducationLab for this course educators will find the following features and resources.

Advanced Data and Performance Reporting Aligned to National Standards

Advanced data and performance reporting helps educators quickly identify gaps in student learning and gauge and address individual and classroom performance. Educators easily see the connection between coursework, concept mastery, and national teaching standards with highly-visual views of performance reports. Data and assessments align directly to national teaching standards, including **International Reading Association's Standards for Reading Proessionals and Common Core,** and support reporting for state and accreditation requirements

Study Plan Specific to Your Text

MyEducationLab gives students the opportunity to test themselves on key concepts and skills, track their own progress through the course, and access personalized Study Plan activities.

The customized Study Plan is generated based on students' pretest results. Incorrect questions from the pretest indicate specific textbook learning outcomes the student is struggling with. The customized Study Plan suggests specific enriching activities for particular learning outcomes, helping students focus. Personalized Study Plan activities may include eBook reading assignments, and review, practice, and enrichment activities.

After students complete the enrichment activities, they take a posttest to see the concepts they've mastered or areas where they still may need extra help.

MyEducationLab then reports the Study Plan results to the instructor. Based on these reports, the instructor can adapt course material to suit the needs of individual students or the entire class.

Assignments and Activities

Designed to enhance students' understanding of concepts covered in class, these assignable exercises show concepts in action (through videos, cases, and/or student and teacher artifacts). They help students deepen content knowledge and synthesize and apply concepts and strategies they have read about in the book. (Correct answers for these assignments are available to the instructor only.)

Building Teaching Skills and Dispositions

These unique learning units help students practice and strengthen skills that are essential to effective teaching. After examining the steps involved in a core teaching process, students are given an opportunity to practice applying this skill via videos, student and teacher artifacts, and/or case studies of authentic classrooms. Providing multiple opportunities to practice a single teaching concept, each activity encourages a deeper understanding and application of concepts, as well as the use of critical thinking skills. After practice, students take a quiz that is reported to the instructor gradebook and performance reporting.

A+RISE activities provide practice in targeting instruction. A+RISE®, developed by three-time Teacher of the Year and administrator, Evelyn Arroyo, provides quick, research-based strategies that get to the "how" of targeting instruction and making content accessible for all students, including English language learners.

A+RISE® Standards2Strategy™ is an innovative and interactive online resource that offers new teachers in grades K-12 just in time, research-based instructional strategies that:

- Meet the linguistic needs of ELLs as they learn content
- Differentiate instruction for all grades and abilities
- Offer reading and writing techniques, cooperative learning, use of linguistic and nonlinguistic representations, scaffolding, teacher modeling, higher order thinking, and alternative classroom ELL assessment
- Provide support to help teachers be effective through the integration of listening, speaking, reading, and writing along with the content curriculum
- Improve student achievement
- Are aligned to Common Core Elementary Language Arts standards (for the literacy strategies) and to English language proficiency standards in WIDA, Texas, California, and Florida.

The Grammar Tutorial provides content extracted in part from *The Praxis Series™ Online Tutorial for the Pre-Professional Skills Test: Writing*. Online quizzes built around specific elements of grammar help users strengthen their understanding and proper usage of the English language in writing. Definitions and examples of grammatical concepts are followed by practice exercises to provide the background information and usage examples needed to refresh understandings of grammar, and then apply that knowledge to make it more permanent.

The Children's and Young Adult Literature Database offers information on thousands of quality literature titles, and the activities provide experience in choosing appropriate literature and integrating the best titles into language arts instruction.

Course Resources

The Course Resources section of MyEducationLab is designed to help you put together an effective lesson plan, prepare for and begin your career, navigate your first year of teaching, and understand key educational standards, policies, and laws.

It includes the following:

- The **Lesson Plan Builder** is an effective and easy-to-use tool that you can use to create, update, and share quality lesson plans. The software also makes it easy to integrate state content standards into any lesson plan.
- The **Certification and Licensure** section is designed to help you pass your licensure exam by giving you access to state test requirements, overviews of what tests cover, and sample test items.

The Certification and Licensure section includes the following:

- **State Certification Test Requirements:** Here, you can click on a state and will then be taken to a list of state certification tests.
- You can click on the **Licensure Exams** you need to take to find:
  - Basic information about each test
  - Descriptions of what is covered on each test
  - Sample test questions with explanations of correct answers
- **National Evaluation Series**™ by Pearson: Here, students can see the tests in the NES, learn what is covered on each exam, and access sample test items with descriptions and rationales of correct answers. You can also purchase interactive online tutorials developed by Pearson Evaluation Systems and the Pearson Teacher Education and Development group.
- **ETS Online Praxis Tutorials:** Here you can purchase interactive online tutorials developed by ETS and by the Pearson Teacher Education and Development group. Tutorials are available for the Praxis I exams and for select Praxis II exams.

Visit www.myeducationlab.com for a demonstration of this exciting new online teaching resource.

Supplements for Instructors and Students for the Eleventh Edition

The following resources are available for instructors to download on **www.pearsonhighered .com/educators.** Instructors enter the author or title of this book, select this particular edition of the book, and then click on the "Resources" tab to log in and download textbook supplements.

- **Instructor's Resource Manual and Test Bank (0-13-337625-7).** The Instructor's Resource Manual and Test Bank includes a wealth of interesting ideas and activities designed to help instructors teach the course. Each chapter includes a chapter-at-a-glance grid, the chapter purpose, underlying concepts, student objectives, vocabulary and key terms, activities and discussion questions, MyEducationLab extension activities, plus test questions for each chapter.
- **PowerPoint Slides (0-13-338590-6).** Ideal for lecture presentations or student handouts, the PowerPoint presentation provides dozens of ready-to-use graphic and text images.
- **MyEducationLab Correlation Guide (0-13-338593-0).** This guide connects chapter sections with appropriate assignable exercises on MyEducationLab.com.
- *TestGen* **(0-13-337624-9).** *TestGen* is a powerful test generator that instructors install on a computer and use in conjunction with the *TestGen* test bank file for this text. Assessments may be created for both print and online testing. *TestGen* is available exclusively from Pearson Education publishers. Instructors install TestGen on a personal computer (Windows or Macintosh) and create tests for classroom testing and for other specialized delivery options, such as over a local area network or on the web. A test bank, which is also called

a Test Item File (TIF), typically contains a large set of test items, organized by chapter and ready for use in creating a test, based on the associated textbook material.

Acknowledgments

We are grateful to the many colleagues and graduate students at the University of North Carolina Charlotte (UNCC) who helped to make this edition possible. A well-deserved "shout out" is due Jean Vintinner, Ph.D., Erin Donovan, and Melissa Sykes for their research-related contributions to this edition. A special thanks to Dr. Jean Vintinner for her revision of Chapter 5, *Planning Instruction*. We would also like to thank Drew Polly, Ph.D., along with graduate students Kim Heintschel, Cindy Hovis, Tracy Maas, Ashley Parker, Laura Rosenbach, Tracy Willey, Betsy Ziskind, Brad Bell, Delon Ferdinand, Heidemarie Klein, Barry Lentz, Kyle Kester, Carrie Roberts, Preston Roundy, and Katie Stover for their contributions to the Voices in the Field feature and strategy examples.

We would be remiss if we did not recognize the outstanding editorial team of Aurora Martinez Ramos, vice president and editor-in-chief for literacy and ELL, and Michelle Hochberg, our editorial assistant on this project. Finally, a well-deserved thank you to our reviewers for their thoughtful suggestions for improving our work: Lasisi Ajayi, San Diego State University; Suzanne Gary Brians, University of Texas at Tyler; Virginia S. Loh, San Diego State University; Ernestine G. Riggs, Loyola University Chicago; and Wolfram Verlaan, Texas A&M University, Corpus Christi.

Content Area Reading

1 Literacy Matters

Effective teachers show students how to think, learn, and communicate with all kinds of texts.

In many ways, the universe serves as a metaphor for the human mind. It is never ending, ever expanding, and unfathomable. So is the human mind. Literacy has a powerful impact on the meaning-making and learning that takes place in the universe of our minds. Through literacy, we begin to see, to imagine, to comprehend, and to think more deeply about images and ideas encountered in all kinds of texts. When it comes to learning in content areas, literacy matters. All teachers have a critical role to play in making a difference in the literate lives of their students. In this chapter, we explore what that role requires for effective teaching in the content areas. And in the process of doing so, we clarify several core concepts related to literacy, teaching, and learning: *teacher*

effectiveness, Common Core State Standards, differentiated instruction, new literacies, adolescent literacy, content literacy/disciplinary literacy, and *reading to learn.*

If you're a content area teacher, or studying to be one, you may be wondering why you're even taking a course that has the terms *reading* and/or *literacy* in its title. No doubt you view your primary role as teaching the core ideas and concepts of your discipline. Content counts! Yet, as a teacher, you also have an important role to play in showing students how to use literacy skills and strategies in your discipline. Literacy is an evolving concept that changes with society over time. Perhaps it's best to think of literacy in terms of the *multiple literacies* that we use to make and communicate meaning. In this book, we explore how to support students' literacies by helping them make and communicate meaning with the various kinds of

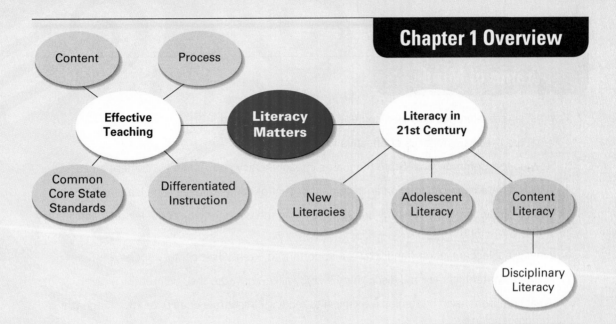

texts—both print and digital—they use in content areas.

Our primary emphasis throughout this book is on reading and writing to learn in middle and high school. Unfortunately, many adolescent learners struggle with academic texts. One of the realities facing teachers across all content areas is that many students make little use of reading and writing as tools for thinking and learning. They either read or write on a superficial level or find ways to circumvent literacy tasks altogether. All too often, adolescent learners give up on reading with the expectation that teachers will impart information through lecture, demonstration, and class discussion. When students become too dependent on teachers as their primary source of information, they are rarely in a position to engage actively in literacy to learn.

This need not be the case. The organizing principle of this chapter underscores the dynamic relationship between literacy and learning: Effective teachers show students how to think, learn, and communicate with all kinds of texts.

Response Journal

Write a "five-minute essay" in your response journal on your initial reaction to the organizing principle.

Study the Chapter Overview. It's your map to the major ideas that you will encounter in the chapter. The graphic display shows the relationships that exist among the concepts you will study. Use it as an organizer. What is the chapter about? What do you know already about the content to be presented in the chapter? What do you need to learn more about?

In conjunction with the Chapter Overview, take a moment or two to study the Frame of Mind questions. This feature uses key questions to help you think about the ideas that you will read about. When you finish reading, you should be able to respond fully to the Frame of Mind questions.

Frame of Mind

1. What is the difference between content and process knowledge?

2. What are the characteristics of effective teaching?

3. How do the Common Core State Standards impact literacy and learning in content areas?

4. Why is differentiated instruction an important aspect of content literacy and learning?

5. What are new literacies and how are they changing the way we think about learning and literacy in the twenty-first century?

6. What is adolescent literacy and why is it important to twenty-first century society?

7. How are content literacy and disciplinary literacy alike? How are they different?

8. What comprehension strategies are critical to reading? What role does prior knowledge play in comprehension?

There are no pat formulas for teachers who want students to develop core concepts and good habits of thinking within a discipline. Nor are there magic potions in the form of instructional strategies that will make a difference with all students, all the time. Teaching is a problem-solving activity: There's just you, the academic texts and instructional strategies that you use, and the students whose lives you touch in the relatively brief time that they are under your wing. Teaching is a daunting but immensely rewarding enterprise for those who are up to the challenge.

Highly effective content area teachers plan lessons that are engaging. These teachers recognize that "engaging the disengaged" is not an easy task. Yet they continually strive to make learning intellectually challenging for the students they are teaching. A top instructional priority, therefore, is to involve students actively in learning the important ideas and concepts of the *content* they are studying. But the effective teacher also knows that an intellectually challenging instructional environment engages students not only in the acquisition of content but also in the *thinking processes* by which they learn that content.

No wonder the classroom is like a crucible, a place where the special mix of teacher, student, and text come together to create wonderfully complex human interactions that stir the minds of learners. Some days, of course, are better than others. The things that you thought about doing and the classroom surprises that you didn't expect fall into place. A creative energy imbues teaching and learning.

Sometimes, however, lessons limp along. Others simply bomb—so you cut them short. The four or so remaining minutes before the class ends are a kind of self-inflicted wound. Nothing is more unnerving than waiting for class to end when students don't have anything meaningful to do.

Consider a high school science teacher's reflection on the way things went in one of her chemistry classes. "Something was missing," she explains. "The students aren't usually as quiet and passive as they were today. Excuse the pun, but the chemistry wasn't there. Maybe the text assignment was too hard. Maybe I could have done something differently. Any suggestions?"

This teacher's spirit of inquiry is admirable. She wants to know how to improve her teaching—how to engage students in learning the important concepts of her chemistry course and how to involve them in thinking like scientists.

 # Effective Teaching in Content Areas

Like all good teachers, the chemistry teacher in the preceding example cares about *what* she does and *how* she does it. *Content* and *process,* after all, are two sides of the same instructional coin. She knows a lot about the *what* of instruction—the content of chemistry—and how to teach that content in ways that develop important ideas and concepts in an intellectually challenging instructional environment. A strong attraction to academic content is one of the reasons teachers are wedded to a particular discipline. Yet it is often much more difficult to teach something than to know that something: "The teacher of the American Revolution has to know both a great deal about the American Revolution and a variety of ways of communicating the essence of the American Revolution to a wide variety of students, in a pedagogically interesting way" (Shulman, 1987, p. 5).

Teaching is complicated. There are no short-cuts to effective teaching in content areas. Often, what to teach (content) and how to teach it (process) represent nagging problems for today's teachers. On one hand, researchers have shown that subject matter mastery is essential for effective teaching (Allen, 2003; Sanders, 2004; Walsh & Snyder, 2004). Indeed, a strong connection exists between teachers' content knowledge preparation and higher student achievement.

The Educational Testing Service (ETS) study *How Teaching Matters* (Wenglinski, 2000) concluded, not surprisingly, that teachers' content knowledge is an important factor in student achievement. Content counts! Student achievement, for example, increases by 40 percent of a grade level in both mathematics and science when teachers have a major or minor in the subject. However, the study also concluded that content knowledge alone is not the only factor necessary to help increase student achievement. Indeed, the classroom instructional practices and strategies of teachers significantly influence student achievement. The study found that students who engage in active, hands-on learning activities and respond to higher-order thinking questions outperform their peers by more than 70 percent of a grade level in mathematics and 40 percent in science. In addition, the study showed that students whose teachers have received professional development training in working with special populations outperform their peers by more than a full grade level. The findings of the ETS study indicate that greater attention, not less, needs to be paid to improving the pedagogical knowledge of teachers and the classroom aspects of teacher effectiveness.

What Makes a Teacher Effective?

The U.S. Department of Education (2010), as well as the National Council on Teacher Quality (2011), readily acknowledges that the "most important factor" in student success is the teacher. When students have access to effective teachers in the classroom, achievement gaps not only can narrow, but students will approach literacy and learning tasks with purpose and enthusiasm. Realistically, however, even in classrooms where teachers are practicing their craft effectively, some students will zone out from time to time or become sidetracked with other matters. Ball and Forzani (2010) put it this way in describing the difference between a tutor working one-on-one with a learner and a teacher working with an entire class of learners:

> Not only do teachers have more learners to understand and interact with, but they also must design and manage a productive environment in which all are able to learn. One student requires a firm hand and a great deal of direction whereas another works best when left to puzzle further on his own. One student is active—tapping her pen, doodling, and rocking on her chair—even while deeply engaged whereas a second is easily distracted (p. 42).

Yet in the presence of an effective teacher most learners will tune in to what they are studying in the classroom—and stay tuned in.

With today's focus on educational reform, teacher effectiveness is closely tied to student achievement. An effective teacher has been defined as one whose students' growth is equivalent to at least one grade level in an academic year (U.S. Department of Education, 2009). An alternative measure suggested by school reformers for determining teacher effectiveness includes classroom observations of teachers working with learners. (Reform Support Network, 2011). Linda Darling-Hammond (2009) expands the notion of teacher effectiveness beyond how well students perform on achievement measures. She suggests that it is important to keep in mind the distinction between *teacher quality* and *teaching quality*. She defines teacher quality as the traits, understandings, and characteristics an effective teacher brings to instruction, including the following:

- Strong general intelligence and verbal ability that help teachers organize and explain ideas, as well as to observe and think diagnostically

- Strong content knowledge

- Knowledge of how to teach others . . . in particular, how to use hands-on learning techniques and how to develop higher-order thinking skills

- An understanding of learners and their learning and development—including how to assess and scaffold learning, how to support students who have learning differences or difficulties, and to support the learning of language and content for those who are not already proficient in the language of instruction

- Adaptive expertise that allows teachers to make judgments about what it is like to work in a given context in response to student needs (Darling-Hammond, 2009, p. 2)

Teaching quality, on the other hand, has more to do with the context of instruction. Quality teaching enables a teacher to meet the demands of a discipline and to provide "strong instruction" that allows a wide range of students to learn.

Pearson and Hoffman (2011) also discuss teaching quality and strong instruction from the perspective of what it means to be a practicing teacher. They describe practicing teachers as *thoughtful, effective, pragmatic,* and *reflective.* In the classroom, the actions of a practicing teacher are guided by ten general "principles of practice" associated with teaching quality. Effective teachers reflect and are guided by these principles in their daily work in the classroom. These principles of practice are summarized in Table 1.1.

Higher levels of student achievement, Pearson and Hoffman (2011) contend, will not result from mandated standards or high-stakes testing alone. While standards and high-stakes assessment are an integral part of today's educational landscape, practicing teachers, who know how to balance content and process in a standards-based curriculum, are the real game changers in the education of twenty-first century learners.

Table 1.1   Ten General Principles of Practice Associated with Quality Teaching

1.	***Principle of Praxis***: Effective teachers act on the understanding that education has the power to transform the individual and society.
2.	***Principle of Purpose***: Effective teachers operate in the moment guided by a clear understanding of *why* they are doing *what* they are doing. There is always a purpose behind their actions in the classroom.
3.	***Principle of Serendipity***: Although effective teachers engage in a variety of instructional practices, they "expect the unexpected" and are open to learning opportunities which may occur within the context of instruction.
4.	***Principle of Exploration***: Effective teachers are continually exploring new practices and making changes in their practices based on their exploration of instructional possibilities in classroom.
5.	***Principle of Reflection***: Effective teachers think about the *what, how,* and *why* of instruction during and after teaching activity. They engage in the process of reflection to solve instructional problems and set goals.
6.	***Principle of Community***: Effective teachers share their classroom knowledge and experiences within and across multiple professional communities as a means of growing professionally and giving back.
7.	***Principle of Service***: Effective teachers serve the learners in their classrooms and their parents.
8.	***Principle of Flexibility***: Effective teachers plan instruction but are flexible in the implementation of lessons. They adapt to unanticipated events or responses in ways that make learning possible.
9.	***Principle of Caring***: Effective teachers care about the learners in their classroom, the disciplinary content that they teach, and the literacy processes they use to make a difference in the lives of students. Caring is necessary to build relationships essential to the teaching/learning transaction.
10.	***Principle of Reward***: Effective teachers find satisfaction and reward in what they do for their students; they value the spontaneity of classroom life, the immediacy of the classroom, the learning they are a part of, and the autonomy of making instructional decisions.

Effective Teachers and the Common Core State Standards

Literacy and learning are challenges in today's classrooms, where the demands inherent in the teaching of content standards can easily lead to "covering" information without much attention given to *how* students with a wide range of skills and abilities acquire core concepts. Balancing content and process in a standards-based curriculum means at the very least:

- Knowing the standards for your content area and grade level
- Making instructional decisions based on authentic assessments throughout the school year about students' abilities to use reading and writing to learn
- Integrating content literacy practices and strategies into instructional plans and units of study

Standards, in a nutshell, are expected academic consequences defining what students should learn and how they should learn it at designated grade levels and in content areas. Since the mid-1990s, a proliferation of state standards have provided a road map to what students *should know* and *be able to do* at each grade level and for each content area.

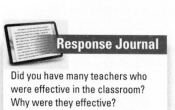

The underlying rationale for the creation of standards is that high learning expectations—clearly stated and specific in nature—will lead to dramatic increases in student achievement. With high learning expectations comes an accountability system based on "high-stakes" testing to determine how well students meet the standards formulated in each content area. Some states tie high-stakes assessment to the threat of grade-level retention for students who perform below predetermined levels of proficiency in critical areas such as reading. We explore in more detail the nature of high-stakes assessment, and explore the types of authentic assessments to improve learning, in Chapter 4.

The United States, unlike most countries, does not have a set of national education standards. Individual states have sole responsibility for determining what teachers should teach and students learn. However, the National Governors Association and the Council of Chief State School Officers recently released the Common Core State Standards (CCSS) for literacy and mathematics. According to the Common Core State Standards Initiative (2010):

> The Common Core State Standards provide a consistent, clear understanding of what students are expected to learn, so teachers and parents know what they need to do to help them. The standards are designed to be robust and relevant to the real world, reflecting the knowledge that our young people need for success in college and careers. With American students fully prepared for the future, our communities will be best positioned to compete successfully in the global economy (p. 11).

The Common Core, adopted by 45 of the 50 states at the time of this writing, is the closest the United States has come as a country to adopting a national curriculum. Because states will be working from the same core standards, the possibility for broadbased sharing of what works in the classroom has never been greater. Since the Common Core does not come with rigid guidelines concerning implementation, it provides local school flexibility to decide how to best implement the standards at various grade levels (Phillips and Wong, 2011).

One of the important dimensions of CCSS is the emphasis on literacy in all content areas. Phillips and Wong (2010) put it this way: "As the Common Core of Standards makes clear, literacy skills cross subject-area boundaries but are not formally taught once students enter the middle grades . . . Think of literacy as the spine; it holds everything together. The branches of learning connect to it, meaning that all core content teachers have a responsibility to teach literacy (pp. 40–41)." The real potential of the Common Core from a literacy perspective is that it positions students to become more active in their use of literacy skills by discovering concepts and processes that lead to independent learning. To become literate in a content area, students must learn how to learn with texts. Integrating these thinking/learning processes into content instruction helps learners to better understand what they are reading about, writing about, talking about in classroom discussion, or viewing on a computer screen or video monitor. Weaving literacy into the fabric of disciplinary study does not diminish the teacher's role as a subject matter specialist. Instead, reading, writing, talking, and viewing are tools that students use to learn with texts in content areas. Who's in a better, more strategic position to show students how to learn with texts in a particular content area and grade level than the teacher who guides *what* students are expected to learn and *how* they are to learn it?

The CCSS Initiative creates high expectations for students to develop their ability to use literacy and language skills to learn in content areas. One of the ultimate goals of Common Core is that students will develop independent learning habits:

> Students must read widely and deeply from among a broad range of high-quality, increasingly challenging literary and informational texts. Through extensive reading of stories, dramas, poems, and myths from diverse cultures and different time periods, students gain literary and cultural knowledge as well as familiarity with various text structures and elements. By reading texts in history/social studies, science, and other disciplines, students build a foundation of knowledge in these fields that will also give them the background to be better readers in all content areas. Students can only gain this foundation when the curriculum is intentionally and coherently structured to develop rich content knowledge within and across grades. Students also acquire the habits of reading independently and closely, which are essential to their future success (Common Core State Standards Initiative, p. 35).

Another major goal of Common Core is that all learners will develop a strong knowledge base across the curriculum:

> Students establish a base of knowledge across a wide range of subject matter by engaging with works of quality and substance. They become proficient in new areas through research and study. They read purposefully and listen attentively to gain both general knowledge and discipline-specific expertise.
>
> They refine and share their knowledge through writing and speaking. They respond to the varying demands of audience, task, purpose, and discipline (Common Core State Standards Initiative, p. 35).

The CCSS Initiative is not without its critics. Tienken (2011), for example, fears that standardization of the curriculum may not meet the needs of a diverse population of U.S. students. Loveless (2011) contends that there is a disconnect between existing national "grade level" tests and CCSS expectations. Some critics argue that top-down mandates for curriculum change are often only vaguely related to day-to-day instruction. Such mandates ignore the professional expertise and thinking of teachers to determine the most effective instructional strategies and methods to teach their students (Lee, 2011). Successful implementation of CCSS will require ongoing professional development to support teachers as they learn how to integrate literacy strategies into their regular instructional routines. This will require a long-term time commitment in school districts where funding for professional development may be limited.

Despite some of the criticism leveled toward CCSS, many educators are hopeful that the Common Core will make a difference in the content knowledge and skills that learners will develop to be successful in college or in careers. Box 1.1, Voices from the Field, captures one teacher's challenge as her school district engages in the implementation of Common Core standards.

Given the wide range of students that teachers encounter daily, *differentiating instruction* will be one of the keys to ensuring the successful implementation of the Common Core.

BOX 1.1

Voices from the Field

Erin, Literacy Coach

Challenge

The Common Core Standards will have a definite impact on how we teach and assess children in the very near future. The document itself is an all-encompassing and at times overwhelming framework of what best practices will look like in classrooms of the future. However, full implementation of the Common Core begins on the classroom level. This is where I come in.

Working for a large school district in a coach/administrator position can be challenging. Not only do you have to be concerned about following the district policy, understanding the curriculum, implementing your administration's common goals but also working with a staff of people who all have their own educational philosophies that should be respected and considered. Keeping all those measures in check is what I do and as the link between administration and the front lines, I feel my job is essential. As such, the implementation of the Common Core Standards is a challenge, to say the least. Once implemented, the Common Core Standards will impact the teachers' daily instruction in a substantial way. The teachers must be able to understand and use the standards in a very different way than they were used to working with our now defunct state standards. Common Core requires a shift in thinking that takes teachers away from teaching bullet points to teaching conceptually. For some of my teachers, that is a pretty big shift.

To complement the district's vision of how Common Core should be implemented, I took a piece

meal approach to professional development and met my share of challenges along the way.

Strategy

The standards are written so that skills and concepts can be vertically aligned across grade levels. They emphasize text complexity and writing across the curriculum. I decided to begin my professional development by showing how argumentative writing can be used in such a way. I showed my staff how the standards "grow up" at each grade level. Then we wrote rubrics based on how each grade level would approach teaching and assessing their standards. Next, we tried to work writing into each subject taught so that the students could practice this argumentative writing task. We had follow up meetings to discuss our successes and further opportunities with implementation. The process seemed to be effective: introduce the concepts, work actively with them, practice them in the classroom, and then provide follow up.

After we worked with writing, we switched to text. Common Core advocates a curriculum that is based on authentic understanding of complex texts. Helping my teachers move away from their "safe" and at times "scripted" text books was the first step of this process. We worked one afternoon in the library to create text sets for the concepts we would be working with in the following semester. The text sets were housed in the library so any teacher working with those concepts could use them. As with writing, we worked toward a vertical alignment and had critical conversations about the leveling and composition of these sets. I was very pleased as I watched the teachers think outside the box by including items such as recipes, song lyrics, newspaper articles, and websites.

Reflection

Any new implementation has its issues. What I learned through this process was how important it was to listen to teachers. They had great ideas about how to use the Common Core and, rather than dictating what we should learn, I learned to wait for their input before designing my professional development. I tried to provide an authentic learning situation, just as I would in my own classroom, so they could walk away with more than just a "make and take." Rather, they walked away with well planned projects, well designed rubrics, and a platform on which they could talk and learn about the Common Core.

Effective Teachers Differentiate Instruction for a Wide Range of Students

Although texts come with the territory, using them to help students acquire content doesn't work well for many teachers. Teaching with texts is more complex than it appears on the surface. As we discuss in Chapter 3, today's classrooms are more diverse than ever before. The wide range of differences is evident in the skills, interests, languages, cultural backgrounds, and funds of knowledge that learners bring to the classroom. Whether you're a novice or a veteran teacher, effective instruction requires the use of *differentiated learning* strategies and a willingness to move beyond *assigning* and *telling* when using texts in the classroom.

Think back to when you were middle or high school students. You probably had teachers who used an instructional strategy for teaching with text that included the following: *Assign* a text to read (usually with questions to be answered for homework) then, in subsequent lessons, *tell* students what the material they read was about, explaining and elaborating on the ideas and information in the text through lecture and question-and-answer routines. The interaction between teacher and students no doubt involved calling on a student to answer a question, listening to the student's response, and then evaluating or modifying the student's response. An assign-and-tell instructional strategy, more often than not, squelches active involvement in learning and denies students ownership of and responsibility for the development of core concepts and processes. Teachers place themselves, either by design or by circumstance, in the unenviable position of dispensing knowledge rather than helping learners to construct knowledge. When teachers become dispensers of knowledge with little attention given to how learners acquire that knowledge, students soon become nonparticipants in the academic life of the classroom.

Response Journal

What do you do as a reader to make meaning and construct knowledge as you interact with a text?

An effective teacher plans instruction and organizes learning opportunities for students so that they will engage actively in developing the core concepts and processes underlying a discipline. Planning is the key to differentiated learning. On the website of Carolyn Tomlinson, one of the leading experts on differentiated instruction, she characterizes differentiation as "responsive teaching" (www.differentiationcentral.com, retrieved March 17, 2012). She explains that it involves preparing in advance for a variety of student needs in order to maximize student learning.

Ongoing formative assessment, a topic we discuss in Chapter 4, allows teachers to make adjustments in their instructional approaches to meet the skill needs, interests, and learning styles of their students. Planning instruction, as we show in Chapter 5, allows teachers to organize learning in ways that will meet the needs of a wide range of students. Differentiating learning through a variety of texts and instructional strategies, which is the main thrust of this book, will actively engage all students in literacy and learning. To use texts and instructional strategies effectively in mixed-ability classrooms, we must first be aware of the powerful bonds that link literacy and learning in a discipline. Let's begin by taking a closer look at some of the meanings attached to the term *literacy*.

Literacy in the Twenty-first Century

To better understand what it means to be literate in a discipline, we need to first examine some of the ways the term *literacy* has been used in our twenty-firstcentury, techno-savvy, media-driven society. Literacy is a dynamic concept that is continually evolving. In the United States and other technologically advanced countries, becoming literate carries with it strong cultural expectations. Society places a premium on literate behavior and demands that its citizens acquire literacy for personal, social, academic, and economic success. But what does it actually mean to be literate in the twenty-first century?

The meaning of *literacy* often fluctuates from one social context to another and from one group to another. For example, the term *computer literacy* has been used in recent times to describe the level of expertise and familiarity someone has with computers and computer applications. *Digital literacy* is often defined as the ability to use digital technology, communication tools, or networks to locate, evaluate, use, and create information. In today's multimedia world, *information literacy* denotes the ability to identify, locate, and access appropriate sources of information to meet one's needs. The broad definition of *media literacy* is even more encompassing in that it refers to someone's ability to access, analyze, evaluate, and produce communication and information in a variety of media modes, genres, and forms. And in the health and wellness field, *health literacy* is a more specific type of information-based competence denoting someone's ability to obtain, process, and understand the basic health information and services needed to make appropriate health decisions.

The above examples are but a few ways the term *literacy* has morphed to characterize someone's level of knowledge or competence in a particular area or subject in a multimodal society. For centuries the most common use of the term *literacy* had been to denote one's ability to read and write a language with competence. Today, however, the dynamic nature of literacy is such that it encompasses more than the ability to read and write black marks on a printed page. Literacy has come to represent a synthesis of language, thinking, and contextual practices through which people make and communicate meaning. Yet the more society evolves the more complex and multidimensional the concept of literacy becomes:

> Today information about the world around us comes to us not only by words on a piece of paper but more and more through the powerful images and sounds of our multi-media culture. Although mediated

messages appear to be self-evident, in truth, they use a complex audio/visual "language" which has its own rules (grammar) and which can be used to express many-layered concepts and ideas about the world. Not everything may be obvious at first; and images go by so fast! If our children are to be able to navigate their lives through this multi-media culture, they need to be fluent in "reading" and "writing" the language of images and sounds just as we have always taught them to "read" and "write" the language of printed communications. (Thoman and Jolls, 2005, p. 8)

As notions of literacy expand with the times, so does the concept of *text*. Literate activity is no longer limited by conventional notions of text (Neilsen, 2006). Texts include not only print forms of communication but also nonprint forms that are digital, aural, or visual in nature. Texts in content area classrooms represent sets of potential meanings and signifying practices, whether the text is a novel in an English class, the instructional conversation that takes place about the novel, or the made-for-television movie based on the novel. Helping students to *think* and *learn* with all kinds of text is an important responsibility of the content area teacher. Johannes Gutenberg's invention of movable type in the fifteenth century resulted in a revolution of ideas. Printed texts in the hands of the masses changed the face of literacy and learning in much the same way that multimodal information and communication technologies (ICT) are creating new literacies and new ways of learning.

New Literacies, New Ways of Learning

The potential for media and technology to make a difference in students' literacy development and learning was evident in the early 1980s, when computers began to play an increasingly important role in classrooms. However, the digital technologies available three decades ago were primitive compared to today's powerful technologies. Today's adolescents represent the first generation of youth who have grown up since the emergence of digital technologies, video games, cell phones, instant messaging, and the World Wide Web. Because they are the first generation to be immersed in ICT for their entire lives, they have at their fingertips more information than any generation in history (Considine, Horton, & Moorman, 2009).

With continuously emerging ICT a reality in the twenty-first century, new literacies are necessary to use ICT effectively and to fully exploit their potential for learning (Kist, 2005; Leu, 2000). The new literacies are grounded in students' abilities to use reading and writing to learn but require new strategic knowledge, skills, and insights to meet the conceptual and technological demands inherent in complexly networked environments. To be sure, the Internet is one of the most powerful ICT extant, and it depends on literacy.

Nevertheless, there are real differences between reading printed texts and reading texts in a digital medium. As Kist (2005, p. 5) explains, printed texts such as books are written for the reader to proceed from the front of the book to the back of the book, reading from left to right, "and most readers of a book will read the text with the order of the words coming in the same order for him or her as for every other reader of that book". However, one reader on the Internet might click on a hyperlink that another online reader would not. As a result, the first online reader would then process the text in a completely different sequence from that of the second reader.

Reading texts in a digital environment is not a linear activity. New literacies, therefore, are crucial in the search for content area information on the Internet and other ICT. As Leu, Leu, and Coiro (2006, p. 1) point out, new literacies allow readers "to *identify* important questions, *navigate* complex information networks to locate important information, *critically evaluate* that information, *synthesize* it to address those questions, and then *communicate* the answers to others. These five functions help to define the new literacies that your students need to be successful with the Internet and other information and communication technologies (ICT)."

What, then, are some of the classroom implications for the development of new literacies? First and foremost, teachers need to help students "learn how to learn" new technologies. From a new literacies perspective, knowing how to learn continuously changing technologies is more critical than learning any particular ICT. Moreover, teachers need to provide instructional support in the development and use of strategies that, among other things, help students critically read and evaluate information. According to Leu (2002, p. 314), learners will need to know how to put into play . . .

> . . . new forms of strategic knowledge necessary to locate, evaluate, and effectively use the extensive resources available within complexly networked ICT such as the Internet. The extent and complexity of this information is staggering. . . . How do we best search for information in these complex worlds? How do we design a Web page to be useful to people who are likely to visit? How do we communicate effectively with videoconference technologies? Strategic knowledge is central to the new literacies.

Response Journal

How proficient are you with the use of new literacies associated with ICT? Are you proficient enough to help students "learn how to learn" ICT such as the Internet? Elaborate.

A teacher should not automatically assume that today's adolescents already are strategic in their use of ICT for academic purposes. The extensive use of ICT by adolescents in social and personal contexts often creates a false sense of competence in an academic context. As Considine, Horton, and Moorman (2009, p. 472) put it, "hands-on is not the same as heads-on" when it comes to making assumptions about how effectively adolescents use ICT to learn.

Print resources, such as textbooks and trade books, in combination with digital texts, sounds, and images create powerful learning environments in an academic discipline. Learning with new literacies, which we will explore in Chapter 2, involves many of the same thinking processes that print forms of text involve. However, teachers who work with adolescent learners in middle and high school may find that some, if not many, of their students struggle with assignments that require thinking and learning with academic text in print or nonprint forms. No wonder *adolescent literacy* is a hot topic in education today (Cassidy & Cassidy, 2009). Let's take a closer look at the concept of adolescent literacy and its implications for thinking and learning with texts.

Adolescent Literacy

According to Bob Wise (2009), president of the Alliance for Excellent Education and a former governor of West Virginia, adolescent literacy is the cornerstone of students' academic success. The literacy learning that takes place in adolescents is of critical importance in preparing them for life in and out of school. The Commission on Adolescent Literacy of the International Reading Association (IRA) asserts that . . .

> . . . adolescents entering the adult world in the 21st century will read and write more than at any other time in human history. They will need advanced levels of literacy to perform their jobs, run their households, act as citizens, and conduct their personal lives. They will need literacy to cope with the flood of information they will find everywhere they turn. They will need literacy to feed their imaginations so they

can create the world of the future. In a complex and sometimes even dangerous world, their ability to read will be crucial. Continual instruction beyond the early grades is needed. (Moore, Bean, Birdyshaw, & Rycik, 1999, p. 3)

In the early grades of elementary school, many students learn basic skills related to reading and writing; however, by fourth grade and on, they need to continue to develop skill and sophistication in the use of literacy strategies and practices specific to different disciplines, texts, and situations. As the emphasis on disciplinary learning increases in middle and high schools, adolescents must develop both confidence in themselves and the thinking processes necessary for academic success in various content areas. Ironically, adolescents often experience difficulty with disciplinary literacy and learning, even though they may regularly use literacies for social purposes outside of school in ethnic, online, and popular culture communities (Moje, 2007).

Since 1992, when periodic National Assessment of Education Progress (NAEP) surveys in reading began for students in grades four, eight, and 12, it has become evident that there is an adolescent literacy crisis in the United States (Alliance for Excellent Education, 2006; Kamil, 2003; Vacca, 1998; Vacca & Alvermann, 1998). Few would argue with the importance of early reading development. Yet the emphasis on learning to read in the primary grades in the United States has served to magnify the lack of attention and commitment given to adolescent learners and their literacy needs.

From a historical perspective, the literacy needs of middle and high school students have received marginal attention by policy makers and curriculum planners. In the latter half of the twentieth century, students who struggled with reading often were identified as "remedial readers" and were assigned to "reading labs" or "remedial reading" classes, where they typically received piecemeal instruction apart from the content areas. As Vacca and Alvermann (1998) indicated, there has been an apparent lack of a national policy and school wide commitment for the ongoing literacy development of learners beyond the primary grades. Recently, however, there have been positive initiatives taking place focusing on the literacy needs of adolescents.

In a landmark report entitled *Reading Next,* Biancarosa and Snow (2004) address the current state of adolescent literacy and identify fifteen critical elements of effective adolescent literacy programs. These elements are highlighted in Box 1.2. In addition, a 2005 federal initiative, the Striving Readers program, provides competitive, discretionary grants to school districts to raise the reading achievement levels of middle and high school-aged students in Title I-eligible schools with significant numbers of students reading below grade level. One of the goals of the Striving Readers program is to enhance reading achievement in middle and high schools through improvements to the quality of literacy instruction across the curriculum.

Teaching adolescents is no easy task. Their lives are complex. Not only are they undergoing great physical changes, but they also are faced with ongoing cognitive, emotional, and social challenges. Adolescents who struggle with literacy in academic disciplines often go through the motions of reading without engaging in the process. Even skilled adolescent readers will struggle with reading sometimes, in some places, with some texts. Some students may lack the prior knowledge needed to connect to important ideas in the text. Others may get lost in the author's line of reasoning, become confused by the way the text is organized, or run into unknown words that are difficult to pronounce, let alone define. Often comprehension problems are only temporary. However, the difference between proficient adolescent readers and those who struggle all the time is this: When proficient readers struggle with text, they know what to do to get out of trouble. They have confidence in themselves as readers and learners. When a text becomes confusing or doesn't make sense, good readers recognize that they have an array of skills and strategies that they can use to work themselves out of difficulty.

Average and above-average adolescent learners, who are usually on track to go to college, might also struggle with reading without their teachers being cognizant of it. Often these students feel helpless about their ability to engage in academic literacy tasks, but go through the motions of "doing" school. Since 1992 periodic national assessments of reading conducted by the National Center for Education Statistics (NCES) show that the majority of U.S. students in grades four, eight, and 12 have obtained, at best, only "basic" levels of literacy. These NAEP surveys for reading (NAEP, 2007) reveal that the vast majority of adolescent learners in grades four and eight have difficulty with complex literacy tasks. For example, they may be able to read with some degree of fluency and accuracy but might not know what to do with text beyond saying the words and comprehending at what is essentially a literal level of performance. In the classroom, these students may appear *skillful* in the mechanics of reading but aren't *strategic* enough in their abilities to handle reading tasks that require interpretation and critical thinking. Throughout this book we explore the role of motivation in the academic lives of adolescents who struggle with school-based literacy even though they are likely to use new literacies *outside* of school for personal and social purposes (Lenters, 2006; Moje, 2007; Moje, Overby, Tysvaer, & Morris, 2008).

The terms *content literacy* and *disciplinary literacy* are frequently used to describe a discipline-centered instructional approach to literacy and learning in content area classrooms. From our perspective, content literacy and disciplinary literacy reflect many of the same instructional attributes, although critics of content literacy pedagogy claim some real differences between the two approaches to literacy and learning (Draper, 2008; Moje, 2007, 2008). In the next section, we explore the common ground between content literacy and disciplinary literacy and discuss how the two concepts may differ in terms of teaching practices.

Content Literacy and Disciplinary Literacy in Perspective

For many years, the term *content area reading* was associated with helping students better understand what they read across the curriculum. However, the concept of content area reading was broadened in the 1990s to reflect the inclusive role language plays in learning with texts. Hence, the relatively new construct of *content literacy* refers to the ability to use reading, writing, talking, listening, and viewing to learn subject matter in a given discipline (Vacca, 2002a). Content literacy involves the use of research-based cognitive learning strategies designed to support reading, writing, thinking, and learning with text. Most recently, the concept of *disciplinary literacy* is having an impact on the way researchers and educators think about literacy and learning in content areas (Buehl & Moore, 2009; Lee, 2004; Moje, 2007, 2008; Shanahan & Shanahan, 2008).

William S. Gray, one of the early titans in the field of reading, articulated the relationship between reading and learning that remains today the underlying rationale for reading in content areas. Not only did he forge the beginnings of content area reading, but he is also credited with what has become an often used, and often confused, mantra in education, "Every teacher is a teacher of reading." More than eighty-five years ago, Gray (1925) published one of the first descriptive studies to identify reading and study skills by content area. He determined that each content area requires different sets of skills for effective reading and study of text material.

Evidence-Based Best Practices   BOX 1.2

Fifteen Elements of Effective Adolescent Literacy Programs

Reading Next, a report to Carnegie Corporation of New York, provides a "vision for action and research" in the development of adolescent literacy programs. The report delineates fifteen elements for improving middle and high school literacy achievement.

1. *Direct, explicit comprehension instruction,* which is instruction in the strategies and processes that proficient readers use to understand what they read, including summarizing, keeping track of one's own understanding, and a host of other practices

2. *Effective instructional principles embedded in content,* including language arts teachers using content-area texts and content-area teachers providing instruction and practice in reading and writing skills specific to their subject area

3. *Motivation and self-directed learning,* which includes building motivation to read and learn and providing students with the instruction and supports needed for independent learning tasks they will face after graduation

4. *Text-based collaborative learning,* which involves students interacting with one another around a variety of texts

5. *Strategic tutoring,* which provides students with intense individualized reading, writing, and content instruction as needed

6. *Diverse texts,* which are texts at a variety of difficulty levels and on a variety of topics

7. *Intensive writing,* including instruction connected to the kinds of writing tasks students will have to perform well in high school and beyond

8. *A technology component,* which includes technology as a tool for and a topic of literacy instruction

9. *Ongoing formative assessment of students,* which is informal, often daily assessment of how students are progressing under current instructional practices

10. *Extended time for literacy,* which includes approximately two to four hours of literacy instruction and practice that takes place in language arts and content-area classes

11. *Professional development* that is both long term and ongoing

12. *Ongoing summative assessment of students and programs,* which is more formal and provides data that are reported for accountability and research purposes

13. *Teacher teams,* which are interdisciplinary teams that meet regularly to discuss students and align instruction

14. *Leadership,* which can come from principals and teachers who have a solid understanding of how to teach reading and writing to the full array of students present in schools

15. *A comprehensive and coordinated literacy program, which is interdisciplinary and interdepartmental and may even coordinate with out-of-school organizations and the local community*

Source: Reading Next: A Vision for Action and Research in Middle and High School Literacy (2004).www.all4ed.org/files/ReadingNext.pdf, pp. 12–13.

These different skill sets are related to one's purpose for reading and the conceptual demands of the text.

Many other researchers in the 1940s, 1950s, and 1960s designed "content-centered" studies to investigate the effectiveness of guiding students' reading within the context of disciplinary instruction. Harold Herber (1964), for example, developed "guide materials" to assist high school physics students in the development of core concepts in their textbook. He found that the students who used "study guides" to read physics text significantly outperformed those students who did not use guides to read the content under study. Herber (1970) later wrote the first comprehensive textbook, *Teaching Reading in Content Areas,* exclusively devoted to content area reading instruction. The guiding principle underlying Herber's book is as powerful today as it was over forty years ago: *Content determines process.* Even though the majority of students learn how to read in elementary school with some degree of proficiency, they must learn how to adapt reading and thinking strategies to meet the peculiarities and conceptual demands of each discipline they study. The shift from skills to learning strategies was first felt in the 1970s and 1980s when numerous research studies were conducted to better understand the role of thinking and learning processes in reading and to validate learning strategies grounded in cognitive principles (Conley, 2008).

Content literacy and disciplinary literacy are extensions of the concept of content area reading, where "content determines process" in a given discipline. The underlying goal of a discipline-specific approach to literacy is to show students how to think and learn with text as they develop a deep understanding of concepts and ideas encountered in texts. Each discipline poses its own challenges in terms of purposes for reading, vocabulary, concepts, texts, themes, and topics. How students read, think, and learn with text more than likely varies from content area to content area: "Even casual observation shows that students who struggle with reading a physics text may be excellent readers of poetry; the student who has difficulty with word problems in math may be very comfortable with historical narratives" (National Council of Teachers of English, 2008).

The big idea behind disciplinary literacy is that literacy development in a discipline is inextricably related to content knowledge and thinking. Doug Buehl (2009, p. 535), a longtime advocate of adolescent literacy and a former social studies teacher and literacy coach in Madison, Wisconsin, argues that middle and high school curricula must focus not only on what students should know and be able to do, but also on how "experts within a discipline read, write, and think". He contends that content area teachers are sometimes frustrated by "generic literacy practices" encountered in professional development workshops that are not relevant to reading and learning in their disciplines.

Buehl (2009, p. 537) advocates for continued research on discipline-specific literacy practices, which seem "to be an especially fertile ground for determining how to mentor students to read, write, and think through the lens of a mathematician, biologist, musician, historian, artist, novelist, and so forth". He cites a statewide project in Wisconsin called Thinking Like a Historian in which history teachers are encouraged to engage in questioning routines around five core themes crucial to thinking and learning with historical text:

1. Cause and effect: "What happened and why?"

2. Change and continuity: "What changed and what remained the same?"

3. Turning points: "How did events of the past affect the future?"

4. Through their eyes: "How did people in the past view their lives and world?"

5. Using the past: "How does studying the past help us understand our lives and world?" (Wisconsin Historical Society, 2009)

In a similar vein, Lee (2004, p. 14) describes disciplinary literacy as "the ability to understand, critique, and use knowledge from texts in content areas". She links disciplinary literacy directly to the needs of culturally diverse adolescent readers who struggle with academic texts and suggests that an important dimension of a discipline-specific approach to literacy is to draw on adolescent learners' "cultural funds of knowledge"—that is, the kinds of knowledge that culturally diverse students bring to learning situations. As we explain in Chapter 3, how teachers adjust instruction to the sociocultural strengths of students in diverse classrooms is an important aspect of literacy and learning in a discipline.

Moje (2007) provides a complex view of disciplinary literacy as she discusses some of the theory, research, and pedagogical practices supporting instructional approaches to disciplinary literacy. She describes one such approach found on the website of the Institute for Learning at the University of Pittsburgh (www.instituteforlearning.org/dl.html):

> This approach to teaching and learning integrates academically rigorous content with discipline-appropriate habits of thinking. The driving idea is that knowledge and thinking must go hand in hand. To develop deep conceptual knowledge in a discipline, one needs to use the habits of thinking that are valued and used by that discipline . . . The ultimate goal of Disciplinary Literacy is that all students will develop deep content knowledge and literate habits of thinking in the context of academically rigorous learning in individual disciplines. (Quoted in Moje, 2007, p. 10)

Others have called for a rethinking of the way literacy is embedded within various disciplinary-specific learning situations. For example, Shanahan and Shanahan (2008) conducted a descriptive research project in which they studied how disciplinary experts (university professors and classroom teachers) from mathematics, history, and chemistry engaged in reading to learn. In the first year of the project, the researchers adapted a pedagogical practice called "think-alouds" to identify the "specialized reading skills" used by the experts to comprehend texts in their respective disciplines. During the think-aloud sessions, the researchers discovered that "[e]ach of the disciplinary experts emphasized a different array of reading processes, suggesting the focused and highly specialized nature of literacy at these levels" (Shanahan & Shanahan, 2008, p. 49).

In the second year of the project, the teams of disciplinary experts studied the viability of generic literacy strategies and explored ways to develop instructional strategies that were discipline-specific. These strategies are similar in intent to the kinds of cognitive-based strategies found in this and other books dealing with literacy and learning across the curriculum. However, the teams of discipline-specific experts modified and adapted generic literacy strategies to meet the textual and conceptual demands inherent in their specific disciplines.

Whether you call it *content area reading, content literacy,* or *disciplinary literacy,* the guiding principle behind each instructional approach remains as powerful today as it has for nearly a century. *Content determines process.* The conceptual demands and structure of a discipline-specific text determines how a reader will interact with that text, make sense of it, and learn from it. As Kamil (2003) concluded, teaching literacy strategies has value for all teachers. However, a disciplinary literacy perspective reminds us that teachers, as subject matter specialists, must also have a solid understanding of the reading, writing, and thinking processes necessary to adapt and modify literacy strategies, tailoring them to meet the conceptual and textual demands of the content under study.

As recent National Assessments of Educational Progress (NAEP) show, far too many adolescents struggle with academic reading tasks (Lee, Grigg, & Donahue, 2007; Perie, Grigg, & Donahue, 2005). Many school districts have begun to use a *tiered* approach to intervention for students who significantly struggle with reading and learning. This approach, known as *Response to Intervention* (RTI), holds much promise for improving literacy and learning across the curriculum. RTI underscores the importance of responsive teaching, assessment, and differentiated instruction in the academic lives of adolescents who struggle with reading. Throughout various chapters of this book, we will highlight RTI and the role it might play in helping students, especially adolescent learners, who struggle with text.

BOX 1.3   # RTI for Struggling Adolescent Learners

Implications for Content Literacy

What is Response to Intervention (RTI) and how does it affect the work of content area teachers? RTI is a relatively new, promising approach to providing the most appropriate instruction, service, and research-based strategy interventions to significantly struggling learners. In response to the growing number of students recommended for special education programs, a new version of the Individuals with Disabilities Education Act was passed in 2004. This act redefines the way students with learning disabilities are identified. Because previous protocols for special education referrals did not require students to have interventions within general education classrooms, it was often difficult to determine whether literacy-related learning problems were due to a student's cognitive disabilities or to a lack of exposure to effective literacy instruction (Johnson, Mellard, Fuchs, & McKnight, 2006).

The goal of RTI, therefore, is to use school wide assessments to identify at-risk learners and to provide various levels of strategy interventions before students fall behind their peers. According to the National Research Center on Learning Disabilities (NRCLD), RTI is "an assessment and intervention process for systematically monitoring student progress and making decisions about the need for instructional modifications or increasingly intensified services using progress monitoring data" (Johnson, Mellard, Fuchs, & McKnight, 2006, p. 2). The International Reading Association (2008) describes RTI as a multi-tiered process that provides services and interventions to struggling learners at increasing levels of intensity. In the RTI instructional framework, all stakeholders are expected to work collaboratively to make instructional decisions. Teachers,

parents, literacy coaches, special education teachers, and additional staff members work together to determine the needs of each student and to plan and deliver appropriate instruction.

RTI is much more prevalent at the elementary school level than at middle and secondary levels. However, many middle and high schools have begun to implement RTI in their school districts. Although there are several RTI models to follow, a three-tier approach to strategy intervention is used in many school districts.

Tier 1

All students in Tier 1 receive high-quality, research-based instruction differentiated to meet their needs, and are screened periodically to identify struggling learners who need additional support. Content area teachers have an important role to play at this level of intervention. Throughout this book, we describe many potentially useful assessment procedures and literacy strategies grounded in cognitive theory and research that support and monitor students' ability to learn with text.

Tier 2

Tier 2 provides targeted intervention for students who have not been successful in classroom learning situations and have not made adequate progress in core curriculum studies. Their progress is monitored frequently to determine whether strategy interventions have been successful. Content area teachers typically receive support, as needed, from literacy coaches and specialists to ensure that students "on the edge" are making adequate progress at their grade level. For example, in some RTI models, students who are at risk of failure are assigned to tutoring centers within a school for more intensive instruction and support. Moreover, handheld electronic devices, which provide more intensive instructional programs for the 10 to 15 percent of students who are at Tier 2, are also being used within content area classrooms to prevent struggling adolescent learners from falling behind their peers.

Tier 3

At this level, students receive individualized, intensive interventions that target the students' skill deficits for the remediation of existing problems and the prevention of more severe problems. Literacy specialists and special education personnel are responsible for providing Tier 3 interventions and work closely with classroom teachers.

 # Reading to Learn

A variety of classroom-related factors influence reading to learn in a given discipline, including:

- The learner's prior knowledge of, attitude toward, and interest in the subject
- The learner's purpose for engaging in reading, writing, and discussion
- The vocabulary and conceptual difficulty of the text material
- The assumptions that the text writers make about their audience of readers
- The text structures that writers use to organize ideas and information
- The teacher's beliefs about and attitude toward the use of texts in learning situations

Writers of texts communicate with readers in the same way that speakers use language to communicate with listeners, or filmmakers use sound and moving images to tell a story or communicate meaning to viewers. Teaching with textbooks or other types of written text involves more than assigning pages to be read, lecturing, or using questions to check whether students have read the material the night before. To use written texts strategically and effectively, you must first be aware of the powerful bonds between reading and knowledge construction. With this in mind, consider how reading to learn relates to meaning-making and text comprehension.

The Role of Prior Knowledge in Reading

In their book *A Good Teacher in Every Classroom,* Darling-Hammond and Baratz-Snowden (2005, pp. 2–3) argue that the conventional view of teaching is simplistic in that teaching is viewed as proceeding through a set curriculum in a manner that *transmits* information from teacher to student. Moreover, they contend that there is much more to teaching than knowing the subject matter that students should learn. Among the many classroom practices characteristic of effective teachers, they "carefully organize activities, materials, and instruction based on students' prior knowledge . . . and engage students in active learning."

Many of the literacy practices and strategies that you will learn about in this book will help you organize instruction around students' prior knowledge and their active engagement in text-related activities. As a result, students will be in a better position to understand the structure of your discipline and the important ideas and concepts underlying the subject matter that you teach.

Not only do readers activate prior knowledge *before* reading but they also use prior knowledge *during* and *after* reading to infer meaning and elaborate on the text content. Good readers don't just read to get the gist of what they are reading unless that is their specific purpose. They use prior knowledge, as well as what they know (or think they know) about the text, to make inferences, to evaluate, and to elaborate on the content. Why is this the case?

Cognitive scientists use the technical term *schema* to describe how people use prior knowledge to organize and store information in their heads. Furthermore, *schema activation* is the mechanism by which people access what they know and match it to the information in a text. In doing so, they build on the meaning they already bring to a learning situation. Indeed, schemata (the plural of schema) have been called "the building blocks of cognition" (Rumelhart, 1982) because they represent elaborate networks of information that people use to make sense of new stimuli, events, and situations. When a match occurs between students' prior knowledge and text material, a schema functions in at least three ways.

First, a schema provides a framework for learning that allows readers to *seek and select* information that is relevant to their purposes for reading. In the process of searching and selecting, readers are more likely to *make inferences* about the text. You make inferences when you *anticipate* content and *make predictions* about upcoming material, or you *fill in gaps* in the material during reading.

Second, a schema helps readers *organize* text information. The process by which you organize and integrate new information into old facilitates the ability to *retain and remember* what you read. A poorly organized text is difficult for readers to comprehend. We illustrate this point in more detail when we discuss the influences of text structure on comprehension and retention in later chapters.

Third, a schema helps readers *elaborate* information. When you elaborate what you have read, you engage in a cognitive process that involves deeper levels of insight, judgment, and evaluation. You are inclined to ask, "So what?" as you engage in conversation with an author.

Reading as a Meaning-Making Process

Language helps a learner to make sense of the world, to understand, and to be understood. As a result, language and meaning cannot be severed from one another. Language isn't language unless meaning-making is involved. Oral language without meaning is mere prattle—a string of senseless, meaningless speech sounds. Written language without meaning is a cipher of mysterious markings on paper.

To be literate in content area classrooms, students must learn how to use reading to construct knowledge in the company of authors, other learners, and teachers. Using reading in the classroom to help students to learn doesn't require specialized training on the part of content teachers, although many of today's middle and high schools employ *literacy coaches* (a topic discussed in Chapter 12) to develop, support, and extend content area teachers' use of literacy strategies. Content literacy practices do not diminish the teacher's role as a subject matter specialist. Instead, reading is a tool students use to construct, clarify, and extend meaning in a given discipline.

Why are you able to read a text such as Lewis Carroll's "Jabberwocky" with little trouble, even though Carroll invents words such as *chortled* and *toves* throughout the poem? Try reading "Jabberwocky" aloud:

JABBERWOCKY

'Twas brillig, and the slithy toves
    Did gyre and gimble in the wabe;
All mimsy were the borogoves,
    And the mome raths outgrabe.

"Beware the Jabberwock, my son!
    The jaws that bite, the claws that catch!
Beware the Jubjub bird and shun
    The frumious Bandersnatch!"

He took his vorpal sword in hand:
    Long time the manxome foe he sought—
So rested he by the Tumtum tree,
    And stood awhile in thought.

And, as in uffish thought he stood,
    The Jabberwock, with eyes of flame,
Came whiffling through the tulgey wood,
    And burbled as it came!

One, two! One, two! And through and through
    The vorpal blade went snicker-snack!
He left it dead, and with its head
    He went galumphing back.

"And hast thou slain the Jabberwock?
    Come to my arms, my beamish boy!
O frabjous day! Callooh! Callay!"
    He chortled in his joy.

'Twas brillig, and the slithy toves
    Did gyre and gimble in the wabe;
All mimsy were the borogoves,
    And the mome raths outgrabe.

What is quickly apparent from your reading of the poem is that going from print to speech is a hollow act unless meaning-making is involved in the transaction.

Try rewriting the poem using your own words. If you and a colleague or two were to compare your rewrites, you undoubtedly would find similarities in meaning, but also important differences. These differences undoubtedly reflect the knowledge of the world—*prior knowledge*—that you as a reader bring to the text as well as the *strategies* you used to make meaning.

Reading as a Strategic Process

Throughout this book, we argue that the real value of reading lies in its uses. Whether we use reading to enter into the imaginative world of fiction, learn with academic texts, meet workplace demands, acquire insight and knowledge about people, places, and things, or understand a graphic on an Internet website, readers, to be successful, must use strategies to meet the demands of the task at hand.

For example, a skilled reader will approach the following passage as a challenge and use a repertoire of reading strategies to construct meaning.

A PLAN FOR THE IMPROVEMENT OF ENGLISH SPELLING*

For example, in Year 1 that useless letter "c" would be dropped to be replased either by "k" or "s," and likewise "x" would no longer be part of the alphabet. The only kase in which "c" would be retained would be the "ch" formation, which will be dealt with later. Year 2 might reform "w" spelling, so that "which" and "one" would take the same konsonant, wile Year 3 might well abolish "y" replasing it with "i" and Iear 4 might fiks the "g/j" anomali wonse and for all.

Jenerally, then, the improvement would kontinue iear bai iear with Iear 5 doing awai with useless double konsonants, and Iears 6–12 or so modifaiing vowlz and the rimeining voist and unvoist konsonants. Bai Iear 15 or sou, it wud fainali bi posibl tu meik ius ov thi ridandant letez "c," "y" and "x"—bai now jast a memori in the maindz ov ould doderez—tu riplais "ch," "sh," and "th" rispektivli.

Fainali, xen, aafte sam 20 iers ov orxogrefkl riform, wi wud hev a lojikl, kohirnt speling in ius xrewawt xe Ingliy-spiking world.

Response Journal

Describe some of the reading strategies you use to successfully complete an academic reading assignment. What are some of the strategies you use for writing essays or papers that will be graded or shared with others?

In order to comprehend text successfully, skilled readers must be able to *decode* or pronounce words quickly and accurately, read with *fluency*, activate *vocabulary knowledge* in relation to the language of the text, and put into play *text comprehension* strategies to understand what they are reading. As Figure 1.1 suggests, decoding, reading fluency, vocabulary, and comprehension are interrelated processes. If readers have trouble decoding words quickly and accurately (e.g., analyzing and recognizing sound–letter relationships), it will slow down their ability to read fluently in a smooth, conversational manner. Moreover, if they struggle to decode words accurately, various reading errors (e.g., mispronunciations, word omissions, and substitutions), if significant, will cause cognitive confusion and limit readers' abilities to bring meaning and conceptual understanding to the words in the text.

When students lack decoding and fluency skills, the act of reading no longer becomes automatic. As you read "A Plan for the Improvement of English Spelling," did the letter substitutions cause you to struggle as a reader? Perhaps. The progressive substitution of letters undoubtedly slowed down your ability to read in a smooth, conversational manner and may even have affected your accuracy in recognizing some words. Just think about some of the students in classrooms today who lack the ability to decode words accurately and read fluently. They may experience difficulty because they read in a slow and halting manner, word-by-word, and have trouble pronouncing words quickly and accurately. They spend so much time and attention on trying to "say the words" that comprehension suffers and, as a result, the reading process breaks down for them. Such students will benefit from *direct, explicit* instruction in decoding and fluency strategies from trained literacy specialists.

Our guess is that the reading process did not break down for you as you read the passage. Even though the substitution of letters slowed down your reading, chances are you were still able to comprehend the passage and construct meaning from it. This is because skilled readers do not use a single strategy to comprehend text. They know how to "think with print" as they

---

*Although on the Internet this passage is widely attributed to Mark Twain, there is uncertainty as to its actual author.

Figure 1.1 Reading Involves the Use of Decoding, Fluency, Vocabulary, and Comprehension Strategies

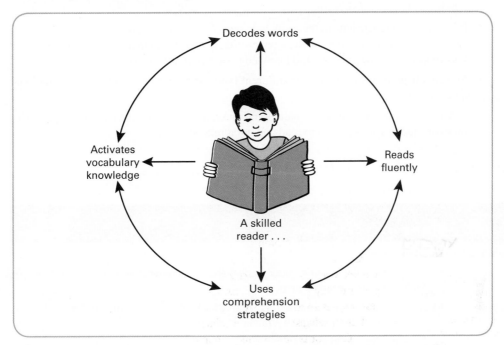

search for and construct meaning from text. Skilled readers have at their command *multiple strategies* for comprehending text.

Reading Comprehension

When skilled readers have difficulty comprehending what they are reading, they often become *strategic* in the way they approach challenging and difficult text. That is to say, good readers have developed *skills* and *strategies* that they use to understand what they are reading. As Duke and Pearson (2002, p. 205) explain, we know a great deal about what good readers do when they read: "Reading comprehension research has a long and rich history . . . much work on the process of reading comprehension has been grounded in studies of good readers." Table 1.2 delineates what good readers do when they engage in the process of comprehending text.

The research-based findings of two influential reports, *The Report of the National Reading Panel* (National Reading Panel, 2000) and the *RAND Report on Reading Comprehension* (RAND Reading Study Group, 2002), indicate that much is known about comprehension instruction. These reports, for example, draw several conclusions about effective comprehension instruction, including the following:

- Instruction can be effective in helping students develop a repertoire of strategies that promotes and fosters comprehension.

- Strategy instruction, when integrated into subject matter learning, improves students' comprehension of text.

- Struggling readers benefit from *explicit instruction* in the use of strategies.
- Vocabulary knowledge is strongly related to text comprehension and is especially important in teaching English learners.
- Effective comprehension strategies include *question generation, question answering routines, comprehension monitoring, cooperative learning, summarizing,* visual displays known as *graphic organizers,* and knowledge of different *text structures.*
- Students benefit from exposure to different types or *genres* of texts (e.g., informational and narrative texts).
- Teachers who provide choices, challenging tasks, and collaborative learning experiences increase students' motivation to read and comprehend texts.

Table 1.2 What Do Good Readers Do When They Comprehend Text?

Characteristics of Good Readers	Strategies of Good Readers
Good readers are:	**Good readers:**
• Active	• Have clear *goals* in mind for their reading and evaluate whether the text, and their reading of it, is meeting their goals.
• Purposeful	• *Look over* the text before they read, noting such things as the *structure* of the text and text sections that might be most relevant to their reading goals.
• Evaluative	• *Make predictions* about what is to come.
• Thoughtful	• Read *selectively,* continually making decisions about their reading—what to read carefully, what to read quickly, what not to read, what to reread, and so on.
• Strategic	• *Construct, revise,* and *question* the meanings they make as they read.
• Persistent	• Try to determine the meanings of *unfamiliar words and concepts* in the text.
• Productive	• Draw from, compare, and *integrate their prior knowledge* with material in the text.
	• Think about the *authors* of the text, their styles, beliefs, intentions, historical milieu, and so on.
	• *Monitor their understanding* of the text, making adjustments in their reading as necessary.
	• *Evaluate the text's quality and value,* and react to the text in a range of ways, both intellectually and emotionally.
	• *Read different kinds of text differently.*
	• *Attend closely* to the setting and characters when reading narrative.
	• Frequently *construct* and *revise summaries* of what they have read when reading expository text.
	• Think about text before, during, and after reading.

Source: Adapted from "Effective Practices for Developing Reading Comprehension" by N. K. Duke and P. D. Pearson, in *What Research Has to Say about Reading Instruction* (pp. 205–242), A. E. Farstrup & S. J. Samuels (eds.). Copyright © 2002 by the International Reading Association. Reproduced with permission of International Reading Association via Copyright Clearance Center.

Throughout Part Two of this book, we will explore a variety of instructional practices that will help students comprehend discipline-specific texts more effectively. Some of these strategies will be useful and highly effective in your specific discipline; some may not. *Content determines process.* How teachers adapt instructional strategies to meet the conceptual demands and peculiarities of their disciplines will be the difference-maker in the literate lives of their students.

Response Journal

Describe the relationships among *reader, text,* and *activity* in the reading comprehension model described in Chapter 2 of the RAND report.

Looking Back | Looking Forward

In this chapter, we invited you to begin an examination of content literacy practices and the assumptions underlying those practices. Teachers play a critical role in helping students use literacy strategies to think and learn with text. Effective teachers make a difference in the literate lives of their students. Therefore, we made a distinction between *teacher qualities* and *teaching quality*. Teacher qualities are the characteristics associated with an effective teacher. Teaching quality, on the other hand, refers to the instructional context and the dynamics underpinning effective teaching in content areas. Effective teachers, for example, differentiate instruction for a wide range of students. Learning with all kinds of text, whether print or digital in nature, is an active process. In today's standards-based educational environment, the pressure to teach content standards well can easily lead to content-only instruction with little attention paid to how students acquire information and develop concepts. The Common Core State Standards Initiative, however, is a step in the right direction. The Common Core acknowledges that teachers must balance content (what they teach) and process (how they teach) as they engage students in thinking and learning with all kinds of texts.

To this end, we explored the role that literacy plays in the acquisition of content knowledge. The concept of literacy must be viewed from a twenty-firstcentury perspective. In an era of digital media, many of today's adolescents have developed "new literacies" that they use for personal and social purposes. New literacies are having a major influence on learning in academic contexts. To shift the burden of learning from teacher to student requires an understanding of the relationships among literacies, texts, and learning across the curriculum. As a result, we attempted to put content literacy and disciplinary literacy practices into perspective, contending that the two approaches to instruction share much common ground. Our emphasis throughout this book is on reading and writing to learn. Learning how to comprehend text across disciplines is what content area reading is all about.

The next chapter puts the spotlight on new literacies in the adolescent lives of twenty-firstcentury learners. Digital texts are highly engaging and interactive. New literacies make it possible to interact with text in ways not imaginable even a short while ago. Literacy-related learning opportunities in multimodal environments are interactive, enhance communication, engage students in multimedia, create opportunities for inquiry, and support socially mediated learning. Whether students are navigating the Internet or interacting with popular media such as video games, an array of learning experiences await them.

Minds On

1. During a job interview, the principal of a middle school asks if you are "highly qualified" for the position. How would you respond?

2. Imagine that during lunch, several teaching colleagues comment that because many students in their courses "can't read," these teachers rarely use books. They argue that students learn content just as well through audiovisual aids and discussions.

Divide a small group of six class members into two smaller groups of three: one representing the teachers who believe books are unnecessary and one representing those who believe books are essential. For ten minutes, role-play a lunchtime debate on the pros and cons of using reading in content areas. After the time has elapsed, discuss the arguments used by the role players. Which did you find valid and with which did you disagree?

3. Your supervisor observes a lesson in which you use a large block of time for students to read. Afterward, the supervisor says that you should assign reading as homework, rather than "wasting" valuable class time. She adds that if you continue with lessons like this, your students will be lucky to finish one or two books over the entire year. Consequently, you request a meeting with the supervisor. What arguments might you bring to this meeting to help convince her of the validity of your approach?

4. Picture a science class of twenty-five students from very diverse backgrounds—different social classes, different ethnicities, and varying achievement levels. Many of the students struggle with text materials. Describe some classroom strategies you might use to respond to struggling readers while maintaining high standards of content learning.

5. Divide your group into two teams, one "pro" and one "con." Review each of the following statements, and discuss, from your assigned view, the pros and cons of each issue.

   a. We read to discover meaning (to understand), as much as we talk to communicate meaning to others (to be understood).

   b. Students need to know the purpose for a text assignment if they are going to read effectively.

   c. Reading strategies are so interrelated that knowledge of them is of little practical value for students.

 # Hands On

1. With a small group, examine the following well-known passage and attempt to supply the missing words. Note that all missing words, regardless of length, are indicated by blanks in the passage.

Besides, Sir, we shall not fight our battles alone. There is a just God, who presides over the destinies of nations, who will raise up friends to fight our _____ for us. The battle, Sir, is not to the strong alone: it is to the vigilant, the active, the _____. Besides, Sir, we have no election. If we were base enough to desire it, it is now too late to retire from the contest.

There is no _____, but in submission or slavery. Our chains are forged. Their _____ may be heard on the plains of Boston! The war is inevitable—and let it come—I repeat, Sir, let it come! It is in vain, Sir, to extenuate the matter. Gentlemen may cry, "Peace! Peace!" But there is no peace. The war has actually begun!

The next gale that sweeps from the North will bring to our ears the clash of resounding _____! Our brethren are already in the field! Why stand we here idle? What is it that the Gentlemen wish? What would they have? Is life so _____, or peace too _____, as to be purchased at the price of chains and _____? Forbid it, Almighty God! I know not what _____ others may take, but as for me, give me _____ or give me death!

After you have filled in the blanks, discuss the processes by which decisions on possible responses were made and any problems encountered. How did prior knowledge of the passage's topic assist your reading process? (After you have completed this experiment, review Patrick Henry's speech at the end of the "Hands On" section in Chapter 5.)

In what ways was your experience similar to that of a student who attempts to decipher a content passage but who has little background knowledge of its content?

2. Bring the following materials to class: a large paper bag, five paper plates, four buttons, three cardboard tubes, scraps of material, six pipe cleaners, three sheets of construction paper, scissors, tape, and a stapler. Your instructor will silently give each group a written directive to create a replica of a living creature (cat, dog, rhinoceros, aardvark, etc.) with no verbal communication permitted.

After your group has constructed its creature, list the communication difficulties, and discuss how each was overcome. Finally, have a spokesperson from each group share these difficulties with the rest of the class.

3. As suggested in the chapter, rewrite Lewis Carroll's poem "Jabberwocky" on page 23 using "real" words.

     Compare your efforts with those of other members of your small group, and discuss the following questions:

   - Why are there differences in the translations?
   - Does your translation change the intended meaning of the poem?

- Do the differences affect your enjoyment of the poem?
- What personal experiences and prior knowledge that you brought to your reading of the poem may have influenced your translation?

eResources

Think about a highly abstract concept, such as *dream* (**www.dreamtree.com**) or *universe* (**www.handsonuniverse.org**), and go to websites devoted to the topics. Bring a physical object to class that represents the concept. Verbally report your criteria for choosing the object to your class.

Explore the website **www.literacymatters.com**. Select a lesson plan sample that is appropriate for the content area and grade level you plan to teach. Discuss how you could adapt this lesson for use in your classroom.

Take a closer look at the Common Core State Standards. Go to the *Common Core State Standards Initiative* online (**www.corestandards.org**) to learn more about the Common Core and the expectations for literacy and learning.

MyEducationLab™

Go to Topic 3: Motivation, the MyEducationLab (**www.myeducationlab.com**) for *Content Area Reading*, where you can:

- Find learning outcomes for Motivation, along with the national standards that connect to these outcomes.
- Complete Assignments and Activities that can help you more deeply understand the chapter content.
- Practice the core teaching skills identified in the chapter with the Building Teaching Skills and Dispositions learning units.
- Check your comprehension on the content covered in the chapter with the Study Plan. Here you will be able to take a chapter quiz, receive feedback on your answers, and then access Review, Practice, and Enrichment activities to enhance your understanding of chapter content.
- Visit A+RISE. A+RISE® Standards2Strategy™ is an innovative and interactive online resource that offers new teachers in grades K–12 just in time, research-based instructional strategies that meet the linguistic needs of English Language Learners (ELLs) as they learn content, differentiate instruction for all grades and abilities, and are aligned to Common Core Elementary Language Arts standards (for the literacy strategies) and to English language proficiency standards in World-Class Instructional Design and Assessment (WIDA), Texas, California, and Florida.
- Use the Online Lesson Plan Builder to practice lesson planning and integrating national and state standards into your planning.

2 Learning with New Literacies

New literacies are transforming the way we read, write, think, communicate, and make meaning.

In a twenty-first century digital culture we live in a socially networked society and have come to rely on our digital devices in much the same way that we rely on friends. The gamut of emotions over losing an Internet connection—much like losing a friend—may range from sadness and regret to puzzlement and frustration. Even anger!

Today's students are digital natives. They have grown up with technologies. Consequently, many learners have developed social media skills and "new literacies" that some parents, best described as "digital immigrants," can only dream of mastering in a lifetime. Many of today's youth are fluent at exchanging emails, texts, instant messages, and social network posts on Facebook or MySpace. Although digital natives have access to and experience with information and communication technologies (ICT), they still have a lot to learn about using ICT for academic purposes. What does this mean for literacy and learning across the curriculum? First, and foremost, it signifies in a very public way that we live in a new media age, where technological advances brought on by the digital forces of electronic devices are transforming the way we communicate, collect information, make meaning, and construct knowledge.

Walk into any middle or high school classroom today and you may very well hear the following snippets of instructional conversations between students:

Jon: Where did you find that list of Revolutionary War battles?

Brittany: I looked it up on Wikipedia.

Danielle: Where did you find out who played Ophelia in that movie?

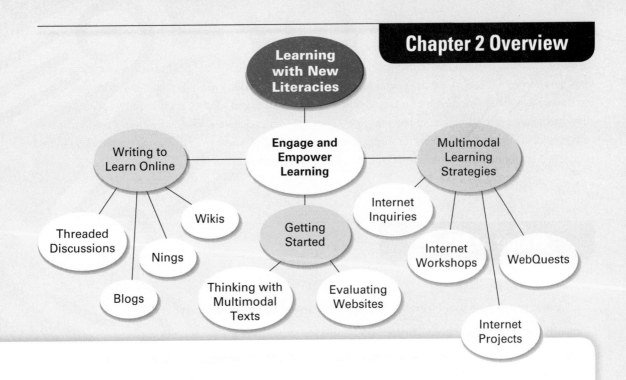

Learning with New Literacies

Engage and Empower Learning

Writing to Learn Online

Threaded Discussions

Wikis

Nings

Blogs

Getting Started

Thinking with Multimodal Texts

Evaluating Websites

Multimodal Learning Strategies

Internet Inquiries

Internet Workshops

WebQuests

Internet Projects

Nate: I found it on the Internet Movie Database.

Andy: How did you find out the title of that poem?

Heather: I Googled the first line of the poem.

These exchanges reflect the types of information gathering students typically engage in as they interact with digital texts in and out of today's content area classrooms. As you can see, even the way we and our students use language is changing! In today's digital world, the names of some search engines have morphed into verbs, as in "I Googled it." Obviously, the ways in which we find information, no matter what the topic, have transformed radically in just a few short years. The Internet has made information accessible to a degree never before imagined. Yet, it is best to heed the advice of Karchmer-Klein and Shinas (2012, p. 291): "As teachers it is necessary to suspend assumptions regarding the technological knowledge and experience students bring to the classroom and instead develop instruction designed to address curriculum goals and students' individual needs."

And therein lies the challenge for teachers in this era of "new literacies": How can we help our students be effective readers and writers when our concept of "literacy" is evolving so rapidly? Even though students may have developed social networking skills, how will we help them find, make meaning of, and evaluate the information available to them via digital media? How do we help young people keep up with the immense changes occurring in digital media when we may have trouble keeping up with these changes ourselves? It simply is not possible to adequately prepare students for reading and writing in the twenty-first century without integrating new literacies into the everyday life of today's classrooms. Web 2.0 is here, and Web 3.0

(whatever that may be) could arrive by the time this book gets into your hands. Are today's schools up to the challenge? While it is important for teachers to show students how to comprehend texts that are page-based, the organizing principle for this chapter suggests that students are also going to need to be interacting more with texts that are screen-based—texts that include not only print but also images, motion, and sound—if they are going to be able to lead fully realized literate lives: New literacies are transforming the way we read, write, communicate, and make meaning.

Frame of Mind

1. What are new literacies?

2. What is different about learning with new literacies? What is the same?

3. Why is learning with new literacies essential for students?

4. What are some instructional strategies that can be used to engage and empower learning through the use of new literacies?

5. How do the roles of teachers change when they make new literacies an integral part of subject matter learning?

Literacy has evolved from a traditional view of print-based reading and writing to one that recognizes the multiplicity of literacies that vary across time and space. Although skilled readers use many of the same strategies online as they do offline, there are also new skill sets and strategies that learners must develop to use new literacies effectively (Coiro and Moore, 2012). The comprehension strategies that we discussed in Chapter 1, for example, are used by learners both online and offline depending on their purposes for reading. When they go online, however, some of the new literacy strategies that learners are likely to use may include generating digital questions, examining search engine results, and making sense of the multimodal aspects of digital text. As Sweeny (2010, p. 122) noted, "Schools need to embrace ICTs so that students are prepared to function in a world where new literacies are the expectation and the norm." No wonder new literacies are changing the instructional landscape for learning in today's classrooms.

New Literacies: An Overview

In a relatively brief period of time, new literacies have impacted the way we think about teaching and learning. Ironically, the first person to use the term *new literacy,* John Willinsky (1990), coined the phrase before the advent of many of the new media that have driven the "new literacies" revolution. Willinsky's idea of a "new" literacy revolved more around a different mind-set for approaching reading and writing in the classroom than around technological advances. He describes classrooms that are driven not by textbooks and teacher talk, but instead by inquiry and student choice—a "new" literacy that wasn't dependent on students regurgitating "right" answers. Of course, the roots of a student-centered concept of curriculum, literacy, and learning can be traced back to the groundbreaking work of John Dewey (1899–1980) and many other educational pioneers and literacy researchers who followed in his footsteps.

A recent line of research—the New Literacy Studies—underscores the importance of "a specific sociocultural approach to understanding and researching literacy" (Lankshear & Knobel, 2003, p. 16). A sociocultural approach views literacy as social practice. That is to say, New Literacy Studies examine literacy as completely situated in all of the many "discourses" (i.e., uses of language) in people's lives—as they act at work, at school, within the family, and in any social situation (Barton & Hamilton, 1998; Street, 1995; Gee, 1996).

As new media became more and more a part of our lives, teachers learned how to surf the Internet and bookmark; in today's classrooms, they're learning how to blog and build a wiki. Being a literate person in today's society involves more than being able to construct meaning from a printed text. A literate person needs to be able to "read" and "write" and learn with texts that have *multimodal* elements such as print, graphic design, audio, video, gesture, and nonstop interaction. In a twenty-first century, media-driven society, a teacher needs to have at least a basic mastery of reading and writing using modes of communication that were previously left to the art, music, theater, and film teachers. Reading and writing aren't just about print anymore, as we move from a page-dominated literacy to a screen-dominated literacy (Kress, 2003).

From the Arts to Media Literacy

Over the past few decades, in a not unrelated development, many educators have advocated for more inclusion of the arts in classrooms. Arts integration advocates such as Eisner (1997) and Greene (1997) have urged teachers to bring into every classroom multiple forms of representation such as painting, music, and theater. Leland and Harste (1994) discuss "ways of knowing" that need to be honored in our classrooms regardless of whether the Internet has brought these arts elements into the everyday lives of readers and writers. Those who have described what arts-integrated classrooms can look like have given us a glimpse into what all classrooms may need to look like when all reading and writing is done in a multimodal environment.

In fact, it is art educator Eliot Eisner who provides us with a particularly useful overarching definition of literacy:

> In order to be read, a poem, an equation, a painting, a dance, a novel, or a contract each requires a distinctive form of literacy, when literacy means, as I intend it to mean, a way of conveying meaning through and recovering meaning from the form of representation in which it appears. (Eisner, 1997, p. 353)

At the same time that some educators were urging arts integration, television had already been an impetus to the development of another key strand of the new literacies movement. Many educators, particularly from the United Kingdom and Australia, called for young people to be educated about the ways of television and all media (Buckingham, 1993), arguing that all students should be exposed to at least the basics of media education, including elements of consumerism as well as production (Buckingham, 2003; Hobbs & Frost, 2003).

Paralleling the work of media educators are the critical literacy theorists who have urged educators to help students explore and examine the power dynamics in the discourses that surround us (Freire, 1970, 2000; McLaren, 1989). Essentially, students need to learn how to be consumers of both "fiction" and "nonfiction" media, and to be able to recognize when they're being manipulated, as when, for example, they see their favorite television character drinking Dr Pepper. Students are now exposed to advertising even when doing simple research for a school project, and are at risk of being "branded" by corporations even when attempting to perform literacy tasks that used to be free of any kind of advertising (Klein, 2000).

Nonlinear Characteristics of New Literacies

Along with the multimodal aspects of the new literacies, there are additional characteristics of reading on the screen that differentiate new literacies from print-based literacy. For example, new media are usually read in a nonlinear fashion. That is to say, the reader may jump from element to element within a digital text in a completely random way. Traditional printed texts such as books are written for readers to proceed from front to back, reading from left to right. However, readers of electronic texts have the option of clicking on any one of a number of hyperlinks that can take them on a path that digresses completely from the path other readers might take. Linear reading, of course, still occurs. Though many adolescents have probably read the latest *Hunger Games* or *Twilight* book, and perhaps even last night's assignments in their textbooks, much of their personal reading now is done with digital texts. As a result, reading is individualized and proceeds in nonlinear fashion, based on the immediate interests and characteristics of the reader (Reinking, 1997).

In addition, a reader can now interact with other readers and even the author of the text being read. A reader no longer has to wait for an author to respond to a letter or to conduct research at the library about a question that comes up. In many cases, a reader can e-mail the author to answer a question (if the author keeps up with e-mail!). Or, if the author is not available, with several keystrokes, the reader is able to find a community of readers via a bookselling site with whom to engage in some social networking revolving around the text. If there were ever a doubt that reading is a socially constructed activity, these characteristics of new media completely negate the stereotype of the lonely reader being "shushed" by the librarian. Though individualized, reading is becoming a truly social and interactive experience.

Linking In-School with Out-of-School Literacies

The literacies that students have access to outside of school are much different than they were even a decade ago. As adolescent learners develop their use of new literacies for personal and social purposes, there seems to be more of a gap between students' in-school literacies and their out-of-school literacies. For example, while students say that they always intend to read books on paper (Scholastic, 2008), there is a general tapering off of print-based reading frequency among adolescents, with an even larger decline in reading among boys, who report they read much less frequently as teenagers than they did as eight-year-olds (Scholastic, 2006). Historically, reading researchers have concentrated more attention on the cognitive side than the affective, motivational side of reading (Guthrie & Wigfield, 1997). This is why it is more critical than ever to continue to make curricular content more relevant, especially in the modes in which content is presented.

There is also an economic argument for using new literacies in the classroom: Helping students to learn with new literacies is part of making sure that they are prepared for life in the twenty-first century. The Pew Internet project reported that 73 percent of respondents (representing 147 million adults) are Internet users, and 55 percent of Americans have broadband access at home as of 2008 (Pew Internet and American Life Study, 2006, 2008). Moreover, the emphasis on new literacies does not necessarily have a negative impact on students' print literacy. Some studies have shown a link between using activities that involve nonprint-dominated materials and an increase in print literacy.

Using activities that involve visual art—another form of text in the classroom, such as the "sketch-to-stretch" activity—has been shown to further students' comprehension of print and learning in general (Bustle, 2004; Hibbing & Rankin-Erickson, 2003; Short, Harste, & Burke, 1996; Whitin, 2002). The sketch-to-stretch activity involves asking students to take a break from reading by stretching and then sketch what is being visualized while reading, thus linking print literacy with visual literacy. (See Chapter 9 for a detailed discussion.)

Many teachers are embracing new literacies, in combination with printed texts, as motivational tools in their classrooms; new literacies, in essence, become "the spoonful of sugar to help the print go down" (Kist, 2005). Read about Melissa's gradual journey into the use of new literacies and technologies in Voices from the Field (see Box 2.1).

BOX 2.1   **Voices from the Field**

Melissa, Secondary School English Teacher

Challenge

I know as a teacher it is essential for me to use new literacies and technologies in the classroom. In fact, I enjoy exploring the language of my learners and love the glimpse of excitement I see when they realize we are "doing something different." Planning creative lessons and activities targeting higher level thinking is generally a pleasant task in my sometimes endless teaching duties. The difficulty emerges in the application and front-loading stages that are required for implementing high-tech tools and technologies in the classroom. User names, passwords, and student codes can be over-whelming to acquire and distribute; computer carts and wireless server set-up almost guarantee off-task behaviors and frantic requests for help from the class techies who are wondering why I don't get it.

The logistics of implementing technology in the classroom can be daunting, but like any purposeful and effective teaching tool, it pays dividends in terms of student focus and retention. As a teacher who recently explored electronic portfolio development using student created websites, I can feel the pain of those educators who neither have the time nor the motivation to "upload" to the new method of teaching. However, projector use and PowerPoint presentations pale in comparison to student-focused programs that encourage a deeper learning than the paper-and-pencil

(continued)

BOX 2.1   (Continued)

world could ever image. Collaboration and experimentation are built-in perks of many educational technologies. Teaching with new technologies is worth it . . . but where to start?

Strategy

As a fellow educator who struggles fitting everything deemed "necessary" into my lessons, I've listed below some "strategies" I learned from my voyage into world of teaching with new technologies.

- Use your resources. I was introduced to the website creation site Weebly by the librarian at my school and found out about Glogster by trolling a colleagues' website set up for student use. Most teachers have some things they do really well—it just is hard to find the time to get together and share that knowledge. Making teacher (or staff) talk a priority can result in gained insight into new technology uses. Not only does this provide access to technology with support, but it also encourages cooperative lesson development and collaboration among professionals. Set aside twenty-five minutes every week to "research" educational websites, technology, and freebies that you can incorporate into your lessons. Sometimes this means I have a "working lunch," but it ultimately is worth the time when I see it results in student engagement and less classroom management issues.

- Explore before teaching. Prior to deciding on the Weebly site, I tried several other "easy" website creators. I quickly found that if it was not simple for me to learn, it would be a nightmare to try and teach students while expecting a focus on content and quality products. Unfortunately, many teachers don't have the luxury of "practice time"; utilize the technology as a means to an end and make the skills taught the focus of the journey. I used a Saturday morning to fool around with the technology I planned on pursuing and learned the basics so I could create an example that could be presented to students as a "gist"—a basic tangible product that helps them focus on the project/lesson

requirements. I also created a short "summary sheet" by copying and pasting from the Help or Frequently Asked Questions section that accompanied the technology I wanted to use. I also cited my references and showed my students how to avoid plagiarism. This freed their minds to critically think about the assignment, not the technology element.

- Don't stress. My students obtain my practiced level of knowledge usually within fifteen minutes of being introduced to the technology I'd like them to use. Many times, they even have previous experience with it outside of the classroom. Don't get caught up in the logistics—without a doubt, there are students in the room that are willing to help others who are struggling. If I got stuck, I worked with my students to troubleshoot, and in the process I modeled investigation skills and trial and error. Sometimes I didn't know how to do what the student intended. The problem would eventually work itself out through collaboration or the student was forced to think creatively around the obstacle. In addition, Google was always a helpful option—basic answers to my questions were many times only a search away, and I used the opportunity as a teachable moment regarding website reliability and validity.

- Start with a set up. If possible, set up a class list with student user names and passwords. Always obtain a list of student e-mails, as e-mails are frequently required for user accounts. Those students that don't have e-mails can easily set up an account for this purpose through a free site. In addition, many websites offer a free limited function educational version for teachers. In some cases, I had students register independently with a specific password so I could access their account if necessary and they could keep it after they moved on. Set up may also include taking the time to create a very basic example for student guidance. This is optional, though helpful because it may aid you in identifying those areas that will present your students problems. If you choose not to do this, make sure to keep some student samples to use for future classes. The great thing about the technology is that these will still be accessible long after the student has moved on. Embrace the learning process. The more I use technology, the more comfortable I become and the more understanding I have regarding what to avoid and what works the best. While teachers don't expect their students to be perfect at the start of a lesson, many educators frequently buy into perfection pressure for themselves. I started my technology trips with basic practices and easy swaps, and then focused on adding something different each marking period. After a while, most of my lessons included some element of technology and I was able to go back and increase the complexity rather than starting from scratch. The initial time spent paid off as I reworked lesson elements, and I didn't have to worry about becoming overwhelmed with new set ups for each new set of students.

Reflection

The use of technology creates layered learning that reaches students in a way that simple instruction and basic practice cannot. My venture into digital portfolios was well worth the time and effort expended. Not only did my students create, collaborate, and connect, but I also enjoyed more time-on-task teaching and less distracted behaviors. Technology implementation can be tough when there's not enough time to figure out what needs to be done. Making teaching with technology an area of exploration and enjoyment rather than another task that must be completed will benefit both students and teachers. It is no secret that teachers can get frustrated because their professional world and expectations are continuously changing; in the world of technology, this is an accepted and positive reality. Embracing digital teaching fully and with gusto was my way to overcome any negative expectations and I'm satisfied with the results.

New Literacies and Content Standards

Knowing how to use new literacies is integral to the strategic knowledge and skills that every student in all content areas will need to develop to be discipline-literate in the twenty-first century. The Common Core State Standards Initiative (2010, p. 7) highlights what is expected of students in today's technologically-driven society:

> Students employ technology thoughtfully to enhance their reading, writing, speaking, listening, and language use. They tailor their searches online to acquire useful information efficiently, and they integrate what they learn using technology with what they learn offline. They are familiar with the strengths and limitations of various technological tools and mediums and can select and use those best suited to their communication goals.

Practically all of the national education associations in the various academic disciplines have developed content standards or statements of principle that implicitly or explicitly acknowledge the use of technologies for information and communication. Actually, new literacies are embedded in more state and national standards than many people assume. Though the term *new literacies* is absent from most state standards within the United States, *media* and *media literacy* are more than likely mentioned. And as Baker (2009) points out, regardless of whether states use the term *media literacy* in their state standards, the topics related to media are present in many subject areas:

- Propaganda and persuasion
- The vocabulary of film and video

- Advertising and marketing
- Bias and objectivity

One of the more comprehensive set of standards for the proficient use of technologies in schools was developed in 2007 by the International Society for Technology in Education (ISTE). The ISTE standards revolve around several broad areas of strategic knowledge and skills: creativity and innovation; communication and collaboration; research and information fluency; critical thinking, problem-solving, and decision-making; digital citizenship; and technology operations and concepts. The standards for each of these areas are outlined in Box 2.2.

Recently the United States Department of Education (2010) published an executive summary of the National Education Technology Plan (NETP) entitled *Transforming American*

ISTE Educational Technology Standards for Students* — BOX 2.2

1. **Creativity and Innovation:** Students demonstrate creative thinking, construct knowledge, and develop innovative products and processes using technology.

   - Apply existing knowledge to generate new ideas, products, or processes
   - Create original works as a means of personal or group expression
   - Use models and simulations to explore complex systems and issues
   - Identify trends and forecast possibilities

2. **Communication and Collaboration:** Students use digital media and environments to communicate and work collaboratively, including at a distance, to support individual learning and contribute to the learning of others.

   - Interact, collaborate, and publish with peers, experts, or others employing a variety of digital environments and media
   - Communicate information and ideas effectively to multiple audiences using a variety of media and formats
   - Develop cultural understanding and global awareness by engaging with learners of other cultures
   - Contribute to project teams to produce original works or solve problems

3. **Research and Information Fluency:** Students apply digital tools to gather, evaluate, and use information.

   - Plan strategies to guide inquiry
   - Locate, organize, analyze, evaluate, synthesize, and ethically use information from a variety of sources and media
   - Evaluate and select information sources and digital tools based on the appropriateness to specific tasks
   - Process data and report results

4. **Critical Thinking, Problem Solving, and Decision Making:** Students use critical thinking skills to plan and conduct research, manage projects, solve problems, and make informed decisions using appropriate digital tools and resources.

   - Identify and define authentic problems and significant questions for investigation
   - Plan and manage activities to develop a solution or complete a project
   - Collect and analyze data to identify solutions and/or make informed decisions
   - Use multiple processes and diverse perspectives to explore alternative solutions

5. **Digital Citizenship:** Students understand human, cultural, and societal issues related to technology and practice legal and ethical behavior.

- Advocate and practice safe, legal, and responsible use of information and technology
- Exhibit a positive attitude toward using technology that supports collaboration, learning, and productivity
- Demonstrate personal responsibility for lifelong learning
- Exhibit leadership for digital citizenship

6. Technology Operations and Concepts: Students demonstrate a sound understanding of technology concepts, systems, and operations.

- Understand and use technology systems
- Select and use applications effectively and productively
- Troubleshoot systems and applications
- Transfer current knowledge to learning of new technologies

*Excerpted from ISTE's Educational Technology Standards for Students, by the International Society for Technology in Education, 2007, Washington, DC: retrieved April 13, 2012, from http://www.iste.org/Libraries/PDFs/NETS-S_Standards.sflb.ashx.

Education: Learning Powered by Technology. The NRPT outlines five goals and goal-specific recommendations to transform education in America through technology. The goals of NEPT revolve around learning, assessment, teaching, a comprehensive infrastructure to improve learning, and student productivity. The goal for learning in all content areas is particularly germane to this chapter: "All learners will have engaging and empowering learning experiences both in and out of school that prepare them to be active, creative, knowledgeable, and ethical participants in our globally networked society (NEPT, 2010, p. 14)." *Engage* and *empower* are the key words for teaching students how to learn with new technologies and new literacies in the twenty-first century.

 Engage and Empower Learning: Getting Started

The Internet is quickly changing the way we think, inquire, communicate, read, and write. This revolutionary way of communicating includes elements of print, visual art, sound, motion pictures, and advertising. Based on a review of new literacies research and a long-term study of classrooms that are embracing new literacies, Kist (2003, 2005, 2007a) has proposed some characteristics of new literacies classrooms:

- New literacies classrooms feature daily work in multiple forms of representation.
- In new literacies classrooms, there are explicit discussions of the merits of using certain symbol systems in certain situations with much choice.
- In new literacies classrooms, there are meta-dialogues, such as think-alouds, by teachers who model working through problems using certain symbol systems.
- In new literacies classrooms, students take part in a mix of individual and collaborative activities.
- New literacies classrooms are places of student engagement in which students report achieving a "flow" state.

There are numerous instructional tools and strategies for using new literacies in content area classrooms. Given the multiplicity of possibilities for online learning, it is reasonable for a teacher to ask, "Where do I begin?" A good starting point is to demonstrate to students how to think critically in a multimodal environment.

Model How to Think and Learn in Multimodal Environments

Most students probably are well aware of the basic conventions of the Web such as the idea of clicking on a link and going to another website. However, one of the most helpful discussions to have with students is to simply have them discuss the differences in thinking and learning about a multimodal text versus reading to learn in a print-based environment. A good way to get the discussion going is to model a typical (that is to say, nonlinear) reading progression on the Internet.

If a student wants to find out about space exploration in the United States, for example, he or she can access NASA's website on the Internet. Within that site, one might click on "Space Shuttle" to inquire into the future of the space program now that the space shuttle mission officially ended in 2012. Click on to various links to find out what the shuttles "will do in retirement" or "what's next" for NASA. You can also click on to a link for a brief overview and history of the space program or digress to videoclips on NASA Television. Later, the reader might click on the "current opportunities" link to find out about many of the lectures and educational projects that NASA offers to students at various grade levels.

The concepts of *hypertext* and *hypermedia* are crucial to understanding the interactions between reader and text in a multimodal environment. Hypertext differs from printed text in that its structure is much less linear. The hypertext format offers a "web" of text that allows the reader to link to other related documents and resources on demand. When sound, graphics, photographs, video, and other nonprint media are incorporated into the hypertext format, the electronic environment is called "hypermedia."

From an instructional perspective, the branching options offered in hypertext and hypermedia serve two important functions: to scaffold students' learning experiences and to enhance and extend thinking. For readers who may struggle with text or with difficult concepts, the resources available on demand in a hypertext environment include pronunciations, definitions, and explanations of keywords and terms, audio versions of the text, video recordings, video files, photographs, graphics, interactive exercises, and student-centered projects.

One of the most profound ways of getting students to fully realize the interactivity of the Web is to give them practice in writing this way, by insisting that they embed hyperlinks in their writing. To get started, students can look at examples of famous texts embedded with hyperlinks, such as the Magna Carta or the Declaration of Independence found at the site called "From Revolution to Reconstruction" (http://odur.let.rug.nl/~usa). Students can then take any text—an excerpt from a textbook or a novel—and type the excerpt into a word processing document, embedding the text with a certain number of hyperlinks. If, for instance, the text mentions Yosemite National Park, students could be shown how to turn the words "Yosemite National Park" into a hyperlink taking them to the official Yosemite site (www.nps.gov/yose). Once students have practice embedding their own writing with hyperlinks, a logical follow-up is a discussion prompted by such questions as: How is reading hypertext different from reading text in a book? How is writing with embedded hyperlinks different from writing with pencil and paper? What are some things that a writer can do when writing in a hypertext environment that can't be done when writing in a paper-based environment? What are the advantages and disadvantages of communicating in each environment?

Show Learners How to Evaluate Websites

Along with the benefits of interactive web texts come the risks of quality control. Because a hyperlink can take the reader to potentially untested sites, students need to be taught from an early age how to evaluate the links they come across and how to use them wisely. There are many models for helping students to search effectively online. Don Leu and his New Literacies Research Team at the University of Connecticut (www.newliteracies.uconn.edu) have come up with a framework for student practice that uses four different lenses when evaluating online resources: (1) examining what bias the site may contain; (2) determining how reliable the site is; (3) determining the accuracy of information on the site; and (4) synthesizing the information presented on the site in a meaningful way (see Figure 2.1).

Figure 2.1   A Framework for Critically Evaluating Websites

Bias and Stance

- Identify, evaluate, and recognize that all websites have an agenda, perspective, or bias.

- Identify and evaluate bias, given a website with a clear bias.

- Identify and evaluate the author of a website whenever visiting an important new site.

- Use information about the author of a site to evaluate how information will be biased at that site.

Reliability

- Investigate multiple sources to compare and contrast the reliability of information. Identify several markers that may affect reliability such as:

    Is this a commercial site?
    Is the author an authoritative source (e.g., professor, scientist, librarian, etc.)?
    Does the website have links that are broken?
    Does the information make sense?
    Does the author include links to other reliable websites?
    Does the website contain numerous typos?
    Does the URL provide any clues to reliability?
    Do the images or videos appear to be altered?

- Understand that Wikipedia is a reasonable, but imperfect, portal of information.

- Identify the general purpose of a website (entertainment, educational, commercial, persuasive, exchange of information, social, etc.).

- Identify the form of a website (e.g., blog, forum, advertisement, informational website, commercial website, government website, etc.) and use this information when considering reliability.

Accuracy

- Evaluate information based on the degree to which it is likely to be accurate by verifying and consulting alternative and/or especially reliable sources.

Synthesize Information

- Understand both the specific information related to the task as well as the broader context within which that information is located.

- Synthesize information from multiple media sources including written prose, audio, visual, video, and/or tables and graphs.

- Separate relevant information from irrelevant information.

- Organize information effectively.

- Manage multiple sources both on- and offline, including:

    Choose tools to meet the needs of managing information, including file folders, electronic file folders, notebooks, e-mail, and so on.
    Cite sources.
    Take notes with paper and pencil, when appropriate.
    Take notes with a word processor, when appropriate.
    Type notes using shortcut strokes such as highlight/cut/copy/paste.

Source: Leu, D.J., Coiro, J., Castek, J., Hartman, D.K., Henry, L.A., & Reinking, D. (2008). Research on instruction and assessment in the new literacies of online reading comprehension. In C.C. Block, S. Parris, & P. Afflerbach (Eds.), *Comprehension instruction: Research-based best practices.* New York: Guilford Press. Reprinted by permission of Guilford Press.

An entertaining and instructive way to help students see how easily readers of the Internet can be misled is to show them some of the well-known hoax sites, such as the MalePregnancy site that purports to follow a man through the first recorded male pregnancy. Students can list and discuss design elements of the hoax sites that make them seem as if they are presenting legitimate information. The following hoax sites can be used to teach students the principle that not all sites that appear to be valid are in fact valid:

- Male Pregnancy: www.malepregnancy.com
- Dihydrogen Monoxide: www.dhmo.org
- McWhortle Enterprises, Inc.: www.mcwhortle.com
- Northwest Tree Octopus: http://zapatopi.net/treeoctopus

BOX 2.3   # RTI for Struggling Adolescent Learners

Strategy Intervention and New Literacies

RTI strategy interventions in Tier 1 and Tier 2 should capitalize on students' use of new literacies. Offering struggling adolescent readers an opportunity to interact with electronic text may lead to greater motivation and engagement in literacy activities. The novelty and variety of using multiple media in the classroom may attract students to reading who had long ago given up the pursuit. Technology, as we'll learn about in this chapter, has created a wealth of new opportunities for learning and has influenced how content area teachers implement instruction. Yet teachers must go beyond incorporating technology into lessons. Adolescent learners facing academic challenges must be taught how to navigate their own learning and think critically while interacting with these resources.

Computers and other electronic devices are both a "facilitator of knowledge and medium for literacy" (Biancarosa & Snow, 2004). Technology allows teachers to plan higher levels of differentiation and to meet the academic needs of a greater number of students during instruction. Electronic databases, such as EBSCO, provide middle and high school students a wealth of information at various degrees of reading difficulty, allowing teachers to find multiple texts related to course content.

For example, EBSCO has created The Student Research Center, a search interface designed specifically for middle and high school students. The Student Research Center provides adolescent learners with appropriate research tools for easily obtaining the information that they seek from EBSCO databases, including electronic magazines, newspapers, biographies, film, and video. Students can also search databases by topic and limit their searches according to appropriate *lexile reading levels* (see Chapter 4 for a discussion of lexile reading levels and other tools for determining the readability or difficulty level of texts).

Through the use of electronic texts, content area teachers can create flexible groups within their classes that allow all students access to text appropriate to their needs and relevant to course objectives. In addition, interactive computer programs, such as PLATO and Academy of Reading, adapt to a student's reading performance by providing text passages that are written at a level consistent with the student's needs. Doing so increases the comprehensibility of the text for the student. Additionally, such programs provide students with immediate feedback on assignments and allow teachers to track student progress towards goals outlined in intervention plans. Some programs that include voice recognition software allow students to record themselves while reading so that miscues can be tracked and appropriate feedback provided. These resources can be useful for providing students with multiple interactions with texts and for offering independent practice (Biancarosa & Snow, 2004).

Strategies for Writing to Learn

Writing is an essential tool in a new literacies classroom. Many of the instructional strategies associated with multimodal learning feature writing in one form or another. As we explain in Chapter 9, writing to learn is an essential component of literacy and learning across all disciplines because students are often expected to represent their knowledge through writing. What makes the new literacies applications different is that the concept of "writing" has expanded to include creating nonprint representations of knowledge, and the texts themselves may be shaped collaboratively over time and distance.

There are many applications for writing with multiple representations of text. Allowing students to represent the content in a Microsoft PowerPoint presentation is one type of writing activity that allows them to think about core ideas and concepts. However, with new literacies, students have at their command the ability to think and learn with content not only using print but also graphics, sound, and video. A common project, for example, in social studies classrooms is to have students do research on local histories, videotaping local participants in historical events, and then uploading their memories to a website devoted to this project. If students are not able to collect their own primary source documents, they can go online to such sites as the Library of Congress's American Memory Project (http://memory.loc.gov/ammem/amhome.html).

Two examples of local history projects can be found at the following websites:

Mound Builder Indians

Charles Russell Elementary, Ashland, Kentucky

http://library.thinkquest.org/CR0212160

Social History of Beverly Public Schools

Beverly High School, Beverly, Massachusetts

www.primaryresearch.org/PRTHB/schoolhistory/about.php

For additional ideas and lessons for multimodal writing, explore the websites in Figure 2.2.

Figure 2.2   Related Read/Write/Think Lesson Plans

These lesson plans elaborate on ideas suggested in this chapter. Read/Write/Think is a joint project of the International Reading Association and the National Council of Teachers of English. See www.readwritethink.org/index.asp for more ideas.

Annotating Poems with Hyperlinks
www.readwritethink.org/lessons/lesson_view.asp?id=36

Blogging About Utopian Societies
www.readwritethink.org/lessons/lesson_view.asp?id=942

Critical Media Literacy: Commercial Advertising
www.readwritethink.org/lessons/lesson_view.asp?id=97

Conducting Collaborative Internet Research: Harlem Renaissance
www.readwritethink.org/lessons/lesson_view.asp?id=252

Examining the Content of Internet Sites
www.readwritethink.org/lessons/lesson_view.asp?id=29

Using Wikis to Catalog Protest Songs
www.readwritethink.org/lessons/lesson_view.asp?id=979

Although we live in a new media age, some educators are concerned that we will lose "book knowledge" as a society; that today's students are so tuned into their mobile phones, iPods, and laptops, they won't know how to speak, write, or read anymore. It's clear, however, that what many people are doing on their digital devices is a form of reading and writing and that these new literacies are shaping our communication in ways we never could have envisioned just twenty years ago. As researchers at the Pew Internet and American Life Project report in their ground-breaking study, *Writing, Technology and Teens*:

> Most teenagers spend a considerable amount of their life composing text, but they do not think that a lot of the material they create electronically is *real* writing. The act of exchanging e-mails, instant messages, texts, and social network posts is communication that carries the same weight to teens as phone calls and between-class hallway greetings. (Lenhart, Arafeh, Smith, & Macgill, 2008, p. i)

Using a combination of focus groups from various regions of the United States and telephone surveys, the Pew research team documented many interesting phenomena about adolescents' personal identities in relation to technology and writing. The role of digital technologies in the lives of adolescents is quite evident in these findings: 75 percent of teens have a cell phone, 93 percent use the Internet, 68 percent of online teens use instant messaging, and nearly 75 percent have created content for the Internet. Figure 2.3 summarizes the Pew findings.

It seems that many educators around the world are indeed realizing the potential of new reading and writing forms. Whether or not we embrace these new forms, the screen-based

Figure 2.3   Writing, Technology, and Teens: Summary of Findings

- Even though teens are heavily embedded in a tech-rich world, they do not believe that communication over the internet or text messaging is writing.
- The impact of technology on writing is hardly a frivolous issue because most believe that good writing is important to teens' future success.
- Teens are motivated to write by relevant topics, high expectations, an interested audience, and opportunities to write creatively.
- Writing for school is a nearly everyday activity for teens, but most assignments are short.
- Teens believe that the writing instruction they receive in school could be improved.
- Nonschool writing, while less common than school writing, is still widespread among teens.
- Multichannel teens and gadget owners do not write any more—or less—than their counterparts, but bloggers are more prolific.
- Teens more often write by hand for both out-of-school writing and school work.
- As tech-savvy as they are, teens do not believe that writing with computers makes a big difference in the quality of their writing.
- Parents are generally more positive than their teen children about the effect of computers and text-based communication tools on their child's writing.
- Teens enjoy nonschool writing and, to a lesser extent, the writing they do for school.

Source: Lenhart, A., Arafeh, S., Smith, A., & Rankin Macgill, A. (April 24, 2008). *Writing, Technology and Teens.* Washington, DC: Pew Internet & American Life Project. Retrieved May 2009, from www.pewinternet.org/~media/Files/Reports/2008/PIP_Writing_Report_FINAL3.pdf. Reprinted by permission.

society to which Kress (2003) referred is now upon us. Learners will need to have practice in navigating the rich sources of communication that are now available in greater abundance and in more alternative forms than ever before. Writing provides many opportunities to learn in a new literacies-centered classroom. Let's take a closer look at some of the communication tools that teachers can use to engage and empower writing to learn.

Threaded Discussions

A potentially powerful online writing to learn strategy makes use of a communication tool known as *threaded discussions*. Threaded discussions are designed to involve students in the exploration of texts and topics under study. In the process of doing so, learners are often engaged in problem solving, reflection, and critical thinking.

In a threaded discussion, small groups of students in a class are connected through a digital medium such as an Internet-based forum or discussion board. *Moodle, Google Groups, Mediawiki, PBWiki,* and *ThinkPad* are some of the more popular, free options that teachers have used for course management, forums, and discussions. Whatever software is used to establish a threaded discussion forum, it is important that the site used is secure and can be accessed only with a password. It should also be easy to navigate and have instructions on how to use and participate in discussions.

When used for instructional purposes, online discussions allow a teacher to post a question or topic for students to read about from various sources and reflect upon. Each small group usually gets a different question or topic for discussion. Within their small groups, learners then respond to the question with their own posts over time. The combined posts comprise a "thread" of conversation; hence the term *threaded discussion.*

Threaded Discussion Groups (TDGs) may be selected by the teacher or self-selected by the students themselves. Each learner in a TDG works individually to inquire into the topic (or respond to a question) and gather information using online and/or offline informational sources. In a literature class, for example, TDGs may be involved in a discussion of a short story or novel; in an American History class, TDGs may be gathering information online, from a textbook and/or supplementary texts in order to respond to a question posted by the teacher; in an eighth-grade science class, students may be studying global warming by searching for information on the Internet. Unlike a chat room where discussion is spontaneous and in real-time, threaded discussions are *asynchronous*; in other words, discussion is not simultaneous as in face-to-face exchanges among participants. Asynchronous threaded discussions allow students the time to search for and gather information as well as read, think, and reflect on the topic or question before responding. As Wolsey (2004, (p. 1)) noted,

> Through threaded discussion groups, students are allowed time to think about their responses . . . and to the comments of other students in the group. In a face-to-face discussion in the classroom, students must wait their turn to speak and do not have time for reflection; in the asynchronous environment of the TDG, students are free to explore the literature, their peers' responses, and their own experiences as they contribute to the discussion.

Within the framework of an asynchronous threaded discussion, a teacher can participate in every group and monitor several groups at once because discussions are not occurring in real time.

Netiquette in Online Discussions

The whole idea behind a threaded discussion is to be collaborative, not combative. Before beginning threaded discussions as a classroom activity, a teacher should review and emphasize the rules of *netiquette* when posting a response online. Netiquette—a "cyber word"—refers to the social code and rules of network communication. The term is derived from the words *network* and *etiquette*. When students are engaged in threaded discussions and other forms of online communication, it is imperative that they follow netiquette rules. First and foremost, they are to treat other students in a TDG with respect and courtesy. They shouldn't attack another student for his or her ideas. This is not to say they can't disagree with another's comments, but they should be respectful of the student who made them. Moreover, no one student should dominate a discussion with multiple posts.

Consider the following netiquette suggestions for student interactions in online forums adapted from Online Student Expectations (retrieved April 26, 2012):

* Respect the privacy of classmates and what they share.

* Ask for clarification if a posting is difficult to understand.

* Recognize that exposure to another group member's response and comments are part of the learning experience, even though you may personally disagree with the comments.

* Before posting a comment, ask whether you would make the same comment in a face-to-face discussion.

* Keep in mind that something that would be inappropriate in a face-to-face classroom discussion is also inappropriate in an online discussion.

Guidelines for Threaded Discussions

Planning instruction, a topic we discuss in detail in Chapter 5, is essential to the success of threaded discussions in the classroom. McVerry (2007) suggests following four stages of implementation which include: organizing the threaded discussion; modeling the skills students need to effectively post online; facilitating and managing the group discussions as they take place online; and assessing the quality of the students' posts. When organizing a threaded discussion, teachers need to ask themselves:

* What are the goals and objectives of the threaded discussion?

* What are the rules and conventions students should follow in making a post?

* How many posts will students be required to make? How long should a post be?

* Will each small group in the class receive the same question or different questions?

* How much choice should students have in how the discussion unfolds?

Providing explicit instruction that models what is expected of students when making posts online is another important instructional component that will help to insure the success of threaded discussions. Begin by walking students through the use of the technology needed to engage in discussions. Also show and discuss models of high quality posts from past classes. Once the threaded discussions begin, continue to model the process by participating in the TDGs with teacher posts that help facilitate the conversations occurring among students.

Facilitating the TDGs is especially important, especially if learners lack confidence, are unsure of themselves, or do not participate fully in the discussions. Some students may lack prior knowledge or interest in the subject under discussion. Others may fear being wrong or lack experience with online communication. Whatever the case, the teacher needs to guide and manage threaded discussions on an ongoing basis to ensure that learners participate successfully and are engaged in higher levels of thinking than merely regurgitating a fact or two.

Several well-established guidelines to facilitate TDGs are suggested below:

- Use one question or topic to begin a threaded discussion.
- Assign a different question or topic to each group in the class.
- Vary the writing approach for responding to questions. For example, learners can respond to topics with comments or opinions supported by text study, they can engage in role-play according to assigned roles, or they can raise reflective questions for further response and study.
- Lead the conversation in order to model effective posting, set the tone for discussion, and keep students focused on the topic.

Allow learners to disagree with a post in a collaborative, not combative manner. In addition to these suggestions, it is important to be specific with instructions. For example, you might instruct learners to respond to a posted question with a paragraph of at least five to eight sentences or more depending on the purpose of the discussion. Also, you might ask learners to respond to other student posts with a minimum of two or three sentences.

Assessing the quality of students' writings in a threaded discussion should be viewed as a culminating learning experience, not a paper-and-pencil test of students' ability to write in this particular medium. In other words, assessment is *authentic*. Engaging in authentic assessment, as we discuss in detail in Chapter 4, is a collaborative experience between teacher and students. The use of a *rubric* is one way to have students play a role in judging the quality of their writing and participation in a threaded discussion. A rubric provides students with a detailed framework and guidelines about what is expected of them in online discussions. As Edelstein and Edwards (2002, retrieved May 1, 2012) contend, a rubric not only evaluates student performance but also improves learning: "A well-written rubric can provide useful feedback regarding the effectiveness of a student's participation in threaded discussions and offer benchmarks against which to measure and document progress."

The design of the rubric depends on the instructional objective(s) for student engagement and learning in the threaded discussion. The teacher develops performance criteria that are directly tied to the lesson's objectives. Each criterion is then judged along several dimensions. Teachers use rubrics to rate student performance; however, students may also use a rubric as a self-assessment tool to improve performance. Figure 2.4 contains a sample rubric that covers the basic criteria for a threaded discussion.

Blogs, Wikis, and Nings

Readers frequently access information from "homemade" collaborative texts found online in the form of *blogs, wikis,* and *Nings*.

Blogs

Blogs, short for *weblogs,* are essentially online journals or diaries that are often personal accounts of life experiences. In many instances, blog readers rely on these stream-of-consciousness accounts for serious information, whether in regard to political races, social issues, or even

Figure 2.4   Rubric Example for a Threaded Discussion

Category	1	2	3	4
Participation and Timeliness	Does not respond to posts in a timely manner	Occasionally responds to posts in a timely manner	Frequently responds to posts within a 24-hour period	Consistently responds to posts within a 24-hour period
Relevance	Comments and opinions do not relate to discussion of content	Most posts are off topic or offer little insight into discussion content	Frequently posts comments related to topic and prompts further discussion of content	Consistently posts comments related to topic and prompts further discussion of content
Content Quality	Does not express ideas clearly; posts are not supported with specific ideas or examples	Minimal development of topic; posts are occasionally supported with specific ideas and examples	Posts are frequently supported with specific ideas and examples	Ideas fully developed and are consistently supported by ideas and examples
Writing Mechanics	Poor spelling and grammar in most posts; posts are hastily written with noticeable errors	Errors in spelling and grammar in some of posts	Few spelling or grammatical errors	Consistently uses grammatically correct language with correct spelling
TOTAL				
COMMENTS:				

weather conditions. Teachers are now assigning students to read preselected blogs related to class projects, make comments on the blogs, and then report back to the class, perhaps in the form of their own student blogs. A class can set up its own blog with space available for each student to have personal *blogspace*. Commonly used sites to host blogs are www.blogger.com and www.typepad.com.

Study how Heidi Whitus, an English teacher from Communication Arts High School, begins the year with a class activity that asks students to perform certain tasks related to media study and respond in the form of a blog (see Figure 2.5).

Blogs can be set up so that only members of the class can access them and only the blog owner can post entries. The teacher can be notified via e-mail each time an entry is posted or comment made so that appropriateness of content can be monitored. Teachers are

Figure 2.5 Heidi Whitus's Blog Assignment

Please do at least one of the following before December 4 and report on it in your blog:

	Advanced	Proficient	Partially Proficient	Not Proficient
Activity 1 Listen to the podcast of "On the Media" at least twice during the semester. You can subscribe to it from iTunes or go to www.onthemedia.org. Summarize the stories you heard on your blog. Be sure to make a note of the dates of the podcasts you listened to.	• More than two shows listened to • Detailed summaries and reflections of both stories • Dates included	• Two or more shows listened to • Summaries of both stories • Dates included	• Two shows listened to • Insufficient summaries of stories • Dates not included	• Fewer than two shows listened to • No summaries of stories • Dates not included
Activity 2 Read the San Antonio *Express-News* **and** a newspaper from another city on at least three different days. Compare the types of stories covered, the amount of advertising, and the kinds of feature stories ("soft" news) in the two papers.	• Read papers on more than three days • Detailed comparison and reflections of both papers	• Read papers on three days • Comparison of both papers	• Read papers on fewer than three days • Slight comparison of both papers	• Read papers on fewer than two days • No comparison of papers
Activity 3 Watch television news from at least three different channels (WOAI, KENS-5, KSAT, PBS, KABB are the local stations, and if you have cable you should also include CNN, FOX News and/or MSNBC); **compare** their approach to broadcast journalism by choosing a specific story and describing the differences in how the different channels cover the story.	• Watched more than three channels • Detailed comparison and reflections of all stories	• Watched three channels • Comparison of all stories	• Watched fewer than three channels • Slight comparison of stories	• Watched fewer than two channels • No comparison of stories
Activity 4 Watch at least two of the following movies about mass media outside of class, and summarize the films and your reflections of them in your blog:	• Watched more than two films • Detailed summaries of all films	• Watched two films • Summaries of both films	• Watched two films • Slight summaries of film	• Watched fewer than two films • No summaries of films

- *All the President's Men*
- *Broadcast News*
- *The China Syndrome*
- *Shattered Glass*
- *Network*
- *Good Night and Good Luck*
- *His Girl Friday*
- *Citizen Kane*

Source: Adapted from Kist, W. (2010). *The socially networked classroom: Teaching in the new media age.* Thousand Oaks, CA: Corwin Press.

using blogs for such functions as classroom management, learning logs and online note-books, class discussions, and, of course, personal expression (Echlin, 2007). When introducing blogs, it's important to establish guidelines for blogging such as those suggested in Figure 2.6.

An interesting blogging project called YouthVoices (http://youthvoices.net) attempts to bring together schools from around the world as students write blog entries and collaborate on various writing activities. The project represents a school-based social network that was started in 2003 by a group of teachers participating in the National Writing Project. Students are also allowed and encouraged to create their own groups about topics as diverse as rap music and world peace. As they communicate with each other online about their various topics of inquiry, students are expected to adhere to some simple but direct rules of conduct:

- Speak directly to the student or teacher whose post you are responding to
- Quote from the post or describe specific details (of an image or video)
- Relate the work to your own experiences or to another text, image, video, or audio that this one reminds you of
- Be encouraging and generous with your remarks; end on a positive note

Following these guidelines leads to a greater citizenship potential for students, as they will increasingly have to collaborate and interact with people online over the course of their lives.

Wikis and Nings

Wikis and Nings are more collaborative in nature, as readers seek to build knowledge on a specific topic and upload the text to a common environment. *Wiki* is a Hawaiian word meaning "fast" and has come to signify a collaboratively built text in which volunteers

Figure 2.6 Student Blogging Guidelines

1. Avoid inappropriate language. When engaging in online discussions of a classroom topic, comments should be related to the content of the post and should not involve gossiping, bullying, "chat talk," or non-content-related explanations or observations.

2. Blog posts should be respectful, constructive, on-topic, and add meaningful content to the online discussion. The goal of classroom-related blogging is to share knowledge of the topic and to advance the online discussion. Whenever possible, end a post with a question so that your readers will have something to think about as they prepare their responses.

3. Approach blogging as an activity that leads to a "published" piece of writing. Resist reacting to a

post without thinking about the topic first, what you already know about the topic, or what questions you might raise to advance the discussion. Then respond to the post, but also take the time to proofread, revise, and edit your comments before you submit them for others to read. Check also for correct spelling and grammar.

4. Avoid providing personal information, photos, or videos with your image in your blogs. Classroom-related sites for blogging may be open to the public to view. You never know who will read your posts.

5. Reply to all or most of your comments. Use references and resources, but do not plagiarize.

contribute facts and help to edit and shape the presentation of the information. Many teachers are using sites such as www.pbwiki.com or www.wikispaces.com to host wikis that they build with their students. Such wiki building can also serve to facilitate a discussion about the pitfalls (and advantages) of using wikis for information: When anyone and everyone can contribute information to a wiki, readers need to make sure the information being read is accurate.

Nings have come on strong since the startup of www.Ning.com in 2004. At this site, readers can join discussions on a growing number of topics and start a social network of their own, focusing on a common topic of interest. Nings are rapidly becoming sources of information for people interested in delving deeply into a topic. Nings and wikis can be set up to engage students with many different topics.

Social studies teacher Tom Daccord set up a wiki combined with a Ning to help students research the presidential race of 2008 as part of the Great Debate Wiki/Ning Project (www .greatdebate2008.wikispaces.com). This project was a collaboration of approximately ten schools across the United States. Students who never met each other face-to-face had the opportunity to collaboratively build a knowledge base about the presidential race and also to make persuasive arguments about their positions. They were assigned to research and collect information on topics related to the candidates' positions and then post them on the wiki. They began the project by exploring several presidential positions assigned by their teachers, but were also encouraged to inquire into other issues related to the candidates' positions. One group of students chose to research the issue of the death penalty, even though this was not a major issue in the presidential campaign. This topic, for whatever reason, generated much research and then much passionate debate, once students moved to the second part of the project. After the positions were thoroughly researched, students went to the Ning and participated and debated in the various forums according to the topics they had researched. The Ning was password-protected, so that only members of the classes involved could make comments.

The advantage of having students document their process via a blog, wiki, and/or Ning is that teachers and students have a running record of the journey taken. Moreover, a teacher has the ability to guide and redirect student thinking, if necessary, via a well-placed blog comment or comment in a Ning forum. The fact that the teacher's comment appears alongside the students' gives a clear visual representation that the teacher and students are colearners.

Strategies for Multimodal Learning

Showing students how to use strategies to think and learn in multimodal environments and participate in threaded discussions, blogs, wikis, and Nings is often initiated within the context of demonstration lessons known as Internet workshops. The Internet workshop allows teachers to model and demonstrate skills and strategies related to new literacies.

Internet Workshops

An Internet workshop is characterized by its flexibility. In some respects, it is similar in purpose to a writing workshop or a reading workshop in an English/language arts classroom (Atwell, 1998). In writing and reading workshops, teachers who use a workshop model in their classrooms set aside regularly scheduled time for students to engage in reading and writing activities. In the process of doing so, students share their reading and writing with others in the class, typically in small-group book discussions or writing response groups. During workshop time, teachers often conduct "minilessons" to respond to content- and process-related issues and problems students are having during reading or writing sessions. Minilessons may also be designed for strategy instruction. In these explicit instructional situations, a teacher may take several minutes or more of workshop time to show students how to use a set of procedures that will help them become more skillful as readers and writers.

Like reading and writing workshops, an Internet workshop provides an instructional framework for students, allowing for regularly scheduled time to engage in activity on the Internet. The activity may range from specific electronic text assignments to individual or group research to collaborative projects on the Internet. For example, a teacher might assign a website or several websites for students to visit. With younger learners, the websites are bookmarked in advance by the teacher so that the class has easy access to them. Students are directed to the website(s) to engage in a content literacy activity in much the same way as they would in a textbook or other print resources. Many of the content literacy activities in this book can be adapted for this purpose.

On other workshop occasions, students may work individually or in collaboration with one another on WebQuests, Internet inquiries, or Internet projects. These instructional strategies are much more extensive than specific assignments on the Internet and may take one to several weeks to accomplish. Regardless of the type of instructional focus, teachers should bring students together intermittently during workshops to share their work or to build strategic knowledge and skills related to the effective use of the Internet as a tool for learning. In these situations, workshop time is devoted to problems students are having searching for information or communicating with others. Internet workshops can also be designed around explicit strategy instruction. For example, a workshop might revolve around using search engines effectively, thinking critically about information, or designing a web page.

Internet Inquiries

The Internet inquiry engages students in research using information sources on the Internet. Inquiries can be conducted individually or collaboratively and often take one or more weeks to complete. Internet inquiries are typically part of larger thematic units and are used in conjunction with Internet workshops. The Internet inquiry broadly follows the tenets of a discovery model for investigating hypotheses or questions. Students are invited to (1) generate questions about a topic or theme under discussion in class, (2) search for information on the Internet to answer the questions, (3) analyze the information, (4) compose a report or some other form of dissemination related to findings, and (5) share findings with the whole class.

Question generation is one of the keys to conducting a successful Internet inquiry. Many teachers use the KWL strategy (what I **K**now, what I **W**ant to learn, and what I did **L**earn) (see Chapter 7) to help students raise questions. Others use brainstorming techniques to generate a list of questions. Whatever strategy is used for generating questions, the questions should come from the students rather than the teacher whenever possible. An Internet workshop minilesson might focus on asking good questions to guide the information search. A teacher may also use workshop time to scaffold instruction on how to use search engines effectively or how to record and analyze information through the use of "inquiry charts" (I-charts) and other tools for recording and analyzing findings (Hoffman, 1992; Randall,1996). In Chapter 5, we provide steps to guide the various phases of any type of inquiry or research investigation.

An Internet Inquiry in Elementary Science

Students in a third-grade elementary classroom have been engaged in a thematic unit related to the study of monarch butterflies. As part of the unit, the class developed a plan for raising monarch butterflies and visited several websites on the Internet related to specific workshop activities that the teacher had planned. The students also read trade books such as *Discovering Butterflies* by Douglas Florian, *Monarch Butterfly* by Gail Gibbons, and *Animal World: Butterflies* by Donna Bailey. As a result of these classroom learning experiences, the class embarked on an Internet inquiry designed around the students' "personal questions" regarding monarch butterflies. The class first brainstormed a list of questions that the teacher recorded on chart paper. Some of the questions included: Do monarch butterflies eat anything besides milkweed? Are monarch butterflies found all over the world? How long do monarch butterflies live? and How many eggs can one monarch butterfly lay? Using the list of questions on chart paper as a guide, each student selected three questions to research. The questions did not have to come from the brainstormed list but could be generated by students as they engaged in their information search on the Internet and from trade books that were available in the classroom.

The teacher conducted an Internet workshop on how to use the search engine Ask.com (www.ask.com). She also explained to students how to use I-charts to record information they found on individual websites or in trade books related to each of their questions. Across the top of the I-chart, each student recorded his or her name and a personal question about monarch butterflies. The remainder of the I-chart was divided into two columns. The left column provided space for a student to record the name of the website or trade book that was used to gather information. The right column was used to record information that students found to answer their questions. Across the bottom of the I-chart was space for students to record "new questions" based on their research.

When students completed their information searches, they collected their I-charts and began analyzing the information to answer their questions. The teacher facilitated the analysis by walking around the room, helping individuals as needs arose. Students used the analysis to create a poster portraying the answers to their questions. The inquiry culminated with a "poster session" in which students shared the information related to their questions.

Internet Projects

An Internet project involves collaborative approaches to learning on the Internet. Often students engage in project learning with other students who may be from different schools in different parts of the country or the world. Other types of projects may involve collaborative interactions between students and experts from various fields. For example, Internet projects are regularly posted on websites such as NASA Quest, where students have the opportunity to discuss space science and many other topics with one another and with NASA personnel.

Many Internet projects are designed by teachers as part of units of study. Advanced planning is essential for teacher-designed projects. Generally the following steps need to be considered:

- *Plan a project for an upcoming unit and write a project description.*
- *Post the project description and time line several months in advance* seeking classroom partnerships with other teachers.
- *Post the project at a location on the Internet where teachers advertise their projects,* such as Global SchoolNet's Internet Project Registry (www.gsn.org/pr/index.cfm).
- *Arrange collaboration details* with teachers in other classrooms who agree to participate.
- *Complete the project using Internet workshop sessions* for project-related activities and e-mail information exchanges with students and teachers in other classrooms involved in the project.

Leu, Leu, and Coiro (2006) provide numerous examples at different grade levels of Internet projects for various content areas that are posted on websites or have been designed by teachers.

WebQuests

WebQuests have become a popular instructional model for engaging learners on the Internet. A WebQuest is a teacher-designed web page that packages various learning tasks and activities for students to complete using Internet resources. WebQuests are typically organized around several components: introduction, task, process, resources, learning advice, and conclusion.

The introduction to a WebQuest provides an overview of the learning opportunity available to the students. Often the introduction places the learner(s) in a hypothetical situation somewhat similar to RAFT (**R**ole of the writer, **A**udience, **F**ormat, **T**opic)writing activities (see Chapter 9). As a result, students are assigned a role and a purpose for engaging in the learning activity. The task component of the WebQuest describes the task(s) students will complete and lists the questions that guide the information search. The process component outlines the steps and procedures students will follow to complete the learning task. The resources component of a WebQuest provides links to information resources on the Internet that students will need to access to complete the learning task. The "learning advice" component provides directions to students on how to organize information, whether in outlines, time lines, graphic organizers (see Chapter 10), notebook entries such as the double-entry journal format (see Chapter 5), or I-charts. And finally, the conclusion to the WebQuest brings closure to the activity and summarizes what students should have learned from participation in the WebQuest.

Looking Back Looking Forward

Digital texts and media are highly engaging and interactive. Hypertext and hypermedia make it possible to interact with text in ways not imaginable even a short while ago. Text learning opportunities in multimodal environments are interactive, enhance communication, engage students in multimedia, create opportunities for inquiry through information searches and retrieval, and support socially mediated learning. Reading and writing with computers has changed the way we think about literacy and learning. Whether students are navigating the Internet or interacting and collaborating with others through threaded discussions, blogs, Nings, and wikis, an array of electronic text learning experiences await them. Various instructional strategies, including Internet workshops, Internet inquiries, Internet projects, and WebQuests are approaches to online learning in various content areas.

In the next chapter, we take a closer look at one type of student who often struggles with content literacy tasks—the English learner. With every passing year, the United States becomes more linguistically and culturally diverse. English learners struggle with academic language and are often tracked in lower ability classes than language majority students. The dropout rate among English learners is alarmingly high. How can content area teachers plan instruction to account for cultural and linguistic differences in their classrooms? Let's read to find out.

Minds On

1. To what extent do you believe students should participate in the selection of documents from websites for use in a content course? Would you answer this question differently for students of various ages?

2. How often have you used digital texts as part of subject matter learning? In your estimation, did the teacher use a digital text assignment to its full potential? If not, in what additional ways might the digital text resource have been explored?

3. Why do many students seem to dislike doing research in a library but are enthusiastic about surfing the Internet for information resources?

4. What are the similarities between learning with new literacies and traditional print texts? What are the differences?

5. What are the barriers facing teachers who want to assign more projects involving new literacies? What are ways to overcome those barriers? Are the benefits worth the effort?

6. What are the challenges of assessing new literacy projects?

Hands On

1. Assign students to write an essay with embedded links. Look at some examples of hypertext such as any Wikipedia article or online text. Discuss with students what is different about writing in a hypertext environment versus a traditional pencil-and-paper environment.

2. Instead of a paper-and-pencil anticipation guide, set up a digital version, in which students e-mail you whether they disagree or agree with statements you have written that preview a text they will be reading. (See Chapter 6 for more details.)

3. Select a recent news event and conduct a search for information resources on the Web. Select several resources and compare them for treatment, reliability, and accuracy. What does it mean to develop a healthy skepticism when interacting with texts on the Web?

4. Using the keywords "Examples of WebQuests," conduct a search on the Internet for teacher-designed WebQuests in the content area of your choice. Evaluate three or four of the WebQuest websites. Based on your search, what are some of the strengths of a WebQuest instructional model? What are some of the weaknesses? Discuss the strengths and weaknesses of these WebQuests in a small group.

5. Search the Global SchoolNet's Internet Projects Registry or other locations similar to it for Internet project descriptions in your content area. Use these project descriptions to guide the development of a project description that you have in mind at a grade level of your choice. Share your project descriptions with others in your group.

eResources

Conduct an Internet inquiry of your own by going to Reading Online (**www.readingonline.org**) and Global SchoolNet's Internet Project Registry (**www.gsn.org/GSH/pr/index .cfm**). Study several reports and Internet projects in your content area.

Find out more about the WebQuest strategy by going to **http:// webquest.org/index.php**. Explore existing WebQuests and consider how you could create a WebQuest for your content area.

MyEducationLab™

Go to Topic 9: Integrating Technology, the MyEducationLab (**www.myeducationlab.com**) for *Content Area Reading*, where you can:

- Find learning outcomes for Integrating Technology, along with the national standards that connect to these outcomes.
- Complete Assignments and Activities that can help you more deeply understand the chapter content.
- Practice the core teaching skills identified in the chapter with the Building Teaching Skills and Dispositions learning units.
- Check your comprehension on the content covered in the chapter with the Study Plan. Here you will be able to take a chapter quiz, receive feedback on your answers, and then access Review, Practice, and Enrichment activities to enhance your understanding of chapter content.
- Visit A+RISE. A+RISE® Standards2Strategy™ is an innovative and interactive online resource that offers new teachers in grades K–12 just in time, research-based instructional strategies that meet the linguistic needs of English Language Learners (ELLs) as they learn content, differentiate instruction for all grades and abilities, and are aligned to Common Core Elementary Language Arts standards (for the literacy strategies) and to English language proficiency standards in World-Class Instructional Design and Assessment (WIDA), Texas, California, and Florida.
- Use the Online Lesson Plan Builder to practice lesson planning and integrating national and state standards into your planning.

3 Culturally Responsive Teaching in Diverse Classrooms

Teachers respond to linguistic and cultural differences by scaffolding instruction in culturally responsive classrooms.

Over the last several decades, political, social, and economic changes have brought an increasingly diverse group of students to U.S. schools from all across the globe. According to the recent census report, the Hispanic population accounted for over one-half of the nation's growth between 2000 and 2010. Similarly, while the 1960's student population was 80 percent Caucasian, today, non-Hispanic Caucasians make up only 57 percent of the U.S. student population (Calderson, Slavin, & Sanchez, 2011). The Common Core State Standards, discussed in Chapter 1, define rigorous skills and knowledge to be acquired by all learners regardless of their cultural or socioeconomic backgrounds. When it comes to teaching and learning with texts in diverse classrooms, we're all in the same boat, and the ship's captain—the teacher—is responsible for the welfare of everyone on board.

Different languages and cultures are gifts in our classrooms; they bring us fresh perspectives and vibrant new ideas that have the potential to animate classroom interactions. Yet teaching with texts is more challenging in today's classroom, where cultural and linguistic diversity has been increasing steadily. More often than not, students from different backgrounds struggle with literacy and learning in academic contexts. As a result, the strengths that they bring to instructional situations often go

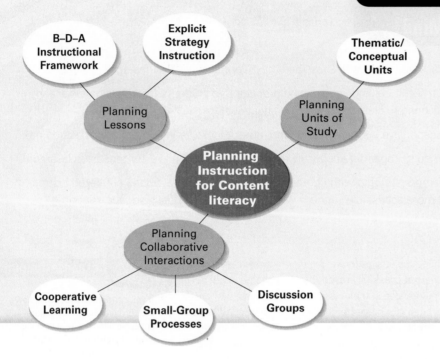

untapped. Literacy educator Lee Gunderson believes we need to make connections between the content that we teach and students' cultures and languages. This concept is often defined as *culturally responsive teaching* or *culturally relevant pedagogy*.

The increasing number of learners whose first language is one other than English demands literacy-related instruction that is strategic and culturally responsive, with high learning expectations for all students so that all students have access to opportunities that will support them in meeting the college and career reading standards emphasized in the Common Core State Standards. The current proposed blueprint for the reauthorization of the Elementary and Secondary Education Act, (U.S. Department of Education, 2010) emphasizes the importance of providing appropriate instruction, a challenging curriculum, and additional supports in order to meet diverse learner needs.

How can teachers be responsive to linguistic and cultural diversity in their classrooms while maintaining high standards for content literacy and learning? Understanding the cultural and linguistic differences between mainstream and nonmainstream learners is an important first step, as the organizing principle of this chapter suggests: Teachers respond to linguistic and cultural differences by scaffolding instruction in culturally responsive classrooms.

Frame of Mind

1. Why are today's classrooms more diverse than they were several decades ago?

2. What are some of the cultural and linguistic differences that students from various racial and ethnic backgrounds bring to classroom learning situations?

3. What is culturally responsive instruction and what does it look like in content area classrooms?

4. What can a teacher do to implement culturally responsive instruction in a content area classroom?

5. Why do English learners struggle with content literacy tasks, and how does sheltered instruction make content more accessible to them while providing additional language support?

The purpose of this chapter is straightforward enough: to help teachers successfully respond to linguistic and cultural differences in their classrooms and to promote academic achievement for all learners. In culturally responsive classrooms, teachers draw on students' backgrounds, languages, and experiences to make connections with the discipline-specific content under study. In doing so, students find that academic experiences are more meaningful in their lives, and therefore, they become more interested and focused on content area learning. This is not a simple process but one that occurs in small increments and through the use of a variety of strategies as teachers and students experience positive results.

Tim Fitzpatrick, a science teacher in an urban high school, captures the essence of culturally responsive instruction by "keeping it real" in his science classes. His voice is featured in Box 3.1. Cindy Hovis, an English language teacher in a rural school district, describes strategies she uses to help her students acquire subject area vocabulary needed for academic achievement. Her voice is featured in Box 3.4.

As diverse learners become more engaged, they are motivated to focus on topics, complete assignments, and contribute to the classroom community with thoughtful questions and appropriate comments (Izzo & Schmidt, 2006; Schmidt & Finkbeiner, 2006).

Response Journal

If you currently are teaching, how would you describe the cultural and linguistic differences of your students? If you are studying to be a teacher, describe the cultural and linguistic differences that existed in your school experiences.

BOX 3.1

Voices from the Field

Tim, High School Science Teacher

Tim Fitzpatrick has been teaching for twelve years in one of the most impoverished urban high schools in his state. More than 95 percent of the students receive free or reduced lunches and 50 percent are labeled as special education or English language learner (ELL). Students in Tim's school identify their cultural backgrounds as European American (10 percent), African American (25 percent), Latino (25 percent), Native American (5 percent), and racially mixed (10 percent). In addition, about 25 percent of the students claim China, Vietnam, Bangladesh, Nigeria, Thailand, Ghana, Sudan, Egypt, Kenya, or Zaire as their countries of origin.

Tim teaches several science courses, including a ninth-grade Survey of Sciences course, Biology, and Environmental Science. English learners are exclusively enrolled in the freshman survey course that includes introductions to chemistry, physics, biology, and earth science. Environmental Science is an elective for all seniors and deals with ecology, weather, and human effects on the natural world. Biology requires a state standardized test at the end of the school year. From Tim's perspective, "Science is a subject that may be easier to teach to ELL students than other content area courses. The sciences have their own languages, new to all of the students. We're also able to use many visuals and hands-on activities."

Keeping It Real

Tim's approach to instruction is culturally responsive: "I keep it real. I use a lot of common sense and dialogue with my students both in and out of the classroom. My student–teacher relationships are a number one priority. I respect my students and constantly ask them to explain to each other and to me. They'll learn more when they are comfortable and know that I care." Tim also communicates regularly with the English as second language (ESL) teacher, since many of his students have had little, if any, formal schooling in their countries of origin and have trouble reading or writing in their home languages. Early in the school year, he makes it a point to label all tools and equipment in the science lab in both English and the students' home languages so they can begin to identify them. Because he sees culture and language as inextricably intertwined, Tim has discovered that recognizing the students' home languages and writing them next to English words is an essential element in his class.

Moreover, Tim attempts to connect culture to content whenever it makes sense to do so:

> Biology is great for drawing upon my students' cultures because of genetics and the study of plant and animal life in their countries of origin. Studying world scientific problems in terms of cultural understandings, such as energy, immunities, birth control, uses and abuses of automobiles are all topics for great discussion and practice communicating. I took my classes to see the Ernie Davis movie *The Express* in the fall, and they were blown away by the racism. It made for great discussions in all of my science classes.

At the beginning of the school year, Tim's classes go through a modified version of the ABCs of Cultural Understanding and Communication in which students develop autobiographic sketches and share aspects of their life stories with one another (see Box 3.2 on page 65). According to Tim, the exercise is well worth the time:

> It takes one class period and students get the message that I welcome dialogue. Students are also encouraged to sit near a different person daily, so they can learn and develop as a learning community. I want them to express their informed opinions . . . not regurgitate facts.

As part of his instructional routines, Tim begins classes with a question for journal writing. For example, he reads a short passage regarding a man being attacked by a mountain lion, explains the meaning of predator and prey, and then asks the students to write about another example, possibly from their own experiences. They then share responses with one another. He also uses Microsoft PowerPoint presentations for

(continued)

BOX 3.1   (Continued)

lectures, designs word walls with technical vocabulary related to the content under study, and uses graphic organizers such as concept maps (see Chapter 8 for further explanations). In addition, Tim is selective about assigning text material to read. He only selects para-graph sections that are most important in text chapters and, if the text is too difficult, he will even rewrite material that is crucial for understanding core concepts.

So now we know what Tim means when he says, "I keep it real."

Most people, other than those who study culture, probably don't think much about what it means to be immersed in a culture, just as fish probably don't think much about what it means to be immersed in water. The term *culture* represents a complex and multidimensional concept at best. Culture has been defined by Peregoy and Boyle (2008) as the shared beliefs, values, and rule-governed patterns of behavior that define a group and are required for group membership. On one level are the surface features of a culture—its foods, dress, holidays, and celebrations. On another level are deeper elements, which include not only values and belief systems but also "family structures and child-rearing practices, language and non-verbal communication, expectations, gender roles, biases—all the fundamentals of life that affect learning" (Díaz-Rico & Weed, 2002, p. 197).

Language and culture are inextricably connected. Native speakers learn language in social settings, and in the process, they also learn their culture's norms for using language. As you might expect, different cultures have different rules that are always culturally defined and culturally specific. When a student's norms differ from the teacher's expectations, communication is often hindered. Because language use is culturally specific, it is easy for teachers not to recognize that language rules are indeed in effect for speakers of other dialects or speakers with different cultural norms for communicating.

Response Journal

Brainstorm a list of words and idiomatic expressions that are specific to a cultural group with whom you identify. Why would someone outside of your cultural group have difficulty understanding these words and expressions?

Culturally Relevant Pedagogy

The rapidly changing demography of the United States and its schools is transforming the country into a society that is increasingly *multicultural*. Guofang Li (2009), for example, explored the extent to which cultural and linguistic diversity prevails in today's classrooms as well as the conflicts and struggles of diverse learners trying to make sense of a curriculum dominated by mainstream European American cultures. Li's book *Multicultural Families, Home Literacies and Mainstream Schooling* provides a powerful lens for better understanding the lives and home practices of underrepresented students and their families.

In diverse classrooms, cultural and linguistic sensitivity is a crucial first step in working with students to meet academic strands. Developing and implementing culturally relevant instructional practices, require that other elements be considered. Brown-Jeffy and Cooper (2011) identify five essential themes in their framework for culturally relevant pedagogy:

1. Identity and achievement
2. Equity and excellence
3. Developmental appropriateness
4. Teaching the whole child
5. Student–teacher relationships

Identity and achievement considers the identity of both student and teacher. It invites teachers to consider the cultural lens through which they see themselves as well as the lens through which students view their own identities. Brown-Jeffy and Cooper (2011, p. 73) point out that, "Cultural awareness does not and should not include colorblindness or race-neutral policies." The home cultures of students should be acknowledged, valued and used as tool for learning.

Equity and excellence emphasizes that students have different learning needs. To be effective, teachers need to recognize that achieving equity doesn't mean that every student receives the same instruction or the same type of support. It means that each student receives what he or she needs in order to understand the concepts presented. Equity and excellence also encompasses the belief that the curriculum area content needs to make sense within those cultures represented in a classroom.

Brown-Jeffy and Cooper's theme of *developmental appropriateness* asks teachers to consider not only whether or not a concept or activity is appropriate for a student's developmental level, but also how the diversity of the student's culture might impact developmental appropriateness. In other words, teachers are encouraged to consider what might be considered culturally appropriate for students from diverse backgrounds.

Teaching the whole child is related to developmental appropriateness, but focuses more on home–school–community collaboration, and fostering a supportive learning community for students from diverse backgrounds. Family and community experiences shape the academic identity of students. Understanding these experiences and influences will help a teacher to be sensitive and responsive to diverse student needs.

Finally, *student–teacher relationships* focus on fostering a classroom atmosphere that communicates a message of genuine concern for individual students and effective interactions between teachers, students, and families.

Sensitivity to cultural and language differences, and a willingness to understand and respond to these differences, enables teachers to teach with greater effectiveness (Sharan, 2010). Similarly, teachers have found that allowing students to interact freely during class discussions is helpful in that it encourages them to explore ideas without the fear of having to speak perfect English. Doing so doesn't minimize the importance of learning Standard English, but rather, analogous to the writing process, it allows students from diverse backgrounds to have brainstorming and drafting time in their verbal interactions. Teaching for cultural understanding will also make a difference in the way diverse learners respond to instruction.

An example of culturally responsive instruction might be seen in how a teacher selects and uses text in his or her classroom. Kim, a middle school language arts teacher, divided her classroom library thematically so that it mirrored the topics she planned to cover in her class. For example, when she was teaching characterization, she created a section in her library that contained books, songs, poems, and graphic novels that provided examples of how writers create and develop characters. Students could then access examples of characterization that were appropriate for their individual reading level and that were of a genre and format of interest to them. In her library, Kim also created buckets of books based on the topics of interest that her students had noted in the reading interest inventory she had asked them to complete early in the school year. So, along with topics, such as characterization, that supported her lesson plans, she had buckets of resources on subjects such as soccer, music, warfare, and art, just to name a few. Her goal was to create a space where students would be motivated to access materials independently.

Teaching for cultural understanding will also make a difference in the way diverse learners respond to instruction.

Teaching for Cultural Understanding

Various instructional perspectives reflect different belief systems related to the teaching of multicultural concepts in today's classrooms. Diaz (2001) describes these perspectives within the context of four distinct instructional approaches. In the *contributions approach,* teachers typically emphasize culturally specific celebrations and holidays within the curriculum, such as Martin Luther King Day. The contributions approach reflects the surface level of a culture but does not make provisions for in-depth study of its deeper elements.

Somewhat related to the contributions approach is an instructional perspective that is additive in nature. The *additive approach* underscores the teaching of various themes related to multicultural concepts and issues. These concepts and issues are integrated into the curriculum through the development of a thematic unit of study, but on the whole the curriculum remains relatively the same throughout the year.

When teachers attempt to help students understand diverse ethnic and cultural perspectives by providing them with ongoing opportunities to read about concepts and events, make judgments about them, think critically, and generate their own conclusions and opinions, they are using a *transformative approach.* This approach, combined with the next one, lends itself well to content literacy strategies that emphasize critical analysis and interpretation. According to Diaz (2001), an extension of the transformative approach involves project learning. The *decision-making/social action approach* provides learners with opportunities to engage in activities and projects related to cultural concepts and issues, particularly those issues and problems dealing with social action.

Teachers need to go beyond limiting the content of instructional lessons to celebrations or one-time-only thematic units related to multicultural concepts. Today's teachers need to provide students with literacy and learning experiences that will provide them with the cross-cultural knowledge and skills they will need as future adults in a nation that has become increasingly diverse. Multicultural literature helps students develop cross-cultural knowledge and skills.

One model used to help teachers become more culturally aware and sensitive to those from diverse backgrounds and experiences is the ABCs of Cultural Understanding and Communication (Schmidt, 1998, 1999b, 2000, 2001, 2003, 2005a,b). Teachers who participate in this process have also adapted the model for their own classrooms. Their students learn to appreciate the differences around them and classrooms become learning communities, a reality often difficult to create in secondary classrooms. Box 3.2 briefly explains the model.

After completing the ABCs model's first four steps, teachers design lesson plans for connecting home, school, and community for children's reading, writing, listening, speaking, and viewing based on numerous modifications of the model. They see ways to develop collaborative relationships with families in an atmosphere of mutual respect, so that students gain the most from their education.

Evidence-Based Best Practices   BOX 3.2

ABCs of Cultural Understanding and Communication

1. Students write their autobiographies, starting with their earliest memories of family traditions, religion, education, victories, defeats, and so forth. The life stories are shared only with the instructor, so personal information may be confidentially included.

2. Teachers interview parents or family members of students who are culturally different from themselves. This occurs on neutral ground, usually not at school. They interview at a local coffee shop, park, or community center. A student's home is also acceptable if the teacher is willing to visit. The teacher begins by asking the family member what he or she would like to see happen in school for the student. The teacher attempts to discover student interests and routines outside of school. The teacher also shares his or her own life experiences at appropriate times during the interview.

3. The teacher then creates a chart comparing and contrasting the life of the family member and the life of himself or herself (the teacher).

4. Next, the teacher analyzes the differences. He or she writes why certain differences are admired and why certain differences make one feel uncomfortable. The purpose of this exercise is to examine one's own culture in relation to the culture of the person interviewed. This helps develop an awareness of ethnocentricity, the idea that your own culture guides your existence.

5. Finally, the teacher begins to make connections by studying the curriculum and exploring ways to make studies meaningful to specific students and their families and communities. Inviting a mother and her new baby into the classroom to discuss human development may be one way to bring relevance to learning. Inviting a new arrival from Puerto Rico to teach a song or dance to the class and discuss the island's geography is another way to include differences. Inviting a carpenter to discuss house framing when students study trigonometry connects school and community in positive, memorable ways.

The ideas depicted in Box 3.2 may be adapted in any content area and are usually implemented at the beginning of a course of study or the school year. Students create lifeline stories depicting key events; interview each other; compare and contrast life stories of famous mathematicians, scientists, and politicians; and use the Internet to explore the reasons for cultural differences related to geography and architecture.

The ABCs of Cultural Understanding and Communication helps teachers learn about family and community values and shows them how to value communities and families.

Integrating Multicultural Literature Across the Curriculum

When teachers use multicultural literature in the classroom, they provide students with texts that not only are engaging but also recognize the unique contributions of each culture and the similarities of the human experience across cultures. At the same time, they help nonmainstream cultures appreciate and value their heritage and give all students the benefits of understanding ways of knowing about the world that are different from their own. Choosing multicultural texts to integrate into the curriculum is no easy task. When selecting multicultural literature Louie (2006) offers the following suggestions for effective teaching practices:

- Consider whether or not the story is an authentic depiction of the culture it intends to represent.
- Consider the perspectives of the diverse characters in the story.
- Identify the characters' perspectives of events and conflicts.
- Encourage students to relate their own experiences to those portrayed in the text.
- Identify values that shape the conflict-resolution strategies used by characters. Discuss how cultural mores and expectations may have influenced a character's decisions and viewpoints.

Multicultural Books: A Closer Look

Multicultural books encompass every genre, including picture books, poetry, fiction, and nonfiction. A defining characteristic of multicultural books is their focus on people of color. These books provide diverse students with rich opportunities not only to see themselves reflected in the books they read but also to appreciate and celebrate the experiences of people of color from the past. As such, multicultural books also provide mainstream students with opportunities to learn about other cultures and peoples. For example, Suzanne Fisher Staples's (1991) *Shabanu: Daughter of the Wind* draws readers into the life of a girl growing up among camel-trading nomads in modern Pakistan. Similarly, Linda Crew's (1991) *Children of the River* portrays the challenges faced by Cambodian immigrants as they work to assimilate into the American culture.

Such books can help students understand cultural norms related to family, morality, sex roles, dress, and values of other cultures. Most importantly, however, multicultural literature brings the people of a particular group into focus and can help students realize that in spite of our differences all people share many common emotions, dreams, and hopes for the future. Through interactions with characters representing a variety of cultures, young people begin to view members of parallel cultures as individuals who are unique, and yet have universal feelings and experiences. Pam Muñoz Ryan's (2000) *Esperanza Rising* is a wonderful coming-of-age novel focused on a "riches to rags" story of a wealthy young Mexican girl and her mother who end up becoming migrant workers in the fields of California. The book is based on the real-life experiences of the author's grandmother. Teenagers can relate to it because it tells a story of identity and family—common themes in all of our lives.

Multicultural books portray members of a wide variety of cultures including African and African American, Asian and Asian American, Native American, Latino, and so on. It is important to note that there is a difference between being Mexican and being Mexican American. When selecting multicultural books for the classroom, teachers must differentiate between these groups. For example, a Mexican person living in Mexico has remarkably different experiences from a Mexican American person living in the United States. Teachers cannot assume, for example, that a modern Mexican American child will be able to relate to a book about Mexico.

Studying the folklore of diverse cultures is a common practice in schools, especially in the lower grades; however, the protagonists of many folktales are adolescents who have much to say to today's young adults. The human dimension of slavery is powerfully told, for example, in Virginia Hamilton's *The People Could Fly* (1985); true multicultural understanding is also enhanced by her compilation of creation myths entitled *In the Beginning* (1988). A host of folktale collections from around the world can add insight to the study of history, social studies, and geography. Folk literature is the "cement" or "mirror" of society (Sutherland & Arbuthnot, 1986, p. 163), and thus gives readers an insider's view of a culture's beliefs and attitudes that is not typically found in textbooks. That said, scholars of multicultural literature such as Cai (1994) caution against using folktales exclusively, a practice that can perpetuate perceptions of exoticism and otherness. Ideally, folktales are typically studied in conjunction with contemporary, realistic depictions of the cultures in question. For example, it would be ideal to pair a substantial library of Chinese folktales about Mulan with more contemporary stories about Chinese American females such as Grace Lin's (2007) *The Year of the Dog* and/or Joyce Lee Wong's (2007) *Seeing Emily*. Historical fiction can provide a lens into the challenges and perspectives of diverse cultures. Gary Paulsen's (1995) *Nightjohn* chronicles the perils faced by a slave who secretly teaches other slaves to read. The story encourages students to consider the empowering potential of the ability to read for both of the characters in the story and for themselves. Similarly, in Helen Hughes Vick's (1998) *Walker of Time,* a Hopi Indian boy goes back in time to view the life from the perspective of the ancients.

Many students in today's ethnically diverse urban classrooms prefer books about young people living in challenging circumstances that may parallel their own experiences. These titles describe teens' personal struggles with drugs, gangs, abuse, and similar issues. Many urban students feel a strong connection with characters in these books, for whom daily survival in today's world is often a challenge. Short story anthologies like *Big City Cool: Short Stories About Urban Youth* (Weiss & Weiss, 2002) contain selections by Walter Dean Myers, Amy Tan, and other authors familiar with what it means to grow up in urban America. Jeffery Canada's (2010) *Fist, Stick, Knife, Gun* chronicles the author's own experiences growing up in the South Bronx and learning the codes of the street. The book provides a vivid depiction of the violence encountered on these urban streets, and offers a glimpse into the inner conflict experiences by those who navigate them.

Fran Buss' (2002) *Journey of the Sparrows* depicts the terrifying journey of Salvadorian immigrants as they seek to cross the U.S. border. The memoir *Always Running: La Vida Loca: Gang Days in L.A.* (Rodriguez, 1993) is what high school teacher Carol Jago calls a "disappearing book"—a book that mysteriously leaves the shelves of her classroom library and seldom returns, which is a clear indicator of its popularity. *Always Running* is the controversial memoir of Luis Rodriguez's life in a gang, which was written in an effort to get his son to leave gang life and create a different future for himself. Other factual books of interest to urban students include Loung Ung's (2000) *First They Killed My Father: A Daughter of Cambodia Remembers*, which graphically portrays one family's struggle to survive the horrors of the Khmer Rouge in Cambodia. In *Voices from the Fields: Children of Migrant Farm Workers Tell Their Stories* (Atkin, 1993), ten Mexican American children of migrant farmworkers describe their lives in their own words. One of the young people featured is a gang member, one an unmarried teenage mother, and one is making plans to attend college and become a physician. The author portrays the uncertainty of their lives, at the same time recognizing the strong bonds that bind these young people to their families.

Research suggests that despite the availability of high-quality and interesting multicultural books, many teachers are not using these books to full advantage. Teachers often cite lack of time and knowledge about these books as reasons for limiting their use (Loh, 2006). Because of the canon or other required readings dictated by the school district, teachers sometimes report that they do not have time or opportunity to expose their students to multicultural books that fall outside of the prescribed curricula.

According to Wills and Mehan (1996), however, diverse experiences need to be viewed as part of the American narrative, not as a separate entity. For example, when teaching a unit on World War II, teachers should also include texts about the Japanese internment such as *Looking Like the Enemy: My Story of Imprisonment in Japanese American Internment Camps* (Gruenewald, 2005) and texts about African American women during this time such as *Bitter Fruit: African American Women in World War II* (Honey, 1999). Considering and studying multiple perspectives about any given topic and/or unit only enhances and deepens the content and cultural knowledge; in this way the lives of our students are further enriched.

To learn more about the many resources for identifying multicultural books for students, teachers can refer to lists and guides developed by the Cooperative Children's Book Center, the North Central Regional Education Laboratory, the American Library Association, and so on. Other sources include magazines such as *BookList, School Library Journal, Kirkus Review,* and the *Horn Book Magazine.* Lastly, teachers can consider books that have won awards such as the Asian/Pacific American Award for Literature, the International Board on Books for Young People (IBBY) Honour List, the Pura Belpre Award, and the Coretta Scott King Award, among others.

Teachers report that they often fear offending other cultures by choosing the "wrong" book. For this reason, some teachers opt out of using multicultural books altogether (Loh, 2006; Bishop, 2003). The resources mentioned above can help teachers select appropriate multicultural books with confidence and avoid the temptation to ignore diversity in our classroom libraries and in our curricula and instruction.

Ways of Knowing in a Culturally Responsive Classroom

It is crucially important to be aware that students from diverse cultural backgrounds bring different ways of knowing, different styles of questioning, and different patterns of interaction to school. For example, different cultures may have different attitudes, expectations, and assumptions about the value of reading and writing and what it means to be a reader and writer. Alicia, a Latina student, didn't want to be a "schoolgirl." To be a schoolgirl meant always having her head in a book, always doing homework. However, Alicia had little trouble getting involved in school activities that revolved around meaningful, collaborative, literacy activities, such as tutoring younger students and writing social studies texts for them (Heath & Mangiola, 1989).

Different cultures may place a different emphasis and value on various cognitive activities and styles of questioning. Some societies, for example, emphasize memorization and analytical thinking over the ability to experiment or to make predictions (Fillmore, 1981). The cognitive styles of culturally diverse students may differ. Heath (1983) discovered that African American students experienced academic difficulty in their classrooms partly because of their lack of familiarity with the kinds of questions they were expected to answer in school. For example, based on family interaction patterns in the African American community that she studied, Heath found that students were not familiar with school questions asking them to describe or identify the attributes of objects or concepts. The students were much more familiar with analogy-type questions comparing one object or concept with another. When teachers became aware of the differences between the kinds of questions they asked and the kinds of questions familiar to the students, they were able to make adjustments in their questioning style. As a result, the teachers noticed a marked contrast in their students' participation and interest in lessons.

Ways of knowing are intertwined with ways of interacting and learning. Rather than emphasize individual competition, some cultural groups prize group interaction, helping one another, and collaborative activity. Reyes and Molner (1991), for example, suggest that cooperative learning is more "culturally congruent" with students from Mexican American backgrounds. The research support for cooperative classroom strategies, especially in diverse learning situations, is impressive (Little Soldier, 1989; Slavin, 1987).

Many students from diverse linguistic and cultural backgrounds are discriminated against not only because of race and language but also because of their struggles to exist in high-poverty areas. The daily struggles to survive in poverty also yield funds of knowledge that are often overlooked in schools. It is each teacher's responsibility to develop relationships that nourish trust. By seriously drawing on students' interests and popular culture, teachers can make connections that demonstrate a respect for students' lives (Payne, 2003; Schmidt, 2005a; Schmidt & Lazar, 2011).

When teaching for linguistic and cultural diversity, motivational activities are based on the same principles as those learned for any successful teaching and learning situation. Teachers must draw on students' prior knowledge and interests. Therefore, family and community cultures and languages, popular culture, and individual student interests are all necessary considerations when motivating students for learning. Teachers differentiate instruction and plan for the inclusion of relevant information in their content areas. Ideas interspersed throughout this book will demonstrate and expound on these motivational principles for engaging diverse groups of students in content area classrooms.

Funds of Knowledge

The powerful role that culture plays in shaping students' behaviors and their knowledge of the world often goes unnoticed in classrooms. The concept of *funds of knowledge* provides a framework to recognize a student's interests and the background knowledge that they bring to content area concepts (Hedges, Cullen, & Jordon, 2011). Convincing students that their experiences are recognized and valued as they approach new learning situations is particularly challenging when "culturally inherited ways of knowing do not match those privileged in the school curriculum" (Zipin, 2009, p. 317).

Response Journal

Think about the funds of knowledge that you possess based on your cultural background and heritage. Describe how you make use (or will make use) of such knowledge in your teaching.

Understanding the sociocultural dynamics of home and community gives us a broader perspective on the worldviews students bring to school. Culturally and linguistically diverse students typically come from working-class families where their individual lives are inseparable from the social dynamics of the household and community in which they live. A teacher who makes a point of understanding the home culture, ethnic background, and community of students is in a better position (1) to understand the kinds of knowledge that culturally diverse students bring to learning situations and (2) to adjust the curriculum to their sociocultural strengths.

Luis Moll (1994) contends that much is to be gained from understanding the "social networks" of the households in a cultural group. These networks are crucial to families, who often engage in exchanging "funds of knowledge." These funds of knowledge may represent occupationally related skills and information that families share with one another as a means of economic survival. Moll argues that the social and cultural resources that students bring to school—their funds of knowledge—are rarely tapped in classroom learning contexts. Using the community's rich resources and funds of knowledge builds on one of students' greatest assets: the social networks established within a cultural group. One such resource is its people. Moll (1994, p. 194) puts it this way: "One has to believe that there are diverse types of people that can be helpful in the classroom even though they do not have professional credentials. Wisdom and imagination are distributed in the same way among professional and nonprofessional groups."

In a middle-level classroom, Mexican American students in Tucson, Arizona, engage in a study of construction which includes inquiry into the history of dwellings and different ways of building structures. The students have access to a wide array of reading materials from the library to focus their investigation: trade books, magazines, newspapers, and reference resources, to name a few. The teacher builds on students' reading by inviting parents and community members to speak to them about their jobs in the construction industry. For example, a father visits the class to describe his work as a mason. Similarly, Cuero (2010) describes the experience of a Mexican-American fifth-grade student who lacked confidence in her reading and writing abilities. For this student, a dialogue journal correspondence with her teacher in her native language of Spanish allowed her to describe her transnational experiences through vivid written expression and a strong voice. The implications of this experience support the importance of validating and including students' home language experiences and the fund of knowledge they might bring to their new academic pursuits.

Showing interest in students' home cultures and ethnic backgrounds builds trust in the classroom. Jackson (1994) believes that building trust with students of diverse backgrounds is a culturally responsive strategy that is often overlooked. One way to create trust may be as simple as learning students' names and pronouncing them correctly, and perhaps having them share the unique meanings and special significance of their first names. Teachers may also invite them to research and share information about their family's ethnic background, using questions suggested by Cover (1989): What generation in the United States do you represent? Are you and your siblings the first of your family to be born in this country? Were you foreign born? From where did you or your ancestors migrate? What made them wish to come here? Does your immediate or extended family practice ethnic or cultural customs which you or they value or with which you or they identify? Do you or your relatives speak your ethnic group's language? What occupations are represented in your family background?

Drawing on Students' Funds of Knowledge Across Content Areas

Drawing on funds of knowledge can help students to make meaningful connections between the often abstract concepts addressed in content area classes and the application of those concepts in the world outside of the classroom. Understanding how individuals in various occupations and professions use the same knowledge and concepts presented in their content area classes helps to make course material more relevant to students. This heightened relevance leads to higher levels of engagement and retention. Hearing the experiences of community and family members can help students to open their minds to future occupations that may be of interest to them.

For the teacher, a first step in this process is to become aware of the experiences and backgrounds of family members and community members that may help students to better understand how content area knowledge can be used. By sending out an electronic or paper survey to family members, teachers can learn the types of jobs in which parents or other family members engage, as well as their hobbies or interests that may have applicability to a particular content area. Family and community members can contribute to content area classrooms in different ways. Some, for example, may be willing to visit the classroom and to serve as a guest speaker on a topic of interest. Schmidt and Ma (2006) suggest ways in which a variety of community members can share their knowledge and talents with students in content areas such as music, art, dance, mathematics, science, culinary arts, and vocational studies. Examples include:

- A local musician can discuss the instruments he or she uses when performing, and may even bring in examples of these instruments for students to see and use.

- An artist can share the different types of materials used in their work or hobby, and can encourage students to explore different ways in which those materials can be used.

- Dancers who represent different cultures such as Latino, African, Asian, or Arabic can show students the dance steps used, as well as the accompanying music, and costumes that help to showcase the history and richness of the culture represented.

- A professional chef, cook, or baker can visit a chemistry class to demonstrate and discuss how various ingredients, such as yeast, sugar, and hot and cold water, interact with one another. Students may then predict the interactions of ingredient combinations of their own creation, and conduct experiments to check the accuracy of their predictions and the connections to chemical formulas they have studied in class.

- An engineer, architect, or tradesman can visit a mathematics class to showcase some of the tools of their respective trades and to explain how knowledge of mathematical concepts is applied when using these tools. A contractor, for example, may discuss how the dimensions pictured on a blueprint are transformed into a full-scale structure.

- A systems engineer from a local company can visit a technology classroom to explain both the hardware and software involved in supporting such a business. In addition, someone in the field of information technology can express to students the need for ongoing professional development to stay up-to-date in the advancements that affect this field.

- Local small-business entrepreneurs can be motivational in the classroom. They can raise awareness for these businesses within the community. They can show students the necessity of a well-rounded education, as owners must handle many areas of the business, such as managing, accounting, and public relations. Also, entrepreneurs embody the creativity required to see what a community needs and finding a way to fill that need.

For a family or community member, serving as an interviewee for students who are researching connections between a content area and a particular occupation could be an alternative to giving a full class demonstration or presentation. Additionally, with proper planning, businesses often allow students to visit their place of employment so that they can observe the profession in action.

Whether they are interviewing people in various professions, participating in the visit of a guest speaker, or visiting a company or business, teachers can help to make these experiences meaningful for students by following a model similar to the Before-During-After (B-D-A) lesson model described in chapter 5. Schmidt and Ma (2006) suggest that, before a presentation, visit, or interview, teachers and students should work together to prepare for the experience by activating students' prior knowledge about the occupation or hobby to be investigated, listing what they would like to learn about how work in that field is carried out, and compiling questions that they might pose to the guest speaker or interviewee. During the presentation, visit, or interview, it is helpful for students to be engaged in the experience by asking questions, making connections to their content area studies, and, if applicable, actively participating in appropriate aspects of the presentation. After the experience, the teacher can continue to encourage students to investigate how new content area concepts may be put to use in occupations about which they have learned. By making connections between units of study in school and the experiences of their family and community members, the relevance of the content area studies can become more apparent.

Characteristics of Culturally Responsive Instruction

Culturally responsive instruction, as you can see, is related to students' ways of knowing, motivation for learning, and their funds of knowledge. In other words, instruction that is responsive to cultural differences in the classroom makes connections with students' backgrounds, origins, and interests to teach the required standards associated with a curriculum. Learning becomes more relevant as teachers draw on students' prior knowledge and experiences. So how can teachers tell that culturally responsive instruction is happening in classrooms?

Research on culturally responsive instruction has discovered seven key characteristics of culturally responsive instruction (Au, 1993; Boykin, 1978, 1984; Ladson-Billings, 1994, 1995; Moll, 1992; Osborne, 1996; Reyhner & Garcia, 1989; Schmidt, 2003, 2005a,b; Tatum, 2005). When lessons in secondary mathematics, social studies, science, language, and English content areas incorporate the seven characteristics, students stay more focused, become invested in what is happening, and actually step onto the road of academic success and social achievement (Tatum, 2000). Additionally, literacy development is promoted, because reading, writing, listening, speaking, and viewing provide the foundation for the seven characteristics of culturally responsive teaching (Schmidt, 2005a,b). These characteristics, with brief definitions, follow (Schmidt, 2003):

1. *High expectations.* Supporting students as they develop the literacy appropriate to their ages and abilities.

2. *Positive relationships with families and community.* Demonstrating clear connections with student families and communities in terms of curriculum content and relationships.

3. *Cultural sensitivity.* Reshaped curriculum mediated for culturally valued knowledge, connecting with the standards-based curriculum as well as individual students' cultural backgrounds.

4. *Active teaching methods.* Involving students in a variety of reading, writing, listening, speaking, and viewing behaviors throughout the lesson plan.

5. *Teacher as facilitator.* Presenting information, giving directions, summarizing responses, and working with small groups, pairs, and individuals.

6. *Student control of portions of the lesson ("healthy hum").* Talking at conversation levels around the topic studied while completing assignments in small groups and pairs.

7. *Instruction around groups and pairs to create low anxiety.* Completing assignments individually, but usually in small groups or pairs with time to share ideas and think critically about the work.

Culturally responsive instruction helps to create classroom learning environments that celebrate languages and cultures (Cazden, 2001; Cummins, 1986; Igoa, 1995; Schmidt, 1998). Literacy coaches support content area teachers in the development of classroom learning environments by providing training around the following ideas and others found in this chapter:

- Label objects in the classroom in two or three languages, such as desk, chair, book, teacher, students, and so on. Have the student or a family member assist the teacher if necessary. Labeling is common in primary classrooms. It works great in secondary classrooms too. A daily practice pronouncing the vocabulary highlights other cultures and languages. The small amount of time necessary to implement this idea not only recognizes linguistic differences but also teaches and brings an awareness to second language learning.

- Invite students or family members to present information or artifacts from their country of origin. Many students have jewelry and art objects they can share. Storytelling in some cultures is a powerful record of history.

- Use paired learning.

- Give opportunities for students to speak, read, or write in their home language each day in school.

- Include visuals wherever and whenever possible, such as videos, overhead transparencies, disposable cameras, and posters when teaching.

- Present opportunities for hands-on classroom experiences and field trips.

- Put up the daily class schedule and provide a predictable environment for learning.

- Have a map of the world or globe for students to view.

- Use choral reading for students with limited English fluency.

- Have bilingual dictionaries available.

- Use nonfiction picture books to teach key concepts in content areas.

- Include different cultures in curriculum topics (e.g., famous Latino chemists, famous Chinese artists).

- Encourage drawing and writing.

- Keep a personal journal.

- Help students keep an assignment pad.

Linguistic Differences in Today's Schools

Linguistic differences among today's student population are strikingly evident in many school districts throughout the United States. From the East Coast to the West Coast, and from the Gulf to the Northern Great Lakes, the increasingly large number of immigrants from non-European nations is influencing how content area teachers approach instruction. It is no exaggeration to suggest that in some urban school districts more than fifty languages are spoken (Banks, 2001).

When immigrant students maintain a strong identification with their culture and native language, they are more likely to succeed academically, and they have more positive self-concepts about their ability to learn (Banks, 2001; Diaz, 2001; Garcia, 2002). Schools, however, tend to view linguistically diverse students whose first language is one other than English from a deficit model, not a difference model. For these English learners, instructional practices currently are compensatory in nature: "That is, they are premised on the assumption that language diversity is an illness that needs to be cured" (Diaz, 2001, p. 159).

In addition, regional variations in language usage, commonly known as dialects, are a complicated issue for teachers. In truth, all English language users speak a dialect of English, which is rooted in such factors as age, gender, socioeconomic status, and the region of the country where one was born and grew up. Even presidents of the United States speak dialects! The difficulty with dialect differences in the classroom is the *value* assigned to dialects—the perceived goodness or badness of one particular language variation over another. Roberts (1985), however, suggests that language variations are neither good nor bad, and that such judgments are often about the people who make them rather than about clarity or precision. Delpit (1988) argues quite convincingly that teachers need to respect and recognize the strengths of diverse learners who use dialects in the classroom.

Dialect Use in the Classroom

Cultural variation in the use of language has a strong influence on literacy learning. Even though students whose first language is not English do not have full control of English grammatical structures, pronunciation, and vocabulary, they can engage in reading and writing activities (Goodman & Goodman, 1978). When students use their own culturally acceptable conversational style to talk and write about ideas they read in texts, they are likely to become more content literate and to improve their literacy skills. Au and Mason (1981), for example, describe how minority Hawaiian learners improved their reading abilities when they were allowed to use their home language to talk about texts.

Language *differences* should not be mistaken for language *deficits* among culturally diverse students. Many of the low-achieving high school students in the rural Georgia classroom that Dillon (1989) studied were African Americans who spoke a dialect commonly referred to as black English vernacular. Black dialect is acquired through family interactions and participation in the culture of the community. The teacher in Dillon's study had much success in leading text-related discussions because of his sensitivity to his students' dialect as a tool for communication in the class. As Dillon put it, the teacher "allowed students to use dialect in his classroom because they were more comfortable with it and more effective communicators" (Dillon, 1989, p. 245).

Similarly, Martinez (2010) states that the use of Spanglish—a blend of Spanish and English among English learners—can be a helpful tool for supporting students' development of academic literacy. By code-switching, for example, where students begin a sentence in one language and switch to the other language, Martinez found that English learners were better able to communicate the nuances of meaning in creative and intelligent ways. The use of Spanglish helped them to draw upon and transfer the language skills that they already possessed.

Shouldn't students from minority backgrounds learn to use standard American English? The question is a rhetorical one. As teachers, our stance toward the use of standard American English is critical. Standard American English, often thought of as the "news broadcast-type" English used in the conduct of business, is the language of the dominant mainstream culture in U.S. society—the "culture of power," according to Delpit (1988). Delpit explains that the rules and codes of the culture of power, including the rules and codes for language use, are acquired by students from mainstream backgrounds through interaction with their families. Minority students, however, whose families are outside the mainstream culture, do not acquire the same rules and codes. If students are going to have access to opportunities in mainstream society, schools must acquaint students from minority backgrounds with the rules and codes of the culture of power. Not making standard American English accessible to students from minority backgrounds puts them at a disadvantage in competing with their mainstream counterparts.

Although it is important for culturally diverse learners to receive explicit instruction in the use of standard American English, *when* and *under what circumstances* become critical instructional issues. All students should understand how cultural contexts influence what they read, write, hear, say, and view. Language arts classes are probably the appropriate place to provide explicit instruction in the functional use and conventions of standard American English. Although becoming proficient in standard American English may be an important school goal for all students, it should not be viewed as a prerequisite for literate classroom behavior (Au, 1993). When it is viewed as a prerequisite, teachers deny students the opportunity to use their own language as a tool for learning. Increasing their command of standard American English, in and of itself, will not improve students' abilities to think critically, "since students' own languages can serve just as well for verbal expression and reasoning" (Au, 1993, p. 130).

English Language Learning

English learners (ELs) are those students who speak English as a nonnative language. Because their home language is that of a minority group—for example, Spanish, Navajo, or Vietnamese—they are considered to be *language minority* students. English learners are, for the most part, the children of immigrants who left their homelands for one reason or another. Some English learners, however, are born in the United States. As Peregoy and Boyle (2001, p. 3) explain:

> Many recent immigrants have left countries brutally torn by war or political strife in regions such as Southeast Asia, Central America, and Eastern Europe; others have immigrated for economic reasons. Still others come to be reunited with families who are already here or because of the educational opportunities they may find in the United States. Finally, many English language learners

were born in the United States and some of them, such as Native Americans of numerous tribal heritages, have roots in American soil that go back for countless generations.

Among recent immigrants, there exist various groups within this newcomer population: Some are highly schooled in their native language but need to learn academic English, vocabulary, and core concepts. Some have limited school experience in their native country, while others may have never attended a school of any kind. It is important for teachers to remember that English learners are not a homogenous group. Calderon, Slavin, and Sanchez (2011) estimate that 80 percent of second-generation immigrant children are classified as long-term English learners in middle and high school, despite having been in the United Stated since kindergarten. Some students are reclassified as general education students as soon as they pass the state assessment, despite the fact that they may not have developed English proficiency across the domains of listening, speaking, reading, and writing. Migrant English learners are another group of ELs that are typically born in the United States, but who lack English proficiency because their families move from state to state picking crops, thus interrupting their educational experiences. Transnational English learners return to their native countries for a portion of the school year, attend school there, and then return to U.S. schools, also creating inconsistencies in their educational experiences.

Bilingual and ESL Programs

English learners vary in their use of English. Some may have little or no proficiency in the use of English. Others may have limited English skills; still others may use English proficiently and are mainstreamed into the regular curriculum. What is language proficiency? It has been defined as "the ability to use a language effectively and appropriately throughout the range of social, personal, school, and work situations required for daily living in a given society" (Peregoy & Boyle, 2001, p. 29). Language proficiency, therefore, encompasses both oral and written language processes, including speaking, listening, reading, and writing.

In the United States, there is an array of instructional programs for English learners. Programs vary greatly, depending on the number of ELs enrolled in a school district. Many with limited English proficiency are placed in bilingual and English as a second language (ESL) programs. Bilingual and ESL programs are designed specifically to meet the academic, cultural, and linguistic needs of English learners until they are proficient enough in English to be mainstreamed into the regular curriculum.

Bilingual programs are designed to teach English and to provide instruction in the core curriculum using the home language of the English learner. Bilingual programs reach only a small percentage of students, despite a growing body of research that suggests that immigrant students who maintain a strong identification with their culture and native language are more likely to succeed academically and have more positive self-concepts about their abilities to learn (Banks, 2001; Diaz, 2001; Garcia, 2002). ESL programs differ from bilingual programs in that they are taught entirely in English in schools where there are many language minority groups represented, making it difficult to implement bilingual instruction.

Bilingual and ESL teachers provide invaluable compensatory services for language minority students with limited English proficiency. When these students are mainstreamed into the regular curriculum, however, they often struggle with content literacy tasks. Let's take a closer look at some of the reasons diverse learners struggle with reading and writing in content area classrooms.

What Makes Content Literacy Difficult for English Learners?

Once they are mainstreamed into the regular curriculum, English learners encounter numerous challenges in learning the English language. Not only must they acquire skills for social uses of English, they must acquire academic skills, across the content areas, in the domains of listening speaking, reading, and writing. The academic language of texts is not the language of conversational speech, but rather it is word knowledge that makes it possible for students to interact with texts that are used across school subject areas (Flynt & Brozo, 2008).

Reading textbooks is one of the most cognitively demanding, context-reduced tasks that minority language students will encounter (Cummins, 1994). The vast variety of subject area vocabulary and the linguistic complexity of the English language makes English language learning particularly challenging for many middle and secondary students. Many educators find it difficult to grasp the magnitude of learning academic English. While many students acquire informal, social English in approximately two to three years, academic English typically takes between five and ten years to master. This can make content area instruction challenging for teachers and students alike (Flynt & Brozo, 2008). Consider the vocabulary of a native English speaker. A five-year-old native English speaker would begin kindergarten with a vocabulary that ranges from 5,000 to 7,000 words (Manyak & Bauer, 2009)—words that a nonnative English speaker would not have in their vocabulary. This initial vocabulary deficit in the language of instruction creates an achievement gap from the beginning that is difficult for English learners to bridge. The gap widens when English instruction is delayed until the middle and secondary years.

The vocabulary load of content area textbooks is particularly challenging for some English learners. To try to understand the complexity involved in learning academic vocabulary, consider the vocabulary of the seemingly simple word *apple*. If you were to list key words or phrases about emotional associations with apples or why you like apples, your list might include basic vocabulary such as:

  apple pie

  sweet

  crunchy

  stem

  cozy kitchen

  pleasant aroma

While the social language of *apple* may seem common and relatively simple to learn, consider what the academic language of *apple* might look like. Consider the language of *apple* from a poet's perspective, and the additional vocabulary and linguistic complexity needed to understand the opening lines of Robert Frost's poem *After Apple-Picking*.

My long two-pointed ladder's sticking through a tree toward heaven still,
  And there's a barrel that I didn't fill

Beside it, and there may be two or three
  Apples I didn't pick upon some bough.

But I am done with apple-picking now.
   Essence of winter sleep is on the night,

The scent of apples: I am drowsing off.

While every content area teacher knows the academic language of his or her subject, we rarely have the time to consider the academic language involved in other content areas. That English learner who leaves poetry class still has to face the academic demands of at least three other content areas. When that same student goes the mathematics class, the language of *apple* may change according to computations or to an economist's perspective: measurements, quart, bushel, tons, yield, symmetry, circumference, crop abundance. When that student goes to science class, the academic language may be from a biologist's perspective and may include vocabulary such as: orchard, botanical information, blossoms, pollination, deciduous, harvest, and pruning. When that student goes to social studies class, the language of *apple* may be from an historian's perspective: immigration of the apple, legend of Johnny Appleseed, John Chapman, and the cultivation of various apple varieties.

As the language of *apple* changes, the demands of academic language and vocabulary become more apparent. When we are aware of this, it is easier to empathize with the English learner who has to face this volume of academic vocabulary and complexity surrounding this single, and previously simple sounding, concept.

Manyak and Bauer (2009) suggest that, in order for English language vocabulary instruction to be effective, schools must implement consistent and intensive vocabulary instruction across grade levels. English learners in particular benefit from vocabulary instruction that presents high-frequency words in phrases and short reading passages designed to improve reading fluency. Effective instruction requires teachers to strike a balance between attention to basic word concepts and the richer vocabulary instruction of their content area.

Researchers have discovered that students learning English as a second language are more capable of comprehending subject area content than previously thought, especially in activity-based classes such as science. They may not be able to easily express ideas orally in English, but when given opportunities to write and answer written questions, they demonstrate clear understandings (Bernhardt, 1998; Bernhardt & Kamil, 1998). Similarly, Ma (2004), in his case study of college-level Korean international students, discovered that they preferred listening activities rather than discussion activities in class. They explained that listening to others in small groups was helpful in hearing multiple perspectives and interpretations necessary for understanding the culture and language of the United States. Additionally, these students relate to a Confucian learning culture (Watkins & Biggs, 1996) that emphasizes deep reflective listening. Unfortunately, they may be placed at a disadvantage in classrooms in the United States, where those who are talkative in discussion groups are privileged (Li, 2005; Pang & Cheng, 1998).

Books for English Learners

English learners have become a recognizable force in today's classrooms. ELs face a triple challenge compared to mainstream students: They need to learn academic content, develop native-like English proficiency, and achieve comfort with American culture. It is important to note that ELs have language, not cognitive, obstacles.

One way to address these challenges is to have ELs interact with authentic trade books. In doing so, teachers can increase students' content and vocabulary knowledge, offer more

BOX 3.3   RTI for Struggling Adolescent Learners

Responding to the Language Needs of English Learners

In recent years, there has been a surge in the percentage of English learners. This population of students is often disproportionately represented in special education programs—not as a result of cognitive disabilities, but rather because of their struggle with using the English language. The overrepresentation of English language learners in special education programs spotlights the need for appropriate materials for assessing and supporting non–English-speaking students (James, 2004). By following RTI guidelines, remediation sensitive to the needs of English language learners should be provided within the classroom to lessen the amount of inappropriate special education referrals.

In an era of high-stakes assessments, it is important that appropriate RTI-related assessment measures be used to evaluate the progress and achievement of students with limited English proficiency. While some states provide standardized assessments in alternate languages, most prominently Spanish, others rely on test modifications or accommodations, such as extended time and alternative placement for testing, the use of a language translation dictionary, or additional support from the test administrator to simplify, reiterate, or read aloud test items. In some cases, students who face language challenges are exempt from testing altogether based on the length of time they have been exposed to English education.

In an effort to uphold the ideals of RTI, assessments should be provided in a language and format

familiar to each English learner so that the results represent the student's abilities rather than language difficulties (James, 2004). For example, classroom teachers can provide texts and trade books in students' native languages; students can be permitted to give their initial response to a reading in their primary language and then translate their work. This allows English learners to fully process reactions to text before attempting to translate their thoughts. When more formal methods of assessment are required, educators can locate resources that will meet the needs of culturally diverse classrooms.

Some examples of assessments provided in alternative languages include the following:

- *The Woodcock-Muñoz Achievement Battery–Revised.* This assessment by Riverside Publishing is parallel to the English language version and measures cognitive abilities and academic achievement.

- *The Native Language Literacy Screening Device.* This assessment created by the New York State Department of Education is available in 26 languages and measures students' literacy levels in their native languages.

- *Spanish Reading Inventory.* This reading inventory written by Jerry L. Johns and published by Kendall Hunt allows teachers to conduct running records with passages in Spanish to determine students' reading levels and plan appropriate instruction.

practice with authentic language, and provide scenarios that describe the life of American teenagers, which will expose ELs to a variety of cultural behaviors and ways of thinking. Books, TV shows, and movies can be excellent venues for ELs to learn about real-life experiences. For example, Jeff Kinney's *Diary of a Wimpy Kid* (Kinney, 2007) can introduce ELs to the dynamics of junior high school hierarchies. The book's humor, simple vocabulary, and graphics will engage ELs, which increases their motivation to read.

Knowing that English learners need additional support with language learning, teachers may find *graphic novels* to be a perfect alternative for these students. Graphic novels, already popular with adolescents for independent reading, combine words with pictures that can support the learning of students for whom English poses particular difficulties. Using graphic novels in the classroom is an increasingly popular way to scaffold ELs' understanding of content. Illustrations in graphic novels provide valuable context clues about the meaning of the written content and offer particular support for students who lack the ability to visualize as they read. Graphic novels are available in a variety of genres, including biographies, fiction, nonfiction, and fantasy. These texts have particular appeal for reluctant readers and can be used to teach a variety of literacy skills including dialogue, inferencing, story elements, literary terms like *writing, satire, irony, parody,* and many more.

Using Will Eisner's (2000) *New York: The Big City,* Kelly Faust developed a lesson for her urban English learners, many of whom had been in this country for only one year. The purpose of the lesson was to further student understanding of story elements and encourage writing. She began the lesson by showing the students six frames of a wordless story from the book on the overhead projector. She then used the think-aloud strategy to point out the events of the story and the ways in which the visual techniques of the illustrator supported it. She reviewed the basic elements of a story with her students, and asked students whether the frames represented a story. Students pointed out that these frames contained characters, setting, and a simple plot. Students then discussed the story with a partner, creating their own version of the events portrayed in the frames. At this point, one team of students dictated their story to the group. Kelly recorded this story on chart paper, so that other students could see the concepts recorded. She modeled for the students how to use quotation marks to designate the exact words of a speaker. At strategic points, Kelly involved specific students in recording the text on paper. Next, Kelly directed the students to identify the characters, the setting, and the events of the plot in the recorded story.

Following this, Kelly presented students with a new series of wordless frames from the Eisner book. She reviewed the think-aloud strategy and students took turns thinking aloud with a partner about the text. Students then worked in teams to draft their own stories on notebook paper. At this point, Kelly conducted minilessons reviewing areas of need reflected in the student drafts. After revising, the students transferred their stories to chart paper and shared them with the class, pointing out the elements of story as reflected in their own writing.

Vocabulary in areas such as mathematics, social studies and science can be overwhelming, causing content to be inaccessible for many English learners. More vocabulary is introduced in social studies and science textbooks than in textbooks used to teach students a foreign language. Using picture books with ELs is a good practice because pictures can aid comprehension (see Box 3.4). Also, the vocabulary and language patterns of picture books are simple, which also aids comprehension. Picture books, including wordless picture books, have been found to support English learners facilitation with the English language, particularly in terms of speaking and listening, as students are invited to explain their interpretation of a story by reading the pictures. Martinez-Roldan and Newcomer (2011) suggest the following strategies for engaging students in wordless picture book reading:

- Use a small group, rather than whole class, format for book discussions.
- Use an assortment of books by the same author to compare techniques and messages.
- Invite open conversations about the text, using open-ended, inferential, and applied questions.
- Invite students to make text predictions.
- Invite students to create annotated pages or to create narrations to accompany their interpretations of the visual images in the book.

Picture Books in Mathematics BOX 3.4

A variety of picture books may be used not only to help young adolescent English learners develop mathematical concepts but also to draw on their prior knowledge and experience (Schmidt & Ma, 2006). Here are several suggestions for using math picture books in middle grade classrooms:

- To spark interest and develop an understanding of mathematical concepts, have English learners read stories about famous mathematicians and cultures that have been mathematically oriented. The Internet provides wonderful leads on famous mathematicians from different cultures.

- Have English learners read math-oriented picture books to younger siblings. Picture books explain in ways that help students understand mathematical concepts. In addition, students may create and design their own math books to be shared in other classrooms and with younger audiences.

- Use math picture books as a strategy for motivating interest in mathematics and providing a greater depth of understanding of mathematical

concepts. Create an area in the classroom to display picture books such as the following:

Burns, M. *The Greedy Triangle*

Heller, R. *More Geometrics*

Wisniewski, D. *RainPlayer*

Tang, G. *Math for All Seasons*

Tang, G. *Math-terpieces*

Tang, G. *The Grapes of Math*

Scieszka, J. *Math Curse*

Schwartz, D. *How Much Is a Million*

Neuschwander, C. *Sir Cumference and the First Round Table*

Seife, C. *Zero: Biography of a Dangerous Idea*

McKellar, D. *Kiss My Math: Showing Pre-Algebra Who's Boss*

These books enhance the study of mathematics with humor and delightful stories and illustrations, bringing added joy to the study of math while encouraging related reading, writing, listening, speaking, and viewing activities.

Additionally, chapter book series such as Mary Pope Osborne's *Magic Tree House* and Jon Scieszka's *Time Warp Trio* bring various science and social studies concepts to life in an easy-to-read but content-rich manner.

English learners need to learn to navigate nonnarrative texts because much of secondary schooling is based on the ability to read this text type. For social studies topics, check out books by Russell Freedman. Freedman includes a lot of primary and secondary sources and illustrations in his works. Furthermore, his books are rich in content but more concise and interesting than textbooks. *Immigrant Kids* (Freedman, 1995), for example, is ideally suited for ELs as are other books about teens who share their struggles. Shaun Tan's wordless graphic novel *The Arrival* (Tan, 2007) depicts the journey of an immigrant who grapples with loneliness and the strangeness of learning a new language and culture. There are also several anthologies that address this topic, such as *First Crossing: Stories About Teen Immigrants* (Gallo, 2007) and *Kids Like Me: Voices of the Immigrant Experience* (Blohm & Lapinsky, 2006). Series such as Ellen Levin's *If You . . .* (e.g., *If Your Name Was Changed at Ellis Island* [1996] and *If You Traveled West in a Covered Wagon* [1992])and David Adler's picture book biographies are also welcome additions to content area learning for ELs.

Teaching for cultural understanding and using multicultural literature create a community of learners within the four walls of the classroom. Within such learning communities, it is important for teachers to understand the ways in which diverse learners "come to know" and to tap into students' "funds of knowledge."

Sheltered Instruction for English Learners

Sheltered instruction does not focus specifically on second language development issues. Instead, teachers often use a variety of instructional aids to let students who have limited skills in reading, writing, listening, and speaking "see" challenging, and often abstract, content visually.

Response Journal

What does the term *sheltered* suggest to you? Why do you think it is used to describe an instructional approach for English learners?

This may be done by contextualizing the learning tasks through hands-on cooperative activities, pictures, relevant media, artistic representations of meaning, and reading-to-learn strategies modeled for the students (Campano, 2007; Haynes, 2007). As a result, sheltered instruction often provides opportunities for nonnative students to learn discipline-specific content while improving their English language skills (Díaz-Rico, 2008; Faltis & Coulter, 2008).

When English learners struggle with content literacy tasks, instruction should be specially designed to meet their academic and linguistic needs, which often include (1) learning grade-appropriate and academically demanding content; (2) learning the language of academic English as reflected in content subjects, texts, and classroom discourse; (3) engaging in appropriate classroom behavior and understanding participation rules and expectations in small groups and whole-class instructional routines; and (4) mastering English vocabulary and grammar (Echevarria, Vogt, & Short, 2008). Sheltered instruction, also known as SDAIE (specially designed academic instruction in English), is an approach to content area learning and language development that provides the instructional support needed to make grade-level content more accessible for ELs while promoting English development (Echevarria & Graves, 2003).

Although the concept of "sheltering" English learners is similar to the concept of scaffolding instruction for all learners who need instructional support to be successful with content literacy tasks, it has been adapted for use in two types of instructional contexts: (1) in mainstreamed, core curriculum classrooms made up of native speakers and nonnative speakers who are at an *intermediate* level of language proficiency and (2) in ESL classrooms made up of nonnative speakers who are at similar levels of language proficiency.

The SIOP Model

One model for sheltered instruction, SIOP (sheltered instruction observation protocol), provides a comprehensive instructional framework that can be used in several ways to shelter instruction for English learners. First, the SIOP model serves as a blueprint for designing lessons that integrate content learning with additional language support for English learners. Second, the SIOP model enhances instructional delivery by making teachers aware of highly effective practices and behaviors that will make a difference in the academic and language development of students. And third, the SIOP model provides an observational framework for rating teachers in sheltered classrooms. Figure 3.1 depicts the major components within the

Figure 3.1 The Sheltered Instruction Observation Protocol (SIOP)

Observer: _____

Date: _____

Grade: _____

Class: _____

Teacher: _____

School: _____

ESL level: _____

Lesson: Multi-day   Single-day

I. Preparation

1. Clearly defined *content objectives* for students
2. Clearly defined *language objectives* for students
3. *Content concepts* appropriate for age and educational background level of students
4. *Supplementary materials* used to a high degree, making the lesson clear and meaningful (graphs, models, visuals)
5. *Adaptation of content* (e.g., text, assignment) to all levels of student proficiency
6. *Meaningful activities* that integrate lesson concepts (e.g., surveys, letter writing, simulations, constructing models) with language practice opportunities for reading, writing, listening, and/or speaking

II. Instruction

(1) Building Background

7. *Concepts explicitly linked* to students' background experiences
8. *Links explicitly made* between past learning and new concepts
9. *Key vocabulary emphasized* (e.g., introduced, written, repeated, and highlighted for students to see)

(2) Comprehensible

10. *Speech* appropriate for students' proficiency level (e.g., slower rate, enunciation, and simple sentence structure for beginners)
11. *Explanation* of academic tasks clear
12. Uses a variety of *techniques* to make content concepts clear (e.g., modeling, visuals, hands-on activities, demonstrations, gestures, body language)

(3) Strategies

13. Provides ample opportunities for student to use *strategies*
14. Consistent use of *scaffolding* techniques throughout lesson, assisting and supporting student understanding
15. Teacher uses a variety of *question types throughout the lesson including those that promote higher-order thinking skills* throughout the lesson (e.g., literal, analytical, and interpretive questions)

(4) Interaction

16. Frequent opportunities for *interactions* and discussion between teacher/student and among students, which encourage elaborated responses about lesson concepts
17. *Grouping configurations* support language and content objectives of the lesson
18. Consistently provides sufficient *wait time for student response*
19. Ample opportunities for students to *clarify key concepts in L1*

(5) Practice/Application

20. Provides *hands-on* materials and/or manipulatives for students to practice using new content knowledge
21. Provides activities for students to *apply content and language knowledge* in the classroom
22. Uses activities that integrate all *language skills* (i.e., reading, writing, listening, and speaking)

(6) Lesson Delivery

23. *Content objectives* clearly supported by lesson delivery
24. *Language objectives* clearly supported by lesson delivery
25. *Students engaged* approximately 90–100% of the period
26. *Pacing* of the lesson appropriate to the students' ability level

III. Review/Assessment

27. Comprehensive *review* of key vocabulary
28. Comprehensive *review* of key content concepts
29. Regularly provides *feedback* to students on their output (e.g., language, content, work)
30. Conducts *assessment* of student comprehension and learning of all lesson objectives (e.g., spot checking, group response) throughout the lesson

Source: Echevarria, J., Vogt, M., & Short, D. (2008). *Making content comprehensible for English language learners: The SIOP model*, 3rd ed. Published by Allyn & Bacon, Boston, MA. Copyright © 2008 by Pearson Education Inc. Reprinted with permission of the publisher.

SIOP model: lesson preparation, instruction, strategies, interaction, practice/application, lesson delivery, and assessment (Echevarria, Vogt, & Short, 2008).

Sheltered instruction is a powerful approach to content area learning and language development. The literacy strategies described throughout this book may be incorporated into instructional routines for students in sheltered or nonsheltered classrooms. Many of these strategies have been recommended by English language educators for use with language minority students (Díaz-Rico & Weed, 2002; Echevarria & Graves, 2003; Echevarria, Vogt, & Short, 2008; Peregoy & Boyle, 2001). In the next section, we highlight several strategies and suggest ways to adapt instruction for diverse learners.

Adapting Instruction in Content Classrooms

Content area teachers are in a strategic position to make adaptations in the way they design and deliver instruction in classrooms with native and nonnative speakers. These adaptations in instructional design and delivery lead to additional language support for English learners, as well as increased learning opportunities in the core curriculum.

Provide Comprehensible Input

Support nonnative speakers in your classroom by showing sensitivity to their language needs. An important component of sheltered instruction is to provide *comprehensible input* for English learners (Echevarria & Graves, 2003). Make content learning comprehensible by simplifying your language when giving directions, leading whole-class discussions, or facilitating small-group interactions. When talking to a class that includes ELs, especially students at a beginning or intermediate level of language proficiency, it may be necessary to speak clearly and speak at a slightly slower rate than you normally would if you had only native speakers in your classroom. During discussions, it may also be necessary to repeat yourself, define new words in a meaningful context, or paraphrase when you use more sophisticated language than ELs can understand. Providing comprehensible input also means being aware of your use of idiomatic expressions and limiting them when students find idiomatic expressions difficult to understand. Moreover, keep in mind that gestures and facial expressions help to dramatize what you are saying during discussion. Barton (1995) reminds teachers not only to simplify and clarify the language they use but also to check for understanding frequently throughout classroom conversations. As we explained earlier in the chapter, scaffold instruction during discussion by supporting students in their use of home languages and their own culturally acceptable conversational styles.

Use Strategies for Vocabulary Development

Linguistically diverse learners, whether they are good or poor readers, will encounter unfamiliar content area vocabulary during reading that may pose comprehension problems for them. In a study of bilingual readers, researchers discovered that good readers focused on increasing vocabulary (Jimenez, Garcia, & Pearson, 1995, 1996). In addition, English learners who struggle as readers benefited from vocabulary strategy instruction (Jimenez & Gamez, 1996). Vocabulary strategy instruction is effective when a teacher helps ELs to develop a few key terms in depth rather than attempting to have them learn many words superficially (Gersten & Jimenez, 1994). Such instruction should take into account strategies and procedures that will help students build meaning for important concept terms.

For example, whenever the opportunity presents itself, it's important to help students recognize and use the relationship between cognates and the context in which they are used. *Cognates* are words that are culturally and linguistically related in both the nonnative speaker's language and in English. As part of cognitive strategy instruction for struggling readers, Latina/o students in a middle school special education classroom were shown how to approximate word meaning through the cognate relationships they encountered in the texts that they were reading. The researchers used a think-aloud strategy, as discussed in the previous chapter, to scaffold instruction (Jimenez & Gamez, 1996, p. 88):

Researcher: You know the word in Spanish, so we can use a Spanish clue to help us figure out what it means. Victor, what does *espectacular* mean?

Victor: That it's useful?

Researcher: It's something very . . .

Sara: Special?

Researcher: Special, you got it! I like this. So (for) something very special, you can say wonderful, *espectacular.* The Spanish clue helped us with *spectacular* because that is exactly the same in English and Spanish. Have you guys heard that word on the radio, *spectacular?* [The researcher writes this on the chalkboard.] That's English, and here's Spanish *espectacular.* The only difference between English and Spanish is that we put an *e* in the front in Spanish. That's exactly the same word. It almost sounds exactly the same, only a little bit different. But when you guys can do this you're taking advantage of your bilingualism and you're using what you already know to help you understand. OK? I think it's really cool when Latino kids do that. That makes a lot of sense to me.

In addition to emphasizing cognate-related vocabulary building, showing linguistically diverse learners how to approximate word meaning through *word structure* and context is another important aspect of vocabulary building. In Chapter 8, we will examine in more detail how to use context and word structure in content classrooms, and explore a variety of strategies for vocabulary and concept development. In Box 3.5, English language teacher, Cindy, explains how she uses an Interactive Word Wall (IWW) to assist English learners in developing an understanding of important vocabulary concepts in their content area classes. Interactive Word Walls support students' concept learning by allowing them to explore, evaluate, reflect on, and apply word meanings (Harmon, Wood, Hedrick, Vintinner, & Willeford, 2009).

Differentiate Between Intensive and Extensive Reading

English learners need to be taught that not all texts need to be read and understood at the same level of detail, and that they may employ different strategies for different reading tasks. Kristin Berry, a tenth-grade global studies teacher, introduced *intensive reading* and *extensive reading* strategies to her interdisciplinary English/global studies class while working on a unit of study about World War II. She followed these four steps to help English learners and native language speakers recognize when to use intensive reading and extensive reading strategies:

1. Kristin required her students to engage in an intensive reading of the core textbook to understand the big picture. They read about Germany's aggression in Europe, Japan's aggression in Asia, diplomacy and the Allied forces, major events and figures, and the fall of Germany and Japan, as well as the relationships among the social, political, military, and economic factors.

BOX 3.5   Voices from the Field

Cindy, Middle Grades ELL Teacher

As a teacher of English learners in a low-SES, rural school district, I often see students who struggle to understand and retain vocabulary necessary for academic achievement. There are many reason why this happens:

- English language students do not always have the prior knowledge or experience needed to understand content area vocabulary.

- Students often lack in-depth vocabulary instruction. For example, they may be instructed to look up vocabulary definitions and copy them down. They write down the first definition or the shortest.

- Inadequate exposures to vocabulary concepts present EL students from learning the nuance of words with various meanings across different content areas.

- Vocabulary instruction and the linguistic complexity of textbooks often bog down EL students.

- Students lack opportunities for engagement and interaction with essential vocabulary.

Strategy

Vocabulary instruction can be tedious unless you provide students with opportunities for engagement and interaction. One of my favorite strategies for helping my EL students with content area vocabulary is the Interactive Word Wall (Harmon, Wood, Hedrick, Vintinner, & Willeford, 2009). An IWW consists of the targeted vocabulary words, an illustration, and a definition. An example of part of the Interactive Word Wall that my students used in a science unit that included the study of trees is pictured below. The size of the IWW can vary widely depending on your purposes and available space. I've used an entire wall for some IWWs and a pocket chart for others.

deciduous		trees that lose their leaves in the fall
conifers		trees that keep their needles all year

| chlorophyll | | the green coloring in leaves |

After introducing the unit to my class, I pass out the vocabulary word cards first and let the students read and post each one on the wall. Next, I pass out the pictures and instruct the students to try to match each picture to the vocabulary word to which they think it corresponds. If they are not sure where a word belongs, I try to help them to make a logical inference based on the information they have. Then, I pass out the definitions and ask the students to match the definitions to the corresponding word and picture combination. Finally, I explain that after we read the text, the students will have an opportunity to revisit the word wall and to make any changes from their original ideas about word/picture/definition correspondence. Through this process, my students have a purpose for reading and a clear focus on the targeted vocabulary. In that respect, this strategy works much the same as an anticipation guide described in Chapter 6. It also allows me to assess my students' prior knowledge of the subject by looking at the correct or incorrect vocabulary matches that they make. As we read the text selection, we discuss and clarify the concepts to be sure that my English learners understand the vocabulary concepts.

Reflection

As my students read the text selection, I often see them glancing at the IWW for clarification and confirmation. And, because students benefit from multiple exposures to vocabulary concepts, we sometimes follow up by having them reconstruct the IWW on a subsequent day, or engage in an extension strategy. In the tree unit example above, I might ask them to diagram and label parts of the tree, or compare and contrast conifer and deciduous trees. My goal is to engage my students by providing opportunities for them to revisit and reuse the targeted vocabulary. In doing so, I seek to implement effective teaching practices that will meet the wide array of needs of my English learners.

2. To help her students comprehend the chapters, Kristin not only worked with them on important vocabulary but also clarified the meaning of difficult sentences through rereading, paraphrasing, summarizing, group discussion, and written response. Through reading intensively, Kristin helped her students develop a solid understanding of the textbook.

3. In collaboration with her language arts colleague, Kristin incorporated a variety of learning activities and assignments into her lessons. She required students to read extensively some of the books that addressed various aspects of the war, such as *The Diary of Anne Frank: Play and Related Readings* (Goodrich & Hackett, 2000), *Night* (Wiesel, 2006), *Rumors of Peace* (Leffland, 1979), and *Summer of My German Soldier* (Greene, 1999). Then Kristin asked her

Figure 3.2 Graphic Organizer for Electromagnetic Energy

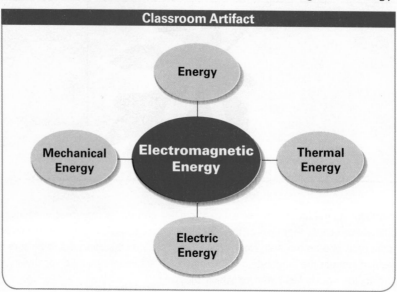

students to select one novel to read for a general understanding. They were to connect what they read with what they had learned from reading the textbook.

4. To help students cope with the large volume of reading, Kristin also gave explicit instruction in the use of two study strategies that we elaborate on in Chapter 10: *skimming* (i.e., reading quickly to grasp the main ideas of a text) and *scanning* (i.e., reading quickly to locate specific detail). These varied reading experiences extended, diversified, and brought life to the textbook.

As a result of Kristin's sheltered approach to instruction, intensive reading and extensive reading helped both English learners and mainstream students learn during the unit of study.

Use the Repeated Reading Strategy

For English learners who are still in the process of developing reading fluency, the *repeated reading strategy* may be a useful intensive reading approach to fully comprehend a content area text across varied grade levels. A three-step reading process may help students better understand a text through the use of repeated readings of text material:

1. The first reading focuses on breaking down the linguistic barriers for the English learners. To begin, each student is required to skim a given text and mark any language item not understood. Before explaining the terms in class, the teacher encourages responses from other students. This is useful in developing students' ability to guess the meaning of a word from its context. The teacher may call students' attention to some "key points." The teacher also helps ELs differentiate between *denotation* (the literal meaning a word has) and *connotation* (the implied or suggested meaning of a word in context). Thus the students will not do a rigid word-for-word interpretation of every sentence in English. It is worth mentioning that because of the linguistic subtleties and intricacies of English figurative expressions, special consideration should be given to the unique difficulty of learning "language forms."

2. The next reading centers on the ideas expressed in the text. Clearly, the students should be allowed more time for this second reading so that they may dwell on the main ideas and important details in the text for in-depth comprehension. As the language form is but a vehicle for carrying meaning, the students should be encouraged to learn how the main ideas, viewpoints, and so on are presented; how the ideas flow from beginning to end; and how all the separate sentences and paragraphs are tightly knitted semantically. In other words, now the central task is to understand the ideas that are presented and the way they are connected in the text.

3. The third stage primarily aims to help students size up how the material is organized in order to have an overview of the text. The organizational pattern; the effect of the style, tone, and attitude achieved; and the basic writing techniques (such as diction and rhetoric) can all be dealt with in this final reading.

After the three readings, students would better know the language forms involved in the text and the ideas these forms express. As a result, students' knowledge of the text is likely to be more comprehensive because of the text-centered method employed throughout the reading process. It is important to remember that the three steps are interchangeable. When used in combination with other group discussion and/or writing activities, the repeated reading strategy would be even more effective.

Use Learning Strategies for Active Engagement

Throughout the remainder of this book, we will be focusing on learning strategies that will engage students in comprehending texts. These strategies can be as simple and straightforward as creating posters for a chapter. This strategy allows teachers to use a variety of group and collaborative activities in different content areas. Betty Vrooman, for example, uses posters with the English learners in her middle school social studies class. She follows these three steps:

1. After her students read a particular chapter, Betty asks them to create a poster to visually represent the main ideas expressed by this chapter. Based on the length and complexity of the chapter, she varies the requirement for the total number of key concepts to be included in a poster, from five to twelve. Her students use illustrations, color, lettering, and so on to present the chapter's information in an inviting and creative manner.

2. Betty's students share their posters in a small group consisting of three to five students (including both English learners and mainstream learners). All members take turns sharing their posters with each other. While sharing, they are encouraged to use the ideas from the poster as "talking points." Betty asks the other students to point out at least one thing that they particularly like in the poster and to offer one suggestion about how to better interpret the chapter's content as well.

3. After the group sharing, Betty invites all students to share in a whole-class session, and each individual student can share some of the highlights from his or her own reading, writing, or group sharing. Meanwhile, she provides further explanation about the main ideas, concepts, or additional background information related to the chapter under study. When needed, she also gives feedback to clarify any unclear points or misunderstandings as reflected from the students' posters or presentations.

In summary, Betty feels that asking her students to create posters for a text they read helps deepen their engagement with the text. The sharing provides further opportunities for both the English learners and mainstream students to exchange ideas about what they thought and understood. This strategy may be easily adjusted for use in other content areas. In each case, the poster helps to support English learners' critical engagement with a text in a socially supported context. Chapter 5 provides a more extended discussion of collaborative learning strategies.

Use Writing Strategies

English learners sometimes get stuck while engaging in specific writing activities. By involving them in a variety of writing strategies, as emphasized in Chapter 9, students will come to view writing as a tool to understand as well as to be understood. One such strategy, "mental composition," is particularly useful in composing an essay or reflecting on a learning task. The strategy helps students, especially ELs, think about what they are going to write without having to worry about "getting it down on paper." It is helpful to introduce this strategy to students by thinking aloud with them and modeling the process. For example, after reading the young adult novel *Walk Two Moons* (Creech, 1996), a seventh-grade language arts teacher, Stephanie, used her response to the novel to model the steps of the mental composition strategy. She wanted the students to understand that a written paper would need to have an introduction, a body, and an ending, so she began the lesson by explaining that the book told the story of a young girl named Salmanca (Sal) Tree Hiddle. Next, she wanted to model for her students how to write the body of her paper. She thought aloud with them about the story structure of this novel, noting that there was a story within a story. One story was about Sal's trip with her grandparents to visit her mother's burial place, and the other story focused on her best friend. Finally, to model how to write the ending of her paper, Stephanie discussed how Sal's journey ended. She also mentioned some of the important issues raised in the novel, such as coping with the death of a family member as a young adolescent. At the end of the lesson, she pointed out that the thought process she had modeled reflected how she might approach the writing of her paper. Then, she invited the students to share how they might approach a written paper based on their reading of this novel.

Stephanie models the procedures for mental composition, or in her words, "seeing a paper unfolding in one's head." She realizes the importance of engaging English learners in actual writing as well. Therefore, in addition to mental composition, she selects some topics to involve her students in practicing brainstorming, planning, drafting, revising, and completing the writing. At the same time, she provides some concrete suggestions to help them generate ideas: journal entries, informal nongraded writing, one-page think pieces, in-class free writing, microtheme paragraphs, practice exam questions/topics, small-group discussions, rewrites, and so on. In other words, mental composition and regular writing become supplementary and complementary.

Mental composition may be adapted for helping students notice varied learning tasks. For example, students may use it to recall what was learned at various stages of reading a novel or text and review what was taught after a particular class. When used in combination with other writing practices, such mental composing promotes active intellectual participation through writing, reading, speaking, and listening across content areas.

Looking Back Looking Forward

The linguistic, cultural, and achievement differences of students contribute to the complexities of classroom diversity. Students of diverse backgrounds (who may be distinguished by their ethnicity, social class, language, or achievement level) often struggle in classrooms. English language learners especially challenge teachers to look for and experiment with instructional strategies that will actively involve them in the life of the classroom. Sheltered instruction makes a difference in the academic and language development of English learners.

The achievement gap for English learners remains prevalent, and signifies the importance of teacher preparation, on-going professional development, and community-wide support for the achievement of English learners. Funding cuts during the economic downturn of recent years have made meeting diverse learner needs increasing challenging. Calderon, Slavin, and Sanchez (2011) point out that collaboration among school faculty and the culti-

vation of home–school connections can help to address students' language, literacy, and core content needs. Teachers reach diverse learners by scaffolding instruction in ways that support content literacy and learning.

In the next chapter, we explore another dimension of standards-based curriculum as we shift our attention to different forms of assessment in the content area classroom. Concern about assessment is one of the major issues in education in the United States today. What role do standardized "high-stakes" assessments play in the lives of classroom teachers? How will the implementation of the Common Core State Standards impact the way in which student learning is assessed? How do authentic forms of assessment inform instructional decisions? How can teachers use portfolios and make decisions about the texts they use? The key to assessment in content areas, as we contend in the next chapter, is to make it as useful as possible. Let's find out how and why this is the case.

Minds On

1. Picture a content area class of twenty-five students from very diverse backgrounds—different native languages, different ethnicities, and varying achievement levels. Describe some classroom strategies you might use to respond to individual differences while maintaining high standards of content literacy and learning.

2. Create a culturally responsive lesson for your content area using the characteristics of culturally responsive instruction described in the chapter.

3. Write your life story from earliest memories to the present. Reflect on your life and your students' lives as you write your autobiography.

Hands On

1. For fifteen minutes in a four-member small group, discuss the topic "how technology might transform popular sports by the year 2125." After the discussion, reflect on how the unique background of each member of the group contributed to the views expressed. Did any of the following factors influence individual participation: background knowledge of sports or technology, past experience playing sports, individual

understanding of sports language or technological applications, or personal definitions of "popular" sports? What parallels might you draw with classroom lessons in which students bring cultural and linguistic differences to the learning activities?

2. Come to class prepared to share a piece of your personal "fund of knowledge"—knowledge and information that your family has passed on—with your

small group. For example, you might share a passed-on craft, a skill, a family hobby, or a recipe. How did this sharing "connect" you to the group and the group to your culture?

3. Teach a culturally responsive content area lesson and reflect on it in writing. Report your process of designing and implementing the lesson in class. How did your students respond to the lesson? What did you learn about culturally responsive instruction from this experience?

4. Interview one of your students' parents. Find out their perspective on their child's approach to reading and writing. What interests does their child have? How might reading and writing in the classroom help to support these interests, while building a facility with the English language? Based on this conversation, what you can do to make learning more interesting or meaningful for your student?

 **eResources**

The following sites are filled with ideas for engaging English learners of all levels: **http://literacyconnections.com/SecondLanguage.php** and **www.literacynet.org/esl**. Browse these sites for engaging activities and suggestions for working effectively with ELs. Adapt those activities and suggestions to content area lessons.

Go to **www.colorincolorado.org**, a bilingual site for educators, administrators, librarians, families, and English learners. Explore the starter-kit on placement, instruction, special services, and assessment, as well as suggestions for teaching and learning across the content areas.

Visit **http://graphicclassroom.blogspot.com** for information on using comics and graphic novels across the curriculum.

Visit the Multicultural Education Internet Resource Guide **(http://jan.ucc.nau.edu/~jar/Multi.html)** and a specialproject of *The Internet TESL Journal* **(http://a4esl.org)**. Explore the various activities available to assist English-learning students.

Go to SIOP Central **(www.cal.org/siop)** to study lesson plans based on the SIOP model.

MyEducationLab™

Go to Topic 1: Diversity, Culture, and Literacy, the MyEducationLab (**www.myeducationlab.com**) for *Content Area Reading*, where you can:

- Find learning outcomes for Diversity, Culture, and Literacy, along with the national standards that connect to these outcomes
- Complete Assignments and Activities that can help you more deeply understand the chapter content.
- Practice the core teaching skills identified in the chapter with the Building Teaching Skills and Dispositions learning units.
- Check your comprehension on the content covered in the chapter with the Study Plan. Here you will be able to take a chapter quiz, receive feedback on your answers, and then access Review, Practice, and Enrichment activities to enhance your understanding of chapter content.
- Visit A+RISE. A+RISE® Standards2Strategy™ is an innovative and interactive online resource that offers new teachers in grades K–12 just in time, research-based instructional strategies that meet the linguistic needs of English Language Learners (ELLs) as they learn content, differentiate instruction for all grades and abilities, and are aligned to Common Core Elementary Language Arts standards (for the literacy strategies) and to English language proficiency standards in World-Class Instructional Design and Assessment (WIDA), Texas, California, and Florida.
- Use the Online Lesson Plan Builder to practice lesson planning and integrating national and state standards into your planning.

4 Assessing Students and Texts

Instructional assessment is a process of gathering and using multiple sources of relevant information about students for instructional purposes.

How effectively are students learning to use reading, writing, talking, and viewing as tools to comprehend and respond to material in content areas? Assessing students and texts to provide this kind of information means that there is a direct connection between teaching and learning . . . between instruction and the improvement of practice. Assessment in content area classrooms means that students and teachers are actively engaged in a process of evaluation and self-evaluation. Instead of measuring learning exclusively by a score on a standardized test or proficiency exam, the learning process includes assessment of authentic tasks.

Teachers and students want useful assessment; that is, they want to make sense of how and what is taught and learned at any given time.

Teachers want to make instructional decisions based on their students' content literacy skills, concepts, and performance. They must also deal with the very real pressure of state and federal mandates for standards-based curriculum and testing. The pressure to simply raise tests scores has caused some researchers and teachers to question the effect of mandated standards and assessments on student learning and on teachers' ability to meet diverse learner needs. More than ever in this high-stakes testing environment there is a clear need to carefully consider what assessments are used, how assessment results are interpreted, and how assessments impact teaching and learning across the content areas.

To understand assessment, you need to differentiate between two major contrasting approaches: a

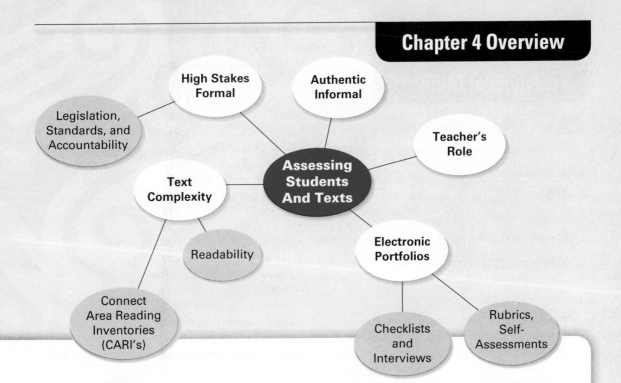

formal, high-stakes approach and an informal, authentic approach. When standards were initially developed by professional organizations and state governments, testing was thought to be necessary to ensure that schools would meet high standards of achievement. Soon, students' performances on state-mandated tests became the focus of debate among educators, policy makers, and constituency groups. The public's attention today is often on this formal, high-stakes approach to assessment. Many teachers, however, have become adept at alternative, authentic assessment practices to help them make decisions about instruction appropriate for each student. As depicted in the graphic organizer, portfolios, observations, anecdotal records, checklists, interviews, inventories, and conferences with students are some of the methods and techniques that make authentic assessment possible.

Assessing for instruction should, first and foremost, provide the opportunity to gather and interpret useful information about students as they learn, including: their prior knowledge; their attitudes toward reading, writing, and subject matter; and their ability to use content literacy to learn with texts. Through the portfolio assessment process—collecting authentic evidence of student work over time—teachers and students gather useful information about an individual's comprehension and response to content area material. The organizing principle of this chapter maintains that assessment should be useful, authentic, and responsive to teacher decision making: **Instructional assessment is a process of gathering and using multiple sources of relevant information about students for instructional purposes.**

Frame of Mind

1. How does assessment help us set instructional goals?

2. How does a formal, high-stakes approach differ from an informal, authentic approach?

3. What have legislators done to try to ensure students' achievement?

4. What are some of the informal assessment strategies teachers use in the context of their classrooms?

5. How can content area teachers involve students in the electronic portfolio process?

6. How might teachers analyze the complexity of texts?

Teachers sometimes know intuitively that what they do in class is working. More often, however, information for making decisions is best obtained through careful observation of students. Their strengths and weaknesses as they interact with one another and with texts can be assessed as they participate in small groups, contribute to class discussions, respond to questions, and complete written assignments. This approach to assessment is *informal* and *authentic*; it is student centered and classroom based. This approach, however, isn't the only one operating in schools today. If teachers are in a school district guided by standards-based curricula, they need to understand the differences between *high-stakes* and *authentic* approaches to assessment.

Response Journal

Write about a time when a teacher had an intuition about you as a student. Was it on target? Off target?

 **Approaches to Assessment**

The two major views of assessment, high-stakes and authentic, are like different sides of the same coin. They represent the almost opposite perspectives of policy makers on one side and teachers on the other. Policy makers are responding to the public demand for assurances that students will leave school well prepared to enter either the workforce or college. Teachers and other educators are calling for better, more authentic assessment practices that will improve instruction and result in learning. As Tierney (1998, p. 378) put it, one focuses on "something you *do to* students," and the other focuses on "something you *do with* them or help them *do for themselves*."

Authentic methods often include some combination of observations, interviews, anecdotal records, and student-selected performances and products. The information gained from an authentic assessment can be organized into a rich description or portrait of your content area classroom or into student *portfolios*. Concerns that emerge, whether about individual students or about the delivery of instructional strategies, are likely to make sense because they come directly from the classroom context and often result from teacher–student or student–student interaction.

Consider how an authentic approach differs from a more formal, high-stakes one. In Table 4.1, the two approaches are compared in several categories. Certainly, there are many gray areas in assessment, where the formal and informal overlap. In this table, however, differences between the two approaches are emphasized. Traditional, formal assessments are product oriented. They are more tangible and can be obtained at predetermined points in time. Authentic assessments are informal and process oriented. The process is ongoing, providing as much information about

Table 4.1 Comparisons of Two Approaches to Assessment

	High-Stakes/Formal	Authentic/Informal
Orientation	Formal; developed by expert committees and test publishers	Informal; developed by teachers and students
Administration	Testing one time performance; paper-and-pencil, multiple-choice; given to groups at one seating	Continuously evolving and intermittent throughout an instructional unit; small group, one on one
Methods	Objective; standardized reading achievement tests designed to measure levels of current attainment; state proficiency testing of content knowledge	Classroom tests, checklists, observations, interviews, and so on, designed to evaluate understanding of course content; real-life reading and writing tasks
Uses	Compare performance of one group with students in other schools or classrooms; determine funding, support for districts and schools; estimate range of reading ability in a class; select appropriate materials for reading; identify students who need further diagnosis; align curriculum; allocate classroom time	Make qualitative judgments about students' strengths and instructional needs in reading and learning content subjects; select appropriate materials; adjust instruction when necessary; self-assess strengths and weaknesses
Feedback Format	Reports, printouts of subtest scores; summaries of high and low areas of performance; percentiles, norms, stanines	Notes, profiles, portfolios, discussions, recommendations that evolve throughout instructional units; expansive (relate to interests, strategies, purpose for learning and reading)

the student as learner as about the product. Together, they permit a more balanced approach through a combination of traditional/formal and authentic/informal practices. The end result is an understanding of *why* particular results are obtained in formal assessment, which informs the *how* of the teacher decision-making process.

High-Stakes Testing: Issues and Concerns

Never have the stakes been higher. With virtually every state adopting content standards in multiple content areas, such as English, mathematics, social studies, and science, standardized testing systems have been mandated, developed, and put in place throughout the United States. Under No Child Left Behind, states were required to use standardized tests results to determine whether schools are achieving adequate yearly progress (AYP). While revisions to No Child Left Behind are widely expected to mitigate the punitive aspects of the original legislation, high-stakes testing is likely to remain.

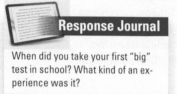

Response Journal

When did you take your first "big" test in school? What kind of an experience was it?

Thus, although standardized testing has been used to evaluate student achievement since Thorndike developed the first standardized tests in the early part of the twentieth century, the amount of mandatory testing has increased. And the stakes—significant rewards and penalties—have risen. Furthermore, in recent years, mandatory tests have been administered to younger and younger students and with greater frequency than ever before (Hoffman et al. 1999).

Several issues and concerns surround the use of high-stakes testing. Proponents of high-stakes testing contend that such testing is a sound strategy to use to ensure that standards are met and students are achieving at an appropriate level of proficiency. They seek to effectively end the practice of social promotion, that is, promoting students from one grade level to the next regardless of whether the students have demonstrated on tests the potential to work successfully at the next grade level. Proponents of high-stakes tests assert that test results can help schools to identify areas of weakness and to allocate resources where they are most needed in order to improve their programs and the performance of individual students (ECS, 2008). Some proponents also point to generally positive popular attitudes about the fairness and utility of standardized testing. For example, despite claims to the contrary, many people believe that standardized tests are inherently fair and scientific (Afflerbach, 2004).

Though use of mandated, high-stakes testing has spread, questions abound about the implications of such tests. One concern centers on the narrowing of the school curriculum as a result of the heavy emphasis placed on test preparation (Nichols & Berliner, 2007, p. 9). As Guilfoyle (2006) explains, "In this culture of 'What gets measured gets done,' the question that begs to be asked [is], 'What happens to what *doesn't* get measured?'." What doesn't get tested can include subjects such as social studies, visual arts, music, and physical education as well as school-sponsored extracurricular activities All too often, these subjects become marginalized. In their study of social studies instruction, Fichett and Heafner (2010) found that an average of 12 minutes a day in elementary grades and 24 minutes a day in the intermediate grades were spent on social studies instruction. Teachers often used time designated for social studies instruction to teach math and reading skills that were to be part of mandated assessments. Similarly, in one California school, for example, funding was dropped for music, art, Spanish, and industrial design classes and students were required to take two periods of core subjects for which high-stakes tests were administered (Zastrow & Janc, 2006).

What about the validity of certain assessment tools? Some studies have raised questions about the reasons behind student gains on state-mandated assessment, suggesting that the scores produced may be substantially higher than the students' understanding of the subject area material (Koretz, 2008). Research has not shown a link between increased standardized testing and increased reading achievement (Afflerbach, 2004). Some researchers suggest that students' improved performances on standardized tests can be attributed not only to achievement but also to factors such as the increased class time spent on test preparation, students' growing familiarity with test questions and procedures, and a large proportion of low-scoring students being exempted from taking tests in order to avoid the sanctions connected with low test scores (Klein, Hamilton, McCaffrey, & Stecher, 2000; Nichols & Berliner, 2007). Additionally, some are concerned that students referred to as "bubble kids"—those who are close to attaining a passing score—receive targeted instruction in order to raise their scores to the required marks, but students whose scores are not close to passing don't receive the instruction they need to progress.

Additional concerns about high-stakes testing include the contention that high-stakes tests require a significant amount of time and resources that could be directed more effectively toward other ways of increasing reading achievement. In addition, although high-stakes tests paint an incomplete picture of students' reading capabilities, students are being labeled at earlier ages based on the result of these test scores (Afflerbach, 2004). High-stakes testing encourages educators to view students as test score "increasers" or test score "suppressors" (Nichols & Berliner, 2008). For students who struggle academically, high-stakes testing can diminish both their self-efficacy for learning and their motivation to attempt academic pursuits. For students who are academically capable, an academic routine centered on achieving a mandated test score often fails to focus on their potential as learners. Nichols and Berliner (2008) point out that research has yet to examine the impact of high-stakes testing on students' attitudes and dispositions toward learning. Other critics claim that, far from being fair, high-stakes testing has led to a disproportionate number of minority and low-income students being retained or dropping out of school (Darling-Hammond, 2003).

School leaders face the challenge of blending student needs with needed scores and have expressed additional concerns about mandated high-stakes tests. Some assert that the tests are not grounded in child development theory, pointing out that students of the same chronological age should not be expected to be at the same point in terms of cognitive development and academic achievement (Mraz, 2000). Others, such as literacy consultant Dorothy Barnhouse (2012, p. 1) express concern that, for some teachers, having their performance evaluated almost solely on the basis of student test scores, results in the scores receiving more emphasis than authentic learner needs. As she explains, "This year, I have seen more and more teaching that is about answers. No inquiry, curiosity, or study. No thinking. Just answers." Some professional organizations, such as the International Reading Association, advise against attaching rewards and penalties to single test scores and encourage the use of multiple measures, which honor the complexity of reading, to inform important decisions (Ransom et al., 1999). The Literacy Researchers Association (formerly the National Reading Conference) recommends that assessment be aligned with classroom curricula and instruction, provide clear suggestions for improved instruction to meet learner needs, and be consistently reviewed and revised by stakeholders, including school boards, teachers, and parents (Afflerbach, 2004). Even the proposed *Reauthorization of the Elementary and Secondary Education Act* (i.e. *No Child Left*

Behind) calls for state accountability systems that "recognize process and growth and reward success rather than only identify failure" (Duncan, 2010, p. 9).

No single test can meet the needs of all groups who require information about school and student performance. Different constituencies need different types of information, presented in different forms, and made available at different times. Policy makers and the general public may benefit from information provided by norm-referenced tests that are administered on an annual basis. Parents, teachers, and students need information specific to individual students on a more consistent basis. Observations, portfolios, samples of student work over time, and conferences about student progress are more effective than standardized tests in providing that type of information. The purpose of the assessment selected, and the goals for its use, should be carefully considered so that the assessment tool selected will ultimately serve to provide information that can be used to improve learning opportunities for all students (Farr, 1992).

Response Journal

Do you feel competent in making assessment part of teaching? What do you think is the best preparation you could receive?

BOX 4.1   RTI for Struggling Adolescent Learners

Identifying Students in Need of Support

RTI should be viewed as a tool for identifying, assessing, and assisting students who need support beyond traditional instruction. Because assessment is one of the cornerstones of RTI, teachers need resources that will help them to identify which students are at risk for failure, pinpoint specific areas of strength and weakness, and offer insight into the effectiveness of instructional strategies (Berman & Biancarosa, 2005). RTI is a process by which students are screened to determine their present level of performance and then intermittently assessed thereafter to determine their progress and reaction to instruction. Furthermore, curriculum-based measurements are used to assess students' progress toward course goals and objectives (Stecker, Fuchs, & Fuchs, 2008). In this chapter, we suggest a variety of assessment tools that will help content area teachers document students' progress and plan appropriate instruction over the course of the school year. The data created by these assessments should drive instructional decision making.

RTI is not simply focused on addressing learning deficits, rather it is a process by which student strengths can be identified in order to support learning across the content areas. Students who may benefit from the RTI process are not only those students deemed "at-risk," but also students who benefit from non-traditional forms of instruction or who need different outlets to present their knowledge of a subject area. Differentiation, as supported by RTI, can be evidenced through changes in the process, the product, or the content of the learning experience (Tomlinson & Strickland, 2005). Teachers are in a strategic position to select materials for whole-class or individualized instruction that align with the needs of the students. Often, trade books and anthologies provided by publishers provide direction on how to match resources to students' abilities through leveling systems such as Lexile scores or grade equivalencies, which analyze difficulty by considering characteristics such as sentence and word length or complexity of vocabulary and syntax. Several informational databases also include the reading levels of texts and articles relevant to subject area topics. This allows content area teachers access to texts of varying levels of difficulty in order to differentiate instruction for their students.

Legislation, Standards, and Accountability

Traditionally, the role of the federal government in educational policy was to provide funding to individual states. Authority over curriculum and assessment was delegated by state policy makers to local school districts. Districts, in turn, relied on teachers and building administrators to make instructional decisions with little guidance or interference from legislative authorities (Massell, Kirst, & Hoppe, 1997). At the turn of the twenty-first century, however, the federal government began to play an increasingly more prominent role in educational policy making.

In 2002, the No Child Left Behind Act (NCLB), a reauthorization of the original Elementary and Secondary Education Act (ESEA) of 1964, instituted new accountability requirements that marked an unprecedented level of federal involvement in K–12 schools. NCLB required states to administer standardized assessments in reading, mathematics, and science to students in grades three through eight and in high school. To meet NCLB requirements, state policy makers were actively engaged in assessing student performance and imposing consequences for schools that did not meet required standards. In order for schools to receive federal funding for education, NCLB required states to develop and implement a standardized accountability program that showed whether their public schools had achieved adequate yearly progress (AYP). AYP was described as "an all or nothing" model (NCDPI, 2008), and the consequences of not achieving AYP were serious. Schools that did not make AYP for two or more consecutive years faced sanctions under the federal law. Those sanctions included losing federal funding, being restaffed, or being closed altogether (Guilfoyle, 2006; Toppo, 2001).

Critics of the legislation contended that, although high standards of educational achievement are desirable, NCLB unfairly penalized schools and actually lowered standards as states adjust their proficiency requirements downward to preserve federal funding, thus giving an illusion of progress when test scores increased (Koretz, 2008). Additional concerns were raised about the disproportionate number of mandates in relation to the actual funding offered to schools to fulfill those mandates (Maguire, 2001). Some even challenged the constitutionality of NCLB, questioning whether the federal government was infringing on states' rights, coercing rather than inducing states to meet requirements in order to receive federal funding (McColl, 2005).

By 2012, many educators and policy makers alike seemed to agree that the one-size-fits-all approach of NCLB was seriously flawed, resulting in more schools failing to meet test score targets than ever before. NCLB narrowed the definition of reading, focusing too heavily on basic reading skills, and deemphasizing high-level thinking skills (Longo, 2010) and balanced literacy instruction (Pruisner, 2009). A new federal administration (in 2008) brought new policy reform efforts. The current proposal to revise the NCLB legislation places a greater emphasis on "investing in teacher quality, community and school partnerships, and overall innovation" (Berry & Herrington, 2011, p. 288). First, the Race to the Top initiative passed in 2009, which launched a competitive grants process intended to motivate states and local school districts to take a different and more aggressive approach to improve public education. The Race to the Top Executive Summary (2009) outlines the following education reform efforts that the initiative was designed to support:

- Adopting standards and assessments that prepare students to succeed in college and the workplace to compete in the global economy
- Building data systems that measure student growth and success, and inform teachers and principals about how they can improve instruction

- Recruiting, developing, rewarding, and retaining effective teachers and principals, especially where they are needed most
- Turning around the lowest-achieving schools

Next, the Common Core Standards, described in Chapter 1, established standards in English language arts, mathematics, and science that are intended to be clearer, higher, aligned with twenty-first century skills, and research-based. A key goal of the Common Core Standards initiative is to ensure that American students are prepared to compete successfully in college and in the global economy. While some have already raised concerns about the curriculum focus of the Common Core and about how the Common Core Standards will be aligned with state standards (Beach, 2011), many states are already working to revise their standards and assessment procedures in order to meet the requirements of the Common Core. For example, North Carolina has launched a five-year effort, North Carolina's Accountability and Curriculum Reform Effort (ACRE) to redefine the Standard Course of Study for K–12 students, as well as statewide assessment programs and the school accountability model. This reform effort seeks to identify the critical knowledge and skills that students need, create assessments that incorporate more open-ended questions and real-world applications, and create a new model for measuring school success in preparing students for college and the workplace (NCDPI, 2012).

Standardized Testing: What Teachers Need to Know

Standardized reading tests are formal, usually machine-scorable, instruments in which scores for the tested group are compared with standards established by an original normative population. The purpose of a standardized reading test is to show where students rank in relation to other students based on a single performance.

To make sense of test information and to determine how relevant or useful it may be, you need to be thoroughly familiar with the language, purposes, and legitimate uses of standardized tests. For example, as a test user, it is your responsibility to know about the norming and standardization of the reading test used by your school district. Consult a test manual for an explanation of what the test is about, the rationale behind its development, and a clear description of what the test purports to measure. Not only should test instructions for administering and scoring be clearly spelled out, but also information related to norms, reliability, and validity should be easily defined and made available.

Norms represent average scores of a sampling of students selected for testing according to factors such as age, sex, race, grade, or socioeconomic status. Once a test maker determines norm scores, those scores become the basis for comparing the test performance of individuals or groups to the performance of those who were included in the norming sample. *Representativeness,* therefore, is a key concept in understanding student scores. It's crucial to make sure that the norming sample used in devising the reading test resembles the characteristics of the students you teach.

Norms are extrapolated from raw scores. A *raw score* is the number of items a student answers correctly on a test. Raw scores are converted to other kinds of scores so that comparisons can be made among individuals or groups of students. Three such conversions—percentile scores, stanine scores, and grade-equivalent scores—are often represented by test makers as they report scores.

Percentile scores describe the relative standing of a student at a particular grade level. For example, the percentile score of 85 of a student in the fifth grade means that his or her score is equal to or higher than the scores of 85 percent of comparable fifth graders.

Stanine scores are raw scores that have been transformed to a common standard to permit comparison. In this respect, stanines represent one of several types of standard scores. Because standard scores have the same mean and standard deviation, they permit the direct comparison of student performance across tests and subtests. The term *stanine* refers to a *sta*ndard *nine*-point scale, in which the distribution of scores on a test is divided into nine parts. Each stanine indicates a single digit ranging from one to nine in numerical value. Thus a stanine of five is at the midpoint of the scale and represents average performance. Stanines six, seven, eight, and nine indicate increasingly better performance; stanines four, three, two, and one represent decreasing performance. As teachers, we can use stanines effectively to view a student's approximate place above or below the average in the norming group.

Grade-equivalent scores provide information about reading-test performance as it relates to students at various grade levels. A grade-equivalent score is a questionable abstraction. It suggests that growth in reading progresses throughout a school year at a constant rate; for example, a student with a grade-equivalent score of 7.4 is supposedly performing at a level that is average for students who have completed four months of the seventh grade. At best, this is a silly and spurious interpretation: "Based on what is known about human development generally and language growth specifically, such an assumption [underlying grade-equivalent scores] makes little sense when applied to a human process as complex as learning to read" (Vacca, Vacca, Gove, et al., 2002).

Reliability refers to the consistency or stability of a student's test scores. A teacher must raise the question, "Can similar test results be achieved under different conditions?" Suppose your students were to take a reading test on Monday, their first day back from vacation, and then take an equivalent form of the same test on Thursday. Would their scores be about the same? If so, the test may indeed be reliable.

Validity, by contrast, tells the teacher whether the test is measuring what it purports to measure. Validity, without question, is one of the most important characteristics of a test. If the test purports to measure reading comprehension, what is the test maker's concept of reading comprehension? Answers to this question provide insight into the *construct validity* of a test. Other aspects of validity include *content validity* (Does the test reflect the domain or content area being examined?) and *predictive validity* (Does the test predict future performance?).

In general, information from standardized tests may help screen for students who have major difficulties in reading, compare general reading-achievement levels of different classes or grades of students, assess group reading achievement, and assess the reading growth of groups of students (Allington & Strange, 1980). However, teachers also need useful information about students' text-related behavior and background knowledge. You would be guilty of misusing standardized test results if you were to extrapolate about a student's background knowledge or ability to comprehend course materials on the basis of standardized reading-test performance. Alternatives to high-stakes, formal assessments are found in an informal, authentic approach to assessment. One of the most useful tools for inquiry into the classroom is observation.

Authentic Assessment: The Teacher's Role

In a high-stakes approach to assessment, the *test* is the major tool; in an authentic approach, the *teacher* is the major tool. Who is better equipped to observe students, to provide feedback, and to serve as a key informant about the meaning of classroom events? You epitomize the process of assessing students in an ongoing, natural way because you are in a position to observe and collect information continuously (Valencia, 1990). Consequently, you become an observer of the relevant interactive and independent behavior of students as they learn in the content area classroom.

Observation is one unobtrusive measure that ranges from the occasional noticing of unusual student behavior to frequent anecdotal jottings to regular and detailed written field notes. Besides the obvious opportunity to observe students' oral and silent reading, there are other advantages to observation. Observing students' appearance, posture, mannerisms, enthusiasm, or apathy may reveal information about self-image. However, unless you make a systematic effort to tune in to student performance, you may lose valuable insights. You have to be a good listener to and watcher of students. Observation should be a natural outgrowth of teaching; it increases teaching efficiency and effectiveness. Instructional decisions based on accurate observations help you zero in on what and how to teach in relation to communication tasks.

Today's teachers are expected to meet the special needs of all students. Consequently, the challenges of teaching diverse learners in the classroom may cause nonspecialist teachers to feel frustrated and unprepared. Understanding and accepting differences in students can, however, lead to effective instructional adaptations. Lynne, a middle school literacy coach, explains how she has used observational assessment to help address the needs of students with behavioral issues that affect their learning:

> I am often asked by teachers for advice on how to address behavioral concerns that they have about particular students. I begin by recommending that they use a Behavior Frequency Observation Checklist as a diagnostic-prescriptive measure to record the instances of inappropriate or inattentive behaviors they observe. I've used the checklist with individual teachers, and also with teachers across subject areas to document student behaviors observed in different content area classes. For example, I've given teachers across content areas the same frequency observation form to document the existence of the targeted behaviors of a particular student or a group of students. This orderly observation and documentation allowed the teachers to determine if the same behaviors occurred across content area classes, or if the behaviors were isolated to a specific class. Based on this documentation, appropriate intervention strategies could be developed and implemented. After an agreed-upon period of time, the frequency checklist can be repeated to determine to what extent intervention strategies were effective.

There are several advantages to using a frequency observation form: the observer can identify specific target behaviors or academic skills; when completed, the form provides objective data about targeted behaviors that can be used when communicating concerns to parents or to school support personnel; data collected can be used to develop intervention strategies to enhance the learning environment for the student; and the form can serve as both a pre-assessment tool to establish a baseline for future intervention and as a post-assessment tool to judge the impact of an intervention. In addition to the basic format for behavior frequency data, Lynne included two other sections: *other pertinent information,* where she noted the reason for the observation as well as any support the student might be receiving in or out of school, and *tentative conclusions,* where she made comments about what she just observed and what to focus on in the next observation. Figure 4.1 illustrates Lynne's observation of Thomas.

Figure 4.1 Behavior Frequency Observation

Classroom Artifact

Student Name: Thomas   Date: October 12, 2012

Start time: 10:00 a.m.   Stop time: 10:30 a.m.

School: Edison Middle School   Grade: 6

Subject: Mathematics

Other pertinent information: Thomas is being observed to determine if a referral for possible ADHD evaluation is appropriate.

Target Behavior	Frequency of Occurrence	Total
Calls out of turn	|||||||||||||	13
Moves out of seat	||||||	6
Distracts others (e.g., drops things, moves the desk, touches others)	||||||||||	10
Makes unnecessary noises (e.g., taps desk, hums)	|||||||	7
Off task (e.g., not working; does not start assignment)	|||||||||||||||	15

Tentative Conclusion: Additional observations across content area classes are recommended.

To record systematic observations, to note significant teaching–learning events, or simply to make note of classroom happenings, you need to keep a notebook on hand or online. Information collected purposefully aids in classifying information, inferring patterns of behavior, and making predictions about the effectiveness of innovative instructional procedures. As they accumulate, these "field notes" provide documentary evidence of students' interactions over periods of time.

Teachers and others who use informal, authentic tools to collect information almost always use more than one means of collecting data, a practice known as *triangulation*. This helps ensure that the information is valid and that what is learned from one source is corroborated by what is learned from another source. A fifth-grade science teacher recounted how he combined the taking of field notes with active listening and discussion to assess his students' current achievement and future needs in the subject:

> I briefly document on individual cards how students behave during experiments conducted individually, within a group, during reading assignments, during phases of a project, and during formal assessments. Knowing which students or what size group tends to enhance or distract a student's ability to stay on task helps me organize a more effective instructional environment. When students meet to discuss their projects and the steps they followed, I listen carefully for strategies they used or neglected. I sometimes get insights into what a particular student offered this group; I get ideas for topics for future science lessons and projects or mini-lessons on time management, breaking up a topic into "chunks," and so on.

BOX 4.2

Voices from the Field

Cindy, Tenth-Grade Social Studies Teacher

Challenge

When preparing my lessons for our reading of *The Kite Runner* with my social studies honor students, I was concerned that many of the complexities presented in that story would be lost on the students if they didn't have a basic understanding of Afghanistan. I decided that I needed to get a sense of what the students already knew, or what they thought they knew, about Afghanistan before we opened the book. I thought that understanding these topics might help them to better comprehend the book we were about to read together.

Strategy

I had, on occasion, used a Frequency Observation Form to record data on students' behavior, but I had not yet adapted it for observations of students' academic skills. I decided to try. I began by listing topics that would be addressed through their reading of the book such as details about Afghan history and culture. Then we engaged in a prereading discussion about these topics. Through their responses during this discussion, which included asking students for a show of hands to indicate how many of them agreed or disagreed with statements about Afghanistan, I was able to gauge the extent to which my students' knowledge and assumptions about Afghanistan were accurate.

Reflection

My Frequency Observation Chart indicated that, prior to reading the book, only four out of twenty students had prior knowledge of Afghanistan that was detailed and accurate. This meant that I had some work to do to help build their background knowledge before I assigned them chapters of the book to read on their own! Knowing that they lacked relevant information on the book's key focus helped me to select strategies and questioning techniques throughout our reading to enhance their knowledge of the topic and to check for comprehension as they read. When we had finished reading and discussing *The Kite Runner,* I revisited the Frequency Observation Chart again to see if my students' understanding of Afghan culture and history had improved. This time, I found that seventeen of the twenty students had acquired knowledge needed to understand the many nuances in the story. Also, I noticed that students' responses during our class discussions were often more insightful than I had expected, and almost all of the students participated in those discussions. Had I simply plunged into reading this book without ascertaining what they already knew or didn't know, I'm not sure that would have happened.

Response Journal

How can parent–teacher conferences make a difference in students' academic performance? What can a teacher do to enhance the effectiveness of these conferences?

In Box 4.2 Cindy, a high school social studies teacher, shares her experience using frequency observation with class discussion.

Informal assessment strategies are useful to teachers during parent–teacher conferences for discussing a student's strengths and weaknesses. They also help build an ongoing record of progress that may be motivating for students to reflect on and useful for their other teachers in planning lessons in different subjects. And finally, the assessments themselves may provide meaningful portfolio entries from both a teacher's and a student's perspective, serving "as the essential link among curriculum, teaching, and learning" (Wilcox 1997, p. 223).

Many students want to establish a personal rapport with their teachers. They may talk of myriad subjects, seemingly unrelated to the unit. It is often during this informal chatter, however, that you find out about the students' backgrounds, problems, and interests. This type of conversation, in which you assume the role of active listener, can provide suggestions about topics for future lessons and materials and help the student's voice emerge.

Discussion, both casual and directed, is also an integral part of assessment. You need to make yourself available, both before and after class, for discussions about general topics, lessons, and assignments. For an assessment of reading comprehension, nothing replaces one-on-one discussion of the material, whether before, during, or after the actual reading. Finally, encourage students to verbalize their positive and negative feelings about the class itself as well as about topics, readings, and content area activities.

A note of caution: It's important to realize that "no matter how careful we are, we will be biased in many of our judgments" (MacGinitie, 1993, p. 559). Yet teachers who observe with any sort of regularity soon discover that they are able to acquire enough information to process "in a meaningful and useful manner" (Fetterman, 1989, p. 88). They can then make reliable decisions about instruction with observation and other techniques in portfolio assessment.

Portfolio Assessment in a Digital Age

A valuable trend that occasionally swings in and out of mandated curricula is portfolio assessment. Now more than ever, portfolios are one of the strongest tools for educators because of the unique opportunity they provide: concretely visualizing student growth over time. Portfolios encourage the incorporation of different types of summative and formative assessments, which allows teachers to incorporate intervention and enrichment as needed. In addition, the combination of technology and student access to online publishing provides a unique opportunity for real-time publication and comprehensive synthesis of reading, writing, responding, and analyzing. Electronic portfolios, sometimes referred to as e-portfolios or digital portfolios, allow students to organize information, highlight skills, and represent their work (Waters, 2007). Unlike blogs and random posts, which are considered personal spaces for expression, e-portfolios are artifact and standard driven. Ideally, an e-portfolio can accompany a student through every year of their schooling, resulting in a visual demonstration of their learning and development even as the student transitions from one school or classroom to another.

As a global, balanced practice in gathering information about students, portfolio assessment is a powerful concept that has immediate appeal and potential for accomplishing the following purposes:

- Providing and organizing information about the nature of students' work and achievements
- Encouraging student management of learning and expectations, as well as reflection and thematic analysis
- Involving students themselves in reflecting on their capabilities and making decisions about their work
- Using the holistic nature of instruction as a base from which to consider attitudes, strategies, and responses
- Assisting in the planning of appropriate instruction to follow
- Showcasing work mutually selected by students and teacher

- Revealing diverse and special needs of students as well as talents
- Incorporating multi-literacies and social technologies that students use outside of the classroom
- Displaying multiple student-produced artifacts over time
- Integrating assessment into the daily instruction as a natural, vital part of teaching and learning
- Expanding both the quality and the quantity of evidence by means of a variety of indicators
- Providing an alternative to the standard paper and pencil assessment routines

Portfolios are vehicles for ongoing assessment, and although they may seem challenging to implement, once developed, they provide teachers with an overview of a student's skills and growth. Many educators recognize that portfolio assessment can extend beyond summative evaluation and instead serve as a formative tool that aids in aligning teaching and assessment in order to facilitate productive learning (Lam & Lee, 2009). Composed of a purposeful collection of artifacts, student learning portfolios examine achievement, effort, improvement, and, most importantly, processes (selecting, comparing, sharing, self-evaluation, and goal-setting) according to Tierney, Carter, and Desai (1991). As such, they lend themselves beautifully to instruction in content areas ranging from math and science to English, history, and health education. Though the content of a portfolio is tailored to a particular subject, the goal and production of the portfolio remains consistent. A benefit that encourages cross-curricular opportunities, the use of portfolios encourages integration and vertical alignment throughout students' school days.

Though teacher assignments and support define the creation of the portfolio, teachers and students collaboratively choose the significant pieces incorporated into student portfolios. Selections represent processes and activities more than products; student assessment is truly focused on the learning rather than the final outcome. A distinct value underlying the use of portfolios is a commitment to students' evaluation of their own understanding and personal development. In addition, electronic portfolios allow students to critique and "teach" through response and interaction with their peers' portfolios. By providing a more in-depth and thoughtful assessment than can be gleaned from on-demand tests alone, the digital portfolio can serve as a comprehensive measure of student knowledge and growth (Tuttle, 2007). In addition to serving as a resource for student and teacher collaboration, digital portfolios have been shown to be an effective source of engagement for students, as they publish their work and monitor their own progress (Waters, 2007).

Contrasting portfolios with traditional assessment procedures, Walker (1991) submits that instead of a contrived task representing knowledge of a subject, portfolios are an "authentic" assessment that measures the process of the construction of meaning. As concepts and skills are developed, the portfolio changes and adapts, supporting areas of growth with structurally sound knowledge. The students make choices about what to include; these choices, in turn, encourage self-reflection on their own development, their own evaluation of their learning, and personal goal setting. In this way, their learning becomes not a reiteration of a predetermined response, but rather a statement of what they have learned, and of what they have yet to learn (Tuttle, 2007). In addition, portfolio sharing provides students with an opportunity to view other ideas and perspectives. Exposing students to alternative examples via peer models encourages evaluation and analysis of material; student portfolios become a resource for textual learning and comprehension.

Adapting Portfolios to Content Area Classes

By making individual adjustments, portfolios can be adapted to serve different learning needs, across the content areas. Techniques such as rubric evaluation, self and peer responses, observing, and use of parent and teacher feedback provide helpful sources of information about students in the classroom. The use of portfolios is in many ways a more practical method of organizing this type of information. While, in some cases, portfolios have earned a reputation for being high maintenance, electronic portfolios make student assessment over time easier for teachers because of their holistic and self-motivating nature. With digitized work, teachers are able to identify examples from a portfolio into meaningful, instructional content (Walters, 2007). Linek (1991) suggests that many kinds of data be collected for a thorough documentation of attitudes, behaviors, achievements, improvement, thinking, and reflective self-evaluation.

Once students take ownership for their portfolio development, the continuous adding and revising of their portfolios incorporates itself into the daily routines of the classroom. For example, students may begin a math course by saying things such as, "What are we learning this for anyway? It's got nothing to do with me and my life." As opportunities are provided for functional application in realistic situations, student comments and attitudes may change over time to, "Boy, I never realized how important this was going to be for getting a job in real life!" Additionally, students may view their portfolio as another form of social networking within the school day. Responses and reviews of other portfolios provide interconnectedness to students' use of the Internet and natural affinity to technology.

Much more than a folder for housing daily work, a record file, or a grab bag, a portfolio is a comprehensive profile of each student's progress and growth. As the emphasis on global competiveness and on meeting Common Core Standards sharpens, portfolio self-reflection encourages students to carefully evaluate which of their work products is representative of their knowledge and skills (Tuttle, 2007). With the incorporation of the Internet and website building, the portfolio itself can be completely electronic. The transition from paper-and-pencil portfolios to digitally designed formats allows student collections to become a place for reflection and growth, not just a collection of artifacts (Hicks, Russo, Autrey, Gardner, Kabodian, & Edington, 2007). Student portfolios can become an exploration of learning, extending outside the realm of standard paper activities and incorporating additional tools of learning and enjoyment including the artistic visuals, music, and video production. Professional associations have endorsed the use of portfolios. For example, if you are preparing to teach a math class, whether it's arithmetic, algebra, or trigonometry, the National Council for Teachers of Mathematics (NCTM) offers assessment guidelines to help teachers to decide with students the types of student work-products that should be part of a portfolio. Box 4.3 outlines a procedure for implementing portfolios.

Melissa, a secondary English teacher, experimented with e-portfolios as a comprehensive evaluation tool for literacy and writing development. Here's how she described the process of implementation that she followed:

> I viewed e-portfolio development as a way to incorporate technology and student multi-literacies with state and county mandated content and researched-based instruction. Once a skeptic of the portfolio, the integration of Common Core Standards required portfolio usage and intimidated me. The organization and filing of the students' papers seemed daunting, and the shuffling of folders and wasted time spent on portfolio development made the understanding of portfolios as an assessment tool nearly impossible. Once I incorporated students' technology skills with the portfolio concept, I was able to see the benefit of the portfolio and even found grading and "paperwork" benefits as well.

Evidence-Based Best Practices

BOX 4.3

Steps in the Implementation of Portfolios

To get started implementing the portfolio assessment process, certain logical steps must be taken and certain decisions need to be made:

1. *Discuss with your students the notion of portfolios as an interactive vehicle for assessment.* Explain the concept and show some examples of items that might be considered good candidates for the portfolio. Provide some examples from other fields, such as art and business, where portfolios have historically recorded performance and provided updates.

2. *Specify your assessment model.* What is the purpose of the portfolio? Who is the audience for the portfolio? How much will students be involved? Purposes, for example, may be to showcase students' best work, to document or describe an aspect of their work over time (to show growth), to evaluate by making judgments using either certain standards agreed on in advance or the relative growth and development of each individual, or to document the process

that goes into the development of a single product, such as a unit of work on the Vietnam era or the Middle East or nutrition.

3. *Decide what types of requirements will be used, approximately how many items, and what format will be appropriate for the portfolio.* Furthermore, will students be designing their own portfolios? Will they include videos or computer disks? Or will they have a uniform look? Plan an explanation of portfolios for your colleagues and the principal; also decide on the date when this process will begin.

4. *Consider which contributions are appropriate for your content area.* The main techniques for assessing students' behavior, background knowledge, attitudes, interests, and perceptions are writing samples, video records, conference notes, tests and quizzes, standardized tests, pupil performance objectives, self-evaluations, peer evaluations, daily work samples, and collections of written work (such as vocabulary activities, graphic organizers, concept maps, inquiry/research projects, and reports).

To begin implementing e-portfolios in my class, I followed certain steps:

*   In order to identify a proper outlet for student e-portfolio and publishing, I started with a general Google search and then focused on researching websites and technologies that were available to me and user-friendly. Both commercial portfolio software and website creation sites offer pros and cons that must be considered in relation to student needs and available technology. Though this process and the initial set-up of the student portfolios were a bit time-consuming, it was time well-spent. Once the student websites to house their portfolios were established and the process of implementing the portfolios was completed, the portfolios themselves became almost entirely student-driven and self-sufficient.

*   I explained the concept of portfolios and discussed why they were important. I emphasized to students their role as a writer and publisher to the Internet world. Students were provided examples of e-portfolios to aid their understanding of acceptable artifacts. I also compared their electronic portfolio to their pages on social media sites and referenced the "upkeep" of their learning and examination as a tool for exploration, where layers are peeled away

to reveal new meaning. Similar to interactive notebooks or day-planners with which the students were already familiar, we discussed as a class digital portfolio organization and the basic elements that must be included. Finally, I encouraged students to utilize one another. Peer and self-generated texts became outlets for understanding and analysis. Student self-maintenance was the driving force—choice and freedom fit within the parameters of their portfolio creation.

- Next, I explained the purposes of our portfolio: to describe a portion of students' work over the quarter, showing how it has improved; to reflect on and evaluate their own work in writing and literacy; and to compile a body of work that can travel with them indefinitely. As a class, we also discussed the usefulness of analysis and reliability—understanding what is significant and owned, versus what is plagiarized and unreliable. For those students that were graduating or applying to further their education, I explained the importance of the "live" portfolio as a reference for their work and accomplishments. In addition, I explained the portfolio as an activity in global connectedness and the students' role as writer, thinker, creator, and evaluator.

- Then we discussed the requirements for our portfolio: to create work and explore literature, literacy, writing, and skills development as an integrated process; to incorporate all levels of learning, as well as venture outside of the classic paper trail of thinking; to incorporate writing as well as multi-media, art, and audio as a means of analysis, response, and understanding; that each student strive to post only the best work that he or she has done; to respond and reflect not only on student's own creation, but also the portfolios and work of others; to add pieces that also conform to standard writing and reading expectations; and at the end of the school year, to evaluate students' overall progress and development.

- I gave examples of the kinds of contributions that would be incorporated: writing, reflections (both self and peer), research findings and sources, projects, videos (both individual creation and those found to connect to student learning), responses to writing prompts, visuals, and audio. In addition, I kept a linked portfolio and posted assignments, classmate examples, and potential prompts for those students who were struggling.

- Finally, we discussed the need for continued updating of portfolio websites and the importance of responding to each other's work. Guidelines were given for posting frequency and topics. All student essays and submitted writing needed to be uploaded on a blog page attached to their website portfolio. All documents and materials that were not created solely by the student required citations or references to illustrate the fact that it was not the student's own work. Students were given examples and a brief tutorial for setting up their web pages. Class time was allocated for students to set up their portfolios. Students were advised that portfolios would be graded periodically for content and growth.

Incorporating electronic portfolios is a continuous process for both students and the instructor. Teachers are encouraged to view portfolio development as part of their planning process, and portfolio writing as a representation of students' critical thinking (Fiedler & Pick, 2004). As the teacher gains a better understanding of technology and potential uses and assignments, the student expectations and portfolios will need to be adapted accordingly. While technological issues may occur, the pedagogical framework remains the same, essentially becoming more efficient and streamlined during the process of digitization since the ability to create, edit, store, and display students' work from any computer with Internet access allows for grading and management outside of the school context (Robins, 2006).

While the lack of paper files is a bonus, the incorporation of the Internet has pros and cons. Plagiarism, copyright violations and Internet guidelines must be explained so students understand the consequences and procedures. Additionally, student incorporation of their social literacies with formal learning may require an adjustment period. Regardless, the electronic portfolio has benefits beyond its classroom application. Not only are digital records of achievement maintained by the students themselves, but also the revision of portfolio material can be as easy as a click of the computer mouse (Lam, 2004). Additionally, grading, growth and comprehension can be monitored in a more precise, less stressful process. Student ownership and response, teacher accessibility, and concrete learning artifacts make the electronic portfolio a tool to try. Figure 4.2, depicts the scoring rubric that Melissa used to assess her students' e-portfolios.

Portfolio contributions can take many forms. Fifth-grade teacher Cherrie Jackman, wanted to experiment with portfolios as an assessment tool for writing and science. An example of a

Figure 4.2 Electronic Portfolio Rubric

	1 Not Demonstrated	2 Developing	3 Proficient	4 Accomplished	5 Distinguished
Artifacts					
Selected Artifacts	Artifacts are unconnected to skills and objectives; selection is based on convenience	Artifacts demonstrate targeted skills and objectives on the basic level	Artifacts clearly demonstrate targeted skills and objectives	Artifacts clearly demonstrate targeted skills and objectives; purposeful selection illustrates deeper understanding and reflection	Artifacts clearly demonstrate extensive understanding of targeted skills and objectives; purposeful selection illustrates reflection and mastery
Variety of Artifacts	All artifacts are of similar form and quality	Artifacts vary in form but quality is similar	Artifacts vary in form and demonstrate growth over time	Artifacts vary in form and quality; consistent growth is evident	Artifacts vary in form and quality; consistent growth is evident, and content illustrates clear growth and development
Mechanics	Spelling and punctuation distracts from the content; editing is not evident	Spelling and punctuation errors are present but do not distract from the content	Spelling and punctuation errors are minor; editing efforts are demonstrated	There are few to no spelling and punctuation errors; editing resulted in revisions that worked	Spelling, punctuation and editing resulted in a work that is ready for publication

	1 Not Demonstrated	2 Developing	3 Proficient	4 Accomplished	5 Distinguished
Reflections					
	No reflection on work is evident; reflections don't include areas of growth or areas of continued effort	Reflections are vague or repetitive; reflections may include areas of growth but don't describe areas of continued effort	Most of the reflections include specific reactions, areas of growth and recognized areas of continued effort	All reflections are specific to selected artifacts; reactions include a clear understanding of areas of growth and noted weakness	All reflections include detailed reactions that are descriptive and insightful; clear understanding of growth and areas of weakness are noted, and goals are set for future work
Multimedia Elements					
Collaboration	There is no connection between student work and peer/audience influences/ comments are not posted	Connections between student work and peer/audience influence is limited	Connections between student work and peer/audience influence is demonstrated in student's revisions and reflections	Connections between student work and peer/audience influence is demonstrated in student's revisions, reflections, and posted elements to extend concepts	Connections between student work and peer/audience influence is strongly linked to student's revisions, reflections, and posted elements to extend concepts; clear connections are drawn between targeted concepts and external information
Graphics, Links, and Twenty-first Century Elements	There are no elements that contribute to understanding of goals; multimedia use is inappropriate and distracting	Some elements that contribute to understanding of goals are present but multimedia use is basic and limited	Elements that contribute to understanding of goals are present; multimedia use is complex and illustrate connections	Elements contribute to understanding of goals and demonstrate complex thinking; multimedia selection is purposeful and complex	Elements clearly demonstrate understanding of goals and make complex connections between objectives; multimedia selection is purposeful, complex, and creative
Publishing Elements					
Organization	There is no organization; portfolio is simply a random collection of student work	Portfolio organization is limited; student work generally illustrates progressive growth and understanding	Portfolio is organized with thought and demonstrates progressive growth and understanding	Portfolio organization is well thought out; collection demonstrates progressive growth and understanding, and order choice is specific to objectives	Portfolio organization shows extensive understanding of growth and progression; order choice demonstrates clear connections between objectives and student reflections

(continued)

Figure 4.2 *(continued)*

	1 **Not Demonstrated**	2 **Developing**	3 **Proficient**	4 **Accomplished**	5 **Distinguished**
Formatting	Text is difficult to read, navigation is confusing, and use of formatting tools is not evident	Text is difficult to read, navigation is basic, and better use of formatting tools is needed	Text is generally easy to read, navigation allows for accessibility, formatting tools are used	Text is easy to read, navigation is well thought out, and creative use of formatting tools is present	Text is appropriately selected for maximum impact, navigation is well planned and creative use of formatting tools makes for maximum effectiveness
Citations	Multimedia is not cited and/or citations are not correctly formatted	Some of the multimedia used is cited with accurate and correct citations	Most of the multimedia is cited with accurate and correct citations	All multimedia is cited with accurate and correct citations	All multimedia and content in the student portfolio is accurate and correctly cited
Formal Language	Portfolio is casual and social networking elements are present	Portfolio uses basic formal language with little social networking elements	Most of the portfolio utilizes formal writing and differs from social networking elements	Formal writing is used throughout the portfolio; social networking elements are not present	Advanced formal writing and vocabulary are utilized; clear distinction between social networking and portfolio creation is evident

portfolio contribution made by one of Cherrie's students is a personal reflection on an experiment done in science class (see Figure 4.3).

As Scott's math teacher discovered, an array of assessment possibilities, including writing conference logs and learning participation inventories, are useful in high school. Figure 4.4 depicts the writing conference log for Scott, developed during a geometry unit on quadrilaterals. First, students were asked to take double-entry journal notes that connected the information they read in their geometry textbook to information presented during class discussions. Next, the students worked together in small groups to create a *semantic feature analysis* (see Chapter 10) that compared and contrasted the characteristics of different types of quadrilaterals. After completing the semantic feature analysis, students were asked to write a paragraph that summarized their findings. Finally, in preparation for a mandatory standardized test, students completed a series of word problems that required them to apply their knowledge of quadrilaterals. They were asked to show their computations and to write a summary explaining how they solved each word problem. In addition to the writing conference log, Scott's teacher also used the learning participation survey, shown in Figure 4.5, to assess Scott's participation throughout the quadrilaterals unit.

Figure 4.3 A Personal Reflection for Science

Experiment:

They're All Wet—Determine what effect soaking seeds has on the time it takes them to sprout. In a group of four, develop an experiment using the scientific procedure. Evaluate your group from a scientific and cooperative point of view.

Reflection:

I selected the experiment "They're All Wet" as my best work in science for a number of reasons.

① My group worked very well together. Everyone was assigned a job (reader, recorder, speaker, organizer), and everyone got to talk.

② We wrote a sound hypothesis and design for our experiment because we took our time and we thought about the process.

③ We kept very good records of our observations, and then everyone participated in telling about them.

④ Even though our experiment did not prove our hypothesis, I learned many things from this experiment (see above).

Next time maybe my results will support my hypothesis, but I did learn the proper way to conduct an experiment.

Checklists and Interviews

Informal assessment techniques, such as checklists, interviews, and content area reading inventories (discussed later in this chapter), are different from natural, open-ended observation. They often consist of categories or questions that have already been determined; they impose an a priori classification scheme on the observation process. A checklist is designed to reveal categories of information the teacher has preselected. When constructing a checklist, you should know beforehand which reading and study tasks or attitudes you plan to observe. Individual items on the checklist then serve to guide your observations selectively.

The selectivity that a checklist offers is both its strength and its weakness as an observational tool. Checklists are obviously efficient because they guide your observations and allow you to zero in on certain kinds of behavior. But a checklist can also restrict observation by limiting the breadth of information recorded, excluding potentially valuable raw data. Figure 4.6 presents sample checklist items that may be adapted to specific instructional objectives in various content areas.

In addition to checklists, observations, logs, and inventories, interviews should be considered part of the portfolio assessment repertoire. There are several advantages of using interviews, "be they *formal*, with a preplanned set of questions, or *informal*, such as a conversation about a book" (Valencia, McGinley, & Pearson, 1990, p. 14). First, students and teachers interact in collaborative settings. Second, an open-ended question format is conducive to the sharing of students' own views. Third, it reveals to what extent students are in touch with their internal disposition toward reading subject matter material.

Figure 4.4　Writing Conference Log

Name: *Scott*

Date: 1-22-09

Title: *Double-entry journal for class notes on quadrilaterals*

Focus of conference: *Self-checking knowledge*

Genre: *Nonfiction*

Progress Observations

Strengths:

- *Scott was able to note the main characteristics of each type of quadrangle.*
- *He consistently spelled most terms correctly, and knew how to find the spelling of unfamiliar terms.*
- *Scott makes connections between new and prior learning.*

Areas to work on:

- *Scott needs more practice organizing information.*
- *Needs to improve his use of punctuation when writing sentences*

Date: 1-15-09

Title: *Comparing the structures of quadrilaterals (Semantic feature analysis and summary paragraph)*

Focus of conference: *Compare/Contrast*

Genre: *Nonfiction*

Progress Observations

Strengths:

- *Is able to identify the types of quadrilaterals (Square, rectangle, rhombus, trapezoid, parallelogram) and compare attributes*
- *Correctly uses the semantic features analysis to compare and contrast*
- *Uses evidence to support his claims about the characteristics of each quadrilateral*

Areas to work on:

- *Work on use of grammar and punctuation when writing summary paragraph*

Date: 1-27-09

Title: *Answering word problems completely and correctly*

Focus of conference: *Practicing for standardized assessments*

Genre: *Nonfiction*

Progress Observations

Strengths:

- *Good application of knowledge of quadrilaterals*
- *Mastery of basic math problem solving*

Areas to work on:

- *Elaborate explanation of work in completing word problems*
- *Consider a problem from multiple perspectives to determine the best answer*
- *Use complete sentences and proper punctuation in formal written responses*

Figure 4.5 Learning Participation Inventory

Name: *Scott*

Observations for work completed January '09	Often	Occasionally	Seldom
1. Shows enthusiasm for learning *Scott always begins work promptly and remains engaged throughout the lesson; makes appropriate connections to previously learned concepts.*	★		
2. Raises questions *Scott asks questions of both the teacher and of his classmates but his questions do not usually make use of higher-order thinking skills.*		★	
3. Listens attentively during discussions *Scott often listens during small-group discussions but tunes out during whole-class instruction.*		★	
4. Shares ideas *Shares his ideas in small-group settings, but seldom participates during whole-class discussions.*			★
5. Responds thoughtfully to the ideas of others *Scott usually considers the perspectives of other students.*	★		
6. Participates in projects enthusiastically *Scott understands how class concepts link together and works hard to make connections between assignments and course goals.*	★		

Observations:

While Scott seems hesitant to share ideas in whole-group settings, once he understands the material and how concepts fit together, he works diligently with classmates in small-group settings to complete assignments.

In general, there are three *types of interviews*: structured and semistructured, informal, and retrospective. As described by Fetterman (1989, pp. 48–50), these types blend and overlap in actual practice.

- *Formally structured and semistructured.* Verbal approximations of a questionnaire; allow for comparison of responses put in the context of common group characteristics; useful in securing baseline data about students' background experiences.

- *Informal.* More like conversations; useful in discovering what students think and how one student's perceptions compare with another's; help identify shared values; useful in establishing and maintaining a healthy rapport.

- *Retrospective.* Can be structured, semistructured, or informal; used to reconstruct the past, asking students to recall personal historical information; may highlight their values and reveal information about their worldviews.

Figure 4.6   Sample Checklist Items for Observing Reading and Study Behavior

Reading and Study Behavior	Fred	Pat	Frank	JoAnne	Jenny	Courtney	Mike	Mary
Comprehension								
1. Follows the author's message	A	B	B	A	D	C	F	C
2. Evaluates the relevancy of facts								
3. Questions the accuracy of statements								
4. Critical of an author's bias								
5. Comprehends what the author means								
6. Follows text organization								
7. Can solve problems through reading								
8. Develops purposes for reading								
9. Makes predictions and takes risks								
10. Applies information to come up with new ideas								
Vocabulary								
1. Has a good grasp of technical terms in the subject under study								
2. Works out the meaning of an unknown word through context or structural analysis								
3. Knows how to use a dictionary effectively								
4. Sees relationships among key terms								
5. Becomes interested in the derivation of technical terms								
Study Habits								
1. Concentrates while reading								
2. Understands better by reading orally than silently								
3. Has a well-defined purpose in mind when studying								
4. Knows how to take notes during lecture and discussion								
5. Can organize material through outlining								
6. Skims to find the answer to a specific question								
7. Reads everything slowly and carefully								
8. Makes use of book parts								
9. Understands charts, maps, tables in the text								
10. Summarizes information								

Grading Key: **A** = always (excellent)
  B = usually (good)
  C = sometimes (average)
  D = seldom (poor)
  F = never (unacceptable)

Rubrics and Self-Assessments

Students need to play a role in the assessment of their own literacy products and processes. Teachers who want to help students get more involved in assessment invite them to participate in setting goals and to share how they think and feel. What are the students' perceptions of their achievements? McCullen (1998, p. 7) described how she begins this process with middle grade students:

> I usually start by envisioning the possible outcomes of each assignment. Then the students and I develop a standard of excellence for each facet of the process and convert the outcomes into a rubric. Thus, before the students begin their research, they know the goals of the assignment and the scope of the evaluation.

Rubrics are categories that range from very simple and direct to comprehensive. Rubrics provide students with detailed, consistent guidelines about the expectations for their papers or projects. Some are designed to help individual students self-assess; often they are designed to be used by small groups or by an individual student and teacher. In Figure 4.7, a basic rubric, sometimes referred to as a *holistic rubric,* serves the dual purpose of involving each student in evaluating the group's work on an inquiry project involving the Internet and in self-evaluating. This type of scoring rubric provides a list of criteria that correspond to a particular grade or point total.

More detailed types of rubrics include *analytic rubrics* and *weighted trait rubrics.* Analytic rubrics break down the total score for an assignment into separate traits on which the assignment will be evaluated. Weighted trait rubrics, although similar to analytic rubrics, assign higher values to some traits than to others. The weighted trait rubric, shown in Figure 4.8, was

Figure 4.7   Rubric for Self-Evaluation

Sixth-Grade Inquiry Project

Name: _____

Directions: Evaluate your performance in each of the following categories. Feel free to make comments about areas of this project in which you believe you were successful and areas in which you thought you could improve

Content	Points Possible	Points Earned	Comments
Selection of topic and identification of subtopics	5		
Planning and organization of project	10		
Annotated bibliography of print resources: thoroughness and focus (minimum 4)	20		
Annotated bibliography of Web resources: thoroughness and focus (minimum 4)	20		
Effective use of time in the computer lab	5		
Presentation of findings to classmates	15		

Figure 4.8   Detailed Rubric for an Inquiry Project on the Five Senses

Group Evaluation	Individual Evaluation
3 • Worked well together every day • Thoroughly completed the lab activity • Developed a well-organized, very neatly presented handout that combined all group members' work, including at least one visual aid • Worked independently on most days	• Used at least four sources, including one website and one traditional source; correctly listed the sources • Thoroughly answered the assigned question • Came up with and answered thoroughly two related questions • Participated in an experiment and engaged in a thoughtful reflection around that experiment • Cooperated with and helped group members every day
2 • Worked well together most days • Completed the lab activity with some effort • Developed a well-organized, fairly neatly presented handout that combined all group members' work; may or may not have included a visual aid • Worked independently on some days	• Used at least three sources, including one website and one traditional source; listed the sources • Thoroughly answered the assigned question • Came up with and tried to answer two related questions • Participated in an experiment and engaged in a thoughtful reflection around that experiment
1 • May or may not have worked well together • Completed the lab activity • Developed a handout that combined all group members' work; did not include a visual aid • Did not work independently	• Used at least two sources; listed the sources • Answered the assigned question • Came up with and tried to answer one related question • Participated in an experiment and engaged in a reflection around that experiment • Cooperated with and helped group members some days
0 • Did not work well together • Did not complete the lab activity • Did not develop a handout that combined all group members' work • Did not work independently	• Used fewer than two sources • Did not answer the assigned question • Did not come up with any related questions • May have participated in an experiment but did not reflect on that experiment • May or may not have cooperated

Grading Scale

- 70 percent of your grade is based on your individual score
- 30 percent of your grade is based on the group score

Final Score	Letter Grade
2.5–3.0	A
2.0–2.4	B
1.4–1.9	C
0.6–1.3	D
Below 0.6	F

developed in a seventh-grade life science class by the teacher and her students for a unit on exploring the five senses. The teacher gave the students copies of the rubric in advance so they could monitor themselves. Using a scale of zero to three, students were graded individually and as part of a group by their teacher and by themselves. Note that 70 percent of the total grade was based on their individual scores, whereas 30 percent was based on the group score. A rubric such as this can be time consuming to develop. Rubrics containing less detail and those developed in partnership with students may take less time to construct. They surely help involve students in monitoring their own learning in an authentic, meaningful way that takes the guesswork out of assessment.

 # Assessing Text Complexity

Evaluating texts and assessing students' interactions with texts are crucial tasks for content area teachers and students—and they call for sound judgment and decision making. One of the best reasons we know for making decisions about the quality of texts is that the assessment process puts you and students in touch with their textbooks. To judge well, you must approach text assessment in much the same manner as you make decisions about other aspects of content area instruction. Any assessment suffers to the extent that it relies on a single source of or perspective on information rather than on multiple sources or perspectives. Therefore, it makes sense to consider evidence in the student's portfolio along with several other perspectives.

One source of information to consider is publisher-provided descriptions of the design, format, and organizational structure of the textbook along with grade-level readability designations. Another information source is your acquired knowledge of and interactions with the students in the class. A third is your own sense of what makes the textbook a useful tool. A fourth source is student perspective, so that instructional decisions are not made from an isolated teacher's perception of the students' perspectives. To complement professional judgment, several measures can provide you with useful information: Content area comprehension inventories, and readability formulas such as Lexile levels, the Fry graph, the cloze procedure, and a content area framework for student analysis of reading assignments. The first order of business, then, if content area reading strategies are to involve students in taking control of their own learning, is to find out how students are interacting with the text.

Content Area Reading Inventories

Teacher-made tests provide another important indicator of how students interact with text materials in content areas. A teacher-made *content area reading inventory* (CARI) is an alternative to the standardized reading test. The CARI is informal. As opposed to the standard of success on a norm-referenced test, which is a comparison of the performance of the tested group with that of the original normative population, success on the CARI test is measured by performance on the task itself. The CARI measures performance on reading materials actually used in a course. The results of the CARI can give a teacher some good insights into *how* students read course material.

Administering a CARI involves several general steps. First, explain to your students the purpose of the test. Mention that it will be used for evaluation only, to help you plan instruction, and that grades will not be assigned. Second, briefly introduce the selected portion of the text to be read and give students an idea direction to guide silent reading. Third, if you want to find out how the class uses the textbook, consider an open-book evaluation, but if you want to determine students' abilities to retain information, have them answer test questions without referring to the selection. Finally, discuss the results of the evaluation individually in conferences or collectively with the entire class.

A CARI can be administered piecemeal over several class sessions so that large chunks of instructional time will not be sacrificed. The bane of many content area instructors is spending an inordinate amount of time away from actual teaching.

A CARI elicits the information you need to adjust instruction and meet student needs. It should focus on students' abilities to comprehend text and to read at appropriate rates of comprehension. Some authorities suggest that teachers also evaluate additional competency areas, such as study skills—skimming, scanning, outlining, taking notes, and so forth. We believe, however, that the best use of reading inventories in content areas is on a much smaller scale. A CARI should seek information related to basic reading tasks. For this reason, we recommend that outlining, note taking, and other useful study techniques be assessed through observation and analysis of student work samples.

Teachers estimate their students' abilities to comprehend text material at different levels of comprehension by using inventories similar to the one shown in Figure 4.9 for American history. The teacher wanted to assess how students responded at literal (getting the facts), inferential (making some interpretations), and applied (going beyond the material) levels of comprehension. At this time you can also determine a measure of reading rate in relation to comprehension.

You can construct a comprehension inventory using these steps:

1. *Select an appropriate reading selection from the second fifty pages of the book.* The selection need not include the entire unit or story but should be complete within itself in overall content. In most cases, two or three pages will provide a sufficient sample.

2. *Count the total number of words in the excerpt.*

3. *Read the excerpt and formulate ten to twelve comprehension questions.* The first part of the test should ask an open-ended question such as, "What was the passage about?" Then develop three or more questions at each level of comprehension.

4. *Prepare a student response sheet.*

5. *Answer the questions.* Include specific page references for discussion purposes after the testing is completed.

While students read the material and take the test, the teacher observes, noting work habits and student behavior, especially of students who appear frustrated by the test. The American history teacher whose inventory is illustrated in Figure 4.9 allowed students to check their own work as the class discussed each question. Other teachers prefer to evaluate individual students' responses to questions first and then to discuss them with students either individually or during the next class session.

Figure 4.9 Sample Comprehension Inventory in American History

General directions: Read pages 595–600 in your textbook. Then look up at the board and note the time it took you to complete the selection. Record this time in the space provided on the response sheet. Close your book and answer the first question. You may then open your textbook to answer the remaining questions.

STUDENT RESPONSE FORM

Reading time: _____ min. _____ sec.

I. *Directions:* Close your book and answer the following question: In your own words, what was this section about? Use as much space as you need on the back of this page to complete your answer.

II. *Directions:* Open your book and answer the following questions.

1. To prevent the closing of banks throughout the country, President Roosevelt declared a national "bank holiday."

 a. True b. False

2. The purpose of the Social Security Act was to abolish federal unemployment payments.

 a. True b. False

3. The National Recovery Administration employed men between the ages of 18 and 25 to build bridges, dig reservoirs, and develop parks.

 a. True b. False

4. President Roosevelt established the Federal Deposit Insurance Corporation to insure savings accounts against bank failures.

 a. True b. False

III. *Directions:* Answers to these questions are not directly stated by the author. You must "read between the lines" to answer them.

1. Give an example of how FDR's first 100 days provided relief, reform, and recovery for the nation.

 _____

2. How is the Tennessee Valley Authority an example of President Roosevelt's attempt to help the poorest segment of American society?

 _____

3. How did the purpose of the Civil Works Administration differ from the purpose of the Federal Emergency Relief Act?

 _____

IV. *Directions:* Answers to these questions are not directly stated by the author. You must "read beyond the lines" to answer them.

1. If FDR had not promoted his New Deal program through his fireside chats, do you think it would have been successful? Why or why not?

 _____

2. Why did FDR's critics fear the New Deal? Do you think their concerns were justified? Why or why not?

 _____

3. Which New Deal program would you call the most important? Why?

 _____

how content area reading materials correspond to students' reading levels so that a compatible match between the two can be made.

The Fry Graph

The readability graph developed by Edward Fry (1977) is a quick and simple readability formula. The graph was designed to identify the grade-level score for materials from grade one through college. Two variables are used to predict the difficulty of the reading material: sentence length and word length. Sentence length is determined by the total number of sentences in a sample passage. Word length is determined by the total number of syllables in the passage. Fry recommended that three 100-word samples from the reading be used to calculate readability. The grade-level scores for each of the passages can then be averaged to determine overall readability. According to Fry, the readability graph predicts the difficulty of the material within one grade level. See Figure 4.10 for the graph and expanded directions for the Fry formula.

Cloze Procedure

The cloze procedure does not use a formula to estimate the difficulty of reading material. Originated by Wilson Taylor in 1953, a cloze test determines how well students can read a particular text or reading selection as a result of their interaction with the material. Simply defined, then, the *cloze procedure* is a method by which you systematically delete words from a text passage and then evaluate students' abilities to accurately supply the words that were deleted. An encounter with a cloze passage should reveal the interplay between the prior knowledge that students bring to the reading task and their language competence. Knowing the extent of this interplay will be helpful in selecting materials and planning instructional procedures. Figure 4.11 presents part of a cloze test passage developed for an art history class. To construct, administer, score, and interpret a cloze test, follow the steps outlined below.

1. *Construction*

   a. Select a reading passage of approximately 275 words from material that students have not yet read but that you plan to assign.

   b. Leave the first sentence intact. Starting with the second sentence, select at random one of the first five words. Delete every fifth word thereafter, until you have a total of fifty words deleted. Retain the remaining sentence of the last deleted word. Type one more sentence intact. For children below grade four, deletion of every tenth word is often more appropriate.

   c. Leave an underlined blank of fifteen spaces for each deleted word as you type the passage.

2. *Administration*

   a. Inform students that they are not to use their textbooks or to work together in completing the cloze passage.

   b. Explain the task that students are to perform. Show how the cloze procedure works by providing several examples on the board.

   c. Allow students the time they need to complete the cloze passage.

Figure 4.10   Fry Readability Graph

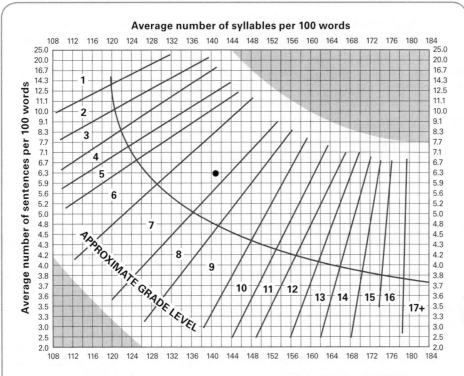

EXPANDED DIRECTIONS FOR WORKING READABILITY GRAPH

1. Randomly select three (3) sample passages and count out exactly 100 words each, beginning with the beginning of a sentence. Do count proper nouns, initializations, and numerals.

2. Count the number of sentences in the 100 words, estimating length of the fraction of the last sentence to the nearest one-tenth.

3. Count the total number of syllables in the 100-word passage. If you don't have a hand counter available, an easy way is simply to put a mark above every syllable over one in each word; then, when you get to the end of the passage, count the number of marks and add 100. Small calculators can also be used as counters by pushing numeral 1, then pushing the + sign for each word or syllable.

4. Enter graph with *average* sentence length and *average* number of syllables; plot dot where the two lines intersect. Area where dot is plotted will give you the approximate grade level.

5. If a great deal of variability is found in syllable count or sentence count, putting more samples into the average is desirable.

6. A word is defined as a group of symbols with a space on either side; thus *1945* is one word.

7. A syllable is defined as a phonetic syllable. Generally, there are as many syllables as vowel sounds. For example, *stopped* is one syllable and *wanted* is two syllables. When counting syllables for numerals and initializations, count one syllable for each symbol. For example, *1945* is four syllables.

Source: Edward Fry, *Elementary Reading Instruction.* Copyright © 1977 by McGraw-Hill Companies. Reprinted by permission.

Figure 4.11 Sample Portion of a Cloze Test

If the symbol of Rome is the Colosseum, then Paris's symbol is without doubt the Eiffel Tower. Both are monuments unique (1) planning and construction; both (2) admiration by their extraordinary (3) and bear witness (4) man's inborn will to (5) something capable of demonstrating (6) measure of his genius. (7) tower was erected on (8) occasion of the World's (9) in 1889. These were the (10) of the Industrial Revolution, (11) progress and of scientific (12). The attempt was made (13) adapt every art to (14) new direction which life (15) taken and to make (16) human activity correspond to (17) new sensibility created by (18) changing times.

Answers to the cloze test sample may be found on page 130.

3. *Scoring*

   a. Count as correct every *exact* word students apply. *Do not* count synonyms even though they may appear to be satisfactory. Counting synonyms will not change the scores appreciably, but it will cause unnecessary hassles and haggling with students. Accepting synonyms also affects the reliability of the performance criteria, because they were established on exact word replacements.

   b. Multiply the total number of exact word replacements by two to determine the student's cloze percentage score.

   c. Record the cloze scores on a sheet of paper for each class. For each class, you now have one to three instructional groups that can form the basis for differentiated assignments (see Figure 4.12).

4. *Interpretation*

   a. A score of 60 percent or higher indicates that the passage can be read competently by students. They may be able to read the material on their own without guidance.

Figure 4.12 Headings for a Cloze Performance Chart

Subject _____

Period _____

Teacher _____

Below 40 percent	Between 40 and 60 percent	Above 60 percent

b. A score of 40 to 60 percent indicates that the passage can be read with some competency by students. The material will challenge students unless they are given some form of reading guidance.

c. A score below 40 percent indicates that the passage will probably be too difficult for students. They will need either a great deal of reading guidance to benefit from the material or more suitable material.

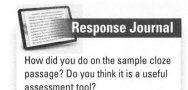

Response Journal

How did you do on the sample cloze passage? Do you think it is a useful assessment tool?

The cloze procedure is an alternative to a readability formula because it gives an indication of how students will actually perform with course materials. Unfortunately, the nature of the test itself will probably be foreign to students. They will be staring at a sea of blank spaces in running text, and having to provide words may seem a formidable task. Don't expect a valid score the first time you administer the test. It's important to discuss the purpose of the cloze test and to give students ample practice with and exposure to it.

Looking Back Looking Forward

Assessing students and texts is a process of gathering and using multiple sources of relevant information for instructional purposes. Two major approaches to assessment prevail in education today: a formal, high-stakes one and an informal, authentic one. Pressure from policy makers and other constituencies has resulted in the adoption of curriculum standards, particularly the Common Core Standards, specifying goals and objectives in subject areas and grade levels. Hence, student performance on state-mandated tests must also be considered by teachers who need to make instructional decisions based on their students' content literacy skills, concepts, and performance.

An informal, authentic approach is often more practical in collecting and organizing the many kinds of information that can inform decisions, including (1) students' prior knowledge in relation to instructional units and text assignments, (2) students' knowledge and use of reading and other communication strategies to learn from texts, and (3) assessment of materials. The use of portfolios and careful observation and documentation of students' strengths and weaknesses as they interact with one another and with content-specific material sheds light on the *why* as well as the *what* in teaching and learning.

In this chapter, the key terms, major purposes, and legitimate uses of standardized tests were presented. Contrasts were drawn between portfolios and testing. As teachers engage learners in a process of portfolio assessment, they make adaptations appropriate for their subject matter and consider issues that have been raised about using portfolios. Suggestions for assessing students' background knowledge included interviews, pretesting, and instructionally based strategies. Interpreting interviews, surveys, scales, and observations, and developing rubrics, logs, and inventories help both teachers and students assess performance, behavior, and perspectives. For insights into how students interact with text material and a measure of performance on the reading materials used in a course, teacher-made content area reading inventories were suggested.

Assessing the difficulty of text material requires both professional judgment and quantitative analysis. Text assessment considers various factors within the reader and the text—the exercise of professional judgment being as useful as calculating a readability formula. Teachers, therefore, must be concerned about the quality of the content, format, organization, and appeal of the material. We supplied several procedures for assessing text difficulty: content area comprehension inventories; readability formulas such as Lexile levels, the Fry graph, and the cloze procedure; and a content area framework for student analysis of reading assignments.

How do teachers incorporate instructional practices and strategies into lessons *before, during,* and *after* assigning texts to read? In the next chapter, we explore the design of content literacy lessons and units of study. These lessons and units bring students and texts together in content learning situations.

Minds On

1. You are planning for the new school year in a district whose scores on the statewide proficiency tests have not shown much improvement. As long as you don't stray from the Common Core Standards, you may use any assessment strategies to meet the needs, abilities, and interests of your students. Outline your plan for instructional assessment.

2. Electronic portfolios are a common tool for assessing and monitoring student's progress in a subject area over time. With a small group of classmates, select a content area and develop a template for an electronic portfolio designed to help you and your students monitor students' progress in a given subject.

3. Imagine that you are a new teacher reviewing the required text you will be using in the fall. Initially, you find the book fascinating, and you are certain it will excite many of your students. Yet after analyzing the work, you discover that its readability appears to be above the reading level of most of your students. How might you use this text effectively?

4. Readability formulas are predictive measures. How do predictive measures differ from performance measures in helping you determine how difficult reading materials will be for your students?

Hands On

1. In groups of three, turn to the "Legislation, Standards, and Accountability" section of this chapter. How has your state (or region or province) taken action to put standards for curriculum content in place? Describe any recent revisions in process or testing procedures or personnel that may affect your local school district. Rewards? Consequences?

2. Develop an observation checklist for the assessment of reading and study behavior in your content area. Compare your checklist with those developed by others in the class for similar content areas. What conclusions might you draw?

3. Each member of your group should locate one sample of text material on the same topic from these sources: an elementary content area text, a secondary content area text, a newspaper, and a popular magazine. Determine the readability of a sample passage from each by using two different readability formulas. Compare your findings by using two additional readability formulas. What conclusions can you draw from the comparison?

4. Two members of your group of four are designated as observers. The other members should collaboratively attempt to solve the following mathematics problem:

   Calculate the surface area of a cylinder that is 12 inches long and 5 inches in diameter.

   Note any observations that you believe might be useful in assessing the group's performance. What types of useful information do observations like these provide?

Answers to Figure 4.11

1. in	5. build	9. Fair	13. to	17. the
2. stir	6. the	10. years	14. every	18. rapidly
3. dimensions	7. The	11. of	15. had	
4. to	8. the	12. conquests	16. every	

eResources

Go to the website for the International Reading Association (**www.reading.org**), select "About IRA," and open the IRA Position Statements (**www.reading.org/General/AboutIRA/PositionStatements.aspx**). Examine IRA's position statement on the rights of students. Read and discuss the ten principles listed and how each relates to authentic assessment.

Go to the website **www.carnegie.org/literacy/national.html**. There you will find information about NAEP scores and state resources. Discuss these scores and resources in the context of other types of assessments used or required in your school.

Read the full text of the IRA's position on high-stakes testing (**www.reading.org/downloads/positions/ps1035_high_stakes.pdf**).

MyEducationLab™

Go to Topic 2: Assessment, the MyEducationLab (**www.myeducationlab.com**) for *Content Area Reading*, where you can:

- Find learning outcomes for Assessment, along with the national standards that connect to these outcomes.
- Complete Assignments and Activities that can help you more deeply understand the chapter content.
- Practice the core teaching skills identified in the chapter with the Building Teaching Skills and Dispositions learning units.
- Check your comprehension on the content covered in the chapter with the Study Plan. Here you will be able to take a chapter quiz, receive feedback on your answers, and then access Review, Practice, and Enrichment activities to enhance your understanding of chapter content.
- Visit A+RISE. A+RISE® Standards2Strategy™ is an innovative and interactive online resource that offers new teachers in grades K–12 just in time, research-based instructional strategies that meet the linguistic needs of English Language Learners (ELLs) as they learn content, differentiate instruction for all grades and abilities, and are aligned to Common Core Elementary Language Arts standards (for the literacy strategies) and to English language proficiency standards in World-Class Instructional Design and Assessment (WIDA), Texas, California, and Florida.
- Use the Online Lesson Plan Builder to practice lesson planning and integrating national and state standards into your planning.

5 Planning Instruction for Content Literacy

Instructional planning brings students and texts together in ways that support content literacy and learning.

Planning is essential, whether fighting a war, leading a country, running a business, or teaching a class of middle or high school learners. When Dwight Eisenhower was asked what the key to victory was during the Normandy invasion of World War II, he minimized the product of planning—the battle plan—noting that "plans are nothing; planning is everything." It was the strategic planning that went into the lead-up to the invasion—the process of thinking through the actions needed for victory—that made the difference between success and failure. It was the thinking through of objectives, activities, unintended consequences, and strategic alternatives in case something went wrong that were of primary concern to Eisenhower and his military commanders. A lack of planning can have short- and long-term damaging results. Without a plan in the classroom, you not only lose instructional time, but you also sacrifice student engagement, motivation, and learning, all of which can be difficult to retrieve.

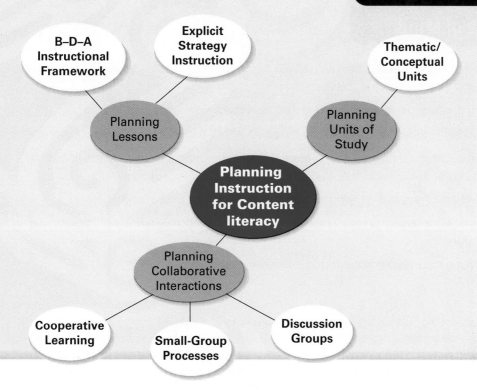

Likewise, the key to content literacy and learning is the forethought that goes into planning *instructional frameworks* that support thinking and learning with text. Engaged learning is the result, quite often, of well-planned lessons and units of study. Someone in the world of business once said that 90 percent of your results come from activities that consume 10 percent of your time. When this saying is applied to an instructional context, the time teachers take to plan engaged learning environments is time well spent. Planning appropriate frameworks for instruction includes the thinking through of text-centered lessons and units of study revolving around what students need to learn, strategies and activities that will facilitate learning, and texts that serve as vehicles for learning. The organizing principle of this chapter underscores the planning of active text learning environments in content area classrooms: Instructional planning brings students and texts together in ways that support content literacy and learning.

Originally written in collaboration with Jean Vintinner, University of North Carolina at Charlotte.

Frame of Mind

1. How can content area teachers plan and design instruction so that students will actively engage in literacy- and subject-related activities?

2. What planning components are involved in explicit strategy instruction?

3. What is involved in designing a text lesson based on a B–D–A instructional framework?

4. How does designing a unit of study help teachers plan a variety of instructional activities that connect literacy and learning as well as explore the interrelatedness of content?

5. How do teachers create an inquiry/research emphasis within units of study?

6. How can teachers incorporate collaborative/cooperative learning activities within lessons and units of study?

7. How are guided discussions different from reflective discussions?

Content literacy has the potential to play an important role in the academic lives of children and adolescents. In order to plan instruction effectively, a teacher needs to be aware of the *explicit* and *functional* dimensions of content literacy. The explicit aspects of content literacy emphasize direct instruction in the development of skills and strategies that enable students to comprehend what they are reading. Instruction is explicit in the sense that teachers overtly engage in the teaching of procedures to develop students' understanding and use of strategies. In a school wide curriculum, the primary responsibility for explicit strategy instruction often falls on the shoulders of reading/language arts teachers and literacy specialists. And this is as it should be. Yet classroom teachers also have a responsibility to show students how to learn with discipline-specific texts, especially those students who struggle with literacy tasks in an academic context.

As crucial as explicit strategy instruction may be to students' literacy development, another equally important dimension of content literacy is the functional nature of strategy use in content areas. Functional instruction emphasizes the application of strategies needed to learn from a variety of print and digital sources of information. When the functional aspects of content literacy are operating in the classroom, the teacher is able to integrate literacy and learning in seamless fashion. To the casual observer in a content area classroom, the functional use of strategies would be difficult to categorize as a "strategy lesson." What the observer might conclude, however, is that the teacher used a variety of instructional activities and strategies that actively engage students in learning the content under study.

Explicit Strategy Instruction

It's hard to use an instructional strategy effectively if teachers aren't truly familiar with what the strategy is meant to do and why. When building this metacognition of strategies, there are three levels of knowledge necessary for both teachers and students to be successful: declarative, procedural and conditional knowledge (Brown, 1987; Jacobs and Paris, 1987; Schraw & Moshman, 1995).

- Declarative knowledge accounts for teachers' and students' understanding of strategies. Before we can hope to effectively implement any strategy, it is important that all parties understand what a strategy is and the skills it is meant to support. If teachers are hoping to build vocabulary, it is unlikely they will achieve results with a strategy meant to support fluency.

- Procedural knowledge refers to teachers' and students' aptitude to execute strategies. Any time students are learning a new strategy or adapting one in a new way, they have little prior knowledge and will require explicit instruction. Teachers need to explain and model the new strategy, often several times or in a variety of ways, before students will be confident and successful at implementing the strategy independently.

- Conditional knowledge is often the last to develop and refers to the ability to determine and select strategies that are most appropriate and effective for the content and task at hand. This requires teachers to know about the intricacies of the content to be studied, as well as the abilities of the students. In order to adequately support student learning and developing the metacognitive skill that allows students to self-select and employ strategies, teachers need to plan based on student characteristics and appropriately scaffold instruction. For example, if students are struggling with the difficulty of the textbook, choosing a strategy that requires them to read independently will most likely lead to frustration. In contrast, teaching them a strategy, such as jigsaw groups (which you will learn about later in this chapter), that allows students to discuss what they read and work collaboratively with classmates, they will more likely be engaged and comprehend more of what they are reading.

Students use strategies to support learning only when they have the appropriate materials, the teacher has created an instructional scenario that prompts and scaffolds proper use, and students are well-versed in both content and strategy expectations (Waters & Kunnmann, 2009). With these ideals in mind, it is up to the teacher to create the most conducive conditions for learning.

When texts serve as tools for learning in content area classrooms, teachers have a significant role to play. That role can be thought of as "instructional scaffolding." Content-literate students know how to learn with texts independently. Yet many students have trouble handling the conceptual demands inherent in text material when left to their own devices to learn. A gap often exists between the ideas and relationships they are studying and their prior knowledge, interests, attitudes, cultural background, language proficiency, or reading ability. Instructional scaffolding allows teachers to support students' efforts to make sense of texts while showing them how to use strategies that will, over time, lead to independent learning. (See Box 5.1 for additional ideas on how to support all learners.)

BOX 5.1 RTI for Struggling Adolescent Learners

Planning, Implementing, and Differentiating Strategies to Meet the Needs of All Learners

Trying to meet the needs of the diverse population in your class can often seem an overwhelming task, but with policies and measures such as Response to Intervention and the Individuals with Disabilities Education Act 2004, it is imperative that teachers find effective ways to scaffold learning to support the development of all students.

When teaching students strategies to support content learning, there are several ways in which you can differentiate both instruction and practice to provide effective scaffolding. Offering flexible grouping opportunities allows teachers to cluster students based on needs and gives students opportunities to work with students of heterogeneous abilities (Tomlinson, 1995). Once students are placed in temporary homogeneous groups, teachers can offer instruction that is specifically tailored to the learning needs of the small group. This may include extended intensive practice with strategies or materials, adapted resources, or additional support in transferring strategy knowledge to a variety of situa-

tions (Ehren, Deschler, & Graner, 2010). When students are placed in groups with students of varied abilities, they can work with and learn from each other.

Another way of implementing strategies while adapting to the different learning abilities and needs in your classroom includes accommodations to the product associated with the strategy (McMackin & Witherell, 2010). While all students may be working on a collaborative activity, the accountability task can be modify to match the abilities of the students: reports may be shorter, students may be allowed to use word processing programs to correct spelling and grammar, or the number of supporting resources may be fewer to allow students with lower reading levels to be successful within the same time limits as the rest of the class.

Overall, strategy instruction supports all students in every content area. With proper planning, teachers can provide whole class instruction on methods that support content while supporting students with diverse learning needs.

Used in construction, scaffolds serve as supports, lifting up workers so that they can achieve something that otherwise would not have been possible. In teaching and learning contexts, scaffolding means helping learners to do what they cannot do at first. Instructional scaffolds support text learners by helping them achieve literacy tasks that would otherwise have been out of reach. Instructional scaffolding provides the necessary support that students need as they attempt new tasks; at the same time, teachers model or lead the students through effective strategies for completing these tasks. Providing "necessary support" often means understanding the diversity that exists among the students in your class, planning active learning environments, and supporting students' efforts to learn with texts. All learners will benefit from explicit, scaffolded instruction in the use of literacy strategies.

Strategy instruction helps students who struggle with text become aware of, use, and develop control over learning strategies (Brown & Palincsar, 1984). Explicit teaching provides an alternative to "blind" instruction. In blind instructional situations, students are taught what to do, but this is where instruction usually ends. Although directed to make use of a set of procedures that will improve reading and studying, students seldom grasp the rationale or payoff underlying a particular strategy. As a result, they attempt to use the

Figure 5.1   Instructional Model for Explicit Strategy Instruction

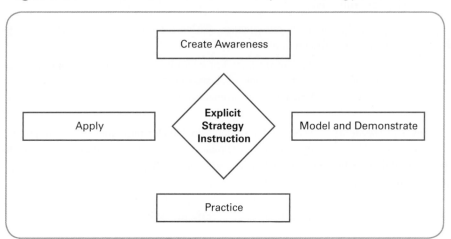

strategy with little basis for evaluating its success or monitoring its effectiveness. Explicit instruction, however, attempts not only to show students *what* to do but also *why, how,* and *when.* Pearson (1982, p. 22) concludes that such instruction helps "students develop independent strategies for coping with the kinds of comprehension problems they are asked to solve in their lives in schools." In addition, explicit strategy instruction can help students independently transfer skills and strategies to unique scenarios (Fuchs et al., 2003) and other content areas (Halpern, 1998).

As Figure 5.1 shows, explicit strategy instruction has several components: *awareness and explanation, modeling and demonstration, guided practice,* and *application.* By way of analogy, teaching students to be strategic readers provides experiences similar to those needed by athletes who are in training. To perform well with texts, students must understand the rules, work on technique, and practice. A coach (the teacher) is needed to provide feedback, guide, inspire, and share the knowledge and experiences that she or he possesses in the same way literacy coaches support teachers.

Strategy Awareness and Explanation

To begin the awareness and explanation stage of explicit strategy instruction, first conduct an informal assessment of students' ability to use a particular literacy strategy. As discussed in Chapter 4, formative assessments are becoming more prevalent in today's classrooms as a means for planning suitable instruction, and often developed by schools or districts to ensure appropriate pacing and equity throughout classrooms. Students should think of the assessment as a "tryout" rather than as some kind of test of their ability to use the strategy. Assessment gives the teacher an opportunity to determine the degree of knowledge that students have about a strategy under discussion. Moreover, it yields insight into how well the students use a strategy to handle a reading task. For these reasons, assessing the use of a strategy should occur in as natural a context as possible. Assessment can usually be accomplished within a single class period if these steps are followed:

1. *Assign students a text passage of approximately 500 to 1,500 words.* The selection should take most students ten to fifteen minutes to read.

2. *Direct students to use a particular strategy.* For example, suppose the strategy involves writing a summary of a text selection. Simply ask students to do the things they normally do when they read a passage and then write a summary of it. Allow adequate time to complete the task.

3. *Observe the use of the strategy.* Note what students do. Do they underline or mark important ideas as they read? Do they appear to skim the material first to get a general idea of what to expect? What do they do when they begin actually constructing the summary?

4. *Ask students to respond in writing to several key questions about the use of the strategy.* For example: What did you do to summarize the passage? What did you do to find the main ideas? Did you find summarizing easy or difficult? Why?

During the awareness step, a give-and-take of ideas takes place between teacher and students. As a result, students should recognize the rationale and process behind the use of the strategy. It is important to first discuss the assessment. Teachers should use their observations and students' reflective responses to the questions for this purpose. Continue the strategy discussion with the following activities:

- Lead a discussion of why the strategy is useful. What is the payoff for students? How does it improve learning?

- Engage in a discussion that explains the rules, guidelines, or procedures for being successful with the strategy.

- Have students experience using the strategy. They can practice the rules or procedures on a short text selection.

Awareness and explanation provide students with a clear picture of the learning strategy. The *why* and *how* are solidly introduced, and the road has been paved for more intensive modeling and demonstration of the strategy.

Strategy Demonstration and Modeling

Once the *why* and a beginning sense of the *how* are established, the students should receive careful follow-up in the use of the strategy. Follow-up sessions are characterized by demonstration through teacher modeling, explanations, practice, reinforcement of the rules or procedures, and more practice. The students progress from easy to harder practice situations and from shorter to longer text selections. The following activities are recommended:

- *Use a smartboard, chart, Microsoft PowerPoint presentation, or overhead transparency to review the steps students should follow.*

- *Demonstrate the strategy.* Walk students through the steps. Provide explanations. Raise questions about the procedures.

- *As part of a demonstration, initiate a think aloud procedure to model how to use the strategy.* By thinking aloud, the teacher shares with the students the thinking processes he or she uses in applying the strategy. Thinking aloud is often accomplished by reading a passage out loud and stopping at key points in the text to ask questions or provide prompts. The questions and prompts mirror the critical thinking required to apply the strategy. Once students are familiar with the think-aloud procedure, encourage them to demonstrate and use it during practice sessions. In Chapter 7, we explain in more detail the role that thinkalouds play in modeling strategies.

Guided Practice

Use trial runs with short selections from the textbook, trade book, or other reference materials. Debrief the students with questions after each trial run: Did they follow the steps? How successful were they? What caused them difficulty? Have them make learning log entries. Often, a short quiz following a trial run shows students how much they learned and remembered as a result of using the study strategy.

The practice sessions are designed to provide experience with the strategy. Students should reach a point where they have internalized the steps and feel in control of the strategy.

Strategy Application

The preceding components of strategy instruction should provide enough practice for students to know *why, how,* and *when* to use the study strategies that have been targeted by the teacher for emphasis. Once students have made generalizations about strategy use, regular class assignments should encourage its application. Rather than assign for homework a text selection accompanied by questions to be answered, frame the assignment so that students will have to apply the strategies they are learning. Repeated practice with strategies will also allow students multiple exposures to content, strengthening their comprehension of both strategies and material and leading to students' ability to independently apply methods. This repetition also allows teachers opportunities to provide immediate and meaningful feedback to students about their understanding of material and strategy use (Blanchowicz et al., 2006).

 **Planning Lessons**

A lesson usually revolves around all of the students in a class reading the same text. Text-centered lessons provide a blueprint for action. Planning in advance of actual practice is simply good common sense. Planning is essential because learners respond well to structure. When reading text, learners need to sense where they are going and how they will get there. Lessons should be general enough to include all students and flexible enough to allow the teacher to react intuitively and spontaneously when a particular plan is put in actual practice. In other words, lessons shouldn't restrict decisions about the instruction that is in progress; instead, they should encourage flexibility and change.

Lesson Plan Formats

Lesson plan formats vary from school district to school district. However, a comprehensive lesson plan undoubtedly will be aligned with standards (sometimes referred to as *benchmarks* in some local and state curricular guides) within a particular content area at a particular grade level. Moreover, a comprehensive lesson plan will not only address the standards in a discipline but also will include instructional goals or objectives, essential questions, assessment, instructional strategies and activities, instructional materials and resources, and technology. What questions do teachers need to consider when planning lessons?

- *Standards (benchmarks).* What local, state, or national standards will be addressed? Common Core State Standards are available for Reading and Math and make accommodations for other content areas. In addition, many states have additional or supplementary objectives for some content areas or special populations.

- *Instructional goals.* What will students need to know and be able to do? What knowledge, attitudes, skills, and strategies will students gain from participation in the lesson?

- *Essential questions.* What "big" questions will generate discussion about the topic under study? What questions will be asked to help students focus on important aspects of the topic?

- *Instructional strategies and activities.* What instructional practices, strategies, and activities will be used in the lesson? How will the learning environment support collaborative interactions among students and active engagement in the topic?

- *Instructional materials and resources.* What textbook assignments, trade books, newspaper and magazine articles, reference materials, electronic texts, and so on will students need to engage in learning?

- *New literacies.* How will the use of new literacies support student learning? How will technology and media extend and enhance the lesson?

- *Assessment.* What assessment tools will be needed to evaluate student learning? Will students engage in self-assessment?

Throughout Part I of this book we have discussed various instructional practices, strategies, and activities to engage students in reading content area text materials. These content literacy practices and strategies fit nicely within the Strategy Awareness and Explanation section of the lesson plan format we just described. Teachers can plan lessons in what we call a B–D–A instructional framework.

B–D–A Instructional Framework

What a teacher does *before reading, during reading,* and *after reading* (B–D–A) is crucial to active and purposeful reading. The B–D–A instructional framework can help teachers incorporate instruction strategies and activities into lessons involving content literacy and learning. A lesson doesn't necessarily take place in a single class session; several class meetings may be needed to achieve the objectives of the lesson. Nor do all the components of a B–D–A lesson necessarily receive the same emphasis in any given reading assignment; the difficulty of the material, students' familiarity with the topic, and your judgment all play a part when you decide on the sequence of activities you will organize. What the structure of a B–D–A instructional framework tells you is that readers need varying degrees of guidance. As we show throughout this book, there are before-reading, during-reading, and after-reading activities that support students' efforts to construct meaning. The components of a B–D–A instructional framework can be examined in Figure 5.2.

Figure 5.2   B–D–A Instructional Framework

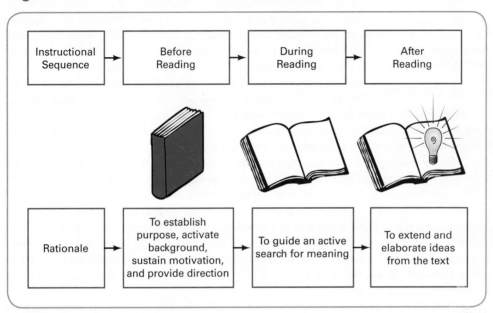

Before-Reading Activities

A B–D–A–centered lesson that includes activity and discussion before reading reduces the uncertainty that students bring to an assignment. Before-reading activities get students ready to read, to approach text material critically, and to seek answers to questions they have generated about the material. The before-reading dimension of a lesson, which is explained in Chapter 6, has also been called the *prereading* phase of instruction. During this instructional phase, a teacher often emphasizes one or more of the following: (1) motivating readers, (2) building and activating prior knowledge, (3) introducing key vocabulary and concepts, and (4) developing metacognitive awareness of the task demands of the assignment and the strategies necessary for effective learning.

A key factor related to motivation is activating students' interest in the text reading. However, concerning how to motivate students, we must first raise a fundamental question: Why should students be interested in this lesson? A teacher may even wish to consider whether he or she is interested in the material! If teachers are going to be models of enthusiasm for students, then the first step is to find something in the material about which to get really excited. Enthusiasm—it is almost too obvious to suggest—is contagious. Another consideration is the relevance of the material to students' lives, both in school and beyond. Relating material as building blocks for future learning can help students understand the purpose and practicality of new material. It is also helpful to explain the importance of new knowledge to possible life and career opportunities for students to appreciate the application of this content in their futures. As well as being a crucial component to student motivation and engagement, this is an essential element of the Common Core State Standards.

Response Journal

Reflecting on your school experience, how did some of your teachers create interest in text readings in the before-reading phase of a text lesson?

Building and activating prior knowledge for a lesson and presenting key vocabulary and concepts are also essential to preparation before reading. In making decisions related to prior knowledge, it's important to review previous lessons in light of present material. What does yesterday's lesson have to do with today's? Will students make the connection to previously studied material? Sometimes several minutes of review before forging on into uncharted realms of learning can make all the difference in linking new information to old. Furthermore, when deciding which vocabulary terms to single out for instruction, we emphasize three questions that should be considered: What keywords will students need to understand? Are all the terms equally important? Which new words carry heavy concept loads?

Before-reading activities may also include discussions that develop an awareness of the reading task at hand and of the strategies needed to handle the task effectively. These are metacognitive discussions. Providing direction is another way of saying that students will develop task knowledge and self-knowledge about their own learning strategies. Helping students analyze the reading task ahead of them and modeling a learning strategy that students will need during reading are two metacognitive activities that quickly come to mind. Here are some general questions to ask in planning for a metacognitive discussion: What are the most important ideas in the lesson? What strategies will students need to learn these ideas? Are the students *aware* of these strategies?

A B–D–A instructional framework also includes provisions for guiding the search for meaning during reading. In other words, students need to be shown how to think with texts as they engage in literacy-related learning, such as setting a purpose for reading, a topic emphasized in Chapters 6 through 10.

During-Reading Activities

Teachers easily recognize the important parts of a text assignment. Most students don't. Instead, they tend to read every passage in every chapter in the same monotonous way. Each word, each sentence, each paragraph is treated with equal reverence. No wonder a disconnect often exists between the text and the reader.

The disconnect between text and reader is especially noticeable in content areas where readers must interact with highly specialized and technical language. Nowhere, for example, is content literacy more challenging for students than in the reading of mathematics texts. Math texts are tersely written in highly condensed language. Students must perceive and decode mathematical symbols, construct meanings for specialized and technical vocabulary and concepts, analyze and interpret relationships, and apply interpretations to the solution of problems.

Study how two mathematics teachers adapt the B–D–A instructional framework to scaffold reader–text interactions during reading. The first teaches pre-algebra classes in a middle school. The students are studying probability, and the objective of the teacher's lesson is to ensure that the class will be able to determine the probability of a simple event. During the before-reading phase of the lesson, the students explore the questions: Why do some sporting events, such as football, use the flipping of a coin to begin a game? Is the coin flip a fair way to decide which team will kick off? The questions tap into the students' prior knowledge and their conceptions (some naive, some sophisticated) of probability.

As part of the lesson, the teacher asks the students to use their math journals to write definitions of several terms associated with probability: *odds, chances, outcomes, events,* and *sample space.* The students' definitions are discussed as the teacher builds on what they know

Figure 5.3   Using a Selective Reading Guide in Math

Before reading, think about the ways in which we have defined *probability* in class discussion. Now compare our definitions with the one in the book. Develop in your own words a definition of *probability* based on what you know and what you have read.

Probability: _____

Now read and define other key terms in this section.

Outcomes: _____

Events: _____

Sample space: _____

Example 1. Read the example and answer the following:

What is the probability of rolling a 5? _____

How do you know? _____

Example 2. Read this example slowly, and when you finish:

Define odds in favor: _____

Example 3. Put on your thinking caps to answer the following:

What are the odds? _____

What is the difference between finding the probability and finding the odds? _____

_____

You're on your own!

Complete problems 1–31 with your study buddy.

to arrive at a set of class definitions of the terms. He then pairs the students in "study buddy" teams and asks them to use what they already know about probability to read the assigned section from the textbook. The "study buddies" read the text section and complete the selective reading guide illustrated in Figure 5.3.

Together, the study buddies discuss the assigned material as they work through the guide. Selective reading guides, as we suggest in Chapter 10, are one way of engaging students in reading by providing a "road map" to the important concepts in the material.

The second teacher, a high school mathematics teacher, also adapts the B–D–A framework to guide students' engagement with the text and to help them make important connections between reading and mathematics. When she first started teaching, she noticed with some dismay that students almost never read the text. Nor did they talk about mathematics with one another. Therefore, she makes a conscious effort to incorporate literacy and cooperative learning principles whenever instructional situations warrant them.

One such situation occurred when her students were studying the concepts of ratio, proportion, and percentage. The focus of the lesson was a section that dealt with the development of scale drawings as an application of proportion. She initiated the lesson by having students take five minutes to write admit slips, a writing-to-learn strategy we introduce in Chapter 9. Admit slips are students' "tickets of admission" to the lesson. The teacher can use them in a variety of ways to find out what students are feeling and thinking as they begin the class period.

The teacher triggered admit slip writing with the prompt: "If you had a younger brother or sister in the sixth grade, how would you describe a scale drawing in words that he or she would understand?" Using half-sheets of paper distributed by the teacher, the students wrote freely for several minutes until instructed to "wind down" and complete the thoughts on which they were working. The teacher collected the admit slips and shared a few of the students' descriptions with the class. The discussion that followed revolved around the students' conceptions of scale drawings and what it means to be "in proportion."

The teacher then formed four-member cooperative groups to guide students' interactions with the text section on scale drawings. Each team was assigned to draw a scale model of the recreation room in its "dream house." First, the teams had to decide what facilities would be included in the recreation room. Once they developed the list of facilities, the team members read the text section and discussed how to develop a scale that would fit all of the facilities into the space provided for each team at the chalkboard. The lesson concluded with the teams describing their scale drawings. The teacher then asked the students to regroup and develop a list of the important ideas related to scale models.

After-Reading Activities

Guidance during reading bridges the gap between students and text so that students learn how to distinguish important from less important ideas, to perceive relationships, and to respond actively to meaning.

Ideas encountered before and during reading may need clarification and elaboration after reading. Post reading activities create a structure that refines emerging concepts. For example, a social studies teacher who was nearing completion of a unit on Southeast Asia asked her students to reflect on their reading by using the activity in Figure 5.4. The writing prompt in part II of the after-reading activity is based on an instructional practice called RAFT, which we describe in Chapter 9. The writing and follow-up discussion refined and extended the students' thinking about the ideas under study. The questions "Who is really best qualified?" and "Who is the specialist in each field?" prompted students to sort out what they had learned. The teacher provided just enough structure by listing topics from various facets of Southeast Asian culture to focus students' thinking and help them make distinctions.

Activities such as the one in Figure 5.4 extend thinking about ideas encountered during reading. Writing activities, study guides, and other after-reading practices are springboards to thinking and form the basis for discussing and articulating ideas developed through reading.

Some More Examples of B–D–A–Centered Lessons

How teachers adapt the B–D–A instructional framework depends on the students in the class, the text that they are studying, and the kinds of activities that will be reflected in the lesson. Following are some examples of text-centered lessons in different content areas at different grade levels. As you study these lessons, notice how the teachers adapt the B–D–A framework in their lessons.

Middle School Physical Education Class

Middle level students were assigned a text on locomotors movement. The text explained the different types of such motion (running, skipping, hopping, and galloping) and the way the body must move for each, as well as the impact exercise can have on overall health. The

Figure 5.4 Postreading Activity for a Southeast Asia Lesson

I. *Directions:* A rice farmer, a Buddhist monk, a government official, and a geographer all feel competent to speak on any of the following topics. Who is really best qualified? Who is the specialist in each field? On the blank line preceding each topic, place the letter of the correct specialist.

A. Rice farmer
B. Buddhist monk
C. Government official
D. Geographer

_____ 1. The forested regions of Thailand
_____ 2. The life of Siddhārtha Gautama
_____ 3   The amount of rice exported each year
_____ 4. The monsoon rains in Southeast Asia
_____ 5. Harvesting rice
_____ 6. The causes of suffering
_____ 7. The art of meditation
_____ 8. The Me Nam River Basin
_____ 9. The amount of rice produced per acre
_____ 10. The pagodas in Thailand
_____ 11. The number of Buddhists living in Bangkok
_____ 12. The virtues of a simple life
_____ 13. The rice festival in Bangkok
_____ 14. The Temple of the Emerald Buddha
_____ 15. The attainment of Nirvana (perfect peace)

II. *Directions:* Pretend you are the rice farmer, the Buddhist monk, the government official, or the geographer. Write a "guest editorial" for the local newspaper revealing your professional attitude toward and opinion about the approaching monsoon season.

teacher's objectives were to (1) involve students in an active reading and discussion of the text and (2) have students enact each of these types of locomotors movement to understand how the body functions. Study how she planned her instructional activities in Figure 5.5.

High School French Class

By way of contrast, study how a high school French teacher taught Guy de Maupassant's short story "L'Infirme" to an advanced class of language students. The story is about two men riding in a train. Henri Bonclair is sitting alone in a train car when another passenger, Revalière, enters the car. This fellow traveler is disabled, having lost his leg during the war. Bonclair wonders about the type of life he must lead. As he looks at the disabled man, Bonclair senses that he met him a few years earlier. He asks the man if he is not the person he met. Revalière is that man. Now Bonclair remembers that Revalière was to be married. He wonders if he got married before or after losing the leg or at all. Bonclair inquires. No, Revalière has not married, refusing to ask the girl to put up with a "deformed" man. However, he is on his way to see her, her

Figure 5.5   B–D–A Activities in a Middle School Physical Education Class

I. Before Reading

A. Before introducing the text, determine what students now know about locomotors skills.

 1. What are the types of locomotors movement?

 2. How does the body function during each type of movement?

 3. How can this type of movement affect an individual's health?

B. Connect students' responses to these questions to the text assignment. Introduce the passage and its premise.

C. Form small groups of four students each, and direct each group to participate in the following situation:

 Pretend that you are trying to come up with a new exercise routine for students at your school. But you do not have any class time or equipment to accomplish your goal. You decide students could get in some cardio getting from their classroom to the lunchroom as quickly and safely as possible. What are some creative and efficient ways they can accomplish this task?

D. Have the students share their group's top five ideas with the class, and write them on the board.

II. During Reading

A. Assign the selection to be read in class.

B. During reading, direct students to note the similarities and differences between their ideas on the board and what they read about locomotors skills.

III. After Reading (Day 2)

A. Discuss the previous day's reading activity. How many of the students' ideas were similar to skills mentioned in the text? How many were different?

B. Extend students' understanding of locomotors skills. Divide the class into groups of four students. Each group is responsible for testing each of the exercise routines brainstormed by the class. Have them practice each type of locomotors skills between class and the cafeteria and measure:

 1. The distance between the classroom and the cafeteria

 2. The ability of students to correctly and carefully execute the skills mentioned in the reading (running, galloping, skipping. and hopping)

 3. Measure their heart rates to determine which skill provided the greatest cardio exercise

Conduct the experiment during lunch time. The students will make notes and take them back to the classroom. Each group's discoveries will be discussed in class.

---

husband, and her children. They are all very good friends. The French teacher formulated five objectives for the lesson:

 1. To teach vocabulary dealing with the concept of "infirmity"

 2. To foster students' ability to make inferences about the reading material from their own knowledge

 3. To foster students' ability to predict what will happen in the story in light of the background they bring to the story

 4. To foster students' ability to evaluate their predictions once they have read the story

 5. To use the story as a basis for writing a dialogue in French

Two of the activities used in the French teacher's plan, the *graphic organizer* and the *inferential strategy,* are explained in depth in later chapters. The steps in the activities section of the lesson plan are outlined in Figure 5.6.

Figure 5.6 A B–D–A Lesson in a High School French Class

I. Before Reading

    A. Begin the lesson by placing the title of the story on the board: "L'Infirme." Ask students to look at the title and compare it to a similar English word (or words). Determine very generally what the story is probably about (a handicapped person).

    B. On the overhead, introduce keywords used in the story by displaying a *graphic organizer:*

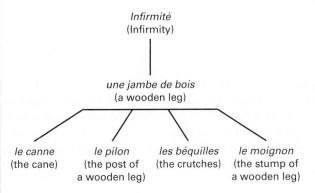

    C. Use the *inferential strategy*. Ask and discuss with the class the following three sets of questions. Have the students write down their responses.

      1. *Vous avez peut-être vu quelqu'un qui est très estropié à cause de la perte d'une jambe ou d'un bras. Qu'est-ce qui traverse votre esprit? De quoi est-ce que vous vous demandez?*

      (You may have seen someone who is very crippled because of the loss of a leg or an arm. When you see such a person, what crosses your mind? What do you wonder about?)

      2. *Dans l'histoire, Bonclair voit ce jeune infirme qui a perdu la jambe. Qu'est-ce que vous pensez traverse son esprit?*

      (In the story, Bonclair sees this crippled young man who has lost his leg. What do you think crosses his mind?)

      3. *Quand vous voyez quelqu'un qui a l'air vaguement familier, qu'est-ce que vous voulez faire? Qu'est-ce que vous faites? Quels sont souvent les résultats?*

      (When you see someone who looks vaguely familiar, what do you want to do? What do you do? What are often the results?)

      4. *Dans cette histoire, Bonclair se souvient vaguement qu'il a fait la connaissance de cet infirme. Prédites ce qu'il fera et prédites les résultats.*

      (In this story, Bonclair remembers vaguely having met this cripple. Predict what he does and the results.)

      5. *Imaginez que vous êtes fiancé(e)à un jeune-homme ou à une jeune femme. Puis vous avez un accident qui vous rend estropié(e). Qu'est-ce que vous feriez? Voudriez-vous se marier? Pourriez-vous compter sur l'autre de vous aimer encore?*

      (Imagine that you are engaged to a young man or woman. Then you have an accident that leaves you crippled. What would you do? Would you still want to marry? Could you still expect the other to love you?)

      6. *Dans notre histoire, Revalière a eu un accident juste avant son marriage. Prédites ce qu'il fera et ce qu'il comptera de la jeune fille Prédites les résultats.*

      (In our story, Revalière has had an accident just before his marriage. Predict what he did and what he expected of the young woman. Predict the results.)

II. During Reading

    A. Assign the reading, instructing the students to keep in mind their prior knowledge and predictions.

    B. Ask them to note possible changes in their predictions.

III. After Reading

    A. After the reading, conduct a follow-up discussion with the class. Relate their predictions to what actually happened, noting how our background knowledge and experience of the world lead us to think along certain lines.

(continued)

Figure 5.6 (*continued*)

B. Have the class form groups of four with at least one male and one female in each group. Establish the following situation:

Une jeune fille vient d'être estropiée dans un accident de natation. Son fiancé lui a téléphoné.Il veut lui parler. Qu'est-ce qu'il veut lui dire? On frappe à la porte. C'est lui.

(A young lady was recently crippled in a swimming accident. Her fiancé has called her. He wants to talk to her. What does he want to talk about? There is a knock at the door. It is he.)

1. Think together, drawing on your past knowledge or experience of situations like this. Write a fifteen- to twenty-line group dialogue in French between the girl and her fiancé. What might he have to tell her? How might she react?

2. Select a male and female student to present the group's dialogue to the class.

These lesson activities all have the same underlying purpose. Each provides a set of experiences designed to move readers from preparation to engagement with the text to extension and elaboration of the concepts in the material under study. How teachers plan instructional activities for content literacy lessons varies by grade level and the sophistication of the students. The same is true of developing plans for a unit of study. In the next section, we go beyond designing and planning lessons to decisions related to thematic learning involving multiple literacy experiences.

Planning Units of Study

Units of study organize instruction around objectives, activities, print and nonprint resources, and inquiry experiences. A unit may be designed for a single discipline or may be interdisciplinary, integrating two or more content areas. In middle schools, where content area teachers are teamed in learning "communities" or "families," opportunities abound to develop interdisciplinary units. Interdisciplinary units require coordination and cooperation by all of the content area teachers teamed within a learning community. Team planning helps students make connections not otherwise possible among many knowledge domains and provides students with multiple exposures to new information, leading to deeper understanding and long term retention (Kamil, 2003). For example, a middle school teaching team organized an interdisciplinary unit around the theme of "Native Americans." They developed a four-week unit in which 130 seventh graders were "born" into one of sixteen Native American tribes. The students inquired into tribal lifestyles from many disciplinary perspectives and participated in a variety of activities to understand life as Native Americans—both emotionally and intellectually.

Components of a Well-Designed Unit

The unit of study is a planning tool that includes (1) a title reflecting the theme or topic of the unit, (2) the major concepts to be learned, (3) the texts and information sources to be studied by students, (4) the unit's instructional activities, and (5) provisions for assessing what students have learned from the unit.

Content Objectives

Content analysis is a major part of teacher preparation in the development of a unit of study. Content analysis results in the *what* of learning—the major concepts and understandings that students should learn from reading the unit materials. Through content analysis, the major concepts become the objectives for the unit. It doesn't matter whether these content objectives are stated in behavioral terms. What really matters is that you know which concepts students will interact with and develop. Therefore, it's important to decide on a manageable number of the most important understandings to be gained from the unit. This means setting priorities; it's impossible to cover every aspect of the material that students will read or to which they will be exposed.

A unit on spatial relationships for a high school art class provides an example of how a teacher planned content objectives, activities, and materials. First, she listed the major concepts to be taught in the unit:

- Humans are aware of the space about them as functional, decorative, and communicative.
- Space organized intuitively produces an aesthetic result, but a reasoned organization of space also leads to a pleasing outcome if design is considered.
- Occupied and unoccupied space have positive and negative effects on mood and depth perception.
- The illusion of depth can be created on a two-dimensional surface.
- The direction and balance of lines or forms create feelings of tension, force, and equilibrium in the space that contains them.
- Seldom in nature is the order of objects so perfect as to involve no focal point, force, or tension.

Instructional Activities and Text Resources

The high school art teacher then developed the activities and identified the texts to be used in the unit (see Figure 5.7). As you study the figure, keep in mind that some of the text-related activities suggested are explored later in this book.

The actual framework of units will vary. For example, you might organize a unit entirely on a sequence of lessons from assignments in a single textbook. This type of organization is highly structured and is even restrictive in the sense that it often precludes the use of various kinds of other literature rich in content and substance. However, a unit of study can be planned so that the teacher will (1) use a single textbook to begin the unit and then branch out into multiple-texts and differentiated activities, (2) organize the unit entirely on individual or group inquiry and research, or (3) combine single-text instruction with multiple-text activities and inquiry.

Branching out provides the latitude to move from a single-text lesson to independent learning activities. The move from single- to multiple-information sources exposes students to a wide range of texts that may be better suited to their needs and interests. By interacting with multiple texts and a variety of authors, students are exposed to a wider range of styles, formats, and vocabulary, which in turn can raise their comprehension of content and increase their vocabulary through repeated and diverse exposure to new words. By engaging with multiple texts on the same topic, students also build valuable critical thinking skills as they learn to

Figure 5.7   Activities and Texts

Text-Related Activities	Texts
1. Graphic organizer	Graham Collier, _Form, Space, and Vision_
2. Vocabulary and concept bulletin board	
3. Prereading	Chapter 3, Collier
4. Prereading	Chapters 6 and 7
5. Art journal	Chapters 6 and 7
6. K-W-L	Chapter 11
7. Vocabulary exercise	Chapter 3
8. Vocabulary exercise	Chapters 6 and 7
9. Vocabulary exercise	Chapter 11
10. Student's choice (list of projects for research study)	H. Botten, _Do You See What I See?_
11. Hands-On	H. Helfman, _Creating Things That Move_
Ink dabs	D. McAgy, _Going for a Walk with a Line_
Straw painting	L. Kaumpmann, _Creating with Space and Construction_
Dry seed arrangement	G. LeFrevre, _Junk Sculpture_
Cardboard sculpture	J. Lynch, _Mobile Design_
Positive-negative cutouts	
Perspective drawing	
Large-scale class sculpture	
Mobiles	
Space frames	_Calder's Universe_
12. Filmstrip	
13. Field trip to studio of a sculptor	
14. Field trip to museum	Displays of artist's works with questionnaires to be filled out about them
15. Learning corner	

assimilation information from several sources, which often provide small vignettes of information or possibly conflicting data (NCTE, 2004, 2006). (See Figure 5.8.)

Unit planning simply provides more options to coordinate a variety of information sources. In single-discipline units, B–D–A activities become an integral part of unit teaching.

Listing texts and resources is an important part of the planning process for a single-discipline unit. One reason a unit is so attractive as a means of organization is that the teacher can go beyond the textbook—or, for that matter, bypass it. A wide array of literature, both narrative and informational, gives students opportunities for an intense involvement in the theme or topic under study. Trade books, digital texts, pamphlets, periodicals, reference books, newspapers, and magazines are all potential alternative routes to acquiring information.

Moreover, the Internet has become a valuable planning resource for teachers in the development of units. You can access many useful ideas for integrating digital texts into units of study.

Figure 5.8 "Branching Out" in a Thematic Unit:
Using a Wide Range of Texts

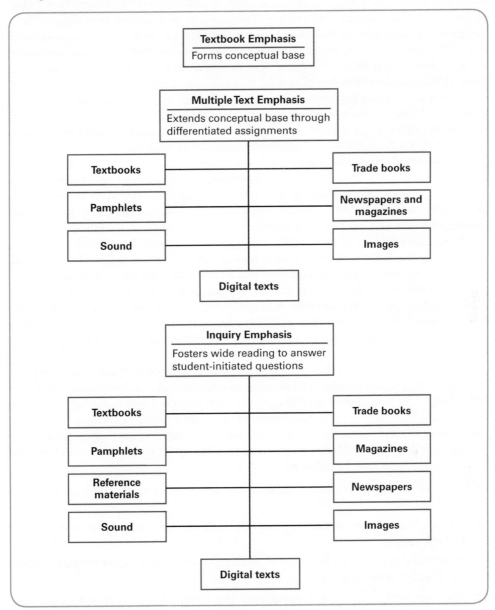

An Inquiry/Research Emphasis in Units of Study

Gathering, organizing, and sharing information are crucial to both academic success and success in our information-rich society. Inquiry should, therefore, play a major role in learning important content, and the process of inquiry should be woven into thematic units of study.

Standards for the English Language Arts (1997, p. 7), developed by IRA and NCTE, describes the fundamental characteristics of inquiry reading as follows: "Students conduct research on issues and interests by generating ideas and questions and by posing problems. They gather, evaluate, and synthesize data from a variety of sources (e.g., print and non-print texts, artifacts, and people) to communicate their discoveries in ways that suit their purpose and audience." Research continues to be an important part of the Common Core State Standards, represented in the all four of their English Language Arts strands, as well as in Literacy in content area strands (National Governors Association for Best Practices, 2010).

How teachers guide inquiry/research projects is the key to a successful unit. The process of inquiry, like the process of writing that we describe in Chapter 9, works best when it occurs in steps and stages. Each stage of an inquiry/research project requires careful support by a teacher. In Box 5.2, we outline the stages and procedures for guiding inquiry/research.

When teachers simply assign and evaluate research reports, students often paraphrase whatever sources come to hand rather than actively pursuing information that they are eager to share with others. Genuine inquiry is an opportunity to build critical thinking skills and is always a messy endeavor characterized by false starts, unexpected discoveries, changes in direction, and continual decision-making. Too much guidance can be as dangerous as too little.

In an in-depth study of two middle school research projects, Rycik (1994) found that teachers may lose their focus on genuine inquiry as they establish procedures for guiding all students to complete a project successfully. The teachers in the study were very concerned with providing sufficient guidance, so they broke down their projects into a series of discrete steps (such as making note cards) that could be taught, completed, and evaluated separately. As the projects moved forward, the teachers gradually came to believe that mastering the procedure for each step was the primary outcome of the project, even more important than learning content information.

Rycik (1994) concluded that inquiry should not be confined to one big research paper because teachers cannot introduce and monitor the wide range of searching, reading, thinking, and writing skills that students need to complete such projects. Good researchers, like good writers, must learn their craft through frequent practice in a variety of contexts. This means that students should research from a variety of sources and express their findings for a variety of audiences in a variety of forms. Some recommendations for integrating research into the classroom routine include the following:

- *Make identifying questions and problems as important in your classroom as finding answers.*

- *Provide frequent opportunities to compare, contrast, and synthesize information from multiple sources.*

- *Present findings of research in a variety of products and formats,* including charts, graphs, and visual or performing arts.

- *Discuss possible sources for information* presented in the class or for answering questions posed by the teacher or students (e.g., personal interviews, diaries, experiments).

The teacher must carefully plan inquiry-centered projects, giving just the right amount of direction to allow students to explore and discover ideas on their own. The research process isn't a do-your-own-thing proposition; budding researchers need structure. Many a project has been wrecked on the shoals of nondirection. The trick is to strike a balance between teacher guidance and student self-reliance. A research project must have just enough structure to give

Evidence-Based Best Practices   **BOX 5.2**

Procedures for Guiding Inquiry/Research Projects

I. Raise questions, identify interests, organize information.
   A. Discuss interest areas related to the unit of study.
   B. Engage in goal setting.
      1. Arouse curiosities.
      2. Create awareness of present levels of knowledge.
   C. Pose questions relating to each area and/or subarea.
      1. "What do you want to find out?"
      2. "What do you want to know about ___?"
      3. Record the questions or topics.
      4. "What do you already know about ___?"
   D. Organize information; have students make predictions about likely answers to gaps in knowledge.
      1. Accept all predictions as possible answers.
      2. Encourage thoughtful speculations in a nonthreatening way.
II. Select materials.
   A. Use visual materials.
      1. Trade books
      2. Magazines, catalogs, directories
      3. Newspapers and comics
      4. Indexes, atlases, almanacs, dictionaries, readers' guides, computer catalogs
      5. Films, slides
      6. Online videos, television programs
      7. Digital texts: CD-ROMs, website documents, online articles and databases, webinars, virtual field trips
   B. Use nonvisual materials.
      1. Audio files
      2. Recorded music or talk
      3. Radio programs or webcasts
      4. Field trips
   C. Use human resources.
      1. Interviews
      2. Letters
      3. On-site visits
      4. Discussion groups
      5. E-mail
      6. Listservs
   D. Encourage self-selection of materials.
      1. "What can I understand?"
      2. "What gives me the best answers?"
III. Guide the information search.
   A. Encourage active research.
      1. Reading
      2. Listening
      3. Observing
      4. Talking
      5. Writing
   B. Facilitate with questions.
      1. "How are you doing?"
      2. "Can I help you?"
      3. "Do you have all the materials you need?"
      4. "Can I help you with ideas you don't understand?"
   C. Have students keep records.
      1. Learning log that includes plans, procedures, notes, and rough drafts
      2. Book record cards
      3. Record of conferences with the teacher
IV. Consider different forms of writing.
   A. Initiate a discussion of sharing techniques.
   B. Encourage a variety of writing forms.
      1. Essay or paper
      2. Lecture to a specific audience
      3. Case study
      4. Story: adventure, science fiction, other genre
      5. Dialogue, conversation, interview
      6. Dramatization through scripts
      7. Commentary or editorial
      8. Thumbnail sketch
V. Guide the writing process.
   A. Help students organize information.
   B. Guide first-draft writing.
   C. Encourage responding, revising, and rewriting.
   D. "Publish" finished products.
      1. Individual presentations
      2. Classroom arrangement
      3. Class interaction

students (1) a problem focus, (2) physical and intellectual freedom, (3) an environment in which they can obtain data, and (4) feedback situations in which to report the results of their research.

A Multiple-Text Emphasis in Units of Study

The literature-based movement in elementary schools serves as a prototype for the use of trade books in middle and high school classrooms. In addition, technology makes it possible to access and explore information sources through digital programs, electronic books, and the Internet. Internet inquiries and WebQuests provide excellent instructional frameworks for inquiry-centered learning. Although textbooks may be used to provide an information base, the foundation for individual and group inquiry into a theme or topic is built on students' use of multiple-information resources, both print and nonprint. Trade books (see Chapter 11) and digital texts, as we explained in Chapter 2, are geared to students' interests and inquiry needs.

Say that in a middle grade classroom, students are engaged in a thematic unit on the environment. What might you observe over several weeks? For starters, the teacher may conduct several whole-class lessons at the beginning of the unit using the textbook to develop a conceptual framework for individual and group investigation. As the weeks progress, however, whole-class activity is less prevalent. Instead, small groups work on research projects or in discussion teams using Jacqueline Kelly's *The Evolution of Calpurnia Tate* (2009), Jean Craighead George's *My Side of the Mountain* (2004), Lynne Cherry's *The Great Kapok Tree: A Tale of the Amazon Rain Forest* (2000), Gary Paulsen's *Woodsong* (1990) and *Hatchet* (1987) and Roy Gallant's *Earth's Vanishing Forests* (1991). Individual students are also working on inquiries with books such as Paul Goble's *I Sing for the Animals* (1991) and Peter Parnall's *Marsh Cat* (1991) and *The Daywatchers* (1984). This gradual release of responsibility (Pearson & Gallagher, 1983) provides enough scaffolding to support students as they learn new content and strategies, but also builds in time for independent practice to support students as they learn to transfer this knowledge and skill to other topics.

In addition, the students are conducting research online, tapping into the rich information resources on the Internet. Several students investigate the websites of Environmental Science, the Rainforest Action Network, and the Global Recycling Network. Others explore software programs: Ozzie's World (Digital Impact), Zug's Adventures on Eco-Island (Zugware), Zurk's Rainforest (Soliel), and Imagination Express: Rainforest (Edmark). One or two students navigate the pages of electronic reference books, such as Grolier's Multimedia Encyclopedia (Grolier).

Toward the end of the unit, the class completes culminating activities, which may involve panel discussions, report writing, and oral presentations in which individuals or groups share knowledge gleaned from the various activities and texts. Tasks like these address all strands of the Common Core State Standards: Reading, Writing, Speaking and Listening, and Language. In this class, what you would observe is that everyone has something to contribute.

Active learning environments within units of study integrate whole-class, small-group, and individual learning activities. Whole-class presentation is an economical means of giving information to students when the classroom context lends itself to information sharing. A whole-class activity, for example, may be used to set the stage for a new thematic unit. The unit introduction, discussion of objectives, and background building can all take place within whole-class structure when the teacher must take on the primary role as content expert.

However, the chief drawback of whole-class presentation is that it limits active participation among students. Although whole-class interaction provokes discussion to an extent, it cannot produce the volume of participation necessary to engage students in active learning situations. A viable alternative supported by a substantial body of research lies in the use of collaborative interactions between teacher and students and among students. These collaborative interactions are grounded in the principles underlying cooperative learning and small-group processes.

Planning Collaborative Interactions

Cooperative learning allows groups of students to pursue academic goals through collaboration in classroom instructional activities. The goals of cooperative learning, therefore, are to foster collaboration in a classroom context, to develop students' self-esteem in the process of learning, to encourage the development of positive group relationships, and to enhance academic achievement (Johnson, Johnson, & Holubec, 1990). Cooperative groups facilitate active participation and should be a primary form of classroom organization when teachers bring students together to comprehend texts. The National Reading Panel's (NRP) review of research on text comprehension identifies cooperative learning as a scientifically supported comprehension strategy (NRP, 2000). We agree with Duke and Pearson (2002), however, who view cooperative learning as an "instructional medium" that facilitates reading comprehension rather than an individual instructional strategy. Within the learning environment created by cooperative groups, students produce more ideas, participate more, and take greater intellectual risks. A cooperative group, with its limited audience, provides more opportunity for students to contribute ideas to a discussion and take chances in the process. The students can try out ideas without worrying about being wrong or sounding dumb—a fear that often accompanies risk taking in a whole-class situation.

Cooperative Learning

Engaged learners are socially interactive. Bringing learners and texts together in social collaboration to engage in discussions may be achieved through the use of cooperative learning groups. Many variations on cooperative group learning are possible. Several cooperative grouping patterns, in particular, work well within the context of content literacy practices and text-related discussions. The cooperative groups described in the following sections give you a feel for how students might collaborate in their interactions with texts and with one another as they extract and construct meaning to make sense out of what they are reading.

Jigsaw Groups

Interdependent team learning with texts may be achieved through *jigsaw groups* (Aronson, 1978). Jigsaw teaching requires students to specialize in a content literacy task that contributes to an overall group objective. Jigsaw groups are composed of students divided heterogeneously into three- to six-member teams. Each student on a team becomes an expert on a subtopic of a theme or topic about which the class is reading. Not only is the student accountable for teaching the other members of the

Response Journal

Describe how you would use the jigsaw strategy in your content area.

group about his or her subtopic but also he or she is also responsible for learning the information other group members provide during the jigsaw discussions.

For example, a science teacher in a middle school engages students in a thematic unit on the solar system. As part of the unit of study, he divides the class into groups of three. Each group will be assigned a different planet in our solar system. One group will be assigned the sun to help complete the solar system as a classroom. Each student within each group will be assigned to become an expert on a particular topic related to their planet or star: size of their planet or star, distance of their planet or star from other planets, and the weather on their planet or star. Once each student has their assigned topic to become an expert in, they will research that topic individually to present with other "experts" in the class who had to research that same topic. As a group they will be given questions about their planet or star that they will have to research together. Students will be given time to gather information about their topic to get familiar with it so they can present to the class at the end. Once completed, the first set of experts regarding the *size* of their planet or star will present the information they gathered, one by one, in front of the class. After which the next group of experts on *distance* will do the same, followed by the group of experts on *weather* and climate conditions. Each of the expert groups has a variety of resource materials and texts made available by the teacher to help them explore and clarify their subtopics. When the members in each of the expert groups complete their tasks, they return to their jigsaw teams to teach and share what they have learned. As a jigsaw member presents his or her findings, the other members listen and take notes in preparation for a unit exam the teacher will give on the overall topic. Each group will then present together one by one the additional information they have gathered regarding their planet or star: How many moons does it have?, Does the planet or star have rings?, How much would you weigh on the planet or star? Students will then turn in their work for assessment and be graded on their participation as well as the work they have gathered. (See Figure 5.9.)

Figure 5.9 Note-Taking Protocol for Solar System Jigsaw

Planet	Size	Distance	Weather	Cool Information
Sun				
Mercury				
Venus				
Earth				
Mars				
Jupiter				
Saturn				
Uranus				
Neptune				
Pluto				

The purpose of a jigsaw group is for the kids to learn how to work together, take responsibility for the topic they are individually assigned, and learn more about their solar system through a way that's fun for them. Some strategic grouping could be used as a teacher, such as grouping a very bright student with a student who needs a lot of help. There are a variety of different ways you can group as a teacher but the overall purpose of the group would be served no matter how a teacher decided to use it.

A theater teacher also finds jigsaw to be useful in involving students in collaborative guided discovery into the four styles of modern theatre. The class is divided into four heterogeneous groups. Each group is assigned one of four theatrical genres: Melodrama, Realism, Absurdism, or Dadaism. Within their groups, each student chooses a subcategory on which they would like to focus their research: key elements and philosophies of the genre, the development of the genre (What caused the movement? How did it evolve from the other artistic movements of its time?), the lasting effects of the genre (What type of impact has the style had on art, culture, and society? Is it still felt today?), the audience reaction (How was the genre first received by audiences and critics?), and the playwrights associated with the genre and their major works

Once research is completed, groups discuss their findings and work together to create a cohesive presentation to be given to the class. In this way, all students will be exposed to all four genres, as well as becoming an expert on their particular subcategory. It's important to note that while subcategories are being researched, students may enter into discussion with other students researching the same subcategory. This would prompt a comparison of the genres. (See Figure 5.10.)

Figure 5.10 Note-Taking Protocol for Modern Theatre Genre Jigsaw

	Melodrama	Realism	Absurdism	Dadaism
Key elements and philosophies of the genre				
The development of the genre (What caused the movement? How did it evolve from the other artistic movements of its time?)				
Lasting effects of the genre (What type of impact has the style had on art, culture, and society? Is it still felt today?)				
Audience reaction (How was the genre first received by audiences and critics?)				
Playwrights associated with the genre and their major works				

Student Teams Achievement Divisions (STAD)

Student teams lend themselves well to content area learning situations that combine whole-class discussion with follow-up small-group activity. The originator of Student Teams Achievement Divisions (STAD) groups, Robert Slavin (1988; 1994), emphasizes the importance of achieving team learning goals but also recognizes that individual performance is important in cooperative groups.

STAD groups work this way: The teacher introduces a topic of study to the whole class, presents new information, and then divides the class into heterogeneous four-member groups of high-, average-, and low-achieving students to engage in follow-up team study. The goal of team study is to master the content presented in the whole-class discussion. The team members help each other by discussing the material, problem solving, comparing answers to guide material, and quizzing one another to ensure that each member knows the material. The students take periodic quizzes, prepared by the teacher, following team study. A team score is determined by the extent to which each member of the team improves over past performance. A system of team awards based on how well students perform individually ensures that team members will be interdependent for learning.

After provided background on the area, a social studies teacher planning a unit on the Italian Renaissance divided the class into heterogeneous teams of five students. Each team was to come together and use maps and other research materials to identify and understand the terms associated with this time period: Florence, Sistine Chapel, Florence Cathedral, St. Peter's Basilica, Siena, Venice, Tuscany, Rome, Arch of Titus, Arch of Constantine, Tempio Malatestiano, and the Last Supper. For each of these terms, teams had to exhibit an understanding of the term, map the associated location, and determine the date of significance. In addition, each team had to complete a short quiz on the Italian Renaissance. Through this process, teams were able to guide their own learning through the structured support of the strategy. (See Figure 5.11.)

Learning Circles

Johnson and colleagues (1990, 1994) underscore the importance of positive interdependence through a cooperative learning model. Similar to STAD, learning circles mesh whole-group study with small-group interactions and discussion. Learning circles may comprise two to six members of varying abilities who come together to share text resources and help each other learn. All of the content literacy activities that we present in this book can be adapted to the type of interdependent learning teams that are suggested by Johnson and colleagues. However, cooperative groups don't run by themselves. You have to plan for the success of positive interdependence by teaching students how to use collaboration skills to work interdependently in teams and then facilitating the group process as students engage in discussion and interaction.

Johnson and colleagues (1990) suggest eighteen steps for structuring learning circles, some of which include specifying content objectives, deciding on the size of the group, assigning students to groups, arranging the room, planning instructional activities and guide material to promote interdependent learning, explaining the academic task, explaining the criteria for success, structuring the division of labor within the groups, structuring individual accountability and intergroup cooperation, monitoring students' behaviors, teaching the skills of collaboration, providing task assistance as needed, evaluating student learning, and assessing how well the teams functioned.

Group brainstorming, prediction, problem solving, mapping, and study strategies, all of which are discussed in Part Two, are easily woven into the fabric of cooperative learning circles.

Figure 5.11 A STAD Project for a Unit on the Italian Renaissance

Teach: Students will be given material to research the Italian Renaissance. We will go over notes in class and divide up into groups of five. Important topics discussed are location, dates, terms, artist names, artwork names, and landmarks.

Team Study: Teams will come together and use maps and other research materials to identify and understand the terms listed below. Map identification is important along with dates and the understanding of terms.

Florence   Sistine Chapel   Florence Cathedral   St. Peter's Basilica   Siena   Venice
Tuscany   Rome   Arch of Titus   Arch of Constantine   Tempio   Malatestiano
Last Supper

Quiz:

1. Who created the *Sistine Chapel*? When was it created and where is it located?

2. Who created the *Last Supper*? When was it created and where is it located?

3. Who created the Arch of Constantine? When was it created and where is it located?

4. Who created the Arch of Titus? When was it created and where is it located?

5. Where did the Renaissance begin and when?

Coming to a group consensus on a variety of discussion tasks is an important outcome in cooperative learning groups. Students need to be shown how to engage cooperatively in consensus building as they decide what conclusions they can or cannot support as a result of their interactions with texts and one another.

Group Investigation

As we explained earlier in this chapter, students can be combined in teams of two to six to collaborate on inquiry topics that interest them within the context of a thematic unit and the major concepts of study. Each group selects a topic and cooperatively plans the inquiry in consultation with the teacher. Each research team, for example, decides how to investigate the topic, which tasks each member will be responsible for, and how the topic will be reported. The groups then conduct the investigation, synthesize their findings into a group presentation, and make their presentation to the entire class. The teacher's evaluation includes individual performance and the overall quality of the group presentation. Examples include the following:

- In Figure 5.12, study how an American history teacher in high school sets up a group investigation project on the Revolutionary War.
- One math teacher showed the relevant applications of trigonometry by creating groups to investigate how different careers use these math skills. Students were places in groups of three and asked to conduct research on the internet on the career of their choice. Each member of the group was given a role:

  Math Expert: Find concepts and theories that are relevant to the chosen career. Examples include Pythagorean Theorem, trigonometric functions, and The Law of Sines

  Researcher: Find applications of trigonometry in their chosen career

  Graphics Designer: Responsible for finding pictures, graphs, and diagrams which illustrate how trigonometry is used in their chosen career

Figure 5.12 A Group Investigation Project for a Unit on the Revolutionary War

Directions: Congratulations! You have been chosen to anchor the new series *TimeLine.* This show features the same type of in-depth interview as *NightLine,* except you have a time machine. You can go back in time and interview someone from the Revolution. To prevent changing the future, here are the rules:

1. Work in pairs. Both of you will do research and write the interview. Decide who will be the interviewer and who the interviewee. Decide on a historical interview date.

2. Your interviewee may be an actual historical figure (e.g., Paul Revere), or you may create a fictional eyewitness to a historical event (e.g., the Boston Tea Party).

3. Your research must be based on at least two sources, only one of which may be an encyclopedia.

A bibliography must be included in the written interview turned in after the presentation.

4. Presentation
   a. Introduce the interviewee and briefly tell why this person is important or interesting.
   b. Your questions must stay within your time frame. You can't ask George Washington if he wants to be president; the office doesn't exist yet. You may ask him if he would like a political office in the future.
   c. The interviewee's answers must be reasonable and based on historical facts from your research.
   d. You are encouraged to include visual aids: pictures, cartoons, maps, props, and costumes.
   e. The interview should last no less than four minutes and no more than ten minutes.

Here is a list of possible subjects, or you may choose your own.

George Washington

Samuel Adams

Crispus Attucks

Thomas Jefferson

John Adams

Benjamin Franklin

Benedict Arnold

Francis Marion, the "Swamp Fox"

Marquis de Lafayette

Charles Cornwallis
    (British general)

Frederick North (British
    prime minister)

King George III

Haym Solomon (financier)

George Rogers Clark

John Dickinson

Thomas Paine

John Locke

Jean-Jacques Rousseau

Abigail Adams

James Arnistead (spy)

Deborah Sampson Gannett
    (soldier)

Patrick Henry

John Hancock

Ethan Allen

Peter Zenger

David Bushnell
    (submarine inventor)

Boston Massacre

Boston Tea Party

Reading and responding to the
    Declaration of Independence as
    a wealthy merchant or planter, a
    poor artisan or farmer, or a slave

Revolutionary battle or campaign of
    your choice

Treaty of Paris

Figure 5.13 A Group Investigation Project for a Unit on Right Triangles and Trigonometry

Description of the strategy: The idea of this group investigation is to show students that trigonometry is important in "real life." The group investigation requires groups of students to show how different careers use trigonometry. For this investigation, students will spend time in the computer lab. Students will be separated by the teacher into heterogeneous groups of three. The teacher will choose a leader of the group. Each group will select a career that uses trigonometry, such as an engineer, crime scene investigator, or construction worker. Once students have chosen a career, they will need to obtain teacher approval. Students will decide what their role will be in this investigation. The three roles are as follows:

Math Expert: Find concepts and theories that are relevant to the chosen career. Examples include Pythagorean Theorem, trigonometric functions, and The Law of Sines.

Researcher: Find applications of trigonometry in their chosen career.

Graphics Designer: Responsible for finding pictures, graphs, and diagrams which illustrate how trigonometry is used in their chosen career.

The teacher provides a list of helpful websites to the students. After students have completed their research, the individuals within the group will meet to discuss how they would like to present the information to the class. The group leader will organize the discussion and handle any disagreements within the group. Creativity is encouraged. The presentation will be done as a group with each student focusing on his role in the investigation. A detailed description of the required presentation will be provided to the students with an attached rubric for individual and group assessments.

To make sure that all students stay focused and understand the activity, the teacher will circulate throughout the classroom and computer lab to check on students' progress. Also, it may be helpful to have poster board, markers, rulers, scissors, and glue available to students for use in their presentations.

After students have completed their research, groups presented their findings to the class. (See Figure 5.13.)

- In Figure 5.14, study how a middle school science teacher creates a fictitious contest to encourage students to complete a group investigation project on the Earth's biomes.

Figure 5.14 A Group Investigation Project for a Unit on the Earth's Biomes for a Middle School Science Class.

This group investigation activity will allow students the opportunity to select a biome that appeals to them and assemble with classmates who share a similar interest. Students will then form a collaborative research group which will ideally consist of between two and six students. As the instructor, I will meet with each research group to discuss the biome they have selected and present them with project guidelines (see below). As inquiry begins, each group will be responsible for deciding how they will investigate their biome. Additionally, each group will be accountable for self-assigning roles for conducting research, agreeing on how to unify their findings, and selecting a formal presentation format. Research will culminate with group presentations to the class, which will be evaluated based upon the quality of the presentation, as well as the contributions of each group member.

Group Investigation Project—The Earth's Biomes

To enrich our unit study of population dynamics, I have created a group investigation project centered on the following biomes:

Rainforest	Desert
Tundra	Temperate Deciduous Forest
Taiga	Grassland

Students will select a biome that appeals to them and assemble with classmates who share a similar interest. I will meet with each group and provide them with the following guidelines:

Project Guidelines

AAA Carolinas is seeking entries from middle school students throughout the region to create an informative and eye-catching advertisement featuring the Earth's biomes. Advertisements can be exhibited in any format

(i.e. a poster, a brochure, a flyer, a pamphlet, a booklet) and must include the following:

- Fauna: describe two native animals and their adaptations needed to survive (include pictures)
- Flora: describe two native plants and their adaptations needed to survive (include pictures)
- Symbiotic relationships: detail two organisms, identify the type of symbiosis, and explain the role each organism plays in the relationship
- Average daily temperatures along with a seasonal temperature graph
- Average daily precipitation along with a seasonal precipitation graph
- Topography
- Geographical location depicted on a world map
- Three recreational activities for visitors
- Appropriate clothing for visitors to pack
- Three fascinating facts about the biome
- Three exciting pictures capturing the essence of the biome
- If applicable, a brief description of any endangered or threatened species within the biome

Your advertisements must contain all the required information, while being factually and grammatically correct. Keep in mind, you are promoting new *AAA Carolina* travel packages to the "Earth's Biomes", so make your final product resourceful and artistically appealing to potential tourists. The advertisement selected as the winner will be featured in all *AAA Carolina* offices to supplement the company's new travel packages. Good Luck!

Small-Group Processes

Small-group learning is complex, and cooperative teams don't run by themselves. Students must know how to work together and how to use techniques they have been taught. The teacher, in turn, must know about small-group processes. The practical question is: How will individual students turn into cooperative groups? Anyone who has ever attempted small-group instruction in the classroom knows the dilemma associated with the question. Many conditions can confound team learning if plans are not made in advance; in particular, teachers must scaffold instruction around such matters as the size, composition, goals, and performance criteria of small groups and the division of labor within a group.

Group Size

The principle of "least group size" operates whenever you form learning teams. A group should be just large enough to include all the skills necessary to solve a problem or complete a task. A group that's larger than necessary provides less chance for individual participation, lower levels of engagement, and greater opportunity for conflict. If too many students are grouped together, there's bound to be a point of diminishing returns. The group size for content area reading should range from two to six members (depending, of course, on the type of reading task). Because most small-group activities involve discussion, three- or four-member groups are probably best.

Group Composition

Homogeneous grouping is often not necessary for discussion tasks. Both intellectual and non-intellectual factors influence a small group's performance, and the relationship between intelligence and small-group performance is often surprisingly low. Experiential and social background, interests, attitudes, and personality contribute greatly to the success of a cooperative group. Grouping solely by reading or intellectual ability shortchanges all students and robs discussion of diversity.

Students who struggle with reading shouldn't be relegated to tasks that require minimal thinking or low-level responses to content material. There is no quicker way to initiate misbehavior than to put students who find reading difficult together in a group. People learn from one another. A student whose background is less extensive than other students' can learn from them. The student who has reading difficulties needs good readers as models. Furthermore, the student who has trouble reading may in fact be a good listener and thinker who will contribute significantly to small-group discussion. This opportunity for flexible grouping also allows teachers to strategically place students in order to best meet their individual needs for a particular task (Tomlinson, 1995).

Group Goals and Tasks

Group learning is goal oriented. How the goals and the paths to task completion are perceived affects the amount and quality of involvement of the team members. If group goals are unclear, members' interest quickly wanes. Goals must also be directly related to the task. The conditions of the task must be clearly defined and must be understood by the individual members of the group.

Therefore, you should explain the criteria for task performance. For example, when students work with reading guides, such as those that are suggested in this book, they should attempt to adhere to such criteria as the following:

- *Each student should read the selection silently and complete each item of the guide individually or with others in the group,* depending on the teacher's specific directions.
- *Each item should be discussed by the group.*
- *If there is disagreement on any item, a group member must defend his or her position and show why there is disagreement.* This means going back into the selection to support one's position.

- *No one student should dominate a discussion or boss other members around.*
- *Each member should contribute something to each group discussion.*

As students work on literacy activities in their groups, the teacher can facilitate performance by reinforcing the criteria that have been established.

Team Building in Cooperative Learning

Groups lack cohesiveness when learning is not cooperative but competitive and when students aren't interdependent in learning but work independently. However, since the 1970s, social scientists and instructional researchers have made great strides in understanding the problems of the competitive classroom. Researchers (Johnson & Johnson 1987; Slavin, 1988) have studied the practical classroom applications of cooperative principles of learning. The bulk of their research suggests that cooperative small-group learning has positive effects on academic achievement and social relationships. Positive interdependence can be achieved through a variety of schemes in which students are rewarded for their individual and collaborative effort (Johnson & Johnson, 1990; Vaca, Lapp, & Fisher, 2011). For example, a social studies teacher attempted to have students adhere to discussion behaviors during their interactions in small groups. (These discussion behaviors were basically the same as those we discussed under performance criteria.) Each small group earned a performance grade for discussing text assignments in a six-week thematic unit. Here's how the group members earned their grades:

- The teacher observed each member in the group to monitor the use of the desired discussion behaviors.
- On Fridays, each group earned a color reward worth a given number of points: green = one point, blue = two points, black = three points, and red = four points. The color that a group earned was based on how well it had performed according to the criteria for discussion.
- Each member of the group received the color (and the points that went with it) that the whole group earned. Therefore, if one or two members of the group did not use the appropriate discussion behaviors, the entire group got a lower point award.
- The color for each student in the class was noted on a learning incentive chart.
- Each week, the small groups changed composition by random assignment.
- The points attached to each color added up over the weeks. When the unit was completed, a specific number of points resulted in a performance grade of A, B, C, or D.

Response Journal

What is your reaction to the point system that the social studies teacher used to create positive interdependence among the small groups in his class?

What happened as a result of the reward system? On the Monday of each week that students were randomly assigned to new groups, they immediately went to the learning incentive chart to check the color received the previous week by each of the other members in their new group. Motivation was high. Group pressure caused individual students who had not received high points the previous week to concentrate on improving their performance in the new group.

Group Roles and Division of Labor

If cooperative groups are to be successful, members must divide the work of the group and understand their different roles within the group. Therefore, consider specifying complementary and interconnected responsibilities that the group must undertake to accomplish a joint task. Johnson and Johnson (1990) define several roles, which may vary by the nature of the task, for example:

- *Leader*. The group leader facilitates the work of the group. Leadership skills include *giving directions* (reviewing instructions, restating the goals of the group, calling attention to time limits, offering procedures on how to complete the task most effectively), *summarizing* aloud what has been read or discussed, and *generating responses* by going beyond the first answer or conclusion and producing a number of plausible answers from which to choose.
- *Reader*. The reader in the group is responsible for reading the group's material aloud so that the group members can understand and remember it.
- *Writer-recorder*. The writer-recorder records the responses of the group on paper, edits what the group has written, and makes sure the group members check this work for content accuracy and completeness.
- *Checker*. The checker makes sure the group is on target by checking on what is being learned by the members. The checker, therefore, may ask individuals within the group to explain or summarize the material being discussed.
- *Encourager*. The encourager watches to make sure that all the members in the group are participating and invites reluctant or silent members to contribute.

If students are to understand the roles and the responsibilities of each role, you will need to develop in them a knowledge and an awareness of each. Discuss each role, demonstrate appropriate behavior and responses, role-play with students, coach, and provide feedback during actual group discussions.

Planning Discussions

Many of the instructional strategies and alternatives in this book are necessarily tied to discussion of one kind or another. Discussion allows students to respond to text, build concepts, clarify meaning, explore issues, share perspectives, and refine thinking. But effective discussions don't run by themselves. For a discussion to be successful, a teacher has to be willing to take a risk or two.

Whenever you initiate a discussion, its outcome is bound to be uncertain, especially if its purpose is to help students think critically and creatively about what they have read. Often a teacher abandons discussion for the safety of recitation, in which the outcome is far more predictable. A text discussion, however, should be neither a quiz show nor, at the opposite end of the continuum, a bull session. Yet, when discussions aren't carefully planned, students often feel an aimlessness or become easily threatened by the teacher's questions. Both being quizzed about text material and simply shooting the bull are apt to close doors on active text learning.

Different purposes for text discussion lead to the use of different types of discussions by content area teachers. *Guided discussions* and *reflective discussions* provide varying degrees of structure for students to talk about text as they interact with one another (Wilen, Ishler, Hutchison, & Kindsvatter, 2004).

Guided Discussion

If your aim is to develop concepts, clarify meaning, and promote understanding, the most appropriate discussion may be *informational*. The main objective of an informational discussion is to help students grapple with issues and understand important concepts. When the discussion task is information centered, teachers use a *guided discussion*.

In a guided discussion, a teacher provides a moderate amount of scaffolding as he or she directs students to think about what they have read through the use of questions and/or teacher-developed guide material. Because the emphasis is on content understanding and clarification, it is important to recognize the central role of the teacher in a guided discussion. Your responsibilities lie in asking questions, in probing student responses when clarifications are needed to extend thinking, in encouraging student questions, and in providing information to keep the discussion on course. The potential problem, however, is domination of the discussion. Alvermann, Dillon, and O'Brien (1988, p. 31) caution that, when overused, this role "can result in a discussion that more nearly resembles a lecture and frequently may confuse students, especially if they have been encouraged to assume more active roles in discussion."

A guided discussion can easily take a *reflective turn*. When teachers consciously shift gears from guided discussion to reflective discussion, their roles in the discussion shift, as explained in the section below.

For example, Creech and Hale (2006, p. 23) explain that discussion can be an important component of an inquiry approach in science classrooms, as teachers model their own problem-solving processes for students: "I model talking aloud about my own thinking processes and encourage students to 'think aloud' about how they make sense of what they are doing. Through this instructional conversation, students learn the *text* includes labs, data, and their own work, and that *reading* is an active problem-solving process."

One example of a structured format for guided discussions is the Paideia Seminar that seeks to integrate critical literacy skills with social interaction around a text (Roberts & Billings, 2011). First, students must prepare for a discussion by reading and considering the chosen text and preparing questions or comments for the group discussion. Students then enter into a guided dialogue about the text and their perceptions and reaction to it. During this time, the teacher and students pose prompts or questions to the group to further the conversation. Once the discussion is complete, teachers prepare an opportunity for students to apply their understanding of the text. Paideia Seminars provide opportunities for students to collaborate to better understand content while building intellectual and social skills (Robinson, 2006).

Reflective Discussion

A reflective discussion is different from a guided discussion in several respects. The purpose of a reflective discussion is to require students to engage in critical and creative thinking as they solve problems, clarify values, explore controversial issues, and form and defend positions. A reflective discussion, then, presumes that students have a solid understanding of the important concepts they are studying. Without a basic knowledge and understanding of the ideas or issues under discussion, students cannot support opinions, make judgments, or justify and defend positions. This type of instruction provides a forum to reflect the diverse perspectives in the classroom (Lester, 1998).

The teacher's role during a reflective discussion is that of participant. As a participant, you become a group member, so that you can contribute to the discussion by sharing ideas and expressing your own opinions: "Teachers can guide students to greater independence in learning by modeling different ways of responding and reacting to issues, commenting on others' points of view, and applying critical reading strategies to difficult concepts in the textbooks" (Alvermann et al., 1988, p. 31).

Creating an Environment for Discussion

Discussion is one of the major process strategies in the content area classroom. Because many of the strategies in this text revolve around discussion of some sort, we offer several suggestions for creating an environment in which discussion takes place, whether in small groups or in the whole class.

Arrange the Classroom to Facilitate Discussion

Arrange the room so that students can see each other and huddle in conversational groupings when they need to share ideas. A good way to determine how functional a classroom is for discussion is to select a discussion strategy that does not require continuous question asking. For example, brainstorming involves a good mixture of whole-class and small-group discussion. Students need to alternate their attention between the board (where the teacher or another student is writing down all the ideas offered within a specified time) and their small groups (where they might categorize the ideas) and back to the front of the room (for comparison of group categories and summarization). If students are able to participate in the various stages of brainstorming with a minimum of chair moving or other time-consuming movements, to see the board, and to converse with other students without undue disruption, the room arrangements are adequate or conducive to discussion.

Encourage Listening

Encourage a climate in which everyone is expected to be a good listener, including the teacher. Let each student speaker know that you are listening. As the teacher begins to talk less, students will talk more. Intervene to determine why some students are not listening to each other or to praise those who are unusually good role models for others. Accept all responses of students positively.

Try starting out with very small groups of no more than two or three students. Again, rather than use questions, have students react to a teacher-read statement (e.g., "Political primaries are a waste of time and money"). In the beginning, students may feel constrained to produce answers to questions to satisfy the teacher. A statement, however, serves as a possible answer and invites reaction and justification. Once a statement is given, set a timer or call time by your watch at two-minute intervals. During each interval, one student in the group may agree or disagree *without interruption*. It is important for students to respectfully consider the perspectives of classmates, so after each group member has an opportunity to respond, the group summarizes all dialogue, and one person presents this summary to the class (Gold & Yellin, 1982, pp. 550–552; Larson, 2000).

Establish a Goal for Discussion

Establish the meaning of the topic and the goal of the discussion: "Why are we talking about railroad routes and how do they relate to our unit on the Civil War?" Also, explain directions explicitly, and don't assume that students will know what to do. Many of the content area reading strategies in this book involve some group discussion. Frequently, strategies progress from independent, written responses to sharing, to comparing those responses in small groups, and then to pooling small-group reactions in a whole-class discussion. Without the guidance of a teacher who is aware of this process, group discussion tends to disintegrate.

Focus the Discussion

Keep the focus of the discussion on the central topic or core question or problem to be solved. Teachers may begin discussions by asking a question about a perplexing situation or by establishing a problem to be solved. From time to time, it may be necessary to refocus attention on the topic by piggybacking on comments made by particular students: "Terry brought out an excellent point about the Underground Railroad in northern Ohio. Does anyone else want to talk about this?" During small-group discussions, one tactic that keeps groups on task is reminding them of the amount of time remaining in the discussion.

Keeping the focus is one purpose for which teachers may legitimately question to clarify the topic. They may also want to make sure that they understood a particular student's comment: "Excuse me, would you repeat that?" Often, keeping the discussion focused will prevent the class from straying away from the task.

Avoid Squelching Discussion

Give students enough think time to reflect on possible answers before calling on someone or rephrasing your question. Moreover, try to avoid answering your own question. (One way to prevent yourself from doing this is to resist having a preset or "correct" answer in your own mind when you ask a question beyond a literal level of comprehension.) Do not interrupt students' responses or permit others to interrupt students' responses. Do, however, take a minute or two for you or a student to summarize and bring closure to a group discussion just as you would in any instructional strategy. Never underestimate the importance of providing appropriate time for students to develop their responses before sharing with the class. Some students may take longer to fully consider how they'd like to respond to questions or prompts. Others may be hesitant to share or lack confidence in their response, so consider allowing students to share ideas with a partner before presenting them to the class. This collaboration allows them to clear up any misunderstandings and gather peer support before engaging the whole group.

Both guided and reflective discussions may be conducted with the whole class or in small groups. A small-group discussion, whether guided or reflective, places the responsibility for learning squarely on students' shoulders. Because of the potential value of collaborative student interactions, we underscore the invaluable contribution of small-group discussions. Small-group learning opportunities help learners contribute ideas to a discussion and take chances in the process. The students can try out ideas without worrying about being wrong or sounding dumb—a fear that often accompanies risk taking in a whole-class situation. Although allowing students to work in small groups may require teachers to allow students to self-direct learning, accountability measures can be put in place to ensure engagement. Each group member can take on a role (as mentioned in the Group Roles and Division of Labor section above) within the group to facilitate and record the group's work. In addition, the teacher may want to develop an open-ended assignment that all groups can complete that will outline their thoughts during the discussion and that will allow the teacher to review all students' work after circulating to facilitate the activity during class.

Looking Back | Looking Forward

Planning is essential for content literacy and learning. It helps teachers to think through the goals, activities, texts, and strategies necessary to support students' learning with text. It also allows teachers to prepare to differentiate instruction for students who may struggle with content or skills. For example, the planning that goes into explicit strategy instruction helps teachers model and show students how to use literacy strategies to learn and provides an opportunity for students to apply this knowledge in a supportive setting, leading to student success. Components of an explicit strategy instructional framework include awareness and explanation, modeling and demonstration, guided practice, and application.

In addition, B–D–A instructional frameworks help teachers to plan instructional activities at critical periods within the reading and discussion of a text that has been assigned to the whole class. This particular lesson structure focuses on what students do *before*, *during*, and *after* reading to facilitate text comprehension. A unit of study, however, helps teachers to organize instructional activities around inquiry projects and multiple texts. Unit planning gives the teacher much more latitude to coordinate resource materials and activities. Unit activities can be organized around the whole class, small groups, or individuals. An effective content classroom, organized around text lessons and units of study, thrives on collaborative interactions between teacher and students and among students and other students. These interactions are grounded in the principles of small-group processes, cooperative learning, and discussion.

In the next chapter, our emphasis turns to kindling student interest in text assignments and preparing them to think positively about what they will read. The importance of the role of prereading preparation in learning from text has often been neglected or underestimated in the content area classroom. Yet prereading activity is in many ways as important to the text learner as warm-up preparation is to the athlete. Let's find out why.

Minds On

1. You have probably seen some variation of the bumper sticker, "If you can read this, thank a teacher." In a small group, sitting in a circle, discuss how you feel about seeing this sticker and what you think it means for content area teachers. Select one member of your group to act as an observer, and use the questions that follow to record group interactions. Allow ten to fifteen minutes for discussion, and then ask the observer to share her or his list of questions and answers with the group.

   Observer's questions:

   a. Who raised questions during group discussion?

   b. Could most of the questions be answered yes or no, true or false?

   c. Who answered the questions?

   d. Who decided who would answer and when they would answer?

   e Who kept the group on task?

   f. Did your seating arrangement change before or after the discussion?

   As a group, discuss the following:

   a. Did the discussion process described by the observer involve the sharing of ideas by group members with no one person asking or answering all the questions?

   b. What were the advantages and disadvantages of having the discussion progress without the rigid protocol of one person deciding who would answer and when?

   c. How would you contrast the effect of the seating in rows used in lecture question-and-answer sessions with the effect of the circle seating used in this discussion?

2. Join together with four or five other individuals who either teach or are planning to teach at approximately the same grade level. Imagine that you have just attended a cooperative learning workshop and you plan to incorporate what you learned into your teaching. What do you consider the single best cooperative activity for your grade level and why? Discuss how

you would implement this approach with a selected topic. List any problems you expect might arise, and explain how you would solve them.

3. Recognizing that students with different abilities and interests learn differently, to what extent should a teacher attempt to organize a class so that all the students in the class will learn the same concepts and information? What modifications could you make to classroom practices and strategies to address the need for differentiation to meet the needs of all learners? Would your answer be the same for a third-grade science class and a high school advanced physics class? What general guidelines can you develop as a group to help a new teacher organize learning to balance course content with individual differences? Also, what type of physical classroom design do you think would best facilitate your philosophy?

 # Hands On

1. Try the following experiment. Roll a standard 8½ by 11-inch sheet of paper into a tube 11 inches long and approximately 1 inch in diameter. Then hold the tube in your left hand and, keeping both eyes open, look through the tube with your left eye. Next, place your right hand, palm toward your face, against the side of the tube approximately half the distance from your eye to the end of the tube. Angle the tube slightly so that the far end of the tube is behind your palm, and a hole should appear in your hand.

   With a small group or individually, brainstorm how you might use this experiment as a prereading activity for a science lesson on the eye.

2. Team up with two other individuals. Designate one member of your group "observer," one "reader," and one "artist." The observer's task will be to make a written record of the actions of the reader and the artist. The artist will draw a triangle described by the reader in the following instructions:

   Draw a triangle so that one side is twice as long as one of the other two. Use one of the small sides as the base, and construct the triangle so that the longest side faces the left side of the paper. Design your triangle so that the longest side is three inches long. Make it exactly three inches if you have a ruler available, or estimate the length if you do not. Finally, assign the letters *a*, *b*, and *c* to each side of the triangle, designating the longest side as *c*.

   After the reader and the artist have completed the drawing, review the notes by the observer, and develop a written record of the intentions or reasons for each action previously recorded. For example, if the observer recorded that the reader turned back to reread the instructions, you might explain that the artist had forgotten a fact that he or she needed to understand.

   Finally, compare observations, make a class list of the learning strategies used by each group, and discuss which are successful approaches for a number of people. From prereading this activity, what conclusions can you draw about the role of metacognition in reading to learn?

3. Bring your favorite book, magazine, poem, song, or drama to class. Develop a prereading activity that would provide the rationale for using this material, and introduce this piece. (This activity can be done in small groups of five or six or with the entire class.)

   Before your presentation, plan a series of entry questions and comments to match what you think others will say in response. Also, because you are introducing this material with a purpose in mind, the discussion should lead your small group to a particular point from which the next activity might begin.

   Be prepared to reach that departure point by a number of alternate routes. Prereading activities and discussions often remain detached from the reading/content activity, so that a novice is tempted to say, "That's enough talking. Let's get to the real lesson." The discussion or activity must be integral to the "real" lesson.

   Following is the complete passage from the exercise at the conclusion of Chapter 1 that could be used for this prereading activity:

   Besides, Sir, we shall not fight our battles alone. There is a just God, who presides over the destinies of nations, who will raise up friends to fight our battles for us. The battle, Sir, is not to the strong alone: it is to the vigilant, the active, the brave. Besides, Sir, we have no election. If we were base enough to desire it, it is now too late to retire from the contest.

There is no retreat, but in submission or slavery. Our chains are forged. Their clanking may be heard on the plains of Boston! The war is inevitable—and let it come—I repeat, Sir, let it come! It is in vain, Sir, to extenuate the matter. Gentlemen may cry, "Peace! Peace!" But there is no peace. The war has actually begun!

The next gale that sweeps from the North will bring to our ears the clash of resounding arms! Our brethren are already in the field! Why stand we here idle? What is it that the Gentlemen wish? What would they have? Is life so dear, or peace too sweet, as to be purchased at the price of chains and slavery? Forbid it, Almighty God! I know not what course others may take, but as for me, give me liberty or give me death!

eResources

Access useful ideas for content literacy lesson plans in your subject area by visiting the following sites: Federal Resources for Educational Excellence (**http://www.free.ed.gov/**), Lessons of Effective Instruction (**http://www.michigan.gov/mde/0,1607,7-140-5235_53792-219150,00.html**), the Ohio Resource Center (**www.ohiorc.org**), and the Content Literacy Information Consortium (CLIC) (**http://curry.edschool.virginia.edu/go/clic**).

Access useful plans for inquiry projects and cooperative learning in your subject area by exploring Lesson Planet (**http://www.lessonplanet.com/lesson-plans/education**), Edutopia (**http://www.edutopia.org/**) and Education World (**www.education-world.com**).

Explore ready-made plans for integrating electronic texts into units by visiting the Web Toolboxes (**www.ed.sc.edu/caw/toolbox.html**) and ReadWriteThink (**http://www.readwritethink.org/classroom-resources/lesson-plans/compare-contrast-electronic-text-90.html**).

MyEducationLab™

Go to Topic 7: Planning for Instruction, the MyEducationLab (**www.myeducationlab.com**) *for Content Area Reading*, where you can:

- Find learning outcomes for Planning for Instruction, along with the national standards that connect to these outcomes.
- Complete Assignments and Activities that can help you more deeply understand the chapter content.
- Practice the core teaching skills identified in the chapter with the Building Teaching Skills and Dispositions learning units.
- Check your comprehension on the content covered in the chapter with the Study Plan. Here you will be able to take a chapter quiz, receive feedback on your answers, and then access Review, Practice, and Enrichment activities to enhance your understanding of chapter content.
- Visit A+RISE. A+RISE® Standards2Strategy™ is an innovative and interactive online resource that offers new teachers in grades K–12 just in time, research-based instructional strategies that meet the linguistic needs of English Language Learners (ELLs) as they learn content, differentiate instruction for all grades and abilities, and are aligned to Common Core Elementary Language Arts standards (for the literacy strategies) and to English language proficiency standards in World-Class Instructional Design and Assessment (WIDA), Texas, California, and Florida.
- Use the Online Lesson Plan Builder to practice lesson planning and integrating national and state standards into your planning.

6 Activating Prior Knowledge and Interest

Organizing Principle

Activating prior knowledge and generating interest create an instructional context in which students will read with purpose and anticipation.

Learning happens. Most people outside the fields of cognitive psychology and education probably give little thought to how it happens or why it happens. Learning is rooted in what we already know. Cognition—the process of knowing—is an active process that takes place in the brain. From a content literacy perspective, the essence of cognitive readiness is to prepare students to make connections between what they know and what they will learn. It is impossible to learn without prior knowledge.

Getting students cognitively ready to learn with text is no easy task. Teachers occasionally are perplexed by the behaviors of students who are capable of acquiring content through lecture and discussions but appear neither *ready* nor *willing* to read to learn. Readiness is a state of mind, a mental preparation for learning, a psychological predisposition. But readiness also entails an emotional stake in the ideas and concepts under scrutiny and a willingness on the part of the students to *want* to engage in learning. Most students, we believe, would like to use reading to learn but don't believe that they have much chance of success.

Students *will* want to read when they have developed a sense of confidence in their ability to use reading to learn. Confident readers connect what they already know to what they are learning. They generate interest in the reading task at hand, even

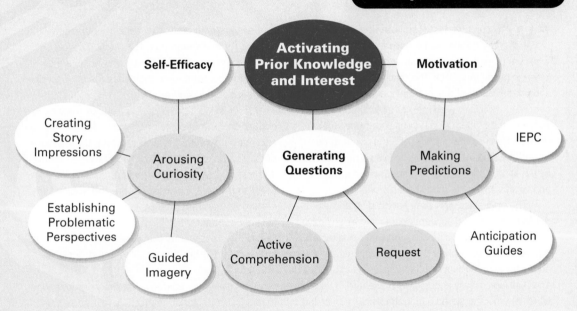

when the text is inherently dry or difficult. Preparing students to think purposefully about what they will read is implicit in the organizing principle for this chapter:

Activating prior knowledge and generating interest create an instructional context in which students will read with purpose and anticipation.

Frame of Mind

1. Why do prereading strategies that activate prior knowledge and raise interest in the subject prepare students to approach text reading in a critical frame of mind?

2. How can meaningful learning be achieved with content area reading?

3. What are the relationships among curiosity arousal, conceptual conflict, and motivation?

4. How and why does a prediction strategy, such as use of an anticipation guide, facilitate reading comprehension?

5. Why is it important for content area teachers to develop a self-efficacy for teaching reading in their subject area?

" W hy can't we just read like in other classes? Why do we always have to think about what we read?" complained an irritated high school junior in his history class. The teacher, who uses and adapts many of the instructional strategies suggested in this book, was momentarily caught off guard by the student's questions. But rather than dismiss them as the rantings of a malcontent, he turned the student's questions into a positive event by initiating a brief discussion about what it means and what it takes "to read like a historian."

The discussion was aimed at building and reinforcing students' concepts of reading as an active search for meaning—a process which, from a historian's perspective, involves detecting bias, analyzing and verifying information, inferring cause and effect, and thinking critically about ideas presented in text. Much of what transpired during the discussion boiled down to this: Active readers think *about* text, think *with* text, and think *through* text. "Historians," the teacher explained with more than a little enthusiasm, "actively search for meaning in everything they read. And that's what I expect from each of you."

Although the classroom incident just described is one of countless little dramas that occur daily in the context of teaching, for us it typifies two of the most powerful realities of content literacy: first, that many students are passive participants when it comes to reading to learn; and second, that caring and knowledgeable teachers can make a difference in the way students approach reading and learn with texts.

For many passive readers, learning with text remains a mysterious process. For most teachers, reading just happens, particularly when there is a strong purpose or a need to read in the first place.

However, a great deal of uncertainty pervades reading for many students. The reading process remains a mystery to students who believe they have limited control over their chances of success with a reading assignment.

You can do a great deal to reduce the lack of control and the uncertainty that students bring to text learning situations. You can take the mystery out of learning with texts by generating students' interest in what they are reading, convincing them that they know more about the subject under study than they think they do, helping them actively connect what they do know to the content of the text, and making them aware of the strategies they need in order to construct meaning.

The challenge content area teachers face with reading to learn is not necessarily related to students' inability to handle the conceptual demands of academic texts. What students can do and what they choose to do are related but different instructional matters. Therefore, you need to create conditions that not only allow students to read effectively but also motivate them to want to read purposefully and meaningfully.

Self-Efficacy and Motivation

When students engage in content literacy activities, some feel confident in their ability to achieve success with reading and writing tasks. Others feel unsure and uncertain. Confident learners exhibit a high level of *self-efficacy* in content literacy situations; unsure learners, a low level. Self-efficacy refers to an "I can" belief in self that leads to a sense of competence. Bandura (1986, p. 391) explains that self-efficacy refers to "people's judgment of their abilities to organize and execute courses of action required to attain designated types of performance." Self-efficacy is not concerned with the skills and strategies students bring to content literacy situations, but rather it focuses on students' estimations of their ability to apply whatever skills and strategies they bring to literacy learning. As Alvermann (2001) explains, self-efficacy contributes to the development of students' literacy identities. Before they can become lifelong readers, students must first view themselves as competent and capable readers.

Self-efficacy is important for supporting teacher effectiveness as well as for developing students' perceptions of themselves as capable readers. Teachers' self-efficacy can impact students' learning (Hoy & Spero, 2005), new and veteran teachers alike need to seek professional development that will support reflective teaching practices and build their own self-efficacy for delivering effective instruction. To help build teacher candidates' sense of self-efficacy, the College of Education at the University of North Carolina at Charlotte uses a post-teaching self-efficacy survey, adapted from the model developed by Tschannen-Moran and Woolfolk (2001), in some of its teacher education programs. Teachers are supported through the use of in-depth clinical experiences, immediate feedback on teaching performance, and tools for self-reflecting on teaching practices. The self-efficacy survey is one tool for encouraging reflective teaching. Sample items from this survey are shown in Box 6.1.

Response Journal

Think about your own self-efficacy as a learner. In which subject, if any, in your academic background have you judged yourself unable to succeed? How has low self-efficacy in the subject affected academic performance?

Self-efficacy and motivation are interrelated concepts. If students believe, for example, that they have a good chance to succeed at a reading task, they are likely to exhibit a willingness to engage in reading and to complete the task. Guthrie and Wigfield's (2000) model of reading engagement calls for instruction that underscores the importance of students' motivation in addition to their growth in conceptual knowledge, their use of comprehension strategies, and their social interaction in the classroom. The National Institute for Literacy (2007) explains that students who are motivated readers share several characteristics: They perceive that they have some level of control over their reading; they apply appropriate strategies in order to make complex reading tasks more manageable; and they display a high level of engagement in their reading experiences.

By the time they enter middle school, students' motivation to read—particularly motivation that comes from their own authentic interests and desires to explore topics through reading—often declines. For struggling readers in particular, this decline in motivation is often compounded by

BOX 6.1

Surveying Teachers' Sense of Self-Efficacy

Efficacy is developed as a self-concept or perception of one's effectiveness in a given situation, rather than as a formal assessment of one's ability or performance (Hoy & Spero, 2005). Providing in-depth clinical experiences, feedback, and tools for self-reflection have been found to have a positive impact on attitudes and self-awareness (Hedrick, McGee, & Mittag, 2000). To support teachers in their effort to reflect on their instructional practices and build self-efficacy for effective teaching, the teacher education programs at UNC Charlotte use a Self-Efficacy Survey, adapted from Tschannen-Moran and Woolfolk (2001). The chart below depicts a sampling of survey items, which can be used as part of professional development for both pre-service and in-service teachers.

(continued)

BOX 6.1 (Continued)

Sample Survey of Teacher Candidate's Sense of Self-Efficacy

Please describe how your perception of your effectiveness as a teacher has changed since the beginning of the semester in terms of your ability to:	Decreased Significantly	Decreased Slightly	Increased Slightly	Increased Significantly
1. plan and design appropriate instructional practices in your content area				
2. implement appropriate instructional practices in your content area				
3. reflect on appropriate instructional practices in your content area				
4. find and implement strategies that will meet the needs of students				
5. find and implement strategies that align with the required curriculum				
6. determine the effectiveness of strategies to convey content knowledge				
7. help your students to think critically				
8. gauge students' comprehension of the concepts you have taught				
9. craft helpful questions for your students				
10. provide appropriate support for struggling students				
11. provide appropriate challenges for very capable students				
12. provide alternative explanations or examples when students are confused				
13. motivate students				
14. make your expectations clear to students				

the assessment and grouping practices common in middle and secondary schools. Some researchers, such as Oldfather and Dahl (1994), suggest that part of this decline in students' motivation may be attributed to the limited emphasis middle and secondary teachers typically place on self-expression and personal response to reading. By fostering a learning environment that is response-centered, teachers can provide students with critical opportunities to explore texts, construct meaning, and make personal connections to content area topics.

Students' motivation for reading and learning with texts increases when they perceive that text is relevant to their own lives and when they believe that they are capable of generating credible responses to their reading of the text (Knickerbocker & Rycik, 2002). Research suggests that, unlike out-of-school reading experiences, in-school reading is often perceived to be uninteresting to many students. One study found that even students who were identified as avid readers outside of school were not necessarily engaged in school reading experiences (Wilson & Kelley, 2010). One factor found to inhibit students' motivation to read centered on their belief that they rarely control what they read during the course of the school day (Daniels &Steres, 2011). A relevant curriculum, engaging instructional strategies, and a school culture that fosters wide reading can help to engage students in reading across the curriculum. Students have been found to be more enthusiastic about in-school reading when the texts used are accessible, interesting, and when they have a choice in the selection of the text (Lapp & Fisher, 2009). Wolk (2010) notes that outside of school, students' reading experiences are increasingly varied, incorporate different media, and often include digital texts which may not be accessible to them in school. He suggests that teachers think broadly about the types of text they use in their content area classes, pointing out that a variety of high interest, high quality texts can serve to engage students in reading, and more likely develop their propensity to become life-long readers. Box 6.2 outlines Wolk's suggestions about possible texts that could be used to engage students in literacy and learning across the content areas.

Evidence-Based Best Practices BOX 6.2

Using a Variety of Texts to Support Reading Engagement

As we pointed out in Chapter 1, textbooks are often the predominant source of reading in the content areas, especially in middle and high school classes. To offer students a wider range of reading materials that have the potential to be both engaging and informative, Wolk (2010) encourages teachers to consider texts beyond the so-called "classics" or traditional texts. He suggests the following text options when selecting texts across content areas:

- *Children's and Young Adult Literature*: This category can include texts that are traditionally thought of as independent reading book, such as Collins'(2010) *The Hunger Games* and Wilson's (2008) *100 Cupboards* series.

- *Graphic Novels and Graphic Memoirs:* No longer relegated to "comic book" status, graphic novels such as McCloud's (2006) *Making Comics: Storytelling Secrets of Comics, Manga, and Graphic Novels* and Josh Neufeld's (2010) *A. D. New Orleans: After the Deluge,* a memoir about six survivors of Hurricane Katrina, graphic novels have evolved into a thought-provoking literary genre.

- *Newspapers:* Local and national newspapers can offer a variety of ideological perspectives on issues of both local and international prominence.

- *Magazines:* In addition to magazines specifically designed for school use, periodicals such as *Boston Review, The New York Times Magazine,* and *Discover* are all potential texts for in-school reading.

- *Literary Magazines:* Steven Spielberg is credited for saying, "It will take a generation of readers to spawn a generation of writers." Literary magazines such as *Kenyon Review* and *Antioch Review* can provide examples of quality writing and literary analysis.

- *Studies and Reports:* Reports, such as those from various centers and government agencies, can provide a basis for investigating a multitude of contemporary topics including criminal justice and immigration. Increasingly, reports such as these are available online.

- *Songs:* Certain song lyrics can help students to make connections to current social and political topics of study.

Bruner (1970, 1990), a pioneer in the field of cognitive psychology, suggested that the mind doesn't work apart from feeling and commitment. Learners make meaning when they exhibit an "inherent passion" for what is to be learned. How people construct meaning depends on their beliefs, mental states, intentions, desires, and commitments. Likewise, Eisner (1991) calls on us to celebrate thinking in schools by reminding us that brains may be born, but minds are made. Schools do not pay enough attention to students' curiosity and imagination. As a result, students disengage from active participation in the academic life of the classroom because there is little satisfaction to be gained from it. Unless students receive satisfaction from schoolwork, Eisner argues, there is little reason or motive to continue to pursue learning: "Thinking . . . should be prized not only because it leads to attractive destinations but because the journey itself is satisfying" (Eisner, 1991, p. 40).

Given the current policy emphasis on accountability and adequate yearly progress as measured by high-stakes assessments (discussed in Chapter 4), teachers often find themselves torn between seeking to increase students' interest in content area subjects by supporting their motivation to learn and simply trying to fulfill externally imposed and even arbitrary achievement targets.

Nevertheless, effective teachers understand the importance of taking the time to make their subject areas relevant to students. In exploring matters of the mind, cognitive activity cannot be divorced from emotional involvement. Meaningful learning with texts occurs when students reap satisfaction from texts and a sense of accomplishment from reading. As Ivey and Fisher (2005, p. 8) explain, "Teachers who understand their students' backgrounds, prior knowledge, interests, and motivations are much more likely to make the connections that adolescents crave."

Teachers can support students' motivation for reading by setting clear goals and expectations for reading, providing students with access to a variety of reading materials, and, when possible, allowing students a level of choice in selecting the texts they read (Brozo & Flyny, 2007; Guthrie & Davis, 2003). Teachers can also give students opportunities to interact with one another through shared reading experiences, and they can guide students in learning how to evaluating their own understanding of a text (Wigfield, 2004; Reed, Schallert, Beth, & Woodruff, 2004).

Two of the most appropriate questions that students can ask about a text are: "What do I need to know?" and "How well do I already know it?" The question "What do I need to know?" prompts readers to activate their prior knowledge to make predictions and set purposes. It gets them thinking positively about what they are going to read. "How well do I already know it?" helps readers search their experience and knowledge to give support to tentative predictions and to help make plans for reading.

As simple as these two questions may seem on the surface, maturing readers rarely *know enough* about the reading process to ask them. "What do I need to know?" and "How well do I already know it?" require *metacognitive awareness* on the part of the learners. However, these two questions, when consciously raised and reflected on, put students on the road to regulating and monitoring their own reading behavior. It is never too early (or too late) to begin showing students how to set purposes by raising questions about the text.

In Chapter 1, we underscored the important role that prior knowledge plays in meaningful learning, so we won't belabor the point here, other than to reaffirm that prior knowledge activation is inescapably bound to one's purpose for reading and learning. As students ready themselves to learn with texts, they need to approach upcoming material in a critical frame of mind. Instructional scaffolding should make readers receptive to meaningful learning by creating a reference point for connecting the given (what one knows) with the new (the material to be learned). A frame of reference signals the connections students must make between the given and the new. They need to recognize how new material fits into the conceptual frameworks they already have. In Box 6.3,

BOX 6.3

Voices from the Field

Drew, Mathematics Coach

Challenge

During a unit on area and perimeter, a fifth grade class-room teacher, Mrs. Little, and I, posed a real-world mathematical task to students to allow them to explore these concepts more deeply. Here is the task they were given:

> *You have 12 yards of fencing to build a rectangular cage for your rabbit. Which dimensions give you the most space inside the cage?*

Students often struggle with solving these types of mathematical tasks for a couple reasons: they struggle to read and make sense of the mathematical situation and, sometimes, they don't know where to begin. In this case, students struggled to distinguish between the concepts of perimeter (the amount of fencing) and area (the space inside).

Strategy

In order to support the students, Mrs. Little and I spent time at the beginning of the lesson activating their prior knowledge by asking them about real-life examples of area and perimeter. We posed questions, such as:

- If we needed to build a fence, how would we determine how much fencing we would need?

- Can you think of other examples where we would need to figure out the distance around something?

- If we needed to put carpet down on the floor of a house, how would we determine how much carpet we would need?

- Can you think of other examples where we would need to figure out how much material we will need to cover a flat surface?

We posed the task to students and provided them with plastic square tiles to begin exploring the task. Initially, students connected the number 12 in the task with the need to grab 12 square tiles. Nearly every student did this and immediately made rectangles.

Some students made a rectangle that was 6 tiles wide and 2 tiles tall, while others made one that was 4 tiles wide and 3 tiles tall. While both used 12 tiles, neither rectangle had a perimeter of 12.

Seeing this misconception, Mrs. Little and I revisited students' understanding of perimeter by asking them a few questions:

> Mrs. Little: Do we know the amount of fencing that we have or the space that we have inside of our pen?
>
> Lisa: We have 12 yards of fencing.
>
> Mrs. Little: So, if we think about fencing, will the amount of fencing be the distance around the rectangle or the space inside?
>
> Oscar: Fencing will go around, so we need to find the distance on the outside of the rectangle.
>
> Polly: If we know that we have 12 yards of fencing, how can we use our tiles to help us?
>
> Jimmy: We can look at the rectangles that we made and then count the distance around each shape.
>
> Mrs. Little: Go ahead and do that.

As students counted the distance around they realized that neither rectangle had a perimeter of 12 units. Rather, the 6×2 rectangle had a perimeter of 16 units, and the 4×3 rectangle had a perimeter of 14 units. Students were confused about how to find a rectangle with a perimeter of 12 units. Mrs. Little asked, "How can we find a rectangle that has a perimeter of 12?" Students started to manipulate the 12 tiles and counted the perimeter of their representations. No students were able to find a rectangle that used 12 tiles and also had a perimeter of 12.

Mrs. Little then asked, "Do we have to use exactly 12 tiles or can we use a different number?" The students all responded, "a different number."

When Mrs. Little asked why that was the case, Samuel commented, "The only thing given to us is that the fencing or perimeter had to be 12. The number of tiles could be different."

Students worked for the next 15 minutes making rectangles out of their tiles that had a perimeter of 12.

(continued)

BOX 6.3 (Continued)

The teacher then asked students to share their solutions on the SMART board by drawing a picture of their rectangle and writing the dimensions. The use of a visual helped struggling students to make sense of their classmates' answers. Table 1 shows the solutions that they came up with.

During the discussion, Mrs. Little had made Table 1 on the SMART board and asked students to talk with their table groups about observations that they had. Tyrone mentioned, "There are two rectangles that have an area of 5 and two that have an area of 8." After Mrs. Little asked him to explain the difference between the two rectangles that had an area of 5, Tyrone said, "One rectangle is 5 by 1 and the other is 1 by 5. When we draw them they have the same dimensions, but one is just twisted around." Tyrone drew a visual up on the SMART Board of the two rectangles to match his explanation.

Last, the entire class was able to explain that the pen with the largest amount of space was a 3 by 3 rectangle, which students called a square. The discussion of this part of the task allowed students to discuss the relationship between squares and rectangles.

Reflection

This lesson allowed fifth grade students to build on their prior knowledge of fencing and carpets to explore a real-world mathematical task about the area and perimeter of rectangles. The use of guiding questions at the beginning of the lesson using real-life examples of area and perimeter provided a foundation that was revisited later in the lesson to address misconceptions. Also, the use of concrete manipulatives (plastic square tiles) and drawings help students to connect the mathematical concepts to representations of those concepts. By having the opportunity to create pictorial representations, students were able to better grasp the difference between area and perimeter and successfully complete the task.

As the Common Core State Standards in Mathematics are implemented in schools, the eight Standards for Mathematical Practice heavily emphasize the need for teachers to build upon students' prior knowledge to help them make sense of the mathematical situations that are embedded in tasks and problems. This task is an example of how students' prior knowledge of fencing and carpeting helped them explore area and perimeter.

Table 1

Width	Length	Area
5	1	5
4	2	8
3	3	9
2	4	8
1	5	5

Drew, a mathematics coach, works with a fifth grade teacher to activate her students' knowledge for and interest in the concepts of area and perimeter. Conceptual conflicts are the key to creating motivational conditions in the classroom (Berlyne, 1965). Should students be presented with situations that take the form of puzzlement, doubt, surprise, perplexity, contradiction, or ambiguity, they will be motivated to seek resolution. Why? The need within the learner is to resolve the conflict. As a result, the search for knowledge becomes a driving motivational force. When a question begins to gnaw at a learner, searching behavior is stimulated; learning occurs as the conceptual conflict resolves itself.

꩜ Arousing Curiosity

Arousing curiosity and activating prior knowledge are closely related instructional activities. Curiosity arousal gives students the chance to consider what they know already about the material to be read. Through your guidance, they are encouraged to make connections and to relate their knowledge to the text assignment. And further, they will recognize that there are problems—conceptual conflicts—to be resolved through reading. Arousing curiosity helps students raise questions that they can answer only by giving thought to what they read.

Creating Story Impressions

Using story impressions is an instructional strategy that arouses curiosity and allows students to anticipate story content. Although teachers use story impressions with narrative text, it may also be used to create "text impressions" in content areas other than English language arts.

Response Journal

How might you adapt story impressions to a content area other than English or history?

The story impressions strategy uses clue words associated with the setting, characters, and events in the story to help readers write their own versions of the story prior to reading. McGinley and Denner (1987, p. 249), originators of the strategy, describe it this way: "Story impressions get readers to predict the events of the story that will be read, by providing them with fragments of the actual content. After reading the set of clues, the students are asked to render them comprehensible by using them to compose a story of their own in advance of reading the actual tale."

Fragments from the story, in the form of clue words and phrases, enable readers to form an overall impression of how the characters and events interact in the story. The clue words are selected directly from the story and are sequenced with arrows or lines to form a descriptive chain. The chain of clue words triggers impressions about the story. Students then write a "story prediction" that anticipates the events in the story.

The story impression example in Figure 6.1 was developed in preparation for students' reading of Jonathan Swift's classic, *Gulliver's Travels*. Based on the terms listed in the story chain, the students generated their prediction. Similarly, the example in Figure 6.2 shows how a high school Spanish teacher, Mr. Roundy, used the story impression strategy with his Spanish class. Mr. Roundy chose a story that he thought many of his students may have heard when they were children: *La Princesa y El Guisante* (*The Princess and the Pea*). He selected ten words directly from the text and asked students to predict what might happen in the story based on their understanding of the words listed. Figure 6.2 shows the story impression his students created in preparation for their reading of *La Princesa y El Guisante*. After they had read the author's version of the story, Mr. Roundy had his students compare and contrast their story impression predications with the text as the author wrote it.

As McGinley and Denner (1987, p. 250) explain, "The object, of course, is not for the student to guess the details or the exact relations among the events and characters of the story,

Figure 6.1 Story Impression for *Gulliver's Travels*

Classroom Artifact

Story Chain	Story Prediction
shipwrecked little people politics corruption giant science useless immortal talking horses insane morals	*After being shipwrecked with a bunch of little people, a traveler, whose interest in politics was obvious but whose past was filled with corruption, decided to live off his giant bank account. He believed that science was useless and had failed him. Knowing he wasn't immortal, he decided to survive his ordeal by talking to sea horses, making people believe that he was insane. That way, he thought, they might not pay attention to his questionable morals.*

Figure 6.2 Story Impression for *La Princesa y El Guisante*

Classroom Artifact

Story Chain	Story Predication
Principe (prince) *Verdad* (truth) *Mundo* (world) *Encontrar* (to find) *Deseo* (desire) *Tempestad* (storm) *Lluvia* (rain) *Ropa* (clothes) *Cama* (bed) *Cuerpo* (body)	*Creo que el Príncipe llega a su casa y encuentra que suesposa, la Princesa, no está y que toda sur opa ha sido dejada en su cama. El anda por el mundo tratando de buscar lo que su corazón anhela, la Princesa, pero nadie le dice la verdad sobre donde ella esta. Creo que la lluvia lo va a cojer.* *(I think that the Prince comes home to find that his wife, the Princess, is missing and all of her clothes have been left on the bed. He is out in the world trying to find his heart's desire, the Princess, but no one will tell him the truth about where she is. I think that the Prince is going to be caught in a rainstorm.)*

but to simply compare his or her own story guess to the author's actual account." Box 6.4 outlines the steps to follow in the story impression strategy.

Establishing Problematic Perspectives

Creating problems to be solved or perspectives from which readers approach text material provides an imaginative entry into a text selection. For example, the teacher's role in creating problematic perspectives is (1) providing the time to discuss the problem, raising questions, and seeking possible solutions before reading and then (2) assigning the reading material that will help lead to resolution and conceptual development.

A social studies teacher and her students were exploring the development of early American settlements in a unit on colonial life. She presented the problem situation to her students as

Evidence-Based Best Practices BOX 6.4

Story Impressions

McGinley and Denner (1987) suggest the following steps to introduce story impressions to the class for the first time:

1. *Introduce the strategy.* Say to the students, "Today we're going to make up what we think this story *could* be about."

2. *Use large newsprint, a transparency, or SMART board to show students the story chain.* (See the left side of Figure 6.1 for an example.) Say, "Here are some clues about the story we're going to read." Explain that the students will use the clues to write their own version of the story and that, after reading, they will compare what they wrote with the actual story.

3. *Read the clues together, and explain how the arrows link one clue to another in a logical order.* Then brainstorm story ideas that connect all of

the clues in the order that they are presented, saying, "What do we think this story could be about?"

4. *Demonstrate how to write a story guess.* Use the ideas generated to write a class-composed story that links all of the clues. Use newsprint, the whiteboard, or a transparency for this purpose. Read the story prediction aloud with the students.

5. *Invite the students to read the actual story silently, or initiate a shared reading experience.* Afterward, discuss how the class-composed version is similar to and different from the author's story.

6. *For subsequent stories, use story impressions to have students write individual story predictions. Or have them work in cooperative teams to write a group-composed story guess.*

shown in Figure 6.3. The series of questions promoted an interest-filled discussion, putting students in a situation in which they had to rely on prior knowledge for responses.

Asking the students in the social studies class to approach reading by imagining that they were early European settlers placed them in a particular role. With the role came a perspective. Creating such a perspective has its underpinnings in a schema-theoretical view of the reading process.

One of the early studies of the Center for the Study of Reading at the University of Illinois pointed to the powerful role of perspective in comprehending text (Pichert & Anderson, 1977). The researchers showed just how important the reader's perspective can be. Two groups of readers were asked to read a passage about a house from one of two perspectives: a burglar

Response Journal

Create a problematic perspective on some topic of study in your content area.

Figure 6.3 A Problem Situation in a U.S. History Class

The time is 1680 and the place is Massachusetts. Imagine that you are early European settlers. You will want to try to think as you believe they may have thought and act as they might have acted. You and your group have petitioned the Great and General Court to be allowed to form a new town. After checking to make sure you are of good character and the land is fertile and can be defended, the court says yes. It grants you a five-mile-square plot of land. As proprietors of this land, you must plan a town. What buildings would you put in first? Second? Third? Later? Why? How would you divide the land among the many people who want to live there? Why? As proprietors, would you treat yourselves differently from the others? Why? How would you run the government?

Figure 6.4 Creating a Perspective in an Auto Mechanics Class

You are the only mechanic on duty when a four-wheel-drive truck with a V-8 engine pulls in for repair. The truck has high mileage, and it appears that the problem may be a worn clutch disk. What tools do you think you will need? What procedures would you follow? Put your answers to these questions under the two following headings.

Tools Needed　　　　　**Procedures**

_____　　_____

_____　　_____

_____　　_____

_____　　_____

_____　　_____

or a house buyer. When readers who held the perspective of a house burglar read the story about going through the house, they recalled different information from those readers who approached the story from the perspective of a house buyer.

Creating a perspective (a role) for the student is one way to get into reading. Students in these roles find themselves solving problems that force them to use their knowledge and experience. In Figure 6.4, a high school teacher created a perspective for students before assigning a reading selection from an auto mechanics manual.

In preparation for reading Golding's book *Lord of the Flies,* an English teacher set up a perspective in which students' curiosity was aroused and their expectations of the story raised:

Imagine that you and your fellow classmates are stranded on an island after your plane has crashed. You cannot find the pilot and have to make some important decisions. What actions will you take once you have an opportunity to process the situation?

The class considered the orienting question. After some discussion, the teacher initiated the activity in Figure 6.5. The students formed small groups, and each group was directed to come to a consensus on the activities they would choose.

Figure 6.5 Creating a Perspective in an English Class

Imagine that your plane crashes, leaving you and the other passengers stranded on an island. From the list below, which activities would you choose to do in order to try to ensure your survival?

_____ 1. Elect a leader.	_____ 8. Relax and try to have fun on the island.
_____ 2. Create a communication device.	
_____ 3. Devise a survival plan with the whole group.	_____ 9. Build a fire.
	_____ 10. Gather wood.
_____ 4. Create a rescue strategy.	_____ 11. Create rules or laws.
_____ 5. Gather tools for hunting.	_____ 12. Purify water for drinking.
_____ 6. Build a shelter.	_____ 13. Simply wait for rescue.
_____ 7. Explore the island.	_____ 14. Create fishing equipment.

From the small-group discussions came the recognition that the values, beliefs, and attitudes readers bring to a text shape their perspective as much as their background knowledge of a topic. For this reason, we suggest that when building the motivation for a text to be read, take into account, where appropriate, an examination of values, attitudes, and controversial issues related to the subject matter.

Guided Imagery

Students' ability to visualize what they are reading is an important component for developing comprehension. Guided imagery allows students to explore concepts by creating mental images (Deshler, Schumaker, Lenz, Bulgren, Hock, & Knight, 2001). Samples (1977) recommends guided imagery, among other things, as a means of:

- Building an experience base for inquiry, discussion, and group work
- Exploring and stretching concepts
- Solving and clarifying problems
- Exploring history and the future
- Exploring other lands and worlds

Figure 6.6 shows a guided imagery example used by Ms. Maas with her sixth-grade middle school science students. As she explained, "My state standards require that my students describe ways in which organisms interact with each other and with non-living part of the environments and investigate factors that determine the growth and survival of organisms." To introduce the concept of symbiosis, Ms. Maas created a guided imagery exercise to help her students visualize and comprehend the importance of a commensal relationship within the marine environment.

Figure 6.6 A Guided Imagery Illustration

Close your eyes . . . start moving your body . . . you are a remora fish swimming through the balmy 83 degree waters of the Coral Sea off the north east coast of Australia. As the cumulus clouds float overhead, intermittent rays of sunlight filter through the turquoise sea water to reveal the vivid colors of the Great Barrier Reef. You encounter danger everywhere as you constantly search for food and shelter. As you swim gracefully past huge outcrops of pink, brain coral, you face a venomous red and white striped lionfish and a blue-ringed octopus. You are quickly growing more tired of swimming and need to find your next meal fast. You decide to venture cautiously away from the protection of the reef. As you swim, you come face to face with a school of poisonous, box jellyfish. You dive down, swimming hard and fast to avoid their enormous tentacles. Up ahead in the deep water, you confront the ocean's top predator: a great white shark. Despite being tired and hungry, you swim eagerly *towards* the shark knowing this is exactly what you have been waiting for: Your next free meal and free ride! You catch up with the shark and quickly attach yourself onto the underside of his body with your large, sucker-like mouth. Now, you can finally rest from swimming and relax from the dangers of the ocean knowing you are more protected attached to the shark than swimming alone in the vast ocean. All of a sudden, you sense you're moving through the water faster. The great white shark is now tailing a school of mackerel. He quickly darts into the mass of fish, devouring several fish in one bite. Ah, at last, your free meal. You swiftly release your grip from the shark's body and gulp up the uneaten scraps of food left behind. As the shark continues to thrash about and consume more, you find yourself quickly becoming full and satisfied. You speedily reattach yourself to the shark's body so as not to miss the ride or any other free meals along the way.

She presented her students with the text shown in Figure 6.6. After her students read and had time to think about the text, she initiated a whole-group discussion prompted by the following questions:

1. What do you think symbiosis means?
2. What were the two species illustrated in this visual exercise, and how did the partners affect one another?
3. Can a symbiotic relationship affect the two partners differently?
4. Did the relationship result in:
   a. Both partners benefiting (mutualism)
   b. One partner benefiting while the other partner was neither helped nor hurt (commensalism)
   c. One partner benefiting while the other partner was harmed (parasitism)
5. Can you think of any other symbiotic relationships found in nature?

Response Journal

Create a guided imagery scenario on a topic of study in your content area.

By introducing the concept of symbiosis through this guided imagery exercise, she was able to arouse her students' interest about the topic, activate their background knowledge, and motivate them to want to continuing learning about these unique and vital relationships that exist in nature.

Guided imagery provided an instructional option to help students connect what they see in their mind's eye to what they will study.

Content area teachers assess students' prior knowledge of and interest in a topic to be studied through authentic instructional practices. Box 6.5 describes an additional instructional strategy, PreP, designed by Langer (1981) to assess students' prior knowledge within an instructional context, and motivate them to learn more about a topic of study.

Evidence-Based Best Practices

BOX 6.5

PreP Procedure

Brainstorming is a key feature of the prereading plan (PreP), which may be used to estimate the levels of background knowledge that students bring to the text assignments.

Before beginning the PreP activity, the teacher should examine the text material for keywords (which represent major concepts to be developed), phrases, or pictures and then introduce the topic that is to be read, following the three-phase plan outlined by Langer (1981, p. 154):

1. *Initial associations with the concept.* In this first phase the teacher says, "Tell anything that comes to mind when . . ." (e.g., ". . . you hear the word *Congress*"). As each student tells what ideas initially came to mind, the teacher jots each response on the board. During this phase, the students have their first opportunity to find associations between the key concept and their prior knowledge. When this activity was carried out in a middle school class, one student, Bill, said, "Important people." Another student, Danette, said, "Washington, D.C."

2. *Reflections on initial associations.* During the second phase of PreP, the students are asked, "What made you think of . . . [the response given by a student]?" This phase helps the students develop awareness of their network of associations. They also have an opportunity to listen to each other's explanations, to interact, and to become aware of their changing ideas. Through this procedure, they may weigh, reject, accept, revise, and integrate some of the ideas that came to mind. When Bill was asked what made him think of important people, he said, "I saw them in the newspaper." When Danette was asked what made her think of Washington, D.C., she said, "Congress takes place there."

3. *Reformulation of knowledge.* In this phase, the teacher says, "Based on our discussion and before we read the text, have you any new ideas about . . . (e.g., ". . . Congress)?" This phase allows students to verbalize associations that have been elaborated or changed through the discussion. Because they have had a chance to probe their memories to elaborate on their prior knowledge, the responses elicited during the third phase are often more refined than those from the first. This time, Bill said, "Lawmakers of America," and Danette said, "The part of the U.S. government that makes the laws."

Through observation and listening during PreP, content area teachers will find their students' knowledge can be divided into three broad levels. On one level are students who have *much* prior knowledge about the concept. These students are often able to define and draw analogies, make conceptual links, and think categorically. On the second level are students who may have *some* prior knowledge. These students can give examples and cite characteristics of the content but may be unable to see relationships or make connections between what they know and the new material. On the third level are students who have *little* background knowledge. They often respond to the PreP activity by making simple associations, often misassociating with the topic.

Making Predictions

Prediction strategies activate thought about the content before reading. Students must rely on what they know through previous study and experience to make educated guesses about the material to be read.

Why an educated guess? Smith (1988, p. 163) defines predicting as the prior elimination of unlikely alternatives. He suggests:

> Readers do not normally attend to print with their minds blank, with no prior purpose and with no expectation of what they might find in the text. . . . The way readers look for meaning is not to consider all possibilities, nor to make reckless guesses about just one, but rather to predict within the most likely range of alternatives. . . . Readers can derive meaning from text because they bring expectations about meaning to text.

You can facilitate student-centered purposes by creating anticipation about the meaning of what will be read.

Anticipation Guides

An anticipation guide is a series of statements to which students must respond individually before reading the text. Their value lies in the discussion that takes place after the exercise. The teacher's role during discussion is to activate and agitate thought. As students connect their knowledge of the world to the prediction task, you must remain open to a wide range of responses. Draw on what students bring to the task, but remain nondirective in order to keep the discussion moving.

Anticipation guides may vary in format but not in purpose. In each case, the readers' expectations about meaning are raised before they read the text. Keep these six guidelines in mind in constructing and using an anticipation guide:

1. *Analyze the material to be read.* Determine the major ideas—implicit and explicit—with which students will interact.

2. *Write those ideas in short, clear declarative statements.* These statements should in some way reflect the world in which the students live or about which they know. Therefore, avoid abstractions whenever possible.

3. *Put these statements in a format that will elicit anticipation and prediction.*

4. *Discuss the students' predictions and anticipations before they read the text selection.*

5. *Assign the text selection.* Have the students evaluate the statements in light of the author's intent and purpose.

6. *Contrast the readers' predictions with the author's intended meaning.*

Adapting Anticipation Guides in Content Areas

A science teacher began a weather unit by introducing a series of popular clichés about the weather. He asked his students to anticipate whether the clichés had a scientific basis (see Figure 6.7). The before-reading discussion led the students to review and expand their concepts of scientific truth. Throughout different parts of the unit, the teacher returned to one or two of the clichés in the anticipation guide and suggested to the class that the textbook assignment would explain whether there was a scientific basis for each saying. Students were then directed to read to find out what the explanations were.

A health education teacher raised expectations and created anticipation for a chapter on the human immunodeficiency virus (HIV) and AIDS. Rather than prepare written statements, she conducted the anticipatory lesson as part of an introductory class discussion. She raised curiosity about the topic by asking students to participate in a strategy known as the "every-pupil response." She told the students that she would ask several questions about becoming infected with HIV. Students were to respond to each question by giving a "thumbs up" if they agreed or a "thumbs down" if they disagreed. The class had to participate in unison and keep their thumbs up or down. After each question, the students shared their reasons for responding thumbs up or thumbs down. The questions were framed as follows: "Is it true that you can contract HIV by:

- Having unprotected sex with an infected partner?"
- Kissing someone with HIV?"

Figure 6.7 Anticipation Guide for Clichés About Weather

Directions: Put a check under "Likely" if you believe that the weather saying has any scientific basis; put a check under "Unlikely" if you believe that it has no scientific basis. Be ready to explain your choice.

Likely	**Unlikely**	
_____	_____	1. Red sky at night, sailors' delight; red sky at morning, sailors take warning.
_____	_____	2. If you see a sunspot, there is going to be bad weather.
_____	_____	3. When the leaves turn under, it is going to storm.
_____	_____	4. If you see a hornet's nest high in a tree, a harsh winter is coming.
_____	_____	5. Aching bones mean a cold and rainy forecast.
_____	_____	6. If a groundhog sees his shadow, six more weeks of winter.
_____	_____	7. Rain before seven, sun by eleven.
_____	_____	8. If a cow lies down in a pasture, it is going to rain soon.
_____	_____	9. Sea gull, sea gull, sitting on the sand; it's never good weather while you're on land.

- Sharing needles with an HIV-infected drug user?"
- Sharing a locker with an infected person?"
- Using a telephone after someone with HIV has used it?"
- Being bitten by a mosquito?"

The verbal anticipation guide created lively discussion as students discussed some of their preconceived notions and misconceptions about HIV and AIDS.

Mathematics teachers also have been successful in their use of anticipation guides. In a pre-calculus class, the teacher introduced the activity shown in Figure 6.8 to begin the trigonometry section of the textbook. She created the anticipation guide to help students address their own knowledge about trigonometry and to create conceptual conflict for some of the more difficult sections of the chapter they would be studying. Figure 6.9 is the anticipation guide that a middle school mathematics teacher used to introduce her class to a unit on graphing, analyzing, organizing, and interpreting data.

Finally, a tenth-grade English teacher developed an anticipation guide for Elie Wiesel's book *Night.* The teacher had been relying mainly on the KWL strategy (what I **K**now, what I **W**ant to learn, and what I did **L**earn)(see Chapter 7) for before-reading and after-reading discussions. She decided, as a change of pace, to use the anticipation guide in Figure 6.10 as an alternative to KWL. She adapted the anticipation guide format by asking students, before reading, to discuss their responses to a series of statements about the Holocaust. After reading *Night,* the students were then asked to revisit their original responses to the statements on the guide and to consider whether their reading confirmed or refuted their prereading responses. For the postreading discussion, the teacher placed a blank version of the anticipation guide on

Figure 6.8 Anticipation Guide for Preconceived Notions about Trigonometry

Directions: Put a check under "Likely" if you believe that the statement has any mathematical truth. Put a check under "Unlikely" if you believe that it has no mathematical truth. Be ready to explain your choices.

Likely	Unlikely	
_____	_____	1. Trigonometry deals with circles.
_____	_____	2. Angles have little importance in trigonometry.
_____	_____	3. Sailors use trigonometry in navigation.
_____	_____	4. Angles can be measured only in degrees.
_____	_____	5. Calculators are useless in trigonometry.
_____	_____	6. Trigonometry deals with triangles.
_____	_____	7. Trigonometry has no application in the real world.
_____	_____	8. Radians are used in measuring central angles.
_____	_____	9. Trigonometry has scientific uses.
_____	_____	10. Radians can be converted to degrees.

Figure 6.9 Anticipation Guide for Graphing Data

Directions: Below is a list of statements related to our new unit on graphing, analyzing, organizing, and interpreting data. Before we begin our unit, look carefully at each statement and indicate in the Before Study column whether or not you believe the statement is true or false. Once we have completed our study, you will review these statements again to see if your ideas about them have changed.

Before Study		Statement	After Study	
T	F	All data can be represented using *line graphs*.	T	F
T	F	*Histograms* are the same as *bar graphs*.	T	F
T	F	*Pie Charts* are used to represent parts of a whole.	T	F
T	F	All graphs require scales for clarity.	T	F
T	F	*Bar Graphs* can show multiple data easily in one graph.	T	F
T	F	*Line Graphs* always result in straight lines.	T	F
T	F	*Histograms* have spaces between each bar.	T	F

Figure 6.10 Anticipation Guide for *Night*

Directions: Read each of the following statements and, in the Before Reading column, place a plus (+) if you agree with the statement and a minus (–) if you disagree. Be prepared to support your responses during our class discussion. Later, after learning about the Holocaust, you will complete the After Reading column to see if any of your initial responses have changed. You'll be asked to discuss why you confirmed or changed your ideas from your before-reading responses.

Before Reading	Statement	After Reading
_____	The Holocaust took place only in Germany.	_____
_____	The Jews had plenty of time to escape so they could have avoided being sent to a concentration camp.	_____
_____	Jews were targeted because of their religion.	_____
_____	Other countries did not know what was happening to the Jews.	_____
_____	People in concentration camps were only killed if they broke a law.	_____
_____	Life in the concentration camps wasn't so bad for those who were too old or too young to work.	_____
_____	Survivors of the Holocaust just want to forget about what happened.	_____
_____	Jews were the only target of Hitler and the Nazis.	_____
_____	The Holocaust took place between WWI and WWII.	_____
_____	The term *Holocaust* was developed by the Jewish prisoners while they were at the camps.	_____

an overhead projector so that the students, as a class, could discuss how their knowledge and beliefs had changed as a result of their reading of *Night*.

Imagine, Elaborate, Predict, and Confirm (IEPC)

Many students, particularly those who struggle with reading, have difficulty creating mental images as they read (Lenihan, 2003). The imagine, elaborate, predict, and confirm (IEPC) strategy encourages students to use visual imagery to enhance their comprehension of a text selection. Figure 6.11 shows how a social studies teacher used the IEPC strategy to help her students to understand Theodore Taylor's book *The Cay*. Wood and Taylor (2005) explain the steps in implementing the IEPC strategy:

1. *Select a text passage or introduction to the text that contains content appropriate for developing imagery.* In the IEPC example illustrated in Figure 6.11, the teacher read a brief

Figure 6.11 IEPC Chart for *The Cay*

I	E	P	C
Being stranded on a desert island; feeling afraid Feeling suspicious of the person with whom you are stranded; wondering if they are going to harm you Being frustrated at not being able to see and not being able to do anything about it Seeing the dark rain clouds gather; wondering how long the storm will last and how strong it will be How will Phillip and Timothy survive?	Phillip and Timothy must have been terrified, especially after their boat was torpedoed. They must have been lonely, starving, exhausted. Phillip was white. Timothy was black. Phillip had been taught that black people were inferior. Will he overcome his prejudice? Phillip has lost his sight. He must feel helpless and angry because he is now dependent on Timothy. The wind is blowing furiously; waves are crashing on the shore; everything is soaked and flooded; it's hard to see or to walk.	Phillip and Timothy will learn to live together on the island. Timothy will help Phillip. Phillip will learn not to judge people by the color of their skin. Timothy and Phillip will survive the hurricane and they will be rescued and returned to civilization. Phillip will learn how to adjust to his blindness and Timothy and Phillip will remain friends.	Phillip disliked Timothy, but had to rely on him. Timothy took care of Phillip; Phillip learned to respect and care about Timothy. Phillip learns through Timothy's actions toward him that racism is wrong; he regains his sight, both physically and emotionally. Timothy dies in the hurricane protecting Phillip. Phillip holds Timothy's hand until he dies. Phillip is able to live because of what Timothy taught him.

synopsis of the text to the students, which introduced them to the basic setting of the story and to the conflict that would develop in its plot.

2. *Imagine.* Have students close their eyes to imagine a scene from the book or text they are going to read. Encourage them to use experiences by thinking about the feelings, sights, smells, and tastes that they associate with the topic. Their images may emanate from the title of the text, a picture from the passage, or a passage read by the teachers. Ask students to share their images with a partner or with the group and to record their images in the "I" column of the IEPC chart. Students who were preparing to read *The Cay* imagined what it might be like to be stranded on a desert island with only one other person, whom they disliked or distrusted. They imagined the frustration that might result from being blind.

3. *Elaborate.* Once the students have heard initial responses from their classmates, ask them to think of additional details associated with the scene they have visualized. Ask questions that will prompt them to elaborate on the original images they described. Record their responses in the "E" column of the IEPC chart. The students preparing to read *The Cay* elaborated on their initial images by talking about what might have led to the dislike and distrust between the boys who were stranded on the island. They also elaborated on what it might feel like to experience a hurricane on the island, as the characters did in the story.

4. *Predict.* Have the students use their initial images and elaboration of those images to make predictions about the text they are going to read. Record those predictions in the "P" column of the IEPC. As Figure 6.11 shows, students offered a range of predictions about what might happen as *The Cay* unfolded and about how the characters might respond to their difficult predicament.

5. *Confirm.* During and after reading, encourage students to recall their predictions. Were they able to confirm their predictions or have they modified their predictions based on what they have learned from reading the text? Record their confirmations and modifications, using a different color marker for each, in the "C" column of the IEPC chart. As they read *The Cay,* the students looked carefully for passages and clues that would help them to identify which of their predictions were accurate and which needed to be modified. After reading the story, the students confirmed that their prediction that Phillip would learn not to judge people by the color of their skin proved to be accurate. In contrast, they recognized that their prediction that the characters would survive the storm together did not match what actually happened in the story.

 # Question Generation

Teaching students to generate their own questions about material to be read is an important pre-reading instructional goal. Teachers need to intentionally select strategies that will engage students in expressing their perceptions and developing understanding of text topics (Cook-Sather, 2002). Neufeld (2005) suggests that, before reading a text, students ask and answer questions that will help them to read with a purpose, to recognize major characteristics of the texts, to activate their prior knowledge, and to make predictions about what they are about to read. By providing opportunities for students to generate questions and seek answers to those questions, teachers can support students in becoming strategic readers.In the following sections, we examine several instructional strategies for engaging students in asking questions for reading.

Active Comprehension

Teachers can use an active comprehension strategy when they *ask questions that beget questions in return*. You might, for example, focus attention on a picture or an illustration from a story or book and ask a question that induces student questions in response: "What would you like to know about the picture?" In return, invite the students to generate questions that focus on the details in the picture or its overarching message.

Or you might decide to read to students an opening paragraph or two from a text selection, enough to whet their appetites for the selection. Then ask, "What else would you like to know about _____?" Complete the question by focusing attention on some aspect of the selection that is pivotal to students' comprehension. It may be the main character of a story or the main topic of an expository text.

Active comprehension questions not only arouse interest and curiosity but also draw learners into the material. As a result, students will read to satisfy purposes and resolve conceptual conflicts that they have identified through their own questions.

ReQuest

ReQuest, sometimes called reciprocal teaching, was originally devised as a one-on-one procedure for a remedial instructional context. Yet this strategy can easily be adapted to content area classrooms to help struggling readers think as they read. ReQuest encourages students to ask their own questions about the content material under study. Self-declared questions are forceful. They help students establish reasonable purposes for their reading. Manzo, Manzo, and Estes (2001) suggest the following steps for implementing the ReQuest strategy:

1. *Both the students and the teacher silently read the same segment of the text.* For students who have difficulty comprehending, Manzo recommends reading one sentence at a time. It can also be helpful to divide a longer, more complex text into smaller, more manageable sections. Then students and teacher can pause at the end of each small section and implement the ReQuest procedure. It is also helpful to inform the students before they begin reading that they will be asking the teacher questions about the text after they have read it.

2. *The teacher closes the book and is questioned about the passage by the students.*

3. *Next there is an exchange of roles.* The teacher queries the students about the text.

4. *On completion of the student–teacher exchange, the students and the teacher read the next segment of the text, pausing at the predetermined stopping point.* Steps 2 and 3 are then repeated.

5. *Students stop questioning and begin predicting.* At a suitable point in the text, when the students have processed enough information to make predictions about the remainder of the assignment, the exchange of questions stops. The teacher then asks prediction questions, "What do you think might happen in the remainder of the text? What has the author said or implied that makes you think so?" Divergent thinking is encouraged.

6. *Students are then assigned the remaining portion of the text to read independently.*

7. *The teacher facilitates a follow-up discussion of the material.*

Although the steps for ReQuest were devised for one-on-one instruction, they can be adapted for the content area classroom where students struggle with texts.

You can modify the ReQuest procedure to good advantage. For example, consider alternating the role of questioner after each question. By doing so, you will probably involve more students in the activity. Once students sense the types of questions that can be asked about a text passage, you might also try forming ReQuest teams. A ReQuest team composed of three or four students can be pitted against another ReQuest team. Your role is to facilitate the multiple actions resulting from the small-group formations.

Our own experiences with ReQuest suggest that students may consistently ask factual questions to stump the teacher or other students. Such questions succeed brilliantly because you are subject to the same restrictions imposed by short-term memory as the students. That you miss an answer or two is actually healthy—after all, to err is human.

However, when students ask only verbatim questions because they don't know how to ask any others, the situation is unhealthy. The sad fact is that some students don't know how to ask questions that will stimulate interpretive or applied levels of thinking. Therefore, your role as a good questioner during ReQuest is to provide a model from which students will learn. Over time, you will notice the difference in the quality of the student questions formulated. Box 6.6 shows how a civics and economics teacher used ReQuest with her class of predominantly English learners.

Evidence-Based Best Practices

BOX 6.6

ReQuest Procedure

In a civics and economics class, a teacher applied the ReQuest strategy to help English learners understand the different branches of government in the United States. She related their understanding of the United States government to that of their native countries.

1. *Both the students and the teacher silently read the same segment of the text.* The teacher and the English learners read a section of the text about the structure of the United States government that outlined the three branches of government—legislative, judicial, and executive.

2. *The teacher closed the book and was questioned about the passage by the students.* The teacher encouraged students to make connections between the information in the text and their experiences with the governments of their native countries. She was prepared to answer questions about the information presented in the reading as well as to assimilate this information with students' existing knowledge of alternative government structures. For example, one student from Mexico noted that, although Mexico has a president, presidential elections in that country are held every six years, rather than every four years as they are in the United States. He went on to point out that there are no opportunities for reelection of a president in Mexico as there are in the United States.

3. *Next there was an exchange of roles.* The teacher then asked students questions about the text and encouraged them to make comparisons between the U.S. government and those of the countries with which they were familiar. For example, the teacher asked students to compare the civil liberties protected by the U.S. Constitution with those that are protected by the governments of their native counties. A student from Mexico referenced the individual and social rights established in the Constitution of Mexico and made comparisons to amendments in the U.S. Constitution.

4. *On completion of the student–teacher exchange, the class and the teacher read the next segment of the text.* Steps 2 and 3 were repeated.

5. *The teacher invited students to make predictions.* At this point in the lesson, the civics and economics teacher asked questions such as, "Now that we know how laws are created, what changes in legislation do you think might lie in the future?"

6. *Students were assigned a subsequent portion of the text to read silently.*

7. *The teacher facilitated a follow-up discussion of the material.*

Looking Back Looking Forward

Meaningful learning with texts occurs when students experience a sense of satisfaction with text and a feeling of accomplishment. In this chapter, the roles that self-efficacy and motivation play in purposeful learning was emphasized. Although some students may be skilled in reading and knowledgeable about the subject, they may not bring that skill and knowledge to bear in learning situations. It takes motivation, a sense of direction and purpose, and a teacher who knows how to create conditions in the classroom that allow students to establish their own motives for reading. One way to arouse curiosity about reading material is to encourage students to make connections among the key concepts to be studied. Another is to create conceptual conflict. Students will read to resolve conflicts arising from problem situations and perspectives and will use guided imagery to explore the ideas to be encountered during reading.

To reduce any uncertainty that students bring to reading material, you can help them raise questions and anticipate meaning by showing them how to connect what they already know to the new ideas presented in the text. The questions students raise as a result of predicting will guide them into the reading material and keep them on course. Anticipation guides, ReQuest, and self-questioning are strategies for stimulating predictions and anticipation about the content.

In the next chapter, we explore ways to guide reading comprehension in the curriculum. A classroom teacher who encourages student engagement in reading brings learners and texts together to explore and construct meaning.

Minds On

1. Suppose you go to your e-reader looking for a good book to read. You look under the "Current Best-Sellers" category. Because you have little familiarity with any of the books, how will you make a selection? How will you anticipate which book is for you? Because students rarely have the opportunity to select their course textbook, what can teachers do to help students make the book "fit"?

2. Divide your discussion group into two subgroups: individuals who are willing to take the position that all of the following statements are correct and those willing to argue that all of the statements are inaccurate. Discuss the pros and cons of each topic for five minutes. After you have finished, bring any items to the class as a whole that you believe could truly have been defended from either view, and be prepared to explain why or under what circumstances.

   a. Students are not qualified to ask their own questions about difficult content material.

   b. The old but still common practice of assigning reading in preparation for a discussion is not always useful.

   c. Just as athletes need to warm up before a contest, readers need to warm up to get ready for a text.

   d. Having students read a variety of materials on the subject matter will only confuse them.

   e. It is pointless to discuss most subjects with students before they read the text, because the varied social and economic backgrounds of the students make it possible for only a few to connect any relevant personal experience to the text subject.

3. Eliot Eisner believed that brains are born but minds are made. What do you believe is the teacher's role in a classroom filled with twenty-five brains waiting to be made into minds? Is the teacher the molder, shaper, and maker—that is, the only active partner? Is the teacher to serve as a model learner, a guide through knowledge, or a facilitator—that is, an equal or superior partner? Or do you see some happy medium? In your group, attempt to reach a consensus on what you consider to be the best role for a teacher in relation to these prompts.

Hands On

1. At the end of a unit of study, or at the end of the semester, use the Self-Efficacy Survey to assess your perception of your own professional growth as a teacher. What did you learn about your own teaching through this exercise? What professional development plans will you make to continue to build your own teaching effectiveness?

2. Team with a group of four or five other students. Before the next class, each member should collect three political cartoons, each using a different newspaper,

magazine, or book. These cartoons may represent current or historical political issues.

When you return to class, share the cartoons you found and discuss the knowledge the reader must already have in order to understand the humor. Select the one cartoon you found most enjoyable and list the background knowledge needed to understand it. When all groups have finished discussing and selecting, have each group read and explain its favorite cartoon to the whole class. As a large group, discuss how this activity illustrates the concept of prior knowledge when reading text. If there are art majors in the class,

ask them to share the role of prior knowledge in viewing works of art.

3. Bring to class a nonfiction book or magazine article on a subject you enjoy. With a partner, develop an Anticipation Guide for your topic. Implement the Anticipation Guide with another team in your class. On completion of the activity discuss as a small group the effectiveness of the prediction and discussion, the successfulness of the learning that occurred, and your perceptions of the usefulness of this activity in a content area classroom.

eResources

Find out more about self-efficacy and motivation by going to a special site created by Emory University (**www.des.emory.edu/mfp/self-efficacy.html**) to broaden the understanding of self-efficacy.

Learn about question generation as a research-based comprehension strategy by going to Intervention Central

(**www.interventioncentral.org/htmdocs/interventions/rdngcompr/qgen.php#topAnchor**). Identify some hints for using question generation as an instructional strategy in class. Explore Intervention Central more thoroughly for other intervention strategies (www.interventioncentral.org).

MyEducationLab™

Go to Topic 8: Study Skills and Strategies, the MyEducationLab (**www.myeducationlab.com**) for *Content Area Reading*, where you can:

- Find learning outcomes for Planning for Instruction, along with the national standards that connect to these outcomes.
- Complete Assignments and Activities that can help you more deeply understand the chapter content.
- Practice the core teaching skills identified in the chapter with the Building Teaching Skills and Dispositions learning units.
- Check your comprehension on the content covered in the chapter with the Study Plan. Here you will be able to take a chapter quiz, receive feedback on your answers, and then access Review, Practice, and Enrichment activities to enhance your understanding of chapter content.
- Visit A+RISE. A+RISE® Standards2Strategy™ is an innovative and interactive online resource that offers new teachers in grades K–12 just in time, research-based instructional strategies that meet the linguistic needs of English Language Learners (ELLs) as they learn content, differentiate instruction for all grades and abilities, and are aligned to Common Core Elementary Language Arts standards (for the literacy strategies) and to English language proficiency standards in World-Class Instructional Design and Assessment (WIDA), Texas, California, and Florida.
- Use the Online Lesson Plan Builder to practice lesson planning and integrating national and state standards into your planning.

7 Guiding Reading Comprehension

Organizing Principle

Teachers guide students' reading by (1) modeling how to read, think, and learn with texts; and (2) scaffolding instruction in the use of comprehension strategies that allow students to learn with text in meaningful ways.

Teachers have observed how some students approach the reading of academic text: They read as fast as they can—eyes skimming over words, fingers flipping through the pages—to glean bits of information here and there in a mad dash to finish the reading assignment! How many times have teachers received one- or two-word answers in response to thoughtful questions about assigned text? Superficial reading of academic text, more often than not, is devoid of thinking and learning.

Effective teachers, of course, always hope for more from their students. They set the bar high by challenging learners to develop ways of thinking that are essential for comprehending text and developing core concepts in a discipline. Through the instructional support they provide, teachers can build students' confidence and competence as readers by showing them how to use comprehension strategies to think deeply about text. A starting point for showing students how to read, think, and learn begins with the understanding that behind a text—whether print-based or nonprint in nature—is a real person doing real work. Writers, for example, believe that they have something worthwhile to say and reasons for saying it. Some write to entertain, others to inform. Authors like us do the latter. When writers of informational texts talk directly to readers as we're doing now, linguists label the process metadiscourse, a mouthful of a word that describes what a writer does to engage the reader in thinking about the text.

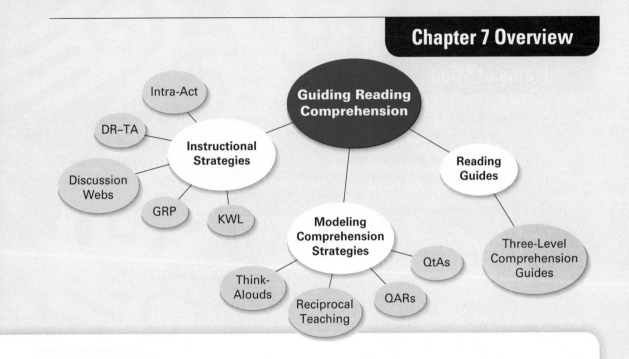

Most readers don't consciously think about what a writer does to draw them into thoughtful interactions with the text. But an effective writer of academic text knows that when readers engage in the process, they think about what they are reading. Whether the reading involves traditional or digital texts, active, engaged reading always involves a dialogue between the reader and the text. As we learned in the previous chapter, engaged readers are motivated, knowledgeable, strategic, and socially interactive. They have much to contribute to the dialogue that takes place in the mind as they interact with texts to construct meaning. Yet in today's diverse classrooms, students may have trouble handling the conceptual demands of difficult text. How does a content area teacher guide comprehension in

ways that model thinking strategies and engage and sustain students in discipline-specific learning, especially if the ideas encountered during reading are complex?

Earlier, we studied how activating prior knowledge before, during, and after reading is a critical instructional component of content literacy lessons. In this chapter, we extend the dialogue on reading comprehension as we explore strategies to think and learn with text. As the organizing principle for this chapter highlights: Teachers guide students' reading by (1) modeling how to read, think, and learn with texts and (2) scaffolding instruction in the use of comprehension strategies that allow students to learn with text in meaningful ways.

Frame of Mind

1. How do think-alouds, reciprocal teaching, QARs, and QtAs model reading/thinking/learning strategies for students as they interact with texts in a discipline?

2. Describe the procedures associated with each of these literacy-related instructional strategies: KWL, KWHL, directed reading–thinking activity (DR–TA), guided reading procedure (GRP), intra-act, and discussion web. How do these instructional strategies support thinking and learning with text? Which of these strategies may be particularly useful when adapted to your content area?

3. Why and when should teachers use reading guides?

4. How can you modify and adapt three-level reading guides to meet the conceptual demands of your discipline?

Although metaphors come and go, one that has been around since the ancient Greeks is as powerful today as it was centuries ago. In Plato's *Theaetetus,* written more than 2,000 years ago, Socrates is asked to explain what it means to think. He responds to his questioner by explaining that when the mind is thinking it is merely talking to itself, asking questions and answering them. Thinking is a conversation. It is a dialogue that you have with yourself in your mind. When a reader engages in a dialogue with text, the conversation metaphor puts an incredibly complex process—reading—into the context of what happens inside the minds of readers.

The conversations that take place between readers and texts transcend time and space. Texts make it possible to bring readers and authors together in content area classrooms. There is a catch, however. Thinking with texts requires students to participate actively in the conversation. A conversation works only when participants are involved and interacting with one another. Everyday conversations, for example, involve an exchange of ideas between two or more parties—a give-and-take dialogue— around topics of mutual interest and relevance.

Learning conversations in content area classrooms have similar characteristics, unless they break down or never get started. Dialogues easily turn into monologues when the transmission of information becomes more important than the sharing of ideas among students, teachers, and texts. Guiding the learning conversations that occur between the reader and the text is the subject of this chapter.

Response Journal

What is your reaction to Socrates' explanation of what it means to think?

Modeling Comprehension Strategies

Students who struggle with text are usually unaware of strategies that will help them more effectively comprehend and make meaning. Content area teachers typically have more content to cover than time in which to teach it all. It is understandable, then, that some teachers view comprehension instruction as an added burden. Comprehension instruction can, however, support, rather than distract from, the teaching of content area concepts. Students' comprehension has been found to improve when teachers explain and model comprehension strategies that can aid students in their reading of content area texts (Biancarosa & Snow, 2006; Ness, 2009). Comprehension instruction has been found to be effective when it is focused on addressing the specific needs of individual students (Pitcher, Martinez, Dicembre, Fewster, & McCormick, 2010), and when students learn how to apply strategies in meaningful contexts with a variety of texts (Rupley, Blair, & Nichols, 2009). In this section, we explain several research-based practices that provide explicit instruction in the use of comprehension strategies (National Reading Panel, 2000). Teachers from various disciplines can, with some modification, incorporate *think-alouds, reciprocal teaching, question–answer relationships (QARs),* and *questioning the author (QtA)* into their instructional routines to show students how to read, think, and learn with discipline-specific texts.

Response Journal

Think-alouds, QARs, and reciprocal teaching are research-based instructional practices. Educators often describe a research-based instructional practice as a "best practice." What does the term *best practice* mean to you?

Using Think-Alouds to Model Comprehension Strategies

In think-alouds, teachers make their thinking explicit by verbalizing their thoughts while reading orally. The think-aloud strategy helps readers clarify their understanding of reading and their understanding of how to use strategies. Students will more clearly understand the strategies after a teacher uses think-alouds, because they can see how a mind actively responds to thinking through trouble spots and constructing meaning from the text (Davey, 1983).

There are five basic steps to follow when using think-alouds. First, select passages to read aloud that contain points of difficulty, ambiguities, contradictions, or unknown words. Second, while orally reading and modeling thinking aloud, have students follow silently and listen to how trouble spots are thought through. Third, have students work with partners to practice think-alouds by taking turns reading short, carefully prepared passages and sharing thoughts. Fourth, have students practice independently. Encourage them to monitor the strategies they use when reading and to reflect on the degree to which they made predictions, formed mental images, recognized analogies that connected to what they read, or used a reading strategy to support their comprehension when the text did not make sense to them. Finally, to encourage transfer, integrate practice with other lessons and provide occasional demonstrations of how, why, and when to use think-alouds. Five points can be made during think-alouds:

1. Students should develop hypotheses by making predictions.
2. Students should develop images by describing pictures forming in their heads from the information being read.

3. Students should link new information with prior knowledge by sharing analogies.

4. Students should monitor comprehension by verbalizing a confusing point.

5. Students should regulate comprehension by demonstrating strategies.

Let's look at how each of these points can be modeled in a middle school earth science class.

Develop Hypotheses by Making Predictions

Teachers might model how to develop hypotheses by making predictions from the title of a chapter or from subheadings within the chapter. Suppose you were teaching with an earth science text. You might say, "From the heading 'How Minerals Are Used,' I predict that this section will tell about things that are made out of different minerals." The text continues:

> Some of the most valuable minerals are found in ores. An **ore** is a mineral resource mined for profit. For example, bauxite (BAWK-sight) is an ore from which aluminum is taken. Iron is obtained from the ore called hematite (HEE-muh-tight). Bauxite and hematite are metallic minerals.
>
> Metallic minerals are metals or ores of metals. Gold, iron, and aluminum are examples of metals. Metals are important because of their many useful properties.
>
> One useful property of many metals is malleability (mal-ee-uh-BIL-uh-tee). **Malleability** is the ability to be hammered without breaking. Malleability allows a metal to be hammered into thin sheets.

Develop Images

To model how to develop imaging, at this point you might stop and say, "I have a picture in my head from a scene I saw in a movie about the Old West. I see a blacksmith pumping bellows in a forge to heat up an iron horseshoe. When the iron turns a reddish orange, he picks it up with his tongs, and he hammers. The sparks fly, but slowly the horseshoe changes shape to fit the horse's hoof." The text continues:

> Another property of many metals is ductility (duk-TIL-uh-tee). **Ductility** is the ability to be pulled and stretched without breaking. This property allows a metal to be pulled into thin wires.

Share Analogies

To model how to link new information with prior knowledge, you might share the following analogies. "This is like a time when I tried to eat a piece of pizza with extra cheese. Every time I took a bite, the cheese kept stretching and stretching into these long strings. It is also like a time when I went to the county fair and watched people make taffy. They got this glob of candy and put it on a machine that just kept pulling and stretching the taffy, but it never broke." The text continues:

> Metals share other properties as well. All metals conduct heat and electricity. Electrical appliances and machines need metals to conduct electricity. In addition, all metals have a shiny, metallic luster.

Monitor Comprehension

To model how to monitor comprehension, you can verbalize a confusing point: "This is telling me that metals have a metallic luster. I don't know what that is. I'm also confused because I thought this section was going to be about things that are made out of different minerals. This is different from what I expected."

Regulate Comprehension

To model how to correct lagging comprehension, you can demonstrate a strategy: "I'm confused about what *metallic luster* means, and I don't know why the authors are talking about this when I expected them to talk about stuff made out of minerals. Maybe if I ignore the term *metallic luster* and keep on reading, I'll be able to make some connections to what I expected and figure it all out." The text continues:

> Very shiny metals, like chromium, are often used for decorative purposes. Many metals are also strong. Titanium (tigh-TAY-nee-um), magnesium (mag-NEE-zee-um), and aluminum are metals that are both strong and lightweight. These properties make them ideal building materials for jet planes and spacecraft.

"Oh, they're talking about properties of metals that make them especially good for making certain things, like aluminum for jets because it is strong and lightweight. Now I understand why they're talking about properties. I'll bet chrome and chromium are just about the same, because I know chrome is the shiny stuff on cars. I think *metallic luster* must mean something like shiny because chromium reminds me of chrome."

Similarly, when preparing to teach a middle school science unit on popular dynamics, Mrs. Maas developed a think-aloud activity for one portion of that unit on "the water cycle." She realized that it was important for students to understand and comprehend the continuous movement of matter through both living and nonliving parts of an ecosystem. The continuous movement, or cycling of matter, is vital to sustain life on Earth. Following the guidelines listed above, she described her implementation of the water cycle think-aloud:

> I presented my students with a text related to the water cycle. To begin our think-aloud activity, I modeled my hypothesis by saying, "From the title, I'm thinking this text is going to focus on water moving between streams, lakes, and oceans since water covers nearly 75 percent of the Earth's surface." As I proceeded with the lesson, students began reading the text and quickly realized that it pertained to water cycling through the ecosystem as either a liquid on land or as a vapor in the atmosphere. They encountered words such as precipitation, condensation, and evaporation. As they continued to read, I encouraged them to develop a mental image of a street in the summer after a rainstorm (precipitation) and the steam rising (evaporation) off the pavement. As we continued to read and learn more about the water cycle, I helped them to create analogies. For example, I compared this cycling of water through an ecosystem to water flowing across a water wheel. The energy created by the water turned the wheel just like energy (sun) drove the water cycle. As we continued to read, we encountered statements and questions that proved confusing. For example, questions such as "if water follows a continuous cycle, why do we need to conserve water?" or "If water becomes polluted, does it stay polluted forever since it remains in a constant and continuous cycle?" As we completed our reading of the text, I encouraged the students to "think-aloud" to support their comprehension of the material. By effectively modeling and implementing think-alouds, I hope to provide my students with one more effective comprehension strategy to further their understanding and appreciation of the content material.

Think-alouds are best used at the beginnings of lessons to help students learn the *what's* and *how's* of constructing meaning with text. The next teaching strategy, *reciprocal teaching*, is an excellent follow-up to think-alouds. Reciprocal teaching helps students learn how to apply the strategy learned during a think-aloud so that they can understand the author's message.

Using Reciprocal Teaching to Model Comprehension Strategies

When using reciprocal teaching, you model how to use four comprehension activities (generating questions, summarizing, predicting, and clarifying) while leading a dialogue (Brown & Palincsar, 1984). Then students take turns assuming the teacher's role. A key to the effectiveness of this strategy is adjusting the task demand to support the students when difficulty occurs. That is, when students experience difficulty, you provide assistance by lowering the demands of the task. As the process goes on, you slowly withdraw support so that students continue learning. When planning a reciprocal teaching lesson, there are two phases. The first phase has five steps:

1. Find text selections that demonstrate the four comprehension activities.
2. Generate appropriate questions.
3. Generate predictions about each selection.
4. Locate summarizing sentences and develop summaries for each selection.
5. Note difficult vocabulary and concepts.

In the second phase, decisions are made about which comprehension activities to teach, based on the students' needs. It also helps determine students' present facility with the activities so that you are prepared to give needed support during the process. Once students are familiar with more than one strategy, reciprocal teaching can be used to model the decision-making process about which strategy to use.

Using Question–Answer Relationships (QARs) to Model Comprehension Strategies

Question–answer relationships (QARs) make explicit to students the relationships that exist among the type of question asked, the text, and the reader's prior knowledge. In the process of teaching QARs, you help students become aware of and skilled in using learning strategies to find the information they need to comprehend at different levels of response to the text (Raphael, 1982, 1984, 1986). Raphael explains the answers to questions can be found in different places:

- *In the Text—Right There:* The words used in the question and the words used for the answer can usually be found in the same sentence.
- *In the Text—Think and Search:* The answer is in the text, but the words used in the question and those used for the answer are not in the same sentence. You need to think about different parts of the text and how ideas can be put together before you can answer the question.
- *In Your Head—Author and You:* The answer is not in the text. You need to think about what you know, what the author says, and how they fit together.
- *In Your Head—On Your Own:* The text got you thinking, but the answer is inside your head; it is not directly answered by the author. You need to think about what you already know about the topic in order to answer the question.

The procedures for learning QARs can be taught directly to students by literacy specialists and can be reinforced by content area specialists. Keep in mind, however, that students may come to your class totally unaware of what information sources are available for seeking an answer, or they may not know when to use different sources. In this case, it is worth several days' effort to teach students the relationship between questions and answers. It may take up to three days to show students how to identify the information sources necessary to answer questions. The following steps, which we have adapted for content area situations, are suggested for teaching QARs:

1. *Introduce the concept of QARs.* Show students a description of the four basic question–answer relationships. We recommend a chart that can be positioned in a prominent place in the classroom. Students may then refer to it throughout the content area lessons. Point out the two broad categories of information sources: "In the text" and "In your head."

2. *Begin by assigning students several short passages from the textbook.* (These should be no more than two to five sentences in length.) Follow each reading with one question from each of the QAR categories on the chart. Then discuss the differences between a "right there" question and answer, a "think and search" question and answer, an "on your own" question and answer, and an "author and you" question and answer. Your explanations should be clear and complete. Reinforce the discussion by assigning several more short text passages and asking a question for each. Students will soon begin to catch on to the differences among the four QAR categories.

3. *Continue the second day by practicing with short passages.* Use one question for each QAR category per passage. First, give students a passage to read along with questions *and* answers *and* identified QARs. Why do the questions and answers represent one QAR and not another? Second, give students a passage along with questions and answers; this time they have to identify the QAR for each. Finally, give students passages, decide together which strategy to use, and have them write their responses.

4. *Review briefly on the third day.* Then assign a longer passage (75 to 200 words) with up to six questions (at least one each from the four QAR categories). First, have students work in groups to decide the QAR category for each question and the answers for each. Next, assign a second passage, comparable in length, with five questions for students to work on individually. Discuss their responses either in small groups or with the whole class. You may wish to work with several class members or colleagues to complete the QAR activity in Box 7.1. It was developed by a high school English teacher as part of a short story unit.

5. *Apply the QAR strategy to actual content area assignments.* For each question asked, students decide on the appropriate QAR strategy and write out their answers.

Once students are sensitive to the different information sources for different types of questions and know how to use these sources to respond to questions, variations can be made in the QAR strategy. For example, you might have students generate their own questions to text assignments—perhaps two for each QAR strategy. They then write down the answers to the questions as they understand them, except that they leave one question unanswered from the "think and search" category and one from the "on your own" or "author and you" category. These are questions about which the student would like to hear the views of others. During the

Evidence-Based Best Practices

BOX 7.1

QAR Awareness in a High School English Class

A high school English teacher develops students' awareness of QARs with the following guided practice activity. The teacher summarizes Roald Dahl's *Lamb to the Slaughter* and asks students to answer a set of questions about the excerpt. The students are also asked to identify the QAR associated with each question.

<u>Summary</u>

> *Mary Maloney is a devoted housewife. Her husband, Patrick Maloney, is a police detective. She takes care of him in an almost suffocating way! He arrives home every evening at 5:00 p.m. Mary has a drink waiting for him and understands how tired he is. She loves the way he walks in the door and the way he looks. She is six months pregnant, but on one evening Patrick tells her some disturbing news. After he tells her, he says something like, "I will make sure you are looked after and I will make sure you have money." Mary always cooks him dinner except on Thursday nights. On one particular Thursday night, Patrick does not want to go out. Mary appears mad after she hears his news. She still decides to cook him dinner. She goes into the basement freezer and gets a leg of lamb. On her way up, she hits Patrick on the back of the head with the frozen lamb. He passes out and dies. She tries to cover up the murder and calls the police, crying. When the police arrive, Mary asks the detective to eat the lamb as that was what Patrick would have wanted. As the detectives eat the lamb, the scene becomes ironic. They say, "I bet the murder weapon is right here under our noses!" Mary listens and giggles.*

1. *Question:* Where did Mary go to get the leg of lamb?

   Answer: _____

   QAR: _____

2. *Question:* Why is Patrick offering to give Mary money?

   Answer: _____

   QAR: _____

3. *Question:* Why did Mary have the detectives eat the lamb?

   Answer: _____

   QAR: _____

4. *Question:* Why did Mary use the leg of lamb to hit Patrick instead of something else?

   Answer: _____

   QAR: _____

5. *Question:* Why did Mary kill Patrick?

   Answer: _____

   QAR: _____

6. *Question:* Why was Mary giggling at the end of the story?

   Answer: _____

   QAR: _____

discussion, students volunteer to ask their unanswered questions. The class is invited first to identify the question by QAR category and then to contribute answers, comments, or related questions about the material.

A second variation involves discussions of text. During question-and-answer exchanges, preface a question by saying, "This question is *right there* in the text," or "You'll have to *think and search* the text to answer," or "You're *on your own* with this one," or "The answer is a combination of the *author and you*. Think about what the author tells us and what we already know to try and come up with a reasonable response." Make sure that you pause several seconds or more for "think time." Think time, or "wait time," is critical to responding to textually implicit and schema-based questions.

Once students are familiar with QARs, they can be used in combination with a variety of interactive strategies that encourage readers to explore ideas through text discussions.

Questioning the Author (QtA)

Questioning the author (QtA) is a comprehension strategy that models for students the importance of asking questions while reading. Beck, McKeown, Hamilton, and Kucan (1997) devised the QtA strategy to demonstrate the kinds of questions students need to ask in order to think more deeply and construct meaning about segments of text as they read. Good readers act on the author's message. If what they are reading doesn't make sense to them, they generate questions about what the author says and means. When students struggle with text, however, they often do not have a clue about generating questions, let alone interacting with the author of text. Enter QtA instruction.

The QtA strategy shows students how to read text closely as if the author were there to be challenged and questioned. QtA places value on the quality and depth of students' responses to the author's intent. It is important that students keep their minds active while reading as they engage in a dialogue with an author. Good readers monitor whether the author is making sense by asking questions such as, "What is the author trying to say here?" "What does the author mean?" "So what? What is the significance of the author's message?" "Does this make sense with what the author told us before?" "Does the author explain this clearly?" These questions are posed by the teacher to help students "take on" the author and understand that text material needs to be challenged.

Through QtA, students learn that authors are fallible and may not always express ideas in the easiest way for readers to understand. QtA builds metacognitive knowledge by making students aware of an important principle related to reading comprehension: *Not comprehending what the author is trying to say is not always the fault of the reader*. As a result, students come to view their roles as readers as "grappling with text" as they seek to make sense of the author's intent.

Planning a QtA Lesson

Planning QtA lessons for narrative or informational texts involves a three-stage process that requires the teacher to (1) identify major understandings and potential problems with a text prior to its use in class, (2) segment the text into logical stopping points for discussion, and (3) develop questions, or *queries,* that model and demonstrate how to "question the author." Box 7.2 examines the planning process.

When using QtA to comprehend stories, pose *narrative queries*. Through the use of narrative queries, students become familiar with an author's writing style as they strive to understand character, plot, and underlying story meaning. The following queries help students think about story characters: "How do things look for this character now?" "Given what the author has already told us about this character, what do you think the author is up to?" Understanding the story plot can be accomplished with queries such as these: "How has the author let you know that something has changed?" "How has the author settled this for us?"

Evidence-Based Best Practices

BOX 7.2

Steps in a QtA Lesson

1. Analyze the text

- *Identify major understandings and potential problems that students may encounter during reading.*
- *Read the text closely and note the author's intent, the major ideas and themes, and any areas or potential obstacles in the material that could affect comprehension.*
- *Reflect on your own comprehension as you read the text.* Note any passages that you re-read or pause to think about, knowing that these sections will most likely be problematic for students.

2. Segment the text

- *Determine where to stop the reading to initiate and develop discussion.* The text segments may not always fall at a page or paragraph break. You may want to stop reading after one sentence to ask a question.

3. *Develop questions*

- *Plan questions that will help students respond to what the author says and means.* These generic questions prompt students' responses to the text and encourage them to dig deeper and make sense of what they are reading. The following question guide will help you frame initiating and follow-up questions at different points in the lesson. Initiating questions at the beginning of the reading draw students' attention to the author's intent, whereas follow-up queries focus the

direction of the discussion and assist students as they integrate and connect ideas. Follow-up questions help students determine why the author included certain ideas.

QTA Question Guide

Initial questions at the beginning of the lesson:

- What is the author trying to say?
- What is the author's message?
- What is the author talking about?

Follow-up questions during reading help students make connections and inferences about the text:

- This is what the author says, but what does it mean?
- How does this text segment connect with what the author has already said?

Follow-up questions during reading help students with difficulties and confusion with the way the author presents information:

- Does the author make sense here?
- Did the author explain this clearly?
- What's missing? What do we need to find out?

Follow-up questions during reading clarify misinterpretations or make students aware that they made an inference (reinforce QARs):

- Did the author tell us that?
- Did the author say that or did you "think and search" to get the answer?

Guiding the QtA Discussion

Beck and colleagues (1997) recommend the use of a variety of "discussion moves" to guide students:

- *Marking:* Draw attention to certain ideas by either paraphrasing what a student said or by acknowledging its importance with statements such as "Good idea" or "That's an important observation."

- *Turning back:* Make students responsible for figuring out ideas and turning back to the text for clarification.

- *Revoicing:* Assist students as they express their ideas; filter the most important information and help students who are struggling to express their ideas by rephrasing their statements.

- *Modeling:* Think aloud about an issue that is particularly difficult to understand; one that students are unable to reach without assistance.

- *Annotating:* Provide information that is not in the text so that students can understand the concepts fully.

- *Recapping:* Summarize the main ideas as a signal to move on in the lesson. Recapping can be done by either the teacher or the students.

The thoughtful use of questions is vital for classroom discussion. As learners actively explore and clarify meaning, guide the discussion as you progress from one text segment to the next. Students can also be encouraged to formulate their own questions as they read a text in order to raise questions as they read, to monitor their comprehension, and to identify gaps that may exist in their expectations for the reading and the actual text. Following is one way to encourage students to ask questions as they read:

1. *Have students listen to or read a portion of the text from the beginning of a selection.*

2. *Ask students to write five to ten questions that they think will be answered by the remainder of the selection.*

3. *Discuss some of the questions asked by the students before reading. Write the questions on the board.*

4. *Have students read to determine whether the questions are answered.*

5. *After reading, ask the students to explain which questions were answered, which weren't, and why not.*

6. *Discuss with students the similarities and differences between their expectations of the reading and the actual text.*

 # Instructional Strategies

Strategies presented in this chapter teach students how to approach reading material with an inquisitive mind. Many of the instructional strategies presented here form a bridge between teacher-initiated guidance and independent learning behavior by students.

In this section, we describe several instructional strategies that engage students in reading, guide their interactions with texts, and help them to clarify and extend meaning. The instructional strategies that follow include (1) *KWL*, which stands for What do you *K*now? What do you *W*ant to know? What did you *L*earn? (2) *discussion webs*, (3) *guided reading procedure (GRP)*, (4) *intra-act*, and (5) *directed reading–thinking activity* (DR–TA). Note the differences as well as the similarities of various instructional strategies emphasized in this section. Each can be adapted to serve any subject matter material.

Think about the kinds of adaptations you will have to make with each instructional strategy to meet the particular needs of your content area.

The KWL Strategy

KWL is an instructional strategy that engages students in active text learning. The strategy begins with what students *know* about the topic to be studied, moves to what the students *want to know* as they generate questions about the topic, and leads to a record of what students *learn* as a result of their engagement in the strategy. Follow-up activities to KWL include discussion, the construction of graphic organizers, and summary writing to clarify and internalize what has been read.

KWL may be initiated with small groups of students or the whole class. When they develop confidence and competence with the KWL strategy, students may begin to use it for independent learning. KWL uses a strategy sheet, such as the one in Figure 7.1. The procedures to follow in KWL revolve around the completion of the strategy sheet as part of the dynamics of student response and discussion.

Procedures for KWL

Here's how the KWL strategy works.

1. *Introduce the KWL strategy in conjunction with a new topic or text selection.* Before assigning a text, explain the strategy. Donna Ogle (1992, p. 271), the originator of KWL, suggests that dialogue begin with the teacher saying

> It is important to first find out what we think we know about this topic. Then we want to anticipate how an author is likely to present and organize the information. From this assignment we can generate good questions to focus on reading and study. Our level of knowledge will determine to some extent how we will study. Then as we read we will make notes of questions that get answered and other new and important information we learn. During this process some new questions will probably occur to us; these we should also note so we can get clarification later.

In the process of explaining KWL, be sure that students understand *what* their role involves and *why* it is important for learners to examine what they know and to ask questions about topics that they will be reading and studying.

The next several steps allow you to model the KWL strategy with a group of learners or the entire class. Some students will find it difficult to complete the KWL strategy sheet on their own. Others will avoid taking risks or revealing what they know or don't know about a topic. Others simply won't be positively motivated. Modeling the KWL strategy reduces the initial risk and creates a willingness to engage in the process. Students who experience the modeling of the strategy quickly recognize its value as a learning tool.

2. *Identify what students think they know about the topic.* Engage the class in brainstorming, writing their ideas on the board or on an overhead transparency. Use the format of the KWL strategy sheet as you record students' ideas on the chalkboard or transparency. It's important to record everything that the students *think* they know about the topic, including their misconceptions. The key in this step is to get the class actively involved in making associations with the topic, not to evaluate the rightness or wrongness of the associations. Students will

Figure 7.1 A KWL Strategy Sheet

K—What I Know	W—What I Want to Know	L—What I Learned and Still Need to Learn

Categories of Information
I Expect to Use

A.   E.

B.   F.

C.   G.

D.

Source: "K-W-L: A Teaching Model That Develops Active Reading in Expository Text" by D. M. Ogle, *The Reading Teacher, 39*(6), 564-5–70. Copyright © 1986 by the International Reading Association. Reproduced with permission of International Reading Association via Copyright Clearance Center.

sometimes challenge one another's knowledge base. The teacher's role is to help learners recognize that differences exist in what they think they know. These differences can be used to help students frame questions.

3. *Generate a list of student questions.* Ask, "What do you want to know more about? What are you most interested in learning about?" As you write their questions on the white board or SMART Board recognize that you are again modeling for students what their role as learners should be: to ask questions about material to be studied.

When you have completed modeling the brainstorming and question-generation phases of KWL, have the students use their own strategy sheets to make decisions about what they personally think they know and about what they want to know more. Students, especially those who may be at risk in academic situations, may refer to the example you have modeled to decide what to record in the first two columns.

4. *Anticipate the organization and structure of ideas that the author is likely to use in the text selection.* As part of preparation for reading, have students next use their knowledge and their questions to make predictions about the organization of the text. What major categories of information is the author likely to use to organize his or her ideas?

The teacher might ask, "How do you think the author of a text or article on _____ is likely to organize the information?" Have students focus on the ideas they have brainstormed and the questions they have raised to predict possible categories of information. As students make their predictions, record these on the board or transparency in the area suggested by the KWL strategy sheet. Then have students make individual choices on their own strategy sheets.

5. *Read the text selection to answer the questions.* As they engage in interactions with the text, the students write answers to their questions and make notes for new ideas and information in the L column of their strategy sheets. Again, the teacher's modeling is crucial to the success of this phase of KWL. Students may need a demonstration or two to understand how to record information in the L column.

Debrief students after they have read the text and have completed writing responses in the L column. First, invite them to share answers, recording these for the group to see. Then ask, "What new ideas did you come across that you didn't think you would find in the text?" Record and discuss the responses.

6. *Engage students in follow-up activities to clarify and extend learning.* Use KWL as a springboard into postreading activities to internalize student learning. Activities may include the construction of graphic organizers to clarify and retain ideas encountered during reading or the development of written summaries.

KWL Examples

In Christa's U.S. history class, students were beginning a study of the Vietnam War. Christa realized that her students would have little, if any, prior knowledge of and attitudes toward the Vietnam War, even though it's still part of our national consciousness. The students, in fact, were acutely aware of the war from recent popular movies and also from relatives who had participated in it.

However, Christa realized that although students might know something about the Vietnam War, they had probably had little opportunity to study it from the perspective of historians. This, then, was Christa's objective as a teacher of history: to help students approach the study of the Vietnam War—and understand the social, economic, and political forces surrounding it—from a historian's perspective.

Therefore, Christa believed that the KWL strategy would be an appropriate way to begin the unit. She believed that it would help students get in touch with what they knew (and didn't know) about the Vietnam War and raise questions that would guide their interactions with the materials that they would be studying.

Christa began KWL knowing that her students were familiar with its procedures, having participated in the strategy on several previous occasions in the class. Following the six steps, the class as a whole participated in brainstorming what they knew about the war and what they wanted to know. Christa recorded their ideas and questions on an overhead transparency and encouraged students' participation by asking such questions as, "What else do you know? Who knows someone who was in the war? What did he or she say about it? Who has read about the Vietnam War or seen a movie about it? What did you learn?"

As ideas and questions were recorded on the transparency, Christa asked the students to study the K column to anticipate categories of information that they might study in their textbook and other information sources that they would be using: "Do some of these ideas fit together to form major categories we might be studying?" She also asked the students to think about other wars they had studied—World Wars I and II, the U.S. Civil War, and the American Revolution: "When we study wars, are there underlying categories of information on which historians tend to focus?"

On completion of the whole-class activity, Christa invited her students to complete their strategy sheets, recording what they knew, what they wanted to find out more about, and what categories of information they expected to use.

Then, for homework, she assigned several sections from a textbook covering the Vietnam War and asked students to work on the L column on their own. Figure 7.2 shows how one student, Clayton, completed his strategy sheet.

Figure 7.2 Clayton's KWL Strategy Sheet on the Vietnam War

K—What I Know	**W**—What I Want to Know	**L**—What I Learned and Still Need to Learn
U.S. lost war protest marches and riots movies made in 1960s jungle fighting POWs guerrilla fighting North and South fighting each other U.S. soldiers suffered the wall in Washington	Why did we go to war? Why did we lose? How many soldiers died? Who helped us? Who was president during war? On whose side were we?	Gulf of Tonkin Resolution made it legal for war but was not legally declared French helped U.S. Nixon withdrew troops because of fighting at home Lottery used to draft soldiers Antiwar movement at home 55,000 Americans died plus thousands of innocent people Kennedy, Johnson, and Nixon were the presidents Fought war to stop communism

Categories of Information I Expect to Use

A. cause

B. results

C. U.S. involvement

D. type of fighting

E.

F.

G.

As part of the next day's class, Christa asked the students to work in groups of four to share what they had found out about the war. They focused on the questions they had raised, as well as on new ideas they had not anticipated. When the groups completed their work, Christa brought the class together. She directed them to open their learning logs and write a summary of what they had learned from participating in KWL. Students used the L column on their strategy sheets to compose the summary. Clayton's summary is shown in Figure 7.3.

In Christa's class, the learning logs serve as history notebooks, in which students can record what they are learning, using a variety of writing-to-learn activities. (We explain learning logs and their uses more fully in Chapter 11.)

A high school math teacher adapted the KWL strategy to support his students' study of the Fibonacci numbers. Fibonacci numbers (a famous sequence of numbers that have been shown to occur in nature) are the direct result of a problem posed by a thirteenth-century mathematician, Leonardo of Pisa, on the regeneration of rabbits. The teacher used a math text from an enrichment unit to clarify and extend students' understanding of the Fibonacci numbers. The text selection, "Mathematics in Nature," illustrates the properties of the Fibonacci numbers and requires students to determine the relationships between these numbers and various phenomena in nature—for example, the leaves on a plant, the bracts on a pinecone, the curves on a seashell, or the spirals on a pineapple.

Before initiating the KWL strategy, the teacher used three props (a toy rabbit, a plant, and a pineapple) to arouse students' curiosity and to trigger their responses to the question, "What do these items have to do with mathematics?" After some exploratory talk, he then asked students, "What do you know about mathematics and nature?" The strategy sheet in Figure 7.4 illustrates the reader–text interactions that occurred as the teacher guided students through the steps in KWL.

The KWL can also be adapted to include other relevant categories. The KWHL—what I know, what I want to know, how I can find the information I need, and what I learned—is one common variation to the original KWL strategy. Figure 7.5 shows an application of a KWHL in a health class. The teacher used this strategy to activate students' prior knowledge about different types of macromolecules and to introduce them to some of the basic vocabulary associated with this topic. While the standard course textbook was the starting point for research to complete the KWHL chart, students were encouraged to consider other sources that they might use to help them learn more about this topic.

Figure 7.3 Clayton's Summary in His Learning Log

> We fought the Vietnam War to stop communism. The U.S. Congress passed the Gulf of Tonkin Resolution, which said it was OK to go to war there, but the war was never declared a war—it was only called a conflict. The French and South Vietnamese people helped us, but it didn't matter. 55,000 Americans died fighting. People protested in the United States. Nixon withdrew the troops because of pressure to end the war at home.

Figure 7.4 A KWL Strategy Sheet in a Math Class

K—What I Know	**W**—What I Want to Know	**L**—What I Learned and Still Need to Learn
planetary motion spirals 4 seasons landscaping geometric designs multiplying populations phases of the moon	What does a pineapple have to do with math? How are growth patterns in plants related to math? How is mathematics specifically related to nature? Where do bees fit?	Pineapples have hexagons on the surface that are arranged in sets of spirals. These spirals are related to Fibonacci numbers. Fibonacci numbers are found in leaf arrangements on plants. The rate that bees regenerate males is related to Fibonacci numbers. Who is this Fibonacci guy? What's the big deal about the "golden ratio"?

Categories of Information
I Expect to Use

A. Animals   E.

B. Plants   F.

C. Solar System   G.

D. Laws of Nature

Figure 7.5 A KWHL Strategy Sheet in a Health Education Class

Macromolecule	What do we know?	What do we want to find out?	How we find out what we want to learn?	What did we learn?
Proteins	– something you can eat – part of the body	– what this has to do with health	– textbook – internet – health magazine	– proteins are made up of amino acids
Lipids				
Polysaccharides				
Nucleic acids				

Discussion Webs

Discussion webs encourage students to engage the text and each other in thoughtful discussion by creating a framework for students to explore texts and consider different sides of an issue in discussion before drawing conclusions. Donna Alvermann (1991) recommends discussion webs as an alternative to teacher-dominated discussions.

The strategy uses cooperative learning principles that follow a think–pair–share discussion cycle (McTighe & Lyman, 1988). The discussion cycle begins with students first thinking about the ideas they want to contribute to the discussion based on their interactions with the text. Then they meet in pairs to discuss their ideas with a partner. Partners then team with a different set of partners to resolve differences in perspective and to work toward a consensus about the issue under discussion. In the final phase of the discussion cycle, the two sets of partners, working as a foursome, select a spokesperson to share their ideas with the entire class.

The discussion web strategy uses a graphic display to scaffold students' thinking about the ideas they want to contribute to the discussion based on what they have read. The graphic display takes the shape of a web. In the center of the web is a question that is central to the reading. The question is posed in such a way that it reflects more than one point of view. Students explore the pros and cons of the question in the No and Yes columns of the web—first in pairs, and then in groups of four. The main goal of the four-member teams is to draw a conclusion based on their discussion of the web. Figure 7.6 illustrates a discussion web used after students had read Sharon Flake's book *The Skin I'm In,* winner of the 1999 Coretta Scott King Award. The book tells the story of Maleeka, a seventh grader in an inner-city school, who is torn between winning the approval of street-smart peers and pursuing her own academic capabilities. The question posed in the discussion web, "Should Maleeka have entered the writing contest?" invites students to consider one dilemma Maleeka faces as she works to resolve these conflicts.

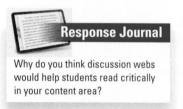

Response Journal

Why do you think discussion webs would help students read critically in your content area?

Procedures for the Discussion Web

Alvermann (1991) suggests an integrated lesson structure for the discussion web strategy that includes the following steps:

1. *Prepare your students for reading by activating prior knowledge, raising questions, and making predictions about the text.*

2. *Assign students to read the selection and then introduce the discussion web by having the students work in pairs to generate pro and con responses to the question.* The partners work on the same discussion web and take turns jotting down their reasons in the Yes and No columns. Students may use keywords and phrases to express their ideas and need not fill all of the lines. They should try to list an equal number of pro and con reasons on the web.

3. *Combine partners into groups of four to compare responses, work toward consensus, and reach a conclusion as a group.* Explain to your students that it is okay to disagree with other members of the group, but they should all try to keep an open mind as they listen to others during the discussion. Dissenting views may be aired during the whole-class discussion.

Figure 7.6   Discussion Web for *The Skin I'm In*

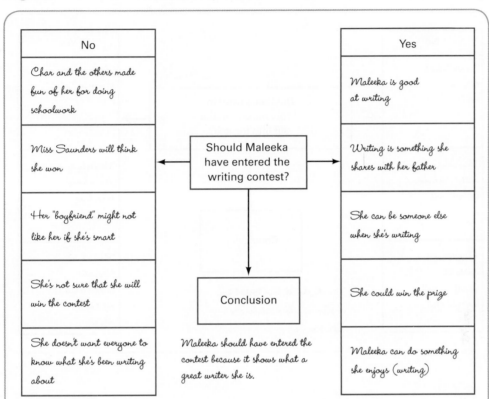

No		Yes
Char and the others made fun of her for doing schoolwork	Should Maleeka have entered the writing contest?	Maleeka is good at writing
Miss Saunders will think she won		Writing is something she shares with her father
Her "boyfriend" might not like her if she's smart		She can be someone else when she's writing
She's not sure that she will win the contest	Conclusion	She could win the prize
She doesn't want everyone to know what she's been writing about	Maleeka should have entered the contest because it shows what a great writer she is.	Maleeka can do something she enjoys (writing)

4. *Give each group three minutes to decide which of all the reasons given best supports the group's conclusion.* Each group selects a spokesperson to report to the whole class.

5. *Have your students follow up the whole-class discussion by individually writing their responses to the discussion web question.* Display the students' responses to the question in a prominent place in the room so that they can be read by others.

The level of participation in discussion web lessons is usually high. The strategy encourages students' individual interpretations of what they are reading and also allows them to formulate and refine their own interpretations of a text in light of the points of view of others. As a result, students are eager to hear how other groups reached a consensus and drew conclusions during whole-class sharing. The strategy works well with informational or narrative texts and can be adapted to the goals and purposes of most content area subjects.

Discussion Web Examples

Donna Mitchell, a music teacher, introduced her middle grade students to components of an opera by having them listen to Wagner's *The Flying Dutchman*. In the discussion, she activated students' prior knowledge of opera using a playbill that she constructed in the form of a modified cloze activity. As part of the lesson, Mrs. Mitchell also had students listen to the overture

Figure 7.7 Discussion Web for *The Flying Dutchman*

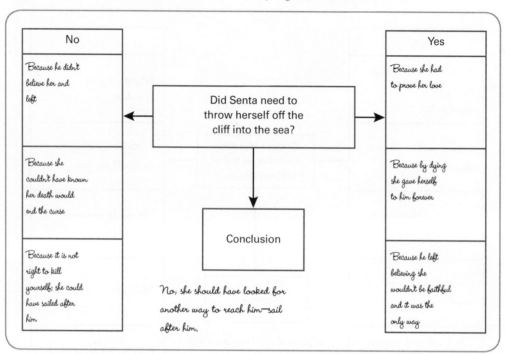

of the opera to set a mood and read to them portions of the story over several days. At the conclusion of the read-alouds, students entered the postreading stage of the lesson as they engaged in a discussion web activity. Study the discussion web in Figure 7.7 completed by one group of students in her class as they grappled with the question, "Did Senta need to throw herself off the cliff into the sea?"

Math teachers might also use the discussion web to help students consider relevant and irrelevant information in story problems. Study the discussion web in Figure 7.8, noting the adaptations the teacher made. In this illustration, the students worked in pairs to distinguish relevant and irrelevant information in the story problem. They then formed groups of four to solve the problem.

Social studies teachers might use the discussion web to help students consider different perspectives on an issue or event. The discussion web in Figure 7.9 asked students to consider whether or not President Truman's decision to drop the atomic bomb on Japan in an effort to end World War II was correct. Working in small groups of four to five, students deliberated that decision from political, ethical, and strategic perspectives. The discussion web illustrates some of the main points that they considered when trying to achieve consensus on the question posed to them.

Guided Reading Procedure (GRP)

The guided reading procedure (GRP) emphasizes close reading (Manzo, 1975). It requires that students gather information and organize it around important ideas, and it places a premium

Figure 7.8 Discussion Web for a Story Problem

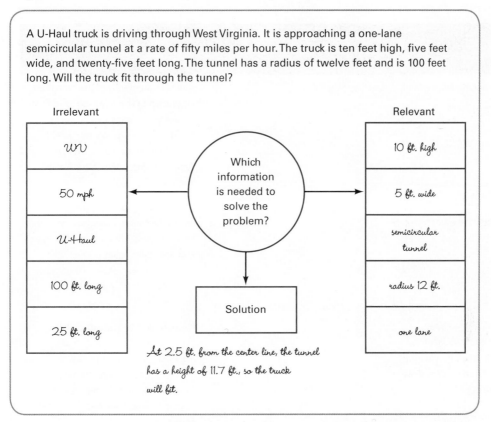

A U-Haul truck is driving through West Virginia. It is approaching a one-lane semicircular tunnel at a rate of fifty miles per hour. The truck is ten feet high, five feet wide, and twenty-five feet long. The tunnel has a radius of twelve feet and is 100 feet long. Will the truck fit through the tunnel?

Irrelevant

WV

50 mph

U-Haul

100 ft. long

25 ft. long

Which information is needed to solve the problem?

Relevant

10 ft. high

5 ft. wide

semicircular tunnel

radius 12 ft.

one lane

Solution

At 2.5 ft. from the center line, the tunnel has a height of 11.7 ft., so the truck will fit.

on accuracy as students reconstruct the author's message. With a strong factual base, students will work from a common and clear frame of reference. They will then be in a position to elaborate thoughtfully on the text and its implications.

Procedures for GRP

Here's how the GRP works.

1. *Prepare students for reading.* Clarify key concepts; determine what students know and don't know about the particular content to be studied; build appropriate background; and give direction to reading.

2. *Assign a reading selection.* Assign 500 to 900 words in the middle grades (approximately five to seven minutes of silent reading); 1,000 to 2,000 words for high school (approximately ten minutes). Provide general purpose to direct reading behavior. For example, "Read to remember all you can."

3. *As students finish reading, have them turn books face down.* Ask them to tell what they remember. Record it on the board in the fashion in which it is remembered.

Figure 7.9   Discussion Web for a Social Studies Class

NO	Should President Truman have dropped the atomic bomb on Japan?	YES
Too many innocent lives would be lost.		It was estimated that the proposed Operation Olympic would have cost as many Japanese casualties as the dropping of the bomb would have caused, as well as many more American casualties in the Pacific Theatre.
The cities of Hiroshima and Nagasaki could have been lost forever.		With the willingness of the Japanese to use mass suicide in the form of Kamikaze pilots on Okinawa and people jumping to their death in Saipan, it was clear that extreme measures were needed to end the war.
Almost 60 cities had been destroyed already in Japan as a result of the war; they might have surrendered in time, if we could just be patient.		Firebombing had already killed 100,000 people in Tokyo, and Imperial Japan still showed no sign of surrender. An atomic bomb may have been the only way of getting the Japanese to surrender.
The only reason we really wanted to drop the bomb was because we wanted to justify spending around $2 billion on its development.	**Conclusion** Dropping the atomic bomb on Hiroshima and Nagasaki was the lesser of two evils for the United States as well as for Japan. No American lives were lost during the dropping of the bombs, and fewer Japanese lives were lost than would have been lost in Operation Olympic. The dropping of the bomb also protected America's political interests.	The bomb halted the war so quickly, which impressed the Soviet Union so much that they didn't request joint occupation of Japan.

4. *Help students recognize that there is much that they have not remembered or have represented incorrectly.* Simply, there are implicit inconsistencies that need correction and further information to be considered.

5. *Redirect students to their books and review the selection to correct inconsistencies and add further information.*

6. *Organize recorded remembrances into some kind of an outline.* Ask guiding, nonspecific questions: "What were the important ideas in the assigned reading? Which came first? What facts on the board support it? What important point was brought up next? What details followed?"

7. *Extend questioning to stimulate an analysis of the material and a synthesis of the ideas with previous learning.*

8. *Provide immediate feedback, such as a short quiz, as a reinforcement of short-term memory.*

A GRP Example

Eighth graders were assigned a reading selection from the music education magazine *Pipeline*. The selection, "Percussion—Solid as Rock," concerns the development and uses of percussion instruments from ancient to modern times.

The teacher introduced the selection by giving some background. She then began a guided discussion by asking students to remember as much as they could as they read the assignment silently. The teacher recorded the collective memories of her students on a white board, so that they could be seen by the group. Then she asked, "Did you leave out any information that might be important?" Students were directed to review the selection to determine whether essential information was missing from the list on the screen. The teacher also asked, "Did you mix up some of the facts on the list? Did you misrepresent any of the information in the author's message?"

These questions are extremely important to the overall GRP procedure. The first question—"Did you leave out any information that might be important?"—encourages a review of the material. Students sense that some facts are more important than others. Further questioning at this point will help them distinguish essential from nonessential information. The second question—"Did you mix up some of the facts on the list?"—reinforces the importance of selective rereading and rehearsal because of the limitations imposed by short-term memory.

Next, the teacher asked the class to study the information recorded on the white board. The teacher directed the students to form pairs and then assigned the following task: "Which facts on the white board can be grouped together? Organize the information around the important ideas in the selection. You have five minutes to complete the task."

On completion of the task, the teacher encouraged students to share their work in whole-group discussion. Their groupings of facts were compared, refined, and extended. The teacher served as a facilitator, keeping the discussion moving, asking clarifying questions, and provoking thought. She then initiated the next task: "Let's organize the important ideas and related information. Let's make a map." Figure 7.10 shows what the students produced.

Response Journal

How is the GRP similar to KWL? How is it different?

Figure 7.10 Semantic Map of "Percussion—Solid as Rock"

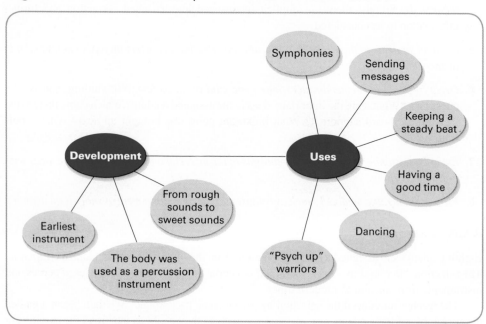

Outlining the mass of information will make students aware of the text relationships developed by the author. In Chapter 10 we explore several outlining procedures, such as semantic mapping, which help students produce the author's main ideas in relation to one another. Producing the author's organizational structure leads to more efficient recall at a later time and lays the groundwork for interpreting and applying the author's message. Once this common framework is developed, your questioning should lead to more divergent and abstract responding by the students.

In the example above, the discussion "took off" after the outline was completed. The teacher asked several reflective questions that helped students associate their previous experiences and beliefs about drumming to the content under discussion. Cognitive performance centered on evaluation and application as students linked what they knew to what they were studying.

The final suggested step in the GRP is a short quiz, mainly to demonstrate in a dramatic way how successful the students can be with the reading material. The quiz should be viewed as positive reinforcement, not an interrogation check. Most of the students in this class earned perfect or near-perfect scores on the quiz—and this is as it should be.

Intra-Act

Intra-act lays the groundwork for reflective discussion. Pivotal to the intra-act strategy is the notion that students engage in a process of valuing as they reflect on what they have read. Hoffman (1979, p. 608) suggests intra-act to provide readers with "the opportunity to experience rather than just talk about critical reading." According to Hoffman, students are more likely to read critically when they engage in a process of valuing. The valuing process allows students to respond actively to a text selection with thought and feeling.

The intra-act procedure can be used with a variety of reading materials—content area text assignments, historical documents, newspaper and magazine articles, narratives, and poetic material. The procedure requires the use of small groups whose members are asked to react to value statements based on the content of the text selection.

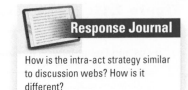

Response Journal

How is the intra-act strategy similar to discussion webs? How is it different?

Procedures for Intra-Act

There are four phases in the intra-act procedure.

1. *Comprehension.* The comprehension phase promotes an understanding of the reading material to be learned. To begin this phase, the teacher follows effective prereading procedures by introducing the text reading, activating and building prior knowledge for the ideas to be encountered during reading, and inviting students to make predictions and speculate on the nature of the content to be learned. Building a frame of reference for upcoming text information is crucial to the overall success of the intra-act procedure.

Before inviting students to read the selection individually, the teacher forms small groups—intra-act teams—of four to six members. The teacher assigns a student from each group to serve as the team leader. The comprehension phase depends on the team leader's ability to initiate and sustain a discussion of the text. The team leader's responsibility is to lead a discussion by first summarizing what was read. The group members may contribute additional information about the selection or ask questions that seek clarification of the main ideas of the selection. The comprehension phase of the group discussion should be limited to seven to ten minutes.

2. *Relating.* The team leader is next responsible for shifting the discussion from the important ideas in the selection to the group's personal reactions and values related to the topic. Many times, this shift occurs naturally. However, if this is not the case, members should be encouraged by the team leader to contribute their own impressions and opinions. Discussion should again be limited to seven to ten minutes.

3. *Valuation.* Once group members have shared their personal reactions to the material, they are ready to participate in the valuation phase of the discussion. The teacher or team leader for each group distributes a game sheet. This game sheet contains a valuing exercise—a set of four declarative statements based on the selection's content. These value statements reflect opinions about the text selection and draw insights and fresh ideas from it. The purpose of the valuing exercise is to have students come to grips with what the material means to them by either agreeing (A) or disagreeing (D) with each statement. Figure 7.11 shows such a game sheet.

4. *Reflection.* The reflection phase of intra-act begins by scoring the game sheet. Group members take turns revealing how each responded to the four statements. As each member tells how he or she responded, the other members check whether their predictions agreed with that member's actual responses. During this phase, the teacher acts as a facilitator, noting how students responded but refraining from imposing a particular point of view on students. Instead, encourage students to reflect on what they have learned. According to Hoffman (1979,

Figure 7.11 Intra-Act Example

Teens and Technology: Is internet socializing a bad thing?

Name: _____

Date: _____

Total Score: _____

Percentage of Correct Predictions: _____

	Jose	*Adrian*	*Jordan*	*Emily*
1. The use of social websites is a waste of time.	A D	A D	A D	A D
2. Participation in social networking websites gives kids valuable skills such as collaboration.	A D	A D	A D	A D
3. Participation in social networking websites develops kids' technical skills like creating a webpage.	A D	A D	A D	A D
4. Social networking can be dangerous.	A D	A D	A D	A D
5. Through the use of social networking websites, students can learn from their peers.	A D	A D	A D	A D

p. 607), "It is very important that during this period students be allowed ample time to discuss, challenge, support and question one another's response. This interaction serves to separate opinions quickly arrived at from sound evaluative thinking."

Intra-act will require several classroom applications before students become accustomed to their roles during discussion. Repeated and extensive participation in intra-act will help students become fully aware of the task demands of the procedure. In the beginning, we recommend that on completion of an intra-act discussion, students engage in a whole-class discussion of the process in which they participated. Help students debrief: "What did we learn from our participation in intra-act? Why must all members of a group participate? How might discussion improve the next time we use intra-act?" Questions such as these make students sensitive to the purpose of the intra-act procedure (problem solving) and the role of each reader (critical analysis).

An Intra-Act Example

After students in a contemporary issues class read Lewin's (2008) article "Teenagers' Internet Socializing: Not a Bad Thing", four students, Jose, Jordan, Adrian, and Emily met as a group to discuss their thoughts and impressions of the text. Jose, the group's team leader, began with a summary of the article and then gave his reactions. Jose stated, "The article suggested that time spent on the Internet is not as bad as some may believe. The Internet provides teens with technology and literacy skills needed in the twenty-first century."

After some discussion about the key points of the article, the team leader shifted the conversation to elicit personal reactions and responses of the group in the relating phase. Jordan reacted to the article by stating, "I think technology is part of our world and we must embrace it. There are many different purposes and benefits of using social media. I use the Internet not only to communicate with my friends in a social way, but also to study for tests, do research, and share ideas."

Adrian replied, "I agree that the Internet, if used appropriately, is a useful tool. We just need to inform our parents because they do not have as much experience and ongoing use with it. I've never talked with strangers online, only my friends; but my parents think that is a major problem with Internet use."

Emily joined the conversation by adding, that she thought too much time spent on the Internet instead of face-to-face interaction reduced personal connections with others and negatively affected social skills.

When time for discussion was over, the valuation phase was initiated. Students were given a game sheet with these five value statements:

1. The use of social websites is a waste of time.

2. Participation in social networking websites gives kids valuable skills such as collaboration.

3. Participation in social networking websites develops kids' technical skills like creating a web page.

4. Social networking can be dangerous.

5. Through the use of social networking websites, students can learn from their peers.

Each student was asked to respond individually to the statements and then predict whether the other members of the group would agree or disagree with each statement. Each student completed his or her own intra-act game sheet. From the discussion, Jose was confident that Adrian would not agree with the first statement because she said that "I agree that the Internet, if used appropriately, is a useful too." Similarly, he thought that Emily would agree because she thought too much time on the Internet could be problematic. He was also pretty sure that Jordan would disagree because he valued the role of technology in today's society. Jose used similar reasons to predict the group members' reactions to other statements.

As part of the reflection phase of intra-act, the group members shared what they learned. Jose found out that most of his predictions were accurate. He was surprised to find out that Adrian agreed somewhat with statement 1, but she explained that, "It's not always a waste of time but when people use it to talk about other people and bully people on social networks, I think it is a waste of time and can have negative consequences." Others agreed with Adrian but thought that the use of the Internet did more good than harm. The debate was typical of the discussion that went on in all the groups as students worked out the ways in which ideas presented in the text fit in with their own attitudes and beliefs.

Directed Reading–Thinking Activity (DR–TA)

The DR–TA fosters critical awareness and thinking by engaging learners in a process that involves prediction, verification, interpretation, and judgment. Much like the QtA, the teacher guides the reading and stimulates thinking through the frequent use of open-ended questions such as "What do you think?" "Why do you think so?" "Can you prove it?" The learning environment for a DR–TA lesson is critical to its success as an instructional practice. The teacher must be supportive and encouraging so as not to inhibit students' participation in the activity. As a rule, avoid inhibiting participation by refuting students' predictions; encourage students to think divergently, using information that is stated or implied in the text to substantiate their predications or interpretations. Wait time is also important. When posing an open-ended question, it is not unusual to pause for two, three, five, or even ten seconds for students to respond. Too often, the tendency is to slice the original question into smaller parts. Sometimes a teacher starts slicing too quickly out of a sense of frustration or anxiety rather than because of students' inability to respond. Silence may very well be an indication that hypothesis formation or other cognitive activities are taking place in the students' heads. So wait—and see what happens.

To prepare for a DR–TA with an informational text, analyze the material for its superordinate and subordinate concepts. What are the relevant concepts, ideas, relationships, and information in the material? The content analysis will help you decide on logical stopping points as you direct students through the reading.

For short stories and other narrative material, determine the key elements of the story: the *setting* (time and place, major characters) and the *events in the plot* (the initiating events or problem-generating situation, the protagonist's reaction to the event and his or her goal to resolve the problem, the set of attempts to achieve the goal, outcomes related to the protagonist's attempts to achieve the goal and resolve the problem, the character's reaction).

Once these elements have been identified, the teacher has a framework for deciding on logical stopping points within the story. In Figure 7.12, we indicate a general plan that may be followed or adapted for specific story lines. Notice that the suggested stopping points come at key junctures in a causal chain of events in the story line. Each juncture suggests a logical stopping point in that it assumes that the reader has enough information from at least one preceding event to predict a future happening or event.

In a high school biology class, students were engaged in a study of a textbook chapter on plant reproduction. Using a DR–TA framework, the teacher guided the students' interactions with the text material. Study an excerpt of the transcript from the beginning cycle of the DR–TA in Figure 7.13.

Figure 7.12 Potential Stopping Points in a DR–TA for a Story Line with One Episode

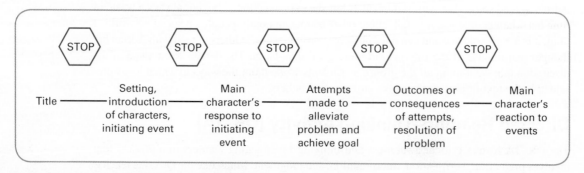

Figure 7.13 Excerpt of a DR–TA Transcript from a Biology Lesson
on Plant Reproduction

Teacher–Student Interactions	Analysis of Lesson
I'D LIKE FOR YOU TO BEGIN BY SCANNING THE HEADINGS, SUB-HEADINGS, PHOTOS, AND CAPTIONS IN THIS SECTION. THEN TELL ME WHAT YOU EXPECT TO FIND IN THIS SECTION. YOU KNOW IT IS ABOUT PLANT REPRODUCTION. WHAT ELSE DO YOU EXPECT TO LEARN?	The teacher directs students to preview a section of text about plant reproduction to activate prior knowledge and set a reading purpose.
S: It happens by bees.	The student's response is based on prior knowledge which she judges to be relevant.
WHY DO YOU SAY BEES?	The teacher encourages the student to elaborate on her response.
S: Well, I think because I know bees go from flower to flower.	
WHAT HAPPENS WHEN BEES GO FROM FLOWER TO FLOWER?	The teacher probes the student for a more detailed response.
S: They get nectar from the flowers.	
HOW DOES THAT HELP WITH PLANT REPRODUCTION?	The teacher again scaffolds the student's response through questioning.
S: It helps spread the pollen from flower to flower.	
WHAT DOES POLLEN HAVE TO DO WITH PLANT REPRODUCTION?	The teacher encourages other students to participate by asking them to analyze the student's hypothesis.
S: It allows them to reproduce asexually.	
DOES ANYONE AGREE OR DISAGREE?	
S: I think she is wrong.	This student's response suggests that he is evaluating the other student's response.
WHY?	The teacher probes for justification of the student's comment.
S: I think there are other ways for plants to reproduce.	The student offers a general statement.
CAN YOU ELABORATE?	The teacher asks for elaboration.
S: Well, I know that plants have both male and female parts so they must reproduce sexually like humans do.	The student provides an explanation for his statement in terms of his prior knowledge.

(continued)

Figure 7.13   (*continued*)

Teacher–Student Interactions

ANYBODY ELSE?

WELL, LET ME GIVE YOU THE FIRST PART OF THE TEXT TO READ AND DETERMINE IF YOUR PREDICTIONS ARE ACCURATE. I WANT YOU TO READ TO THE BOTTOM OF THE PAGE AND THEN I WANT YOU TO GO TO THE TOP OF THE NEXT PAGE. IT WILL BE THE VERY TOP PARAGRAPH. COVER UP WHAT'S BELOW IT WITH YOUR PAPER. READ THAT FAR AND STOP.

(Students read silently)

Analysis of Lesson

The teacher does not point out the validity or lack of validity of either student's response. She recognizes that each student is thinking critically by tapping prior knowledge and connecting it with the new text. Students will then read on to determine clues to justify the concepts they have hypothesized. The teacher remains consistent as a facilitator of the discussion.

As you examine the transcript, note that teacher–student interactions are recorded in the left column of the box. The teacher's questions and comments are printed in capital letters, followed by the students' responses in lowercase letters. An analysis of the DR–TA lesson as it evolved is printed in the right column.

The transcript shows how the students used prior knowledge and text structure (discussed in Chapter 10) to anticipate the information that the text would reveal. As they shared what they expected to find, the students engaged in analyzing their pooled ideas. Their interactions with the teacher illustrate how a DR–TA instructional framework creates a need to know and helps readers declare purposes through anticipation and prediction making.

Once the purposes were established, the teacher assigned a section of the text chapter to be read. Although the students' predictions were amiss in the initial cycle of questioning, the teacher chose not to evaluate or judge the predictions. She recognized that as readers interact with the text, more often than not they are able to clarify their misconceptions for themselves.

Reading Guides

What exactly is a reading guide? It has sometimes been compared to a "worksheet"—something students complete after reading, usually as homework. But reading guides do more than give students work to do. Guides, like worksheets, may consist of questions and activities related to the instructional material under study. One of the differences, however, between a reading guide and a worksheet is that students respond to the questions and activities in the guide *as* they read the text, not after. A reading guide provides instructional support as students need it. Moreover, a well-developed guide not only influences content acquisition but also prompts higher-order thinking.

Guides help students comprehend texts better than they would if left to their own resources. Over time, however, text learners should be weaned from this type of scaffolding as they develop the maturity and

Response Journal

When you were a student, how helpful were worksheets in comprehending a text assignment?

the learning strategies to interact with difficult texts without guide material. With this caveat in mind, let's explore the use of one type of reading guide that scaffolds learning at different levels of understanding: three-level comprehension guides.

Comprehension Levels

Because reading is a thoughtful process, it embraces the idea of levels of comprehension. Readers construct meaning at various levels of thinking and conceptual difficulty (Herber, 1978). Figure 7.14 shows the different levels of comprehension.

At the *literal level,* students *read the lines* of the content material. They stay with print sufficiently to get the gist of the author's message. In simple terms, a literal recognition of that message determines what the author says. Searching for important literal information isn't an easy chore, particularly if readers haven't matured enough to know how to make the search or, even worse, haven't determined why they are searching in the first place. Most students can and will profit greatly from being shown how to recognize the essential information in the text.

Knowing what the author says is necessary but not sufficient in constructing meaning with text. Good readers search for conceptual complexity in material. They read at the *interpretive level—between the lines.* They focus not only on what authors say but also on what authors mean by what they say. The interpretive level delves into the author's intended meaning. How readers conceptualize implied ideas by integrating information into what they already know is part of the interpretive process. Recognizing the thought relationships that the author weaves together helps readers make inferences that are implicit in the material.

From time to time throughout this chapter, you have probably been trying to read us—not our words but us. And in the process of responding to our messages, you probably raised questions similar to these: "So what? What does this information mean to me? Does it make sense? Can I use these ideas for content instruction?" Your attempt to seek significance or relevance in what we say and mean is one signal that you are reading at the *applied level.* You are reading *beyond the*

Figure 7.14 Levels of Comprehension

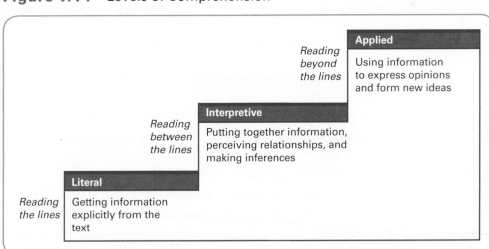

lines. Reading at the applied level is undoubtedly akin to critical reflection and discovery. When students construct meaning from text at the applied level, they know how to synthesize information—and to lay that synthesis alongside what they know already—to evaluate, question the author, think critically, and draw additional insights and fresh ideas from content material.

Three-Level Comprehension Guides

The levels-of-comprehension model that we have just introduced lends itself well to the development of guide material to engage students in reading. A three-level guide provides the framework in which students can interact with difficult texts at different levels of comprehension. One of the best ways to become familiar with the three-level guide is to experience one. Therefore, we invite you to participate in the following demonstration.

Preview the three-level guide in Figure 7.15. Then read "The Case of the Missing Ancestor." And then complete the three-level guide as you read the text or after reading.

Figure 7.15   Three-Level Guide for "The Case of the Missing Ancestor"

I. *Directions:* Check the statements that you believe say what the author says. Sometimes, the exact words are used; at other times, other words may be used.

_____ 1. The Germans discovered the fossilized remnants of the Neanderthal man and the Heidelberg man.

_____ 2. Charles Dawson found a human skull in a gravel pit in Piltdown Common, Sussex.

_____ 3. Charles Dawson was a professional archaeologist.

_____ 4. The fossil, labeled *Eoanthropus dawsoni,* became known as the Piltdown man.

_____ 5. The discovery of the Piltdown man was acclaimed as an important archaeological find.

_____ 6. Dental evidence regarding the Piltdown man was ignored.

II. *Directions:* Check the statements that you believe represent the author's *intended* meaning.

_____ 1 The English scientific community felt left out because important fossils had been found in other countries.

_____ 2. Good scientific practices were ignored by the people working with the Piltdown fossils.

_____ 3. Many scientists said that Piltdown was important because they wanted England to be important.

_____ 4. Dawson wanted to make himself famous, so he constructed a hoax.

III. *Directions:* Check the statements you agree with, and be ready to support your choices with ideas from the text and your own knowledge and beliefs.

_____ 1. Competition in scientific research may be dangerous.

_____ 2. Scientists, even good ones, can be fooled by poorly constructed hoaxes.

_____ 3. People often see only what they want to see.

_____ 4. A scientific "fact" is not always correct simply because many scientists believe strongly in it; theories are always open to question.

THE CASE OF THE MISSING ANCESTOR

From the mid-1800s to the early 1900s, Europeans were actively searching for early ancestors. The Germans dug up the fossilized remnants of Neanderthal man and Heidelberg man. The French discovered not only ancient bones but also cave paintings done by early humans.

England, Charles Darwin's home, had no evidence of ancient ancestors. English scientists—both professionals and amateurs—began searching for fossils. Scarcely a cave was left unexplored; scarcely a stone was left unturned. Many scientists asked workers in gravel pits to watch for fossils.

In 1912, Charles Dawson, a part-time collector of fossils for the British Museum, wrote to Dr. Arthur Smith Woodward, keeper of the Natural History Department at the British Museum. Dawson claimed that a human skull he had found in a gravel pit in Piltdown Common, Sussex, "would rival Heidelberg man." Soon Woodward was digging in the gravel pit with Dawson and other eager volunteers. They found a separate jaw that, though apelike, included a canine tooth and two molars, worn down as if by human-type chewing. Flints and nonhuman fossils found at the same dig indicated that the finds were very old.

Despite arguments by some scientists that the jaw came from a chimpanzee or an orangutan, the discoverers reconstructed the skull and connected the jaw to it. They named the fossil *Eoanthropusdawsoni,* Dawson's "Dawn man," and said that it was much older than Neanderthal man. The find came to be known as Piltdown man.

The finds were X-rayed. One dental authority was suspicious of the canine; he said it was too young a tooth to show such wear. However, such contrary evidence was ignored in the general surge of enthusiasm. So the Piltdown man was acclaimed as an important find, a human in which the brain had evolved more quickly than the jaw.

Beginning in the 1940s, the bones were subjected to modern tests. It is now believed that the skull was from a modern human and the jaw was from a modern ape, probably an orangutan. The animal fossils and flints were found to be very old, but not the types that have been found in England. Apparently, they had been placed in the gravel pit to make the finds more convincing. Why were the scientists and others fooled so easily? Perhaps the desire to find an "ancestor" may have interfered with careful scientific observation. (Alexander, 1986)

Several comments are in order on your participation in the three-level guide demonstration. First of all, note that the three-level format gave you a "conscious experience" with comprehension levels as a process. Note also that as you proceeded through the process, you responded to and manipulated the important explicit and implicit ideas in the material. You may have sensed the relatedness of ideas as you moved within and among the levels.

Why did we direct you first to preview the guide and then to read the material? Because surveying helps create a predisposition to read the material. Previewing helps reduce the reader's uncertainty about the material to be read. You know what is coming. When we asked you to read the guide first, we hoped to raise your expectations about the author's message. By encountering some of the ideas before reading, you are in a better position to direct your search for information in the reading material that may be relevant.

You probably noted also that the declarative statements did not require you to produce answers to questions. Rather, you had to make decisions among likely alternatives; it's easier to recognize possible answers than to produce them.

Notice, too, that in a very positive way, the statements can serve as springboards for discussion and conversation about the content. Were students to react to guides *without* the opportunity to discuss and debate responses, the instructional material would soon deteriorate into busywork and paper shuffling.

Response Journal

What do you think is the difference between responding to statements at different levels of comprehension versus responding to questions?

A final comment: Your maturity as a reader is probably such that you didn't need structured guidance for this selection, particularly at levels I and II. If you make the decision that certain segments of your text can be handled without reading guidance, don't construct guide material. A three-level guide is a means to growth in reading and growth through reading. It is not an end in itself.

Constructing Three-Level Comprehension Guides

Don't be misled by the apparent discreteness of comprehension levels. The term *levels* implies a cognitive hierarchy that may be more apocryphal than real. A reader doesn't necessarily read first for literal recognition, then interpretation, and finally application—although that may appear to be a logical sequence. Many readers, for instance, read text for overarching concepts and generalizations first and then search for evidence to support their inferences.

It is important to recognize that in reading, levels are probably interactive and insepa-rable. Nevertheless, the classroom teacher attempts to have students experience each aspect of the comprehension process as they read content material. In doing so, students adapt strategies as they interact with the material. They get a feel for the component processes within reading comprehension. They come to sense in an instructional setting what it means to make inferences, to use information as the basis for those inferences, and to rearrange or transform acquired understandings into what they know already in order to construct knowledge.

If guides were to be used with every text assignment every day, it would become counter-productive. One math teacher's evaluation of a three-level guide crystallizes this point: "The students said the guide actually helped them organize the author's ideas in their minds and helped them understand the material. I think the guide was successful, but I would not use it all the time because many of the assignments don't lend themselves to this type of activity." The three-level guide is only one instructional aide that helps students grow toward mature reading and independent learning.

Finally, we urge you also to consider guides as tools, not tests. Think of each statement in a three-level guide as a prompt that will initiate student discussion and reinforce the quality of the reader's interaction with text.

Before constructing a guide, the teacher has to decide the following: What important ideas should be emphasized? What are the students' competencies? What depth of understanding are the students expected to achieve? What is the difficulty of the material? Having made these decisions, consider these five guidelines:

1. *Begin construction of the guide at level II, the interpretive level.* Analyze the text selection, asking yourself, "What does the author mean?" Write down in your own words all infer-ences that make sense to you and that fit your content objectives. Make sure your statements are written simply and clearly (after all, you don't want to construct a guide to read the guide).

2. *Next, search the text for the propositions and explicit pieces of information needed to support the inferences you have chosen for level II.* Put these into statement form. You now have level I, the literal level.

3. *Decide whether you want to add a distractor or two to levels I and II.* We have found that a distractor maintains an active response to the information search, mainly because students

sense that they cannot indiscriminately check every item and, therefore, must focus their information search more carefully.

4. *Develop statements for level III, the applied level.* Such statements represent additional insights or principles that can be drawn when relationships established by the author are combined with other ideas outside the text selection itself but inside the heads of your students. In other words, help students connect what they know already to what they read.

5. *Be flexible and adaptive.* Develop a format that will appeal to you and your students. Try to avoid crowding too much print on the reading guide.

A Three-Level Comprehension Guide Example

The format of a three-level guide will vary from one content area to another. The classroom example that follows serves only as a model. As you study it, think of ways that you will be able to adapt and apply the three-level construct to your discipline-specific materials. A middle grade teacher constructed the three-level guide in Figure 7.16 as part of a health unit. Notice how she uses question–answer relationships (QARs) as cues to direct students' responses. Students completed the guide individually and then discussed their responses in small groups.

Figure 7.16   Three-Level Guide for a Health Lesson

I. Right There! What did the author say?

Directions: Place a check on the line in front of the number if you think a statement can be found in the pages you read.

_____ 1. Every human being has feelings or emotions.

_____ 2. Research workers are studying the effects on the body of repeated use of marijuana.

_____ 3. You should try hard to hide your strong emotions, such as fear or anger.

_____ 4. Your feelings affect the way the body works.

_____ 5. You are likely to get angry at your parents or brothers or sisters more often than at other people.

II. Think and Search! What did the author mean?

Directions: Check the following statements that state what the author was trying to say in the pages you read.

_____ 1. Sometimes you act in a different way because of your mood.

_____ 2. Your emotional growth has been a continuing process since the day you were born.

_____ 3. The fact that marijuana hasn't been proved to be harmful means that it is safe to use.

_____ 4. Each time you successfully control angry or upset feelings, you grow a little.

(continued)

Figure 7.16 (*continued*)

III. On Your Own! Do you agree with these statements?

Directions: Check each statement that you can defend.

_____ 1. Escaping from problems does not solve them.

_____ 2. Decisions should be made on facts, not fantasies.

_____ 3. Getting drunk is a good way to have fun.

BOX 7.3 # Voices from the Field

Think-Alouds Across Content Areas
Kim, Lead Teacher

Challenge

Classrooms I see today consist of students reading at a wide variety of levels. For example, one fifth-grade class in my school has two students reading at a second-grade level, four students reading at a third-grade level, a handful reading on a fourth-grade level, the majority reading on grade level, and three students reading on a sixth-grade level or above. My job as a lead teacher is to help my colleagues with reading instruction across content areas. Given the wide range of reading levels of students, this is often a challenging task. To make grade level material accessible to students, I encourage teachers to incorporate think-alouds into their content area instruction.

Strategy

To apply the think-aloud strategy when teaching a unit on migration, one fifth-grade teacher chose an article on the topic of migration. She displayed the article on the SMART Board as she modeled the think-aloud:

She read the first paragraph aloud to the students and said, "Wow! 45,000 miles is 60 trips around the earth in the bird's lifetime. That is a long way to travel for such a tiny bird. I wonder what their path might look like as they're traveling. Let's read on to see if the author gives us more information."

Then she continued reading aloud to the students, stopping after the second section to model how she was making sense of the text: "So, I'm learning about how scientists are using tracking devices called geolocators to track the birds' flight. I'm still wondering about their trip. Let's read on to see if the author gives us more detail."

After reading the next section, she thought aloud again, "Now I'm learning about the trek the birds are making. I learned that they stopped in the middle of the Atlantic Ocean to eat, and then they went down the coast of South America. Let's draw that on our map." On the world map displayed in the classroom, she began to chart the migration of the birds as described in the article.

After she had read the last paragraph, the teacher noted, "It's interesting that the birds did not go the shortest way home isn't it? They went all over the Atlantic. Let's add what that might look like on our map." The teacher drew her interpretation of the trek. "How else could that have looked, I wonder? Maybe like this..." She drew another route on the map. "The author told me why they fly back like this in the article. Why is that?" She involved the students in a discussion about migration and what they learned from thinking aloud as the text was read.

Reflection

Some of my colleagues struggled with finding time to incorporate read-alouds into their already packed schedules. In the middle grades, they tried to carve out 15-20 minute blocks two or three times each week for read aloud time, during which they incorporated think-alouds. In order for think-alouds to be successful, they need to be carefully planned. My suggestion to teachers was to share the planning. For example, they worked with their grade-level team members to divide the planning for think-alouds within a single unit. Then, each teacher shared his or her think-aloud plan with the other team members. In a six-person team, they were able to have think-alouds for the entire unit without overburdening any one teacher with the planning for this strategy. By using the think-aloud strategy, teachers were able to model effective comprehension strategies, including predicating, visualizing, summarizing, and confirming. They encouraged their students to transfer the use of the think-aloud strategy to their independent reading.

Looking Back | Looking Forward

Strategy-centered classrooms are places where students learn how to learn. Teachers support students' efforts to make meaning by guiding reading comprehension and modeling how to think and learn with texts. To this end, we explored several research-based comprehension strategies that show students how to be active, thoughtful readers: think-alouds, question–answer relationships (QARs), reciprocal teaching, and questioning the author (QtA). When these strategies are adapted to meet the textual and conceptual demands of a discipline, they not only model comprehension strategies but also engage learners in meaningful talk and discussion about the content under study.

Several comprehension-centered instructional strategies were also suggested to guide students' interactions with texts. These strategies are designed to help students clarify and extend meaning as they engage in reading. For example, KWL is a meaning-making strategy that engages students in active text learning and may be used with small groups of students or with an entire class. KWL comprises several steps that help learners examine what they know, what they want to know more about, and what they have learned from reading; KWHL offers a variation on this strategy, asking students to also consider how they might find the information they need. The directed reading–thinking activity (DR–TA) was also described. DR–TA revolves around three guiding questions: (1) What do you think? (2) Why do you think so? (3) Can you prove it? The guided reading procedure (GRP) encourages close reading of difficult text, whereas the discussion web and intra-act strategies lay the groundwork for reflective discussion following the reading of text material.

In addition to comprehension strategies, teacher-prepared reading guides may also be used to guide reading. Three-level comprehension guides allow learners to interact with text, constructing meaning at different levels of thinking: literal, interpretive, and applied. In the next chapter, we focus on the building blocks of comprehension in a discipline: developing technical vocabulary and concepts. In particular, we examine the relationship between the vocabulary of a content area—its special and technical terms—and its concepts. How can a teacher help students to interact with the language of a discipline and, in the process, show them how to define, clarify, and extend their understanding of the concepts under study?

Minds On

1. Why and how will the instructional strategies that you have studied help you guide students in reading?

2. With a small group, create an intra-act guide sheet for this chapter. After you have finished, discuss any insights into reading gained from this activity.

3. Picture a content area class of twenty-five to thirty students (your choice of grade level and subject) from diverse backgrounds. Describe how you would use discussion webs and KWL strategies while maintaining high standards of content literacy and learning.

4. Select a popular book, film, or song that most members of your small group know. Discuss each of the following levels of comprehension communicated in that work: (a) literal (in the lines), (b) interpretive (between the lines), (c) applied (beyond the lines).

Hands On

1. Without sharing perceptions, each member of your group should read this short paragraph and follow the directions.

   An artist was talking enthusiastically about one of her favorite paintings to several people visiting the gallery when a woman approached her and offered to purchase the work. The owner of the gallery removed the painting from the wall. The painting was snatched from her hands, and the woman bolted through the front door into a waiting van, which sped down the street through a nearby red light and vanished into the night.

   Using the paragraph as a reference, respond to each of the following statements, in the order presented, by circling T (for true), F (for false), or ? (for unable to determine from the paragraph). Once you have characterized a statement as true, false, or questionable, you cannot change your answer.

   a. The artist talked about one of her paintings. T F ?

   b. The thief was a woman. T F ?

   c. The crime appeared to be premeditated. T F ?

   d. This type of theft seems unlikely. T F ?

   e. The owner removed the painting from the wall. T F ?

   f. The owner was the artist. T F ?

   g. The woman who bolted through the door stole the painting. T F ?

   h. The person who snatched the painting from the owner's hands was the artist. T F ?

   i. A robbery didn't occur. T F ?

   Discuss the variety of possible answers based on your responses. What does this activity tell you about reader–text interactions?

2. Select a short informational article in a magazine or book, and make copies for each member of your group. Have each member of the group choose one of the following instructional strategies: (1) KWL (What do you *know?* About what do you *want to know* more? What did you *learn?*); (2) GRP (guided reading procedure); (3) intra-act; (4) DR–TA (directed reading–thinking activity); and (5) a discussion web. If there are more than five members in your group, duplicate strategies as needed.

   Using the same article, design a lesson around the strategy you have chosen and make copies to share with the members of the group. As you review the four different lessons prepared by your colleagues, what comparisons and contrasts can you make between these instructional strategies?

3. Select a short informational article in a magazine or book, and bring copies for each member of your

group. Have each member of the group discuss the merits of one of the following instructional strategies: (1) guided discussion, (2) discussion web, (3) KWL/KWHL, and (4) a three-level reading guide. If there are more than four members in your group, duplicate strategies as needed.

Using the same article, design a lesson around the strategy you have discussed and make copies to share with the members of the group. As you review the four different lessons prepared by your colleagues, what comparisons and contrasts can you make between these instructional strategies?

eResources

The following site is filled with ideas for engaging students in reading: **www.readingrockets.org**. Explore the site for ideas and research on how to support students' motivation to read. Discuss your findings in small groups.

The National Reading Panel's focus on research-based strategies serves as a landmark in reading education. Review the Panel's findings on text comprehension (**www.nichd.nih .gov/publications/nrp/findings.cfm**).

Use the keywords "QtA" or "Questioning the Author" and "KWL" or "KWL Strategies" to search for these two powerful comprehension strategies. Consider how you might use these strategies in your content area. Reading Quest provides examples for KWL (**www.readingquest.org/strat /kwl.html**)and QtA (**www.readingquest.org/strat/qta .html**).

MyEducationLab™

Go to Topic 5: Comprehension, the MyEducationLab (**www.myeducationlab.com**) for *Content Area Reading*, where you can:

- Find learning outcomes for Comprehension, along with the national standards that connect to these outcomes.
- Complete Assignments and Activities that can help you more deeply understand the chapter content.
- Practice the core teaching skills identified in the chapter with the Building Teaching Skills and Dispositions learning units.
- Check your comprehension on the content covered in the chapter with the Study Plan. Here you will be able to take a chapter quiz, receive feedback on your answers, and then access Review, Practice, and Enrichment activities to enhance your understanding of chapter content.
- Visit A+RISE. A+RISE® Standards2Strategy™ is an innovative and interactive online resource that offers new teachers in grades K–12 just in time, research-based instructional strategies that meet the linguistic needs of English Language Learners (ELLs) as they learn content, differentiate instruction for all grades and abilities, and are aligned to Common Core Elementary Language Arts standards (for the literacy strategies) and to English language proficiency standards in World-Class Instructional Design and Assessment (WIDA), Texas, California, and Florida.
- Use the Online Lesson Plan Builder to practice lesson planning and integrating national and state standards into your planning.

Developing Vocabulary and Concepts

Organizing Principle

Teaching words well means giving students multiple opportunities to develop word meanings and learn how words are conceptually related to one another in the texts they are studying.

There is a strong connection between vocabulary knowledge and reading comprehension. If students are not familiar with most words they meet in print, they will undoubtedly have trouble understanding what they read. It has been suggested that words are the building materials students need to construct meaning as they read and learn with text. Technical vocabulary—words unique to a content area—are often unfamiliar to students, but are particularly important for disciplinary thinking and learning. The more experience students have with unfamiliar words and the more exposure they have to them, the more meaningful the words will become.

Vocabulary is as unique to a content area as fingerprints are to a human being. A content area is distinguishable by its language, particularly the technical terms that label the concepts undergirding the subject matter. Teachers know they must do something with the language of their content areas, but they often reduce instruction to routines that direct students to look up, define, memorize, and use content-specific words in sentences. Such practices divorce the study of vocabulary from an exploration of the subject matter. Learning vocabulary becomes an activity in itself—a separate one—rather than an integral part of learning academic content. Content area vocabulary must be taught *well enough* to remove potential barriers to students' understanding of texts in content areas. The organizing principle underscores the main premise of the chapter: **Teaching words well**

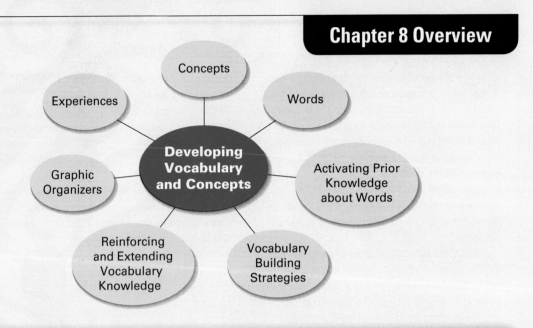

means giving students multiple opportunities to develop word meanings and learn how words are conceptually related to one another in the texts they are studying.

Frame of Mind

1. Why should the language of an academic discipline be taught within the context of concept development?

2. What are the relationships among experiences, concepts, and words?

3. How can a teacher activate what students know about words and help them make connections among related words?

4. How do graphic organizers help students anticipate and understand important concepts in content area texts?

5. How do activities for vocabulary and concept development help students refine their knowledge of special and technical vocabulary?

6. How can knowledge of word structure help students to understand word meanings?

Fridays always seemed to be set aside for quizzes when we were students. And one of the quizzes most frequently given was the vocabulary test: "Look up these words for the week. Write out their definitions and memorize them. Then use each word in a complete sentence. You'll be tested on these terms on Friday."

Our vocabulary study seemed consistently to revolve around the dull routines of looking up, defining, and memorizing words and using them in sentences.

Such an instructional pattern resulted in meaningless, purposeless activity—an end in itself, rather than a means to an end. Although there was nothing inherently wrong with looking up, defining, and memorizing words and using them in sentences, the approach itself was too narrow for us to learn words in depth. Instead, we memorized definitions to pass the Friday quiz—and forgot them on Saturday.

Having students learn lists of words is based on the ill-founded notion that the acquisition of vocabulary is separate from the development of ideas and concepts in a content area. Teaching vocabulary often means assigning a list of words rather than exploring word meanings and relationships that contribute to students' conceptual awareness and understanding of a subject. Once teachers clarify the relationship between words and concepts, they are receptive to instructional alternatives.

Response Journal

What were some of your experiences with vocabulary instruction in content areas?

One clarification that's quickly made involves the types of reading vocabulary found in textbooks. Three types of vocabulary are evident. The first type, *general vocabulary,* consists of everyday words with widely acknowledged meanings in common usage. The second, *special vocabulary,* is made up of words from everyday life, general vocabulary that take on specialized meanings when adapted to a particular content area. The third type, *technical vocabulary,* consists of words that have usage and application only in a particular subject matter field.

Special and technical terms are particularly bothersome when they're encountered in content material. Your participation in the demonstration in Figure 8.1 will illustrate why special and technical terms are likely candidates for vocabulary instruction in content areas. If your responses are similar to those of classroom teachers who have participated in this activity, several predictable outcomes are likely.

First of all, it is relatively easy for you to identify the content areas for several of the lists. Your knowledge and experience probably trigger instant recognition. You have a good working concept of many of the terms on these easy lists. You can put them to use in everyday situations that require listening, reading, writing, or speaking. They are your words. You own them.

Second, you probably recognize words in a few of the lists even though you may not be sure about the meanings of individual words. In lists 4 and 9, for example, you may be familiar with only one or two terms. Yet you are fairly sure that the terms in lists 4 and 9 exist as words

Figure 8.1   Vocabulary Demonstration Words in Content Areas

Directions: In each of the nine blanks, fill in the name of the content area that includes all the terms in the list below:

1. _____	2. _____	3. _____
nationalism	forestry	metaphor
imperialism	ornithology	allusion
naturalism	zoology	irony
instrumentalism	biology	paradox
isolationist	entomology	symbolism
radicalism	botany	imagery
fundamentalist	bacteriology	simile
anarchy	protista	

4. _____	5. _____	6. _____
prestissimo	centimeter	graffles
adagio	milligram	folutes
larghetto	deciliter	lesnics
presto	millisecond	raptiforms
allegro	kilometer	cresnites
largo	decimeter	hygrolated
andante	kilogram	loors
tempo	millimeter	chamlets

7. _____	8. _____	9. _____
trans fat	octagon	auricle
glycogen	hemisphere	ventricle
monosaccharide	decagon	tricuspid
hydrogenation	hexagon	semilunar
enzymes	bisect	apex
lyzine	equilateral	mitral
cellulose	quadrilateral	aorta
	pentagon	myocardium

despite the fact that you may not know what they mean. Your attitude toward these kinds of words is analogous to your saying to a stranger, "I think I've met you before but I'm not sure." Several of the words from the lists may be in your "twilight zone;" you have some knowledge about them, but their meanings are a "bit foggy, not sharply focused." *Trans fat* in list 7 is a case in point for some of us who have heard the term used in television commercials and may even have purchased foods with trans fat at the supermarket. Nevertheless, our guess is that we would be hard pressed to define or explain the meaning of trans fat with any precision.

Finally, in one or two cases a list may have completely stymied your efforts at identification. There simply is no connection between your prior knowledge and any of the terms. You probably are not even sure whether the terms in one list really exist as words.

Which content area did you identify for list 6? In truth, the terms in this list represent nonsense. They are bogus words that were invented to illustrate the point that many of the content terms in textbooks look the same way to students that the nonsense words in list 6 look to you. You're able to pronounce most of them with little trouble but are stymied when you try to connect them to your knowledge and experience. Students are stymied this way every day by real words that represent the key concepts of a content area.

The words in these lists (except list 6) are actually taken from middle and high school textbooks. Just think for a moment about the staggering conceptual demands we place on learners daily as they go from class to class. Terminology that they encounter in content material is often outside the scope of their normal speaking, writing, listening, and reading vocabularies. Special and technical terms often do not have concrete referents; they are abstract and must be learned through definition, application, and repeated exposure.

Your participation in this activity leads to several points about word knowledge and concepts in content areas. The activity is a good reminder that every academic discipline creates a unique language to represent its important concepts. This is why teaching vocabulary in content areas is too important to be incidental or accidental. Key concept words need to be taught directly and taught well.

Informational texts used in content area classes typically bring with them more challenging vocabulary demands than narrative or literary texts (Pearson, Hiebert, & Kamil, 2007). Providing students with direct instruction in vocabulary has been found to influence comprehension of text more than any other factor (Bromley, 2007). Students shouldn't be left to their own devices or subjected to the vagaries of a look up-and-define strategy as their only access to understanding the language of an academic discipline. Verbalizing a dictionary definition of a word and learning it by rote are quite different from encountering that word in a reading situation and constructing meaning for it based on conceptual knowledge and prior experiences.

Selecting specific vocabulary words for meaningful, direct instruction from the plethora of potential words that might be studied in a subject area can be a challenge for teachers. As Ganske (2012, p. 211) explains, "Different situations require different levels of word knowledge." To provide guidance in selecting words on which to focus, Beck, McKeown, and Kucan (2002) categorize vocabulary words according to three tiers or levels:

Tier 1: Tier 1 words are basic high-frequency and high-utility words that are commonly used in everyday language. Tier 1 might include words such as *friend, move, eat,* and *home.* Native language speakers typically don't require direct instruction to understand Tier 1 words.

Tier 2: Tier 2 words are also high-frequency and high-utility words; however, words in this category are more commonly used by advanced or mature language users. Words such as *scalding, reprimand, clarify,* and *escapade* are examples of Tier 2 words. Vocabulary instruction is often needed in order for students to understand the meanings of these words.

Tier 3: Tier 3 words are low-frequency words, but words that are needed to understand a content area material. Tier 3 words are part of the language of a subject area and, as the vocabulary demonstration in Figure 8.1 illustrated, unique and integral to each subject area. Examples of Tier 3 words include *Declaration of Independence, nucleus, quadratic equation,* and *palette.* Tier 3 words are those for which direct instruction is often required in content area classes.

In this chapter, we will show how to teach words well within the framework of subject matter learning. Teaching words well removes potential barriers to reading comprehension.

It is no wonder that research has documented a strong link between vocabulary development and reading comprehension (National Reading Panel, 2000; Pressley, 2002a). Knowledge of word meanings, and the ability to use that knowledge effectively, contributes significantly to a student's reading and listening comprehension (Curtis & Longo, 2001). When teachers understand *how* students acquire knowledge of vocabulary concepts, vocabulary instruction can be effectively integrated within the context of subject area learning (Blachowicz, Fisher, Ogle, & Watts-Taffe, 2006).

Teaching words well involves helping students make connections between their prior knowledge and the vocabulary to be encountered in text and providing them with multiple opportunities to define, clarify, and extend their knowledge of words and concepts during the course of study. To begin, let's explore the connection that links direct experience to concepts and words. Understanding these connections lays the groundwork for teaching words, with the emphasis on learning.

Experiences, Concepts, and Words

Words are labels for concepts. A single concept, however, represents much more than the meaning of a single word. It may take thousands of words to explain a concept. However, answers to the question, "What does it mean to know a word?" depend on how well we understand the relationships among direct experiences, concepts, and words.

Learning the meaning of new terms by reading definitions is only minimally effective. Concepts are learned by acting on and interacting with the environment. Students learn concepts best through direct, concrete, purposeful experiences (Nagy, 1988). Learning is much more intense and meaningful when it develops through firsthand experience. However, in place of using direct experience, which is not always possible, students can develop and learn concepts through various levels of improvised or vicarious experience, which is often feasible in a classroom setting.

What Are Concepts?

Concepts create mental images, which may represent anything that can be grouped together by common features or similar criteria: objects, symbols, ideas, processes, or events. In this respect, concepts are similar to schemata. A concept hardly ever stands alone; instead, it is bound by a hierarchy of relationships. As a result, "most concepts do not represent a unique object or event but rather a general class linked by a common element or relationship" (Johnson & Pearson, 1984, p. 33).

Bruner, Goodnow, and Austin (1977) suggest that we would be overwhelmed by the complexity of our environment if we were to respond to each object or event that we encountered as unique. Therefore, we invent categories (or form concepts) to reduce the complexity of our environment and the necessity for constant learning. For example, every feline need not have a different name; each is known as a *cat*. Although cats vary greatly, their common characteristics cause them to be referred to by the same general term. Thus, to facilitate communication, we invent words to name concepts.

Concept Relationships: An Example

Consider your concept for the idea of a *garment*. What pictures comes to mind? Your image of the process of creating a garment might differ based on your experience with clothing, your interest level or even your purpose for creating the garment. Maybe you base your idea on why you need the garment, how you will use it, or your skill level as a designer. Each student's experiences and understanding will vary as they take on the task of understanding the process behind planning and making their own garment. Nevertheless, for any concept, we organize all our experiences and knowledge into conceptual hierarchies according to *class, example,* and *attribute* relationships. As part of the family and consumer science curriculum, students in an introductory apparel course learned that the concept of a *garment* is really made of a series of decisions that can be categorized according to the results of each decision. These relationships are shown in Figure 8.2.

In any conceptual network, class relations are organized in a hierarchy consisting of superordinate and subordinate concepts. In Figure 8.2 the superordinate concept is creating a garment. *Pattern, trimming,* and *fabric* represent the three classes of decisions one will have to make when constructing a garment. They are in a subordinate position in this hierarchy. Each decision is then broken down into the smaller steps that must be considered to inform the larger class. These decisions are subordinate to their classes.

For every concept, there are examples. An *example* is a member of any concept being considered. Class-examples relations are complementary. For example, in order to decide on the season for which you will create your garment, you must weigh all four options—summer, spring, winter, and fall. When considering these subordinate levels, one must ask, what do they have in common? Obviously, each listed is a season and the season would have an influential effect on the fabric choices one makes for their garment. This helps the learner focus on *relevant attributes,* the features, traits, properties, or characteristics common to every example of a particular group. In this case, the relevant attributes which are common to making a decision about fabric are that all examples listed are seasons. An attribute is said to be *critical* if it is a characteristic that is necessary for every class member to possess. An attribute is said to be *variable* if it is shared by some by not all examples of this class. Looking at making a fabric choice we see that we will consider purpose, cost, and season. Their commonalities help us construct the garment in our mind and make appropriate choices so that the garment matches our needs. That is critical: all factors must impact our fabric choice. They also have variable characteristics. For example, *how* will they impact our fabric choice? Cost concerns a budget, purpose concerns how it will be used, and season concerns when it will be used.

This brief discussion illustrates an important principle: *teachers can help students build conceptual knowledge of context terms and ideas by teaching and reinforcing the concept words in relation to other concept words.* This key instructional principle plays itself out in content area classrooms whenever students are actively making connections among the key words in a lesson or unit of study.

 # Using Graphic Organizers to Make Connections Among Key Concepts

At the start of each chapter, we have asked you to use a "chapter overview" to organize your thoughts about the main ideas in the text. These ideas are presented within the framework of a *graphic organizer,* a diagram that uses content vocabulary to help students anticipate concepts

Figure 8.2 A Concept Hierarchy Based on Class Relations—*Apparel*

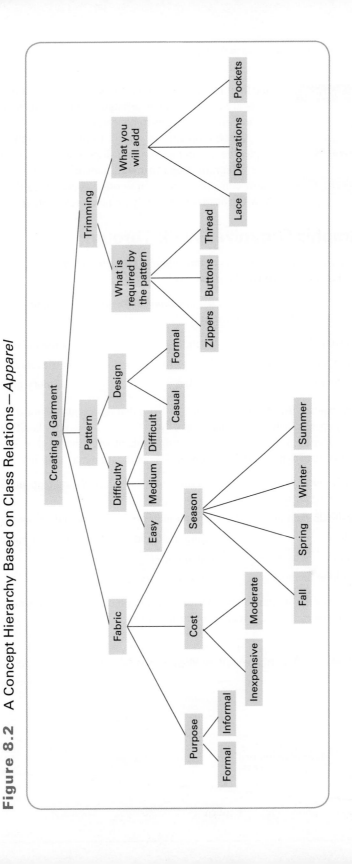

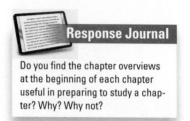

Response Journal

Do you find the chapter overviews at the beginning of each chapter useful in preparing to study a chapter? Why? Why not?

and their relationships to one another in the reading material. These concepts are displayed in an arrangement of key technical terms relevant to the important concepts to be learned.

Graphic organizers vary in format. One commonly used format to depict the hierarchical relationships among concept words is a "network tree" diagram. Keep in mind, network tree graphic organizers always show concepts in relation to other concepts. Let's take a closer look at how to construct and apply graphic organizers in the classroom.

A Graphic Organizer Walk-Through

Suppose you were to develop a graphic organizer for a text chapter in a high school psychology course. Let's walk through the steps involved.

1. *Analyze the vocabulary and list the important words.* The chapter yields several important words, including the following:

episodic memory	encoding	semantic memory
short-term memory	long-term memory	retrieval
sensory memory	storage	memory processes

2. *Arrange the list of words.* Choose the word that represents the most inclusive concept; the one superordinate to all of the others. Next, choose the words classified immediately under the superordinate concepts and coordinate them with one another. Then choose the terms subordinate to the coordinate concepts. Your diagram may look like Figure 8.3.

3. *Add to the scheme vocabulary terms that you believe the students understand.* You add the following terms:

flashbulb memories	explicit memory	organizational systems
echoic	riding a bicycle	tip-of-the tongue phenomenon
iconic	visual codes	schema
working memory	acoustic codes	

4. *Evaluate the organizer.* The interrelationships among the key terms may look like Figure 8.4 once you evaluate the vocabulary arrangement.

Figure 8.3   Arrangement of Words on Memory in a Psychology Test

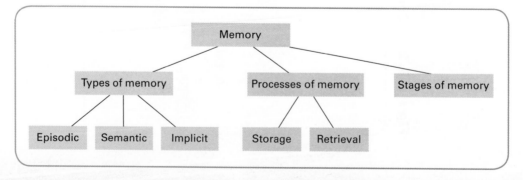

Figure 8.4 Arrangement of Words on Memory After Evaluation of Organizer

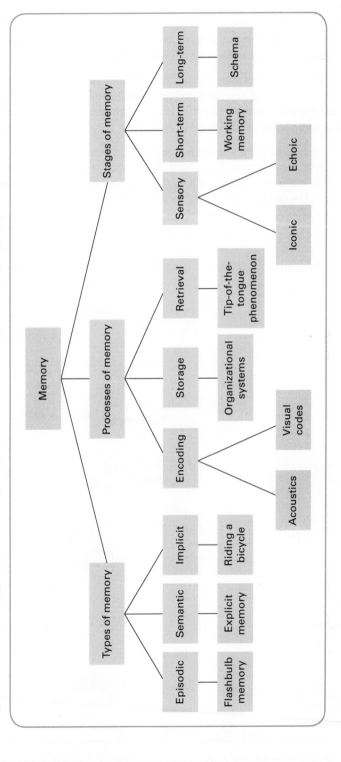

5. *Introduce the students to the learning task.* As you present the vocabulary relationships shown on the graphic organizer, create as much discussion as possible. Draw on students' understanding of and experience with the concepts the terms label. The discussions you will stimulate with the organizer will be worth the time it takes to construct it.

6. *As you complete the learning task, relate new information to the organizer.* This step is particularly useful as a study and review technique. The organizer becomes a study guide that can be referred to throughout the discussion of the material. Students should be encouraged to add information to flesh out the organizer as they develop concepts more fully.

A graphic organizer can be used to show the relationships in a thematic unit in a chapter or chapter subsection. Notice how the graphic organizer in Figure 8.5, developed for a high school business class, introduces the students to corporate infrastructure. This organizer can be used to facilitate discussion on the hierarchy of business roles, responsibilities at different levels of an organization, or ethical business practices. The organization chart can also be used to facilitate students' development of their own mock business.

Figure 8.5   A Graphic Organizer for a Business Organizational Chart

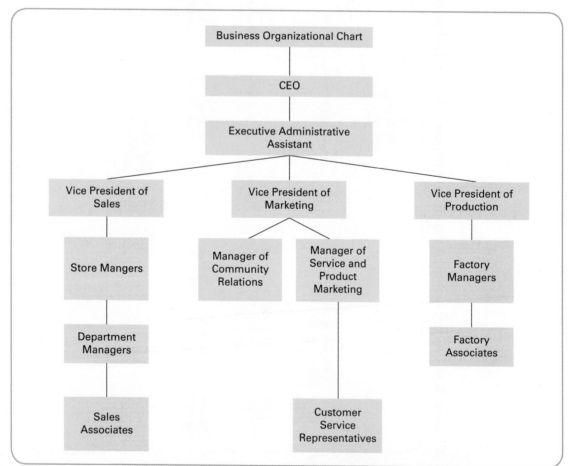

Figure 8.6 A Graphic Organizer for Types of Media in Art

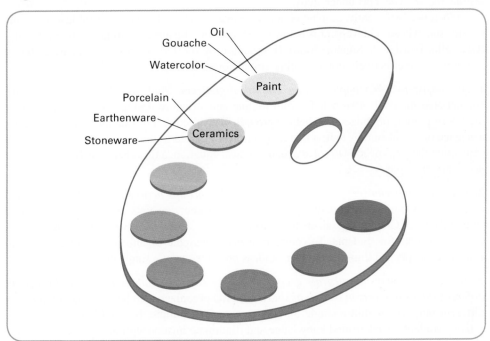

An art teacher used Figure 8.6 to show relationships among types of media used in art. She used an artist's palette rather than a tree diagram. After completing the entries for paint and ceramics herself, the teacher challenged her students to brainstorm other media that they had already used or knew about and to provide examples; she used the open areas on the palette to record students' associations.

When concepts are related to one another in terms of a chronological or linear order, the graphic organizer may be presented in the form of a time line (Parker & Jarolimek, 1997). Time lines can be used when subject area material requires students to understand a sequence of events or the procedural order required to complete a given task. Figure 8.7 shows a time line used in an art history class to illustrate some of the major periods relevant to that content area.

Graphic organizers are easily adapted to learning situations in the elementary grades. For class presentations, elementary teachers often construct organizers on large sheets of chart

Figure 8.7 A Time Line for Art History

1200s–1300s	1400s–1500s	1600s–1700s	1800s	1900s
Individualism in Italian Art	Italian Renaissance	Baroque Period of Europe	Romanticism, Impressionism, Abstract Art	Modernism

paper or on bulletin boards. Still other elementary teachers draw pictures with words that illustrate the key concepts under study.

When used efficiently, graphic organizers have been found to be powerful learning tools for students whose achievement is below grade level or who are exhibiting learning difficulty (Guastello, Beasley, & Sinatra, 2000). Baxendell (2003) offers the following research-based suggestions for effectively implementing graphic organizers:

1. *Be consistent when implementing graphic organizers.* Students who struggle to learn content area material often benefit from routine and structure. Using standard and familiar models of graphic organizers can help to provide that structure. For example, when reviewing a science or social studies unit, a tree diagram may be used to organize key concepts. When explaining the steps needed to solve a mathematical equation, a flowchart may best outline the necessary procedures.

2. *Use graphic organizers to coherently depict relationships between concepts.* For graphic organizers to be understandable, connections between concepts need to be clear and straightforward. Graphic organizers that are cluttered or disorganized can confuse, rather than clarify, concepts for students. To construct coherent graphic organizers, use clear labels to connect concepts and limit the number of ideas presented in any single graphic organizer.

3. *Seek creative ways to integrate graphic organizers across content areas and throughout different stages of a lesson or unit of study.* Graphic organizers can be used and adapted for different purposes within a single unit. They can, for example, be used before reading to activate students' background knowledge and illuminate misconceptions students may have about the topic to be studied. Graphic organizers can also be used during reading to clarify and synthesize concepts and after reading as a form of review. Encouraging students to incorporate illustrations into their graphic organizers can enhance their understanding of the content.

Showing Students How to Make Their Own Connections

Graphic organizers may be used by teachers to build a frame of reference for students as they approach new material. However, in a more student-centered adaptation of the graphic organizer, the students work in cooperative groups and organize important concepts into their own graphic representations.

To make connections effectively, students must have some familiarity with the concepts in advance of their study of the material. In addition, student-constructed graphic organizers presume that the students are aware of the idea behind a graphic organizer. If they are not, you will need to give them a rationale and then model the construction of an organizer. Exposure to teacher-constructed graphic organizers from past lessons also creates awareness and provides models for the instructional strategy.

To introduce students to the process of making their own graphic organizers, follow these steps:

1. *Type the keywords and make copies for students.*

2. *Have them form small groups of two or three students each.*

3. *Distribute the list of terms and a packet of three- by five-inch index cards to each group.*

4. *Have the students write each word from the list on a separate card.* Then have them work together to decide on a spatial arrangement of the cards that depict the major relationships among the words.

5. *As students work, provide assistance as needed.*

6. *Initiate a discussion of the constructed organizer.*

Before actually assigning a graphic organizer to students, you should prepare for the activity by carefully analyzing the vocabulary of the material to be learned. List all the terms that are essential for students to understand. Then add relevant terms that you believe the students already understand and that will help them relate what they know to the new material. Finally, construct your own organizer.

The form of the student-constructed graphic organizer will undoubtedly differ from the teacher's arrangement. However, this difference in and of itself should not be a major source of concern. What is important is that the graphic organizer support students' abilities to anticipate connections through the key vocabulary terms in content materials.

Activating What Students Know about Words

Graphic organizers may be used to (1) activate students' prior knowledge of the vocabulary words in a text assignment or unit of study and (2) clarify their understanding of concepts as they study text. From a strategy perspective, students need to learn how to ask the question, "What do I know about these words?" When you use graphic organizers before reading or talking about key concepts, help the students build strategy awareness by exploring key terms before assigning text to read. In addition, consider the use of a quasi-instructional/informal assessment strategy, known as Knowledge Rating (Blachowicz & Fisher, 1996), illustrated in Box 8.1 on page 255.

Word Exploration

Word exploration is a *writing-to-learn* strategy that works well as a vocabulary activity. Before asking students to make connections between the words and their prior knowledge, a biology teacher asked them to explore what they knew about the concept of *natural selection* by writing in their learning logs.

A word exploration activity invites students to write quickly and spontaneously, a technique called *freewriting,* for no more than five minutes, without undue concern about spelling, neatness, grammar, or punctuation. The purpose of freewriting is to get down on paper everything that students know about the topic or target concept. Students write freely for themselves, not for an audience, so the mechanical, surface features of language, such as spelling, are not important.

Word explorations activate schemata and jog long-term memory, allowing students to dig deep into the recesses of their minds to gather thoughts about a topic. Examine one of the word explorations for the target concept *natural selection*:

> Natural selection means that nature selects—kills off or does away with—the weak so only the strong make it. Like we were studying in class last time, things get so competitive, even among us for grades, jobs, and so on. The homeless are having trouble living—they have no place to call home except the street and nothing to eat. That's as good an example of natural selection as I can think of for now.

The teacher then has several of the students share their word explorations with the class, either reading them verbatim or talking through what they have written, and notes similarities and differences in the students' concepts. The teacher then relates their initial associations to the concept and asks the students to make further connections: "How does your personal understanding of the idea of *natural selection* fit in with some of the relationships that you see?"

Brainstorming

An alternative to word exploration, brainstorming is a procedure that quickly allows students to generate what they know about a key concept. In brainstorming, the students can access their prior knowledge in relation to the target concept. Brainstorming involves two basic steps that can be adapted easily to content objectives: (1) The teacher identifies a key concept that reflects one of the main topics to be studied in the text, and (2) students work in small groups to generate a list of words related to the concept in a given number of seconds.

List–Group–Label

Hilda Taba (1967) suggests an extension of brainstorming that she calls "list–group–label." When the brainstorming activity is over and *lists* of words have been generated by the students, have the class form learning teams to *group* the words into logical arrangements. Then invite the teams to *label* each arrangement. Once the list–group–label activity is completed, ask the students to make predictions about the content to be studied. For example, you might ask, "How does the title of the text (or thematic unit) relate to your groups of words?" or "Describe why you decided to group certain words together on one list rather than place them on a different list."

Wood (2001) suggests list–group–label–write as a variation of the original list–group–label strategy. Once they have completed the *list, group,* and *label* steps in the strategy, ask students, working individually or in pairs, to *write* a sentence or paragraph using the words from one of the lists. This writing task provides students with an opportunity to synthesize their understanding of how the words are related. It also illuminates important background knowledge that students bring to the text or unit, as well as any misconceptions that will need to be addressed as their study of the topic proceeds.

A teacher initiated a brainstorming activity in her high school geometry class. The students, working in small groups, were asked to list in four minutes as many words as possible that were related to geometry. Then the groups shared their lists of geometry words as the teacher created a master list on the board from the individual entries of the groups. She also wrote three categories on the board—Angles, Shapes, and Measures—and asked the groups to classify each word from the master list under one of the categories. Here's how one group organized some of the words from the master list:

ANGLES	SHAPES	MEASURES
acute	polygon	circumference
right	trapezoid	protractor
obtuse	triangle	radius
	circle	area
	square	perimeter

Note that in this example, the teacher provided the categories. She recognized that students needed the additional structure to be successful with this particular task. As a result of the activity, students were able to share what they knew with other members of the class and the teacher was able to identify gaps in students' understanding of concepts that could be addressed through subsequent readings and class discussions.

Word Sorts

Like brainstorming, word sorts require students to classify words into categories based on their prior knowledge. However, unlike brainstorming, students do not generate a list of words for a target concept. Instead, the teacher identifies the keywords from the unit of study and invites the students to sort them into logical arrangements of two or more.

A word sort is a simple yet valuable activity. Individually or in small groups, students literally sort out technical terms that are written on cards or listed on an exercise sheet. The object of word sorting is to group words into different categories by looking for shared features among their meanings. According to Gillet and Kita (1979, pp. 541–542), a word sort gives students the opportunity "to teach and learn from each other while discussing and examining words together."

Gillet and Kita (1979) also explain that there are two types of word sorts: the *open sort* and the *closed sort*. Both are easily adapted to any content area. In the closed sort, students know in advance of sorting what the main categories are. In other words, the criterion that the words in a group must share is stated. In a middle grade music class, students were studying the qualities of various "instrument families" of the orchestra. The music teacher assigned the class to work in pairs to sort musical instruments into four categories representing the major orchestral families: strings, woodwinds, brass, and percussion. Figure 8.8 represents the closed sort developed by one collaborative "think–pair–share" group. Similarly, Figure 8.9 shows how a science teacher applied the close sort strategy to a unit on macromolecules.

Open sorts prompt divergent and inductive reasoning. No category or criterion for grouping is known in advance of sorting. Students must search for meanings and discover relationships among technical terms without the benefit of any structure.

Figure 8.8   Closed Sort for Musical Instruments

Strings (bow or plucked)	Woodwinds (single or double reed)	Brass (lips vibrate in mouthpiece)	Percussion (sounds of striking)
Violin	Flute	Trumpet	Timpani
Viola	Piccolo	Trombone	Bass drum
Cello	Oboe	French horn	Chimes
Harp	Clarinet		Xylophone
	Saxophone		Bells
	Bassoon		Triangle
			Snare drum

Figure 8.9 Closed Sort for a Science Unit on Macromolecules

General	Carbohydrates	Lipids	Proteins	Nucleic Acids
Organic	Monosaccharide	Fatty acids	Amino acid	Nucleotide
Inorganic	Disaccharide	Glycerol	Hydrogen bond	Purine
Monomer	Starch	Hydrophobic	Polypeptide	Pyrimidine
Polymer	Glycogen	Saturated fat	Denaturation	Ribonucleic acid
Dehydration synthesis	Cellulose	Unsaturated fat	Activation energy	Deoxyribonucleic acid
Hydrolysis	Polysaccharide	Steroid	Peptide bond	Nitrogenous base
Anabolic	Fructose	Cholesterol	Enzyme	Adenine
Catabolic	Glucose		Catalyst	Guanine
Macromolecule	Maltose		Substrate	Cytosine
Polymerization	Sucrose		Active site	Thymine
				Uracil

Study how an art teacher activated what students knew about words associated with pottery making by using the open word sort strategy. She asked the high school students to work in collaborative pairs to arrange the following words into possible groups and to predict the concept categories in which the words would be classified:

jordan	lead	Cornwall stone	sgraffito
ball	chrome	cone	roka
antimony	slip	wheel	leather
cobalt	scale	bisque	hard
mortar	kaolin	stoneware	oxidation

Three categories that students formed were *types of clay, pottery tools,* and *coloring agents.* Open word sorts can be used before or after reading. Before reading, a word sort serves as an activation strategy to help learners make predictive connections among the words. After reading, word sorts enable students to clarify and extend their understanding of the conceptual relationships.

Knowledge Ratings

Text previewing strategies have been found to support students' comprehension (Bruns, Hodgson, Parker, & Fremont, 2011). As the procedure implies, knowledge ratings get readers to analyze what they know about a topic. Blachowicz (1986) recommends that teachers present students with a list of vocabulary in a survey-like format in which students must analyze each word individually, as in the two examples in Box 8.1.

BOX 8.1

Two Examples of Knowledge Ratings

Knowledge Rating*

How much do you know about these words?

	Can Define	Have Seen/Heard	?
exponent	X		
intersection	X		
domain			X
intercept		X	
slope		X	
parabola			X
origin		X	
vertex		X	
irrationals	X		
union		X	
coefficient		X	

*From a unit on quadratic functions and systems of equations in a high school math class.

Knowledge Rating*

How much do you know about these words?

	A Lot!	Have Seen/Heard	Not Much
publication design			
color schemes			
font schemes			
layout			
page content			
background fill			
website options			
design gallery			

*From a newspaper unit using Microsoft Publisher in a middle school language arts class.

A follow-up discussion might revolve around questions such as these: Which are the hardest words? Which do you think most of the class doesn't know? Which are the easiest ones? Which will most of us know? Students should be encouraged within the context of the discussion to share what they know about the words. In this way the teacher can assess and get some idea of the state of knowledge the class brings to the text reading or a larger unit of study.

These procedures are all a part of prereading preparation. Naturally it would be foolhardy to use all of these procedures at one time, but one or two in combination set the stage for students to read with some confidence in and competence with the language of the text.

Defining Words in the Context of Their Use

Before considering a variety of extension activities that put students in the position of clarifying and refining their knowledge of words and concepts, consider two strategies that permit text learners to define words in relation to the contexts in which they are used: the vocabulary self-collection strategy (VSS) and concept of definition (CD) procedure. By using a variety of instructional strategies for building content area vocabulary, teachers can help students to recognize when they do not understand a concept and know how they might apply different strategies to aid in their understanding of seemingly unfamiliar terms. Box 8.2 explains how one teacher helped her students to monitor their comprehension of concepts in their reading. Additionally, the VSS and concept of definition word maps (CD word maps) are two instructional strategies that make students aware of and build learning strategies for defining words. Both activities invite students to use their texts to determine how words are defined in their natural context.

stop when they reach an unknown word, and to write those words on an index card. If they are able to use a strategy they have learned to determine the meaning of the unknown word, the student can indicate that with a "star" on the card. If they are unable to determine the meaning, they can bring the card to the teacher's attention during the next class meeting, giving the teacher an opportunity to explicitly teach or re-teach the concept.

Several teachers who attended Betsy's in-service session tried this strategy with their students. One reported that it had "opened her eyes" to what struggling readers experience when they have a limited Tier II vocabulary. Another indicated that she never realized just how difficult it could be to comprehend a text when so many words were unfamiliar. A third teacher said she was saddened when she thought about what daily classroom life must be like for struggling

middle-grade readers, especially since she knew that very few ask for help, but simply sit, trying in blend in, hoping that no one will notice.

One teacher reported that, after meeting with a small group of students to preview the Tier II words she had selected, she noticed that all four students kept the index cards with them and referred to them while reading. As one student explained, she now "pays attention to the words," and when she encounters a word she does not know, she "just has to find out what it means." Vocabulary instruction is most effective when students are taught using explicit instruction and given multiple opportunities to experience words in context and with student-friendly definitions (Beck, McKeown, & Kucan, 2002). This simple strategy allows teachers to implement effective vocabulary instruction that incorporates each of those elements.

Vocabulary Self-Collection Strategy

Vocabulary self-collection strategy promotes the long-term acquisition of language in an academic discipline (Haggard, 1986). As a result of the repeated use of the strategy, students learn how to make decisions related to the importance of concepts and how to use context to determine what words mean. The VSS strategy has been found to be effective for teaching word meaning in context to students across ability levels (Harmon, Hedrick, Wood, & Gress, 2005) and for helping students to build independence as word learners (Ruddell & Shearer, 2002). VSS begins once students read and discuss a text assignment. The teacher asks students, who are divided into teams, to nominate one word that they would like to learn more about. The word must be important enough for the team to share it with the class. The teacher also nominates a word. Here are several suggested steps in VSS:

1. *Divide the class into nominating teams of two to five students.* Together the students on a nominating team decide which word to select for emphasis in the text selection.

2. *Present the word that each team has selected to the entire class.* A spokesperson for each team identifies the nominated word and responds to the following questions:

   a. *Where is the word found in the text?* The spokesperson reads the passage in which the word is located or describes the context in which the word is used.

   b. *What do the team members think the word means?* The team decides on what the word means in the context in which it is used. They must use information from the surrounding context and may also consult reference resources.

   c. *Why did the team think the class should learn the word?* The team must tell the class why the word is important enough to single out for emphasis.

To introduce VSS to the students, the teacher first presents his or her nominated word to the class, modeling how to respond to the three questions. During the team presentations, the teacher facilitates the discussion, writes the nominated words on the board with their meanings, and invites class members to contribute additional clarifications of the words.

To conclude the class session, students record all the nominated words and their meanings in a section of their learning logs or in a separate vocabulary notebook. These lists may be used for review and study. As a consequence of VSS, the teacher has a set of student-generated words that can be incorporated into a variety of follow-up vocabulary activities, as suggested in the next section.

Concept of Definition Word Maps

Although VSS provides opportunities to define and explore the meanings of words used in text readings, many students are not aware of the types of information that contribute to the meaning of a concept. Nor have they internalized a strategy for defining a concept based on the information available to them. In addition, words in a text passage often provide only partial contextual information for defining the meaning of a concept.

Concept of definition (CD) word maps provide a framework for organizing conceptual information in the process of defining a word (Schwartz, 1988; Schwartz & Raphael, 1985). Conceptual information can be organized in terms of three types of relationships:

The general class or category in which the concept belongs

The attributes or properties of the concept and those that distinguish it from other members of the category

Examples or illustrations of the concept

CD word map instruction supports vocabulary and concept learning by helping students internalize a strategy for defining and clarifying the meaning of unknown words. The hierarchical structure of a concept has an organizational pattern that is reflected by the general structure of a CD word map. In the center of the CD word map, students write the concept being studied. Working outward, they then write the word that best describes the general class or superordinate concept that includes the target concept. The answer to "What is it?" is the general class or category. Students then provide at least three examples of the concept as well as three properties by responding, respectively, to the questions, "What are some examples?" and "What is it like?" Comparison of the target concept is also possible when students think of an additional concept that belongs to the general class but is different from the concept being studied. Figure 8.10 provides an example of a CD word map for the word *tiger*.

Response Journal

Select a concept from your content area and develop a CD word map for it.

Schwartz (1988) recommends a detailed plan for modeling CD word maps with students. The plan includes demonstrating the value of CD word mapping by connecting its purpose to how people use organizational patterns to aid memory and interpretation; introducing the general structure of a CD word map, explaining how the three probes define a concept, walking students through the completion of a word map; and applying CD word mapping to an actual text selection.

Two caveats are relevant to CD word map instruction: CD word maps work best with concept words that function as nouns, but the procedure may be used, with some adaptation, with action words as well. Also, a potential misuse of CD word mapping occurs when teachers reproduce a general CD word map on the copier and expect students to define lists of words at the end of a text chapter. This is not the intent of CD word map instruction. Instead, students should

Figure 8.10   CD Word Map for the Word *Tiger*

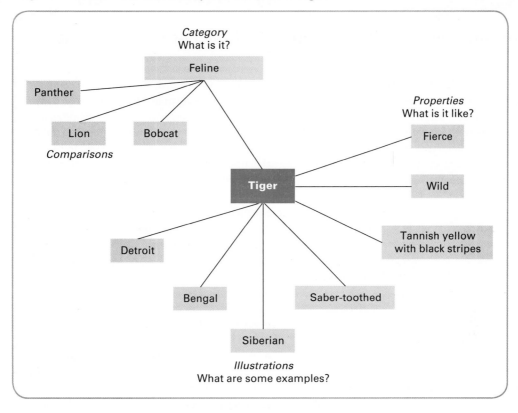

internalize the process through demonstration and actual use, applying it as they need it in actual text learning. Ultimately, the goal of CD word map instruction is to have students own the strategy of defining unknown words in terms of category, property, and example relationships.

 # Reinforcing and Extending Vocabulary Knowledge and Concepts

Students need many experiences, real and vicarious, to develop word meanings and concepts. They need to use, test, and manipulate technical terms in instructional situations that capitalize on reading, writing, speaking, and listening. In having students do these things, you create the kind of natural language environment that is needed to extend vocabulary and concept development. Various vocabulary extension activities can be useful in this respect. Box 8.3 explains how the RTI framework can help teachers to adjust instruction to meet the diverse learning needs of students.

These activities should be completed individually by students and then discussed either in small groups or in the class as a whole. The oral interaction in team learning gives more students a chance to use terms. Students can exchange ideas, share insights, and justify responses in a nonthreatening situation.

BOX 8.3   RTI for Struggling Adolescent Learners

Responsiveness to Vocabulary and Concept Development

As the vocabulary strategy interventions in this chapter suggest, using a single approach to vocabulary and concept development, such as a traditional dictionary definition approach, will not adequately meet the learning needs of all students or the standards of individualized and intensive instruction as outlined by RTI directives. Vocabulary instruction within the RTI framework can be modified to aptly address disparate student needs. For example, vocabulary instruction can be differentiated through the words chosen for study, pronunciation supports, decoding strategies, application of definitions, and the teaching of relationships to underscore the context of more complex words (Vaughn, Cirino, Wanzek, Wexler, Fletcher, & Denton, 2010). Adolescent learners, whether or not they are part of the RTI process, require instruction that is responsive to both their learning needs and their developmental level (Fuchs, Fuchs, & Compton, 2010) .

Some of the most successful strategies help students understand the importance of new vocabulary as it relates to their overall comprehension (Vaughn, 2010). RTI provides a framework for educators to create lessons so that students can learn vocabulary concepts as they relate to their understanding of the complete text. Struggling readers need both *direct* and *indirect* instruction to learn new vocabulary and concepts that can lead to improved comprehension (Bromley, 2007).

RTI requires classroom interventions to be "research based". While much is left to be learned about how students learn and retain new concepts, it is essential that teachers seek strategies that are shown to provide students with varied approaches to learning, using, and retaining new concepts, while improving their overall comprehension (Duff, Fieldsend, Bowyer-Crane, & Hulme, 2008). For Tier 1 accommodations, direct instruction may include whole class or small group instruction. For more intensive interventions, instruction should be based on a particular student's needs. Each intervention should be designed so that its impact can be assessed on a weekly or bi-weekly basis. The fidelity of the interventions, the assessments, and the analysis of the data to inform future instructional decisions, contributes to the success of RTI and supports thoughtful vocabulary instruction that allows each student to experience growth.

Semantic Feature Analysis (SFA)

Semantic feature analysis (SFA) establishes a meaningful link between students' prior knowledge and words that are conceptually related to one another. The strategy requires that you develop a chart or grid to help students analyze similarities and differences among the related concepts. As the SFA grid in Figure 8.11 illustrates, a topic or category (in this case, properties of quadrilaterals) is selected, words related to that category are written across the top of the grid, and features or properties shared by some of the words in the column are listed down the left side of the grid.

Students analyze each word, feature by feature, writing Y (yes) or N (no) in each cell of the grid to indicate whether the feature is associated with the word. Students may write a question mark (?) if they are uncertain about a particular feature.

A variation of a semantic feature analysis used in a computer science class is depicted in Figure 8.12. In developing this SFA, the teacher listed different types of web browsers down the left side of the grid. Words related to features that might be present in particular web browsers were listed across the top of the grid. Students were asked to use a plus sign (+) to indicate that a feature was present in a particular type of web browser or a minus sign (−) to indicate

Figure 8.11 A Semantic Feature Analysis for Geometry

Directions: Determine which of these properties is found in the four quadrilaterals listed. Mark "Y" or "N" in each box.

	Parallelogram	Rectangle	Rhombus	Square
Diagonals bisect each other.				
Diagonals are congruent.				
Each diagonal bisects a pair of opposite angles.				
Diagonals form two pairs of congruent triangles.				
Diagonals form four congruent triangles.				
Diagonals are perpendicular to each other.				

Figure 8.12 A Semantic Feature Analysis for Computer Applications

Directions: Determine which of these properties is found in the web browsers listed.

	RSS Support	Support for Active X	Google Search from Toolbar	Tabbed Browsing	Pop-Up Blocking	Themes/ Skins
Firefox						
Internet Explorer						
Opera						
Safari						

that a feature was not present. The teacher and her students revisited this SFA periodically throughout the course to update it as newer versions of some web browsers became available. Doing so led to class discussions on topics such as the marketing of web browsers, different ways that web servers ensure the security of customers who communicate and shop online, and technology's influence on the way people conduct everyday tasks such as information gathering, shopping, and bill paying.

As a teaching activity, SFA is easily suited to before- or after-reading instructional routines. If you used it before reading to activate what students know about words, recognize that they can return to the SFA after reading to clarify and reformulate some of their initial responses on the SFA grid. In Box 8.4, Voices from the Classroom, read how Tracy devised an effective SFA strategy for her biology class.

BOX 8.4 Voices from the Classroom

Tracy, Tenth-Grade Biology Teacher

Challenge

I noticed that students in my biology class seemed to have difficulty retaining information about specific concepts and vocabulary. Therefore, I wanted to incorporate strategies that would engage students more actively in learning important biology terms. In the past, I've had my students create vocabulary posters as part of their homework assignments. When studying the human body systems, students illustrated a given concept or term with a drawing, clip art, or a photo to help them remember the information. For example, when learning about the functions of the heart, some students represented this concept with an illustration of a pump, including a gasoline pump, bike pump, or even someone pumping iron. Students spent a lot of time on the assignment and enjoyed the activity but they didn't seem to remember the concepts and the vocabulary.

Strategy

In order to help students process the connections between a given concept and its meaning, I continued to incorporate the homework assignment of illustrating the vocabulary word. However, this time, I asked students to add some written explanation of why they made their decision to illustrate the concept the way they did. For example, if a student used a balloon to illustrate the bladder, I would expect them to write something about how the bladder is like a balloon (i.e., because it can stretch and hold things). By writing-to-learn, I hoped that students would be able to add the information to their long-term memory. More recently, I used the Semantic Feature Analysis as an informal assessment to see what students had learned so far about our topic of the excretory system. I began by creating a chart, shown below, with specific vocabulary, facts, and concepts chosen to summarize the topic we had been studying. I modeled the activity first by doing an example with my students. Then, they continued independently by analyzing each concept and marking the column with a + or − to indicate if the words were conceptually related to one another. They did well on those.

Excretory System	Lungs	Skin	Kidneys	Liver
Excretes water				
Excretes urea				
Excretes carbon dioxide				
Excretes urine				

Reflection

After enhancing the vocabulary illustration activity with a written component and by incorporating the Semantic Feature Analysis, students in my biology class were better able to create a meaningful link between concepts, their meanings, and their relationships to various body systems. Their performance on a quiz showed that students consistently had a better recall and a better understanding of the terms and concepts. When we reviewed for the quiz, the students seemed more confident in their answers where previously they tended to fish for the information and responses. Scores on the quiz itself improved compared to scores on previous quizzes. Even the typically struggling students scored 90 percent or above. Prior to using the Semantic Feature Analysis as a learning tool, these students performed inconsistently on assessments with scores ranging from 70 percent to 100 percent. Now the majority were at a mastery level.

Students were engaged during the Semantic Feature Analysis activity. They viewed it as a puzzle or game, and it was easy and fun for them to complete it. The novelty of the activity helped too. There was not a lot of writing, but they had to know the information in order to complete the activity successfully. Perhaps in the future, I will have students write a statement after completing the Semantic Feature Analysis to explain their thinking and to tie all of the information together. I have also created a Semantic Feature Analysis to review for the midterm exam. I hope that organizing and categorizing information will help students spark their memory and summarize the information learned in class.

Review for Midterm	Nervous System	Endocrine System
Carries electrical messages		
Carries chemical messages		
Carries messages on neurons		
Carries messages in blood stream		
Controls reactions to stimulus		
Involves brain and spinal cord		
Involves glands		
Message must jump over gap known as synapse		
Neurotransmitter must fit receptors on dendrite		
Involves hormones		
Involves receptors		
Involves target cells		
Hormones must fit receptor on target cell		
Involves neurotransmitters		
Involves dendrites		
Involves axons		
Message travels slower (minutes, hours, days)		
Message travels very fast (less than one second)		

Categorization Activities

Vocabulary extension exercises involving categorization require students to determine relationships among technical terms much as word sorts do. Students are usually given four to six words per grouping and asked to do something with them. That something depends on the format used in the exercise. For example, you can give students sets of words and ask them to circle in each set the word that includes the others. This exercise demands that students perceive common attributes or examples in relation to a more inclusive concept and to distinguish superordinate from subordinate terms. Following is an example from an eighth-grade social studies class.

Directions: Circle the word in each group that includes the others.

1. government   2. throne
   council   coronation
   judges   crown
   governor   church

A variation on this format directs students to cross out the word that does not belong and then to explain in a word or phrase the relationship that exists among the common items, as illustrated in the following example.

Directions: Cross out the word in each set that does not belong. On the line above the set, write the word or phrase that explains the relationship among the remaining three words.

1. _____   2. _____
   drama   time
   comedy   character
   epic   place
   tragedy   action

Figure 8.13   The Concept Circle

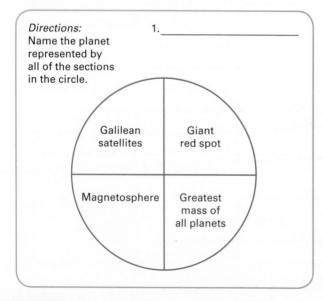

Concept Circles

One of the most versatile activities we have observed at a wide range of grade levels is the concept circle. Concept circles provide still another format and opportunity for studying words critically—for students to relate words conceptually to one another. A concept circle may simply involve putting words or phrases in the sections of a circle and directing students to describe or name the concept relationship among the sections. The example in Figure 8.13 is from a middle grade science lesson.

In addition, you might direct students to shade in the section of a concept circle containing a word or phrase that *does not relate* to the words or phrases in the other sections

Figure 8.14 A Variation on the Concept Circle

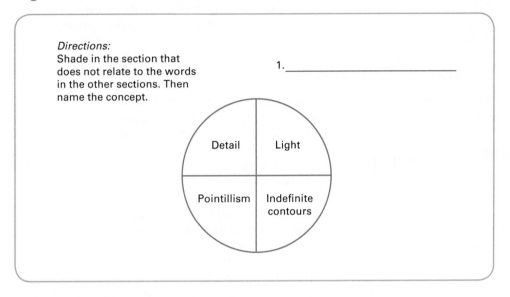

Figure 8.15 Another Variation on the Concept Circle

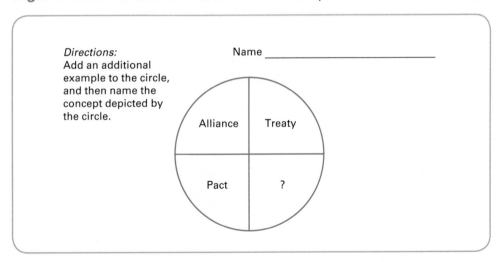

of the circle and then identify the concept relationships that exist among the remaining sections (see Figure 8.14).

Finally, you can modify a concept circle by leaving one or two sections of the circle empty, as in Figure 8.15. Direct students to fill in the empty section with a word or two that relates in some way to the terms in the other sections of the concept circles. Students must then justify their word choice by identifying the overarching concept depicted by the circle.

As you can see, concept circles serve the same function as categorization activities. However, students respond positively to the visual aspect of manipulating the sections in a circle. Whereas categorization exercises sometimes seem like tests to students, concept circles are fun to do.

Vocabulary Triangles

Vocabulary triangles are another visual tool for providing students with opportunities to consider the relationships among word concepts, and to apply those concepts in meaningful ways. Vocabulary triangles can be adapted for use across different content areas and for use with different levels of learners (Digby & Mayers, 1993). Figure 8.16 shows a vocabulary triangle used by a high school English teacher to help her students review and apply vocabulary concepts that had been discussed during their reading. She selected the words *elude, diabolical,* and *larceny* and placed each word in a corner of the triangle. Students were then asked to write sentences connecting the words from two corners of the triangle. Figure 8.17 shows how one student connected the words *elude* and *diabolical, diabolical* and *larceny,* and *larceny* and *elude,* creating a separate sentence for each word pair. By the time they had completed the triangle, students had applied each word twice in relation to another concept from their reading. Finally, as shown in Figure 8.18, students created one sentence that combined all three words from the triangle.

Figure 8.16   Vocabulary Triangle

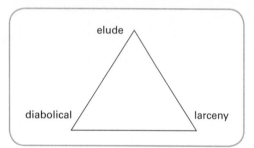

Figure 8.17   Vocabulary Triangle with Paired Sentences

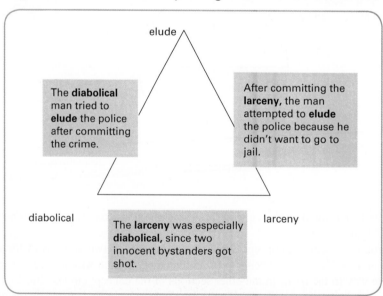

Magic Squares

The magic square activity is by no means new or novel, yet it has a way of reviving even the most mundane matching exercise. We have seen the magic square used successfully in elementary and secondary grades as well as in graduate courses. Here's how a magic square works. An activity sheet has two columns, one for content area terms and one for definitions or other distinguishing statements such as characteristics or examples (see Figure 8.19). Direct students to match terms with definitions. In doing so, they must take into account the letters signaling the terms and the numbers signaling the definitions. The students then put the number of a definition in the proper space (denoted by the letter of the term) in the "magic square answer box." If their matchups are correct, they will form a magic square. That is, the numerical total will be the same for each row across and each column down the answer box. This total forms the puzzle's "magic number." Students

Figure 8.18 Vocabulary Triangle with Combined Sentence

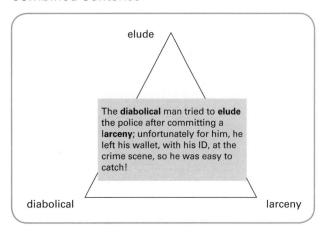

elude

The **diabolical** man tried to **elude** the police after committing a **larceny**; unfortunately for him, he left his wallet, with his ID, at the crime scene, so he was easy to catch!

diabolical   larceny

Figure 8.19 Magic Squares: Analyzing Food Labels

Directions: Select the best answer for each of the terms from the numbered definitions. Put the number in the proper space in the magic square box. If the totals of the numbers are the same both across and down, you have found the magic number!

A. Serving size
B. Servings per container
C. Calories
D. Fat, cholesterol, sodium
E. Fiber, vitamins
F. Trans fats, protein, and sugars
G. Percent daily value
H. 2,000
I. Footnote

1. Provides recommended dietary information for important nutrients, including fats, sodium, and fiber
2. The nutrients listed first should be limited
3. How many portions are in a package
4. Eating enough of these nutrients can improve your health and help reduce the risk of some diseases and conditions
5. Provides a measure of how much energy you get from a serving of this food
6. Recommendations for key nutrients but only for a 2,000 calorie daily diet
7. Influences the number of calories and all the nutrient amounts listed on the top part of the label
8. Recommended daily caloric intake
9. Nutrients without a percent daily value

A	B	C
D	E	F
G	H	I

Source: Information taken from the FDA website: www.cfsan.fda.gov/~dms/foodlab.html.

Figure 8.20 A Model of Magic Square Combinations

7	3	5
2	4	9
6	8	1

0*   15**

10	8	6
2	9	13
12	7	5

4*   24**

7	11	8
10	12	4
9	3	14

5*   26**

9	2	7
4	6	8
5	10	3

1*   18**

9	7	5
1	8	12
11	6	4

3*   21**

16	2	3	13
5	11	10	8
9	7	6	12
4	14	15	1

0*   34**

19	2	15	23	6
25	8	16	4	12
1	14	22	10	18
7	20	3	11	24
13	21	9	17	5

0*   65**

2	7	18	12
8	5	11	15
13	17	6	3
16	10	4	9

0*   39**

* Foils needed in answer column

**Magic number

need to add up the rows and columns to check if they're coming up with the same number each time. If not, they should go back to the terms and definitions to reevaluate their answers.

The magic square exercise in Figure 8.19 is from a family and consumer studies class. Try it. Its magic number is 15. Analyze the mental maneuvers that you went through to determine the correct number combinations. In some cases, you undoubtedly knew the answers outright. You may have made several educated guesses on others. Did you try to beat the number system? Imagine the possibilities for small-group interaction.

Many teachers are intrigued by the possibilities offered by the magic square, but they remain wary of its construction: "I can't spend hours figuring out number combinations." This is a legitimate concern. Luckily, the eight combinations in Figure 8.20 make magic square activities easy to construct. You can generate many more combinations from the eight patterns simply by rearranging rows or columns (see Figure 8.21).

Notice that the single asterisk in Figure 8.20 denotes the number of foils needed so that several of the combinations can be completed. For example, the magic number combination of 18 requires one foil in the number 1 slot that will not match with any of the corresponding items in the matching exercise. To complete the combination, the

Figure 8.21 Variations on Magic Square Combinations

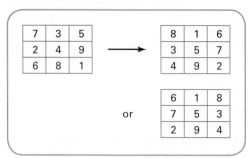

number 10 is added. Therefore, when you develop a matching activity for combination 18, there will be ten items in one column and nine in the other, with item 1 being the foil.

# Vocabulary-Building Strategies

Showing learners how to construct meaning for unfamiliar words encountered during reading helps them develop strategies needed to monitor comprehension and increase their own vocabularies. Demonstrating how to use *context, word structure,* and the *dictionary* provides students with several basic strategies for vocabulary learning that will last a lifetime. With these strategies, students can search for information clues while reading so that they can approximate the meanings of unknown words. These clues often reveal enough meaning to allow readers who struggle with text to continue reading without "short-circuiting" the process and giving up because the text does not make sense.

You can scaffold the use of vocabulary-building strategies before assigning material to be read. If one or more words represent key concepts—and the words lend themselves to demonstration—you can model the inquiry process necessary to construct meaning. The demonstration is brief, often lasting no more than five minutes. There are three types of demonstrations that will make students aware of vocabulary-building strategies. The first is to model how to make sense of a word in the context of its use, the second involves an analysis of a word's structure, and the third combines context and word structure. Usually these demonstrations require the use of visuals, such as an overhead transparency or a whiteboard. After the brief demonstration, guide students to practice and apply the strategy that you just modeled so that they can become proficient in its use.

Using Context to Approximate Meaning

Constructing meaning from context is one of the most useful strategies at the command of proficient readers. Showing readers who struggle how to make use of context builds confidence and competence and teaches the inquiry process necessary to unlock the meaning of troublesome technical and general vocabulary encountered during reading. Using context involves using information surrounding a difficult word to help reveal its meaning. Every reader makes some use of context automatically. Strategy instruction, however, is needed when the text provides a *deliberate context* to help the reader with concept terms that are especially difficult. Often the text author will anticipate that certain words will be troublesome and will provide information clues and contextual aids to help readers with meaning. In these instances, students will benefit from a strategy that allows them to use the deliberate context to construct meaning.

The use of context is mostly a matter of inference. Inference requires readers to see an explicit or implicit relationship between an unfamiliar word and its context or to connect what they know already with the unknown term. It can't be assumed that students will perceive these relationships or make the connections on their own. Most students who struggle with text simply don't know how to use a deliberate context provided by an author. Three kinds of information in particular are useful to struggling readers: *typographic, syntactic, semantic,* and *logographic* clues and cues.

Typographic Clues

Typographic or format clues make use of footnotes, italics, boldface print, parenthetical definitions, pictures, graphs, charts, and the like. A typographic clue provides a clear-cut connection
and a direct reference to an unknown word. Many students tend to gloss over a typographic
aid instead of using it to spotlight the meaning of a difficult term. The teacher can rivet attention to these aids with minimal expenditure of class time.

For example, consider the way a science teacher modeled a strategy for revealing the
meaning of the word *enzymes,* which was presented in boldface type in the text. Before assigning a text section titled "Osmosis in Living Cells," the teacher asked students to "turn to page
241." Then he asked, "Which word in the section on osmosis stands out among the others?"
The students quickly spotted the word *enzymes.* "Why do you think this word is highlighted
in boldface type?" he asked. A student replied, "I guess it must be important." Another student
said, "Maybe because it has something to do with osmosis—whatever that is." The teacher
nodded approvingly and then asked the class to see if they could figure out what *enzymes* meant
by reading this sentence: "Chemical substances called **enzymes** are produced by cells to break
down large starch molecules into small sugar molecules."

The science teacher continued the demonstration by asking two questions: "What are
enzymes?" and "What do they do?" The students responded easily. The teacher concluded the
walk-through with these words: "Words that are put in large letters or boldfaced print are
important. If you pay attention to them as we just did, you will have little trouble figuring out
what they mean. There are four other words in boldfaced type in your reading assignment.
Look for them as you read and try to figure out what they mean."

Syntactic and Semantic Clues

Syntactic and semantic clues in content materials should not be treated separately. The grammatical relationships among words in a sentence or the structural arrangement among sentences
in a passage often helps clarify the meaning of a particular word.

Syntactic and semantic clues are much more subtle than typographic clues. Table 8.1
presents a summary of the most frequently encountered syntactic and semantic clues.

Help students visualize the inquiry process necessary to reveal meaning. For example, if
a *definition clue* is used, as in this example from Table 8.1 ("Entomology is the study of insects,
and biologists who specialize in this field are called entomologists") it may be appropriate first
to display the term. During the modeling discussion, you can then show how *is* and *are called*
provide information clues that reveal meaning for *entomology* and *entomologists.* A simple
strategy would be to cross out *is* and *are called* in the sentence and replace them with equal
signs (=):

Entomology ~~is~~ = the study of insects, and biologists who specialize in this field ~~are called~~ = entomologists.

A brief discussion will reinforce the function of the verb forms *is* and *are called* in the
sentence.

The definition clue is the least subtle of the syntactic and semantic clues. However, all the
clues in Table 8.1 require students to make inferential leaps. Consider one of the examples from
the mood and tone clue: "The tormented animal screeched with horror and writhed in pain as
it tried desperately to escape from the hunter's trap." Suppose this sentence came from a short
story about to be assigned in an English class. Assume also that many of the students would
have trouble with the word *tormented* as it is used in the sentence. If students are to make the

Table 8.1   Syntactic and Semantic Contextual Clues

Type of Clue	Explanation	Examples
Definition	The author equates the unknown word to the known or more familiar, usually using a form of the verb *be*.	*Entomology* **is** the study of insects, and biologists who specialize in this field **are called** *entomologists*. A *critical review* **is** an attempt to evaluate the worth of a piece of writing.
Linked synonyms	The author pairs the unknown word with familiar synonyms or closely related words in a series.	Kunte Kinte was the victim of **cruel, evil,** *malevolent,* and **brutal** slave traders. The senator from Connecticut possessed the traits of an honest and just leader: **wisdom, judgment,** *sagacity.*
Direct description: examples, modifiers, restatements	The author reveals the meaning of an unknown word by providing additional information in the form of appositives, phrases, clauses, or sentences.	*Example clue:* Undigested material **such as fruit skins, outer parts of grain, and the string-like parts of some vegetables** forms *roughage.* *Modifier clues:* Pictographic writing, **which was the actual drawing of animals, people, and events,** is the forerunner of written language. *Algae,* **nonvascular plants that are as abundant in water as grasses are on land,** have often been called "grasses of many waters." *Restatement clue:* A billion dollars a year is spent on *health quackery.* **In other words, each year in the United States, millions of dollars are spent on worthless treatments and useless gadgets to "cure" various illnesses.**
Contrast	The author reveals the meaning of an unknown word by contrasting it with an antonym or a phrase that is opposite in meaning.	You have probably seen animals perform tricks at the zoo, on television, or in a circus. Maybe you taught a dog to fetch a newspaper. **But learning tricks—usually for a reward—is very different from** *cognitive problem solving.* It wasn't a *Conestoga* like Pa's folks came in. **Instead, it was just an old farm wagon drawn by one tired horse.**
Cause and effect	The author establishes a cause-and-effect relationship in which the meaning of an unknown word can be hypothesized.	The *domestication* of animals probably began when young animals were caught or strayed into camps. **As a result, people enjoyed staying with them and made pets of them.** A family is *egalitarian* **when both husband and wife make decisions together and share responsibilities equally**.
Mood and tone	The author sets a mood (ironic, satirical, serious, funny, etc.) in which the meaning of an unknown word can be hypothesized.	A sense of *resignation* engulfed my thoughts as **the feeling of cold grayness was everywhere around me**. The *tormented* animal **screeched with horror and writhed in pain as it tried desperately to escape** from the hunter's trap.

*Italics denote the unknown words. Boldface type represents information clues that trigger context revelation.

connection between *tormented* and the mood created by the information clues, the teacher will have to ask several effective clarifying questions.

The demonstration begins with the teacher writing the word *tormented* on the board. She asks, "You may have heard or read this word before, but how many of you think that you know what it means?" Student definitions are put on the board. The teacher then writes the sentence on the board. "Which of the definitions on the board do you think best fits the word *tormented* when it's used in this sentence?" She encourages students to support their choices. If none fits, she will ask for more definitions now that students have seen the sentence. She continues questioning, "Are there any other words or phrases in the sentence that help us get a feel for the meaning of *tormented*? Which ones?"

The inquiry into the meaning of *tormented* continues in this fashion. The information clues (*screeched with horror, writhed in pain, desperately*) that establish the mood are underlined and discussed. The teacher concludes the modeling activity by writing five new words on the board and explaining, "These words are also in the story that you are about to read. As you come across them, stop and think. How do the words or phrases or sentences surrounding each word create a certain feeling or mood that will allow you to understand what each one means?"

When modeling the use of context in Table 8.1, it's important for students to discover the information clues. It's also important for the teacher to relate the demonstration to several additional words to be encountered in the assignment. Instruction of this type will have a significant cumulative effect. If students are shown how to use contextual clues for two or three words each week, over the course of an academic year they will have 80 to 120 applications in the process.

Logographic Cues

Logographs are visual symbols that represent a word. When paired with vocabulary instruction, logographs can become logographic cues (Beers, 2003) to support students' understanding of vocabulary concepts. Logographic cues are visual aids that students create to help them learn vocabulary concepts. On the front of a note card, students write the vocabulary word they are trying to learn; on the back of the note card, students write the definition in their own words, as well as their own visual representation of the word based on its meaning. The visualization required in generating their own cue, can help students to understand and retain vocabulary concepts, and to make connections between their own image of a concept and its definition (Harvey & Goudvis, 2007). Logographic cues are particularly effective in content areas such as science because they help students to see abstract concepts, such as atoms and protons, in ways that make sense to them. By taking the time to think logically about a word and to create a visual representation for it, students are more likely to understand and remember its meaning.

Context-Related Activities

Readers who build and use contextual knowledge are able to recognize fine shades of meaning in the way words are used. They know the concept behind the word well enough to use that concept in different contexts. In the following sections, we suggest two ways to extend a student's contextual knowledge of content area terms.

Modified Cloze Passages

Cloze passages can be created to reinforce technical vocabulary. However, the teacher usually modifies the procedure for teaching purposes. Every *n*th word, for example, needn't be deleted. The modified cloze passage will vary in length. Typically, a 200- to 500-word text segment yields sufficient technical vocabulary to make the activity worthwhile.

Should you consider developing a modified cloze passage on a segment of text from a reading assignment, make sure that the text passage is one of the most important parts of the assignment. Depending on your objectives, students can supply the missing words either before or after reading the entire assignment. If they work on the cloze activity before reading, use the subsequent discussion to build meaning for key terms and to raise expectations for the assignment as a whole. If you assign the cloze passage after reading, it will reinforce concepts attained through reading.

On completing a brief prereading discussion on the causes of the Civil War, an American history teacher assigned a cloze passage before students read the entire introduction for homework. See how well you fare on the first part of the exercise.

What caused the Civil War? Was it inevitable? To what extent and in what ways was slavery to blame? To what extent was each region of the nation at fault? Which were more decisive—the intellectual or the emotional issues?

Any consideration of the (1) of the war must include the problem of (2). In his second inaugural address, Abraham Lincoln said that slavery was "somehow the cause of the war." The critical word is "(3)." Some (4) maintain that the moral issue had to be solved, the nation had to face the (5), and the slaves had to be (6). Another group of historians asserts that the war was not fought over (7). In their view, slavery served as an (8) focal point for more fundamental (9) involving two different (10) of the Constitution. All of these views have merit, but no single view has won unanimous support.
(Answers can be found on page 278.)

OPIN

OPIN is a meaning-extending vocabulary strategy developed by Frank Greene of McGill University. OPIN provides another example of context-based reinforcement and extension. OPIN stands for *opinion* and also plays on the term *cloze*.

Here's how OPIN works. Divide the class into groups of three. Distribute exercise sentences, one to each student. Each student must complete each exercise sentence individually. Then each group member must convince the other two members that his or her word choice is the best. If no agreement is reached on the best word for each sentence, each member of the group can speak to the class for his or her individual choice. When all groups have finished, have the class discuss each group's choices. The only rule of discussion is that each choice must be accompanied by a reasonable defense or justification. Answers such as "Because ours is best" are not acceptable.

OPIN exercise sentences can be constructed for any content area. Following are sample sentences from science, social studies, and family and consumer studies:

SCIENCE

1. A plant's _____ go into the soil.

2. The earth gets heat and _____ from the sun.

3. Some animals, such as birds and _____ are nibblers.

SOCIAL STUDIES

1. We cannot talk about _____ in America without discussing the homeless.

2. The thought of _____ or revolution would be necessary because property owners would fight to hold on to their land.

3. Charts and graphs are used to _____ information.

FAMILY AND CONSUMER STUDIES

1. Vitamin C is _____ from the small intestine and circulates to every tissue.

2. Washing time for cottons and linens is eight to ten minutes unless the clothes are badly _____.

(Answers can be found on page 278.)

OPIN encourages differing opinions about which word should be inserted in a blank space. In one sense, the exercise is open to discussion, and as a result, it reinforces the role of prior knowledge and experiences in the decisions that each group makes. The opportunity to "argue" one's responses in the group leads not only to continued motivation but also to a discussion of word meanings and variations.

Word Structure

In addition to emphasizing context as a vocabulary-building strategy, showing learners how to approximate word meaning through word structure is another important aspect of vocabulary building. A word itself provides information clues about its meaning. The smallest unit of meaning in a word is called a *morpheme*. Analyzing a word's structure, *morphemic analysis,* is a second vocabulary-building strategy that students can use to predict meaning. When readers encounter an unknown word, they can reduce the number of feasible guesses about its meaning considerably by approaching the whole word and identifying its parts. When students use morphemic analysis in combination with context, they have a powerful strategy at their command. The relationship between morphology knowledge and vocabulary development appears to be reciprocal: Students who have acquired larger vocabularies tend to have a greater understanding of morphology, and building an understanding of morphology helps students to expand their vocabularies (Kieffer & Lesaux, 2007).

Student readers often find long words daunting. A long or polysyllabic word falls within one of four categories:

1. *Compound words made up of two known words joined together.* Examples: *commonwealth, matchmaker.*

2. *Words containing a recognizable stem to which an affix (a prefix, combining form, or suffix) has been added.* Examples: *surmountable, deoxygenize, unsystematic, microscope.*

3. *Words that can be analyzed into familiar and regular pronounceable units.* Examples: *undulate, calcify, subterfuge, strangulate.*

4. *Words that contain irregular pronounceable units so that there is no sure pronunciation unless one consults a dictionary.* Examples: *louver, indictment.*

Content vocabulary terms from categories 1 and 2 (compound words and recognizable stems and affixes) are the best candidates for instruction. You can readily demonstrate techniques for predicting the meanings of these words because each of their isolated parts will always represent a meaning unit.

In some instances, a word from category 3 may also be selected for emphasis. However, there is no guarantee that students will bring prior knowledge and experience to words that comprise the third category. Long phonemically regular words lend themselves to syllabication. Syllabication involves breaking words into pronounceable sound units or syllables. The word *undulate,* for example, can be syllabicated (un-du-late). However, the syllable *un* is not a meaning-bearing prefix.

Many words from category 3 are derived from Latin or Greek. Students who struggle with texts will find these words especially difficult to analyze for meaning because of their lack of familiarity with Latin or Greek roots. Occasionally, a word such as *strangulate* (derived from the Latin *strangulatus*) can be taught because students may recognize the familiar word *strangle.* They might then be shown how to link *strangle* to the verb suffix *-ate* (which means "to cause to become") to hypothesize a meaning for *strangulate.* Unfortunately, the verb suffix *-ate* has multiple meanings, and the teacher should be quick to point this out to students. This procedure is shaky, but it has some payoff.

Words from category 2 warrant instruction, because English root words are more recognizable, obviously, than Latin or Greek ones. Whenever feasible, teach the principles of structural word analysis using terms that have English roots. Certain affixes are more helpful than others, and knowing which affixes to emphasize during instruction will minimize students' confusion.

The most helpful affixes are the combining forms, prefixes, or suffixes that have single, invariant meanings. (See Appendix A.) Many other commonly used prefixes have more than one meaning or have several shades of meaning. Because of their widespread use in content terminology, you should also consider these variant-meaning prefixes for functional teaching. (See Appendix B for a list of prefixes with varying meanings.)

The tables of affixes are resources for you. Don't be misled into thinking that students should learn long lists of affixes in isolation to help in analyzing word structure. This approach is neither practical nor functional. We recommend instead that students be taught affixes as they are needed to analyze the structure of terms that will appear in a reading assignment.

For example, an English teacher modeled how to analyze the meaning of *pandemonium* before students were to encounter the term in an assignment from *One Flew over the Cuckoo's Nest.* She wrote the word on the board—pan*demon*ium—underlining the English base word *demon,* and asked students for several synonyms for the word. Student responses included *witch, devil, monster,* and *wicked people.*

Then she explained that *-ium* was a noun suffix meaning "a place of." "Now let's take a look at *pan.* Sheila, have you ever heard of the Pan American Games? They are similar to the Olympics, but what do you think is a major difference between the Olympics and the Pan American Games?" Sheila and several students responded to the question. A brief discussion led the students to conclude the Pan American Games, like the Olympics, are a series of athletic contests; however, unlike the Olympics, only countries in North, Central, and South America and the Caribbean participate in the Pan American Games. The teacher affirmed the students' conclusions and noted that Pan American means quite literally, "all the Americas." Further discussion centered around the word *panoramic.* Through this process, relating the known to the unknown, students decided that *pan* meant "all."

"Now, back to *pandemonium.* 'A place of all the demons.' What would this place be like?" Students were quick to respond. The demonstration was completed with two additional points. The teacher asked the class to find the place in *One Flew over the Cuckoo's Nest* where *pandemonium* was used and read the paragraph. Then she asked them to refine their predictions of the meaning of *pandemonium.* Next the teacher discussed the origin of the word—which the English poet John Milton coined in his epic poem *Paradise Lost.* Pandemonium was the capital of hell, the place where all the demons and devils congregated—figuratively speaking, where "all hell broke loose."

Using the Dictionary as a Strategic Resource

The use of context and word structure are strategies that give struggling readers insight into the meanings of unknown words. Rarely does context or word structure help learners derive precise definitions for keywords. Instead, these vocabulary-building strategies keep readers on the right track so that they are able to follow a text without getting bogged down or giving up.

There are times, however, when context and word structure reveal little about a word's meaning. In these instances, or when a precise definition is needed, a dictionary is a logical alternative and a valuable resource for students.

Knowing when to use a dictionary is as important as knowing how to use it. A content teacher should incorporate dictionary usage into ongoing plans but should avoid a very common pitfall in the process of doing so. When asked, "What does this word mean?" the teacher shouldn't automatically reply, "Look it up in the dictionary."

To some students, "Look it up in the dictionary" is another way of saying "Don't bug me" or "I really don't have the time or the inclination to help you." From an instructional perspective, that hard-to-come-by teachable moment is lost whenever we routinely suggest to students to look up a word in a conventional or electronic dictionary.

One way to make the dictionary a functional resource is to use it to verify educated guesses about word meaning revealed through context or word structure. For example, if a student asks you for the meaning of a vocabulary term, an effective tactic is to bounce the question right back: "What do you think it means? Let's look at the way it's used. Are there any clues to its meaning?" If students are satisfied with an educated guess because it makes sense, the word need not be looked up. But if students are still unsure of the word's meaning, the dictionary is there.

When students go into a dictionary or an online vocabulary site to verify or to determine a precise definition, more often than not they need supervision to make good decisions. Keep these tips in mind as you work on dictionary usage.

1. *Help students determine the "best fit" between a word and its definition.* Students must often choose the most appropriate definition from several. This poses a real dilemma for young learners. Your interactions will help them make the best choice of a definition and will provide a behavior model for making such a choice.

2. *If you do assign a list of words to look up in a dictionary, choose them selectively.* A few words are better than many. The chances are greater that students will learn several key terms thoroughly than that they will develop vague notions about many.

3. *Help students with the pronunciation key in a glossary or dictionary as the need arises.* This does not mean, however, that you will teach skills associated with the use of a

pronunciation key in isolated lessons. Instead, it means guiding and reinforcing students' abilities to use a pronunciation key as they study the content of your course.

Vocabulary development is a gradual process, "the result of many encounters with a word towards a more precise grasp of the concept the word represents" (Parry 1993, p. 127). If this is the case, students who struggle with demanding text material will benefit from vocabulary-building strategies that make use of context clues, word structure, and appropriate uses of reference tools such as the dictionary.

Looking Back | Looking Forward

A strong relationship exists between vocabulary knowledge and reading comprehension. In this chapter, we shared numerous examples of what it means to teach words well: giving students multiple opportunities to build vocabulary knowledge, to learn how words are conceptually related to one another, and to learn how they are defined contextually in the material that students are studying. Vocabulary activities provide students the multiple experiences they need to use and manipulate words in different situations. Conceptual and definitional activities provide the framework needed to study words critically. Various types of concept activities—such as semantic feature analysis, concept of definition word maps, word sorts, categories, concept circles, and magic squares—reinforce and extend students' abilities to perceive relationships among the words they are studying.

In the next chapter, we underscore the interrelationships between reading, thinking, and writing processes as we explore the role of writing in content area learning. The ideas presented in the chapter are intended to show how writing activity can and must go beyond "mechanical uses" in the content classroom.

Minds On

1. A few of your students come to you and ask why they aren't using dictionaries to help them learn vocabulary words as they did last year. What is your response? Justify your response.

2. Each of the following statements should be randomly assigned to members of your group. Your task with your drawn statement is to play the devil's advocate. Imagine that you are in a conference with other teachers, all of whom have the same students in their classes. One member of the teaching team, represented by the other members of your discussion group, makes the statement you've selected, and you totally disagree. Argue to these teachers why you believe this statement is false. Members of the teaching team must respond with counterarguments, using classroom examples for support whenever possible.

   a. Students who are interested and enthusiastic are more likely to learn the vocabulary of a content area subject.

   b. Students need to know how to inquire into the meanings of unknown words by using context analysis and dictionary skills.

   c. An atmosphere for vocabulary reinforcement is created by activities involving speaking, listening, writing, and reading.

   d. Vocabulary reinforcement provides opportunities for students to increase their knowledge of the technical vocabulary of a subject.

   e. Vocabulary taught and reinforced within the framework of concept development enhances reading comprehension.

f. Vocabulary knowledge and reading comprehension have a strong relationship.

Were there any statements that you had difficulty contradicting? If so, pose these to the class as a whole, and solicit perspectives from other groups.

3. Your principal notices that your history class spends a lot of time working in pairs and groups on vocabulary, and she doesn't understand why this is necessary "just to learn words." As a group, compose a letter to her explaining the importance of student interaction in learning the vocabulary of any content area.

Hands On

1. Working in small groups of four or five students from the same or related content areas, have each student interview two teachers from the same content area about the type of vocabulary strategies used by the teacher to help students understand content area concepts. Ask teachers about how they apply some of the strategies from this chapter and note those strategies that seem to be particularly useful for certain content areas. Did the teachers adapt any of the strategies? Did they use additional vocabulary building strategies? When all interviews are complete, discuss your findings with the small group. How might the information from these interviews inform your vocabulary instruction practices as a content area teacher?

2. Examine the following list of vocabulary words taken from this chapter:

Tier 1 words	comprehension
Tier 2 words	semantic feature
Tier 3 words	analysis
concept	concept circles
word sorts (open, closed)	OPIN
	word puzzles
brainstorming	magic squares
semantic word maps	prior knowledge
knowledge ratings	modified cloze passages
syntactic and semantic contextual aids	

Team with three other members of the class, and with this list of words, each create one of the following:

a. Two conceptually related activities, such as a set of concept circles and a closed word sort

b. A context activity that presents the key concept words in meaningful sentence contexts

c. A semantic word map or a semantic feature analysis

Follow this activity with a discussion of the advantages and disadvantages of each approach and of the appropriate time during a unit to use each.

ANSWERS TO CLOZE PASSAGE

1. causes   **2.** slavery   **3.** somehow   **4.** historians
5. crisis   **6.** freed   **7.** slavery   **8.** emotional
9. issues   **10.** interpretations

POSSIBLE ANSWERS TO OPIN EXERCISES

Science: **1.** roots   **2.** radiation   **3.** rodents
Social Studies: **1.** poverty   **2.** violence   **3.** organize
Family and Consumer Studies: **1.** absorbed   **2.** soiled

eResources

Discovery Education offers a site that allows users to create word puzzles (**http://puzzlemaker.discoveryeducation .com**). Design a puzzle based on vocabulary words from a chapter of a content area text. Seek out vocabulary-building strategies in your content area by using the keywords "vocabulary + lessons + (content area)" to conduct an Internet search. Many links will come up. Consider the value of each site and identify the best sites.

TeacherVision offers downloadable graphic organizers for immediate use (**www.teachervision.fen.com/graphic-organizers/printable/6293.html**). Explore the Internet further for content-specific graphic organizers by using the keywords "graphic organizers + (content area)."

MyEducationLab™

Go to Topic 6: Vocabulary, the MyEducationLab (**www.myeducationlab.com**) for *Content Area Reading*, where you can:

- Find learning outcomes for Vocabulary, along with the national standards that connect to these outcomes.
- Complete Assignments and Activities that can help you more deeply understand the chapter content.
- Practice the core teaching skills identified in the chapter with the Building Teaching Skills and Dispositions learning units.
- Check your comprehension on the content covered in the chapter with the Study Plan. Here you will be able to take a chapter quiz, receive feedback on your answers, and then access Review, Practice, and Enrichment activities to enhance your understanding of chapter content.
- Visit A+RISE. A+RISE® Standards2Strategy™ is an innovative and interactive online resource that offers new teachers in grades K–12 just in time, research-based instructional strategies that meet the linguistic needs of English Language Learners (ELLs) as they learn content, differentiate instruction for all grades and abilities, and are aligned to Common Core Elementary Language Arts standards (for the literacy strategies) and to English language proficiency standards in World-Class Instructional Design and Assessment (WIDA), Texas, California, and Florida.
- Use the Online Lesson Plan Builder to practice lesson planning and integrating national and state standards into your planning.

9 Writing Across the Curriculum

Organizing Principle

Writing activates learning by helping students to explore, clarify, and think deeply about the ideas and concepts they encounter in reading.

Writing, thinking, and good old-fashioned hard work are tied together in ways that cannot be disentangled.

But writing is also a daunting process for many of us. As Gene Fowler, another well-known twentieth-century journalist and author put it: "Writing is easy. All you do is sit staring at a blank sheet of paper until the drops of blood form on your forehead." Whether today's students put pen to paper or create digital texts, *academic writing* can be an intimidating process at times, but it is also an indispensible tool for thinking and learning in content area classrooms. No wonder teachers use a variety of informal and formal writing activities to activate thinking and learning in their disciplines.

In other chapters, we have recommended instructional strategies involving writing to support students' thinking and learning with all kinds of texts. In this chapter, however, our intent is to highlight and reaffirm the powerful learning opportunities that arise whenever teachers connect reading and writing in their classrooms. A classroom environment that supports reading and writing invites students to explore ideas, clarify meaning, and construct knowledge. When reading and writing are taught in tandem, the union influences content learning in ways not possible when students read without writing or write without reading. When teachers invite a class to write before or after reading, they motivate students to use writing to think about what they will read and to think more deeply about the ideas they have read.

Sometimes reading and writing are taught in classrooms as if they bear little relationship to each

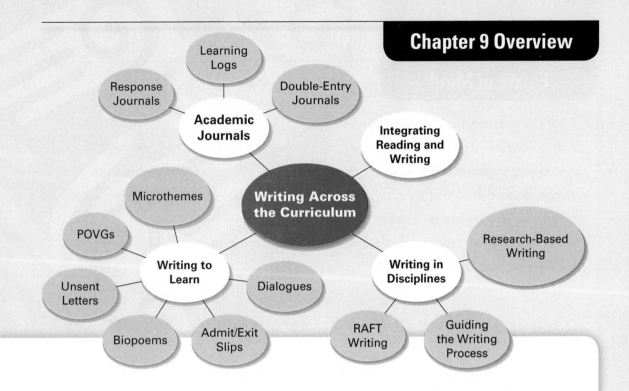

other. The result has often been to sever the powerful bonds for meaning-making that exist between reading and writing. There's little to be gained from teaching reading apart from writing. The organizing principle reflects this notion: Writing activates learning by helping students to explore, clarify, and think deeply about the ideas and concepts they encounter in reading.

Frame of Mind

1. Why emphasize writing to learn in content areas?

2. Why integrate writing and reading?

3. How might teachers create occasions for students to write to read and to read to write?

4. How can teachers use exploratory writing activities to motivate students to read and write?

5. How can teachers use journals to connect writing and reading?

6. How can teachers develop essay writing assignments through RAFT activities?

7. Why and how do teachers guide the writing process?

Several years ago, a teacher shared with us a letter from her grandmother, affectionately known as "Granma Z." Granma Z was living in a nursing home and into the tenth decade of her life. She wrote crookedly across the lines of her writing paper:

> Dear Betty,
>
>   Well Lyle got me a tablet with lines Ardella said use it anyway. We have another lady here now—In her 80, yrs—I am not feeling so good getting old age pains I guess I rode down town to day with Lyle—any way—And it wont be long till I cant write any more. Got my nose almost on the paper now. Joe is all thru as manager now and they are taking a vacation. well news are scarce so will close. I owe Conie a letter too
>   From Granma Z.
>   How is Grama Ethel doin?

Granma Z is "old school." Writing with pen and paper is important to her, even as she approaches 100 years old. Although her eyesight is failing and she physically struggles to get her thoughts on paper, she keeps on writing to her loved ones. It's worth it! Her writing is riddled with spelling and grammatical errors; yet Granma Z has a strong need to communicate and to stay in touch with her family.

Social writing is as important to Granma Z as it is to today's youth. The social writing of adolescents, however, has not been without its controversies. There is a prevailing societal notion that texting, instant messaging, or posting on Facebook are harming adolescents' ability to use language effectively in their writing. Whether or not this is the case, writing for social purposes is an integral part of students' lives today (Sweeny, 2010). Although the majority of today's adolescents do not identify social writing as "real writing," they do recognize the importance of academic writing in their school lives (Lenhart, Arafeh, Smith, & Macgill, 2008). Unfortunately, students often perceive academic writing tasks to be limited in scope; that is, short responses to homework questions—a conclusion that many writing researchers have formed since the 1980s (National Commission on Writing, 2003).

There are at least three good reasons for teachers to take a hard look at the role of writing in content area classrooms. First, writing improves thinking. Second, it facilitates learning. Third, writing is closely connected to reading. Students in content literacy situations need varied and frequent

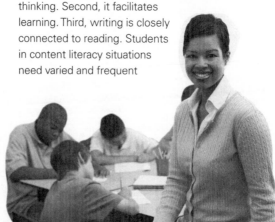

experiences with writing and reading as tools for learning. As Cooper (2012) contends, writing is an essential tool for learning because it engages students in the texts that they are reading and empowers learning. As a result, learners often have a greater depth of understanding when they write about what they are reading. Content area teachers usually have second thoughts about assigning writing in their classrooms because of preconceived notions of what the teaching of writing may entail. Teachers of every discipline share in the responsibility of showing students how to think and write as scientists, historians, mathematicians, and literary critics do. When students engage in writing as a way of knowing, they are thinking on paper or screen (Moore, Moore, Cunningham, & Cunningham, 2006).

Write to Read, Read to Write

There is no better way to think about a subject than to have the occasion to read and write about it. However, reading and writing don't necessarily guarantee improved thinking or learning. Students can go through the motions of reading and writing, lacking purpose and commitment, or they can work thoughtfully to construct meaning, make discoveries, and think deeply about a subject. One way to think about the reading–writing connection is that they both draw upon students' prior knowledge and cognitive processes (Moss and Lapp, 2012). In other words, reading and writing help us to understand what we already know; what we don't think we know that we actually do know; and what we don't know until we have engaged in the process of meaning-making. Classrooms that integrate reading and writing lend encouragement to students who are maturing as readers and writers and provide instructional support so that readers and writers can play with ideas, explore concepts, clarify meaning, and elaborate on what they are learning.

Reading and Writing as Composing Processes

Reading and writing are acts of composing because readers and writers are involved in an ongoing, dynamic process of constructing meaning. Composing processes are more obvious in writing than in reading: The writer, initially facing a blank page or screen, constructs a text. The text is a visible entity and reflects the writer's thinking on paper. Less obvious is the "text"—the configuration of meanings—that students compose or construct in their own minds as they read.

Think of reading and writing as two sides of the same coin. Whereas the writer works to make a text sensible, the reader works to make sense from a text. As a result, the two processes, rooted in language, are intertwined and share common cognitive and sociocultural characteristics. Both reading and writing, for example, involve purpose, commitment, schema activation, planning, working with ideas, revision and rethinking, and monitoring. Both processes occur within a social, communicative context. Skilled writers are mindful of their content (the subject about which they are writing) and also of their audiences (the readers for whom they write). Skilled readers are mindful of a text's content and are also aware that they engage in transactions with its author.

BOX 9.1 ▸ **RTI for Struggling Adolescent Learners**

Responsive Teaching for At-Risk Writers

Students who struggle with academic learning tasks typically find writing activities difficult to accomplish. Increasingly intensive instruction linked to specific skills and strategies is often needed before struggling learners are able to successfully complete independent writing activities. RTI models encourage schools to support at-risk writers by incorporating strategy instruction across the curriculum. In this chapter, we will provide many Tier 1 strategy interventions to help content area teachers in disciplinary learning situations.

If students continue to struggle with writing after Tier 1 instruction, typical Tier 2 accommodations might include explicit small-group or individualized strategy instruction to produce abbreviated writing assignments. This is especially useful for students with specific writing disabilities. When students have difficulty writing, it is helpful to break down assignments into smaller, more manageable tasks. Teachers can modify the requirements of a particular writing assignment or divide writing prompts into a series of adapted steps, allowing struggling writers to focus on a single idea or concept. Struggling writers also benefit from the use of computers to explore ideas as well as to check documents for spelling and grammar, allowing them to focus on content rather than proofreading. Voice recognition software supports students who face physical and cognitive challenges that impede their ability to write.

As we demonstrate in this chapter, writing to learn activities can also be used to support other types of literacy interventions. *Learning logs* can help students monitor their own comprehension and implement fix-up strategies when they encounter reading difficulties. *Exploratory writing* allows students to identify gaps between their prior knowledge and text content. Structured assignments such as *double-entry journals* allow students to process content from multiple perspectives, or at multiple times, to aid in comprehension.

The relationships between reading and writing have been a source of inquiry by language researchers since the mid-1970s (Close, Hull, & Langer, 2005). Several broad conclusions about the links between reading and writing can be drawn: Good readers are often good writers, and vice versa; students who write well tend to read more than those who do not write well; wide reading improves writing; and students who are good readers and writers perceive themselves as such and are more likely to engage in reading and writing on their own.

Why connect reading and writing in instructional contexts? From a content literacy perspective, writing about ideas and concepts encountered in texts will improve students' acquisition of content more than simply reading without writing. When reading and writing are taught in concert, the union fosters problem solving and makes thinking and learning more powerful than if reading or writing is engaged in separately.

Reading and Writing as Exploration, Motivation, and Clarification

When teachers integrate writing and reading, they help students use writing to *think about what they will read* and to *understand what they have read*. Writing may be used as a motivational tool to catapult students into reading. It is also one of the most effective ways for students to understand something they have read. Teachers can put students into writing-to-read or reading-to-write situations because the writing process is a powerful tool for exploring and clarifying meaning.

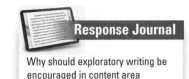

Response Journal

Why should exploratory writing be encouraged in content area classrooms?

Writers engage in a process of exploration and clarification as they go about the task of making meaning. They progress from exploring meaning to clarifying it as they continue to work with a piece of writing. A writer's first efforts are an initial attempt to think on paper or screen. The more writers work with ideas put on paper or screen, the more they are able to revise, rethink, and clarify what they have to say about a subject.

Occasions to write on content subjects before reading and after reading create opportunities to learn content in concert with reading. Students who experience the integration of writing and reading are likely to learn more content, to understand it better, and to remember it longer. This is the case because writing, whether before or after reading, promotes thinking, but in different ways. Writing a summary after reading (see Chapter 10), for example, is likely to result in greater understanding and retention of important information. However, another type of writing—let's say an essay—may trigger the analysis, synthesis, and elaboration of ideas encountered in reading and class discussion.

The International Network of Writing Across the Curriculum (INWAC), an informal community of teachers, researchers, and institutions who champion the development and use of writing strategies in content areas, identifies two major instructional components for disciplinary writing: writing to learn (WTL) and writing in disciplines (WID). Let's take a closer look at each component. How are they alike? How are they different?

Writing to Learn (WTL)

Instructional activities that support WTL are by their very nature short and informal writing tasks. The writing that these activities produce is often tentative and unfinished. When students engage in WTL, they explore ideas and clarify what they are thinking about in relation to a subject under study. Before reading, WTL activities help students tap into prior knowledge and make connections between the "old" (what they already know) and the "new" (what they will be learning about). For example, many content area teachers combine a prereading activity such as brainstorming with five or so minutes of "quick-writing," in which students write freely and spontaneously on what they know and on what they hope to learn from more in-depth reading and study. After reading, quick-writing activities such as *microthemes* are useful in helping students to summarize and extend their thoughts about a subject.

WTL should not be confused with *learning to write*. Students learn to write formally from the time they enter school and continue learning to write throughout their lives. Language arts and English teachers, entrusted with the primary responsibility for students' writing development, teach learners how to engage in the process of writing as a central component of learning to write. In this chapter, we discuss the content area teacher's role in guiding the writing process when students are engaged in more elaborate writing assignments such as essays and research papers.

A variety of instructional activities may be used for WTL, including microthemes, point of view guides (POVGs), unsent letters, biopoems, and admit/exit slips. Having students write regularly in various kinds of journals is also an important component of writing to learn in content area classrooms.

Microthemes

More isn't necessarily better when getting students to think and learn by writing. In fact, brevity is the key to writing an effective microtheme. A microtheme is a brief piece of writing that results in a great deal of thinking (Bean, Drenk, & Lee, 1982). Think of microthemes as mini-essays. Teachers often require students to write a microtheme on one side of an index card or half-sheet of paper. A five- by eight-inch index card is a lot less threatening for students than the prospect of writing a full-blown essay.

Microthemes can be assigned for a variety of purposes, including analyzing and synthesizing information and ideas encountered in reading, writing summaries, or taking a stand on an important issue. In a biology class, for example, students were involved in an ecological study of organisms in short river communities along the western coast of Florida. One of the readings dealt with community relationships in the life of river turtles. As part of the unit, the teacher assigned a variety of WTL activities, including microthemes. One of the microthemes helped students to reflect on and synthesize information related to river turtle life. After much discussion of the topic, the teacher distributed index cards and assigned the following microtheme in the form of two questions: What relationships to other organisms does an adult river turtle have in this river community? How do these relationships differ from those of a young river turtle?

Before writing, students were asked to jot down notes and key points from the text and class discussions that they might use in the microtheme. Since words were at a premium, students had to be concise, yet complete. Here's what Jaycee wrote on her index card:

> Adult river turtles have both direct and indirect relationships with other organisms in this river community. Direct relationships include eating many of the plants that grow in the river. Other organisms eat and live off of the river turtle. Leeches suck on their blood like vampires while other animals eat the turtles eggs. When there in the water river turtles can be food for certain fish, herons, and even a kind of snapping turtle. Indirect relationships are when turtles compete for a food source like tape grass with another organism. Young river turtles differ from adult river turtles. Young turtles can be carnivorous as well as herbivorous. They are also more likely to be eaten by preteters than adult turtles. When both young and adult turtles die they become food for decomposers that return all the substances in the turtles body to the nonliving world.

Jaycee's microtheme is fairly fact-laden and accurate in its description of direct and indirect relationships. Although she has some spelling errors (i.e., *preteters*) and grammatical miscues, these are to be expected in quick-writing activities. Jaycee and her classmates shared their microthemes in "study buddy" groups and also had an opportunity to raise questions in a whole-class follow-up discussion. The teacher then gave students an opportunity to make content changes or add information to their index cards. Although a grade is not assigned to individual microthemes, the teacher has students save their themes to use as "study cards" for unit tests. Other teachers may choose to grade microthemes by assigning points based on a scale of one to five, with five being rated as excellent.

POVGs

A POVG (point of view guide) connects writing to reading in a creative, nonthreatening manner (Wood, 1988; Wood, Lapp, Flood, & Taylor, 2008). POVGs are designed to trigger thoughtful reading and writing by having students "get inside the skin" of a character or a subject under study. Several key characteristics of POVGs include the following:

- POVGs are questions presented in an *interview* format that allow students to think about text from different points of view and perspectives.
- POVGs encourage *speculation, inferential thinking,* and *elaboration* by placing students in *role-play* situations.
- POVGs engage students in writing to learn by having them *actively contribute their own experiences* to the role.
- POVGs require *first-person* writing on the part of students as they respond to a situation.

POVGs can fit into a microtheme format or stand alone as a writing-to-learn activity. In the sample microtheme above, Jaycee's language is formal, textbook-like, and somewhat stilted. However, POVG writing usually results in more informal, playful language as students assume a role and write in the first person. Jaycee's biology teacher also adapts a microtheme format to include POVG-type responses. In the unit on turtle life in a river community, notice how the teacher switched from very academic questions in the microtheme example to a role-play situation:

> Situation: You are about to be interviewed as if you are a young river turtle living in a river community along the west coast of Florida.
> Question: As a young river turtle, what is your typical day like?

Before writing their responses on index cards, students are assigned to read the text and take notes. Notice how Jaycee's language changes as she assumes the role of a young river turtle:

> I get up in the morning thinking about the long day ahead of me. When I leave my veggie pad, the first thing I do is pick up the newspaper and check out the obitcheries to see how the musk turtles are doing. They been having it rough lately. Then I go to the local resterant where I feed on snails, worms, and water insects. As I make my way back to my pad I don't got any fears until I see my mom and dad chomping away at the only thing that will protect me later in life. Tape grass! At this point, I'm thinking, Is this good parental behavior? After a hard days work, I go back home and dream of the day I become an adult. Will I do the same thing to my kids?

The structure of a POVG is easily adapted to learning situations in science, social studies, history, or English language arts. In a high school American history class, students are studying the Great Depression. They have been assigned to read about how farmers from the Great Plains fled to California during the Dust Bowl of the 1930s. The teacher's POVG establishes a situation for writing based on three questions:

> It's 1936. You were a farmer in Oklahoma during the Dust Bowl in which "the land just blew away." The bank foreclosed on your farm and you and your family were forced to move west to California in search of work and a new life. You have been living in California for two years. You are about to be interviewed by a writer from *Collier's Magazine*. First read the text and then write your responses fully for each of the questions in the first person.
>
> 1. What was it like when you reached California? Describe how you were treated.
>
> 2. What kind of farm work did you find in California? Was it different from what you expected in your former life as a farmer in Oklahoma?
>
> 3. Why did you give up migrant farming to move to a "shacktown" called "Okieville"? Describe what life was like for you and your family in Okieville.

Unsent Letters

Like POVGs, the WTL activity known as *unsent letters* establishes a role-play situation in which students are asked to write letters in response to the material they are studying. The activity requires the use of imagination and often demands that writers engage in interpretive and evaluative thinking (Smith, 2002). In a middle school language arts class, students were reading the historical novel, *Number the Stars,* by Lois Lowry. The story is about the Holocaust during World War II and is set in the city of Copenhagen during the third year of the Nazi occupation of Denmark. Lowry tells the story from the point of view of ten-year-old Annemarie Johansen. The plot revolves around Annemarie and her best friend Ellen Rosen, who is Jewish and eventually escapes to Sweden with her family. The teacher invites her class to write an unsent letter from Annemarie to Ellen twenty years after the war ends. Here's what one student writes:

> Dear Ellen,
>   How is Sweden? I'm doing fine. I hope you are too. The war ended 20 years ago but I am still heart-broken because of what the Nazis did. Remember that time when you were sleeping over and the Nazis barged in my apartment. I'm sorry I had to break your necklace, but I think it was worth it. I am married to a guy named Peter, not the Peter we know but another one. My name now is Annemarie Harrison. Do you like it? I have two kids, Ellen and Billy. I moved to America and live in a place called Vero Beach in Florida. It's so peaceful here. I wish it was like that back then, so you wouldn't have had to leave.
>   Sincerely your best friend,
>   Annemarie
>   P.S. Please write back!

An unsent letter is a non-threatening way to have students demonstrate their knowledge about a topic under study. In a pre-calculus class, the teacher asked his students to write a friend an unsent letter describing what they have learned about right triangles. Here's what Max wrote to his buddy Nugget:

> Hey Nugget,
>   Right triangles are very easy to understand. If you have two legs of the triangle you use the Pythagorean Theorem to find the hypotenuse ($a^2 + b^2 = c^2$). If you have one leg and the hypotenuse, you can find the second leg by plugging the number eight into the formula. You can also find the six trig. functions of the right triangle by using the lengths of the sides, or known angles, but you have to remember to put them in relation to r (which is the hyp.).
>   It's helpful to know about the properties of right triangles. Using them, you can find angles of depression and of elevation to objects above or below you. Unfortunately sometimes they are confusing.
>   P.S. You are a loser if you are really curious about right triangles! ☺

Biopoems

Unsent letters direct students' thinking with particular audiences in mind. Biopoems, by contrast, require students to play with ideas using language in a poetic framework. A *biopoem* allows students to reflect on large amounts of material within a poetic form. The biopoem follows a pattern that enables writers to synthesize what they have learned about a person, place, thing, concept, or event under study. For example, study the following pattern for a person or character:

Line 1. First name

Line 2. Four traits that describe character

Line 3. Relative ("brother," "sister," "daughter," etc.) of _____

Line 4. Lover of _____ (list three things or people)

Line 5. Who feels _____ (three items)

Line 6. Who needs _____ (three items)

Line 7. Who fears _____ (three items)

Line 8. Who gives _____ (three items)

Line 9. Who would like to see _____ (three items)

Line 10. Resident of _____

Line 11. Last name

Response Journal

What is your reaction to the use of a biopoem as a writing-to-learn activity?

Biopoems help students to organize, review, and summarize what they have learned in a concise and creative manner. Following is an example of how a chemistry teacher adapted biopoems to the subject of the Periodic Table of Elements.

The Periodic Table

Columns called families, rows called periods, arranged by atomic number

Mendeleev's child

Lover of electrons, protons, and neutrons

Who feels the heat caused by sodium in water, the lightness of argon, and the weight of platinum

Who needs all the attention I can give

Who fears computers, Ipads, and TVs

Who gives gases, metalloids, and more information than I can remember

Who would like to tell us all about the world and likes it when more elements are added

Resident of my chemistry textbook of Elements

A geometry teacher adapted the biopoem format for use in her class. Students were assigned to write a biopoem to describe the characteristics of a concept they were studying. Here's how one student described a trapezoid:

Trape

I've got two legs, two bases, and four angles.

My family includes sister Square and brothers Rhombus and Rectangle.

I need one pair of parallel sides and each pair of base angles to be congruent.

I fear two pairs of parallel sides and also fear only three sides to it.

I would like to see the pyramids in Egypt some day.

Resident of Polygon

Zoid

Biopoems, as you can see, help students to synthesize their learning as they play with ideas in a format that provides an alternative to prose writing.

Admit Slips and Exit Slips

Admit slips are brief comments written by students on index cards or half-sheets of paper at the very beginning of class. The purpose of the admit slip is to have students react to what they are studying or to what's happening in class. Students are asked to respond to questions such as:

What's confusing you about _____?

What problems did you have with your text assignment?

What would you like to get off your chest?

What do you like (dislike) about _____?

The admit slips are collected by the teacher and read aloud (with no indication of the authorship of individual comments) as a way of beginning class discussion. Admit slips build a trusting relationship between teacher and students and contribute to a sense of community in the classroom.

In an algebra class, where students had been studying complex numbers, the teacher asked the class to use admit slips to explain difficulties students had with one of their homework assignments. One student wrote, "I didn't know where to start." Several other students made similar comments. The teacher was able to use the written feedback to address some of the problems that students had with the assignment.

An *exit slip,* as you might anticipate, is a variation on the admit slip. Toward the end of class, the teacher asks students for exit slips as a way of bringing closure to what was learned. An exit slip question might require students to summarize, synthesize, evaluate, or project.

In the algebra class, exit slips were used toward the end of the class to introduce a new unit on imaginary numbers. The teacher asked students to write for several minutes as they reflected on the question "Why do you think we are studying about imaginary numbers after we studied the discriminant?" One student wrote, "Because the discriminant can be negative and I didn't know what kind of a number $\sqrt{-1}$ was. I guessing [*sic*] it must be imaginary. Right?" The teacher was able to sort through the exit slip responses and use them to introduce the new unit.

The several minutes devoted to exit slip writing are often quite revealing of the day's lesson and establish a direction for the next class.

 **Academic Journals**

Because journals serve a variety of real-life purposes, not the least of which is to write about things that are important to us, they have withstood the test of time. Artists, scientists, novelists, historical figures, mathematicians, dancers, politicians, teachers, children, athletes—all kinds of people—have kept journals. Some journals—diaries, for example—are meant to be private and are not intended to be read by anyone but the writer. Sometimes, however, a diary makes its way into the public domain and affects readers in powerful ways. Anne Frank, probably the world's most famous child diarist, kept a personal journal of her innermost thoughts, fears, hopes, and experiences while hiding from the Nazis during World War II. Having read her diary, who hasn't been moved to think and feel more deeply about the tragic consequences of the Holocaust?

Other journals are more work related than personal in that writers record observations and experiences that will be useful, insightful, or instructive. In more than forty notebooks, Leonardo da Vinci recorded artistic ideas, detailed sketches of the human anatomy, elaborate plans for flying machines, and even his dreams. Novelists throughout literary history have used journals to record ideas, happenings, and conversations that have served to stimulate their imaginations and provide material for their writing. Even in a professional sport such as baseball, it is not unusual for hitters to keep a log of their at-bats: who the pitcher was, what the situation was (e.g., runner on base or bases empty), what types of pitches were thrown, and what the outcome of each at-bat was.

Response Journal

Why do people journal?

Academic journals also serve a variety of purposes. They help students generate ideas, create a record of thoughts and feelings in response to what they are reading, and explore their own lives and concerns in relation to what they are reading and learning. Academic journals create a context for learning in which students interact with information personally as they explore and clarify ideas, issues, and concepts under study. These journals may be used as springboards for class discussion or as mind stretchers that extend thinking, solve problems, or stimulate imagination. All forms of writing and written expression can be incorporated into academic journal writing, from doodles and sketches to poems and letters to comments, explanations, and reactions.

Three types of journals in particular have made a difference in content literacy situations: *response journals, double-entry journals,* and *learning logs*. Each of these can be used in an instructional context to help students explore literary and informational texts. Teachers who use academic journals in their classes encourage students to use everyday, expressive language to write about what they are studying, in the same way that they encourage students to use talk to explore ideas during discussion. When expressive language is missing from students' journal writing, the students do not experience the kind of internal talk that allows them to explore and clarify meaning in ways that are personal and crucial to thinking on paper or on screen.

When writing in academic journals, students need not attempt to sound "academic," even though they are writing about ideas and information of importance in various disciplines. Like the writing activities previously discussed in this chapter, journal entries need to be judged on the writer's ability to communicate and explore ideas, not on the quality of handwriting or the number of spelling and grammatical errors in the writing. Journal writing underscores informal learning. It relieves teachers of the burden of correction so that they can focus on students' thinking, and it creates a nonthreatening situation for students who may be hesitant to take risks because they are overly concerned about the mechanics of writing (e.g., handwriting, neatness, spelling, and punctuation).

Response Journals

Response journals create permanent records of what readers are feeling and thinking as they interact with texts. A response journal allows students to record their thoughts about texts and emotional reactions to them. Teachers may use prompts to trigger students' feelings and thoughts about a subject or may invite students to respond freely to what they are reading and doing in class. Prompts include questions, visual stimuli, read-alouds, or situations created to stimulate thinking. An earth science teacher, for example, might ask students to place themselves in the role of a water molecule as they describe what it's like to travel through the water cycle. Examine how Mike, a low-achieving ninth grader who didn't like to write, responded in his journal entry:

My name is Moe, its short for Molecule. I was born in a cloud when I was condensed on a dust particle. My neverending life story goes like this.

During Moes life he had a great time boncing into his friends. He grew up in the cloud and became bigger and heavier. Moe became so heavy that one night lightning struck and he fell out of his cloud as a raindrop. He landed in a farmers field where this leavy plant sucked him up. Moe became a small section of a leave on the plant and their he absorbed sunlight and other things. One day a cow came by and ate Moes leave. He was now part of the cow.

Well you can guess the rest. The farmer ate the cow and Moe became part of the farmer. One day the farmer was working in the field, he started sweating and thats when Moe escaped. He transpirated into the air as a molecule again. Free at last he rejoined a group of new friends in a cloud and the cycle went on.

Mike's teacher was pleased by his journal entry, mechanical errors and all. On homework questions, he usually wrote short, incoherent answers. In this entry, however, he interacted playfully with the information in the text and demonstrated his understanding of the water cycle.

In a high school senior elective psychology course, students were studying Sigmund Freud's theory of psychoanalysis. The teacher used a response journal format to help students apply the concepts of *id, ego,* and *superego* to real-life experiences. In their response journals, students were asked to respond to the following situation: As you enter the classroom, you notice a copy of the key to the test you are going to take. Your teacher is nowhere to be found. What is your id, ego, and superego telling you to do? What action will you take? Why? Here's what one student wrote:

As I walk into the classroom and notice that my teacher isn't in the room, my Id tells me "quick memorize the key before she comes back, you know you didn't study for the test last night and this is the only way you are going to pass. My Ego tells to look at the key, but just make it look like I'm waiting for her at her desk when she comes back in—she won't think I looked at it. My Superego tells me it is wrong to cheat and even if I did get an A on the test I would feel guilty. I would never be able to look at her in the eye again. In the end I would probably look at the key so quickly on the desk (because I would be so nervous of getting caught) I wouldn't even notice any of the answers.

Character Journals

Role-playing is an excellent prompt for response journal writing. A history or an English teacher, for example, may invite students to assume the role of a historical or fictional character and to view events and happenings from the character's perspective. In an American history class, students keep journals of events that took place in American history from the perspective of a fictitious historical family that each student created. The families witness all of the events that take place in American history and write their reactions to these events. The teacher scaffolds the journal writing assignment with the guidesheet shown in Figure 9.1. Study the guidesheet, and then read several entries from one student's journal in Figure 9.2.

Sketchbooks in Art

A high school art teacher incorporates a sketchbook into his courses to guide students' thinking and responses to what they are learning and studying in class. As an introduction to the

Figure 9.1   A Guidesheet for Historical Character Journals

To help you develop your historical character, use the information that you have gained about the American colonies and your own background knowledge.

Who is your character?

1. What is your character's name? How old is your character? Is he or she married? (*Note:* How old were people when they married during his or her time?)

   _____

2. Who else is in your character's family? How old is each of these people? (*Note:* What happened to a lot of children during this time?)

   _____

3. Where does your character live?

   _____

4. What does your character do for a living? Is he or she rich or poor?

   _____

5. What religion is your character? What attitude does he or she have toward religion?

   _____

6. How much education does your character have?

   _____

7. Was your character born in the United States, Europe, or Africa? If he or she was born in Europe, in what country?

   _____

8. How does your character feel about people who are "different" in skin color, religion, social or economic class, or nationality?

   _____

   a. Skin color? (*Note:* This may depend on where he or she lives.)

      _____

   b. Religion?

      _____

   c. Social or economic class?

      _____

   d. Nationality?

      _____

9. How does your character feel about being part of a colony instead of living in an independent country?

   _____

Figure 9.2   Historical Character Journal Entries

Classroom Artifact

1770

My name is Victoria Black and I'm thirteen years old. We are a Protestant family and we attend church regularly. It's a social as well as religious occasion for us. We stay all day and my mother gossips with all of the neighbors. I've made a few friends there but usually I stay with my sister. I have long blond hair and sparkling blue eyes in my mother's words. I'm learning how to take care of the home and cook lately. My mother says it's important because soon enough I'll be married. I think she wants me to marry one of the boys from town whose father is a popular lawyer. I have an older sister Sarah who is fifteen and has just gotten married. My parents are Mathew and Elizabeth Black, they are becoming older and mother has been sick lately. We worry very much for them and say prayers daily. We live on Mander Plantation in Trenton, Pennsylvania, where my father grows cotton and some tobacco. We have many indentured servants which we treat very nicely. I've become close with a couple of them. Usually when servants' time has expired my father will give them some land to start up their lives. Because we are more north we haven't any African slaves yet. My father is planning a trip out east to buy some slaves later this month. I'm still not sure if buying people is the right thing to do but my brother told me he doesn't think they're real people. I don't know how my father feels on this, he must think it's alright. My father is very confused about what's going on with the British. He doesn't understand why the colonists think they even have a chance at fighting and winning with the British. He thinks the war will be over in no time.

1778

I'm married now to William Brown, a new lawyer for Pennsylvania. We have two children, Mary and Richard Brown. They are still both very young, Mary is six and Richard is four and I'm expecting another soon! William is for the Revolutionary War. He feels the Brits are not being sensible with their laws for us. The taxation has bothered us greatly. Each week we scramble for money. Even though William is a lawyer, it's still hard to get started and receive reasonable wages. The British have also gone too far with the quartering act. We had British soldiers knock on our door last week asking for food. William was outraged. He says we have to have a revolution and win, if we want to survive and live happily. William said things are just going to get worse and worse. I don't think things could get any worse. I do worry about this war, for my brothers and William. Hopefully neither of them will be in the militia. We are already hearing of some battles, which sound awful. We are starting to go to church and pray every day now for our family and country.

1779-1781

William and my brothers are going to be in the militia. I'm very worried for them. William feels what he's doing is right for the country. We seem to be winning some of the battles, which is

Figure 9.2 *(continued)*

> *surprising. The women and children from our church gather every day and pray for our brothers and husbands. We all try our hardest to stay on our feet and have enough food for everyone. Some weeks it's difficult. We feel that all of our money is going to taxes. We pray that the end will be here soon. I had a baby boy which we named Daniel Brown. It will be hard to raise these children alone. Before William goes to the militia I'm going to visit my mother, she's dying and I'd like to say goodbye to her.*

sketchbook, the class discusses reasons for keeping a sketchbook, which the teacher adapted from a model used by McIntosh (1991):

- *What should you include in your sketchbook?* New ideas, sketches, concepts, designs, redesigns, words, notes from class, drawings to show understanding, reflections on the class, questions that you have, and new things you've learned.

- *When should you include entries in your sketchbook?* (1) After each class; (2) anytime an insight or a design idea or question hits you; (3) anytime, so keep the sketchbook handy and visible in your work area.

- *Why should you draw and write in your sketchbook?* (1) It will record your ideas and ideas you might otherwise forget; (2) it will record and note your growth; (3) it will facilitate your learning, problem solving, idea forming, research, reading, and discussion in class.

- *How should you write and draw entries in your sketchbook?* You can express yourself in sketches and drawings; in single words, questions, or short phrases; in long, flowing sentences; in designs and redesigns; in diagrams, graphs, and overlays; or in colors.

- *Remember, the sketchbook is yours, and it reflects how perceptive you are with your ideas and how creative you are in your thought processes!*

Math Journals

Math teachers use response journals in a variety of ways. They may invite students to write a "math autobiography" in which they describe their feelings and prior experiences as math learners. Rose (1989, p. 24) suggests the following prompt for a biographical narrative in math:

> Write about any mathematical experiences you have had. The narratives should be told as stories, with as much detail and description as possible. Include your thoughts, reactions, and feelings about the entire experience.

If students need more scaffolding than the prompt, Rose recommends having them complete and write elaborations on sentences, such as:

My most positive experience with math was _____

My background in math is _____

I liked math until _____

Math makes me feel _____

If I were a math teacher, I'd _____

The content of math journals may also include exploratory writing activities, summaries, letters, student-constructed word problems and theorem definitions, descriptions of mathematical processes, calculations and solutions to problems, and feelings about the course. Examine, for example, the journal entries in Figures 9.3 and 9.4.

Double-Entry Journals (DEJs)

A double-entry journal (DEJ) is a versatile adaptation of the response journal. As the name implies, DEJs allow students to record dual entries that are conceptually related. In doing so, students juxtapose their thoughts and feelings according to the prompts they are given for making the entries. To create a two-column format for a DEJ, have students divide sheets of

Figure 9.3 Journal Entry in Response to the Prompt, "What Goes Through Your Mind When You Do a Proof?"

Classroom Artifact

October 7

When I look at something I have to prove, the answer is always so obvious to me, I don't know what to write. This confuses me more because then I just write down one thing. Even though I understand it, no one else could. I don't use postulates & theorems because I have no idea which is which. So if you gave me a proof, I could probably prove it, but just not mathematically using big words.

Figure 9.4 Journal Entry in Response to the Prompt, "Explain to Someone How to Bisect an Angle"

Classroom Artifact

9/4

How to Draw a Bisected Angle

Make an acute angle. Label it $\angle ABC$ — making Point A on one ray, B at the vertex, or point where rays meet, and C on the other ray. Now, with a compass, draw an arc of any measurement which will cross both rays. Next, use your compass to measure the distance between the two points you made by making the arc and keep the measurement locked on your protractor. Now, put the point of your compass on one of the arc points and make a slash in the middle of the angle. Do the same from the other dot on the other ray. The slash marks should cross in the center. Make a point where the slashes cross. Label it Point D. Draw a ray starting at Point B going through Point D. $\overrightarrow{BD}$ now bisects $\angle ABC$.

notebook paper in half lengthwise. As an alternative, younger writers may need more room to write their entries than a divided page allows. They find that it is easier to use the entire left page of a notebook as one column and the right page as the other column.

DEJs serve a variety of functions. In the left column of the journal, students may be prompted to select words, short quotes, or passages from the text that interest them or evoke strong responses. In this column, they write the word, quote, or passage verbatim or use their own words to describe what is said in the text. In the right column, the students record their reactions, interpretations, and responses to the text segments they have selected.

As part of a science unit on the solar system, for example, middle level students used double-entry journals as an occasion to explore their own personal meanings for the concept of the solar system. In the left column, they responded to the question, "What is it?" In the right column, the students reflected on the question, "What does it mean to you?" Study the entries that three of the students wrote in the "What is it?" column. Then compare the three corresponding entries from the right column, "What does it mean to you?"

WHAT IS THE SOLAR SYSTEM?	What Does It Mean to You?
It is nine planets, along with asteroid belts, stars, black holes, and so on.	The solar system is a mystery to me. I know the planets and stuff, but how did it come into being? Galileo had something to do with the solar system, but I'm not sure exactly what. I would like to find out more about it.
It is planets and stars. Earth is the third planet from the sun. It is the only planet with water. Stars are huge—many much greater than the sun in size.	The solar system reminds me of a white-haired scientist who is always studying the big vast opening in the sky. When I look at the sky at night I see tiny twinkling lights. People tell me that they're planets but I think they're stars. I see constellations but I don't recognize them. I am not a white-haired scientist yet.
The nine planets are not very interesting to me and I won't bother to go through them. But I did memorize the order of the planets by this sentence. *My very eager mother just served us nine pizzas.* Take the beginning letters to remind you of each planet.	When I think about what the solar system means to me, I think about an unknown universe, which could be much larger than we think it is. I start to think about science fiction stories that I have read, alien beings and creatures that are in the universe some place.

In an eighth-grade language arts class, the teacher and his students were engaged in a unit on the Yukon and Jack London's *Call of the Wild*. As part of the core book study of London's classic novel about the adventures of a sled dog named Buck, the teacher arranged for a sled dog team demonstration by a group of local residents who participate in dog sledding as a hobby. His class was excited by the demonstration, which took place on the school's grounds. The next day, the class used double-entry journals to reflect on the experience. In the left column, they responded to the question, "What did you learn from the demonstration?" In the right column, they reflected on the question, "How did the demonstration help you better understand the novel?" Examine some of the students' entries in Figure 9.5.

Figure 9.5 Entries from a Double-Entry Journal Assignment for *The Call of the Wild*

Classroom Artifact	
What did you learn from the demonstration?	How did the demonstration help you better understand the novel?
I learned that although dogs just look big and cuddly they really can work. When people take the time they can teach their dog anything. Yet that saying also applies to life. **[Alex]**	I never realized how hard it was for Buck to pull the sled. It takes a lot of work.
It was excellent. I learned that the owners and the dogs were a family and extremely hard workers. I learned how hard a race could be and the risk involved. I'm glad I got to see the dogs and their personalities. **[Marcus]**	It proved to me how Buck needed to be treated with praise and discipline and equality. That way you get a wonderful dog and a companion for life.
I learned about how they trained their dogs and that they need as much or more love and attention as they do discipline. **[Jennifer]**	It helped me understand the book better because it showed how unique Buck is compared to the other dogs. Also what a dog sled looks like and what Buck might have looked like. It made the story come alive more.

Learning Logs

Learning logs are similar to online threaded discussions, which were explained in Chapter 2. Like threaded discussions, learning logs add still another dimension to personal learning in content area classrooms (Bangert-Drowns, Hurley, & Wilkinson, 2004). The strategy is simple to implement but must be used regularly to be effective. As is the case with response and double-entry journals, students keep an ongoing record of learning *as it happens* in a notebook. They write in their own language, not necessarily for others to read but to themselves, about what they are learning. Entries in logs influence learning by revealing problems and concerns.

There is no one way to use learning logs, although teachers often prefer allowing five or ten minutes at the end of a period for students to respond to process questions such as, "What did I understand about the work we did in class today?" "What didn't I understand?" "At what point in the lesson did I get confused?" "What did I like or dislike about class today?" The logs can be kept in a box and stored in the classroom. The teacher then reviews them during or after school to see what the students are learning and to recognize their concerns and problems.

Students may at first be tentative about writing and unsure of what to say or reveal—after all, journal writing is reflective and personal. It takes a trusting atmosphere to open up to the teacher. However, to win the trust of students, teachers refrain from making judgmental or evaluative comments when students admit a lack of understanding of what's happening in class. If a trusting relationship exists, students will soon recognize the value of logs.

 # Writing in Disciplines

WTL activities, as we have shown, provide students with numerous informal opportunities to explore and clarify ideas and concepts. A second instructional component of academic writing—known as writing in disciplines (WID)—involves more formal, elaborate, and well-thought-out writing on the part of students. Although there are aspects of academic writing that cut across all disciplines, each discipline has its specific *writing forms, styles,* and *conventions* that students must consider and follow as they engage in WID assignments. As the Writing in the Disciplines website put it, "The demands of writing a history paper or a sociology paper are, as most students quickly discover, very different from those of writing an English essay or business report" (Writing in the Disciplines, 2001).

As important as a research paper is to learning in most, if not all, disciplines, other forms of writing are also essential: position papers, progress reports, lab and field reports, interpretive essays, reviews, project proposals, and journal or newspaper articles. Table 9.1 provides an extensive listing of writing forms that are an integral part of WID writing assignments.

RAFT Writing

The key to thoughtful writing begins with the design of the assignment itself. The teacher's primary concern should be how to make an assignment *explicit* without stifling interest or the spirit of inquiry. An assignment should provide more than a subject to write on. This is where RAFT can make a difference in students' approach to writing.

Table 9.1 Some Discourse Forms for Content Area Writing

Category	Examples	Category	Examples
Media	Stories or essays for local papers School newspaper stories Interviews Radio scripts TV scripts	Anecdotes and stories	From experience As told by others Of famous people Of places Of content ideas Of historical events
Technology	Blogs Wikis Nings Google Docs Threaded discussion groups Listservs Multimodal texts YouTube videos Internet projects WebQuests	Creative writing	Plays Poems Songs and ballads Fantasy Adventure Science fiction Historical fiction Historical "you are there" scenes Children's books Dramatic scripts
Reviews	Books Films Television programs Documentaries	Science notes	Observations Science notebook Reading reports Lab reports
Letters	Personal reactions Observations Public/informational Persuasive To public officials To imaginary people From imaginary places	Visual	Poster displays Cartoons and cartoon strips Photos and captions Collages and montages Mobiles and sculptures How-to slides
Position papers	National concerns Local issues School issues Historical problems Scientific issues	Math	Story problems Solutions to problems Record books Notes and observations
Business writing	Memos Résumés Technical reports Proposals	Reference materials	Booklets Fact books or fact sheets Dictionaries and lexicons
Opinion writing	Commentaries Editorials Written debates Responses and rebuttals Responses to literature	Other	Requests Journals and diaries Biographical sketches Guess who/what descriptions Demonstrations Puzzles and word searches Prophecy and predictions Dialogues and conversations

RAFT is an acronym that stands for *role, audience, form,* and *topic.* RAFT allows teachers to create *prompts* for many types of discipline-specific writing assignments (Holston & Santa, 1985). What constitutes an effective writing prompt for academic assignments? Suppose you were assigned one of the following topics to write on, based on text readings and class discussion:

- Batiking
- The role of the laser beam in the future
- Nuclear disarmament

No doubt, some of you would probably begin writing on one of the topics without hesitation. Perhaps you already know a great deal about the subject, have strong feelings about it, or can change the direction of the discourse without much difficulty. Others, however, may resist or even resent the activity. Your questions might echo the following concerns: "Why do I want to write about any of these topics in the first place?" "For whom am I writing?" "Will I write a paragraph?" "A book?" The most experienced writer must come to grips with questions such as these, and with even more complicated ones: "How will I treat my subject?" "What role will I take?" If anything, the questions raise to awareness the *rhetorical context*—the writer's *role,* the *audience,* the *form* of the writing, and the writer's *topic*—that most writing assignments should provide. A context for writing allows students to assess the writer's relationship to the subject of the writing (the topic) and to the reader (the audience for whom the writing is intended).

Response Journal

Develop a RAFT writing activity for a topic in your content area.

A good writing activity, then, *situates* students in the writing task. Instead of asking students to write about how to batik, give students a RAFT.

> To show that you understand how batiking works, imagine that you are giving a demonstration at an arts-and-crafts show. Describe the steps and procedures involved in the process of batiking to a group of onlookers, recognizing that they know little about the process but are curious enough to find out more.

This example creates a context for writing. It suggests the writer's role (the student providing a batiking demonstration), the writer's audience (observers of the demonstration), the form of the writing (a how-to demonstration), and the topic (the process of batiking). RAFT writing prompts contrived situations and audiences in the context of what is being read or studied. However, they are far from trivial, nonacademic, or inconsequential. Instead, when students "become" someone else, they must look at situations in a nontraditional way. After writing, they can compare different perspectives on the same issue and examine the validity of the viewpoints that were taken.

Or take, as another example, the nuclear disarmament topic:

> The debate over nuclear disarmament has countries and people taking different sides of the argument. There are some who argue that nuclear proliferation will lead to nuclear war or nuclear terrorism. There are others who contend that the nuclear arms race is the only way to maintain peace in the world.
>
> You have been selected to write a position paper for the class in which you debate your side of the argument. Another student has been selected to defend an opposing position. The class will then vote on the more persuasive of the two positions. Once you have investigated the issue thoroughly, write a paper to convince as many classmates as possible that your position is the better one.

As you can see from the two examples, each creates a lifelike context, each identifies a purpose and an audience, and each suggests the writer's stance and a format—that is, a demonstration or a position paper. In each case, students will not necessarily make the assumption

BOX 9.2   Voices from the Field

Ashley, Eighth-Grade Lead Science Teacher

Challenge

Science teachers in my school struggle to incorporate writing into the curriculum. Although students need to understand how to write within a discipline, I noticed that my students' preferred a kinesthetic approach to science rather than composing a lab report. That's when it clicked for me that I could combine the two approaches to help maximize learning opportunities for my students while helping them use writing in meaningful ways within the science discipline. By using the RAFT strategy (role, audience, form, and topic) and science experiments together, students were able to physically engage with the science concept first by conducting experiments. Later, they were able to write about them using the literacy strategy. Using this method allows students to develop a context for writing by first participating in a lab activity, and then applying what they had learned through RAFT.

Strategy

Initially, my students were not thrilled with having another writing assignment outside of their language arts class. Other teachers were not as receptive to the idea either because they did not feel comfortable "teaching language arts" in their science classes. I figured the only way to create buy-in from both the teachers and students was to conduct a little experiment myself. I was teaching a unit on microbiology and the students had just spent the last two classes refreshing their memories on parts of the cell. In previous years, most students had simply memorized the information to perform well on the test, but had not retained the concepts. This year, my students engaged in an edible cell lab, which included Jell-O and other various treats to construct prokaryotic cells (cells with no nuclear membrane) and eukaryotic cells (cells with a true nucleus). Upon completion of the lab, I modeled for the students how to develop a RAFT writing activity based upon the

cell experiment. My role was that of the nucleus and my audience was the other parts of the cell. I used a memo format on the topic of controlling the processes of the cell. I took the position that there were some parts of the cell that were not doing their job and, as their boss, I put a memo in each of their boxes as a friendly reminder.

The students and teachers responded overwhelmingly well to the wit and humor I included in my memo, and the students were eager to begin their own RAFT scenarios even before I could finish the instructions. A rather creative response came from a student who chose the role of the endoplasmic reticulum. This particular part of the smallest living organism is responsible for moving material around the cell, so the student decided to use the customers of the UPS delivery service as the audience. The student created a set of instructions on how to track your package (cell material) as it is being delivered to its final destination. In another example, a student included the use of the mitochondria (role) speaking to an audience of gym members. The student created a recipe (format) describing how to use energy to get the best workout possible or, in cellular terms, release energy for other cell functions. I used this technique several times over the course of the year, and my students showed improvement in their class assignments test scores, and, most importantly, their retention of the concepts.

Reflection

As with other strategies, RAFT is not without its limitations. Not every student showed an interest, and students who struggled with reading and writing in general found some frustrations with this technique as well. However, using the RAFT method in science classes was an innovative way to get students engaged in the writing process. I believe that this technique not only helped me grow as an educator, but it served as a reminder that, as teachers, we should constantly search for innovative strategies to help our students learn across the disciplines. I would advise other teachers to use this activity to differentiate based on students' ability levels. Some students may need more assistance with the writing process so you might consider using leading statements where students are allowed to fill in the blank. Over time students can become more comfortable with this strategy and, with your guidance, continue to advance their knowledge of the technique and the class material. Additionally, some of the vocabulary terms can be quite difficult for students to understand, therefore making the RAFT process more complicated. I would advise other teachers to be sure that students are equipped with basic knowledge of relevant vocabulary concepts before proceeding with RAFT.

that the teacher is the audience, even though ultimately the teacher will evaluate the written product. Box 9.2, Voices from the Field, describes how Ashley, a middle school science teacher, adapts RAFT in her classrooms.

Research-Based Writing

Research projects pave the way for writing at every stage of the process, whether writing involves drawing up a project schedule, choosing a topic, formulating research questions, making an outline, taking notes, preparing a first draft, revising and editing, or completing the paper. Teachers who carefully plan research projects give just the right amount of direction to allow students to explore and discover ideas on their own. Research isn't a do-your-own-thing proposition. Novice researchers need structure. A research project must have just enough structure to give students (1) a problem focus, (2) physical and intellectual freedom, (3) an environment in which they can obtain data, and (4) guidance in writing and reporting the results of their research. See Box 5.1 on page 136 to review an outline of various aspects of the procedures for guiding research projects.

Ideally, research arises out of students' questions about the topic under study. A puzzling situation may arouse curiosity and interest. We recommend using questions such as the following to initiate research:

How is _____ different from _____? How are they alike?

What has changed from the way it used to be?

What can we learn from the past?

What caused _____ to happen? Why did it turn out that way?

What will happen next? How will it end?

How can we find out?

Which way is best?

What does this mean to you? How does this idea apply to other situations?

As a result of questioning, students should become aware of their present level of knowledge and the gaps that exist in what they know. They can use the questioning session to identify a problem. You might ask, "What do you want to find out?" During the planning stage of a research project, the emphasis should be on further analysis of each individual or group problem, breaking it down into a sequence of manageable parts and activities. The teacher facilitates by helping students to clarify problems. As students progress in their research, data collection and interpretation become integral stages of the inquiry. Students will need the physical and intellectual freedom to investigate their problems. They will also need an environment—a library or media center—where they will have access to a variety of informational materials, including print and electronic sources.

The teacher's role during data collection and interpretation is that of a resource. Your questions will help the students interpret data or perhaps raise new questions, reorganize ideas, or modify plans: "How are you doing? How can I help? Are you finding it difficult to obtain materials? Which ideas are giving you trouble?" This role is very similar to that of guiding the actual writing of the research project.

Guiding the Writing Process

Getting started with the actual writing of a paper or research report can be difficult, even terrifying. Waiting until the night before to write a paper is not good strategy! One of the teacher's first instructional tasks is to make students aware that the writing process occurs in stages. It's the rare writer who leaps in a single bound from an idea-in-head to a finished product on paper. The stages of the writing process may be defined broadly as *discovery, drafting, revising,* and *publishing.* Table 9.2 presents an overview of these stages.

These stages are by no means neat and orderly. Few writers proceed from stage to stage in a linear sequence. Instead, writing is a *recursive* process; that is to say, writing is a back-and-forth activity. As teachers we want to engage students in the use of discovery strategies to explore and generate ideas and make plans before writing a draft, but once they are engaged in the physical act of composing a draft, writers often discover new ideas, reformulate plans, rewrite, and revise.

Discovery: Getting It Out

What students do before writing is as important as what they do before reading. Discovery strategies involve planning, building and activating prior knowledge, setting goals, and getting ready for the task at hand. In other words, discovery refers to everything that students do before putting words on paper for a first draft. The term *prewriting* is often used interchangeably with *discovery,* but it is somewhat misleading because students often engage in some form of writing before working on a draft.

Discovery is what the writer consciously or unconsciously does to get energized and motivated—to get ideas out in the open, to explore what to say and how to say it: What will I include? What's a good way to start? Who is my audience? What form should my writing take? Scaffolding the use of discovery strategies in a classroom involves any support activity or

Table 9.2 Stages in the Writing Process

Discovery
- Exploring and generating ideas
- Finding a topic
- Making plans (Audience? Form? Voice?)
- Getting started

Drafting
- Getting ideas down on paper
- Sticking to the task
- Developing fluency and coherence

Revising
- Revising for meaning
- Responding to the writing
- Organizing for clarity
- Editing and proofreading for the conventions of writing, word choice, syntax
- Polishing

Publishing
- Sharing and displaying finished products
- Evaluating and grading

experience that motivates a student to write, generates ideas for writing, or focuses attention on a particular subject. Students can be guided to think about a topic in relation to a perceived audience and the form that a piece of writing will take. A teacher who recognizes that the writing process must slow down at the beginning will help students discover that they have something to say and that they want to say it.

Response Journal

What kinds of discovery strategies do you use to get started with an important writing assignment?

Getting started on the right foot is what the discovery stage is all about. Generating talk about an assignment or research project before writing buys time for students to gather ideas and organize them for writing. Discussion before writing is as crucial to success as discussion before reading.

Drafting: Getting It Down

The drafting stage involves getting ideas down on paper in a fluent and coherent fashion. The writer drafts a text with an audience (readers) in mind.

If students are primed for writing through discovery strategies, first drafts should develop without undue struggle. The use of in-class time for drafting is as important as allotting in-class time for reading. In both cases, teachers can regulate and monitor the process much more effectively. For example, while students are writing, a teacher's time shouldn't be occupied grading papers or attending to other unrelated tasks.

The drafting stage should be a time to confer individually with students who are having trouble using what they know to tackle the writing task. Serve as a sounding board or play devil's advocate: "How does what we studied in class for the past few days relate to your topic?" or "I don't quite understand what you're getting at. Let's talk about what you're trying to say."

Revising: Getting It Right

Revising a text is hard work. Student writers often think that *rewriting* is a dirty word. They mistake it for recopying—emphasizing neatness rather than an opportunity to rethink a paper. This is why good writing often reflects good rewriting. From a content area learning perspective, rewriting is the catalyst for clarifying and extending concepts under study. Revising text hinges on the feedback students receive between first and second drafts.

Response Journal

When you write a draft of an academic writing assignment, do you seek feedback before revising it? If not, why not? As a skilled writer, do you need feedback from a peer or an instructor?

Teacher feedback is always important, but it's often too demanding and time consuming to be the sole vehicle for response. It may also lack the *immediacy* that student writers need to "try out" their ideas on an audience—especially if teachers are accustomed to taking home a stack of papers and writing comments on each one. The "paper load" soon becomes unmanageable and self-defeating. An alternative is to have students respond to the writing of other students. By working together in "response groups," students can give reactions, ask questions, and make suggestions to their peers. These responses to writing-in-progress lead to revision and refinement during rewriting.

Once feedback is given on the content and organization of a draft, students can begin to edit and proofread their texts for spelling, punctuation, capitalization, word choice, and syntax. Accuracy counts. Cleaning up a text shouldn't be neglected, but student writers in particular must recognize that concern about proofreading and editing comes toward the end of the process.

Publishing: Going Public

When students put the time and efforts to edit, revise, and proofread, their writing deserves to be shared with others. The "publishing" stage of the writing process gives student writers an audience so that the writing task becomes a real effort at communication—not just another assignment to please the teacher. When the classroom context for writing encourages a range of possible audiences for assignments (including the teacher), the purposes and the quality of writing often change for the better. When students know that their written products will be presented publicly for others to read, they develop a heightened awareness of audience. Teachers need to mine the audience resources that exist in and out of the classroom. Some possibilities for sharing finished products include the following:

- Oral presentations to the class
- Class publications such as newspapers, magazines, anthologies, and books
- Room displays
- A secure class website for class members and parents

Looking Back | Looking Forward

In this chapter, we focused on writing to emphasize the powerful bonds between reading and writing. Content area learning, in fact, is more within the reach of students when writing and reading are integrated throughout the curriculum. The combination of reading and writing in a classroom improves achievement and instructional efficiency. When students write in content area classrooms, they are involved in a process of manipulating, clarifying, discovering, and synthesizing ideas. The writing process is a powerful strategy for helping students gain insight into course objectives.

The uses of writing have been noticeably limited in content area classrooms. Writing has often been restricted to noncomposing activities such as filling in the blanks on worksheets and practice exercises, writing one-paragraph-or-less responses to study questions, or taking notes. The role of writing in content areas should be broadened because of its potentially powerful and motivating effect on thinking and learning.

Because writing promotes different types of learning, students should have many different occasions to write. Students should participate in exploratory writing activities, journal-keeping, and discipline-specific forms of writing. Informal writing activities, such as the unsent letter, place students in a role-playing situation in which they are asked to write letters about the material being

studied. Additional activities include biopoems, microthemes, POVGS, and admit/exit slips. Journals, one of the most versatile writing-to-learn strategies, entail students' responding to text as they keep ongoing records of learning while it happens, in a notebook or loose-leaf binder. When students use response journals, double-entry journals, or learning logs, they soon learn to write without the fear of making mechanical errors. Students should also engage in RAFT writing assignments that are task explicit. An explicit RAFT assignment helps students determine the role, the audience, the form of the writing, as well as the topic.

Moreover, writing should be thought of and taught as a process. When students develop process-related writing strategies, they will be in a better position to generate ideas, set goals, organize, draft, and revise. The writing process occurs in stages; it is not necessarily a linear sequence of events but more of a recursive, back-and-forth activity. The stages of writing explored in this chapter were defined broadly as discovery, drafting, revising, and publishing. Discovery-related writing strategies motivate students to explore and generate ideas for the writing, set purposes, and do some preliminary organizing for writing. As students discover what to write about, they draft ideas into words on paper or on the computer screen.

Drafting itself is a form of discovery and may lead to new ideas and plans for the writer. Revising strategies help students to rethink what they have drafted, making changes that improve both the content and organization of the writing. Publishing involves celebrating and displaying finished products. The next chapter examines what it means to study. Studying texts requires students to engage in purposeful independent learning activities. Organizing information, summarizing chunks of information, taking notes, and conducting and reporting inquiry-centered research are examples of learner-directed strategies.

 # Minds On

1. Each member of your group should select one of the following roles to play: (a) a language arts teacher who believes that correct mechanics are the heart of good writing, (b) a science teacher who assigns students a variety of writing-to-learn projects, (c) a history teacher who believes that writing is the job of the language arts department, (d) a math teacher who uses math journals to aid in students' comprehension, and (e) an administrator who lacks a philosophical view and is listening to form an opinion.

   Imagine that this group is eating lunch in the faculty lounge at a middle school where you teach. The language arts teacher turns to the science teacher and says, "My students were telling me that in the writing assignment you gave, you told them not to worry about mechanics, that you were interested mainly in their content and form. I wish you wouldn't make statements like that. After all, I'm trying to teach these kids to write correctly." Continue the discussion in each of your roles.

2. What strategies do you believe would be most useful in making writing assignments meaningful for learning?

3. Your group should divide into two teams, one pro and one con. Review each of the following four statements, and discuss from your assigned view the pros and cons of each issue. After you have discussed all four statements, take an "agree" or "disagree" vote on each statement, and discuss what you really believe about the issue.

   a. We write to discover meaning (to understand) and to communicate meaning to others (to be understood).

   b. Writing is an incidental tool in learning and relatively unconnected to reading.

   c. Writing to learn is a catalyst for reading and studying course material.

   d. Students need to know the writer's role, audience, form, and topic for a writing assignment.

4. At the start of the chapter, we wrote, "When reading and writing are taught in tandem, the union influences content learning in ways not possible when students read without writing or write without reading." Drawing on your experience and the text, discuss some specific examples that support this thesis.

 # Hands On

1. In the center of a blank sheet of paper, write the name of the first color that comes to your mind. Circle that color. Let your mind wander, and quickly write down all descriptive words or phrases that come to your mind that are related to that color word. Connect the words logically, creating clusters. Next, see what images these relationships suggest to you. Write a piece (a poem, a story, or an essay) based on your clusters. Exchange papers, and in pairs, comment on

   a. The best phrase in your partner's piece

   b. What needs explanation or clarification

   c. The central idea of the piece

   With your partner, discuss how this exercise illustrates the characteristics of writing to learn.

2. Work with a partner. For this activity, write down seven pairs of rhyming words, and then recopy the pairs, alternating words (e.g., hot, see, not, me). Next, give your list of rhymes to your partner and have him or her write lines of poetry, using each word on the list as the final word in a line of the poem.

Your task is to observe the other during this activity and to record the characteristics of the other's approach to writing. For example, you might describe the writer pausing, sighing, gazing off, writing hurriedly, scratching out, and erasing. At the end of the activity, share your written description with the partner you observed to see if your observations match the writer's own perceptions.

Switch roles with your partner and repeat the exercise. What did you learn from both observing and being observed as a writer?

3. Take part in the following activities:

a. Brainstorm by clustering associations with the topic "writing in school."

b. Use this cluster to write a first draft of your experiences with writing in school.

c. Meet with a small group. Share your draft by reading it aloud to your group. Receive formative evaluation on your piece, and respond to the writing presented by others in your group. Make notes about possible changes that might be made in a second draft of your piece.

d. Revise your draft.

e. Describe for the class your experiences during this activity. Was this a helpful process? Discuss implications for your own teaching.

 # eResources

The following site contains thousands of story problems for enhancing critical thinking and problem-solving skills: **www.mathstories.com**. Many of the problems are based on children's literature. Browse the site and, working in small groups, write your own story problems based on content area topics of interest.

Use the keywords "double-entry journal," "double-entry journal + classroom lessons," and "RAFT writing strategies" to complete a search of these powerful writing strategies. Consider how you might use these strategies in your content area. Of all the sites that come up in your searches, identify the sites with the most complete information and lessons.

MyEducationLab™

Go to Topic 4: Writing, the MyEducationLab (**www.myeducationlab.com**) for *Content Area Reading*, where you can:

- Find learning outcomes for Writing, along with the national standards that connect to these outcomes.
- Complete Assignments and Activities that can help you more deeply understand the chapter content.
- Practice the core teaching skills identified in the chapter with the Building Teaching Skills and Dispositions learning units.
- Check your comprehension on the content covered in the chapter with the Study Plan. Here you will be able to take a chapter quiz, receive feedback on your answers, and then access Review, Practice, and Enrichment activities to enhance your understanding of chapter content.
- Visit A+RISE. A+RISE® Standards2Strategy™ is an innovative and interactive online resource that offers new teachers in grades K–12 just in time, research-based instructional strategies that meet the linguistic needs of English Language Learners (ELLs) as they learn content, differentiate instruction for all grades and abilities, and are aligned to Common Core Elementary Language Arts standards (for the literacy strategies) and to English language proficiency standards in World-Class Instructional Design and Assessment (WIDA), Texas, California, and Florida.
- Use the Online Lesson Plan Builder to practice lesson planning and integrating national and state standards into your planning.

10 Studying Text

CHAPTER 9

Multigenre Lab

Studying text helps students make connections and think more deeply about ideas encountered during reading.

Studying text is an active, persistent, demanding process that takes place inside the head. It requires not only concentrated effort but also reflective thinking. Through a growing array of technologies including search engines and online texts, students have more information available to them than ever before. However, it is becoming increasing difficult for many students to discern relevant knowledge from less important details in the texts that they encounter. Thinking deeply and carefully about texts is an essential part of effective studying that can increase understanding of subject matter.

Students need to understand their reasons for studying, whether their purposes involve acquiring, organizing, summarizing, or using information and ideas. Studying text requires students to be strategic in their approach to text and topics. They need to be deliberate in their plans, conscious of their goals, and clear about how to apply strategies that will enable them to understand and remember both main ideas and supporting details. Putting study strategies to good use is directly related to students' knowledge and awareness of what it means to study. As they become more aware of studying text, students look for *structure*—how the important information and ideas are organized in text—in everything they read.

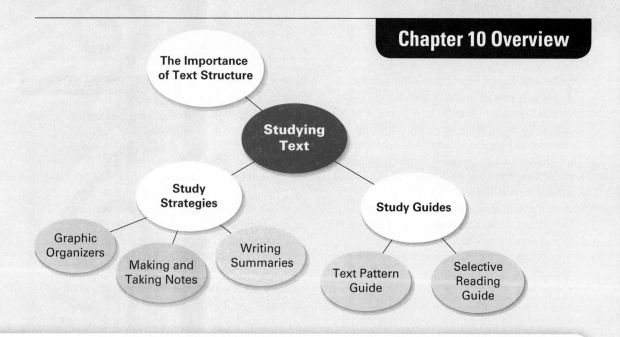

The organizing principle suggests that one important aspect of studying is to show students how to use the structure of ideas in text to their advantage:

Studying text helps students make connections and think more deeply about ideas encountered during reading.

Frame of Mind

1. How is internal text structure different from external text structure?

2. How do graphic organizers help students make connections among important ideas?

3. What note-taking frameworks and procedures can you model for your students?

4. How can you show students how to summarize information?

5. What are study guides? How can you develop study guides using the levels-of-comprehension construct and text patterns?

The poster caught our attention immediately. It had just gone up on the bulletin board in Julie Meyer's classroom. "School Daze: From A to Z" defined significant school activities in the lives of students, each beginning with a letter of the alphabet. The entry for the letter *S* just happened to be the subject of this chapter. It read, "STUDY: *Those precious moments between texting, video games, movies, sports, food, personal grooming, and general lollygagging when one opens one's school books—and falls asleep.*"

Though some students might agree that study is a quick cure for insomnia, few of us would deny that studying texts is one of the most frequent and predominant activities in schools today. The older students become, the more they are expected to learn with texts.

It's not uncommon to find a teacher prefacing text assignments by urging students to "study the material." And some students do. They are able to study effectively because they know what it means to *approach* a text assignment: to *analyze* the reading task at hand, to *make plans* for reading, and then to *use strategies* to suit their purposes for studying. Students who approach texts in this way achieve a level of independence because they are in charge of their own learning.

Other students, less skilled in reading and studying, wage a continual battle with texts. Some probably wonder why teachers make a big deal out of studying in the first place. For them, the exhortation to "study the material" goes in one ear and out the other. Others try to cope with the demands of study, yet they are apt to equate studying texts with rote memorization, cramming "meaningless" material into short-term memory.

Whenever teachers urge students to study, they probably have something definite in mind. Whatever that something is, it shouldn't remain an ambiguous or unattainable classroom goal. All too often, the problem for students is that they aren't aware of what it means to study, let alone to use study strategies.

Today's students need to learn how to work smart. Working smart involves knowing when and when not to take shortcuts; it's knowing how to triumph over the everyday cognitive demands that are a natural part of classroom life.

Knowing how to work smart requires time and patience. Studying is a process that is learned inductively through trial and error and the repeated use of different strategies in different learning situations. And this is where teachers have a role to play. Through the instructional support you provide, students discover that some strategies work better for them than others in different learning situations.

More often than not, however, students will tell you that they study to pass tests. Fair enough. They are quick to associate studying with memorizing information. A concept of study that includes retention has merit. But too many students spend too much time using up too much energy on what often becomes their only strategy: rote memorization. Rote memorizing leads to short-lived recall of unrelated bits and pieces of information. Alternatives to rote memorization should be taught and reinforced when and where they count the most: in a content area classroom.

Studying text *is* hard work. Cultivating a repertoire of study strategies to "get the important ideas straight in your head" is essential. Showing students how to distinguish important from less important ideas is one of the key aspects of studying texts effectively.

Response Journal

How is studying a text different from reading it?

The Importance of Text Structure

Authors impose structure—an organization among ideas—on their writing. Perceiving structure in text material improves learning and retention. When students are shown how to see relationships among concepts and bits of essential information, they are in a better position to respond to meaning and to distinguish important from less important ideas.

Educational psychologists from Thorndike (1917) to Kintsch (1977) and Meyer and Rice (1984) have shown that text structure is a crucial variable in learning and memory. Likewise, for more than fifty years, reading educators have underscored the recognition and use of organization as essential processes underlying comprehension and retention (Herber, 1978; Niles, 1965; Salisbury, 1934; Smith, 1964).

The primary purpose of many content area texts is to provide users with information. To make information readily accessible, authors use external and internal structural features. *External text structure* is characterized by a text's overall instructional design—its format features. Its *internal text structure* is reflected by the interrelationships among ideas in the text as well as by the subordination of some ideas to others.

External Text Structure

Printed and electronic texts contain certain format features—organizational aids—that are built into the text to facilitate reading. This book, for example, contains a *preface,* a *table of contents, appendixes,* a *bibliography,* and *indexes.* These aids, along with the *title page* and *dedication,* are called the *front matter* and *end matter* of a book. Of course, textbooks vary in the amount of front and end matter they contain. These aids can be valuable tools for prospective users of a textbook. Yet the novice reader hardly acknowledges their presence in texts, let alone uses them to advantage.

In addition, each chapter of a textbook usually has *introductory* or *summary statements, headings, graphs, charts, illustrations,* and *guide questions.* By learning how to attend to text features, students can identify the important information and increase their comprehension of the text (Bluestein, 2010).

Organizational aids, whether in electronic or printed texts, are potentially valuable—if they are not skipped or glossed over by readers. Headings, for example, are inserted in the text to divide it into logical units. Headings strategically placed in a text should guide the reader by highlighting major ideas.

Within a text, authors use an internal structure to connect ideas logically in a coherent whole. Internal text structure might vary from passage to passage, depending on the author's purpose. These structures, or patterns of organization, within a text are closely associated with informational writing. Read Box 10.1 to learn how a high school reading specialist used several strategies to help build a student's understanding of text structure, and, in turn, his understanding of texts in a world history course.

Response Journal

Why do some students ignore external organizational aids as tools for studying?

BOX 10.1

Voices from the Field

Betsy, High School Reading Specialist

Challenge

I was asked to work with a ninth-grade student, Stephen, who was struggling in his world history class. No one seemed to know why he was struggling in this particular class. I met with Stephen and together we went through his notebook, assignments, and tests; and we discussed how the class was conducted. Stephen explained that the teacher generally went over the course material in a lecture format, and the students were supposed to "take notes." No specific structure or guidance was given for doing so. Students spent any remaining class time completing textbook readings and answering questions from an accompanying workbook.

My first inclination was to teach Stephen note-taking strategies so that he could gain the most from the teacher's lectures. However, when I reviewed his notes, they appeared to be sufficiently comprehensive and well organized. Additionally, I noticed that the assessments and assignments on which he had performed poorly appeared to be based primarily on the textbook readings. This observation led me to look at how Stephen approached informational text. I began by asking him to show me what he does when he begins to read a new chapter. I noticed that he simply opened the book to the chapter, settled in, and read through the entire chapter. Next, he opened the workbook read a question and began flipping through pages in an attempt to find the answer. He had particular difficulty with questions that required him to attend to specific text features, such as tables, maps, or illustrations. I concluded that what Stephen needed was to learn effective study strategies.

Strategy

In order to try to increase his comprehension of text, I decided to teach Stephen to notice and use text features using the text feature strategy from Boushey and Moser (2009). Using clear acetate sheets and Vis-à-vis markers, we worked with one portion of the text as I modeled circling all of the text features including headings, maps, illustrations, timelines, and tables. I also wrote brief notes on what I learned from each one of these figures. Next, I guided Stephen in applying the same procedure to a different portion of the text. Then, he tried it on his own.

Once Stephen was independently attending to text features during a text preview as well as during reading, I wanted to teach him how to use the structure of the text to help him comprehend the main idea of each text section. Since he was not actually reading the headings, I decided to teach him a strategy for using those headings to aid his identification of important and interesting details. I taught him how to turn the heading of each section into a question, For example, if a heading reads, "The Causes of the Russian Revolution," the reader turns the heading to the question, "What were the causes of the Russian Revolution?" Using sticky-note strips, I taught Stephen how to mark the parts of the following text that answered that question and only that question. I modeled two sections, then worked through a section with Stephen, and finally asked him to work through the next section on his own.

As Stephen's next class assessment was fast approaching I introduced one last strategy: rereading. When reading dense informational text and trying to comprehend lengthy passages, students can sometimes lose meaning and be unable to identify where their understanding broke down. Chunking text into smaller parts and rereading those parts can be a helpful fix-up strategy.

Reflection

As Stephen completed the assignments related to the unit we worked on together, his grades steadily improved. I spoke with him after he received his unit test grade, and I asked him what had changed for him. Stephen told me that no one had ever told him that text features were that important and that the answers to question can often be found there. He also told me he was surprised by how much it had helped to think about the headings and to use the "question strategy." He did say that, while he didn't really like to reread, he saw that is was important to try to remember to do so when something in the text didn't make sense.

The use of these strategies helped Stephen to improve his comprehension of informational text. It is often surprising to me how many middle and high school students have not been taught, or don't remember, the importance of attending to text features, especially headings. Informational texts can be difficult for students in so many ways. Providing them with strategies for identifying and understanding important concepts, and reinforcing those strategies across subjects and grade levels, can help to improve students' understanding of content area texts.

Internal Text Structure

Content area texts are written to inform. This is why exposition is the primary mode of discourse found in informational texts. This is not to say that some authors don't, at times, attempt to persuade or entertain their readers. They may. However, their primary business is to *tell, show, describe,* or *explain*. It stands to reason that the more logically connected one idea is to another, depending on the author's informative purpose, the more coherent the description or explanation is.

Skilled readers search for structure in a text and can readily differentiate the important ideas from less important ideas in the material. Research has shown that good readers know how to look for major thought relationships (Frey & Fisher, 2010). They approach a reading assignment looking for a predominant *text pattern* or organization that will tie together the ideas contained throughout the text passage.

Text patterns represent the different types of logical connections among the important and less important ideas in informational material. A case can be made for five text patterns that seem to predominate in informational writing: *description, sequence, comparison and contrast, cause and effect,* and *problem and solution*. The following sections contain descriptions and examples of these text structures.

Description

The description text pattern involves providing information about a topic, concept, event, object, person, idea, and so on (facts, characteristics, traits, features), usually qualifying the listing by criteria such as size or importance. This pattern connects ideas through description by listing the important characteristics or attributes of the topic under consideration. The description pattern is one of the most common ways of organizing texts. Here is an example:

> There were several points in the fight for freedom of religion. One point was that religion and government should be kept apart. Americans did not want any form of a national church as was the case in England. Americans made sure that no person would be denied his or her religious beliefs.

Sequence

The sequence text pattern involves putting facts, events, or concepts into a sequence. The author traces the development of the topic or gives the steps in the process. Time reference may be explicit or implicit, but a sequence is evident in the pattern. The following paragraph illustrates the pattern:

> The space shuttle program began in 1972 when NASA's intent to build a reusable space shuttle system was announced. The first shuttle orbital flight, *Columbia,* took place in 1981. Over the next thirty years, the space shuttle program flew 135 missions, concluding with the final mission, *Atlantis,* in 2011.

Comparison and Contrast

The comparison and contrast text pattern involves pointing out likenesses (comparison) and/or differences (contrast) among facts, people, events, concepts, and so on. Study this example:

> Castles were built for defense, not comfort. In spite of some books and movies that have made them attractive, castles were cold, dark, gloomy places to live. Rooms were small and not the least bit charming. Except for the great central hall or the kitchen, there were no fires to keep the rooms heated. Not only was there a lack of furniture, but what was there was uncomfortable.

Cause and Effect

The cause and effect text pattern involves showing how facts, events, or concepts (effects) happen or come into being because of other facts, events, or concepts (causes). Examine this paragraph for causes and effects:

> The fire was started by sparks from a campfire left by a careless camper. Thousands of acres of important watershed burned before the fire was brought under control. As a result of the fire, trees and the grasslands on the slopes of the valley were gone. Smoking black stumps were all that remained of tall pine trees.

Problem and Solution

The problem and solution text pattern involves showing the development of a problem and one or more solutions to the problem. Consider the following example:

> The growing amounts of trash produced over the years, and the limitations of landfills to handle that trash has been a serious concern in recent years. It is estimated that on average, each American produces 4.5 pounds of trash per day, with approximately 67 percent of that being sent to landfills (EPA, 2009). There are several concerns about landfill use including the fact that not all materials decompose, and dangerous chemicals can be leaked from landfills into the air and water. Recycling and composting offer helpful solutions to some of the problems of landfills. In addition to environmental benefits, recycling and composting can create new jobs.

Signal Words in Text Structure

Authors often showcase text patterns by giving readers clues or signals to help them figure out the structure being used. Readers usually become aware of the pattern if they are looking for the signals. A signal may be a word or a phrase that helps the reader follow the writer's thoughts.

Figure 10.1 shows signal words that authors often use to call attention to the organizational patterns just defined.

Awareness of the pattern of *long stretches* of text is especially helpful in planning reading assignments. In selecting from a passage of several paragraphs or several pages, teachers first need to determine whether a predominant text pattern is contained in the material. This is no easy task.

Figure 10.1   Signal Words and Phrases Used in Various Text Structures

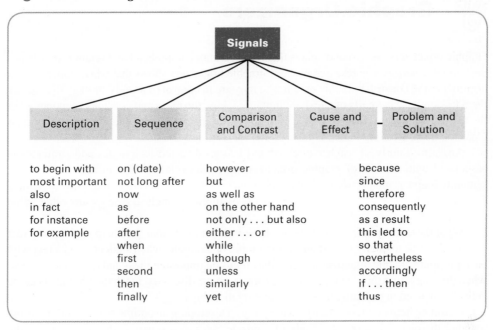

	Signals			
Description	Sequence	Comparison and Contrast	Cause and Effect	Problem and Solution
to begin with	on (date)	however	because	
most important	not long after	but	since	
also	now	as well as	therefore	
in fact	as	on the other hand	consequently	
for instance	before	not only . . . but also	as a result	
for example	after	either . . . or	this led to	
	when	while	so that	
	first	although	nevertheless	
	second	unless	accordingly	
	then	similarly	if . . . then	
	finally	yet	thus	

Informational writing is complex. Authors do not write in neat, perfectly identifiable patterns. Within the individual paragraphs of a text assignment, several kinds of thought relationships often exist. Suppose an author begins a passage by stating a problem. In telling about the development of the problem, the author *describes* a set of events that contributed to the problem. Or perhaps the author *compares* or *contrasts* the problem under consideration with another problem. In subsequent paragraphs, the *solutions* or attempts at solutions to the problem are stated. In presenting the solutions, the author uses heavy description and explanation. These descriptions and explanations are logically organized in a *sequence*.

The difficulty that teachers face is analyzing the overall text pattern, even though several types of thought relationships are probably embedded in the material. Analyzing a text for a predominant pattern depends in part on how clearly an author represents the relationships in the text.

There are several guidelines to follow for analyzing text patterns. First, survey the text for the most important idea in the selection. Are there any explicit signal words that indicate a pattern that will tie together the ideas throughout the passage? Second, study the content of the text for additional important ideas. Are these ideas logically connected to the most important idea? Is a pattern evident? Third, outline or diagram the relationships among the superordinate and subordinate ideas in the selection. Use the diagram to specify the major relationships contained in the text structure and to sort out the important from the less important ideas.

Students must learn how to recognize and use the explicit and implicit relations in the text patterns that an author uses to structure content. When readers perceive and interact with text organization, they are in a better position to comprehend and retain information.

Graphic Organizers

Graphic organizers are visual displays that help learners comprehend and retain *textually important information*. The research base for graphic organizers shows that when students learn how to use and construct graphic organizers, they are in control of a study strategy that allows them to identify what parts of a text are important, how the ideas and concepts encountered in the text are related, and where they can find specific information to support more important ideas (National Reading Panel, 2000).

An entire family of teacher-directed and learner-directed techniques and strategies is associated with the use of graphic organizers to depict relationships in text: word maps, semantic maps, semantic webs, flowcharts, concept matrices, and tree diagrams, to name a few. Although it is easy to get confused by the plethora of labels, a rose by any other name is still a rose.

What these techniques and strategies have in common is that they help students interact with and outline textually important information. For example, when students read a text with an appropriate graphic organizer in mind, they focus on important ideas and relationships. And when they construct their own graphic organizers, as we discussed in Chapter 8, they become actively involved in outlining those ideas and relationships.

Outlining helps students clarify relationships. Developing an outline is analogous to fitting together the pieces in a puzzle. Think of a puzzle piece as a separate idea and a text as the whole. Outlining strategies can be used effectively to facilitate a careful analysis and synthesis of the relationships in a text. They can form the basis for critical discussion and evaluation of the author's main points.

Problems arise when students are restricted in the way they must depict relationships spatially on paper or on a screen. The word *outlining* for most of us immediately conjures up an image of the "correct" or "classic" format that we have all learned at one time or another but have probably failed to use regularly in real-life study situations. The classic form of outlining has the student represent the relatedness of information in linear form:

  I. Main Idea

    A. Idea supporting I
      1. Detail supporting A
      2. Detail supporting A
        a. Detail supporting 2
        b. Detail supporting 2

    B. Idea supporting I
      1. Detail supporting B
      2. Detail supporting B

  II. Main Idea

This conventional format represents a hierarchical ordering of ideas at different levels of subordination. Roman numerals signal the major or superordinate concepts in a text section; capital letters, the supporting or coordinate concepts; Arabic numbers, the supporting or subordinate details; and lowercase letters, the subordinate details.

Some readers have trouble using a restricted form of outlining. Initially, at least, they need a more visual display than the one offered by the conventional format. And this is where graphic organizers can play a critical role in the development of independent learners.

To show students how to use and construct graphic organizers, begin by assessing how students usually outline text material. Do they have a sense of subordination among ideas? Do they have strategies for connecting major and minor concepts? Do they use alternatives to the conventional format? Make them aware of the rationale for organizing information through outlining. The jigsaw puzzle analogy—fitting pieces of information together into a coherent whole—works well for this purpose. Assessment and building awareness set the stage for illustrating, modeling, and applying the strategies. Box 10.2 outlines the steps used to build strategic knowledge and skills related to students' use of graphic organizers.

Evidence-Based Best Practices   **BOX 10.2**

Graphic Organizers

To introduce students to various kinds of graphic organizers that may be applicable to texts in your content area, Jones, Pierce, and Hunter (1988–1989) suggest some of the following steps:

1. *Present an example of a graphic organizer that corresponds to the type of outline you plan to teach.* For example, suppose that a text that students will read is organized around a cause and effect text pattern. First, preview the text with the students. Help them discover features of the text that may signal the pattern. Make students aware that the title, subheads, and signal words provide them with clues to the structure of the text. Then ask questions that are pertinent to the pattern—for example, "What happens in this reading?" "What causes it to happen?" "What are the important factors that cause these effects?"

2. *Demonstrate how to construct a graphic outline.* Suppose that math students have completed a reading about the differences between isosceles triangles and isosceles trapezoids. Show them how to construct a *Venn diagram* to map how they are alike and different. Next, refer to the comparison and contrast questions you raised in the preview. Guide students through the procedures that lead to the development of the Venn

diagram: First, on an overhead transparency (or using a doc cam or Smart Board), present an example of a partially completed Venn graphic. Second, have students review the text and offer suggestions to help complete the graphic. The accompanying graphic display shows a class-constructed rendering of the Venn diagram. Third, develop procedural knowledge by discussing when to use the Venn graphic and why.

3. *Coach students in the use of the graphic outline and give them opportunities to practice.* If other texts represent a particular text pattern that you have already demonstrated with the class, encourage students individually or in teams to construct their own graphic outlines and to use their constructions as the basis for class discussion.

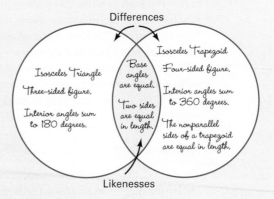

Differences

Isosceles Triangle
Three-sided figure.

Interior angles sum to 180 degrees.

Base angles are equal.
Two sides are equal in length.

Isosceles Trapezoid
Four-sided figure.

Interior angles sum to 360 degrees.

The nonparallel sides of a trapezoid are equal in length.

Likenesses

Using Graphic Organizers to Reflect Text Patterns

Students can be shown how to construct maps and other types of visual displays to reflect the text patterns authors use to organize ideas. Such organizers can provide a visual tool that illustrates the connections among concepts (Bulgren, Marquis, Lenz, Schumaker, & Deshler, 2009). According to Jones, Pierce, and Hunter (1988–1989, p. 21), "A fundamental rule in constructing graphic organizers is that the structure of the graphic should reflect the structure of the text it represents."

Jones and her colleagues recommend a variety of possible graphic organizer representations that reflect different text patterns. These "generic" outlines are illustrated in Appendix C. What follows are examples of how some of these outlines might be developed in content area classrooms.

Comparison and Contrast Matrix

In addition to the Venn diagram and graphic organizers, a teacher can show students how a comparison and contrast pattern serves to organize ideas in a text through the use of a matrix outline. A comparison and contrast matrix shows similarities and differences between two or more things (people, places, events, concepts, processes, etc.). Readers compare and contrast the target concepts listed across the top of the matrix according to attributes, properties, or characteristics listed along the left side. Study the two examples of a comparison and contrast matrix in Figure 10.2. High school students used the biology example to outline the likenesses and differences of fungi and algae. Precalculus students used the matrix outline to compare and contrast conic sections (parabola, ellipse, and hyperbola).

Problem and Solution Outline

This graphic representation depicts a problem, attempted solutions, the result or outcomes associated with the attempted solutions, and the end result. It works equally well with narrative or informational texts to display the central problem in a story or the problem and solution text pattern. Figure 10.3 illustrates a problem and solution outline developed by students as part of a class reading of *Monster* by Walter Dean Myers. In studying characterization and plot, students were asked to evaluate the choices made by the main character in the story, Steve. The book is written as a screenplay created by Steve to explain his experience awaiting trial for the murder of a store owner during a robbery, for which Steve may or may not have been serving as a lookout. Throughout the book, Steve reevaluates his decision to be at the store in the first place, and struggles with the perception many have of him as a consequence of his possible participation in the robbery. The students completed a problem and solution outline to analyze the impact that Steve's choices may have had on his life. The teacher introduced the outline. Students worked in pairs to complete the outline and then shared their responses with the whole class.

Network Tree

The network tree is based on the same principle as the graphic organizers introduced in Chapter 8 and used in the chapter organizers in this book. That is to say, it represents the network of relationships

Figure 10.2 Comparison and Contrast Matrices for Biology (a) and Precalculus (b)

(a)

	Fungi	Algae
Body Structure		
Food Source		
Method of reproduction		
Living environment		

(b)

	Parabola	Ellipse	Hyperbola
Sketch two examples			
Equation in standard form			
Special characteristics			
Foci (focal points)			
Line(s) of symmetry			

Figure 10.3 Problem and Solution Outline for
Walter Dean Myers's *Monster*

Problem	*Who* has the problem?	
	Steve Harmon	
	What was the problem?	
	Should he be a lookout during the robbery or should he stand up to his friends?	
	Why was it a problem?	
	If he stands up to his friends he could get beaten up; if he serves as the lookout someone else could get hurt and he could go to jail	
Solutions	**Attempted Solutions**	**Outcomes**
	Steve goes to the store but doesn't commit to being the lookout	Steve ended up getting caught and going on trial
	Steve claims he is not guilty during the trial	Everyone wonders if he is innocent or just trying to get out of trouble
	End Result	
	Steve finds himself on trial for murder and is upset that everyone thinks he is a "monster" for getting involved in a robbery that results in murder. Even though he ends up being found not guilty, Steve knows some people will always believe he was guilty and that he made bad decisions.	

that exists between superordinate concepts and subordinate concepts. It can be used to show causal information or to describe a central idea in relation to its attributes and examples. Notice how math students explored relationships in the quadratic formula by using the network tree illustrated in Figure 10.4.

Figure 10.4   Network Tree for the Quadratic Formula

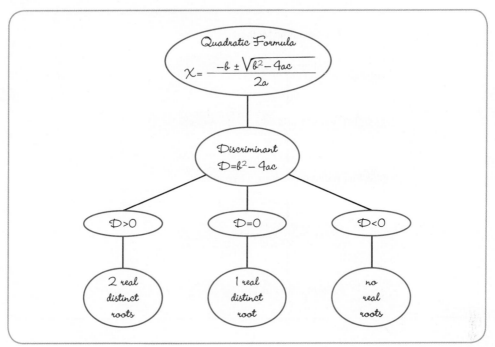

Series of Events Chain

The series of events chain may be used with narrative material to show the chain of events that lead to the resolution of conflict in a story. It may also be used with informational text to reflect the sequence pattern in a text. It may include any sequence of events, including the steps in a linear procedure, the chain of events (effects) caused by some event, or the stages of something. Scientific and historical texts are often organized in a sequence pattern and lend themselves well to this type of graphic display. A science class, for example, might be asked to map the sequence of steps in the scientific method by using a series of events chain. After reading about the scientific method, students might make an outline similar to the one in Figure 10.5.

In an English class, students read an excerpt from *My Bondage and My Freedom,* by Frederick Douglass, the famous American slave, abolitionist, and journalist. Douglass writes about the reasons for and purposes of the Negro spirituals that slaves sang and the effects that these songs had on his life. The teacher assigned the text selection to be read in class and then divided the students into learning circles (four-member teams) to work through the sequence of events that had led to Douglass's hatred of slavery. The series of events chain in Figure 10.6 illustrates the work of one of the learning circles.

Appendix C illustrates additional types of graphic organizers that may be adapted to different content areas.

Figure 10.5   Series of Events Chain for the Scientific Method

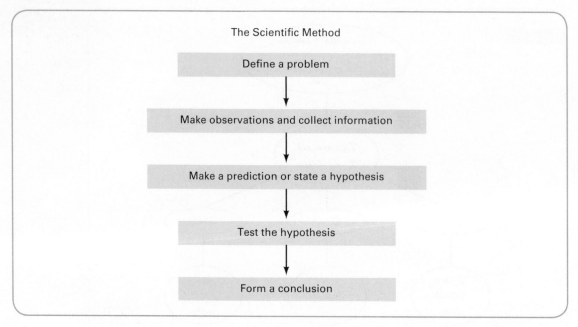

Using Questions with Graphic Organizers

Closely associated with the use of graphic organizers is an instructional scaffold that involves questioning. Graphic organizers and questions related to them go hand in hand. Buehl (1991), for example, lists the types of questions associated with the problem and solution, cause and effect, and comparison and contrast patterns.

 PROBLEM AND SOLUTION

1. What is the problem?

2. Who has the problem?

3. What is causing the problem?

4. What are the effects of the problem?

5. Who is trying to solve the problem?

6. What solutions are attempted?

7. What are the results of these solutions?

8. Is the problem solved? Do any new problems develop because of the solutions?

 CAUSE AND EFFECT

1. What happens?

2. What causes it to happen?

Figure 10.6   Series of Events Chain for an Excerpt from *My Bondage and My Freedom*

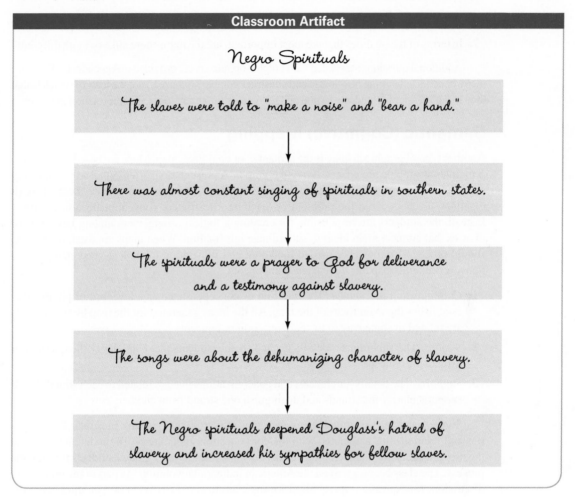

3. What are the important elements or factors that cause this effect?

4. How are these factors or elements interrelated?

5. Will this result always happen from these causes? Why or why not?

6. How would the result change if the elements or factors were different?

COMPARISON AND CONTRAST

1. What items are being compared and contrasted?

2. What categories of attributes can be used to compare and contrast the items?

3. How are the items alike or similar?

4. How are the items not alike or different?

5. What are the most important qualities or attributes that make the items similar?

6. What are the most important qualities or attributes that make the items different?

7. In terms of the qualities that are most important, are the items more alike or more different?

Additional questions associated with graphic organizers are provided in Appendix C. There are many benefits to learning how to use and construct graphic organizers, not the least of which is that they make it easier for students to find and reorganize important ideas and information in the text.

Semantic (Cognitive) Mapping

Another type of graphic display is the semantic, or cognitive, map. Maps are based on the same principles as graphic organizers. A popular graphic representation, often called a *semantic map* or a *cognitive map,* helps students identify important ideas and shows how these ideas fit together. Teachers avoid the problem of teaching a restricted, conventional outline format. Instead, the students are responsible for creating a logical arrangement among keywords or phrases that connect main ideas to subordinate information. When maps are used, instruction should proceed from teacher-guided modeling and illustration to student-generated productions. A semantic map has three basic components:

1. *Core question or concept.* The question or concept (stated as a keyword or phrase) that establishes the main focus of the map. All the ideas generated for the map by the students are related in some way to the core question or concept.

2. *Strands.* The subordinate ideas generated by the students that help clarify the question or explain the concept.

3. *Supports.* The details, inferences, and generalizations that are related to each strand. These supports clarify the strands and distinguish one strand from another.

Students use the semantic map as an organization tool that visually illustrates the categories and relationships associated with the core question under study. To model and illustrate the use of a semantic map, a middle school social studies teacher guided students through the process. The class began a unit on the American industrial revolution. As part of the prereading discussion, four questions were raised for the class to consider: What do you think were the most important factors that impacted the American industrial revolution? How did they impact the industrial revolution? What did these factors have in common? How were they different?

Then, the teacher assigned the material, directing the students to read with the purpose of confirming or modifying their predictions about the impacting factors. After reading, the students formed small groups. Each group listed everything its members could remember about the factors on index cards, placing one piece of information on each card. On the Smart Board, the teacher wrote, "Factors impacting the American industrial revolution" and circled the phrase. She then asked students to provide the main strands that helped answer the question and clarify the concept, "What were the factors that impacted the American industrial revolution?" The students responded by contrasting their predictions to the explanations in the text assignment. The teacher began to build the semantic map on the Smart Board by explaining how the strands help students answer the questions and understand the main concepts.

Next, she asked the students to work in their groups to sort the cards they had compiled according to each of the strands depicted on the semantic map. Through discussion, questioning, and

Figure 10.7 Factors Surrounding the American Industrial Revolution

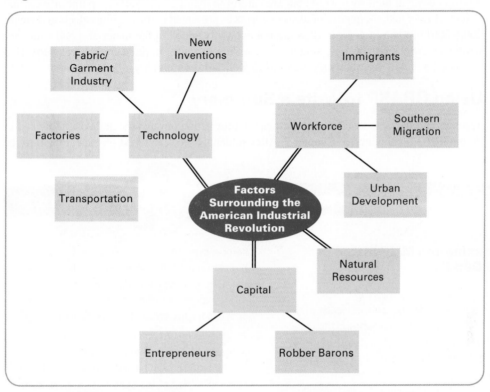

think-aloud probes, the class began to construct the semantic map shown in Figure 10.7. Some teachers prefer to distinguish the strands from supports through the use of lines or bolded text. Some teachers also find it helpful to use different colors to distinguish one strand from another.

With appropriate modeling, explanation, and experience, students soon understand the why, what, and how of semantic maps and can begin to develop maps by themselves. We suggest that the teacher begin by providing the core question or concept. Students can then compare and contrast their individual productions in a follow-up discussion. Of course, text assignments should also be given in which students identify the core concept on their own and then generate the structures that support and explain it. In addition to using graphic outlines, teachers can develop study guides (discussed later in this chapter) to help students discern text patterns.

 # Writing Summaries

Summarizing involves reducing a text to its main points. To become adept at summary writing, students must be able to discern and analyze text structure. If they are insensitive to the organization of ideas and events in expository or narrative writing, students will find it difficult to distinguish important from less important information. Good summarizers, therefore, guard against including information that is not important in the text passage being condensed. Immature text learners, by contrast, tend to *retell* rather than condense information, often including in their summaries interesting but nonessential tidbits from the passage. Good summarizers write in their own words but are careful to maintain the author's point of view and to stick closely to the sequence of ideas or events as presented in the reading selection (Friend, 2000–2001). When important ideas are not explicitly stated in the material, good summary writers create their own topic sentences to reflect textually implicit main ideas. Box 10.3 outlines the "rules" to follow in developing a well-written summary.

Using GRASP to Write a Summary

Teachers can show students how to summarize information through the guided reading procedure (GRP), as explained in Chapter 7. After students have read a text passage, they turn the

Evidence-Based Best Practices   **BOX 10.3**

Differentiating the Main Idea from the Details

When reading and writing expository text, it is often difficult for students to differentiate the main idea from supporting details, and to understand the relationship between the two. For example, a student may be able to identify the main idea in a subsection of a text, but may not differentiate cause from effect, or fact from opinion. Montelongo, Herter, Ansaldo, and Hatter (2010, p. 658) developed a four-part lesson cycle to help students make these types of connections when reading and writing expository text. As the authors explain, "Students must know the interrelationships among the topics, main ideas, and supporting details of paragraphs if they are going to comprehend and remember the important points the author is making." Montelongo, Herter, Ansaldo, and Hatter suggest the following instructional steps:

1. *Introduce vocabulary words.* Select vocabulary words that are essential for understanding the text. Use strategies, such as those described in Chapter 8, to engage students in understanding concepts rather than in memorizing definitions. Encourage students to focus on the context of the vocabulary words.

2. *Identify text structures.* Introduce, or revisit, the different types of internal text structures discussed in this chapter: description; sequence; comparison and contrast; cause and effect; and problem and solution. Work with students to help them identify the main idea and supporting details by identifying the signal words that correspond to the text structure of a particular passage.

3. *Practice using a modified sentence completion activity.* Provide the students with a fill-in-the-blanks worksheet-type page containing 10–12 sentences. Half of the sentences should be related to each other and, when placed in the correct order, form an expository paragraph. The remaining sentences should be unrelated to the topic at hand. Students should try to complete each sentence using an appropriate vocabulary word, and then find the related sentences and assemble them into an expository paragraph. The resulting paragraph should contain one main idea and several supporting details. Montelongo, Herter, Ansaldo, and Hatter point out that, to complete this activity successfully, students will need to review all of the sentences, as opposed to simply identifying the first sentence as the one that states the main idea.

4. *Rewrite the text.* Ask students to rewrite the paragraph they assembled in the previous step, using their own words. They may, for example, use their own synonyms in place of the author's words, or they may add their own supporting details to the text.

books face down and try to remember everything that was important in the passage. What they recall is recorded by the teacher on the whiteboard. Seize this opportune moment to show students how to delete trivial and repetitious information from the list of ideas on the board. As part of the procedure, the students are given a chance to return to the passage, review it, and make sure that the list contains all of the information germane to the text.

When this step is completed, the teacher then guides the students to organize the information using a graphic outline format. Here is where students can be shown how to collapse individual pieces of information from a list into conceptual categories. These categories can be the bases for identifying or creating topic sentences. The students can then integrate the main points into a summary.

Figure 10.8 shows how students in one science class adapted the GRP to summarize information they recalled from an article they read about planets. Following a model developed by Hayes (1989), the teacher modeled the development and writing of an effective summary by guiding students through a procedure called GRASP (guided reading and summarizing procedure). After following the initial steps of the GRP, the teacher recorded students' initial recollections of what they had read in the article on planets. Then, after rereading, students' additions and corrections to their first recollections were recorded.

Figure 10.8 Details Remembered from an Article on the Planets

Students' First Recollections	Additions or Corrections
Ptolemy thought the planets orbited the Earth	Orbited the Sun
Kepler found that the planets orbited in a specific pattern	Pattern is elliptical
Nine planets in our solar system	Currently, there are eight planets (Pluto was downgraded)
Planets consistently orbit the sun from a certain distance	Order: Mercury, Venus, Earth, Mars, Jupiter, Saturn, Uranus, Neptune
Mathematicians can calculate the movements of the planets	Movement was previously thought to be controlled by gods. Movements based on geometry and based on pull of gravity
Many planets have smaller bodies (moons) that orbit around them	Moons orbit Mars, Jupiter, Saturn, Earth, Uranus, Neptune, and Pluto

Figure 10.9   The Planet Summary, as Revised by the Students

While once Ptolemy thought that we had nine planets and they ~~circled~~ *orbited* around the Earth, we now know our solar system is a group of eight planets that ~~circle~~ *orbit* the sun in ~~a circle~~ *an ellipse*. Some planets also have ~~things~~ smaller bodies *, called moons,* moving around them.

The students then organized the information from these notes into the following categories: the planets, the movement of the planets, and changes in beliefs about the planets. These categories, along with the subordinate information associated with each, became the basis for writing the summary. The teacher walked the students through the summary-writing process as a whole class. First, the students were asked to contribute sentences to the summary based on the outline information that they had organized together. Then the teacher invited their suggestions for revising the summary into a coherent message. Figure 10.9 displays part of the completed summary, as revised by the class.

Polishing a Summary

As you can see from the revised summary in Figure 10.9, a good summary often reflects a process of writing *and* rewriting. Teaching students how to write a polished summary is often a neglected aspect of instruction. When students reduce large segments of text, the condensation is often stilted. It sounds unnatural. We are convinced that students will learn and understand the main points better and retain them longer when they attempt to create a more natural-sounding summary that communicates the selection's main ideas to an audience—for example, the teacher or other students. Rewriting in a classroom is often preceded by *response* to a draft by peers and teacher. We dealt in much more detail with responding and revising in Chapter 9. Here, however, let us suggest the following:

- *Compare a well-developed summary that the teacher has written with the summaries written by the students.* Contrasting the teacher's version with the student productions leads to valuable process discussions on such subjects as the use of introductory and concluding statements; the value of connectives, such as *and* and *because,* to show how ideas can be linked; and the need to paraphrase—that is, to put ideas into one's own words to convey the author's main points.

- *Present the class with three summaries.* One is good in that it contains all the main points and flows smoothly. The second is OK; it contains most of the main points but is somewhat stilted in its writing. The third is poor in content and form. Let the class rate and discuss the three summaries.

- *Team students in pairs or triads, and let them read their summaries to one another.* Student response groups are one of the most effective means of obtaining feedback on writing in progress.

- *In lieu of response groups, ask the whole class to respond.* With prior permission from several students, discuss their summaries. What are the merits of each one, and how could they be improved in content and form?

The real learning potential of summary writing lies in students' using their own language to convey the author's main ideas.

 # Making Notes, Taking Notes

Effective study activities for acting on and remembering material involve making notes as well as taking notes. Notes can be written on study cards (index cards) or in a learning log that is kept expressly for the purpose of compiling written reactions to and reflections on text readings.

Note making should avoid verbatim text reproductions. Instead, notes can be used to paraphrase, summarize, react critically, question, or respond personally to what is read. Whatever form the notes take, students need to become aware of the different types of notes that can be written and should then be shown how to write them.

Text Annotations

Text annotations describe the different kinds of notes students can write. Several are particularly appropriate for middle grade and secondary school students. For example, read the following passage. Then study each of the notes made by a high school student, shown in Figures 10.10 through 10.13.

> The Bill of Rights was a compromise which helped support people's rights under the Constitution. It allowed the government to create new laws so that the Constitution could be flexible as the nation progressed. However, the Constitution itself would not change, so it could maintain its original framework and intention. James Madison proposed the Bill of Rights and helped convince Congress to support the first nine amendments.
>
> Under the first amendment, people received freedom to speak against the government and assemble so that they might address issues they found unfair. As we will see with many of the amendments, while they propose freedom they also seek to limit and define the freedom. For example, you cannot yell "bomb" on an airplane, as that might impact the safety of the passengers on the flight.
>
> The Bill of Rights also limits the power of government. It helps define what fair punishment is, when you or your home can be searched, and tries to guarantee a fair trial while providing a lawyer to anyone who cannot afford one.
>
> To date, there have been seventeen amendments added to the Constitution since the Bill of Rights was written. Some define voting rights, while others give the government a right to tax its people. Good or bad, the Bill of Rights provides a space for America to address new issues that may arise as times change and new needs must be met.

The *summary note,* as you might surmise, condenses the main ideas of a text selection into a concise statement. Summary notes are characterized by their brevity, clarity, and conciseness. When a note summarizes expository material, it should clearly distinguish the important ideas in the author's presentation from supporting information and detail. When the summary note involves narrative material, such as a story, it

Figure 10.10 A Summary Note

The Bill of Rights safeguards people's rights and allows the Constitution to be changed as needs change. Nine original amendments were part of the original Bill of Rights; seventeen more have been added.

Figure 10.11 A Thesis Note

> The Bill of Rights helps the Constitution to remain flexible while sticking to its roots. It protects the people and safeguards their rights, but also limits freedoms in order to maintain safety and fairness.

Figure 10.12 A Critical Note

> The Bill of Rights helps the Constitution to remain flexible to address the changing needs of the American people. I think the Bill of Rights is a good start, but it really doesn't go far enough. The author lists the amendments that I think are necessary for anyone to live in a democratic society, but I know we still have problems. How are we enforcing the Bill of Rights? Many times, you hear of people being stopped and searched for reasons that may not be clear to them. I don't think that's what Madison intended when he first suggested this change to the Constitution.

should include a synopsis containing the major story elements. Examine the example of a summary note from a student's note card in Figure 10.10.

The *thesis note* answers the question "What is the main point the author has tried to get across to the reader?" The thesis note has a telegram-like character. It is incisively stated yet unambiguous in its identification of the author's main proposition. The thesis note for a story identifies its theme. Study the example in Figure 10.11.

The *critical note* captures the reader's reaction or response to the author's thesis. It answers the question "So what?" In writing critical notes, the reader should first state the author's thesis, then state the reader's position in relation to the thesis, and finally, defend or expand on the position taken. See Figure 10.12.

The *question note* raises a significant issue in the form of a question. The question is the result of what the reader thinks is the most germane or significant aspect of what he or she has read. See Figure 10.13.

Showing students how to write different types of notes begins with assessment; leads to awareness and knowledge building, modeling, and practice; and culminates in application. First, assign a text selection and ask students to make whatever notes they wish. Second, have the class analyze the assessment, share student notes, and discuss difficulties in making notes. Use the assessment discussion to make students aware of the importance of making notes as a strategy for learning and retention. Third, build students' knowledge for note making by helping them recognize and define the various kinds of text notes that can be written.

As part of a growing understanding of the different types of notes, students should be able to tell a well-written note from a poorly written one. Have the class read a short passage, followed by several examples of a certain type of note, one well-written and the others flawed in some way. For example, a discussion of critical notes may include one illustration of a good critical note, one that lacks the note maker's position, and another that fails to defend or develop the position taken.

Figure 10.13 A Question Note

> Has the Bill of Rights worked? The author lists several ways the Bill of Rights seems to have been effective. For example, it protects freedom of speech, limits the power of government, and works to ensure a fair trial. Without these basic rights protected, it would have been hard to ensure the pursuit of happiness as a reality for all Americans.

Note-Taking Procedures

Walter Pauk's (1978) response to the question, "Why take notes?" is profound in its simplicity: "Because we forget." More than 50 percent of the material read or heard in class is forgotten in a matter of minutes. A system of taking and making notes triggers recall and supports retention. When teaching students how to take notes, modeling and practice should follow naturally from awareness and knowledge building. Teachers can guide students through the process of making and taking different types of notes by sharing their thought processes. For example, a teacher might show how a note is written and revised using a think-aloud procedure. Students can then practice note making individually and in peer groups of two or three. Peer-group interaction is typically nonthreatening and can lead to notes that can be duplicated, compared, and evaluated by the class with teacher direction.

To facilitate the application of note-taking procedures to reading tasks across content areas, we suggest that students write notes regularly and in a variety of forms, such as learning logs, study cards, or on their computers. Note-taking procedures can take many forms. In this section, we highlight a few of those forms: reading logs, annotations, T-notes, and Cornell notes.

Reading Logs

Notes written in reading logs serve two purposes: They can aid students in organizing and synthesizing important information as they read a text and they can serve as a tool for clarifying and reviewing text material. Gomez and Gomez (2007) suggest double-entry reading logs as note making tools that can help students organize key details about complex topics and help teachers to gain information about student learning that can aid them in planning subsequent instruction. Students can, for example, use an argument/evidence double-entry reading log, shown in Figure 10.14, to distinguish main ideas or arguments found in a text from the evidence presented to support each main idea or argument. Similarly, a vocabulary or concept double-entry reading log, shown in Figure 10.15, can be used to help students identify those vocabulary concepts that they find difficult to understand. They can use the left-hand column of the double-entry log to list challenging terms and the right-hand column to write their interpretations of those terms. Later, following class discussions or additional readings that clarify these terms, students can revisit their double-entry logs by adding or revising the information they contain.

Figure 10.14   Argument/Evidence Double-Entry Reading Log

Main ideas or arguments from a text:	Evidence to support each main idea or argument:

Figure 10.15 Vocabulary/Concept Double-Entry Reading Log

Challenging terms from the text:	My interpretation of each term:

Annotations

Annotations can be used as a cognitive literacy strategy across content areas to help students to understand text structure, identify and analyze important concepts, and communicate their understanding of those concepts (Pressley, 2006). Zywica and Gomez (2008) applied text annotation as part of their multiyear Adolescent Literacy Support Project. They found the strategy to be particularly useful when charts, graphs, and illustrations are frequently embedded in the text. The text annotation system they described was designed to help students to identify different components within a single text. As they read, students mark the text with annotation symbols that represent key concepts, questions, or transition points. Some of the text annotation symbols that students used as they read an article for a science class included the following:

- A rectangle around key content vocabulary
- A triangle around difficult or confusing words
- A double underline for main ideas or important points
- A single underline for supporting evidence
- An arrow for procedural words
- An asterisk for transition words
- A question mark for confusing information

We recommend that teachers model the use of annotations and gradually introduce annotation symbols to students by selecting symbols that are most appropriate for organizing and understanding a particular text. Students should not be expected to use all of the annotation symbols at their disposal when reading a single text. As Zywica and Gomez remind us, the purpose of annotating text is to provide a framework to support students' understanding of concepts presented in a text, not to create busywork in addition to the reading. The text annotation procedure can be conducted as a whole-class activity, in which students take turns identifying various components of a text that is visible to the group through an overhead projector or whiteboard. Students can also work in pairs or in small groups to annotate a text, and in doing so can deliberate about correctly identifying elements such as the main ideas and supporting evidence.

T-Notes

T-notes provide a simple but effective framework for organizing information presented in texts. As Burke (2002) explains, teachers can adapt T-notes to help students compare and contrast concepts or to identify patterns across texts. The T-note example pictured in Figure 10.16 was used as a note-taking device for a text selection about different systems of government in a high school civics and economic class. Students used the left-hand side of the T-note to record information from the text that pertained to important points about capitalism; they used the right-hand side to record information in the text that pertained to communism. At the bottom of the T-note, they wrote a statement in which they summarized their understanding of the main idea presented in their reading.

Cornell Notes

A tried and true note-taking procedure common in many schools is the Cornell system developed by Walter Pauk in 1966. Cornell notes, as they are commonly called, can be used both as a note-taking procedure for recording important information during class

Figure 10.16   T-Note for Systems of Government

Name _____	Date _____
Subject _____	Period _____

Systems of Government

Capitalism	Communism
• Wealth is privately owned	• Wealth is commonly owned
• Market economy; laissez-faire	• Society regulates production to ensure everyone is equal
• Free trade; consumers have choice	• Communist state controls production and eliminates choice
• Means for industrialization of many countries in 19th and 20th centuries	• Communists believed industrialization and capitalism caused poor conditions of working class
• Adam Smith is the "father" of capitalist ideals	• Karl Marx is the "father" of communism
• Can lead to monopolies	• People work for common good
• People work for personal advancement	• Eliminates economic and social classes
• Allows people to change their social station by working hard	

In this box, write a summary statement that shows your interpretation of what you have read.

While communism allows everyone to work together toward an equitable society, capitalism allows everyone an opportunity to make a better life through hard work and perseverance.

lectures and as a study tool to review and extend concepts covered in class. Figure 10.17 shows the basic framework of Cornell notes. Students write details from a class lecture in the right-hand column. Soon after the lecture, students use the left-hand column to record questions or list key concepts that are based on the detailed notes they wrote during the lecture. Once students have had time to respond to those questions and to reflect on the material, they can use the space at the bottom of the page to write a summary statement, a synthesis of key points covered, or additional questions they need to address. Pauk and Ross (2007) recommend that students follow the sequence below when using Cornell notes:

1. *Record.* During a class lecture, record the important points addressed in the lecture in the right-hand column.

2. *Question.* As soon after the class as possible, use the left-hand column to develop questions about the material based on the notes you have written in the right-hand column.

3. *Recite.* Cover the notes you have taken during class and try to answer the questions you have written.

4. *Reflect.* Reflect on the material by asking and answering questions such as: How does this new information fit with what I already know? What new information have I acquired? Why is this information important?

5. *Review.* Spend time every week reviewing your notes. This consistent and sequential review of the material can help you to form connections and to analyze thoroughly the concepts presented. Consistent review can also aid in preparing for a unit assessment.

Figure 10.17 Cornell Notes

Name _____   Date _____

Topic _____   Subject _____

Questions or key concepts based on lecture notes or reading:	Important details from class lecture or reading:

A summary statement, list of key points learned from the lecture or reading, or questions from your reflection that you still need to address:

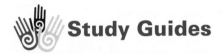

Study Guides

Note-taking procedures such as T-notes and Cornell notes can provide a study guide framework that helps students better comprehend texts. Over time, as students develop the maturity and the learning strategies to interact with difficult texts, the need for study guides is typically reduced. Until that time, however, study guides can provide students with support for navigating complex content area texts. In Chapter 7, we suggested the use of three-level comprehension guides for scaffolding learning at different levels of understanding. Text pattern guides and selective reading guides are also useful for helping students study difficult text.

Text patterns are difficult for some readers to discern, but once students become aware of the importance of organization and learn how to search for relationships in text, they are in a better position to use information more effectively and to comprehend material more thoroughly.

Text Pattern Guides

A study guide based on text patterns helps students perceive and use the major text relationships that predominate in the reading material. As you consider developing a study guide for text patterns, you may find it useful first to read through the text selection and identify a predominant pattern; and second, to develop an exercise in which students can react to the structure of the relationships represented by the pattern.

A middle school teacher prepared a matching activity to illustrate the cause and effect pattern for students who were studying a unit titled "The Native American: A Search for Identity." One reading selection from the unit material dealt with Jenny, an adolescent member of the Blackfoot tribe, who commits suicide.

The teacher asked, "Why did Jenny take her life?" The question led to a before-reading discussion. The students offered several predictions. The teacher then suggested that the reading assignment was written in a predominantly cause and effect pattern. He discussed this type of pattern, and the students contributed several examples. Then he gave them the study guide in Figure 10.18 to complete as they read the selection.

The class read for two purposes: to see whether their predictions were accurate and to follow the cause and effect relationships in the material. Notice that the social studies teacher included page numbers after the causes listed on the guide. These helped students focus their attention on the relevant portions of the text. First, the students read the selection silently; then they worked in groups of four to complete the study guide.

A second example, the comparison and contrast study guide in Figure 10.19, shows how the format of a guide will differ with the nature of the material (in this case, narrative) and the teacher's objectives. Juniors in an English class used the study guide to discuss changes in character in the story "A Split Cherry Tree."

Figure 10.18   Cause–Effect Study Guide for "The Native American: A Search for Identity"

Directions: Select from the Causes column at the left the cause that led to each effect in the Effects column at the right. Put the letter of each effect next to its cause in the space provided.

Causes	Effects

Causes

_____ 1. Jenny takes an overdose of pills (p. 9).

_____ 2. The buffalo herds have been destroyed, and hunger threatens (p. 10).

_____ 3. Native Americans remain untrained for skilled jobs (p. 10).

_____ 4. The temperature reaches 50 degrees below zero (p. 10).

_____ 5. There are terrible living conditions (no jobs, poor homes, and so on) (p. 10).

_____ 6. Pride and hope have vanished from the Blackfeet (p. 11).

_____ 7. Because we're Native Americans (p. 12).

_____ 8. The old world of the Native Americans is crumbling and the new world of the whites rejects them (p. 13).

_____ 9. The attitude of the Bureau of Indian Affairs (p. 13).

Effects

a. Unemployment rate for the Blackfeet is about 50 percent.

b. The first victim of this life is pride.

c. Blackfeet have become dependent on whites' help for survival.

d. Blackfeet turn to liquor.

e. Native Americans are robbed of their self-confidence

f. They are always downgraded.

g. Eighty percent of the Blackfeet must have governmental help.

h. *Hope* is a word that has little meaning.

i. She kills herself.

Figure 10.19   Comparison–Contrast Study Guide for "A Split Cherry Tree"

Directions: Consider Pa's attitude (how he feels) toward the following characters and concepts. Note that the columns ask you to consider his attitudes toward these things twice—the way he is at the beginning of the story (pp. 147–152) and the way you think he is at the end of the story. Whenever possible, note the page numbers on which this attitude is described or hinted.

Characters and Concepts	Pa's Attitude at the Beginning of the Story	Pa's Attitude at the End of the Story
Punishment		
Dave		
Professor Herbert		
School		
His own work		
His son's future		
Himself		

Selective Reading Guides

Selective reading guides show students how to think with print. The effective use of questions combined with signaling techniques helps model how readers interact with text when reading and studying.

The premise behind the selective reading guide is that, though teachers understand how to process information from their own content area, students do not yet possess the necessary processing skills. A selective reading guide can help to guide students' reading of content area texts. Figure 10.20 illustrates how a selective reading guide was used by a marketing teacher in one Career and Technical Education (CTE) department as he guided his students toward developing consumer awareness and an understanding of a market economy. His selective reading guide for a chapter from Clark, Sobel, and Basteri's text *Marketing Dynamics* uses both written questions and signals to help students in processing material from their text.

For struggling readers, teachers add a visual dimension to the guide. Study the guide in Figure 10.21, developed by a middle school science teacher. Notice how he guides students through the life functions of bacteria by using various kinds of cues, signals, and statements. The guide provides location cues to focus students' attention on relevant segments of text, speed signals to model flexibility in reading, and mission statements that initiate tasks that help students think and learn with texts.

Figure 10.20   Selective Reading Guide for a Marketing Class

Chapter 20: Internet as Place

Page 365: Read the introduction. List the ways in which students can use the Internet to support their school work.

Page 366: What is e-commerce? List several examples of businesses that rely on e-commerce.

Page 368: Use a Venn diagram to compare and contrast a dot-com business with a traditional business.

Pages 370–376: Skim the section on "The Internet as Retail Place." List both the positive and negative attributes of online shopping.

Page 376, Figure 29.9: The Better Business Bureau website illustrated in the text gives guidelines for responsible practices for online businesses. Based on your experiences with online shopping, what additional guidelines would you add to this list?

Page 376: The author states that many customers prefer to shop in traditional stores. Do you agree? Do you prefer to shop online or in traditional stores? Why?

Pages 379–381: Skim the section "Future of e-tailing." List the advantages and disadvantages of online shopping. Which do you think will have a more powerful impact on customers in the future?

Figure 10.21 A Reading Road Map

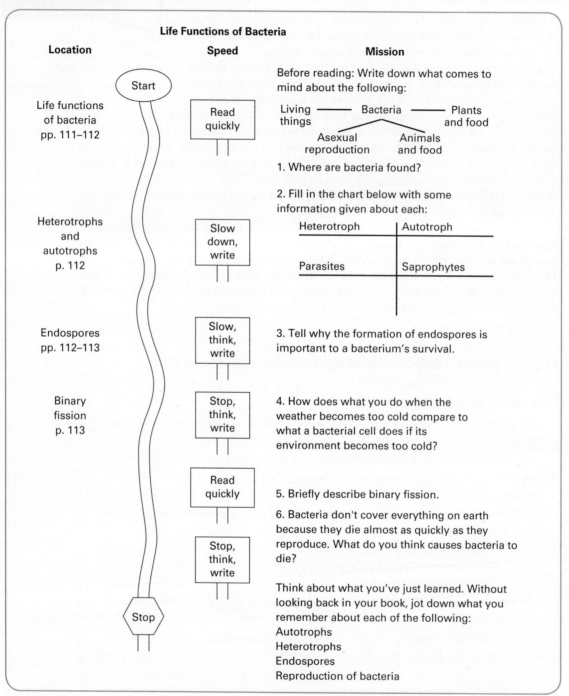

Life Functions of Bacteria

Location	Speed	Mission

Start

Life functions of bacteria pp. 111–112

Read quickly

Before reading: Write down what comes to mind about the following:

Living things —— Bacteria —— Plants and food

Asexual reproduction / Animals and food

1. Where are bacteria found?

2. Fill in the chart below with some information given about each:

Heterotroph	Autotroph
Parasites	Saprophytes

Heterotrophs and autotrophs p. 112

Slow down, write

Endospores pp. 112–113

Slow, think, write

3. Tell why the formation of endospores is important to a bacterium's survival.

Binary fission p. 113

Stop, think, write

4. How does what you do when the weather becomes too cold compare to what a bacterial cell does if its environment becomes too cold?

Read quickly

5. Briefly describe binary fission.

6. Bacteria don't cover everything on earth because they die almost as quickly as they reproduce. What do you think causes bacteria to die?

Stop, think, write

Stop

Think about what you've just learned. Without looking back in your book, jot down what you remember about each of the following:
Autotrophs
Heterotrophs
Endospores
Reproduction of bacteria

Looking Back Looking Forward

Teaching students how to study texts involves showing them how to become independent learners. In this chapter, we used the role that text structure plays to illustrate how you can teach students to use learner-directed strategies that involve constructing graphic organizers, writing summaries, and making and taking notes.

Understanding how authors organize their ideas is a powerful factor in learning with texts. Because authors write to communicate, they organize ideas to make them accessible to readers. A well-organized text is a considerate one. The text patterns that authors use to organize their ideas revolve around description, sequence, comparison and contrast, cause and effect, and problem and solution. The more students perceive text patterns, the more likely they are to remember and interpret the ideas they encounter in reading.

Graphic organizers help students outline important information that is reflected in the text patterns that authors use to organize ideas. The construction of graphic organizers allows students to map the relationships that exist among the ideas presented in text. This strategy is a valuable tool for comprehending and retaining information.

Students who engage in summarizing what they have read often gain greater understanding and retention of the main ideas in text. Students need to become aware of summarization rules and to receive instruction in how to use these rules to write and polish a summary.

Notes are part of another useful strategy for studying text. Making notes allows students to reflect on and react to important ideas in text.

In addition to the development of study strategies, teachers develop study guides to engage students in text comprehension and learning. With the use of guides, teachers provide instructional support to allow students to interact with and respond to difficult texts in meaningful ways. We explored and illustrated two types of guides: text pattern guides and selective reading guides. Text pattern guides help students to follow the predominant text structures in reading assignments. Selective reading guides show students how to think with text by modeling reading behaviors necessary to read effectively. How do teachers incorporate instructional practices and strategies into lessons *before, during,* and *after* assigning texts to read? In the next chapter, we explore the use of trade books in content literacy lessons and units of study. Trade books, like digital texts, are an alternative to textbooks.

Minds On

1. A member of the board of education has been quoted as saying that she is opposed to "spoon-feeding" high school students. After a board meeting one evening, you have an opportunity to talk with her. You explain that there is a difference between "spoon-feeding" students and helping them to "work smart." As a group, discuss how you might justify supporting students' studying through the use of techniques such as graphic organizers, summaries, and note taking.

2. Following an in-service program on using graphic organizers, you notice that some teachers in your building are preparing a semantic map for every assignment, whereas others, who say they don't have time, never use them. Your principal asks you, as a member of a team, to prepare a one-page sheet of guidelines for the use of graphic organizers in which you suggest when, why, and how various graphic displays should be used. What would you include in this guide?

3. Imagine that your group is team-teaching an interdisciplinary unit on the Civil War. Each member of your group should select (a) a content area and (b) one of the text patterns described in this chapter (sequence, comparison and contrast, problem and solution, cause and effect, or description). After reviewing some materials on the art, history, music, politics, science, mathematics, and literature of the Civil War, discuss how you might make use of a selected text pattern to teach a concept.

4. As part of an effort to improve school achievement in content area subjects, the curriculum director of your school system has suggested implementing a

mandatory study skills course for all high school first-year students. As a team, compose a memo explaining why and how studying can be effectively taught when content area teachers are also involved in the delivery of instruction.

5. The basic premise of a study guide is to provide instructional support for students for whom the text is too difficult to handle independently. How might guides be especially well suited to below-level students who have low self-esteem and little confidence in their ability to meet success with content material? In what ways will the purpose of meeting the individual needs of academically at-risk students be better served through their use? Provide specific examples when possible.

6. Reflect on the use of study guides in each of the content areas. Do you agree or disagree with the following statements:

   a. Study guides provide students with direction and organization for their reading.

   b. Study guides give students the chance to respond to texts in meaningful ways.

   c. Study guides are not meant to be used every day or with every reading assignment; that would reduce their effectiveness.

   d. Levels of comprehension are not as discrete as they may seem, but their division and treatment as separate entities are necessary to address various aspects of comprehension.

   e. If students become used to the support study guides offer, they will always be teacher dependent.

7. If a study guide is offered as an independent activity, students will get little out of it; failure will be just as frequent as with the traditional question-laden worksheet. Students need to be led through the use of study guides, sometimes working independently, sometimes working together. Reflect on the role of the content teacher in designing and using guides for learning.

Hands On

1. Design a semantic map for a science lesson on the characteristics of the planets. Create what you consider the most effective design for that specific content.

2. Using either problem and solution, cause and effect, or comparison and contrast, construct a graphic organizer for a passage from an informational text. Share your representation with members of your group, and discuss how some topics seem appropriate for one specific organizational pattern, whereas others might be organized in a variety of ways.

3. Distribute one card to each member of the class. Ask the students to write down the name of an individual they believe has made a significant contribution to society. Emphasize that the contribution may be in either a specific area of knowledge (art, music, science, literature, politics) or a nonspecific area such as acts of humanitarianism or environmental activism.

   Next, announce that the task of the class will be to create clusters of cards with names that have a common focus. Give each student in the class three minutes to find one partner whose card name relates to his or her own. Then have each team of partners locate another team whose names can be classified together. Explain that, if necessary, groups may redefine their common focus to create clusters. As a whole class, share the focus categories developed by each group.

   Finally, repeat the process, but do not allow any group to use the same common focus. Discuss how this activity relates to the process of outlining.

4. Imagine that one of your colleagues asks students to write summaries of what they are reading in class but does not provide explicit instruction on how to summarize a text effectively. You have observed that many of your colleague's students are frustrated by the task or are simply copying summaries written by other students. With a member of your group, create a dialogue in which you discuss some instructional alternatives that will lead students to writing summaries effectively. As a group, discuss the suggestions you found effective and recommend some others that might help students work smart.

5. In a small group, read a short selection from a current news story, magazine article, textbook selection, or electronic media source. Write examples of the different kinds of notes that can be made from the text. Compare your group's notes with those of other groups, and discuss the different thinking tasks each type of note required, as well as the further use of each note in a classroom teaching situation.

6. In a small group, compile a list of study strategies that the group members use as well as the purposes for which they are used. Categorize the strategies into different groupings according to their perceived purposes. Display the strategies on an overhead or a whiteboard for a discussion of commonalities and suggestions for studying texts.

eResources

Find more examples of graphic organizers by going to the Graphic Organizer Index at **www.graphic.org/goindex .html**. Conduct your own Internet search using the keywords "semantic maps + lesson plans." Go to Lesson Planet (**www.lessonplanet.com**) to see what comes up when you search for semantic mapping on this site.

MyEducationLab™

Go to Topic 8: Study Skills and Strategies, the MyEducationLab (**www.myeducationlab.com**) for *Content Area Reading*, where you can:

- Find learning outcomes for Study Skills and Strategies, along with the national standards that connect to these outcomes.
- Complete Assignments and Activities that can help you more deeply understand the chapter content.
- Practice the core teaching skills identified in the chapter with the Building Teaching Skills and Dispositions learning units.
- Check your comprehension on the content covered in the chapter with the Study Plan. Here you will be able to take a chapter quiz, receive feedback on your answers, and then access Review, Practice, and Enrichment activities to enhance your understanding of chapter content.
- Visit A+RISE. A+RISE® Standards2Strategy™ is an innovative and interactive online resource that offers new teachers in grades K–12 just in time, research-based instructional strategies that meet the linguistic needs of English Language Learners (ELLs) as they learn content, differentiate instruction for all grades and abilities, and are aligned to Common Core Elementary Language Arts standards (for the literacy strategies) and to English language proficiency standards in World-Class Instructional Design and Assessment (WIDA), Texas, California, and Florida.
- Use the Online Lesson Plan Builder to practice lesson planning and integrating national and state standards into your planning.

11 Learning with Trade Books

The use of trade books in content areas helps to extend and enrich the curriculum.

The more we think about what we read, the more we learn. More than 100 years ago, Theodore Parker noted that "the books that help you the most are those which make you think the most." That observation still rings true. Even though today's adolescents are immersed in a digital culture, books are assuming a more dynamic role in their lives. With the help of movies and other media, we have seen an explosion in adolescents' reading for pleasure. People of all ages have succumbed to the magic of J. K. Rowling's *Harry Potter* novels; they have continued to voraciously consume her books, even after watching the last of her blockbuster movies. Stephenie Meyer's *Twilight* series and Suzanne Collins's *Hunger Games* have sparked the same phenomenal response among adolescents. These books

fly off the shelves in major bookstores. Today's adolescents are spending hours engaged in an array of literacy pursuits—many involving new literacies—as we suggested in Chapter 2. Literacy clearly plays an important role in their lives. So, why aren't these same students clamoring for books in the classroom?

Today's classrooms must align books with the contemporary needs and interests of diverse student populations. By becoming more knowledgeable about trade books, teachers can better equip themselves to meet the academic, linguistic, social, and emotional needs of today's students. Books are made to be read for a variety of purposes, not the least of which is to learn. Books also serve as vehicles for change, social justice, and agency. Trade books, the subject of this chapter, should not be confused with textbooks. Trade books are published for distribution to the general

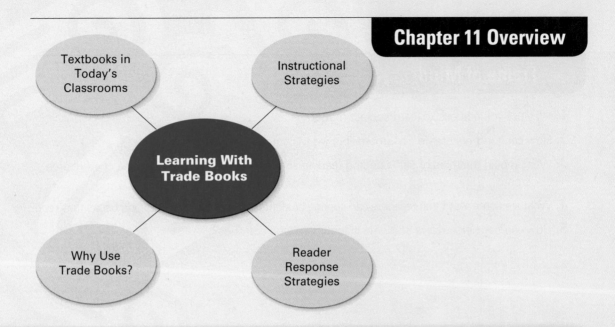

- Textbooks in Today's Classrooms
- Instructional Strategies
- Learning With Trade Books
- Why Use Trade Books?
- Reader Response Strategies

public through booksellers. On the other hand, text-books are distributed directly to school districts and selected by school boards and other policy makers. It's important to acknowledge that textbooks do play an important role in content area learning; however, they also have their limitations.

We make the case that in today's rapidly changing classrooms, textbooks by themselves are not enough. Students need access to a range of reading materials, and trade books provide a veritable mother lode of fiction and informational texts that connect to curricular areas and state standards. Trade books—whether picture books, fiction, nonfiction, or poetry—have the potential to motivate students with intense involvement in a subject and the power to develop in-depth understanding in ways not imagined a few years ago. Furthermore, by engaging students in active response to trade books, we heighten their interest and understanding of text content. By introducing students to trade books that reflect the contemporary realities of diverse cultures and classes, we increase their self-awareness and cultural understanding. We also engage students whose cultures and realities may not be represented in the canon or in textbooks.

Should textbooks be abandoned? Certainly not. Our point in this chapter is to underscore the value of integrating a variety of print and multimedia environments into the curriculum. The organizing principle for this chapter looks beyond the often limiting role of textbooks in content areas: **The use of trade books in content areas help to extend and enrich the curriculum.**

Originally written in collaboration with Barbara Moss and Virginia Loh, San Diego State University.

Frame of Mind

1. Why use trade books to learn subject matter?

2. How can teachers create classroom libraries in content area classrooms?

3. What should the roles of self-selected reading and teacher read-alouds be in the content area classroom?

4. What are some ways that teachers can engage students in responding to the trade books they read?

5. How can teachers involve students in inquiry-related activities?

Content area teaching often involves the use of one type of text—the textbook—often to the exclusion of other types of texts. Textbooks are more the rule than the exception in most classrooms. For many teachers, textbooks are classroom tools that serve as blueprints for learning in particular content areas. In a standards-driven environment, they provide coverage of content in particular disciplines that may well appear on high-stakes tests of some kind. Time constraints in a standards-driven curriculum are real. Teachers feel enormous pressure to cover a certain amount of content in a specified amount of time before students move on to the next chapter or unit of study. Teachers who operate under time constraints often view textbooks as efficient informational resources that support what students are studying in a particular subject at a particular time. When a textbook is the only source of information in a particular content area class, students come to connect the content of a particular subject with what are sometimes dull, lifeless textbooks. When the textbook becomes the curriculum, students are often denied the range of perspectives and opportunities for critical thinking.

In order to nurture a culture of reading, students need trade books in their content area classrooms as well as textbooks. In today's rapidly changing classrooms, learners are expected to read both print-based and electronic books. Electronic books, popularly known as *e-books* or *digital books,* are trade books (or textbooks) that are digitalized to be read on computers or other electronic devices known as *e-readers*. E-readers, such as the Kindle or Nook, and tablet computers, such as the iPad, are becoming more commonplace in classrooms as schools transition from print-based books to e-books and eTextbooks. Whether print-based or digital in nature, students need books that captivate them, nurture their souls, and capitalize on their interests. Readers need books that let them see themselves and satisfy their need to know about the world around them. In many ways, the content area classroom is the perfect place for students to connect with books because it affords students opportunities to build webs of meaning about a topic through a variety of sources. Through such experiences, students engage in meaning-making by evaluating information,

Response Journal

Based on your own school experiences, what do you believe are some of the problems associated with textbook-only instruction?

connecting ideas across sources, comparing and contrasting information, and reflecting on meaning. In this chapter, we explore the role of trade books in the classroom as well as the unique ways in which responses to trade books can enhance and extend content learning experiences. In general, we also make a case for using trade books—trade books that reflect the contemporary realities of our students, that present multiple perspectives, and that advocate for agency and change.

 # Why Use Trade Books?

Trade books, rich in narrative and informational content, can provide a valuable complement to most textbooks. Trade books can transport students to different places and times in ways that textbooks can't. Trade books can also relate experiences and perspectives that may have been excluded in textbooks. Learning with trade books involves exposure to many different genres and forms, all of which are potential sources of information for the active learner. Teaching trade books using a critical literacy framework allows teachers to push students to read the world (Freire, 1970/2000), and ultimately learn about their place in this world. For example, a nonfiction or fiction trade book has the potential to be a magnifying glass that enlarges and enhances the reader's personal interactions with a subject. When teachers use textbooks and trade books in tandem, they help learners think critically about content and, perhaps more importantly, they also help them think about the larger questions of the world.

A major emphasis in the Common Core State Standards (CCSS) is the use of trade books assembled as *text sets*—books related to a topic of study that are written at varying levels of text complexity—to help students understand the depth of the issues covered. According to the CCSS:

> There is evidence that current standards, curriculum, and instructional practice have not done enough to foster the independent reading of complex texts so crucial for college and career readiness, particularly in the case of informational texts. (www.corestandards.org, 2010)

The use of trade books in the classroom can challenge and stimulate student thinking on a range of important issues with particular relevance to the world today, including immigration, globalization, mathematical concepts, scientific inquiry, and much more. Fang (2010), for example, contends that inquiry is the cornerstone of science and that science curricula should include the development of students' ability to access information, comprehend concepts, and produce science texts. Trade books provide an ideal vehicle for accomplishing such goals. Of course, a science teacher, or any teacher for that matter, should not use trade books just for the sake of using trade books. Schroeder, et al. (2009) suggest that in a discipline such as science, teachers must first determine if trade books match the goals of the curriculum and whether they support the goals of scientific literacy.

It is imperative that teachers place thought-provoking books in the hands and minds of students. As Aidan Chambers (1973) notes, good literature both comforts and subverts. As adolescents seek to construct and establish their identities, trade books with social justice themes may help give them a sense of agency and also help them empathize, which is a motivating factor needed for social change (Goodman, 2002). Furthermore, teachers need to acknowledge the power of trade books and guide students toward a more critical lens. According to critical literacy theorists (Bean & Moni, 2003; Foss, 2002; Morgan, 1997), texts position the readers to assume a stance; in order to develop citizens and future leaders, teachers need to teach students how to think critically.

Today's trade books can provide an effective complement to textbooks in virtually any subject. The best trade books overcome many of the limitations of content area texts discussed in the previous section. They provide depth, considerate and accurate information, material at a variety of reading levels, and motivation for learning. For example, high-quality trade books can supply the depth of information that space limitations prevent textbooks from providing. Consider the brief textbook treatment of World War I you might find in a history text. Many outstanding trade books provide in-depth accounts of that event in history, such as *The First World War* (Keegan, 2003). Making a case for using picture books in secondary classrooms, *Faithful Elephants* (Tsuchiya, 1988) offers a different perspective on World War II, encouraging empathy and cross-cultural understanding. Trade books can fulfill the need for story and provide the emotional dimension so lacking in textbooks. Unlike textbooks, they move students' minds and their hearts.

In addition, trade books, nonfiction titles in particular, often contain information that is written and organized in ways that make information more interesting and accessible. The best nonfiction books are more than "baskets of facts"; they speak to young readers personally through informal, engaging writing styles. Their clear, reader-friendly explanations of scientific principles or processes can be extremely helpful to students. In addition, authors of trade books take enormous pains to ensure accuracy. In a speech in Columbus, Ohio, Jim Murphy explained that *each fact* in his award-winning nonfiction title *The Great Fire* (Murphy, 1998) was checked for accuracy at least three times. Similarly, authors of multicultural trade books cite deliberate and diligent research of a variety of sources in order to produce culturally authentic works (Loh, 2006).

Trade books can help teachers differentiate instruction by meeting the range of reading levels in their classrooms. By using a variety of trade books at different levels, teachers can match students with books they can read. Instead of having all students read the same textbooks, students can read a variety of different trade books about a particular topic. This allows teachers to give students books at their independent reading levels, a practice that has been associated with gains in achievement.

Furthermore, exposure to nonfiction literature gives students much needed practice reading expository text, which unlike narrative, does not typically involve characters, plots, or settings. This type of text is typically less familiar to students than narrative and more difficult for them to read. The reality is that many students do not know how to read to learn with informational texts because their school experiences have been limited to textbook-only reading. For some students the only historical, mathematics, or science materials they will ever read in a lifetime are in textbooks.

Trade books help readers at all levels develop greater understanding of content-related concepts. Historical fiction titles, for example, provide a framework for remembering, understanding, and evaluating historical content. The same holds for content in science and other subject areas. Popular science books, both fact and fiction, provide background knowledge for science concepts covered in class and help students relate these concepts to their everyday lives.

Finally, trade books have the power to motivate students to read more. The compelling visual qualities of today's nonfiction books make them many students' favorite out-of-school reading. Authors of nonfiction not only inform but also entertain. Consider, for example, *Phineas Gage: A Gruesome but True Story About Brain Science* (Fleischman, 2002). In 1848, Phineas Gage had a three-and-a-half-foot iron rod blasted through his head and survived. Despite his recovery, Gage's personality underwent a drastic transformation. He changed from a reliable, respected foreman to an unpredictable and temperamental man who eventually lost his job. The focus of the book is not simply on what happened to Gage, but on what neurologists have learned and continue to learn today about the workings of the human brain. Because of its lively writing and extraordinary visuals, this amazing book provides background information about the human brain in a format sure to motivate even those students who have little initial interest in the topic.

Authors of fiction engage students through characters that remind readers of themselves and their peers. Many titles address students' emotional needs because they are written from the viewpoint of students. People of all ages and backgrounds are attracted to books that speak to them in some personal way. For many female students, for example, Ann Brashares's (2001) best-selling *Sisterhood of the Traveling Pants* collection speaks of the powerful bonds of friendship and its potential to transform lives. For males of any ethnicity, but especially Native Americans, Sherman Alexie's (2007) *The Absolutely True Diary of a Part-Time Indian* speaks of the trials and tribulations of forging multiple cultural identities. Today's young adult literature is more edgy than in the past, and one could argue, more representative of today's teens. Because of this, today's young adult books are likely to appeal to a wider audience than ever before and, as a result, teens will be more likely to read such books.

Capturing students' attention and promoting the habit of lifelong reading provide a major rationale for using trade books. Of all the goals for literacy instruction, there is none more critical than creating students who read independently. Independent reading provides practice and pleasure, and develops passion for books. It affords students an opportunity to "get lost in a book"—to be so engaged in reading that one loses track of time, of place, of everything but the power of a text to transport and transform us. Repeated experiences that involve true engagement with books help students develop a love of reading that may last a lifetime. When students are given opportunities to interact with quality trade books, they have a better chance of becoming lifelong readers. Textbooks alone cannot motivate students to continue their learning, particularly in the case of reluctant or academically diverse readers, who are often frustrated and defeated by textbooks in the first place. As Melissa, a high school English teacher, suggests in Box 11.1, there is no substitute for a good book.

BOX 11.1 Voices from the Field

Melissa, High School English Teacher

Challenge

As an English teacher in a low-performing high school, it is important students buy into the idea that what they are doing is connected to their lives in some way, and it is essential that students feel they are working with a text that is part of "real world" reading as opposed to the worksheet realm of textbook regurgitation. Required by my school district to utilize designated texts and follow Common Core State Standards in my lesson and unit planning, incorporation of trade books can seem like yet another element that must be present in my already overcrowded curriculum. However, the use of trade books allows for easy connections between nonfiction texts and literature and offers students the opportunity to read texts that have significance outside the classroom. Additionally, the identification, collection, and incorporation of trade books is deceivingly easy when approached with an open mind and willingness to adapt lessons to ensure student interest is increased and unmotivated learners are offered alternative access to literary concepts and understanding.

Strategy

One of my first steps was to streamline the skills I wanted students to master through my lessons. Instead of focusing on individual concepts that I would introduce through various means, I focused on planning units with trade books that allowed the collection of desired skills to be explored through novels, resulting in a deeper understanding of concepts. Instead of using short stories from the textbook to demonstrate various literary and writing devices, I had students identify elements as they developed throughout a novel, avoiding the choppy, disjointed approach that many times results from textbook organization. This approach allowed for more holistic exposures to litera-ture and stimulated identification of trends and developing elements over time. By making use of novels and texts outside of the textbook, I was able to cover the curriculum in a relevant context that permitted plenty of practice and encouraged generalization of skills beyond the English classroom.

The use of trade books also allows for students to seek out their own texts related to the focus of the lesson. By providing students the opportunity to select supplemental texts that were relevant and interesting, I encouraged the students to take ownership of their learning and provided opportunities for them to become the "experts" in the class. Though textbooks provide related excerpts or articles that connect with the covered content, incorporation of different forms of trade books not only can provide different lenses through which to view concepts and skills but also can allow students to explore aspects of the curriculum to which they have personal connections. While it was initially intimidating to incorporate student supplemental finds, I soon found that planning general activities became more enjoyable for the students since they were exploring texts in which they had an interest.

Though student choice was important, a large part of the Common Core State Standards is the incorporation of nonfiction texts and historical documents with the curriculum. Initially a challenge, it was this requirement that really illustrated the benefit of trade books. Trade books allowed me to present many facets of concepts and explore cross-curricular ideas within my one-subject classroom. Alternatively, students were exposed to texts and counter-arguments that were timely and relevant to the skills being taught and their lives and community. By incorporating nonfiction accounts and historical perspectives, the students gained deeper insight and I was able to meet my necessary standards and objectives without completely overhauling previous lessons that also had value. Simple tweaks to my plans to recognize the place of trade books not only exposed the students to more nonfiction, but also allowed students to mesh context and content in a way that made sense.

Reflection

Through the use of literature and multiple text types, I've been able to engage my typically unmotivated textbook learners in reading, writing, and thinking about a variety of texts that explore different concepts and perspectives. Providing students with short, engaging texts that built their background knowledge, stimulated discussion, and were relevant to the students' own lives, prevented textbook "burnout" and encouraged proactive student behaviors. Throughout the process, I utilized the school librarian, various websites, and even some educational foundations to obtain funds to purchase trade books. I found that many trade books are accessible via donation sites like Swap.com, and many times single copies of books will be offered to schools for a small fee. As I increase my comfort level and build my understanding of the use of trade books, I begin to use the textbook less and less and incorporate multiple trade books with more and more frequency.

Learning with Trade Books

When students have opportunities to learn with trade books, they are in a position to explore and interact with many kinds of texts, both fiction and nonfiction. Today's trade books are better than ever. They are written by authors in touch with the emotions and experiences of today's young people and address an enormous range of themes and genre. They present characters and events from virtually every ethnic and cultural group in accurate and meaningful circumstances and settings.

Today's trade books offer teachers a variety of genres, ranging from easy-to-read titles using engaging formats to extremely sophisticated explorations of complex topics. Trade books can serve the needs of every student in every academic area. The greatest challenge for teachers is deciding which books to choose from the enormous selection available. Figure 11.1 provides a list of references to help teachers select good books for their classrooms.

Figure 11.1 Trade Book Selection Guide for Children and Adolescents

The ALAN Review (Assembly on Literature for Adolescents, National Council of Teachers of English). Published three times a year; articles and "Clip and File" reviews. Urbana, IL: National Council of Teachers of English. http://scholar.lib.vt.edu/ejournals/ALAN

Appraisal: Children's Science Books for Young People. Published quarterly by Children's Science Book Review Committee. Reviews written by children's librarians and subject specialists.

Association for Library Service to Children. (1995). *The Newbery & Caldecott Awards: A Guide to The Medal and Honor Books.* Chicago: American Library Association. Provides short annotations for the winners and runners-up of ALA-sponsored awards.

www.ala.org/ala/alsc/awardsscholarships/literaryawds/literaryrelated.htm

Book Links: Connecting Books, Libraries, and Classrooms. Published six times a year by the American Library Association to help teachers integrate literature into the curriculum; bibliographies in different genres and subjects; suggestions for innovative use in the classroom. www.ala.org/ala/productsandpublications/periodicals/booklinks/booklinks.htm

Booklist. Published Twice Monthly by the American Library Association. Reviews of children's trade books and nonprint materials (video, audio, and computer software). Approximate grade levels are given;

(continued)

Figure 11.1 (*continued*)

separate listing for nonfiction books. www .ala.org/ala/booklist/booklist.htm

Books for the Teenage Reader. Published Annually by the Office of Young Adult Services, New York Public Library. Recommendations from young adult librarians in the various branches of the New York Public Library. http://teenlink.nypl.org/bta1.cfm

Bulletin of the Center for Children's Books. Published monthly by the University of Chicago Press; detailed reviews and possible curriculum uses are noted. http: //bccb.lis.uiuc.edu

Carter, B. (2000). *Best Books for Young Adults* (2nd ed.). Chicago: American Library Association. This classic book contains lists of 1,800 books arranged by topics including animals, romance, and survival.

Children's Books: Awards and Prizes. New York: Children's Book Council. Award-winning titles as well as state "Children's Choice" awards for exemplary trade books. www.cbcbooks.org

Christenbury, L. (Ed.). (1995). *Books for you: A Booklist for Senior High Students* (11th ed.). Urbana, IL: National Council of Teachers of English. Provides annotations for both fiction and nonfiction written for students, organized into fifty categories.

Friedberg, J. B. (1992). *Portraying persons with disabilities: An Annotated Bibliography of Non-Fiction for Children and Teenagers* (2nd ed.). New Providence, NJ: Bowker. Provides comprehensive listings of nonfiction dealing with physical, mental, and emotional disabilities.

Gillespie, J. T., & Barr, C. (2004). *Best Books for High School Readers: Grades 9–12.* Englewood, CO: Libraries Unlimited. Lists 12,000 fiction and nonfiction titles published between 2001 and 2003, recommended in at least two sources and organized thematically.

Gorman, M. (2003). *Getting graphic: Using Graphic Novels to Promote Literacy with Preteens and Teens.* New York: Linworth Publishing. Provides an introduction to teaching with graphic novels and includes a bibliography of fifty graphic novels suitable for sixth grade, as well as suggestions for using these books in the classroom.

Helbig, A., & Perkins, A. R. (2000). *Many peoples, one land: A Guide to New Multicultural Literature for Children and Young Adults.* Westport, CT: Greenwood Press. Provides an extensive listing of titles featuring African Americans, Asian Americans, Hispanic Americans, and Native Americans.

The Horn Book Magazine. Published Six Times a Year by Horn Book, Inc.; articles by noted children's authors, illustrators, and critics on aspects of children's literature, including its use in the classroom. Nonfiction books are reviewed in a separate section. www .hbook.com/publications/magazine/default.asp

International Reading Association. "Children's Choices," a list of exemplary, "reader-friendly" children's literature, is published every October in *The Reading Teacher.* www .reading.org/resources/tools/choices_childrens.html

McClure, A. A., & Kristo, J. (Ed.). (2002). *Adventuring with Books: A Booklist for Pre-K–Grade 6* (13th ed.). Urbana, IL: National Council of Teachers of English. Summaries of hundreds of books arranged by genre and topic within content areas.

Miller-Lachman, L. (1992). *Our Family, Our Friends, Our World: An Annotated Guide to Significant Multicultural Books for Children and Teenagers.* New Providence, NJ: Reed Publishing. Comprehensive reference work includes 1,000 of the best English-language fiction and nonfiction multicultural books published since 1970. Each chapter introduces a culture, a map of the region, and an annotated list of books for preschool through grade twelve.

Notable Children's Trade Books in the Field of Social Studies. National Council for the Social Studies. Published yearly in the spring issue of *Social Education;* annotates notable fiction and nonfiction books, primarily for children in grades K–8. www .socialstudies.org/resources/notable

Outstanding Science Trade Books for Students K–12. National Science Teachers Association. Published each year in the spring issue of *Science and Children;* contains information consistent with current scientific

Figure 11.1 (*continued*)

knowledge; is pleasing in format; illustrated; and is nonsexist, nonracist, and nonviolent.

Rand, D., & Parker, T. T. (2000). *Black Books Galore! Guide to Great African American Children's Books About Girls*. New York: Jossey-Bass. Featuring 360 books arranged alphabetically by title, this book provides descriptions, notes awards, and spotlights well-known authors and illustrators.

Rosow, L. V. (1996). *Light 'n Lively Reads for ESL, Adult and Teen Readers*. Englewood, CO: Libraries Unlimited. Books are arranged in seventeen different thematic units. Each unit lists picture books,

thin books, challenging books, book chapters and "strong passages," newspaper and magazine articles, and suggested activities related to each theme.

School Library Journal. Published by R. R. Bowker; articles on all aspects of children's literature, including its use in content areas; reviews by school and public librarians. www.schoollibraryjournal.com

Totten, H. L., & Brown, R. W. (1995). *Culturally Diverse Library Collections for Children*. New York: Neal-Schuman. Includes annotations on Native Americans, Asian Americans, Hispanic Americans, and African Americans.

Nonfiction Books

Nonfiction trade books have, in recent years, moved from the shadows into the spotlight of literary excellence. Nonfiction books, which include informational books and biographies, are not glorified textbooks. They connect with readers through writing that is not strictly objective

Evidence-Based Best Practices   **BOX 11.2**

Appreciating Art and Artists Through the Use of Trade Books

Today's nonfiction trade books offer teachers rich opportunities to involve students in learning about artists and analyzing their works. Art teacher Carole Newman has found many ways to create literacy activities that serve to extend student learning in her middle school art classes. One project that she typically involves her students in is the study of the lives and work of famous artists. This project combines reading, writing, and artistic expression. She begins this project by providing her students with a wide array of artists' biographies. These include books from the *Lives of the Artists* series, artists' biographies by Jan Greenberg and Diane Stanley, and many others. Some of the artists that students study

include Diego Rivera, Frida Kahlo, Marc Chagall, Pablo Picasso, Jackson Pollack, Edgar Degas, Claude Monet, Georgia O'Keeffe, and so on.

Students identify an artist they wish to learn about, and select and read a book about the artist's life. Students are required to identify five important facts about the artist's life and prepare an in-depth analysis of two of the artist's works. As part of this analysis, students record their observations about the works in a learning log. Finally, students create their own artwork, employing the style and media used by the artist under study. They share their findings through group presentations where they present information about the artists and their works as well as their original artistic creations.

in tone and literal in content, but that engages contemporary readers. These books contain elements of fiction that flesh out historical details and provide an element of entertainment. This "new journalism" (Donelson & Nilsen, 1997) represents the kind of meaty material that entertains students at the same time it informs.

For many students, nonfiction is the literature of choice for out-of-school reading. Many students report a fascination with facts and a "need to know" that drives their reading choices. Despite its popularity, nonfiction seldom makes its way into content area classrooms. Because of this, nonfiction trade books are a largely untapped resource with great potential for motivating readers. By using nonfiction trade books in the classroom, teachers can bridge the gap between students' in- and out-of-school reading, and capitalize on their interest in this genre.

The wide array of nonfiction books available for the classroom can help teachers enliven classroom instruction in every content area. No single book will satisfy all readers, but teachers will find many titles that can spark student learning. Using nonfiction in the classroom can:

- Deepen student knowledge of real people, places, and phenomena of the present and the past
- Provide in-depth, up-to-date information
- Help students see how knowledge in different domains is organized, used, and related
- Develop student familiarity with the language and vocabulary of a discipline
- Improve student comprehension of expository text, a skill required for survival in the Information Age
- Provide insights into contemporary issues of interest to teens that get little attention in textbooks

The range of topics available, the variety of formats, and the varying levels of difficulty make these books an indispensable resource for content area classrooms. Topics addressed in nonfiction trade books range from art to zoology. Formats range from encyclopedic treatments of topics like David Macaulay's (2008) *The Way We Work*, which describes the design and functions of the human body, to tightly focused, narrowly defined topics such as Karen Beil's (1999) *Fire in Their Eyes: Wildfires and the People Who Fight Them*.

There are outstanding biographies and autobiographies of all sorts of people, including rock stars (*John Lennon: All I Want Is the Truth* [Partridge, 2005]), writers (*e.e. cummings: A Poet's Life* [Reef, 2006]), athletes (Lance Armstrong and Sally Jenkins's [2001] *It's Not About the Bike: My Journey Back to Life*), composers (*This Land Was Made for You and Me: The Life and Songs of Woody Guthrie* [Partridge, 2002]), scientists (*Genius: A Photobiography of Albert Einstein* [Delano, 2005]), artists (*Chuck Close, Up Close* [Greenberg & Jordan, 1998]), and ordinary teens who find themselves in extraordinary situations (*A Long Way Gone: Memoirs of a Boy Soldier* [Beah, 2007], the tragic account of a former child soldier in Sierra Leone). There are books that recount real-life adventures such as *Shipwreck at the Bottom of the World: The Extraordinary True Story of Shackleton and the* Endurance (Armstrong, 1998) and *Team Moon: How 400,000 People Landed Apollo 11 on the Moon* (Thimmesh, 2006). Other titles address contemporary issues of concern to people the world over, including AIDS, climate change, and homelessness. There are collections of interviews written with young readers in mind such as *Colors of Freedom: Immigrant Stories* (Bode, 2000), which presents the voices of teen immigrants from such places as Afghanistan, El Salvador, India, Cuba, and China. In addition, there are first-person accounts of teens who make disastrous mistakes, such as *Hole in My Life* (Gantos, 2002), about a teenager who discovered his passion for writing in prison and went on to become a beloved children's author. Figure 11.2 lists additional nonfiction titles useful for various content areas.

Figure 11.2 Nonfiction Trade Books for Content Area Classrooms

Science

Burns, L. G. (2007). *Tracking Trash: Flotsam, Jetsam, and The Science of Ocean Motion*. Boston: Houghton Mifflin.

Dash, J. (2000). *The Longitude Prize*. New York: Farrar, Straus & Giroux.

Delano, M. F. (2005). *Genius: A Photobiography of Albert Einstein*. Washington, DC: National Geographic.

Dendy, L. (2005). *Guinea pig scientists: Bold Self-Experimenters in Science and Medicine*. New York: Henry Holt.

Dingle, A. (2007). *The Periodic Table: Elements with Style*. Boston: Houghton Mifflin/Kingfishers.

Farrell, J. (2005). *Invisible Allies: Microbes that Shape Our Lives*. New York: Farrar, Straus & Giroux.

Fleischman, J. (2002). *Phineas Gage: A Gruesome But True Story About Brain Science*. Boston: Houghton Mifflin.

Giblin, J. (1995). *When Plague Strikes: The Black Death, Smallpox, AIDS*. New York: HarperCollins.

Jenkins, S. (2002). *Life on Earth: The Story of Evolution*. Boston: Houghton Mifflin.

Pearce, F. (2007). *Earth then and Now*. New York: Firefly.

Thimmesh, C. (2000). *Girls Think of Everything: Stories of Ingenious Inventions by Women*. New York: Houghton Mifflin.

Thimmesh, C. (2006). *Team Moon: How 400,000 People Landed Apollo 11 on The Moon*. New York: Houghton Mifflin.

Social Studies

Armstrong, J. (2002). *Shattered: Stories of Children and War*. New York: Knopf.

Bartoletti, S. C. (2001). *Black potatoes: The story of The Great Irish Famine, 1845–1850*. Boston: Houghton Mifflin.

Bitton-Jackson, L. (1997). *I Have Lived a Thousand Years: Growing Up in The Holocaust*. New York: Simon & Schuster.

Bode, J. (2000). *The colors of Freedom: Immigrant Stories*. New York: Franklin Watts.

Calabro, M. (1999). *The Perilous Journey of The Donner Party*. New York: Clarion Books.

Cooper, M. (2002). *Remembering Manzanar: Life in a Japanese Relocation Camp*. New York: Clarion Books.

Deem, J. M. (2005). *Bodies from The Ash: Life and Death in Ancient Pompeii*. Boston: Houghton Mifflin.

Fleming, C. (2008). *The Lincolns: A Scrapbook Look at Abraham and Mary*. New York: Schwartz & Wade Books.

Hoose, P. M. (2001). *We Were There, Too! Young People in U.S. History*. New York: Farrar, Straus & Giroux.

Oppenheim, J. (2006). *Dear Miss Breed: True Stories of The Japanese American Incarceration During World War II and A Librarian Who Made A Difference*. New York: Scholastic.

Raddatz, M. (2007). *The Long Road Home: A Story of War and Family*. New York: Penguin.

Schanzer, R. (2004). *George vs. George: The American Revolution as Seen From Both Sides*. Washington, DC: National Geographic.

Art and Music

Beckett, W. (1999). *My Favorite Things: 75 Works of Art from Around the World*. New York: Abrams.

Byrd, R. (2003). *Leonardo, Beautiful Dreamer*. New York: Dutton.

Greenberg, J., & Jordan, S. (2004). *Andy Warhol: Prince of Pop*. New York: Delacorte.

Greenberg, J., & Jordan, S. (1998). *Chuck Close: Up Close*. New York: DK.

Grody, S., & Prigoff, J. (2007). *Graffiti LA: Street Styles and Art*. New York: Harry N. Abrams.

Marsalis, W. (1995). *Marsalis on Music*. New York: Norton.

Mühlberger, R. (1993). *What Makes a Monet a Monet?* New York: New York Metropolitan Museum of Art/Viking.

Myers, W. D. (2006). *Jazz*. New York: Holiday House.

(continued)

Figure 11.2 (*continued*)

Health and Physical Education

Armstrong, L., & Jenkins, S. (2001). *It's not About the Bike: My Journey Back to Life*. New York: Berkley Books.

Blumenthal, K. (2005). *Let me play! The Story of Title IX: The Law that Changed the Future of Girls in America*. New York: Atheneum.

Canfield, J. (2000). *Chicken Soup for the Sports Fan's Soul: 101 Stories of Insight, Inspiration and Laughter in the World*. Deerfield, FL: HCI.

Chryssicas, M. K. (2007). *Breathe: Yoga for teens*. DK.

Shivack, N. (2007). *Inside out: Portrait of an Eating Disorder*. New York: Simon & Schuster.

Perhaps the greatest difficulty teachers face when selecting nonfiction for the classroom is deciding which books to choose from the large number available. An important point to keep in mind is that variety truly is the spice of life where reading and learning are concerned. No one book will satisfy all readers. The point of using nonfiction trade books in the classroom is to expose students to more than one point of view in a way that is both informational and readable. Although many nonfiction books sound like textbooks packaged in pretty covers, teachers can select quality books by considering the five A's:

1. The **A**uthority of the author
2. The **A**ccuracy of text content
3. The **A**ppropriateness of the book for its audience
4. The literary **A**rtistry
5. The **A**ppearance of the book (Moss, 2003, pp. 123–124)

Table 11.1 suggests questions teachers can consider in relationship to each of the five A's as they select nonfiction books.

Classroom uses for nonfiction are limitless but are most often thought of in reference to student report writing or inquiry projects. Nonfiction trade books have many other excellent uses as well. For example, they can help students consider multiple perspectives related to a particular issue.

One interesting way to use nonfiction involves pairing fiction with nonfiction. Judy Hendershot involved her middle graders in reading the historical novel *Out of the Dust* (Hesse, 1997) as part of a social studies unit on the Depression. During this time she read aloud the nonfiction title *Children of the Great Depression* (Freedman, 2005). Through this pairing of fiction with nonfiction, students developed a deeper understanding of the experiences of the children who suffered through the greatest economic downturn in American history. The first title exposes students to the harsh experiences of the female narrator during this time. The second provides a somewhat wider view, helping students understand the causes of the Depression as well as its impact on children across the country.

Response Journal

Select several nonfiction trade books related to your discipline. Use the five A's to evaluate the books, and identify one title that you think represents a quality book. Explain why you made the choice you did, what content-related objectives the book could help you meet, and how you might use the book in your classroom.

Picture Books

All too often, middle and high school teachers think of picture books as suitable only for the primary grades. However, the picture book format is broad and has, particularly recently, been adapted for students of all ages.

Table 11.1   The Five A's for Evaluating Nonfiction Trade Books

Criteria	Questions to Ask
Authority	Does the author identify and credit experts consulted during the research process?
Accuracy	Is text content accurate?
	Are maps, graphs, charts, and other visual aids presented clearly?
	Does the author distinguish between facts and theories?
Appropriateness	Is information presented in ways appropriate to the intended audience?
	Does the author show respect for the reader?
	Is information effectively organized?
Literary Artistry	Does the book have literary artistry?
	Does the author use literary devices to make information come alive?
	Is the author's style engaging?
Attractiveness	Is the appearance and layout of the book likely to entice readers?

Source: B. Moss. (2003). *Exploring the Literature of Fact: Children's Nonfiction Trade Books in the Elementary Classroom.* New York: Guilford Press. Reprinted by permission of Guilford Press.

Picture books encompass every genre and cover a wide range of subjects. They can be used to enhance instruction in every content area.

In picture books, art and text work together to tell a story. Picture books typically average around thirty-two pages in length, and their illustrations represent a wide range of media from collage to cut paper. These books are works of art that can represent an area of study in and of themselves. Picture books are more than visual feasts though; they contain the rich vocabulary and lyrical language characteristic of the finest literature. Picture books fall into four general categories: wordless books, picture books with minimal text, picture storybooks, and illustrated books.

1. *Wordless books.* Illustrations tell the story completely; no text is involved. Tom Feelings's (1995) *The Middle Passage: White Ships/Black Cargo* portrays the cruel experience of slavery through powerful illustrations that transcend the need for words.

2. *Picture books with minimal text.* The illustrations in these books continue to tell the story, but words are used to enhance the pictures. *Mysteries of Harris Burdick* (Van Allsburg, 1984) is an example of a book with minimal text.

3. *Picture storybooks.* Interdependent story and illustrations are central to the telling of the tale. *Show Way* (Woodson, 2005), which describes an African American family's tradition of making quilts originally designed as secret maps for runaway slaves, is an excellent example of a picture storybook in which illustration and text work together to create a seamless whole.

Evidence-Based Best Practices

BOX 11.3

Linking Physical Education with Literacy Learning

Teacher Tona Wilson at Monroe Clark Middle School in San Diego makes literacy learning an integral part of her physical education classes. She uses read-alouds on a regular basis, for example, to teach students concepts related to health and physical education. She often reads aloud from books such as *Wilma Unlimited* (Krull, 2000) or *Chicken Soup for the Sports Fan's Soul* (Canfield, 2000). She regularly reads short newspaper and magazine articles about current events related to sports. These read-alouds provide a rich source for discussion and help students recognize the importance of health and physical education in their everyday lives.

Tona uses her strong knowledge of trade books related to sports to encourage her students to read in school and out of school. In order to become better acquainted with her students' sports-related interests, Tona has each student complete a survey about their sports-related preferences and extracurricular activities. This provides her with information that enables her to recommend particular titles to her students that relate to their interests in soccer, baseball, dance, or field hockey. She regularly consults with reading teachers at the school who provide assistance in locating books for students with particular interests.

Another literacy-related activity Tona involves her students in is a research project she calls "bioboards." Bioboards involve her students in using trade books to research sports figures from the past or present. Students are required to locate information related to the person's life and (1) create a time line of the sport figure's life, (2) identify great sports moments in his or her life, (3) research the schools the person attended and sports participation in school, and (4) create color pictures depicting selected events and write captions explaining each picture. Each student displays his or her information on an 11-by-17-inch board and presents it to the other members of the class.

As they learn about different types of games, students regularly engage in shared and guided reading activities that teach them about the history, rules, and methods of scoring. They then work with partners incorporating what they have learned about these games to create their own new games, such as racquetball soccer. In these and many other ways, Tona Wilson helps her students see the many values of literacy as they learn about health and physical education.

---

4. *Illustrated books*. These have more words than pictures, but the illustrations illuminate the text in important ways. A stunning example is Kadir Nelson's (2008) *We Are the Ship*. This amazing book was the 2008 winner of the Coretta Scott King Award, which recognizes an African American author and illustrator of outstanding books for children and young adults. Nelson, an extraordinary artist and storyteller, tells the story of the Negro Baseball Leagues from the 1920s to the 1940s. His breathtaking illustrations portray the forgotten players of that time with grace and strength.

Many picture books suitable for middle and high school students are written to appeal to all age groups. Increasingly, however, picture books are written specifically with older readers in mind. Walter Dean Myers's (2002) *Patrol: An American Soldier in Vietnam* provides a vivid example of this trend. This unusual and gripping book combines mixed-media collages with a riveting poem about a young soldier's fear, confusion, and fatigue. Its in-depth focus and emotional content help readers connect with the realities of war for the typical foot soldier.

Picture books can scaffold student understanding of a range of topics through formats that intrigue rather than intimidate. Picture books provide students with background knowledge about people, places, events, and experiences. They can ground students in cognitive concepts critical for understanding a variety of content area subjects. Because picture books with a multicultural focus are increasing in availability, they can also provide rich opportunities for promoting cultural diversity.

Picture books are a particularly rich resource for struggling readers and English language learners. Illustrations aid comprehension, and the manageable length and limited amount of print in picture books enhance their appeal to students for whom reading is a challenge. Because of their accessible format, picture books can motivate these students to read, and independent, enjoyable reading experiences can lead to reading that continues after the bell has rung, an important correlate to increased reading achievement.

Picture books lend themselves to use in virtually every content area. Math and science concepts can come alive though illustrated nonfiction picture books. *Go Figure! A Totally Cool Book About Numbers* (Ball, 2005) takes a lively look at the history of mathematics, number theory, logic, and more through puzzles and problems to solve. *Anno's Math Games II* (Anno, 1989) inspires critical analysis of the notion of sets and logical possibilities presented in the detailed illustrations. The science-related biography *The Man Who Made Time Travel* (Lasky, 2003) relates the story of John Harrison, who devoted thirty-five years of his life to solving the problem of tracking longitude in shipboard navigation. *Gregor Mendel, the Friar Who Grew Peas* (Bardoe, 2006) gives glimpses of the life and work of a man whose name is known to every biology student.

Picture books can also build bridges between the past and present. Many excellent titles focus on events surrounding World War II. In *Hidden Child* (2005), Isaac Millman describes his childhood in France as a Jewish boy hiding from the Nazis. *Home of the Brave* (Say, 2002) presents an enigmatic, haunting view of the internment of the Japanese during World War II. In *The Butter Battle Book* (1984), Dr. Seuss explores the illogical nature of war and poses the question, "Which country will 'push the button' first?"

When author and illustrator Peter Sís's (2007) teenaged children asked him to describe his own youth, Sís responded with an extraordinary combination of graphic novel and picture book, *The Wall: Growing Up Behind the Iron Curtain*. Because words alone could not tell the story, he used period photographs, crosshatch drawings, and journal entries to describe the conflict between his need to pursue his creative instincts and the oppressive communist government in Czechoslovakia. The book provides a vivid portrayal of a world of darkness unimaginable to most of today's students, and could give world history classes a personal glimpse of life under a totalitarian regime.

Illustrated picture books are useful in the English classroom as well. Bruce Coville's (1997) *William Shakespeare's Macbeth* provides an easy-to-read complement to Shakespeare's original work. A similar picture book adaptation of *The Necklace* is also available. Picture book versions of poems are increasingly popular, and combine traditional texts with dramatic illustrations. The vivid illustrations in *Cremation of Sam McGee* (Service, 1986), for example, provide an interesting visual counterpart to this tale of the Yukon during the Gold Rush.

Illustrated books also deal with individuals who have made significant contributions to the arts. Kathleen Krull's *Lives of the Musicians: Good Times, Bad Times (and What the Neighbors Thought)* (1993) and *Lives of the Artists: Masterpieces, Messes (and What the Neighbors Thought)* (1995) give lighthearted, amusing glimpses of well-known musicians and artists.

Each thumbnail sketch is only a few pages long, making them ideal for short read-alouds in music and art classes.

These picture books and countless others can be integrated into your content area. They can be used with older students as interesting schema builders, anticipatory sets to begin lessons, models for quality writing, motivators for learning, read-alouds, and springboards into discussion and writing. Figure 11.3 provides examples of picture books useful for content area classrooms at all grade levels.

Figure 11.3 Picture Books for Middle and High School Classrooms

Aliki. (1999). *William Shakespeare and The Globe*. New York: HarperCollins.

Bunting, E. (1984). *Smoky Night*. Ill. D. Diaz. Orlando, FL: Harcourt Brace.

Burleigh, R. (1997). *Hoops*. Ill. S. T. Johnson. San Diego, CA: Silver Whistle.

Chekhov, A. (1991). *Kashtonka*. Trans. R. Povear. Ill. B. Moser. New York: Putnam.

Coville, B. (1997). *William Shakespeare's Macbeth*. Ill. G. Kelly. New York: Dial.

deMaupassant, G. (1993). *The Necklace*. Ill. G. Kelly. New York: Creative Editions.

Feelings, T. (1995). *The Middle Passage: White Ships/ Black Cargo*. New York: Dial.

Fox, M. (2000). *Feathers and Fools*. Ill. N. Wilton. San Diego, CA: Voyager.

Garland, S. (1993). *The Lotus Seed*. Ill. T. Kiuchi. San Diego, CA: Harcourt.

Giblin, J. (1994). *Thomas Jefferson: A Picture Book Biography*. Ill. M. Dooling. New York: Scholastic.

Golenbock, P. (1990). *Teammates*. Ill. P. Bacon. San Diego: Harcourt Brace Jovanovich.

Goodall, J. (1979). *The Story of An English Village*. New York: Atheneum.

Hoyt-Goldsmith, D. (1994). *Day of the Dead: A Mexican-American Celebration*. Ill. L. Migdale. New York: Holiday House.

Igus, T. (1998). *I See the Rhythm*. San Francisco: Children's Book Press.

Innocenti, R. (1985). *Rose Blanche*. San Diego, CA: Creative Editions.

Krull, K. (1993). *Lives of the Musicians: Good Times, Bad Times (And What the Neighbors Thought)*. Ill. K. Hewitt. San Diego, CA: Harcourt Brace.

Krull, K. (1995). *Lives of the Artists: Masterpieces, Messes (And What the Neighbors Thought)*. Ill. K. Hewitt. San Diego, CA: Harcourt Brace.

Krull, K. (1997). *Lives of the Athletes: Thrills, Spills (and what The Neighbors Thought)*. Ill. K. Hewitt. San Diego, CA: Harcourt Brace.

Krull, K. (2000). *Wilma Unlimited: How Wilma Rudolph Became The World's Fastest Woman*. Ill. D. Diaz. San Diego, CA: Harcourt Brace.

Krull, K. (2003). *Harvesting Hope: The Story of Cesar Chavez*. San Diego, CA: Harcourt.

Lasky, K. (1994). *The Librarian Who Measured the Earth*. Ill. K. Hawkes. Boston: Little, Brown.

Lasky, K. (2003). *The Man Who Made Time Travel*. Ill. K. Hawkes. New York: Farrar, Straus & Giroux.

Lauber, P. (1996). *Hurricanes: Earth's Mightiest Storms*. New York: Scholastic Press.

Lindbergh, R., & Brown, R. (1992). *A View From the Air: Charles Lindbergh's Earth and Sky*. New York: Viking.

Lowe, S. (1990). *Walden*. Ill. R. Sabuda. New York: Philomel.

Macauley, D. (1973). *Cathedral: The Story of its Construction*. Boston: Houghton Mifflin.

Macauley, D. (1998). *The New Way Things Work*. Boston: Houghton Mifflin.

Maruki, T. (1980). *Hiroshima no Pika*. New York: Lothrop, Lee & Shepard.

Myers, W. D. (2002). *Patrol: An American Soldier in Vietnam*. New York: HarperCollins.

Noyes, A. (1983). *The Highwayman*. Ill. C. Mikolaychak. New York: Lothrop, Lee & Shepard.

Peacock, L. (1998). *Crossing the Delaware: A History in Many Voices*. Ill. W. L. Krudop. New York: Atheneum.

Polacco, P. (1994). *Pink and Say*. New York: Scholastic.

Price, L. (1990). *Aida*. Ill. L. & D. Dillon. San Diego, CA: Harcourt Brace.

Rappaport, D. (2001). *Martin's Big Words: The Life of Dr. Martin Luther King, Jr.* Ill. B. Collier. New York: Hyperion.

Raschka, C. (1997). *Mysterious Thelonious*. New York: Orchard.

Ryan, P. M. *When Marian sang: The True Recital of Marian Anderson*. Ill. B. Selznick. New York: Scholastic.

Rylant, C. (1984). *Waiting to Waltz: A Childhood*. Ill. S. Gammell. New York: Bradbury.

Say, A. (2002). *Home of the Brave*. Boston: Houghton Mifflin.

Service, R. (1986). *The Cremation of Sam McGee*. Ill. T. Harrison. New York: Greenwillow.

Seuss, Dr. (1984). *The Butter Battle Book*. New York: Random House.

Simon, S. (1990). *Oceans*. New York: Morrow Junior Books.

Stanley, D. (1996). *Leonardo da Vinci*. New York: Morrow.

Stanley, D. (2000). *Michelangelo*. New York: HarperCollins.

Tsuchiya, Y. (1988). *Faithful Elephants: A True Story of People, Animals and War*. Trans. T. Kykes. Ill. Ted Lewin. Boston: Houghton Mifflin.

Van Allsburg, C. (1984). *Mysteries of Harris Burdick*. Boston: Houghton Mifflin.

Wisniewski, D. (1996). *Golem*. New York: Clarion Books.

Yolen, J. (1992). *Encounter*. Ill. D. Shannon. San Diego, CA: Harcourt Brace Jovanovich.

Fiction Books

Fiction entices readers to interact with texts from a number of different perspectives that are impossible to achieve in nonfiction alone. Genres such as fantasy, traditional works (e.g., folktales and myths), historical fiction, and realistic fiction help readers step outside their everyday world for a while to consider a different subject or perspective. In doing so, readers learn to see the world through a different lens, a skill that is necessary for personal and societal change and development.

For some students, fiction books are better bait than nonfiction books, which some students perceive as too similar to textbooks. Students tend to read books about protagonists who are the same age or older; rarely do they read books in which the protagonist is younger. Crossover novels, books that appeal to both teenagers and adults and that are marketed to both audiences (Hunt, 2007), have blurred the lines between young adult and adult literature. Crossover novels break from the tradition of young adult fiction through their (1) extended length, (2) sophisticated language, (3) unique narrative formats, (4) challenging vocabulary, (5) inclusion of adult characters, and (6) mature themes and topics. According to Hunt (2007), "The crossover novel requires more serious concentration from young readers and helps move them from the pleasures of light reading to the pleasures of literary reading."

Books such as Khaled Hosseini's (2007) *A Thousand Splendid Suns* and Jeanette Walls's (2006) *The Glass Castle: A Memoir* are good examples of this trend. They demonstrate high standards of literary quality yet appeal to a young adult audience. In recognition of the appeal of the crossover phenomenon, the American Library Association now recognizes ten adult books annually that have special appeal to teenage readers through its Alex Awards.

One contributing factor to the increase in fiction reading could be the popularity of movie adaptations. Students tend to read books that have been made into movies. This is easily corroborated in major bookstores; following the release of the movies, bookshelves are stocked with copies of the original texts. Popular young adult books such as *Coraline* (Gaiman, 2006), *Holes* (Sachar, 1998), *Speak* (Anderson, 1999), *The Sisterhood of the Traveling Pants* (Brashares, 2001), and many more have been made into successful motion pictures. It is relevant to note that there have also been several occasions in which movies have been adapted into books. In the classroom, teachers can encourage critical discussions of the similarities and differences in plot and character development by studying the author's and the film director's decisions.

Currently, fantasy is a hot genre for teens. Stories about vampires, dragons, and superheroes never cease to engage and amaze young adult readers. Although fantasy seems an unlikely addition to the required reading list in a content area classroom, consider the possibilities for a moment. Jane Yolen's series *The Pit Dragon Trilogy* (1996), which takes place on a planet called Austar IV, provides young readers with much to consider about the need to improve and change modern social conditions. Nancy Farmer's (2002) *The House of the Scorpion*, set in a futuristic society, offers a profound perspective on cloning and immigration. We can see ourselves more objectively when we consider our lives from the distance of these stories. In this way, fantasy and science fiction books can serve as a springboard for deeper discussions about big ideas.

Poetry and drama provide fascinating insights into a myriad of topics. From Nikki Grimes's (2002) *Bronx Masquerade*, about urban high school students who share their writing in a poetry slam, to Naomi Shihab Nye's (2002) *19 Varieties of Gazelle: Poems of the Middle East*, these genres provide personal glimpses into the human experience. *A Wreath for Emmett Till,* Marilyn Nelson's (2005) moving tribute to the life of the African American boy who was the victim of a racially motivated murder in 1955, is an extraordinary work. This series of fifteen sonnets is multilayered and unsparing in its honesty.

Poetry titles like *Big Talk: Poems for Four Voices* (Fleischman, 2000), *Joyful Noise: Poems for Two Voices* (Fleischman, 1988), and *Math Talk: Mathematical Ideas in Poems for Two Voices* (Pappas, 1993) have real performance potential in the secondary classroom. The poems in each of these titles were designed to be read aloud. English teachers might use these books as models for students to create their own poems in multiple voices. Poetry slams, too, can provide a motivating and engaging way to engage teens in writing and reading their own poetry.

Other texts provide classroom performance opportunities as well. Gary Soto's (1997) *Novio Boy: A Play* is a lighthearted story about young love in a Mexican American community, with realistic characters and familiar situations that students will identify with. For teachers who don't want to tackle group plays, Chamber Stephens's (2002) *Magnificent Monologues for Teens* provides single-character sketches covering a range of topics of interest to teens. Also, the 2007 Newbery winner, *Good Masters! Sweet Ladies!: Voices from a Medieval Village* (Schlitz, 2007) offers a wide range of monologues from the perspectives of medieval youth.

Realistic fiction books run the gamut from problem realism, to sports stories, to mysteries, to adventure, to romance. Young adults have long gravitated toward titles about young people engaged in personal struggles; they like to read stories that reflect their trials and tribulations, real and perceived. *The First Part Last* (Johnson, 2003), for example, is a powerful novel that describes a teenaged father struggling to raise an infant on his own. *When Zachary Beaver Came to Town* (Holt, 1999) is the poignant story of Toby, a boy in a small Texas town, who befriends Zachary, "the world's fattest boy," and discovers that his own problems aren't as bad as they seem. *Jerk, California* (Friesen, 2008) describes a teenage boy who survives the torment of living with Tourette's syndrome and discovers the truth about his real father and a family he has never known.

The popularity and demand for "edgy" books, ones that address serious subjects such as sex, drugs, abuse, and so on, suggests that today's young people crave books that speak to them and not about them or for them. Teens want to read authentic stories about real dramas and traumas. *Go Ask Alice* (Anonymous, 1971) has compelled young readers for more than three decades with its story of a teen addict whose life is spiraling out of control. *Impulse* by Ellen Hopkins (2008) reveals the inner turmoils of three teens placed in a psychiatric hospital after failed suicide attempts. *Speak* by Laurie Halse Anderson (1999) is about a girl dealing with date rape. *Skud* (2004) by Dennis Foon addresses male violence and *Paranoid Park* (2008) by Blake Nelson is about an accidental homicide.

Realistic fiction is a perennial teen favorite; historical fiction, while less popular, has the potential to give the past a pulse. Historical fiction can put a human face on history in ways that textbooks can't. Through vicarious involvement in the lives of characters who never actually existed, but who are placed in times and places that actually did, teens can participate in the most triumphant or the most terrible moments in history. Laurie Halse Anderson's (2000) *Fever 1793* is a dramatic account of a little-known historical event, the yellow fever epidemic in Philadelphia, and demonstrates how a young woman's strength of character helped her survive events that turn her world upside down. Markus Zusak's (2007) *The Book Thief* reveals a compelling story of Nazi Germany during World War II, as narrated by Death. Another extraordinary book set during the time of the Holocaust is *The Boy in the Striped Pajamas* (Boyne, 2006), the unlikely story of a friendship between two children in a concentration camp, one an inmate and one the child of the commandant. This is historical fiction at its best—a moving story of the power of friendship in a world gone mad.

Many worthy works of fiction are found on the annual *Young Adults' Choices List,* sponsored by the International Reading Association. This list reflects the book choices of teens themselves, including titles dealing with social and political issues, such as drunk driving, women's rights, death, and war. The host of fiction books available can do much to enhance and clarify the content curriculum. An author's ability to bring lifelike characters into sharp focus against a real-world setting results in compelling reading. Showing students how authors use different points of view toward history is explored in Box 11.4.

Books for Unmotivated Readers

Meeting the needs of reluctant readers is a perennial challenge for all teachers. Now more than ever before, however, there are easy-to-read titles on a range of topics relevant to today's content area classroom. In addition to picture books, reluctant readers often respond positively to short books (those with fewer than 100 pages), series books, and graphic novels.

Short but intriguing fiction titles such as *Stuck in Neutral* (Trueman, 2001) are sure to captivate those readers who do not readily connect with books. Shawn McDaniel, the main character and narrator of the story, has cerebral palsy and cannot walk, talk, or focus his eyes. As the story progresses, the reader comes to understand the strange world that Shawn inhabits, a world rich

Evidence-Based Best Practices   **BOX 11.4**

Exploring Different Points of View Toward Historical Events

The use of trade books can help expose students to a variety of perspectives in relationship to particular historical events. Students typically study world explorers as part of social studies at both the middle and high school levels. The use of trade books can offer perspectives about historical events beyond those provided in the textbook. By providing students with a wide variety of texts, they can reflect on the ways in which history is not only reported but also interpreted by writers. Consider, for example, the events surrounding Christopher Columbus's discovery of the New World. Trade books from the historical fiction, nonfiction, and picture book genres provide dramatically different portrayals of that event.

Social studies teacher Robert Wells involves his students in examining these different points of view. He uses six different biographies and historical fiction titles for this lesson. Two of these are *Pedro's Journal* (Conrad, 1991), a fictionalized account of Columbus's voyage, narrated by Pedro, a ship's boy who accompanied Columbus on his journey, and Jane Yolen's

Encounter (1992), an account of Columbus's arrival told from the point of view of a Taino Indian boy.

Robert divides students into groups based on the books they are reading and directs students to look at each book's account of the events of October 12, 1492. He focuses groups' reading, asking them to think about the following questions as they read: What are the events that take place as Columbus lands? What is the author's point of view toward Columbus? How does the author describe the native people Columbus meets? What is Columbus's attitude toward the natives?

After students have read their books, Robert leads the whole class in completing a data chart that compares the answers to the questions found in each of the books. The students then engage in a discussion about why the accounts of the same events are different. They reflect on the sources each author used to create the account, as well as the reasons authors who consulted the same sources might provide different accounts. Through this discussion, students gain understanding of the idea of history as interpretation, rather than fact.

Response Journal

How can trade books help you address the needs of reluctant readers in the classroom? What advantages might they have over textbooks?

with experiences that he is unable to communicate to others. As the story progresses, Shawn becomes increasingly concerned about his father's attitude toward him, and he panics when he begins to think that his father is considering killing him to stop his suffering. This moving book raises a number of issues related to euthanasia and is sure to provoke interesting discussions.

Dozens of other fiction and nonfiction titles can captivate reluctant readers. In *Thirteen Reasons Why* (Asher, 2007), a teenage girl sends her classmate a package of cassette tapes that explain her recent suicide. Clay and other teens within her circle of friends are forced to consider how their actions may have contributed to her death. Series books continue to have great appeal for reluctant readers; fantasy and romance titles are particularly popular with teens who may not love to read. The *Star Wars, Cirque du Freak, Circle of Magic,* and *Young Wizards* series help satisfy teen interests in fantasy. The *Luxe* series, teen romance books set at the turn of the century, is popular with female teen readers. Informational series such as Dorling Kindersley's *Eyewitness Books* are extremely appealing to students who enjoy reading about the real world.

Graphic novels are an incredibly rich resource for reluctant readers. Graphic novels employ sophisticated relationships among words and images that can promote critical thinking in ways that words alone cannot. They can be particularly useful for students who find it difficult to visualize what is happening in a text; the graphics support the text and help students get at the meaning of the text. They can also be useful for those students who reject the texts typically found in classrooms. The unique combination of the visual and verbal may be the catalyst that turns a reluctant reader into a ravenous one. Finally, for students who are "Generation Visual" (Lyga, 2004)—that is, they spend most of their time "wired" in some way, whether playing video games or exploring MySpace—these books can provide a familiar visual format.

Graphic novels can engage students in both fictional and factual topics, particularly when they are as well written as Art Spiegelman's (1986) *Maus: A Survivor's Tale*. In this book, the story of the Holocaust is vividly told with the Nazis depicted as cats and the Jewish people as mice. Rather than detracting from the seriousness of the subject, the cartoon format lends force to the plight of the Nazis' victims. More recent graphic novels that are popular with students include *American Born Chinese* (Yang, 2008), which won the highly coveted Michael L. Printz award for young adult literature. This sophisticated text is made up of three individual plotlines: one focused on Chinese folk hero Monkey King; one focused on Jin Wang, an Asian American middle school student who doesn't fit in at school; and one focused on the plight of Danny, a teenager shamed by his Chinese cousin. Gareth Hinds's (2007) *Beowulf* uses full-color illustrations and mixed media to relate this legendary story to a modern audience. *Malcolm X: A Graphic Biography* (Helfer, 2006) describes the events of its subject's life with drama and conflict.

Instructional Strategies for Using Trade Books

A recent study of exemplary content area instruction found a key commonality among effective teachers: All of them used multiple texts with a range of formats and difficulty levels (Allington & Johnston, 2002). These teachers capitalized on the myriad uses for trade books in the content area classroom and used them to enhance and extend students' content area literacy learning. This section will identify ways that teachers can organize students for literature study. Virtually all of these ways of using literature can enhance objectives for student learning in every content area.

Creating Classroom Libraries and Text Sets

Several key components are necessary to create a multitext content area classroom. First and foremost, content area teachers need to acquire books related to their content area. These books can be used to stock classroom libraries, both for large- and small-group reading and for individual inquiry. Locating books for these purposes is always a challenge, but resourceful teachers have found that library book sales, garage sales, and book clubs such as Scholastic and Trumpet are good resources for obtaining inexpensive books.

A classroom library is a critical component of a multitext classroom. By creating a classroom library of books at a range of reading levels and in a variety of genres including picture books, poetry, historical fiction, biography, and informational books, teachers increase students' access to books and help motive them to learn. Other resources such as magazines and newspapers are equally appropriate for inclusion in a content area classroom library. To meet the diverse reading needs and interests of today's students, as well as the variety of ways that trade books can be used in the content area classrooms, classroom libraries should include a wide range of titles, addressing a variety of topics and reading levels.

What kinds of books might be found in a classroom library in an American history class? Good choices include survey books about history such as *A History of Us* (Hakim, 1999), the highly acclaimed series by Joy Hakim that speaks directly to students about historical events using a conversational style. Historical fiction, for example Avi's (2008) *The Seer of Shadows*, combines history with a thrilling story, in this case, the Victorian obsession with the spirit world and a photographer who hatches a scheme to get rich quick by exploiting that obsession. Titles by authors such as Ann Rinaldi and Russell Freedman could add to this collection. The nonfiction *5,000 Miles to Freedom: Ellen and William Craft's Flight from Slavery* (Fradin & Fradin, 2006) uses photographs, letters, and newspaper accounts to document the true adventure of the Crafts as they escaped from slavery to freedom in the North. Easy-to-read picture book biographies, such as *The Amazing Life of Benjamin Franklin* (Giblin, 2000), also have a place in the classroom library. Hundreds of informational titles could round out such a collection, including books by renowned young adult authors like Jim Murphy and many others.

> **Response Journal**
>
> Create a text set of six books related to your discipline. Be sure to select books from a variety of genres and difficulty levels. Describe the books you selected and why you chose those particular books. What kinds of connections exist across the texts? How might you use the books to capitalize on those connections?

However, these titles, excellent as they are, might not appeal to less motivated students. Middle and high school students enjoy books with humor and comic books. For that reason, the teacher might consider *Cartoon History of the United States* (Gonick, 1991), a satirical vision of American history. Other amusing titles, including *So You Want to Be President?* (St. George, 2000) and *Explorers Who Got Lost* (Sansevere-Dreher, Dreher, & Renfro, 1994), debunk some of the myths about our presidents and famous explorers of the past. Magazines like *National Geographic World, Cobblestone,* or *Time for Kids* could round out such a collection.

In addition to a range of titles broadly related to a content area discipline, teachers will want to create text sets related more specifically to particular units of study within a content area. Text sets involve assembling a variety of titles that span a range of difficulty levels and include a range of resources, including books as well as other sources such as magazines, websites, newspaper articles, and so on. A sample text set related to the Civil War appears in Figure 11.4. These text sets can be used in myriad ways: for independent, self-selected reading, individual inquiry, or idea circles.

Self-Selected Reading

Organized, systematic efforts to make independent reading central in the lives of students are essential. Such experiences can create adolescents who want to continue reading after the bell has rung and "read like a wolf eats," as author Gary Paulsen describes the ravenous hunger for books that consumes book lovers. All too often, in today's standardized test-driven culture, we forget the importance of independent reading. Hundreds of studies document the fact that the more time students spend reading, the higher their reading achievement. To encourage reading and demonstrate its importance, many secondary schools provide uninterrupted sustained silent reading time, sometimes referred to as SSR time or DEAR (Drop Everything and Read). At one San Diego high school, a separate twenty-five minute period is allocated each day for sustained silent reading time. During this time, everyone—teachers, students, and even custodial workers at the school site—reads. Uninterrupted sustained silent reading time lets students

Figure 11.4   Text Set on the Civil War

Picture Books

Ackerman, N. (1990). *The Tin Heart.* Ill. Michael Hays. New York: Atheneum. This picture book describes the effect of the Civil War on the friendship of two young girls who live on opposite sides of the Mason-Dixon line.

Lyon, G. E. (1991). *Cecil's Story.* Ill. P. Catalanotto. New York: Orchard. A picture book title that describes the apprehensions of a young boy whose father may need to leave home to serve in the Civil War.

Turner, A. (1987). *Nettie's Trip South.* Ill. Ron Himler. New York: Macmillan. A young girl travels south during the 1850s and discovers firsthand the horrors of slavery.

Winter, J. (1992). *Follow the Drinking Gourd.* New York: Dragonfly. Slaves escape to freedom through the lyrics of a folk song that provide directions for following the Underground Railroad.

Plays

Davis, O. (1978). *Escape to Freedom: A Play About Frederick Douglass.* New York: Viking Penguin. This compelling play exposes young readers to the incredible life of Frederick Douglass.

Folktales

Hamilton, V. (1985). *The People Could fly.* Ill. L. & D. Dillon. New York: Knopf. A collection of American Black folktales narrated in authentic dialect.

Nolen, J. (2005). *Big Jabe.* Ill. Kadir Nelson. New York: Amistad. A tall tale about an African American baby who improves life for the slaves on a plantation.

Historical Fiction

Hahn, M. D. (2005). *Hear the Wind Blow.* New York: Clarion Books. The story of a thirteen-year-old Virginia boy whose life is changed forever when a Confederate soldier he hides in his home is discovered by the Yankees.

Hansen, J. (1986). *Which Way Freedom?* New York: Walker. Describes the life of an escaped slave who serves in the Civil War.

Hunt, I. (1964) *Across Five Aprils.* New York: Follett. Describes how the Creighton family of southern Illinois struggled with the impact of the Civil War.

Reeder, C. (1989). *Shades of Gray.* New York: Macmillan. Twelve-year-old Will Page, the orphaned son of a Confederate soldier, must live with his Uncle Jed, who refused to fight for the Confederacy.

Nonfiction

Armstrong, J. (2005). *Photo by Brady: A Picture of the Civil War.* New York: Atheneum. Armstrong tells the fascinating story of the life of Brady and his indelible mark on history.

Fleming, T. (1988). *Band of Brothers: West Point in the Civil War.* New York: Walker. Describes men who were friends and classmates at West Point and later served in the Civil War, often fighting against one another.

Lester, J. (1968). *To be a Slave.* Ill. T. Feelings. New York: Dutton. Using the actual words of his subjects, Lester portrays life as it existed for slaves in this country.

Murphy, J. (1990). *The Boys' War.* New York: Clarion Books. Diaries, letters and original photographs tells the story of young boys who participated in the Civil War.

Silvey, A. (2008). *I'll Pass for Your Comrade: Women Soldiers in the Civil War.* New York: Atheneum. Describes the women who posed as men to fight in the Civil War and how they coped with daily life as soldiers in a world dominated by men.

Warren, A. (2009). *Under Siege: Three Children at the Civil War Battle for Vicksburg.* New York: Farrar, Straus & Giroux. Uses primary sources to tell the story of children who survived this battle by living in a cave.

Websites

American Memory—Primary Source Photographs of the Civil War

http://memory.loc.gov

The Civil War Home Page—Comprehensive Website Related to the Civil War www.civilwar.com

practice reading and read for their own purposes and pleasure. Students self-select materials other than their textbooks. They can read books, magazines, or newspapers from home or obtain texts from the school or classroom library that relate to personal interests.

Providing access to a range of text types during sustained silent reading time can increase student motivation for reading, because it involves letting students read about topics of interest to them. Silent reading of self-selected books is an effective way to promote the type of engaged reading that has been shown to increase achievement (Guthrie, Schafer, & Huang, 2001).

Simply providing time for SSR, however, may not be sufficient to ensure that students benefit from this time. Pilgreen (2000) identifies eight factors of SSR success: (1) access to books, (2) appealing books that address student interests, (3) classroom environments that encourage reading as a social activity, (4) encouragement from teachers and parents, (5) staff training in SSR, (6) nonaccountability in terms of tests of knowledge or book reports, (7) follow-up activities that can encourage further reading, and (8) distributed time to read that includes short periods of fifteen to twenty minutes at least twice a week. Fisher (2004) argues that SSR programs should not consist of isolated instances in which certain teachers engage students in reading, but rather needs to be school-wide initiatives that represent a larger emphasis on staff development, collaboration between teachers and students, and effective administrative leadership.

Effective sustained silent reading programs have a number of benefits:

- They increase the amount of time students spend reading during the school day.
- They help students develop interest in a subject.
- They build knowledge that helps students read and learn more about a topic.
- They provide a basis for researching a particular topic.
- They familiarize students with different formats and genres used to report information that can be models for their own research and writing. (Worthy, Broaddus, & Ivey, 2001)

Teacher Read-Alouds

Students in Maria Prieto's ninth-grade English class read excerpts from *The Diary of Anne Frank* (Frank, 1967) in their literature anthology every year. This year she decided to enrich her students' study of the diary by reading aloud the informational book *Anne Frank: Beyond the Diary* (van der Rol & Verhoeven, 1993). This visually appealing text contains background on the Frank family, including their move from Germany to Amsterdam, photographs of the diary itself, artifacts, maps of the "secret annex," and a heartbreaking primary source document—the Nazis' typewritten list of Frank family members targeted for arrest. Maria described her use of the book in the following way:

> Before my students start reading the diary, I read aloud Chapters 1 and 2. These chapters provide important background about Anne's life and information about Hitler's rise to power. I put the map of the "secret annex" that appears in the book on the document camera to give students a spatial understanding of the place where the Franks and the van Daans lived. Then my students read the diary. After they've completed their reading of the diary, I read chapters which describe how the Frank family was arrested and the later discovery of the diary. Finally, I read the section of the book that describes Anne's life after the arrest at the concentration camp at Bergen Belsen. After each reading, I passed the book around so that students could more closely examine the photographs. They were very interested in the book. I put several copies of the book in the classroom library and a number of students read it on their own after reading the diary.

This example demonstrates a number of purposes that content area read-alouds can accomplish. First, read-alouds can provide important background information that enhances student understanding of assigned readings. Maria's use of the map of the secret annex, for example, helped students visualize the setting for Anne Frank's experiences. Secondly, the read-aloud extended and enhanced the content in the diary itself by describing the rest of Anne Frank's tragic story. Third, reading aloud can spur student interest in a topic. After hearing a book read aloud, students are much more likely to pick up books this topic, and related ones, on their own.

Reading aloud is considered by many experts to be the single most important activity in developing student literacy ability, regardless of age. Reading aloud provides literary experiences in a supportive context and exposure to the various forms of written language, both narrative and expository. As students listen to literature, they subconsciously absorb its rhythms, structures, and cadences. Read-alouds give struggling readers access to information in the more difficult texts commonly used in content area classrooms.

In addition, read-alouds provide a way for teachers to demonstrate for students the mental processes used to make sense of what they are reading. These processes can become evident to students through many of the strategies described in this book, including think-alouds, directed reading–listening activities, and many others. Read-aloud experiences should go beyond brief isolated experiences during which the teacher reads and students listen. These "bigger" read-aloud experiences should be interactive, with students actively engaged in thinking, questioning, clarifying, and summarizing texts (Ivey, 2002). Finally, read-alouds provide opportunities for response to literature that can lead to engagement and further understanding of content. These will be described in the following section.

Based on hundreds of read-aloud experiences, Barbara Erickson (1996) offers the following guidelines for middle and high school teachers who wish to incorporate reading aloud in their classes:

- Hold students' interest
- Stimulate discussion
- Reflect authors from many cultures
- Match the social and emotional levels of the listeners

Erickson also suggests that teachers prepare for read-alouds carefully by first practicing the work. She recommends that initial read-alouds last no longer than fifteen minutes. Furthermore, she advocates using pictures and props to heighten student interest and increase understanding of text content.

Read-alouds can include books from a variety of genres, including poetry, short stories, fiction, nonfiction, magazine articles, or even plays. Sharon Creech's (2001) *Love That Dog* is a perfect read-aloud for an English class; it uses free verse to explore the ways that poetry helps a young boy express his grief about losing his beloved dog. The poetic picture book *I See the Rhythm* (Igus, 1998) is an ideal music class read-aloud. This stunning book traces the history of African American music through dramatic visuals and rhythmic poetry. An outstanding read-aloud for a world history class studying ancient civilizations is *Bodies from the Ash* (Deem, 2005). This title provides fascinating glimpses of life in ancient Pompeii, based on the clues provided by the plaster cast remains of the unfortunate men, women, and children who died there.

At the beginning of a science lesson, an excerpt from a book read aloud to the class or a picture book can provide an enjoyable preview of the lesson's contents. In this way, trade books play a supporting role by introducing a part of or perspective on the lesson that entices students to want to learn more. The verbal imagery of the text or the visual stimuli of picture books appeal to all age groups and should help to activate schemata that are crucial to further learning. For example, an excellent introduction to a study of the planets is Elaine Scott's (2007) *When Is a Planet Not a Planet? The Story of Pluto.* In this clearly written text she outlines the history of the discovery of the planets and compares the work of scientists today with those of the past. Her explanation of modern-day scientists' skepticism surrounding Pluto's status as a planet and their development of new definitions for the term provide current information about what constitutes of a planet and the existence of dwarf planets.

Response Journal

Identify a read-aloud book that you might use to introduce a unit or topic of study. Plan a lesson around the book, identifying follow-up discussion questions that you might use after you have read the book aloud.

Read-alouds need not be cover to cover. Reading excerpts from books, magazines, newspaper articles, or web pages can sometimes be more effective than longer read-alouds. "Bits and pieces" read-alouds include reading picture captions from nonfiction titles to provide "sneak previews" of books. Short read-alouds focusing on biographical profiles from any of the Kathleen Krull *Lives of* books, for example, can provide an engaging way to interest students in artists, musicians, presidents, and so on.

Group Models for Studying Trade Books

As teachers become increasingly convinced of the value of using literature in content area classrooms, they will want students to experience literature in increasingly varied ways. They may decide that students can benefit from "breaking out" of the textbook to engage in reading trade books, or they may use literature in connection with units of study. Many teachers use the additional time provided by block scheduling to engage students in reading and discussing trade books. One of the most challenging aspects of using literature in the classroom—whether fiction or nonfiction—is grouping students for instruction. The grouping pattern of choice depends on the teacher's and students' goals and purposes for using the literature. The following sections will explain four different grouping models that teachers might wish to use as they involve students in studying content-related literature.

Whole-Group/Single-Book Model

Sometimes teachers want all students in a class to have a common reading experience centered on the same book. On these occasions they may use a whole-group model in which all students read the same book. Science teacher Ken Blake wanted to extend his textbook's treatment of outer space and space travel. He decided to involve his students in reading *Team Moon: How 400,000 People Landed Apollo 11 on the Moon* (Thimmesh, 2006).

Because this was the first time he had used literature to supplement the textbook, he decided to use the whole-group/single-book model. He purchased twenty-five copies of the book, and each student read the book. Students then participated in large- and small-group discussions about a variety of topics, including the work of the astronauts during the flight and the discoveries they made as they explored the moon. Students also compared and contrasted information in their textbook to that found in this book. They considered the challenges posed by the expedition and debated the importance of sending astronauts for further explorations of the moon.

Small-Groups/Multiple-Books Model

A second model for using literature is the small-groups/multiple-books model. With this model, students work in small groups to read different books related to a common theme. Alan Trent used multiple copies of several fiction and nonfiction titles to supplement textbook content and enrich his students' study of the Civil War. Students formed groups based on their selection of one of four different books: *Hear the Wind Blow* (Hahn, 2003), *The War Within: A Novel of the Civil War* (Matas, 2001), *Fields of Fury: The American Civil War* (McPherson, 2002), and *The Boys' War: Confederate and Union Soldiers Talk About the Civil War* (Murphy, 1990). Students read and discussed each title in their small groups over a two-week period. Using the jigsaw strategy, students then formed new groups in which they shared their information. They then shared the information obtained from one another with the larger group through creative extensions, including projects, dramatic presentations, and debates.

Response Journal

Identify three different trade books related to your discipline that students could read in small groups. Select titles that provide different points of view about a particular topic or issue related to your content area. Identify two ways that students in each group might share the perspective provided by the book they read with other members of the class.

Individual Inquiry Model

Individual inquiry is an increasingly popular method to involve students in research by letting them explore issues of personal interest. As part of inquiry experiences, students generate ideas and questions and pose problems. Through their research projects, students investigate topics and collect, analyze, and organize information. Students later present this information through a project or report. By using several sources about the same topic, students can examine multiple points of view and evaluate the accuracy of information.

Inquiry projects can combine fiction with nonfiction. In an inquiry project with high school students, English teacher Joan Kaywell (1994) linked fiction and nonfiction books. Her class first generated a list of problems affecting today's teens such as anorexia nervosa, stress, suicide, pregnancy, sexual abuse, and so on. The class narrowed the number of topics to five and formed inquiry groups based on each topic. At this point, each student in a group selected and read a different young adult novel related to the identified problem.

After reading their novels, students used nonfiction materials to conduct research about the problem posed in their novel. Each student found at least one nonfiction source and cited a minimum of ten facts related to the topic. Students then reconvened in small groups where they pooled these facts and selected twenty-five facts to be included in an information sheet about the problem. They discussed source credibility, recency, and relevancy of information as they narrowed down their lists. They then presented this information to the larger group.

 # Reader Response Strategies

Reader response refers to the way a person reacts to hearing or reading a piece of literature. It describes the unique interaction that occurs between a reader's mind and heart and a particular literary text (Hancock, 2007). Reader responses are dynamic, fluid, and varied. Different readers construct different meanings from texts; no two readers interpret the same work in the same way.

Why should content area teachers be interested in responses to literature? Research suggests that students grow in several different areas when engaged in response-based activities:

- They develop ownership of their reading and their responses.
- They make personal connections with literature.
- They gain appreciation for multiple interpretations and tolerance for ambiguity.
- They become more critical readers and attain higher levels of thinking and richer understanding of literature.
- They increase their repertoire of responses to literature.
- They begin to view themselves as successful readers.
- They develop greater awareness of the literary quality of a work. (Spiegel, 1998)

Involving students in response to literature can help content area teachers meet many important goals related to developing student thinking skills. Response activities can help to develop critical thinkers: Students who can examine different sides of an argument respond more thoughtfully to texts and more thoroughly understand the ways texts work.

Response-centered classrooms can help students grow in their understanding and appreciation of nonfiction just as surely as fiction. Teachers often assume that nonfiction literature will elicit only efferent responses, but studies have found that readers do respond aesthetically to nonfiction (Hancock, 2007). Effective teachers guide students' responses to biographies and informational books in ways that encourage both efferent and aesthetic responses. By providing a supportive context and engaging activities that promote both oral and written responses, teachers can extend and deepen students' literary experiences with both nonfiction and fiction.

The rest of this chapter is devoted to examples of instructional strategies teachers can use to promote responses to literature. Strategies for promoting responses range from writing to drama to inquiry-driven idea circles. All of the strategies described are designed to help teachers encourage meaningful student responses, both aesthetic and efferent, to the excellent literature available today. Through reader response experiences, students can make personal connections between texts and their lives, reflect on what these books have to teach them, and deepen their involvement with literature.

Writing as a Reader Response

Writing in response to reading, whether fiction or nonfiction, allows learners to share their thoughts and feelings about a text. It can help students construct meanings of texts at the same time it improves writing fluency. Writing in response to nonfiction can evoke feelings and enhance learning of text content. As noted in Chapter 9, "writing to learn" can help students think about what they will be reading or reflect on what has been read. It can improve understanding of difficult concepts, increase retention of information, prompt learners to elaborate on and manipulate ideas, and help them gain insight into the author's craft. Notice in Figure 11.5 how a high school English teacher uses the RAFT writing to learn strategy to help students think more deeply about trade books they have been reading related to a unit on Shakespeare's *Macbeth*. RAFT, as you recall from Chapter 9, is a strategy which helps students understand their role as writer, their audience, the format of their work, and the topic of their writing.

Figure 11.5   RAFT Writing to Learn Strategy for *Macbeth* Unit

Role	Audience	Format	Topic
Writer	Readers of Bruce Coville's *William Shakespeare's Macbeth*	Narrative	Create text to accompany Coville's pictorial depiction telling the story of *Macbeth* from the perspective of one of the following characters: Macbeth, Lady Macbeth, or one of Banquo's future kings. Write original narrative using original dialogue from the play; text must match Coville's visuals.
Felance	Facebook Readers	Facebook Page	Construct a Facebook page as Felance that is read by the villagers in Macbeth's kingdom. Include residents' posts and friends' replies regarding Macbeth's rule and the events that occur as a result of his greed. Use Goodall's *The Story of an English Village* to ensure you are writing to your audience and your inferences match the context of the time period.
TMZ Celebrity Reporter	Internet web page readers	Online article	Plan a celebrity-style news article exposing the Macbeths and investigating the changes that occurred as a result of Macbeth's rule. Also comment on the murder and mayhem that marked his rise to power. Compare Alan Bold's *Scotland's Kings & Queens* historical accounts with Macbeth's actions and reign.
MTV Director	Renaissance television viewers	Storyboard with script	Compose a newscast to be played on local MTV stations providing warnings about the BLACK DEATH and identifying symptoms and methods of prevention. In a "special report" illustrating connections to modern plagues, predict the effect of a new plague of your creation. Use Giblin's *When Plague Strikes: The black death, smallpox, and AIDS* to guide your work.
Artist	Globe Theater attendees	Symbolic artistic representation	Interpret the plot, theme, tone, and character emotions in Shakespeare's *Macbeth*. Using Aliki's *William Shakespeare and the Globe*, design a piece of symbolic artwork that would be present on the stage as scenery.

A variety of written response activities encourages students to think in different ways. Some response activities described in this section focus on helping students respond emotionally to texts, others on helping them process information or record what they have learned. Some of the activities are formal, while others are informal in nature.

Reflective Writing

One of the many excellent ideas presented in Stephanie Harvey and Anne Goudvis's (2007) *Strategies That Work* is the idea of asking students to use writing to reflect on the mental connections they make between the texts they are reading and their own lives. As students grow in sophistication, they develop the ability to recognize the mental connections they make between the texts they read and other texts, as well as between the texts they are reading and the wider world. Harvey and Goudis refer to these connections as *text-to-self, text-to-text,* and *text-to-world* connections, respectively. It is possible for students to make these connections with books from any genre.

Text-to-self connections arise when readers feel personal connections with text events or character's emotions. Harvey recommends using memoirs or realistic fiction to help students develop skills in making text-to-self connections, because reader identification with characters can be particularly strong in these types of texts. Saying "It reminds me of. . ." can prompt students to reflect on these types of connections.

Text-to-text connections involve connecting ideas across texts. The concept of *text* can be broadened here; students might connect text content to a movie or song, for example. These connections include comparing characters' personalities and actions, story events and plot lines, and lesson themes or messages in stories; finding common themes, writing styles, or perspectives in an author's work; and comparing the treatment of common themes by different authors.

Text-to-world connections are the most sophisticated connections students can make. With these types of connections, students reflect on the relationship between the content of the text and the wider world. This could include connections related to world events, issues, or concerns.

Post-It Notes

Harvey recommends that teachers use think-alouds and other text demonstrations to model for students how readers naturally create these connections. After this modeling occurs, students can begin to record the various kinds of connections on Post-it notes as they read, jotting down words or phrases that explain the thoughts or feelings that occur to them as they read. As they read and record these connections, students can code text-to-self connections (T–S), text-to-text connections (T–T), and text-to-world connections (T–W). Students should not focus solely on recording and categorizing their connections, but should reflect on how the connection has led them to greater understanding of the text. These notes can serve as the basis for rich postreading discussions about the kinds of thinking students have done as they read. In addition, these notes can often evolve into longer written pieces.

Expository Texts as Models for Writing

Students need a variety of writing experiences in the classroom, including experience in writing nonnarrative texts. One way to involve students in informational writing is by having them use information trade books as models for their own writing. These books can serve as models for brief, short-term writing experiences or extended, long-term experiences.

The Important Book (Brown, 1949), though a picture book, can serve as a model for information writing in many content areas. Each paragraph of this book states an important characteristic or main idea about a common object. This trait is followed by supporting details that further enhance the description of the object and then a restatement of the main idea. Leslie Hughes, a middle school science teacher, used this text structure during a review of a unit on oceans. The teacher read the model to the class and provided students with the following text frame:

The important thing about _____ is _____.

Students then formed writing groups and were assigned particular topics related to oceans. They identified the main ideas related to their topic and inserted it into the text frame. They provided supporting details and concluded the writing with a restatement of the main idea. An example of one student's effort follows:

The important thing about a tide pool is that it contains a community of plants and animals. Tide pools are left in rocky basins and shallow hollows as low tide causes ocean water to go back out to sea. These basins of sea water contain plants, crabs, periwinkles, and other plant and animal life. But the important thing about tide pools is that they contain a community of plants and animals.

Dozens of nonfiction books can provide models for inquiry-related writing. *My Season with Penguins: An Antarctic Journal* (Webb, 2000) is a field journal maintained by biologist Sophie Webb. This title could serve as a model for students' own field journals in a science class. Examples of books that model the use of interviews and oral history abound. One of the finest is *Oh Freedom! Kids Talk About the Civil Rights Movement* (King & Osborne, 1997). This book was actually created by young people; the students interviewed friends, family members, and neighbors who told the story of the civil rights movement from their own per-spectives. The result is an amazing oral history of that turbulent time. Teachers could involve students in conducting their own oral history interviews related to topics of study in a social studies class.

Process Drama as a Heuristic

Responding to literature through drama provides a wealth of opportunities for enhancing student engagement in learning. *Process drama* experiences allow students to establish an imaginary world in which they experience fictional roles and situations. Process drama differs from other forms of drama in that it does not involve the use of scripts; instead students them-selves compose and rehearse episodes that continue over time, and audience is integral to the process (O'Neill, 1995). Like reading, drama requires that students make meaning based on the reading that they have done. However, with drama, this meaning-making takes on a visual component. That is, students externalize the visual images they create from a text and incor-porate thought, language, and movement to demonstrate their learning. Through drama, they enter the world of the text, whether fiction or nonfiction, which lets students observe and reflect on that world.

Students reshape learning obtained through print into a dramatic form. Dramatic activities encourage changes in student thinking and promote positive experiences with literature. Many struggling readers have difficulty creating mental images as they read. Dramatic activities scaffold this image making in a motivating and meaningful way.

These activities can generate interest and help students enter a text, seeing and feeling the emotions of the characters or experiencing the events described. By combining reading with dramatic experiences, teachers help students enhance their oral language skills through listen-ing and speaking, thereby developing vocabulary and reading fluency. Dramatic activities encourage learners to listen for cues and learn to use their voices to convey emotion. In addition, they help students develop self-confidence and cooperative learning skills. These activities also offer a natural entry point into the world of writing; students can move from simply dramatizing the words of others to creating their own scripts that can be performed.

For many students, drama heightens understanding of the often dense and complex expository material found in today's nonfiction. It can enhance student understanding of both technical vocabulary and specific content-related concepts. It can motivate students to explore the content of these books more deeply. Most of all, it can bring abstract information to life, making it concrete and therefore comprehensible, which can be particularly helpful for struggling readers or English language learners.

Dramatic responses to literature have other benefits as well. Responses of this type require in-depth familiarity with the text to be dramatized. Generally learners need repeated exposure to a text before they can formulate a response to it. This repeated exposure could be particularly beneficial for struggling readers.

Improvisational Drama

Improvisational drama involves students in active response to literature and encourages them to use their imaginations. It is beneficial for students of all ages, many of whom find dramatic play extremely motivating. Improvisational responses to fiction and nonfiction help students mediate texts in ways that make them interesting, memorable, and comprehensible. When creating improvisational drama, teachers create structures that allow students to explore important themes found in the books they read. In one scene in *The Giver* (Lowry, 1993), for example, Jonas and the Giver talk about the fact that Jonas could be lost and that all his received memories could be released on people who have never experienced painful memories. In an improvisation based on this book, students could assume roles as members of the society and receive memories for the first time. They could describe this event and the feelings they experience as a result of it (Temple, Martinez, Yokota, & Naylor, 2005). Through this dramatic activity, students deepen their understanding of *The Giver* and the people whose lives it explores. Such experiences provide a nice change of pace in the classroom. Students not only enjoy these activities but also appear to retain much of the information presented as a result of the dramatizations.

Other more structured forms of dramatic response can sensitize students to expository text organization. For example, after reading *The Heart and Blood (How Our Bodies Work)* (Burgess, 1988), a middle grade teacher involved her students in a dramatic activity designed to demonstrate the sequence by which blood flows through the heart. One half of the class carried red sheets of construction paper to represent oxygenated blood and the other carried blue to represent deoxygenated blood. Eight students then paired up to act as valve gatekeepers. Student desks were arranged in the shape of the heart, and stations represented the lungs and other body parts. Students moved around the room, simulating the flow of blood through the heart and other organs, then wrote about the activity in their learning logs (Moss, 2003).

Pantomime

Pantomime is another form of response useful with content-related texts. It requires learners to communicate using their bodies, without relying on verbal communication. Students might enjoy creating pantomimes in response to Aliki's (1983) *A Medieval Feast*. This particular book contains many scenes that students could pantomime, including depictions of turning boars on the spit, fencing fields, and sounding trumpets (Stewig & Buege, 1994). Nicholas Reeves's (1992) *Into the Mummy's Tomb* could stimulate dramatizations of building of the pyramids, the burial of Tutankhamen, the process of mummification, or the purposes of the artifacts found in the tomb.

Tableau

Tableau or snapshot drama is another motivational dramatic response activity. Tableaus are silent performances that involve three-dimensional representations. A tableau typically involves no movement, talking, or props, only gestures. Students freeze moments in time and demonstrate the physical or emotional relationships and character gestures or activities. Typically, teachers give students time to plan their tableau in small groups. Each group comes to the front of the class and the teacher gives a "one, two, three, freeze" cue. The audience then discusses the tableau, offering their interpretations of what they see.

This activity works extremely well with all kinds of texts, including poetry, fantasies, realistic fiction, biographies, or information books. For example, small groups could create tableaus related to selected poems from Cynthia Rylant's (1984) *Waiting to Waltz*. Or, small groups of students could select and read different texts related to a common theme and select a scene to dramatize. Each person in the group would assume a role in the drama. After practicing, students could create their "frozen moments." The other students in the class could then attempt to identify the scene portrayed.

Reader's Theatre

Reader's theatre differs from process drama in that it involves oral presentation of a script by two or more readers. No props, costumes, or memorization of lines is required. Students must, however, read their parts fluently, with appropriate dramatic flair. Reader's theatre is often used with folktales or narrative text, but can be used with nonfiction as well.

Information books and biographies with dialogue are easily adapted to this format, but picture books, short stories, or excerpts from longer books can also be quite effective. The following guidelines can help teachers adapt nonfiction texts to a reader's theatre script:

1. Select an interesting section of text containing the desired content.
2. Reproduce the text.
3. Delete lines not critical to the content being emphasized, including those that indicate that a character is speaking.
4. Decide how to divide the parts for the readers. Assign dialogue to appropriate characters. With some texts, it will be necessary to rewrite text as dialogue or with multiple narrators. Changing third-person point of view to first-person (I or we) can create effective narration.
5. Add a prologue to introduce the script in story-like fashion. If needed, a postscript can be added to bring closure to the script.
6. Label the readers' parts by placing the speaker's name in the left-hand margin, followed by a colon.
7. After the script is finished, ask others to read it aloud. Students can then make revisions based on what they hear. Give students time to read and rehearse their parts (Young & Vardell, 1993).

An obvious next step is to involve students in selecting books from which they can develop their own reader's theatre scripts. Through this activity, learners develop critical thinking skills, make decisions, work cooperatively, and practice the process of revision.

Idea Circles

Another excellent way for students to respond to trade books is through the use of idea circles. Idea circles represent the small-group/multiple-text model of organizing the classroom for literature study. They involve students in small-group peer-led discussions of concepts fueled by reading experiences with multiple texts (Guthrie & McCann, 1996). Idea circles are an ideal way to promote peer-directed conceptual understanding of virtually any aspect of content area learning. This conceptual learning involves three basic ingredients: facts, relationships between facts, and explanations.

Idea circles not only engage students in learning about science and social studies, but they also require engagement in a variety of literacy activities, including locating information, evaluating the quality and relevance of information, summarizing information for their peers, and determining relationships among information found in a variety of sources. They require that students learn to integrate information, ideas, and viewpoints. In addition, they involve students in a variety of important collaborative processes including turn taking, maintaining group member participation, and coaching one another in the use of literacy strategies (Guthrie & McCann, 1996).

Idea circles share some things in common with literature circles. Like literature circles, they involve three to six students in directed small-group discussions. Like literature circles, idea circles are peer led and involve student-generated rules. However, idea circles involve students in discussion surrounding the learning of a particular concept, rather than a discussion centering on a single literary text. In literature circle discussions, students may have conflicting interpretations of a piece of literature. With idea circles, students work together to create a common understanding of a concept by constructing abstract understanding from facts and details. Another difference between literature circles and idea circles is in the use of texts. With literature circles, students all read and respond to a single text. With idea circles, each student may interact with a different text in preparation for the group discussion. Then during the discussion, students share the unique information that they have found. Furthermore, idea circle discussions require the use of informational rather than literary texts.

The teacher begins the idea circle experience by presenting students with a goal in the form of a topic or question. An example of a question might be, "What is a desert?" Before the idea circle meets, students can either read extensively from relevant informational trade books or read and discuss their findings concurrently. Information that students bring to the group comes from prior experiences and discussions with others, as well as from their readings. In their groups, students exchange facts, discuss relationships among ideas, and offer explanations. As this linking together of facts continues, students create a conceptual framework around a topic or question. Individuals offer information, check it against the information found by others, and discuss topics more deeply. Students continually challenge one another regarding the accuracy and relevance of their information. Through this checking, students are encouraged to search for information, comprehend the texts being used, and synthesize information from multiple sources. When conflicts arise, students search their sources to clarify conflicting information. Ultimately, the group must weave together the important details that all students contribute.

Getting Started with Idea Circles

Here's how to use idea circles in your classroom:

1. Decide whether to engage the entire class in idea circles simultaneously or start with a single team and gradually add more.

2. Identify appropriate topics of study. The topic should be interesting, explanatory, and expansive. In addition, the topic should contain natural categories or subtopics.

3. Set clear goals for what each group should accomplish during their discussions. Students may complete data charts, semantic maps, or other graphic organizers.

4. Provide students with a rich array of trade books and other resources at a variety of levels related to the topic under study.

5. Make sure students have read and learned about the topic before participating in the idea circle.

6. Post student-generated interaction rules so that students know how to function in their groups.

When used as part of a unit of study, idea circles are most effective when placed at the middle or end of a unit.

During a social studies exploration of the mound-building tribes in Ohio, teacher Ann Craig involved her students in an inquiry project using idea circles. She divided students into three different groups, with each assigned to study a different mound-builder tribe—the Hopewells, the Adenas, and the Fort Ancient. Ms. Craig focused student inquiry through questions like these: "What were some of the purposes of the mounds?" "Where did each tribe live in Ohio?" "Why are they no longer in existence?" Students consulted a variety of different sources, including trade books, textbooks, websites, and so on, to locate answers to these questions. Finally, the groups were reconfigured so that each contained an Adena expert, a Hopewell expert, and a Fort Ancient expert. The final product for the idea circle was for each group to complete a data chart comparing and contrasting each of the three tribes.

Using Technology to Respond to Literature

Today's students are technology savvy. They have grown up with cell phones, the Internet, and iPods. They memorized e-mail addresses before house addresses. Teenagers spend a great deal of time on the Internet, communicating, networking, and gaming. As we stated in Chapters 1 and 2, teachers need to understand that these activities are acts of literacy. Students are reading and writing and critically thinking, even as they "play." To maintain student interest and to use what they already know, teachers can capitalize on students' digital immersion to further their learning and comprehension of texts. Teachers may even be able to raise the status of reading in the personal lives of students.

Students are forming book clubs (among other clubs) on social networks such as Facebook. Such venues enable students from a variety of places to participate in online discussions about anything. The efficacy of book clubs relies on the contributions of members; as people negotiate thoughts, opinions, and interpretations, greater understanding is achieved. Teachers can set up an Internet community of readers and facilitate reading discussions that go beyond the classroom. Per social networking norms, responses are brief and unedited, but the key here is quantity, not necessarily quality. Also, the comments are documented and can be saved for future analysis. In the classroom, teachers can ask students to elaborate and explicate.

Blogging and Threaded Discussions

Blogging about books and threaded discussions, as we discussed in Chapter 2, can also be effective. For example, two popular blogging sites for adolescents are LiveJournal (www.livejournal.com) and Blogger (www.blogger.com). As we saw in earlier chapters, many students write and read blogs on a daily basis. These blogs may not necessarily be about books, as people blog about anything and everything under the sun. However, teachers can encourage students to blog about books and also to read other people's blogs about books. All bloggers also have a space for comments and questions. Again, it is customary to write many short responses. The idea is to help students build momentum around reading and writing about reading. For this generation, it is probably easier to build a sense of community via the Internet.

The fan fiction sites are fascinating, especially www.fanfiction.net. Fan fiction is a phenomenon that was around long before the Internet; however, it is becoming a popular vehicle for young readers and writers. Essentially, fans write fictional pieces in the same vein as their idols and publish these pieces online. For example, *Harry Potter* fans have the opportunity to make up fiction about the famous magician; fans have written about Harry's married life with Ginny, his early years with the Dursleys, his inner monologues, and so on, in the manner of J. K. Rowling. In this manner, fans can fill in gaps, write from the perspective of secondary characters, and/or extend or elaborate on specific scenes. Fans can also write literary crossovers (e.g., Harry Potter in Dante's *Inferno*).

There are rules for fan fiction. Fans cannot contribute pieces "out of canon," meaning fans must be true to the author or genre. Pieces generally include the following components: disclaimer, peer-review process (space for comments), rating, short commentary about context, and a request for reviews. True to their stage of development, adolescent fan fiction writers want approval and feedback. These writers are doing everything that we want them to do in the classroom: They are negotiating and navigating texts and they are writing and revising based on critical feedback. Why not make this a classroom assignment?

Google Docs

Google Docs is another great tool for encouraging collaborative writing. The key to using these various Internet practices is to recognize that users, in this case our adolescent students, are seeking attention and collaboration by participating and contributing to a social and public network. That being said, Google Docs allows students to work on and to share a single doc. All one needs is a gmail.com address, which is free of charge. All the members of a Google group have access to Google Docs and can actively view and make changes to a particular document in real time.

Technology allows us to extend learning beyond the four walls of the classroom; it also gives us an opportunity to connect with our students and to motivate them. It provides students with choices about when and where they log in. As active members of their respective Internet communities, students experience pride of ownership in their writing and thoughts. Teachers do need to explain the advantages and disadvantages of making personal lives and thoughts public, as teenagers tend to forget that their published words have permanence.

Looking Back Looking Forward

As you can see, books have the power to expand our vision, link us with people from the past, present, and future, and widen our vision of the world. The dialogue that is created between a book and its reader can be a powerful one—it can confuse or perplex us, unnerve us, move us to laughter or tears, or urge us to social action. It can satisfy our curiosity or make us see old ideas in completely new ways. By complementing textbook content with trade books and involving students in opportunities to respond to those books, we can help to ensure that students view the work of the scientist, the historian, or the musician as more than just knowing the facts about a topic—recognizing that such work involves interpretation, reflection, and consideration of multiple points of view.

Trade books in content area classrooms can extend and enrich information across the curriculum. Textbooks generally are unable to treat subject matter with the depth and breadth necessary to fully develop ideas and concepts and engage students in critical inquiry. Trade books have the potential to capture students' interests and imagination in people, places, events, and ideas.

Whereas textbooks compress information, trade books provide students with intensive and extensive involvement in a subject. Trade books offer students a variety of interesting, relevant, and comprehensible text experiences. With trade books, students are likely to develop an interest in and an emotional commitment to a subject. Trade books are schema builders. Reading books helps students generate background knowledge and provides them with vicarious experiences. Many kinds of trade books, both nonfiction and fiction, can be used in tandem with textbooks.

Access to books within the content area classroom helps ensure that students are exposed to content in a variety of formats. By creating classroom libraries, providing time for reading, and reading aloud to students, teachers increase the possibility that students will become lifelong readers.

By involving students in reading and responding to trade books through writing, drama, and inquiry activities such as idea circles, teachers move students from the solitary act of reading to building community around texts through peer interaction. In sharing their responses to literature, whether written or oral, students learn to reflect more deeply on the meanings of texts and connect more personally to the texts that they read. They begin to see that reactions to texts are as varied as the students in a particular classroom, and that by understanding each person's response to a text we come to understand our humanity and ourselves more fully.

In the concluding chapter of this book, we focus our attention on the role of the *literacy coach* as an instructional support for teachers. The literacy coach often collaborates with a school wide academic team to develop and implement a comprehensive plan to increase students' academic achievement. The work of literacy coaches varies from school to school. Often, however, it involves organizing professional development workshops for content area teachers, observing and providing feedback on classroom instruction, modeling effective literacy strategies, and leading all teachers in ongoing reflection and inquiry about their classroom practices.

Minds On

1. Read this statement: "One way of thinking about a textbook is that it takes a subject and distills it to its minimal essentials. In doing so, a textbook runs the risk of taking world-shaking events, monumental discoveries, profound insights, intriguing and far-away places, colorful and influential people, and life's mysteries and processes and compressing them into a series of matter-of-fact statements." Can you think of a book you have read that opened new or more perspectives on a topic of which you had previously had only textbook knowledge? What do you believe is the ideal balance between the use of textbooks and the use of fiction books, nonfiction books, and picture books in a content classroom?

2. To what extent do you believe students should participate in the selection of documents from websites for use in a content course? Would you answer this question differently for students of various ages?

3. You are one of only a few content area teachers in your school who regularly reads aloud to their students. After observing you, your principal suggests that teacher read-alouds represent a waste of instructional time that might be used more profitably. Write a letter to the principal that provides a thoughtful response to this criticism.

4. Reflect on some of the reader response activities you have experienced as a student, either in middle school, high school, or college. These could include discussions, dramatic activities, writing, or other types of activities. How did participation in these kinds of activities influence your understanding of or reaction to the text you were studying?

Hands On

1. Select two nonfiction trade books that you are considering for use in the classroom. The two titles should relate to the same topic—preferably one your students are actually studying. Read the two books, and analyze them in terms of their quality, using the criteria identified in Table 11.1. Which book do you think is more appropriate for use in the classroom and why? Then compare the two titles in terms of their treatment of the topic. How are they alike? How are they different? In what ways do they support or extend information provided in the textbook? Come to class prepared to share your analysis.

2. Select two picture books that you might coordinate with a particular unit you now teach or with a unit you have planned or observed. Explain why you chose these particular books and how you will use them to motivate your students. Describe the activities that will follow the initial use or reading of the book.

3. Create a text set consisting of at least six titles related to a topic of study in your classroom. Select at least one of the books from the text set and plan a read-aloud lesson using the book. Then, decide how your students might respond to the book through discussion, writing, or drama. Come to class prepared to read the book and have your classmates participate in the response activity.

eResources

There are many websites that will help you locate books of interest to your students. Visit one of the following sites that provide useful information on children's literature: the Children's Literature Web Guide (**www.ucalgary .ca/~dkbrown**) and the Assembly on Literature for Adolescents Review (ALAN Review) (**http://scholar.lib .vt.edu/ejournals/ALAN**). Browse these sites for informa-

tion relevant to your content area. Share your findings in small groups and discuss the ways teachers might use these sites.

To find lesson plans and resources for using literature, go to **www.cloudnet.com/~edrbsass/edadolescentlit.htm**. Explore the various lessons for your own content area.

MyEducationLab™

Go to Topic 8: Study Skills and Strategies, the MyEducationLab (**www.myeducationlab.com**) for *Content Area Reading*, where you can:

- Find learning outcomes for Study Skills and Strategies, along with the national standards that connect to these outcomes.
- Complete Assignments and Activities that can help you more deeply understand the chapter content.
- Practice the core teaching skills identified in the chapter with the Building Teaching Skills and Dispositions learning units.
- Check your comprehension on the content covered in the chapter with the Study Plan. Here you will be able to take a chapter quiz, receive feedback on your answers, and then access Review, Practice, and Enrichment activities to enhance your understanding of chapter content.
- Visit A+RISE. A+RISE® Standards2Strategy™ is an innovative and interactive online resource that offers new teachers in grades K–12 just in time, research-based instructional strategies that meet the linguistic needs of English Language Learners (ELLs) as they learn content, differentiate instruction for all grades and abilities, and are aligned to Common Core Elementary Language Arts standards (for the literacy strategies) and to English language proficiency standards in World-Class Instructional Design and Assessment (WIDA), Texas, California, and Florida.
- Use the Online Lesson Plan Builder to practice lesson planning and integrating national and state standards into your planning.

12 Supporting Effective Teaching with Professional Development

Organizing Principle

Participating in planned, collaborative, ongoing and inquiry-based professional development leads to professional growth and improved instruction.

Attracting effective teachers and initially preparing them for success is not enough. They deserve quality support to meet the demands of educational reform. As do professionals in many fields from medicine to management, they face a never-ending need for continuing improvement in their practice. Whether a teacher is looking up websites for a student learning about ecosystems in Panama, admonishing an unruly class, or meeting with colleagues on implementing a chunk of the Common Core State Standards (CCSS), improved student learning is the goal. The quest of effective teachers is to show *all* students how to think, learn, and communicate with all kinds of texts as they work toward that goal . . . including those who don't give us good results. Students progress at varying rates and levels as they develop core concepts. Consequently, teachers employ a variety of strategies to engage and challenge all learners; no small task—one even more daunting for those just beginning their teaching careers.

Teachers are at different stages in their careers, and at different levels of expertise in their craft. The National Council for Accreditation of Teacher Education (NCATE, 2009) describes these differences as a continuum of education preparation and development. First, teachers acquire subject matter and general knowledge; next, they refine their content knowledge and build a foundation of pedagogical knowledge and skills; then, they work as a student teacher or intern, often receiving an initial or novice teaching license in the process. As they continue to build their experience and skills, teachers progress to

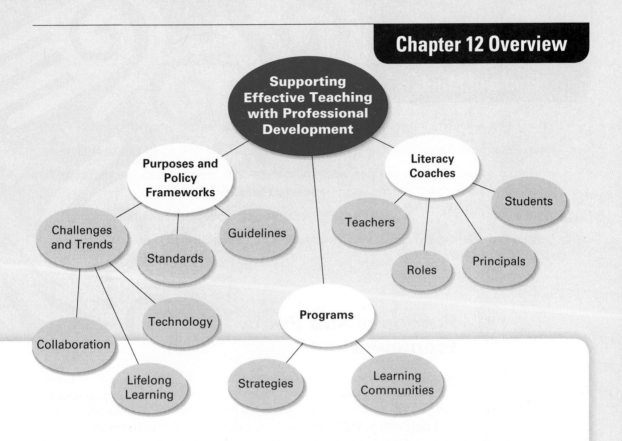

securing a professional license, and can eventually achieve advanced licensure in an area of specialization. Ongoing or sustained professional development is essential for progressing through the more advanced levels of this continuum. In many districts, teacher mentors or literacy coaches provide support. They understand that diversity exists among teachers too, and plan for active and meaningful adult learning in professional learning communities. Literacy coaches often provide "job-embedded" professional development as ongoing teacher support (Bean, 2011). Their leadership role in support of effective teaching and teachers is underscored in this chapter.

Also in this chapter, we lay out purposes and guidelines, contributing to policy frameworks which shape effective professional learning and leadership. We address the importance of direction and response to needs, challenges, and trends that impact the teaching profession. Strategies, personnel, and programs that illustrate how to differentially support effective teaching and teachers are also offered. The organizing principle serves to emphasize our overall focus: Participating in planned, collaborative, ongoing, and inquiry-based professional development leads to professional growth and improved instruction.

Frame of Mind

1. Why is it more important than ever to participate in ongoing professional development?

2. What are some of the main purposes, guidelines, and standards for professional development?

3. How are the roles of literacy coaches, teachers, and principals changing today in support of professional development and the school learning community?

4. What are strategies for inquiry-based professional learning in support of effective teaching?

5. Describe some expanding opportunities in programs for collaborative professional learning, both formal and informal.

Purposes and Policy Frameworks

Are you paying attention when your flight attendant reviews what to do in case of an emergency? You know, the part where they say, "Place the drop-down mask over your own nose and mouth before assisting anyone else." When you think about it, this makes perfect sense; an adult would then be dependable when helping a child or another person with their mask. Perhaps educators, especially classroom teachers on the "front lines", should use this as an analogy. Actively participating in professional development is a major way to get the necessary support (oxygen) teachers need so that they are then able to help others. This is a primary and legitimate purpose for professional development. And, given the growing needs and challenges of our schools and students, quality support for contemporary educators is hardly an option.

Consider some key purposes that drive professional development on a continuum, ranging from the institutional to personal/professional. As illustrated in Figure 12.1, an institutional purpose might be improved student achievement following successful implementation of CCSS in the state and school district. Given the CCSS emphasis on literacy in content areas, and the absence of rigid guidelines for implementation, teachers and other school leaders are positioned to determine strategies for effective teaching.

Figure 12.1 Purposes of Professional Development

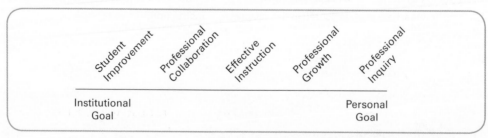

Moving along this continuum, teachers with varying levels of expertise and experience are at different points in their careers. Their professional growth and change calls for participation in a "wide range of professional development, from teacher induction to curriculum support and study groups focused on specific subject areas (Jaquith, A., et al., 2010, p. 3). Their professional growth, through collaboration, reflection and inquiry, mirrors the underlying rationale for the creation of standards for students—that higher learning expectations bring along an accountability system which can, when authentic, improve learning of teachers as well as students. The result: Improved instruction and more effective teaching.

Guidelines

Over the last two decades, to prepare and support educators to meet the demands of educational reform, equitable, persistent, and quality professional development opportunities have been called for by the U.S. Department of Education (1999). With the overall mission of helping all students achieve high standards of learning and development, these principles were proffered:

- Focus on teachers as central to student learning, yet include the school community
- Focus on individual, collegial, and organizational improvement
- Respect and nurture the leadership capacity of principals, teachers, and others
- Reflect the best available research and practice in teaching, learning, and leadership
- Enable teachers to develop further expertise in subject content, strategies, and technology
- Promote continuous inquiry and improvement embedded in daily school life
- Plan collaboratively with those who will participate in and facilitate development
- Require substantial time and other resources
- Be driven by a coherent long-term plan
- Be evaluated ultimately by its impact on teacher effectiveness and student learning

In more recent educational reform, the U.S. Department of Education (USDE) introduced *Race to the Top (RTTT)* (2009), providing $4.35 billion to eleven states and the District of Columbia to address the need to prepare students for college and careers by (1) adopting rigorous academic standards, (2) creating data systems to inform instruction, (3) recruiting and developing effective teachers and principals, and (4) turning around low performing schools. As acknowledged in *RTTT,* an essential component for realizing all of these goals is professional development tailored to meet the individual needs of teachers and principals through a common language of instructional practices using data gathered from teacher and student performance.

In 2012, USDE proposed Project RESPECT. This effort is in response to our country's need to effectively prepare students to perform competitively in the global market. Its main focus is teachers who have had limited classroom experience with diverse populations. RESPECT, or Recognizing Educational Success, Professional Excellence, and Collaborative Teaching, aims ultimately to create an environment in which "teaching becomes a respected profession." This program proposes to:

- Increase earning potential for teachers; link compensation to effective teaching outcomes
- Increase opportunities for professional development and collaboration

- Raise levels of job satisfaction and overall appreciation for the profession of teaching. To this end, President Obama proposed a $5 billion grant program to support reform at state and district levels. Competitors must propose novel change for teachers at all levels of experience and address the six elements of the RESPECT program:
  - Attracting top-tier talent and preparing them for success
  - Creating a professional career continuum with competitive compensation
  - Creating conditions for success
  - Evaluating and supporting the development and success of teachers and leaders
  - Getting the best educators to the students who need them most
  - Sustaining a new and improved system (USDE, 2012, RESPECT Program Proposal)

Standards

Professional educational associations in all subject areas and levels of schooling have spent considerable time and effort, often in concert with other broad-based national groups, such as the National Council for Accreditation of Teachers and many others, in a process of developing standards for professionals. A major voice in content area literacy, the International Reading Association (IRA) offered its latest Standards for Reading Professionals in 2010. Standard 6, Professional Learning and Leadership, is based on a commitment by all reading professionals to lifelong learning. Professionals learn in many different ways, for example, individual learning through activities such as reading, pursuing advanced degrees, and attending professional meetings. Major assumptions cited by the IRA Standards 2010 Committee in developing this standard included these elements for effective professional learning: evidence-based practices, inclusive and collaborative instruction, focus on content, responsive to the range of diversity and to research on adult learning (International Reading Association, 2010).

 # Challenges and Trends

Teaching is tough. Most people probably have some notion that is true. But did any of us think it would come to this? Teachers leaving the profession in their first five years. Teachers retiring at their first opportunity. Salaries reduced by sudden shifting of higher costs for benefits to teachers. Communities letting scores of teachers go, along with fire, police, and other safety personnel. And, the diminishing of teacher status as we "scapegoat" them as the cause of a society-wide failure (Blow, 2011).

Is it any wonder that a major federal/state education initiative is labeled "Project RESPECT?" At this critical point in national, state, and local struggles over resources and needs, educators are addressing issues and rebuilding an environment in which teaching is a respected profession and teachers have an enhanced role in their classrooms. Teaching *all* students means choosing to work with those who struggle developmentally, socially, or academically in one or more subjects or, in some cases, across the board. Therefore, effective teachers look for results which demonstrate improvement in their students' progress. They accept that this is not going to be easy. Consequently, they participate in lifelong learning opportunities to better equip themselves to deal with the ongoing challenges.

Lifelong Learning

Content area teachers, perhaps more so than others, are motivated to stay informed about the latest trend or information, and often go online to access new information and interact with others in their subject field. Their implicit "commitment to professional learning is important, not because teaching is of poor quality and needs to be 'fixed' but because teaching is so *hard* we can always improve it. No matter how good a lesson is, we can always make it better. . . . Every teacher has the responsibility to be involved in a career-long quest to improve practice." (Danielson, 2010–2011, p. 37)

On a related note, one of the skills content area teachers try to foster in their students is that of becoming lifelong learners. By modeling those habits of learning, they can both guide students and enrich the personal and professional knowledge base from which they teach. It follows that, at the very least, teacher voices, preferably of those at different career stages, need to be heard in the planning stages of professional development. Both the second year geometry teacher and the veteran Spanish teacher bring a valid mix of experience and ideas to the table. This type of collaboration contributes to the perceived usefulness of a planned activity and its authenticity. All teachers, regardless of their field or the age of their students, need to make a commitment to lifelong learning.

Collaboration

Educators have a reputation for generosity in offering their insights and expertise to one another, especially their newer colleagues. Hence, collaboration has been part of school life for a very long time. Colleagues have informally shared "materials and insights, particularly with those less experienced than they" (Danielson, 1996, p. 113). What is the essence of collaboration? Often, it's *conversation,* colleagues sitting down together and engaging in serious face to face dialogue about the 'stuff' of teaching. Today, it also includes teachers messaging one another in text or e-mail; social networking with an expanding group of teacher friends as the professional conversation goes on-line.

In an effort to improve the performance of teachers, and in turn students, a more recent agenda revolves around improving the instruments and procedures for the evaluation of teachers. In fact, Danielson's (2010/2011) Framework for Teaching, a widely accepted tool for evaluating the quality of instruction, places emphasis on the need for explicit *conversations between teachers and administrators*. The intent is to use a common language to describe instructional practices as a tool for professional reflection and development. Its projected outcomes are more effective professional development opportunities and greater student performance. As literacy coaches confer with teachers, described later in the chapter, more possibilities emerge to plan ways to effectively support student learning, especially for those who struggle in middle and high school content areas.

Finally, a report of case studies of programs in four states having high levels of teacher participation in professional development identified key, shared characteristics in implementing effective professional learning programs (Jacquith, A. et al., 2010). All have:

- Leadership with stakeholder partners
- Infrastructure of local and state frameworks of standards
- Resources with state funding avenues
- Intermediaries and outside providers

These four states also produced improvements in student achievement as measured in the 2009 National Assessment of Educational Progress (NAEP). How do these states with relatively high levels of participation in effective professional learning ensure the *quality* of these initiatives? According to this report, "it is equally critical to couple state efforts with professional associations and intermediary organizations" (Jacquith, A. et al., 2010, p. 3). Or, put more succinctly: *collaboration*.

Technology

Today's teachers are the first generation of educators to teach the first generation of students who have grown up immersed in, not perplexed by, information and communication technologies (ICT). These students virtually embraced a video game, DVD, cell phone, smartphone, ipad, instant messaging, and the World Wide Web, along with their teddy bears. Yet, they still need help in "learning how to learn" new technologies, as well as reading critically and evaluating information—to barely scratch the surface of this challenging trend. And, just as standards and policy drive the curriculum and instruction of students and teachers, new literacies, described in Chapters 1 and 2, are also imbedded in the professional development of teachers.

Joining the conversation today brings teachers to a wealth of online sites, ranging from school district information updates and sharing, to state and federal education department invitations to participate. Professional association websites, including special interest groups, and numerous other education information outlets, both non- and for-profit, welcome teachers and other interested people to engage in discussion or simply observe. Among the choices are Twitter and other RSS feeds, blogs, and professional networks.

One day in March, John White and other Rural Education team members were answering questions on Twitter about students in rural communities being least likely to enroll in postsecondary education and career training. Topics being discussed included: "How do you educate a student about getting stuck with loans/debt for decades?" and "How do you educate on the risks?"

Drop in, as we did, on *Homeroom: the Official Blog of the U.S. Department of Education* (http://www.ed.gov/blog/) and you will find hundreds of useful topics. Homeroom is intended as a place for collecting new ideas and suggestions. Among the many choices to find colleagues' input in Homeroom at the time we explored it were: English Learners, Compensating great teachers, and P–12 Reform. Part of the larger US DE website, Homeroom connects you with other colleagues but can quickly link you with, for example, the popular searches. There are literally hundreds of keyword choices to explore if you are curious and have the time.

For more focused conversation with colleagues about teaching there are forums on all aspects of literacy, some offering links to related resources. Edutopia, for instance, gives educators a forum for discussion on literacy in content areas (http://.edutopia.org/blog/literacy-instruction-across-curriculum-importance). Other excellent opportunities to connect and collaborate locally

Table 12.1 Professional Association Conversation Blogs: Sampling

Association Content Area	Blog
Math education	http://nctmonline.ning.com/
Science education	http://nstacommunities.org/blog
Language Arts education	http://ncteinbox.blogspot.com/
Social Studies	http://connected.socialstudies.org/SOCIALSTUDIES/Blogs1/ViewBlogs/
English Language Learners	http://blogs.edweek.org/edweek/learning-the-language/
Foreign Language	http://community.actfl.org/Home/
Physical Education	http://www.pelinks4u.org/naspeforum/cgi-bin/discus/discus.cgi
Art Education	http://naea.typepad.com/naea/

and nationally are through blogs set up for teachers and other education leaders by the majority of professional education associations. Refer to Table 12.1 for a partial listing from this 'corner of the blogosphere.'

Another digital outlet for sharing resources and ideas among students/teachers and teachers/teachers is a *professional learning network (PLN)*. Literacy teachers, for example, have numerous network tools from which to choose. A few that zero in on professional learning are:

- Engage (engage.reading.org), International Reading Association
- Connect (connect.nwp.org), National Writing Project
- Classroom 2.0 (www.classroom20.com)

Technology is of paramount importance to the support of effective teaching and professional development. Both a tool and a topic, it plays a critical role in strategies and programs for informal and formal teacher learning, and shared leadership responsibilities of teachers, principals, and literacy coaches.

Literacy Coaches

As teaching becomes even more challenging, with the need to differentiate instruction in order to improve the learning of every student, one logical solution is to better support teachers in the workplace with literacy coaches. This type of ongoing, job-embedded support of effective teaching typically aims at improving both literacy instruction and learning in the content areas (Bean, 2011, p. 315–316). Yet, as integral as literacy coaches have become in many schools, shifts in funding availability directly affect district allocation of resources, in turn placing in jeopardy the positions of those with more experience and advanced degrees.

Roles and Expectations for Literacy Coaches

To support teachers in meeting the needs of diverse adolescents, districts hire literacy coaches whose primary role is to provide continuing professional development for teachers. Although the new role of the literacy coach is similar to the role that some reading professionals held in secondary schools as early as the 1960s and 1970s, when schools with federal grant funds hired reading specialists to provide "resource" assistance to other teachers (Anders, 2002), today literacy coaches often have more multifaceted roles than their predecessors. As Sturtevant (2003) and Toll (2005) explain, literacy coaches in middle and high schools are seen as teacher leaders and may be expected to do the following:

- Mentor individual teachers
- Model and observe in classrooms
- Work with study groups and teacher teams
- Lead a school wide literacy council
- Advise administrators on the school literacy program
- Collaborate with literacy coaches in other schools
- Administer and monitor literacy assessments
- Work with parents and/or community groups

The list of potential responsibilities for literacy coaches can be overwhelming, especially when one considers that middle and high schools with hundreds or thousands of students often have only one literacy coach. In other schools, the position of literacy coach may be held by a professional who also has teaching responsibilities. The Alliance for Excellent Education, an education advocacy group in Washington, D.C., recommends that schools hire one coach for every twenty teachers, for maximum effectiveness (Hall, 2004); this appears unrealistic at the time of this writing in 2012. It remains important for educators in local districts and schools to create school plans that clarify what is expected of literacy coaches (NASSP, 2005). Coaches should participate in this process and the outcomes should be communicated to all constituency groups, including teachers and administrators.

Mraz, Algozzine, and Kissel (2009) describe the roles of the literacy coach as:

Helping Teachers Plan for Instruction. Effective instruction is not as simple as selecting a content area textbook and then assigning students to read and answer questions at the end of each chapter. Effective instruction requires teachers to be knowledgeable and reflective about their instructional practice and the research that informs it. Teachers must apply that knowledge to their instructional decision-making process in order to meet the diverse learning needs of students. Through ongoing collaboration and problem solving, literacy coaches can help teachers to plan reflective and effective instruction for all students. Read Box 12.1, for an overview of the broad role coaches play in RTI for Struggling Adolescent Learners.

Supporting Teachers in Developing Manageable Routines. This includes organizing materials needed for instruction, scheduling time productively, and creating an engaging learning environment. Literacy coaches also help teachers prepare for instruction by offering support and advice on setting and communicating expectations and rules to students, communicating the consequences of desired and undesired behaviors, and handling disruptions effectively and efficiently.

Helping Teachers Deliver Instruction. This involves presenting content, monitoring student learning, and adjusting instruction. Each of these elements can be supported by effective coaching. Once plans for content area instruction have been developed, literacy coaches work with teachers to implement those lessons.

BOX 12.1 RTI for Struggling Adolescent Learners

The Role of Literacy Coaches

As we emphasize throughout this chapter, literacy coaches provide essential leadership for schools to address the needs of all learners, including struggling readers and writers. RTI in practice increases the need for literacy coaches and specialists in schools (IRA, 2008; Stecker, Fuchs, & Fuchs, 2008). Because RTI requires schools to implement evidence-based practices and prepare effective teachers, literacy coaches serve a valuable role in offering professional development to faculty and staff. Literacy coaches, as we discuss in detail in this chapter, can organize workshops and study groups to help teachers understand the variety of reasons students may struggle with reading in content area classes.

Understanding the learner and the nature of the reading tasks required in content area curricula is the first step toward developing instruction that helps students become more successful in meeting the literacy demands of school. A next step would be to help teachers develop expertise in using appropriate literacy strategies in their teaching. For example, after learning the importance of activating and building background knowledge, study group members might explore different types of anticipatory activities to use with their classes. Literacy coaches could then model lessons for teachers in different grade levels or in different content areas and observe and conference with teachers as they try out new ideas. Literacy coaches could also work with small groups of teachers or individuals to look at student work samples and assess what types of difficulties students are having. Although instruction focused on literacy improvement in the content classroom would benefit all students, significantly strug-

gling adolescent learners would arguably gain the most through new access to core curriculum texts that previously may have been beyond their grasp.

Moreover, we contend that literacy coaches can provide leadership in professional collaboration among specialists in the school. At many middle and high schools, individual and small-group instruction for struggling learners is provided by a mix of special education teachers, English to Speakers of Other Languages (ESOL) teachers, speech language pathologists, certified reading teachers, paraprofessionals, and volunteer tutors. Literacy coaches, as leaders of the school literacy program, can provide an invaluable service by encouraging communication among these groups and by helping them work together to provide effective services for students. Coaches can also work collaboratively with library and media specialists to develop a collection of print and technological resources to meet the needs of struggling readers, and they can help teachers review potential materials and programs designed for struggling readers before purchases are made.

At a whole-school level, literacy coaches often organize literacy leadership teams (NASSP, 2005). Literacy teams conduct assessments about the overall literacy achievement and needs of different groups of learners and then systematically plan ways to support both student learning and the professional development of teachers. Although struggling readers are a diverse group and can be defined in a wide variety of ways, all students in middle or high school who struggle to meet course expectations due to difficulties in reading need specialized attention in the school literacy plan.

Promoting a Collaborative Environment. In addition to working with individual teachers, literacy coaches play an important role in the creation of an environment that values teamwork. As Mraz, Algozzine, and Kissel (2009, p. 12) explain, "The teacher–coach relationship is reciprocal: Teachers learn from coaches, coaches learn from teachers and both learn from students." Effective literacy coaches foster collaborative environments by encouraging teachers to share their insights, knowledge, beliefs, and experiences during coaching conversations and professional development sessions.

Promoting Reflective Inquiry. Effective literacy coaches encourage teachers to think reflectively about their teaching practice. That is, literacy coaches encourage teachers to review the instructional decisions they have made and to determine the extent to which those decisions were effective for their students.

Using Data to Guide Instructional Decisions. Coaches collaborate with teachers to gather and examine data. Analysis of these data, which can include both formal and informal assessments, such as those described in Chapter 4, helps assess the degree to which student learning outcomes have been achieved. Several factors contribute to effective assessment practices. These include monitoring student understanding and engaged time, maintaining records of students' progress, informing students about their progress, using data to make decisions, and making judgments about students' performance (Algozzine & Ysseldyke, 2006).

Literacy Coaches, Teachers, and Principals

There are several ways in which literacy coaches work with teachers, principals, and other school constituents to enhance literacy instruction. Together, they build learning communities, an important component of effective professional development and school life. School learning communities are teams of people who share knowledge, engage in periodic reviews of achievements or challenges, and work together to improve the overall learning of students (DuFour, 2003).

Building Learning Communities: A Closer Look

The literacy coach facilitates a collaborative learning environment by working with various participants who contribute to the development of student learning. The community participants may include principals, directors, and assistant principals; teachers, both veterans and newcomers; and parents and caregivers. Principal support, however, cannot be overstated. The principal's understanding and backing is one of the "key factors leading to coaching success" (Bean, 2011, p. 321). After all, principals oversee teacher and specialist job responsibilities, and instructional time allocation, in addition to "validating" the role of those who work with teachers.

Principals who are supportive and knowledgeable about instructional leadership may actively collaborate with literacy coaches, even taking the lead in building a school learning community that promotes effective professional development. We meet such a principal in Voices from the Field, Box 12.2.

BOX 12.2   # Voices from the Field

Laura, Middle School Principal

Challenge

The passing of the national Common Core State Standards (CCSS) marks a drastic change in expectations for educators. Unlike the standardized tests associated with No Child Left Behind (NCLB) and state mandated assessments such as the North Carolina's End of Grade (EOG) tests that required vast amounts of instructional time be devoted to the rote teaching of test-taking skills, the new CCSS require that teachers teach students how to think critically and to explain their thinking at much higher levels. The new standards are designed very differently than the previous curricula used in my state, holding teachers in all content areas responsible for teaching students literacy skills in reading, writing, speaking and listening, and language. This change in design requires instructional leaders to think differently about literacy across the school.

I am a middle school principal of an urban school with 1200 students. Our school has traditionally scored above average on the state assessments, but data indicate that we have continuously struggled to challenge our highest level students. Our school is unique in that we have a well-established reading program where each student has personal goals to meet each quarter. The students and parents have embraced this program, and it is not unusual to see students walking down the hall or sitting in the cafeteria with their nose in a book. While we are proud of the reading culture we have established, we realize that we need to expand literacy beyond our current reading program, which focuses heavily on fictional literature.

Strategy

As a school, we decided to implement the new CCSS, by focusing on the language arts standards that address informational texts and argumentative writing. Our goal this year was to provide ongoing professional development to the staff to ensure that they under-stood content literacy and the new CCSS, and to provide them with strategies they could immediately and effectively incorporate into their lessons.

Throughout the year, we provided differentiated professional development to our teachers based around informational text and argumentative writing. We focused on three main areas; academic vocabulary, literacy in technology sources (i.e. internet websites, blogs, videos, etc.), and pre-reading strategies that "hook" students. Each of these areas aligns with the four areas of literacy skills required by the CCSS. Our focus on providing teachers with quality professional development on how to improve literacy skills in all content areas has had a positive effect on the quality of the lessons teachers designed by teachers and the level of comprehension by students. It is evident from walkthroughs, observations, and student work samples that students are more comfortable looking at various forms of texts and have improved their understanding about how to interpret the information.

Previously, teachers struggled to find nonfictional materials that were grade appropriate and engaging for students and therefore rarely included them in their lesson plans. Now that teachers understand the importance of different types of text, they have been exposing students to nonfiction articles that are both challenging and of high interest. And, to increase the level of rigor of the lessons and meet our school goals, the teachers are posing questions from the texts that encourage students to think critically and justify their stance towards many different issues. Teachers have also begun to expose students to a wider variety of topics that are relevant to their content or connect their content to other areas. For example, I recently observed a language arts class that was discussing a current event article on the exploration of Mars. The class had just read a science fiction story about space, and the students were able to make clear connections between the two texts. In a Spanish class, the students read an article about bull riding and discussed it in relation to Spanish culture and traditions. In a social studies class, the students were studying the political cartoons in the magazine and were required to explain how it related to their current study of Constitutional rights. Each of these lessons also incorporated new vocabulary in real world settings. As a school, we have noticed an increase in the students' ability to apply the new words across content areas because they are connected to real life, not an abstract idea or single setting.

Reflection

As a principal, I've been excited about the new focus on informational texts across the content areas. I have noticed a marked difference in the students' ability to make connections between classes and topics. Not only are the students becoming increasingly aware of national and international events and able to explain the causes and effects of many topics, they are beginning to see the connections between "real life" and the content they are learning. These connections would not have been possible without effective teaching practices supported by professional development.

The focus on increasing writing and reading in all courses has had an observable impact on the level of rigor in teacher's lessons. By mid-year, teachers were comfortable creating and assigning argumentative writing strategies with a pro/con article included from each issue. Teachers are consistently designing activities that require students to take a stance and to use evidence from an article and other sources to defend their opinion. In addition, teachers are demonstrating how to read graphs, political cartoons, and data sets related to different content areas. I firmly believe that our students will be better prepared to meet the expectations set forth in the CCSS, and to meet expectations outside the classroom, through their investigations of real-world issues across the content areas. From my perspective, supportive and sustained professional development for teachers has contributed to these improvements.

When teachers within the school community get together in meaningful and productive ways, as we see in Laura's school, they have successfully collaborated to do the following:

- Strengthen their own professional knowledge
- Problem solve
- Celebrate successes and acknowledge challenges
- Build community
- Enhance instruction
- Discover ways to meet individual student needs (Mraz, et al., 2009).

Though the school as a whole may strive to be a cohesive learning community, different constituencies within the school community might come together for different purposes at different times. For example, learning communities can include teacher–coach, teacher–teacher, and principal–coach interactions. Here's how one middle school learning community worked: A group of six teachers met voluntarily each month throughout the school year to discuss the successes and challenges they experienced as they worked to develop integrated units among content area classes. As part of their conversation about how to effectively address the changes brought about by this integration initiative, the group members, led by the literacy coach, read Moore and Whitfield's (2008) article "Musing: A Way to Inform and Inspire Pedagogy Through Self-Reflection." After reading and discussing the article with colleagues, Jen Boysko, a fifth-grade teacher, wrote the following:

I feel that I reflect on my lessons constantly. It seems as if I am always thinking about what I might say next, or how that lesson could have been different. I recognize that, as an educator, reflecting plays a crucial part in being successful. I did not realize, however, that there are levels of reflecting. When I *react,* I usually just discuss what happened in class that day with a coworker or peer. Unfortunately, I seem to react more to frustrating situations or when I know a lesson was not delivered well. I need to reflect more on things that did go well so that I can continue that behavior or habit, and even possibly improve on it. I *elaborate* those reflections at grade-level meetings when I compare strategies in the classroom with what other teachers are doing. It often takes me back to what I already did, and where I need to go. I *contemplate* insights and thoughts about a classroom situation, both academic and social, to seek out further assistance from my peers or school facilitators. Reflecting is not always an easy process. Realizing that change is needed and moving forward with an action plan is far more difficult than just thinking about it.

At their next meeting together, Jen shared some of her insights about reflective teaching, and the group together talked about their own experiences with the change process and brainstormed advice for moving forward.

Conferring with Teachers

"The most beneficial learning activities are those that are embedded in the work that educators do" (Easton, 2008, p. 748). Examples of embedded learning activities include book studies, lesson analysis, study groups, data analysis, classroom visits, and teacher–coach conversations. Schools and districts undertaking major projects or changes increasingly include teachers and literacy coaches in designing, planning, and implementing these new ideas, which often require a considerable investment of time and mental energy. When viewed as authentic professional growth opportunities, however, professional educators find the time to become involved. In addition to the personal knowledge and experience gained through participation, teachers and literacy coaches are able to interact with one another on a level different from that of the classroom, thereby making an enhanced contribution to the education of students.

Professional knowledge is enriched when teachers and coaches come together to discuss instructional practices. These conversations are at the heart of literacy coaching. Rapport and trust are created when literacy coaches and teachers engage in meaningful conversations (Blachowicz, Obrochta, & Fogelberg, 2005). Teacher–coach conferences can serve several purposes. For example, teachers and coaches may work to connect a school or district wide literacy initiative to classroom instruction, or coaches and teachers may engage in genuine inquiry about strategies that could support student learning in content area classes. These conferences provide the literacy coach with an opportunity to establish a relationship of trust by listening carefully, maintaining confidentiality, and following through on coaching commitments (Bean & DeFord, 2007). Through collaborative dialogue with teachers, coaches can promote a shared vision of the school's literacy goals, use student data to inform instructional decisions, and encourage instructional discussions to continue through ongoing professional development (Shanklin, 2006).

Mraz, Algozzine, and Kissel (2009) suggest that coaches use five phases when conducting conferences with teachers, keeping in mind that a conference should be a dialogue between the teacher and the coach, not a lecture or evaluation on the part of the coach:

1. *Ask questions.* These initial questions can be related to the lesson, to student responses, or to connections between the lesson observed and the broader curriculum or unit of study.

2. *Explain what the coach notices.* State observations, objectively describing behaviors and events without imposing a judgment on what was observed.

3. *Offer a coaching point when it is appropriate to do so.* If there are several areas for which coaching points could be offered, select one as the main priority.

4. *Brainstorm next steps.* The coach and the teacher should determine together next steps for both the teacher and the coach. For example, the teacher and the coach may agree on a particular strategy that the teacher would like to try in class; a time should be scheduled for a follow-up conference to discuss the successes and challenges of this strategy application.

5. *Link to literature.* Suggest and locate practitioner and research articles or books concerning an aspect of literacy learning that is relevant to the teacher; offer to read and discuss these with the teacher at a later time.

Literacy Coaches and Students

In supporting the work of teachers, literacy coaches can play an important part in developing programs that directly affect students. The following examples describe how the work of a literacy coach can support struggling readers, English language learners, and effective overall assessment practices within a school.

Supporting Struggling Readers

Literacy coaches provide essential leadership for schools to address the needs of all learners, including their struggling readers. On a whole-school level, literacy coaches often organize literacy leadership teams (NASSP, 2005). This team can conduct a needs assessment about the overall literacy achievement and needs of different groups of learners and then systematically plan ways to support both student and teacher learning. Although "struggling readers" are a diverse group and can be defined in a wide variety of ways, all students in middle and high school who struggle to meet course expectations due to difficulties in reading need special attention in the school literacy plan.

Teachers' professional development should also be addressed, based on teachers' questions and concerns as well as the students' needs identified by the school needs assessment. Literacy coaches can organize workshops and study groups to help teachers understand the variety of reasons students may struggle with reading in content area classes. Understanding learners and the nature of the reading tasks required in content courses is a first step toward developing instruction that helps students become more successful in meeting literacy demands. A next step would be to help teachers develop expertise in using appropriate literacy strategies in their teaching. For example, after learning the importance of activating and building background knowledge, study group members might explore several types of anticipatory activities to use with their classes. Literacy coaches can then model lessons for teachers in different grade levels or in different content areas, and observe and conference with teachers as they try out new ideas.

Literacy coaches can also work with small groups of teachers or individuals to look at students' work samples and assess what types of difficulties students are having. Although instruction focused on literacy improvement in the content classroom would benefit all students, those who are struggling to comprehend content area texts will arguably gain the most through new access to a curriculum that previously may have been beyond their grasp.

Literacy coaches also can provide leadership in collaboration among specialists in the school. Learners who struggle in reading may have one or more classifications, such as "learning disabled." At many secondary schools, individual and small-group instruction for struggling readers is provided by a mix of special education teachers, ESOL teachers, speech-language pathologists, certified reading teachers and specialists, paraprofessionals, and volunteer tutors. Literacy coaches, as leaders of the school literacy program, can provide an invaluable service by encouraging communication among these groups and by helping them work together to provide effective services for students. Coaches can also work collaboratively with library and media specialists to develop a collection of print and technological resources to meet the needs of struggling readers, and they can help teachers review potential materials or programs designed for struggling readers before purchases are made.

Supporting English Language Learners

Literacy coaches can provide support for English learners in a variety of ways. First, they can ensure that their school's literacy plan considers the needs of these students. As García and Godina (2004, p. 306) note, "few school districts have developed coherent programs of instruction at the middle and high school levels to address the various needs of English language learners." Students learning English at the secondary level are a widely varied group, and details related to cultural, educational, and language background are important to consider. For example, some students arrive in the United States or Canada as teens with a history of limited formal schooling in their home countries; some of them have experienced great trauma in war-torn countries before their arrival. Others enter school with educational backgrounds similar to their North American counterparts. Some English learner students are not new immigrants, but have been in English language programs for a number of years.

It is also important for coaches and literacy councils to understand features of their school's English language program and how it may affect student achievement. Information related to how students are assessed, assigned to ESL or bilingual education classes, and transitioned to general education classes is important to consider. Specialist teachers who work with English learners should, of course, participate on the school literacy council and can provide valuable information on both student needs as well as regulations that affect services for this population.

In addition, the literacy coach can collaborate with the ESL or bilingual education teachers to create a program that helps all teachers in the school understand the needs of English learners. In many schools, content teachers are likely to have students with a range of levels of English proficiency in their classrooms. This may be a new circumstance for many content teachers, who can benefit from workshops and study groups that explore the best ways to merge content teaching with support for the English learner. Content teachers may need assistance from coaches, for example, in locating appropriate materials, understanding students' background knowledge, and learning appropriate strategies for teaching and assessment. ELL and bilingual education teachers may also benefit from the literacy coach's help in adding to their repertoire of strategies for improving the reading, writing, and communication of their students.

Literacy coaches also can assist their school in building communication with the families of their English learners and helping the school's program become more culturally responsive. For example, as coaches successfully advocate for the use of materials representing a wide variety of cultural groups, all students can expand their understanding of the world and see themselves in the curriculum. Many literacy coaches have been effective in supporting English learners and others by creating links that extend beyond the school. This might include developing internships that lead to jobs or college, or bringing business people, government employees, or college students to the school to serve as mentors or tutors.

Supporting Effective Assessment Practices

As part of providing literacy program leadership, a literacy coach can play an important role in a school's assessment program. First, it is important that the literacy coach work with the school's administrators and literacy council to conduct an assessment of the overall needs of their school. This assessment might include a survey of teachers related to their knowledge of teaching practices and views on school improvement; a review of standardized test scores for different grade levels and subpopulations; interviews with school leaders and representatives of different departments; and focus groups of students and parents that discuss students' literacy practices, goals, and needs. The literacy council can also evaluate the current assessment program, taking time to consider whether it provides information that truly informs teaching and learning. With these data, the literacy council can make recommendations about ways the school could better meet the needs of students in literacy and learning.

Moreover, literacy coaches working directly with teachers and teams of teachers can help them select, create, and use assessments to their best advantage. Teachers may need to update their knowledge on principles of assessment, including the purposes of different types of assessments and ways to interpret assessment information for parents and students. Although teachers in many secondary schools feel great pressure related to statewide high-stakes tests, as Afflerbach (2004, p. 386) notes, most high-stakes tests receive money, media attention, and time "all out of proportion to the benefits they provide." Because of this, coaches need to encourage teachers to use a wide variety of assessments that give useful information to inform instruction. Departmental meetings, school wide workshops, or smaller study groups may be helpful in this regard. Teachers may also benefit from one-on-one work with literacy coaches to review students' work samples and discuss what they show about students' literacy skills and understanding of course concepts. This discussion, in turn, provides a catalyst for the coach and teacher to consider teaching strategies that might be beneficial. Adolescent students can also participate in self-reflection on their own progress, possibly using portfolios that include work from a term or a year.

 **Programs and Strategies**

As resources shrink and the press for core curriculum and effective teaching for all learners grows, the culture of professional development is changing in ways that call for more collaboration, conversation, and technology use. We've selected two different types of programs to share: one school-based and somewhat informal, and the other formally connecting state agency and professional association. Each has achieved a high level of communication and collaboration, with multiple strategies supporting effective teachers working toward improvement.

School-based Programs

Chets Creek Elementary School in Jacksonville, Florida is an immersion program in on-going professional development. Chets Creek teachers are "virtually immersed in collaborative learning activities" embedded in the normal course of a school day, according to Heitin (2009). She interviewed Dayle Timmons, a Florida Teacher of the Year and special education teacher/ K–1 literacy coach. Dayle writes about many of the learning activities in her blog, Timmons Times. In it are video-lesson studies, weekly classroom tutorials, teacher wikis, and so on, all taking place at Chets Creek, a national model for the America's Choice School Design.

Philosophy

Professional development should be embedded within the school day and relate to what teachers are actually teaching. It should be part of what is happening every day, rather than occur outside of the school day, with sessions weeks or months apart.

Planning

Ten people form the leadership team comprised of administrators and lead teachers. They meet weekly for one and a half hours as a "think tank," generating ideas about what teachers need, what they want, and making sure to include the first year and 'seasoned' teachers.

Time

Teachers have daily common planning time for their grade level. Slightly larger class sizes, and everyone giving up one planning day a week make it possible for a once a week professional development session for everyone at that grade level. And, one day every other week, students are released early, making time available for whole school sessions.

Opportunities

- Book study groups (principal pays) meet once a week to discuss the book they have chosen. This offers a chance for teachers who are not usually together to get to know one another.

- Book of the Month has the principal buying a specific book for every classroom; she then brings the whole faculty together to demonstrate a strategy that teachers are to use in their classrooms. Often, the follow up to extend the strategy involves technology.

- Bring your own laptop to the IT person who, once a week at a designated time will teach whatever it is teachers want to know. This may include e-mailing tips, how to do something specific with a blog, or how to post a video for a NING community.

- Weekly grade level and subject specific meetings.

- Attend conferences when possible. Blogging about conference sessions helps teachers who could not attend the conference know what attendees were learning.

- Social networking on NING for a group interested in standards-based education. From all over the world, people post comments, questions, and videos among the more than 450 members. Teachers might converse with teachers in Bangkok or New Zealand on the same day; teachers often share what they heard or read with each other.

School Culture

It took time for teachers to "buy in." Over the years, teachers who were uncomfortable with an open door approach within a positive, risk-taking culture, left. Those who are at Chets Creek now want to be part of what has become the kind of environment conducive to learning and growing.

State Agency/Professional Association Partnership

Leadership in Reading Network (LiRN) is a partnership of The Minnesota Reading Association (MRA), the Minnesota Department of Education (MDE), and the Minnesota Center for Reading Research (MCRR) to provide professional development for the state's literacy leaders. Now in year four, this is a growing initiative to provide professional development to a broad spectrum of literacy leaders in the state. Learning together are classroom teachers, literacy coaches, reading specialists, district curriculum professionals, and administrators. A past MRA president and secondary learning/reading specialist, Julianne Scullen, described the program in *Reading Today* (October/November, 2011) which is recapped in the sections below.

Purposes

Seeking new ways to engage teachers in professional conversations, the partnering of the MRA, MDE, and MCRR resulted in LiRN, a growing initiative which provides three full days of professional development to literacy leaders "of all kinds" (Reading Today, 2011, p. 4). Rather than sending one teacher per school or school district to a workshop or conference, only to return to buildings with new ideas soon "lost due to lack of time and support to make effective and strategic changes," additional colleagues are included, which is necessary for collaboration.

Action Plan

LiRN members are requested to bring a guest, free of charge, to each workshop. For instance, a teacher might invite an administrator when the topic is building a culture of literacy. Between learning sessions throughout the day, time and guidance is given to facilitate meaningful conversation among team members. When teams return to work, they have a plan in hand to begin using their new information and ideas.

Opportunities

- One prominent focus is content area literacy instruction, with guests including science, social studies, math, and other subject area teachers. They are provided training in embedding literacy strategies into content curriculum by leaders in their respective fields. Rejoining colleagues/LiRN members, content teachers participate in team discussion.
- Another high interest topic is English learners; LiRN members will invite an ESL teacher or ESL specialist.
- When the focus is Systems of Intervention, administrators will be the special guests.

Time/Resources

LiRN recognizes the importance of time/resources in two ways. First, the built-in time for collaboration among all team members during each day's sessions is nonnegotiable. Second, the resources intended for each participant's professional library are woven into the fabric of the day's agenda. Speakers mention them throughout the day, thus adding to the likelihood the materials/information will be used in the near future.

Future Outlook

This working partnership creates a connection among research, practical application, and standards. The collective partners are united in the effort to facilitate the smooth flow of information through the channels directly to the classroom "to continually enhance instructional practices" (Reading Today, 2011, p. 5). This in turn should help Minnesota educators realize two major goals: building leadership capacity and increasing student achievement.

Professional Development Strategies

Continuing trends of collaboration and technology call for the use of a variety of support strategies to accomplish the goals of the high-quality professional development critical to meet the challenges of effective teaching. Many strategies are mentioned in previous sections, especially in the descriptions of two different kinds of professional development programs: Chets Creek and Minnesota.

High-quality professional development is no longer regarded as a one-stop workshop or isolated event. It is, as Renyi (1998, pp. 73–74) described, "an ethos—a way of being where learning is suffused throughout the teachers' working lives." Box 12.3, Voices from the Field, describes one high school's effort to implement a high-quality professional development initiative in order to improve reading across content area classes.

Teachers who want a successful content area reading program in their school need more than knowledge and enthusiasm if this important aspect of instruction is to become a reality. Certain support strategies can be used to increase success as colleagues engage in what can best be described as a process of change. As teachers work together to grow professionally, it is essential that change initiatives receive necessary support. One way to begin this process is to conduct a needs assessment, such as the one pictured in Figure 12.2, to determine the learning priorities that teachers have for their students and their own professional growth. Such an assessment can guide the work of the literacy coach or principal as individual and school wide literacy goals are pursued. During professional development, relevant experiences, such as the strategies listed in Figure 12.3, need to be provided by teachers and for teachers who want to grow in their ability to deliver content area reading instruction. The literacy coach or principal can facilitate the application of these strategies, incorporating them into informal school and district programs as well as in more formal, state agency affiliated professional development programs.

Professional Inquiry and Growth

When effective teachers reflect on their students' progress and their own teaching practice, they often engage in collaborative classroom research, a powerful form of professional development. As classroom teachers inquire into the teaching and learning going on in their

BOX 12.3 # Voices from the Field

Jean, High School Literacy Coach

Challenge

In an era of high-stakes accountability, pressure falls on teachers to ensure that students understand subject area material and can demonstrate that knowledge effectively on mandated standardized tests. This can be a tall order for secondary students who struggle with basic reading, let alone with the highly specialized subject area texts and multiple transitions throughout the day, with each course and each teacher having different requirements and different instructional approaches. In our school, we have found that many students struggle to comprehend curriculum materials and to meet the wide ranging demands of high school courses.

Strategy

To support students as they strive to understand content and to streamline the transitions within the school day, our school created a school wide professional development initiative for teachers in learning and applying effective strategies for content area reading. Because so few of our high school teachers had received substantive coursework on content area reading strategies in their preservice preparation programs, many were either unaware of what strategies were available to them, or unsure of how to incorporate them into courses that were already filled to the brim with required content.

To begin our initiative, teachers, literacy coaches, and school administrators worked together to form a school-wide reading program that was integrated across content areas and engaged all members of the school community as both learners and teachers:

English teachers showed other teachers how to administer and analyze an informal reading inventory; literacy coaches modeled how to assess students' reading ability and how to differentiate instruction so that content area texts would be accessible to students of varying reading levels; the school media specialist provided a workshop on how to locate supplemental curriculum materials to match students' reading levels; each content area team investigated and selected reading strategies that they believed would best support their specialized course content. Throughout the school year, teachers formed peer support teams to discuss their successes and challenges encountered when implementing new content area reading strategies. In addition to the informal conversations that occurred among teachers throughout the school year, literacy coaches provided formal content area reading workshops as part of ongoing professional development.

Reflection

Some teachers remained resistant to the additional responsibility of reading instruction in content area classrooms. However, most teachers were responsive to this professional development initiative, particularly when they observed growth in their students' understanding of subject area material. Their efforts were concentrated, consistent, and supported by peers and administrators. Having a degree of control over the strategies they selected and the manner in which they used them seemed to give teachers a voice throughout this initiative and a sense of autonomy over the application of strategies in their courses. In my book, that's as good as it gets!

classrooms, they generate questions they want to answer, gather evidence, and share results with other teaching colleagues. This is also called *action research*, a strategy for professional development that not only has 'staying power,' but also may be experiencing a renewal due to teaching workforce transition. With many current teachers facing retirement, school districts are seeking ways to develop programs to build professional knowledge and aptitude for new teachers. Appropriately, site-based "action research encourages school personnel to

Figure 12.2 Sample Needs Assessment Survey

Welcome to the new semester. As we begin to make our professional development plans for the coming months, we would like to know what area or topics interest you the most. For each of the items listed below, please indicate your interest in including that topic in this semester's professional development plan using the following scale:

1 = I am comfortable with this topic and do not need a lot of help in this area.

2 = I would like to refresh or refine my knowledge of this topic.

3 = This is a priority for me and I would like to learn a lot more about it.

Topic	Interest Level		
Integrating new literacies into my teaching	1	2	3
Assessing student performance	1	2	3
Locating appropriate texts	1	2	3
Applying strategies for enhancing student engagement	1	2	3
Applying strategies for activating students' background knowledge	1	2	3
Applying strategies for vocabulary learning	1	2	3
Applying study strategies	1	2	3
Applying strategies for improving students' writing	1	2	3

Figure 12.3 Strategies to Support Change

- Peer collaboration to develop instructional strategies and assessments
- Observations in one another's classrooms in one's own or another building
- Mentoring programs for new teachers or experienced teachers who are new to a grade level
- Small-group seminars that include time for reflective dialogue
- Reading and discussion of professional literature with colleagues
- Peer support teams (peers share questions, concerns, and ideas for solutions as they seek to implement changes in their teaching and literacy programs)
- Peer coaching (feedback is given to teachers by teachers as strategies are applied with students)
- Lesson demonstrations
- Guided practice (a literacy coach leads participants in applying strategies)
- Opportunities to attend conferences or to hear speakers on topical issues
- Follow-up sessions related to conferences or workshops attended
- Threaded discussions
- A professional development website where teachers can share resources, ideas for lesson plans, and relevant data

systematically develop a question, gather data, and then analyze the data to improve their practice" (Gilles, Wilson & Elias, 2010, p. 91).

Action research revolves around writing, dialogue, and problem solving. It can be helpful, even motivating, to content area teachers who try many of the instructional strategies suggested in this book. They gain experience with innovations while receiving support from colleagues, potentially changing their own teaching, hence, growing professionally.

Taking responsibility for one's own adult learning is a logical next step for effective teachers, who are likely to experience a variety of professional development opportunities over the course of their careers. An early-career teacher might spend more time and energy trying out various techniques in the classroom, often dealing with classroom management issues. A 15- year veteran teacher down the hallway might be looking for some innovative, alternative ways to contribute to the profession to avoid burnout issues. Whether novice or veteran, putting together an individual, personal/professional plan for growth and inquiry can be a beneficial experience for any teacher engaged in effective teaching.

Following are some ideas to consider, include, discard, or modify in building an individual plan:

- One of the first steps might be finding a comfortable way to write down random thoughts, concerns, questions, and reflections whenever there is a chance to do so. Reading the entries every so often can provide insights into thinking.

- Finding a like-minded colleague from the same or another school with whom to share happenings/insights revealed in the journal can be powerful. This can initiate conversations, furnish each teacher with fresh perspectives, and generate new ideas to use in the classroom.

- Once colleagues "know one another," they may meet in person if feasible, network face to face, or continue to converse online either with each other or a broader community.

- If in a graduate school course or a professional development series, seek out several people you might like to interact with to "compare notes" about grade level or subject specific developments.

- Apply for membership in a national professional association, such as National Council of Teachers of Mathematics, and take full advantage of services offered: subscriptions, newsletters, conferences, special interest groups, and service opportunities. Stay abreast of current thinking in your field while learning practical, often hands-on, ideas for teaching without feeling overwhelmed.

- Join the state affiliate of an education association where there are often more opportunities for service, leadership, and even publishing.

- If given the opportunity to participate in grant writing for a project that you are interested in, and you foresee connections to your students' needs, teaching, or career goals, think of this as an avenue for growth.

- Write a proposal (individually or jointly) to present for your organization's state or national conference. If accepted, you will be invited to attend, enjoy, and learn with colleagues.

Looking Back | Looking Forward

We considered in this chapter why and how effective teaching depends on supporting effective teachers with quality, differentiated professional development throughout their careers. When professional development opportunities and programs are planned, collaborative, ongoing, and based on inquiry, teaching to help all students improve becomes an attainable goal. Currently, content area teachers face the need to incorporate Common Core State Standards into the curriculum, provoking a more institutional purpose for professional development; they are responsible for meeting the needs of all learners in subject areas. Teachers require support to deliver instructional programs and techniques, and opportunities to engage in inquiry for their own professional growth—a more personal goal.

Teachers, principals, and literacy coaches are key leaders whose roles have changed to incorporate new and recurring challenges and trends. They influence instructional practices designed to serve the diverse literacy needs of students, including struggling readers and English language learners, and they can guide assessment practices used within the school. By building learning communities, conferring with each other, and supporting the planning of a variety of professional development programs and strategies, they create powerful learning environments for all members of the school community.

Ours is a time in which technology is both a tool and topic for furthering the learning of all students and teachers. When incorporated into instruction intended for students and professional development for teachers, technology enriches the learning community and makes goals more attainable. Effective teachers don't sidestep the "difficult" student in order to work with those more likely to score well on tests. They expect improvement in everyone, including themselves.

The roles and titles of literacy coaches have changed over the years, and standards and expectations for literacy coaches have emerged that bring more consistency to the work of literacy coaches. Literacy coaches contribute to inquiry-based professional development in content area classrooms that leads to professional growth for teachers and improved instruction for students. Literacy coaches influence instructional practices designed to serve the diverse literacy needs of students, including struggling readers and English language learners, and they can guide the assessment practices used within the school. By building learning communities, conferring with teachers, and supporting ongoing professional development, literacy coaches create powerful learning environments for all members of the school community. Reflecting on her own professional journey, high school teacher Sarah Van Wyhe explained:

> The experiences I've had and the knowledge I've gained over the past year have made me think how the next thirty might be. Doors may open to different job opportunities, and some I may try to walk through. Right now, I will stay in Mobile Unit #13 that welcomes around eighty teenagers Monday through Friday, one hundred eighty days a year. The difference will be that, when they walk through my door, I will be better able to prepare them for a bright future. I will be a more reflective practitioner who seeks research-based best practices to use in my classroom. I will be confident all my students can learn when taught effective strategies that go with them when they leave. I hope to apply what I have learned, and will continue to learn, in order to become a more effective teacher every day. I will share what I can with my coworkers, they will share ideas with me, and together we will help to shape the future.

Minds On

1. Reflect on a time when you teamed with a literacy coach, a teacher, or principal on a project. What were some of the benefits students and teachers derived from the collaboration? What were some of the drawbacks?

2. Examine the following professional development needs: (a) to become familiar with research and to use it to inform instructional practices, (b) to reconsider one's own beliefs in order to come to a better understanding of teaching practices, and (c) to ex-

plore alternative strategies for improving one's teaching and learning. Where would you place your own professional needs and how do they compare with those of others in your group?

3. Imagine that you are part of a committee in charge of planning a professional development program for teachers in your school. How would you determine what that professional development program should encompass? What factors would you consider as you prepared to implement that program?

Hands On

1. Think of a content area class that you have recently observed. If you were a literacy coach preparing to conduct a conference with the teacher of that class, what questions and comments would you include in that conference? How would you structure the conference so that it was supportive and interactive?

2. Team with several people in the class to develop ideas that could be used by a literacy coach, lead teacher, or principal to support teachers in your school as they work to meet the needs of struggling readers and English language learners.

3. Review the summary of the USDE's RESPECT program. Discuss its six elements and, based on them, propose a novel change to improve teachers' job satisfaction. Focus on your own school or situation, and/or choose a specific level of experience.

eResources

Select an article from the Literacy Coaching Clearinghouse website (**www.literacycoachingonline.org**) and discuss with colleagues how the article connects to the work of literacy coaches in your school or district. What suggestions would you offer for enhancing the work of the coach based on the article you read?

Explore the collection of NCTE's online resources for literacy coaches (**www1.ncte.org/store/books/language/118000 .htm**) and select resources that are most relevant to your content area. Explain how you might incorporate the resources you selected into your content area instruction.

MyEducationLab™

Go to the MyEducationLab (**www.myeducationlab.com**) for *Content Area Reading*, where you can:
- Find learning outcomes along with the national standards that connect to these outcomes.
- Complete Assignments and Activities that can help you more deeply understand the chapter content.
- Practice the core teaching skills identified in the chapter with the Building Teaching Skills and Dispositions learning units.
- Check your comprehension on the content covered in the chapter with the Study Plan. Here you will be able to take a chapter quiz, receive feedback on your answers, and then access Review, Practice, and Enrichment activities to enhance your understanding of chapter content.
- Visit A+RISE. A+RISE® Standards2Strategy™ is an innovative and interactive online resource that offers new teachers in grades K–12 just in time, research-based instructional strategies that meet the linguistic needs of English Language Learners (ELLs) as they learn content, differentiate instruction for all grades and abilities, and are aligned to Common Core Elementary Language Arts standards (for the literacy strategies) and to English language proficiency standards in World-Class Instructional Design and Assessment (WIDA), Texas, California, and Florida.
- Use the Online Lesson Plan Builder to practice lesson planning and integrating national and state standards into your planning.

Appendix A

Affixes with Invariant Meanings

Affix	Meaning	Example
Combining Forms		
anthropo-	man	anthropoid
auto-	self	autonomous
biblio-	book	bibliography
bio-	life	biology
centro-, centri-	center	centrifugal
cosmo-	universe	cosmonaut
heter-, hetero-	different	heterogeneous
homo-	same	homogeneous
hydro-	water	hydroplane
iso-	equal	isometric
lith-, litho-	stone	lithography
micro-	small	microscope
mono-	one	monocyte
neuro-	nerve	neurologist
omni-	all	omnibus
pan-	all	panchromatic
penta-	five	pentamerous
phil-, philo-	love	philanthropist
phono-	sound	phonology
photo-	light	photosynthesis
pneumo-	air, respiration	pneumonia
poly-	many	polygon
proto-	before, first in time	prototype

Affix	Meaning	Example
pseudo-	false	pseudonym
tele-	far	television
uni-	one	unicellular

Prefixes

Affix	Meaning	Example
apo-	separate or detached from	apocarpous
circum-	around	circumvent
co-, col-, com-, con-, cor-	together or with	combine
equi-	equal	equivalent
extra-	in addition	extraordinary
intra-	within	intratext
mal-	bad	malpractice
mis-	wrong	mistreatment
non-	not	nonsense
syn-	together or with	synthesis

Noun Suffixes

Affix	Meaning	Example
-ana	collection	Americana
-archy	rule or government	oligarchy
-ard, -art	person who does something to excess	drunkard, braggart
-aster	inferiority or fraudulence	poetaster
-bility	quality or state of being	capability
-chrome	pigment, color	autochrome
-cide	murder or killing of	insecticide
-fication, -ation	action or process of	classification, dramatization
-gram	something written or drawn	diagram
-graph	writing, recording, drawing	telegraph, lithograph
-graphy	descriptive science of a specific subject or field	planography, oceanography
-ics	science or art of	graphics, athletics
-itis	inflammation or inflammatory disease	bronchitis
-latry	worship of	bibliolatry
-meter	measuring device	barometer
-metry	science or process of measuring	photometry
-ology, -logy	science, theory, or study of	phraseology, paleontology

Affix	Meaning	Example
-phobia	fear	hypnophobia
-phore	bearer or producer	semaphore
-scope	instrument for observing or detecting	telescope
-scopy	viewing, seeing, or observing	microscopy
-ance, -ation, -ion, -ism, -dom, -ery, -mony, -ment, -tion	quality, state, or condition; action or result of an action	tolerance, adoration, truism, matrimony, government, sanction
-er, -eer, -ess, -ier, -ster, -ist, -trix	agent, doer	helper, engineer, countess, youngster, shootist, executrix

Adjective Suffixes

Affix	Meaning	Example
-able, -ible	worthy of or inclined to	debatable, knowledgeable
-aceous, -ative, -ish, -ive, -itious	pertaining to	impish, foolish, additive, fictitious
-acious	tendency toward or abundance of	fallacious
-est	most	greatest
-ferous	bearing, producing	crystalliferous
-fic	making, causing, or creating	horrific
-fold	multiplied by	fivefold
-form	having the form of	cuneiform
-ful	full of or having the quality of	masterful, useful, armful
-genous	generating or producing	androgenous, endogenous
-ic	characteristic of	seismic, microscopic
-less	lacking	toothless
-like	similar to	lifelike
-most	most	innermost
-ous, -ose	possessing, full of	joyous, grandiose
-wise	manner, direction, or positions	clockwise

Appendix B

Commonly Used Prefixes with Varying Meanings

Prefix	Meaning	Example
ab-	from, away, off	abhor, abnormal, abdicate
ad-	to, toward	adhere, adjoin
ante-	before, in front of, earlier than	antecedent, antediluvian
anti-	opposite of, hostile to	antitoxin, antisocial
be-	make, against, to a great degree	bemoan, belittle, befuddle
bi-	two, twice	biped, bivalve
de-	away, opposite of, reduce	deactivate, devalue, devitalize
dia-	through, across	diameter, diagonal
dis-	opposite of, apart, away	dissatisfy, disarm, disjointed
en-	cause to be, put in or on	enable, engulf
epi-	upon, after	epitaph, epilogue, epidermis
ex-	out of, former, apart, away	excrete, exposition
hyper-	above, beyond, excessive	hyperphysical, hypersensitive
hypo-	under, less than normal	hypodermic, hypotension
in-, il-, im-, ir-	not, in, into, within	inept, indoors
inter-	between, among	interscholastic, interstellar
neo-	new, young	neophyte, neo-Nazi
ortho-	straight, corrective	orthotropic, orthopedic
per-	through, very	permanent, perjury
peri-	around, near, enclosing	perimeter, perihelion
post-	after, behind	postwar, postorbital

Prefix	Meaning	Example
pre-	before, in place, time, rank, order	preview, prevail
pro-	before, forward, for, in favor of	production, prothorax, pro-American
re-	again, back	react, recoil
sub-, sur-, sug-, sup-	under, beneath	subordinate, subsoil, substation
super-	above, over, in addition	superhuman, superlative, superordinate
syn-	with, together	synthesis, synchronize
trans-	across, beyond, through	transatlantic, transconfiguration, transaction
ultra-	beyond in space, excessive	ultraviolet, ultramodern
un-	not, the opposite of	unable, unbind

Appendix C

Graphic Organizers with Text Frames

Graphic organizers are visual illustrations of verbal statements. Frames are sets of questions or categories that are fundamental to understanding a given topic. Here we show nine "generic" graphic forms with their corresponding frames. Examples of topics that could be represented by each graphic form are also given. These graphics show at a glance the key parts of the whole and their relations, helping the learner to comprehend text and solve problems.

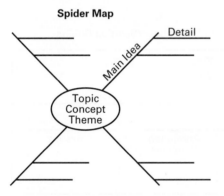

Spider Map

Detail

Main Idea

Topic
Concept
Theme

Used to describe a central idea: a thing (a geographic region), process (meiosis), concept (altruism), or proposition with support (experimental drugs should be available to AIDS patients). Key frame questions: What is the central idea? What are its attributes? What are its functions?

Used to describe the stages of something (the life cycle of a primate); the steps in a linear procedure (how to neutralize an acid); a sequence of events (how feudalism led to the formation of nation-states); or the goals, actions, and outcomes of a historical figure or character in a novel (the rise and fall of Napoléon). Key frame questions: What is the object, procedure, or initiating event? What are the stages or steps? How do they lead to one another? What is the final outcome?

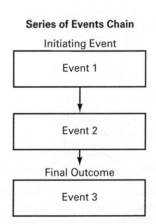

Series of Events Chain

Initiating Event

Event 1

Event 2

Final Outcome

Event 3

417

Used for time lines showing historical events or ages (grade levels in school), degrees of something (weight), shades of meaning (Likert scales), or ratings scales (achievement in school). Key frame questions: What is being scaled? What are the end points?

Continuum/Scale

Low   High

Compare/Contrast Matrix

	Name 1	Name 2
Attribute 1		
Attribute 2		
Attribute 3		

Used to show similarities and differences between two things (people, places, events, ideas, etc.). Key frame questions: What things are being compared? How are they similar? How are they different?

Used to represent a problem, attempted solutions, and results (the national debt). Key frame questions: What was the problem? Who had the problem? Why was it a problem? What attempts were made to solve the problem? Did those attempts succeed?

Problem/Solution Outline

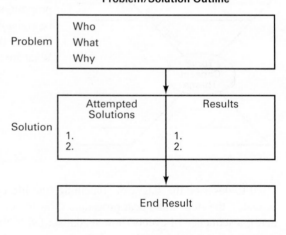

Problem — Who / What / Why

Solution — Attempted Solutions: 1. 2. / Results: 1. 2.

End Result

Network Tree

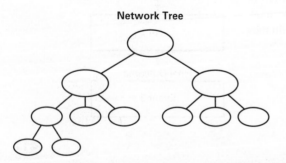

Used to show causal information (causes of poverty), a hierarchy (types of insects), or branching procedures (the circulatory system). Key frame questions: What is the superordinate category? What are the subordinate categories? How are they related? How many levels are there?

Used to show the nature of an interaction between persons or groups (European settlers and Native Americans). Key frame questions: Who are the persons or groups? Did they conflict or cooperate? What was the outcome for each person or group?

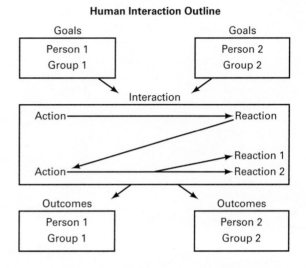

Human Interaction Outline

Used to show the causal interaction of a complex event (an election, a nuclear explosion) or complex phenomenon (juvenile delinquency, learning disabilities). Key frame questions: What are the factors that cause X? How do they relate? Are the factors that cause X the same as those that cause X to persist?

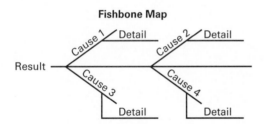

Fishbone Map

Used to show how a series of events interact to produce a set of results again and again (weather phenomena, cycles of achievement and failure, the life cycle). Key frame questions: What are the critical events in the cycle? How are they related? In what ways are they self-reinforcing?

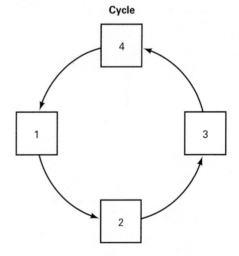

Cycle

References

Abrams, S. (2000). *Using journals with reluctant writers: Building portfolios for middle and high school students.* Thousand Oaks, CA: Corwin Press.

Ackerman, N. (1990). *The tin heart.* Ill. M. Hays. New York: Atheneum.

Adlit.org. (2008). Brian Selznick. Retrieved March 1, 2009, from www.adlit.org/transcript_display/19677.

Afflerbach, P. (2004). *National Reading Conference policy brief: High-stakes testing and reading assessment.* Oak Creek, WI: National Reading Conference.

Alexander, P. (1986). *Silver Burdett biology.* Morristown, NJ: Silver Burdett.

Alexie, S. (2007). *The absolutely true diary of a part-time Indian.* New York: Little, Brown.

Algozzine, B., & Ysseldyke, J. E. (2006). *Effective instruction for students with special needs.* Thousand Oaks, CA: Corwin Press.

Aliki. (1983). *A medieval feast.* New York: Crowell.

Aliki. (1999). *William Shakespeare and the Globe.* New York: HarperCollins.

Allen, M. B. (2003). *Eight questions on teacher preparation: What does the research say?* Denver, CO: Education Commission of the States.

Alliance for Excellent Education. (2006). *Policy brief: Why the crisis in adolescent literacy demands a national response.* Washington, DC: Author.

Allington, R., & Johnston, P. H. (Eds.). (2002). *Reading to learn: Lessons from exemplary fourth-grade classrooms.* New York: Guilford Press.

Allington, R. L., & Strange, M. (1980). *Learning through reading in the content areas.* Lexington, MA: Heath.

Alvarez, M. C. (1996). Explorers of the universe: Students using the World Wide Web to improve their reading and writing. In B. Neate (Ed.), *Literacy saves lives* (pp. 140–145). Herts, UK: United Kingdom Reading Association.

Alvermann, D. E. (1991). The discussion web: A graphic aid for learning across the curriculum. *Reading Teacher, 45*(2), 92–99.

Alvermann, D. E. (2001). Reading adolescents' reading identities: Looking back to see ahead. *Journal of Adolescent & Adult Literacy, 44,* 676–690.

Alvermann, D. E., Dillon, D. R., & O'Brien, D. G. (1988). *Using discussion to promote reading comprehension.* Newark, DE: International Reading Association.

Alvermann, D. E., & Moore, D. W. (1991). Secondary school reading. In P. D. Pearson, R. Barr, M. L. Kamil, & P. Mosenthal (Eds.), *Handbook of reading research* (2nd ed., pp. 951–983). New York: Longman.

Alvermann, D. E., Swafford, J., & Montero, K. M. (2004). *Content area literacy instruction for the elementary grades.* Boston: Allyn & Bacon.

Ames, L. J. (1986). *Draw fifty cars, trucks, and motorcycles.* Garden City, NY: Doubleday.

Anders, P. L. (2002). Secondary reading programs: A story of what was. In D. L. Schallert, C. M. Fairbanks, J. Worthy, B. Maloch, & J. V. Hoffman (Eds.), *51st yearbook of the National Reading Conference* (pp. 82–93). Oak Creek, WI: National Reading Conference.

Anderson, D. L. (1999). *Using projects in the mathematics classroom to enhance instruction and incorporate history of mathematics.* Paper presented at the National Council of Teachers of Mathematics annual conference, San Francisco, CA.

Anderson, L. H. (1999). *Speak.* New York: Farrar, Strauss & Giroux.

Anderson, L. H. (2000). *Fever 1793.* New York: Simon & Schuster.

Anderson, R. C., & Freebody, P. (1981). Vocabulary knowledge. In J. T. Guthrie (Ed.), *Comprehension and teaching: Research perspectives* (pp. 77–117). Newark, DE: International Reading Association.

Anderson-Inman, L., & Horney, M. (1997). Electronic books for secondary students. *Journal of Adolescent & Adult Literacy, 40*(6), 486–491.

Anno, M. (1989). *Anno's math games II.* New York: Philomel.

Anonymous. (1971). *Go ask Alice.* New York: Simon Pulse.

Applebee, A. N. (1991). Environments for language teaching and learning: Contemporary issues and future directions. In J. Flood, J. M. Jensen, D. Lapp, & J. R. Squire (Eds.), *Handbook of research on teaching the English language arts* (pp. 549–558). New York: Macmillan.

Armbruster, B. B. (2000). Responding to informative prose. In R. Indrisano & J. R. Squire (Eds.), *Perspectives on writing: Research, theory, and practice.* Newark, DE: International Reading Association.

Armbruster, B. B., & Anderson, T. H. (1985). Frames: Structure for informational texts. In D. H. Jonassen (Ed.),

Technology of text (pp. 331–346). Englewood Cliffs, NJ: Education Technology Publications.

Armstrong, J. (1998). *Shipwreck at the bottom of the world: The extraordinary true story of Shackleton and the* Endurance. New York: Crown.

Armstrong, J. (2002). *Shattered: Stories of children and war.* New York: Knopf.

Armstrong, L., & Jenkins, S. (2001). *It's not about the bike: My journey back to life.* New York: Berkley Books.

Aronson, E. (1978). *The jigsaw classroom.* Beverly Hills, CA: Sage.

Aronson, M. (1998). *Art attack: A short cultural history of the avant-garde.* New York: Clarion Books.

Artley, A. S. (1975). Words, words, words. *Language Arts, 52,* 1067–1072.

Asher, J. (2007). *Thirteen reasons why.* New York: Penguin.

Atkin, S. B. (1993). *Voices from the fields: Children of migrant farmworkers tell their stories.* Boston: Little, Brown.

Atwell, N. (1990). Introduction. In N. Atwell (Ed.), *Coming to know: Writing to learn in intermediate grades* (pp. xi–xxiii). Portsmouth, NH: Heinemann.

Atwell, N. (1998). *In the middle: New understandings about writing, reading, and learning* (2nd ed.). Portsmouth, NH: Heinemann.

Au, K. H. (1993). *Literacy instruction in multicultural settings.* Orlando: Harcourt Brace.

Au, K. H., & Mason, J. M. (1981). Social organizational factors in learning to read: The balance of rights hypothesis. *Reading Research Quarterly, 17*(1), 115–152.

Avi. (2008). *The seer of shadows.* New York: HarperCollins.

Baker, F. W. (2009). *State standards which include elements of media literacy.* Retrieved February 5, 2009, from www.frankwbaker.com/state_lit.htm.

Baker, J. (1991). *Window.* New York: Greenwillow.

Baker, L. (1991). Metacognition, reading, and science education. In C. M. Santa & D. E. Alvermann (Eds.), *Science learning: Processes and applications* (pp. 12–13). Newark, DE: International Reading Association.

Baker, L., & Brown, A. (1984). Cognitive monitoring in reading. In J. Flood (Ed.), *Understanding reading comprehension* (pp. 21–44). Newark, DE: International Reading Association.

Ball, D., & Forzani, F. M. (2010). Teaching skillful teaching. *Educational Leadership*, *68*(4), 40–45.

Ball, D. L., & Forzani, F. M. (2011). Building a common core for learning to teach and connecting professional learning to practice. *American Educator*, *35*(2), 38–39.

Ball, J. (2005). *Go figure! A totally cool book about numbers.* New York: DK Children.

Ballard, R. D. (1988). *Exploring the Titanic.* New York: Scholastic.

Bamford, R. A., & Kristo, J. V. (Eds.). (1998). *Making facts come alive: Choosing quality nonfiction literature K–8.* Needham Heights, MA: Christopher Gordon.

Bandura, A. (1986). *Social foundations of thought and action: A social cognitive theory.* Englewood Cliffs, NJ: Prentice Hall.

Bangert-Drowns, R. L., Hurley, M. M., & Wilkinson, B. (2004). The effects of school-based writing-to-learn interventions on academic achievement: A meta-analysis. *Review of Educational Research, 74,* 29–58.

Banks, A. B. (2008). *An introduction to multicultural education* (4th ed.). Boston: Pearson.

Banks, J. A. (2001). *Cultural diversity and education: Foundations, curriculum, and teaching* (4th ed.). Boston: Allyn & Bacon.

Bardoe, C. (2006). *Gregor Mendel: The friar who grew peas.* New York: Abrams Books.

Barnes, D. (1995). Talking and learning in the classroom: An introduction. *Primary Voices K–6, 3*(1), 2–7.

Barnitz, J. G. (1994). Discourse diversity: Principles for authentic talk and literacy instruction. *Journal of Reading, 37*(7), 586–591.

Barnhouse, D. (2012, April 23). How testing is hurting teaching. *The New York Times.* Retrieved from http://www.nytimes.com.

Barrentine, S. J. (1999). *Reading assessment: Principles and practices for elementary teachers.* Newark, DE: International Reading Association.

Barron, R. F. (1969). The use of vocabulary as an advance organizer. In H. L. Herber & P. L. Sanders (Eds.), *Research in reading in the content areas: First report* (pp. 29–39). Syracuse, NY: Syracuse University Reading and Language Arts Center.

Barron, R. F., & Earle, R. (1973). An approach for vocabulary development. In H. L. Herber & R. F. Barron (Eds.), *Research in reading in the content areas: Second report* (pp. 51–63). Syracuse, NY: Syracuse University Reading and Language Arts Center.

Barron, R. F., & Stone, F. (1973, December). *The effect of student constructed graphic post organizers upon learning of vocabulary relationships from a passage of social studies content.* Paper presented at the meeting of the National Reading Conference, Houston, TX.

Bartoletti, S. C. (2001). *Black potatoes: The story of the great Irish famine, 1845–1850.* Boston: Houghton Mifflin.

Bartoletti, S. C. (2006). *Hitler youth: Growing up in Hitler's shadow.* New York: Scholastic.

Barton, D., & Hamilton, M. (1998). *Local literacies: Reading and writing in one community.* London: Routledge.

Barton, J. (1995). Conducting effective classroom discussions. *Journal of Reading, 38*(5), 346–350.

Baxendell, B. W. (2003). Consistent, coherent, creative: The 3 C's of graphic organizers. *Teaching Exceptional Children, 35,* 46–53.

Beach, R. W. (2011). Issues in analyzing alignment of language arts common core standards with state standards. *Educational Researchers, 40*(4), 179–182.

Beah, I. (2007). *A long way gone: Memoirs of a boy soldier.* New York: Farrar, Straus & Giroux.

Beals, M. P. (1995). *Warriors don't cry: A searing memoir of the battle to integrate Little Rock.* New York: Washington Square Press.

Beaman, B. (1985). Writing to learn social studies. In A. R. Gere (Ed.), *Roots in sawdust: Writing to learn across the disciplines* (pp. 50–60). Urbana, IL: National Council of Teachers of English.

Bean, J. C., Drenk, D., & Lee, F. D. (1982). Microtheme strategies for developing cognitive skills. In C. W. Griffin (Ed.), *New directions for teaching and learning.* San Francisco: Jossey-Bass.

Bean, R. M. (2004). Promoting effective literacy instruction: The challenge for literacy coaches. *The California Reader, 37*(3), 58–63.

Bean, R. M. (2011). The reading coach: Professional development and literacy leadership in the school. In T. V. Rasinski (Ed.), *Rebuilding the foundation: Effective reading instruction for 21st century literacy* (pp. 315–336). Bloomington, IN: Solution Tree Press.

Bean, R. M., Cassidy, J., Grumet, J. E., Shelton, D. S., & Wallis, S. R. (2002). What do reading specialists do? Results from a national survey. *The Reading Teacher, 55*(8), 736–744.

Bean, R. M., & DeFord, D. (2007). *Do's and don'ts for literacy coaches: Advice from the field.* Retrieved November 1, 2007, from the Literacy Coaching Clearinghouse website, www.literacycoaching online.org.

Bean, T. W. (2001). An update on reading in the content areas: Social constructionist dimensions. *Reading Online, 5*(5). Retrieved October 5, 2005, from www.reading online.org/articles/art_index.asp?HREF=handbook/bean/index.html.

Bean, T. W., & Moni, K. (2003). Developing students' critical literacy: Exploring identity construction in young adult fiction. *Journal of Adolescent & Adult Literacy, 46*(8), 638–648.

Beatty, P. (1987). *Charley Skedaddle.* New York: Morrow.

Beck, I. L., McKeown, M. G., Hamilton, R. L., & Kucan, L. (1997). *Questioning the author: An approach for enhancing student engagement in text.* Newark, DE: International Reading Association.

Beck, I. L., McKeown, M. G., & Kucan, L. (2002). *Bringing words to life: Robust vocabulary instruction.* New York: Guilford Press.

Beebe, B. F. (1968). *African elephants.* New York: McKay.

Beers, K. (2003). *When kids can't read, what teachers can do.* Portsmouth, NH: Heinemann.

Beil, K. M. (1999). *Fire in their eyes: Wildfires and the people who fight them.* San Diego: Harcourt Brace.

Berger, M. (1986). *Atoms, molecules, and quarks.* New York: Putnam.

Berlyne, D. E. (1965). *Structure and direction of thinking.* New York: Wiley.

Berman, I., & Biancarosa, G. (2005). *Reading to achieve: A governor's guide to adolescent literacy.* Washington, DC: National Governor's Association for Best Practices.

Bernhardt, E. B. (1998). Socio-historical perspectives on language teaching in modern America. In H. Byrnes (Ed.), *Perspectives in research and scholarship in second language learning* (pp. 39–57). New York: Modern Language Association.

Bernhardt, E. B., & Kamil, M. L. (1998). Literacy instruction for non-native speakers of English. In M. Graves, B. Graves, & C. Watts (Eds.), *Teaching reading in the 21st century* (pp. 432–475). Boston: Allyn & Bacon.

Berry, K., & Herrington, C. (2011). States and their struggles with NCLB: Does the Obama blueprint get it right? *Peabody Journal of Education, 86,* 272–290.

Betts, E. (1950). *Foundations of reading* (rev. ed.). New York: American Book Company.

Biancarosa, G., & Snow, C. (2004). *Reading next: A vision for action and research in middle and high school literacy.* Report to Carnegie Corporation of New York. Washington, DC: Alliance for Excellent Education. Retrieved June 25, 2007, from www.all4ed.org/publications/ReadingNext/ReadingNext.pdf.

Bishop, R. S. (2003). Reframing the debate about cultural authenticity. In D. L. Fox & K. G. Short (Eds.), *Stories matter: The complexity of cultural authenticity in children's literature* (pp. 25–37). Urbana, IL: National Council of Teachers of English.

Bitton-Jackson, L. (1997). *I have lived a thousand years: Growing up in the Holocaust.* New York: Simon & Schuster.

Blachowicz, C. (1986). Making connections: Alternatives to the vocabulary notebook. *Journal of Reading, 29,* 643–649.

Blachowicz, C., & Fisher, P. (1996). *Teaching vocabulary in all classrooms.* Columbus, OH: Merrill.

Blachowicz, C., Obrochta, C., & Fogelberg, E. (2005). Literacy coaching for change. *Educational Leadership, 62*(6), 55–58.

Blachowicz, C. Z., Fisher, P. J. L., Ogle, D., & Watts-Taffe, S. (2006). Vocabulary: Questions from the classroom. *Reading Research Quarterly, 41*(4), 524–539.

Bleich, D. (1978). *Subjective criticism.* Baltimore: Johns Hopkins University Press.

Blohm, J. M., & Lapinsky, T. (2006). *Kids like me: Voices of the immigrant experience.* Boston: Intercultural Press.

Blow, C. M. (2011, September 2). In honor of teachers. *The New York Times.* Retrieved from www.nytimes.com.

Blumenthal, K. (2005). *Let me play: The story of Title IX: The law that changed the future of girls in America.* New York: Atheneum.

Bluestein, N.A. (2010). Unlocking text features for determining importance in expository text: A strategy for struggling readers. *The Reading Teacher, 63*(7), 597–600.

Bode, J. (1989). *New kids on the block: Oral histories of immigrant teens.* New York: Franklin Watts.

Bode, J. (2000). *Colors of freedom: Immigrant stories.* New York: Franklin Watts.

Boushey, G., & Moser, J. (2009). *The CAFÖ book: Engaging all students in daily literacy assessment and instruction.* New York: Stenhouse.

Boykin, A. W. (1978). Psychological/behavioral verve in academic/task performance: Pre-theoretical considerations. *Journal of Negro Education, 47*(4), 343–354.

Boykin, A. W. (1984). Reading achievement and the social-cultural frame of reference of Afro-American students. *Journal of Negro Education, 53*(4), 464–473.

Boyne, J. (2006). *The boy in the striped pajamas.* New York: Fickling.

Brashares, A. (2001). *Sisterhood of the traveling pants.* New York: Delacorte.

Britton, J. (1970). *Language and learning.* London: Allen Lane.

Bromley, K. (2007). Nine things every teacher should know about words and vocabulary instruction. *Journal of Adolescent and Adult Literacy, 50*(7), 528–537.

Brown, A. L. (1978). Knowing when, where, and how to remember: A problem of metacognition. In R. Glaser (Ed.), *Advances in instructional psychology* (pp. 117–175). Mahwah, NJ: Erlbaum.

Brown, A. (1987). Metacognition, executive control, self-regulation, and other more mysterious mechanisms. In Weinert, F., and Kluwe, R. (Eds.). *Metacognition, motivation, and understanding* (pp. 65–116). Hillsdale, NJ: Erlbaum.

Brown, A. L., Bransford, J. W., Ferrara, R. F., & Campione, J. (1983). Learning, remembering, and understanding. In J. Flavell & E. Markham (Eds.), *Handbook of child psychology* (pp. 393–451). New York: Wiley.

Brown, A. L., & Palincsar, A. S. (1982). Inducing strategic learning from texts by means of informed, self-control training. *Topics in Learning and Learning Disabilities, 2,* 1–17.

Brown, A. L., & Palincsar, A. S. (1984). Reciprocal teaching of comprehension-fostering and comprehension-monitoring activities. *Cognition and Instruction, 1,* 117–175.

Brown, D. (1987). *Principles of language learning and teaching.* Englewood Cliffs, NJ: Prentice Hall.

Brown, M. W. (1949). *The important book.* Ill. L. Weisgard. New York: Harper & Row.

Brown-Jeffy, S., & Cooper, J. E. (2011). Toward a conceptual framework of culturally relevant pedagogy: An overview of the conceptual and theoretical literature. *Teacher Education Quarterly, 38*(1), 65–84.

Brozo, W. G. (1989). Applying a reader response heuristic to expository text. *Journal of Reading, 32,* 140–145.

Brozo, W. G. (1990). Learning how at-risk readers learn best: A case for interactive assessment. *Journal of Reading, 33,* 522–527.

Brozo, W. G., & Flyny, E. S. (2007). Content literacy: Fundamental toolkit elements. *Reading Teacher, 61*(2), 192–194.

Brozo, W. G., & Tomlinson, C. M. (1986). Literature: The key to lively content courses. *Reading Teacher, 40,* 288–293.

Bruce, B. C. (2002). Diversity and critical social engagement: How changing technologies enable new modes of literacy in changing circumstances. In D. E. Alvermann (Ed.), *Adolescents and literacies in a digital world* (pp. 1–18). New York: Peter Lang.

Bruner, J. (1961). The act of discovery. *Harvard Educational Review, 31,* 21–32.

Bruner, J. (1970). The skill of relevance or the relevance of skills. *Saturday Review, 53.*

Bruner, J. (1986). *Actual minds, possible worlds.* Cambridge, MA: Harvard University Press.

Bruner, J. (1990). *Acts of meaning.* Cambridge, MA: Harvard University Press.

Bruner, J., Goodnow, J., & Austin, G. (1977). *A study of thinking.* New York: Science Editions.

Bruns, M. K., Hodgson, J., Parker, D. C., & Fremont, K. (2011). Comparison of the effectiveness and efficiency of text previewing and preteaching keywords as small-group reading comprehension strategies with middle school students. *Literacy Research and Instruction, 50,* 241–252.

Buckingham, D. (1993). *Reading audiences: Young people and the media.* Manchester, UK: Manchester University Press.

Buckingham, D. (2003). *Media education: Literacy, learning and contemporary culture.* Cambridge, UK: Polity.

Buehl, D. (1991, Spring). Frames of mind. *The Exchange: Newsletter of the IRA Secondary Reading Interest Group,* pp. 4–5.

Buehl, D. (2009). Linking research to practice in disciplinary instruction: An interview by David Moore. *Journal of Adolescent and Adult Literacy, 52*(6), 535–537.

Buehl, D., & Moore, D. (2009). Linking research to practice in disciplinary instruction. *Journal of Adolescent and Adult Literacy, 52*(6), 535–537.

Bulgren, J. A., Marquis, J. G., Lenz, B. K., Schumaker, J. B., Deshler, D. D. (2009). Effectiveness of question exploration to enhance students' written expression of content knowledge and comprehension. *Reading & Writing Quarterly, 25,* 271–289.

Bunting, E. (1994). *Smoky night.* Ill. D. Diaz. Orlando, FL: Harcourt Brace.

Burgess, J. (1988). *The heart and blood (How our bodies work).* Englewood Cliffs, NJ: Silver Burdett.

Burke, J. (2002). *Tools for thought: Graphic organizers for your classroom.* Portsmouth, NH: Heinemann.

Burleigh, R. (1997). *Hoops.* Ill. S. T. Johnson. San Diego, CA: Silver Whistle.

Buss, F. (2002). *Journey of the Sparrows.* London: Puffin.

Bustle, L. S. (2004). The role of visual representation in the assessment of learning. *Journal of Adolescent & Adult Literacy, 47,* 416–423.

Cai, M. (1994). Images of Chinese and Chinese Americans mirrored in picture books. *Children's Literature in Education, 25,* 169–191.

Calabro, M. (1999). *The perilous journey of the Donner Party.* New York: Clarion Books.

Camp, G. (1982). *A successful curriculum for remedial writers.* Berkeley: National Writing Project, University of California.

Campano, G. (2007). *Immigrant students and literacy: Reading, writing, and remembering.* New York: Teachers College Press.

Canada, J. (2010. *Fist, stick, knife.* Saratoga Springs, NY: Beacon Press.

Canfield, J. (2000). *Chicken soup for the sports fan's soul: 101 stories of insight, inspiration and laughter in the world.* Deerfield, FL: HCI.

Calderon, M., Slavin, R., & Sanchez, M. (2011). Effective instruction for English learners. *The Future of Children, 21*(1), 103–127.

Carlo, M. S., August, D., McLaughlin, B., Snow, C. E., Dressler, C., Lippman, D. N., Lively, T. J., & White, C. E. (2004). Closing the gap: Addressing the vocabulary needs of English-language learners in bilingual and mainstream classrooms. *Reading Research Quarterly, 39*(2), 188–215.

Carr, E., & Ogle, D. (1987). K-W-L Plus: A strategy for comprehension and summarization. *Journal of Reading, 30,* 626–631.

Carter, B. (2000). *Best books for young adults.* Chicago: American Library Association.

Carter, B., & Abrahamson, R. F. (1990). *Nonfiction for young adults: From delight to wisdom.* Phoenix, AZ: Oryx Press.

Cassidy, J., & Cassidy, D. (2009, February/March). What's hot in adolescent literacy. *Reading Today, 26*(4), 1, 8, 9.

Cazden, C. (2001). *Classroom discourse: The language of teaching and learning.* Portsmouth, NH: Heinemann.

Chambers, A. (1973*). Introducing books to children.* London: Heinemann.

Chang, I. (1991). *A separate battle: Women and the Civil War.* New York: Scholastic.

Chekhov, A. (1991). *Kashtanka.* Trans. R. Povear. Ill. B. Moser. New York: Putnam.

Cherry, L. (2000). *The great kapok tree: A tale of the Amazon rain forest.* San Diego: Harcourt.

Clark, B., Sobel, J., & Basteri, C. G. (2006). *Marketing dynamics.* Tinley, IL: Goodheart-Wilcox.

Clark, R. P. (1987). *Free to write: A journalist teaches young writers.* Portsmouth, NH: Heinemann.

Clary, D., Oglan, V., & Styslinger, M. (2008). *It is not just about content: Preparing content area teachers to be literacy leaders.* Retrieved February 12, 2009, from the Literacy Coaching Clearinghouse website, www .literacycoachingonline.org.

Close, E. A., Hull, M., & Langer, J. A. (2005). Writing and reading relationships in literacy learning. In R. Indrisano & J. A. Paratore (Eds.), *Learning to write, writing to learn: Theory and research in practice* (pp. 67–79). Newark, DE: International Reading Association.

Coiro, J. (2003). Reading comprehension on the Internet: Expanding our understanding of reading comprehension to encompass new literacies. *Reading Teacher, 56,* 458–464.

Coiro, J. & Moore, D.W.(2012). New literacies and adolescent learners: An interview with Julie Coiro. *Journal of Adolescent & Adult Literacy, 55,* 6, 551–553.

Collins, J. L. (1997). *Strategies for struggling writers.* New York: Guilford Press.

Collins, S. *The Hunger Games.* NY: Scholastic.

Common Core State Standards Initiative (2010). Common Core State Standards for English language arts & literacy in history/social studies, science, and technical subjects. Washington, DC: CCSSO & National Governors Association.

Cone, M. (1992). *Come back, salmon: How a group of dedicated kids adopted Pigeon Creek and brought it back to life.* Photo. S. Wheelwright. San Francisco: Sierra Club Books for Children.

Congressional Digest. (1999, August–September). The federal role in education: 1999–2000 policy debate topic. *Congressional Digest, 193.*

Conley, M. (2008). Cognitive strategy instruction for adolescents: What we know about the promise, what we don't know about the potential. *Harvard Educational Review, 78*(1), 84–106.

Conrad, P. (1991). *Pedro's journal.* New York: Scholastic.

Considine, B., Horton, J., & Moorman, G. (2009). Teaching and reading the millennial generation through media literacy. *Journal of Adolescent and Adult Literacy, 52*(6), 471–481.

Cook-Sather, A. (2002). Authorizing students' perspectives: Toward trust, dialogue, and change in education. *Educational Researcher, 31*(4), 3–14.

Cooney, T., Bell, K., Fisher-Cauble, D., & Sanchez, W. (1996). The demands of alternative assessment: What teachers say. *Mathematics Teacher, 89,* 484–487.

Cooper, A. (2012) Today's technologies enhance writing in mathematics. *The Clearing House, 85,* 80–85.

Cooper, M. (2002). *Remembering Manzanar: Life in a Japanese relocation camp.* New York: Clarion Books.

Cope, B., & Kalantzis, M. (Eds.). (2000). *Multiliteracies: Literacy learning and the design of social futures.* London: Routledge.

Cover, R. (1989). *Cultural diversity training.* A paper presented at a conference on issues in multicultural education, Chapel Hill, NC.

Coville, B. (1997). *William Shakespeare's Macbeth.* Ill. G. Kelly. New York: Dial.

Creech, J., & Hale, G. (2006). Literacy in science: A natural fit, promoting student literacy through inquiry. *The Science Teacher, 73*(2), 22–27.

Creech, S. (1996). *Walk two moons.* New York: HarperCollins.

Creech, S. (2001). *Love that dog.* New York: HarperTrophy.

Crew, L. (1991). *Children of the river.* NY: Laurel Leaf Press.

Crue, W. (1932, February). Ordeal by cheque. *Vanity Fair.*

Crutcher, C. (1989). *Athletic shorts.* New York: Greenwillow.

Crystal, D. (2008a). *Txting: The Gr8 Db8.* Oxford, England: Oxford University Press.

Crystal, D. (2008b). Texting. *English Language Teaching (ELT) Journal, 62*(1), 77–83.

Cummins, J. (1981). The role of primary language development in promoting educational success for language minority students. In J. Cummins (Ed.), *Schooling and language minority students: A theoretical framework* (pp. 3–49). Los Angeles: Evaluation, Dissemination, and Assessment Center, California State University at Los Angeles.

Cummins, J. (1986). Empowering minority students: A framework for intervention. *Harvard Educational Review, 56*(1), 18–36.

Cummins, J. (1994). The acquisition of English as a second language. In K. Spangenberg-Urbschat & R. Pritchard (Eds.), *Kids come in all languages: Reading instruction for ESL students* (pp. 36–62). Newark, DE: International Reading Association.

Curry, J. (1989). The role of reading instruction in mathematics. In D. Lapp, J. Flood, & N. Farnan (Eds.), *Content area reading and learning: Instructional strategies* (pp. 187–197). Upper Saddle River, NJ: Prentice Hall.

Curtis, M. E., & Longo, A. M. (2001). Teaching vocabulary to adolescents to improve comprehension. *Reading Online, 5*(4). Retrieved August 8, 2005, from www.readingonline.org/articles/art_index.asp?HREF=curtis/index.html.

Cuero, K. K. (2010). Artisan with words: Transnational funds of knowledge in a bilingual Latin's narratives. *Language Arts, 87*(6), 427–436.

Dahl, R. (1995). *Lamb to the slaughter.* NY: Penguin Books.

Daniels, H. (1994). *Literature circles: Voice and choice in book clubs and reading groups* (2nd ed.). York, ME: Stenhouse.

Daniels, E., & Steres, M. (2011). Examining the effects of a school-wide reading culture on the engagement of middle school students. *Research in Middle Level Education, 35*(2), 1–12.

Danielson, C. (1996). *Enhancing professional practice: A framework for teaching.* Alexandria, VA: Association for Supervision and Curriculum Development.

Danielson, C. (2010/2011). Evaluations that help teachers learn. *Educational Leadership, 68*(4), 35–39. Retrieved February 5, 2013, from www.ascd.org/publications/educational-leadership/dec10/vol68/num04/Evaluations-That-Help-Teachers-Learn.aspx.

Danzer, G. A. (2007). *The Americans: Reconstruction to the 21st century.* New York: McDougall Littell.

Darling-Hammond, L. (2003). Standards and assessments: Where we are and what we need. *Teachers College Record.* Retrieved April 10, 2008, from www.tcrecord. org/Content.asp?ContentID=11109.

Darling-Hammond, L., & Baratz-Snowden, J. (2005). *A good teacher in every classroom: Preparing the highly qualified teachers our children deserve.* San Francisco: Jossey-Bass.

Dash, J. (2000). *The longitude prize.* New York: Farrar, Straus & Giroux.

Davey, B. (1983). Think aloud: Modeling the cognitive processes of reading comprehension. *Journal of Reading, 27,* 44–47.

Davis, O. (1978). *Escape to freedom: A play about Frederick Douglass.* New York: Viking Penguin.

Dean, Z. (2007). *The A-List.* New York: Poppy.

Deem, J. M. (2005). *Bodies from the ash: Life and death in ancient Pompeii.* Boston: Houghton Mifflin.

Deighton, L. (1970). *Vocabulary development in the classroom.* New York: Teachers College Press.

Delano, M. F. (2005). *Genius: A photobiography of Albert Einstein.* Washington, DC: National Geographic.

Delpit, L. D. (1988). The silenced dialogue: Power and pedagogy in educating other people's children. *Harvard Educational Review, 58,* 280–298.

deMaupassant, G. (1993). *The necklace.* Ill. G. Kelly. New York: Creative Editions.

Deshler, D., Schumaker, B., Lenz, K., Bulgren, J., Hock, M.,& Knight, J. (2001). Ensuring content-area learning by secondary students with learning disabiulities. *Learning Disabilities Research and Practice, 16*(2), 96–108.

Dessen, S. (2006). *That summer.* New York: Viking.

Dessen, S. (2009). *Lock and key.* New York: Puffin.

Dewey, J. (1899/1980). *The school and society.* Carbondale: Southern Illinois University Press.

Diaz, C. F. (2001). *Multicultural education for the twenty-first century.* New York: Longman.

Díaz-Rico, L. T. (2008). *Strategies for teaching English learners* (2nd ed.). Boston: Pearson.

Díaz-Rico, L. T., & Weed, K. Z. (2002). *The crosscultural, language, and academic development handbook: A complete K–12 reference guide.* Boston: Allyn & Bacon.

Digby, C., & Mayers, J. (1993). *Making sense of vocabulary.* Englewood Cliffs, NJ: Prentice Hall.

Dillon, D. R. (1989). Showing them that I want them to learn and that I care about who they are: A micro-ethnography on the social organization of a secondary low-track English-reading classroom. *American Educational Research Association Journal, 26,* 227–259.

Dillon, S. (2005, August 23). Connecticut sues the U.S. over school testing [Electronic version]. *The New York Times.*

Dole, J. (2004). The changing role of the reading specialist in school reform. *The Reading Teacher, 57,* 462–471.

Donelson, K. L., & Nilsen, A. P. (1997). *Literature for today's young adults* (5th ed.). New York: Longman.

Draper, R. J. (2008). Redefining content area literacy teacher education: Finding my voice through collaboration. *Harvard Educational Review, 78*(1), 60–83.

Dreher, P. (2000). Electronic poetry: Student-constructed hypermedia. *English Journal, 90*(2), 68–73.

Duff, F., Fieldsend, E., Bowyer-Crane, C., & Hulme, C. (2008). Reading with vocabulary intervention: Evaluation of an instruction for children with poor response to reading intervention. *Journal of Research in Reading, 31*(3), 319–336.

Duffelmeyer, F. A., & Baum, D. D. (1992). The extended anticipation guide revisited. *Journal of Reading, 35*(8), 654–656.

Duffy, G. G. (1983). From turn taking to sense making: Broadening the concept of reading teacher effectiveness. *Journal of Educational Research, 76,* 134–139.

DuFour, R. (2003). Building a professional learning community. *School Administrator, 60*(5), 13–18.

DuFour, R., & Eaker, R. (1998). *Professional learning communities at work: Best practices for enhancing student achievement.* Reston, VA: Association for Supervision and Curriculum Development.

Duke, N. K., & Pearson, P. D. (2002). Effective practices for developing reading comprehension. In A. E. Farstrup & S. J. Samuels (Eds.), *What research has to say about reading instruction* (3rd ed., pp. 205–242). Newark, DE: International Reading Association.

Duncan, A. (2010). *A Blueprint for reform: The reauthorization of the Elementary and Secondary Education Act.* Washington DC: U. S. Department of Education.

Dyer, D. (1997). *Jack London: A biography.* New York: Scholastic.

Eanet, M., & Manzo, A. V. (1976). REAP: A strategy for improving reading/writing/study skills. *Journal of Reading, 19,* 647–652.

Easton, L. B. (2008). From professional development to professional learning. *Phi Delta Kappan, 89*(10), 755–759, 761.

Echevarria, J., & Graves, A. (2003). *Sheltered content instruction: Teaching English-language learners with diverse abilities* (2nd ed.). Boston: Allyn & Bacon.

Echevarria, J., Vogt, M., & Short, D. J. (2008). *Making content comprehensible for English language learners: The SIOP model* (3rd ed.). Boston: Allyn & Bacon.

Echlin, H. (2007). *Digital discussion: Take your class to the Internet.* Retrieved September 8, 2008, from www .edutopia.org/whats-next-2007-Blog.

Edelstein, S. & Edwards, J. (2002). If you build it, they will come: Building learning communities through learning discussions. *Online Journal of Distance Learning Administration, V* (1). Available at www.westga .edu/~distance/ojdla/spring51/edelstein51.html.

Educational Technology Standards for Students (2007). Washington, D.C.: International Society for Technology in Education. Available at http://www .iste.org/Libraries/PDFs/NETS-S_Standards.sflb.ashx.

Edwards, P. (1967). *Equiano's travels: The interesting narrative of the life of Olaudah Equiano or Gustavus Vassa, the African.* New York: Praeger.

Ehren, B. J., Deshler, D. D., & Graner, P. S. (2010). Using the Content Literacy Continuum as a Framework for Implementing RTI in Secondary Schools. *Theory Into Practice, 49*(4), 315–322

Eisner, E. (1997). Cognition and representation: A way to pursue the American dream? *Phi Delta Kappan, 78,* 349–353.

Eisner, E. W. (1985). *The educational imagination: On the design and evaluation of school programs* (2nd ed.). New York: Macmillan.

Eisner, E. W. (1991). The celebration of thinking. *Maine Scholar, 4,* 39–52.

Eisner, W. (2000). *New York: The big city.* New York: DC Comics.

Environmental Protection Agency (2009, Nov.) *Municipal solid waste generation, recycling, and disposal in the United States.: Detailed tables and figures for 2008.* Washington DC: Office of Resource Conservation and Recovery.

Epstein, S., & Epstein, B. W. (1978). *Dr. Beaumont and the man with a hole in his stomach.* New York: Coward McCann & Geoghegan.

Erickson, B. (1996). Read-alouds reluctant readers relish. *Journal of Adolescent & Adult Literacy, 40*(3), 212–215.

Evans, C. W., Leija, A. J., & Falkner, T. R. (2001). *Math links: Teaching the NCTM 2000 standards through children's literature.* Englewood, CO: Teacher Ideas Press.

Faltis, C. J., & Coulter, C. A. (2004). *Teaching English learners and immigrant students in secondary schools.* Upper Saddle River, NJ: Pearson.

Fang, Z. (2010). Improving middle school students' science literacy through reading infusion. *The Journal of Educational Research, 103*(4), 262–273.

Farmer, N. (2002). *The house of the scorpion.* New York: Atheneum/Richard Jackson.

Farr, R. (1992). Putting it all together: Solving the reading assessment puzzle. *Reading Teacher, 46,* 26–37.

Farr, R., & Tone, B. (1998). *Assessment portfolio and performance* (2nd ed.). Orlando, FL: Harcourt Brace.

Farrell, J. (2005). *Invisible allies: Microbes that shape our lives.* New York: Farrar, Straus & Giroux.

Feelings, T. (1995). *The middle passage: White ships, black cargo.* New York: Dial.

Fetterman, D. M. (1989). *Ethnography step by step.* Thousand Oaks, CA: Sage.

Fichett, P., & Heafner, T. (2010). A national perspective on the effects of high-stakes testing and standardization on elementary social studies marginalization. *Theory and research in social education, 38*(1), 114–130.

Fiedler, R., & Pick, D. (2004). Adopting an electronic portfolio system: Key considerations for decision makers. In M. Simonson (Ed.). *Association for Educational Communication and Technology International Conference Proceedings.* (pp. 167–181). Bloomington, IN: AECT.

Fillmore, L. (1981). Cultural perspectives on second language learning. *TESL Reporter, 14,* 23–31.

Finn, P. (1999). *Literacy with an attitude: Educating working class students in their own self-interest.* Albany: SUNY Press.

Fisher, D. (2004). Setting the "opportunity to read" standard: Resuscitating the SSR program in an urban high school. *Journal of Adolescent & Adult Literacy, 48,* 138–149.

Fisher, D., & Frey, N. (2003). Writing instruction for struggling adolescent readers: A gradual release model. *Journal of Adolescent & Adult Literacy, 46,* 396–405.

Fisher, D., Frey, N., & ElWardi, R. (2005). Creating independent writers and thinkers in secondary schools. In R. Indrisano & J. A. Paratore (Eds.), *Learning to write, writing to learn: Theory and research in practice.* Newark, DE: International Reading Association.

Flanigan, K., & Greenwood, S. C. (2007). Effective content vocabulary instruction in the middle: Matching students, purposes, words, and strategies. *Journal of Adolescent & Adult Literacy, 51*(3), 226–238.

Flavell, J. H. (1976). Metacognitive aspects of problem solving. In L. B. Resnick (Ed.), *The nature of intelligence* (pp. 38–62). Mahwah, NJ: Erlbaum.

Flavell, J. H. (1981). Cognitive monitoring. In P. Dickson (Ed.), *Communication skills.* Orlando, FL: Academic Press.

Flynt, E.S., & Brozo, W. G. (2008). Developing academic language: Got words? *The Reading Teacher, 61*(6), 500–502.

Fleischman, J. (2002). *Phineas Gage: A gruesome but true story about brain science.* Boston: Houghton Mifflin.

Fleischman, P. (1988). *Joyful noise: Poems for two voices.* New York: HarperCollins.

Fleischman, P. (2000). *Big talk: Poems for four voices.* New York: Candlewick.

Fleming, T. (1988). *Band of brothers: West Point in the Civil War.* New York: Walker.

Foon, D. (2004). *Skud.* Canada: Groundwood Books.

Foss, A. (2002). Peeling the onion: Teaching critical literacy with students of privilege. *Language Arts, 79*(5), 393–403.

Fox, M. (2000). *Feathers and fools.* Ill. N. Wilton. San Diego, CA: Voyager.

Fradin, D., & Fradin, J. (2006). *5,000 miles to freedom: Ellen and William Craft's flight from slavery.* Washington, DC: National Geographic.

Frank, A. (1967). *Anne Frank: The diary of a young girl.* New York: Doubleday.

Freedman, R. (1995). *Immigrant kids.* New York: Puffin.

Freedman, R. (2000). *Give me liberty! The story of the Declaration of Independence.* New York: Holiday House.

Freedman, R. (2005). *Children of the Great Depression.* New York: Clarion Books.

Freeman, E. B., & Person, D. G. (1998). *Connecting informational children's books with content area learning.* Boston: Allyn & Bacon.

Freire, P. (1970/2000). *Pedagogy of the oppressed.* New York: Continuum.

Frey, N., & Fisher, D. (2012). If you want to help students organize their learning: Fold, think, and write with three-dimensional graphic organizers. D. Lapp, & B. Moss (Eds.). *Exemplary instruction in the middle grades: Teaching that supports engagement and rigorous learning* (pp. 310–320). NY: Guilford.

Friend, R. (2000–2001). Teaching summarization as a content area strategy. *Journal of Adolescent & Adult Literacy, 44,* 320–329.

Friesen, J. (2008). *Jerk, California.* New York: Penguin.

Frost, Robert. (1915). *North of Boston.* New York: Henry Holt and Company.

Fry, E. (1977). Fry's readability graph: Clarifications, validity, and extension to level 17. *Journal of Reading, 21,* 242–252.

Fuchs, L., Fuchs, D., & Compton, D. (2010). Rethinking response to intervention at middle and high school. *School Psychology Review, 39*(1), 22–28.

Fuchs, L. S., Fuchs, D., Prentice, K., Burch, M., Hamlett, C. L., Owen, R., Hosp, M. & Jancek, D. (2003). Explicitly teaching for transfer: Effects of third-grade students' mathematical problem solving. *Journal of Educational Psychology, 95*(2), 293–305.

Fulton, M., & Porter, M. (2000). *Common state strategies to improve student reading.* Denver, CO: ECS.

Gagne, R. (1970). *The conditions of learning.* New York: Holt, Rinehart, and Winston.

Gaiman, N. (2006). *Coraline.* New York: HarperCollins.

Gallant, R. A. (1991). *Earth's vanishing forests.* New York: Macmillan.

Gallo, D. R. (2007). *First crossing: Stories about teen immigrants.* Cambridge, MA: Candlewick Press.

Gambrell, L. B. (1980). Think-time: Implications for reading instruction. *Reading Teacher, 33,* 143–146.

Ganske, K. (2012). If you want students to learn vocabulary move beyond copying words. In D. Lapp, & B. Moss (Eds.). *Exemplary instruction in the middle grades* (pp. 205–224). NY: Guilford.

Gantos, J. (2002). *Hole in my life.* New York: Farrar, Straus & Giroux.

Garcia, E. (2002). *Student cultural diversity: Understanding and meeting the challenge* (3rd ed.). Boston: Houghton Mifflin.

García, G. E., & Godina, H. (2004). Addressing the literacy needs of adolescent English language learners. In T. Jetton & J. A. Dole (Eds.), *Adolescent literacy research and practice* (pp. 304–320). New York: Guilford Press.

Garland, S. (1993). *The lotus seed.* Ill. T. Kiuchi. San Diego, CA: Harcourt.

Gee, J. P. (1996). *Social linguistics and literacies: Ideology in discourses* (2nd ed.). London: Falmer Press.

Gere, A. R. (Ed.). (1985). *Roots in the sawdust: Writing to learn across the disciplines.* Urbana, IL: National Council of Teachers of English.

Gersten, R., & Jimenez, R. (1994). A delicate balance: Enhancing literature instruction for students of English as a second language. *Reading Teacher, 47,* 438–449.

Giblin, J. (1994). *Thomas Jefferson: A picture book biography.* Ill. M. Dooling. New York: Scholastic.

Giblin, J. C. (1995). *When plague strikes: The Black Death, smallpox, AIDS.* New York: HarperCollins.

Giblin, J. C. (2000). *The amazing life of Benjamin Franklin.* Ill. M. Dooling. New York: Scholastic.

Giblin, J. (2000). More than just the facts: A hundred years of children's nonfiction. *The Horn Book, 76,* 413–424.

Giblin, J. (2002). *The life and death of Adolf Hitler.* New York: Clarion Books.

Gilles, C., Wilson, J., & Elias, M. (2010). Sustaining teachers' growth and renewal through action research, induction programs, and collaboration. *Teacher Education Quarterly, 37*(1), 91–108.

Gillet, J., & Kita, M. J. (1979). Words, kids, and categories. *Reading Teacher, 32,* 538–542.

Goble, P. (1991). *I sing for the animals.* New York: Bradbury.

Gold, P., & Yellin, D. (1982). Be the focus: A psycho-educational technique for use with unmotivated learners. *Journal of Reading, 25*(5), 550–552.

Golenbock, P. (1990). *Teammates.* Ill. P. Bacon. San Diego, CA: Harcourt Brace Jovanovich.

Gomez, L. M., & Gomez, K. (2007). Reading for learning: Literacy supports for 21st century work. *Phi Delta Kappan, 89*(3), 224–228.

Gonick, L. (1991). *Cartoon history of the United States.* New York: HarperCollins.

Goodall, J. (1979). *The story of an English village.* New York: Atheneum.

Goodlad, J. (1984). *A place called school.* New York: McGraw-Hill.

Goodman, D. J. (2000). Motivating people from privileged groups to support social justice. *Teachers College Record, 102,* 1061–1086

Goodman, K., & Goodman, Y. (1978). *Reading of American children whose language is a stable rural dialect of English or a language other than English.* Washington, DC: National Institute of Education. (ERIC Document Reproduction Service No. ED173754)

Goodrich, F., & Hackett, A. (2000). *The diary of Anne Frank: Play and related readings.* New York: Dramatists Play Service.

Graham, S. (2005). Strategy instruction and the teaching of writing: A meta-analysis. In C. A. MacArthur, S. Graham, & J. Fitzgerald (Eds.), *Handbook of writing research.* New York: Guilford Press.

Gray, W. S. (1925). *Summary of investigations related to reading* (Supplementary Educational Monographs, No. 28). Chicago: University of Chicago Press.

Gredler, M. E., & Johnson, R. L. (2004). *Assessment in the literacy classroom.* Boston: Pearson.

Greenberg, J., & Jordan, S. (1998). *Chuck Close: Up close.* New York: DK.

Greene, B. (1999). *Summer of my German soldier.* New York: Puffin Books.

Greene, M. (1997). Metaphors and multiples: Representation, the arts, and history. *Phi Delta Kappan, 78,* 387–394.

Greenlee-Moore, M. E., & Smith, L. L. (1996). Interactive computer software: The effects on young children's reading achievement. *Reading Psychology, 17,* 43–64.

Griffin, G. A. (1991). Interactive staff development: Using what we know. In A. Lieberman & L. Miller (Eds.), *Staff development for education in the '90s* (pp. 243–258). New York: Teachers College Press.

Grimes, N. (2002). *Bronx masquerade.* New York: Speak.

Grove, N. (1981, March). Wild cargo: The business of smuggling animals. *National Geographic, 159,* 287–315.

Gruenewald, M. M. (2005). *Looking like the enemy: My story of imprisonment in Japanese American internment camps.* Troutdale, OR: New Sage Press.

Guastello, E. F., Beasley, T. M., & Sinatra, R. C. (2000). Concept mapping effects on science content comprehension of low-achieving inner-city seventh graders. *Remedial and Special Education, 21,* 356–365.

Guilfoyle, C. (2006). NCLB: Is there life beyond testing? *Educational Leadership, 64*(3), 8–13.

Gunderson, L. (2007). *English-only instruction and immigrant students in secondary schools: A critical examination.* Mahwah, NJ: Erlbaum.

Gunderson, L. (2009, February). *Where are the English Language Learners?* Paper presented at English Language Learner Institute at the Annual Convention of the International Reading Association, Phoenix, AZ.

Guth, N. D., & Pettengill, S. S. (2005). *Leading a successful reading program: Administrators and reading specialists working together to make it happen.* Newark, DE: International Reading Association.

Guthrie, J. T., & Davis, M. H. (2003). Motivating struggling readers in middle school through an engagement model of classroom practice. *Reading and Writing Quarterly, 19,* 59–85.

Guthrie, J. T., & Humenick, N. M. (2004). Motivating students to read: Evidence for classroom practices that increase reading motivation and achievement. In P. McCardle & V. Chhabra (Eds.), *The voice of evidence in reading research* (pp. 329–354). Baltimore: Brookes.

Guthrie, J. T., & McCann, A. D. (1996). Idea circles: Peer collaborations for conceptual learning. In L. B. Gambrell & J. F. Almasi (Eds.), *Lively discusssions! Fostering engaged reading* (pp. 87–105). Newark, DE: International Reading Association.

Guthrie, J. T., Schafer, W. D., & Huang, C. (2001). Benefits of opportunity to read and balanced instruction on the NAEP. *Journal of Educational Research, 94,* 145–162.

Guthrie, J. T., & Wigfield, A. (1997). Reading engagement: A rationale for theory and teaching. In J. T. Guthrie & A. Wigfield (Eds.), *Reading engagement: Motivating readers through integrated instruction* (pp. 1–12). Newark, DE: International Reading Association.

Guthrie, J. T., & Wigfield, A. (2000). Engagement and motivation in reading. In M. Kamil, P. Mosenthal, P. D. Pearson, & R. Barr (Eds.), *Handbook of reading research, Vol. III* (pp. 403–424). Mahwah, NJ: Erlbaum.

Hadaway, N. L., Vardell, S. M., & Young, T. A. (2002). *Literature-based instruction with English language learners.* Boston: Allyn & Bacon.

Haggard, M. R. (1986). The vocabulary self-collection strategy: Using student interest and world knowledge to enhance vocabulary growth. *Journal of Reading, 29,* 634–642.

Hahn, M. D. (2003). *Hear the wind blow.* New York: Clarion Books.

Hakim, J. (1999). *A history of US.* New York: Oxford University Press.

Hall, B. (2004). *Literacy coaches: An evolving role.* Retrieved October 21, 2006, from www.carnegie.org/reporter/09literacy/index.html.

Halliday, M., & Hasan, R. (1976). *Cohesion in English.* London: Longman.

Halpern, D. F. (1998). Teaching critical thinking for transfer across domains: Dispositions, skills, structure training, and metacognitive monitoring, *American Psychologist, 53*(4), 449–455.

Hamilton, V. (1985). *The people could fly: American black folktales.* New York: Knopf.

Hamilton, V. (1988). *In the beginning: Creation stories from around the world.* Orlando, FL: Harcourt Brace.

Hancock, M. (2007). *A celebration of literature and response: Children, books, and teachers in K–8 classrooms* (3rd ed.). New York: Prentice Hall.

Hancock, M. R. (1993). Exploring and extending personal response through literature journals. *Reading Teacher, 46,* 466–474.

Hansen, J. (1986). *Which way freedom?* New York: Walker.

Harmon, J. M., Hedrick, W. B., Wood, K., & Gress, M. (2005). Vocabulary self-selection: A study of middle-school students' word selections from expository texts. *Reading Writing Quarterly, 26,* 313–333.

Hamon, J. M., Wood, K. D., Hedrick, W. B., Vintinner, J., & Willeford, T. (2009). Interactive word walls: More than just reading and writing on the walls. *Journal of Adolescent & Adult Literacy, 52*(5), 398–408.

Hart, P. D., & Teeter, R. M. (2002). *A national priority: Americans speak on teacher quality.* Princeton, NJ: Educational Testing Service.

Harvey, S. (1998). *Nonfiction matters: Reading, writing, and research in grades 3–8.* Portland, ME: Stenhouse.

Harvey, S., & Goudvis, A. (2000). *Strategies that work: Teaching comprehension to enhance understanding.* York, ME: Stenhouse.

Harvey, S., & Goudvis, A. (2007). *Strategies that work: Teaching comprehension for understanding and engagement.* York, ME: Stenhouse.

Hayes, D. A. (1989). Helping students grasp the knack of writing summaries. *Journal of Reading, 33,* 96–101.

Haynes, J. (2007). *Getting started with English language learners: How educators can meet the challenge.* Alexandria, VA: Association for Supervision and Curriculum Development.

Healy, M. K. (1982). Using student response groups in the classroom. In G. Camp (Ed.), *Teaching writing: Essays from the Bay Area writing project* (pp. 266–290). Portsmouth, NH: Boyton-Cook.

Heath, S. (1983). *Ways with words: Language, life, and work in communities and classrooms.* Cambridge, MA: Harvard University Press.

Heath, S., & Mangiola, L. (1989). *Children of promise: Literate activity on linguistically and culturally diverse classrooms.* Washington, DC: National Education Association.

Hedges, H., Cullen, J., & Jordon, B. (2011). Early years of curriculum: Funds of knowledge as a conceptual framework for children's interests. *Journal of Curriculum Studies, 43*(2), 185–205.

Hedrick, W. B., McGee, P., & Mittag, K. (2000). Preservice teacher learning through one-on-one tutoring: Reporting perceptions through email. *Teaching and Teacher Education, 16,* 47–63

Heitin, L. (2009). Grassroots professional development. Retrieved February 5, 2013, from http://www.edweek.org/tsb/articles/2009/03/16/02timmons.ho2.html.

Helfer, A. (2006). *Malcolm X: A graphic biography.* New York: Farrar, Straus & Giroux.

Herber, H. L. (1964). Teaching reading and physics simultaneously. In J. A. Figurel (Ed.), *Improvement of reading through classroom practice. Proceedings of the 9th Annual Convention of the International Reading Association, 9,* 84–85.

Herber, H. L. (1970). *Teaching reading in content areas.* Englewood Cliffs, NJ: Prentice Hall.

Herber, H. L. (1978). *Teaching reading in content areas* (2nd ed.). Upper Saddle River, NJ: Prentice Hall.

Hesse, K. (1997). *Out of the dust.* New York: Scholastic.

Hibbing, A. N., & Rankin-Erickson, J. L. (2003). A picture is worth a thousand words: Using visual images to improve comprehension for middle school struggling readers. *Reading Teacher, 56,* 758–770.

Hickam, H. (1998). *Rocket boys.* New York: Delacorte.

Hicks, T., Russo, A., Autrey, T., Gardner, R., Kabodian, A., & Edington, C. (2007). Rethinking the purposes and processes for designing digital portfolios. *Journal of Adolescent & Adult Literacy, 50*(6), 450–458.

Hiebert, E. (2011). Using multiple sources of information in establishing text complexity. *Reading Research Report #11.03.* Santa Cruz, CA: TextProject, Inc.

Hinds, G. (2007). *Beowulf.* New York: Candlewick.

Hobbs, R., & Frost, R. (2003). Measuring the acquisition of media-literacy skills. *Reading Research Quarterly, 38,* 330–355.

Hobbs, W. (1989). *Bearstone.* New York: Atheneum.

Hoffman, J. V. (1979). The intra-act procedure for critical reading. *Journal of Reading, 22,* 605–608.

Hoffman, J. V. (1992). Critical reading/thinking across the curriculum: Using I-charts to support learning. *Language Arts, 69,* 121–127.

Hoffman, J. V., Au, K. H., Harrison, C., Paris, S. G., Pearson, P. D., Santa, C. M., Silver, S. H., & Valencia, S. W. (1999). High-stakes assessments in reading: Consequences, concerns, and common sense. In S. J. Barrentine (Ed.), *Reading assessment: Principles and practices for elementary teachers* (pp. 21–34). Newark, DE: International Reading Association.

Holston, V., & Santa, C. (1985). RAFT: A method of writing across the curriculum that works. *Journal of Reading, 28,* 456–457.

Holt, K. W. (1999). *When Zachary Beaver came to town.* New York: Holt.

Homer, C. (1979). A direct reading-thinking activity for content areas. In R. T. Vacca & J. A. Meagher (Eds.), *Reading through content* (pp. 41–48). Storrs: University Publications and the University of Connecticut Reading-Language Arts Center.

Honey, M. (1999). *Bitter fruit: African American women in World War II.* Columbia: University of Missouri Press.

Hoose, P. M. (2001). *We were there, too! Young people in U.S. history.* New York: Farrar, Straus & Giroux.

Hopkins, E. (2008). *Impulse.* New York: Margaret K. McElderry.

Hosseini, K. (2007). *A thousand splendid suns.* New York: Riverhead.

Hoy, A. K., & Spero, R. B. (2005). Changes in teacher efficacy during the early years of teaching: A comparison of four measures. *Teaching and Teacher Education, 21,* 343–356.

Hoyt-Goldsmith, D. (1994). *Day of the Dead: A Mexican-American celebration.* Photo. L. Migdale. New York: Holiday House.

Huey, E. (1908). *The psychology and pedagogy of reading.* New York: Macmillan.

Hunt, I. (1964). *Across five Aprils.* New York: Follett.

Hunt, J. (2007, March/April). Redefining the young adult novel. *Horn Book.* 2007. Retrieved February 14, 2009, from www.hbook.com/magazine/articles/2007/mar07_hunt.asp.

Hymes, D. (1972). On communicative competence. In J. Pride & J. Holmes (Eds.), *Sociolinguistics.* Harmondsworth, UK: Penguin.

Hynd, C. R., McNish, M. E., Guzzetti, B., Lay, K., & Fowler, P. (1994). *What high school students say about their science texts.* Paper presented at the annual meeting of the College Reading Association, New Orleans.

Igoa, C. (1995). *The inner world of the immigrant student.* Mahwah, NJ: Lawrence Erlbaum.

Igus, T. (1998). *I see the rhythm.* San Francisco: Children's Book Press.

Innocenti, R. (1985). *Rose Blanche.* San Diego, CA: Creative Editions.

International Reading Association. (1999a). *Adolescent literacy position statement.* Newark, DE: Author.

International Reading Association. (1999b). *High-stakes assessments in reading: A position paper of the International Reading Association.* Newark, DE: Author.

International Reading Association. (2005). *Standards for middle and high school literacy coaches.* Newark, DE: Author. Retrieved March 1, 2006, from www.reading.org/downloads/resources/597coaching_standards.pdf.

International Reading Association. (2006). *Standards for reading professionals.* Retrieved July 6, 2006, from www.reading.org/styleguide/standards_reading_profs.html.

International Reading Association. (2006). *Standards for middle and high school literacy coaches.* Newark, DE: Author.

International Reading Association. (2008). *Implications for reading teachers in response to intervention (RTI).* Retrieved October 9, 2008, from www.reading.org/downloads/resources/rti0707_implications.pdf.

International Reading Association and National Council of Teachers of English. (1997). *Standards for the English language arts.* Newark, DE: Author.

Ivey, G. (2002). Getting started: Manageable literacy practices. *Educational Leadership, 60,* 20–23.

Ivey, G., & Broaddus, K. (2001). "Just plain reading": A survey of what makes students want to read in middle school classrooms. *Reading Research Quarterly, 36,* 350–377.

Ivey, G., & Fisher, D. (2005). Learning from what doesn't work. *Educational Leadership, 63*(2), 8–15.

Izzo, A., & Schmidt, P. R. (2006). A successful ABC's in-service project: Supporting culturally responsive teaching. In P. R. Schmidt & C. Finkbeiner (Eds.), *ABC's of cultural understanding and communication: National and international adaptations* (pp. 19–42). Greenwich, CT: Information Age Publishing.

Jackson, F. (1994). Seven strategies to support culturally responsive pedagogy. *Journal of Reading, 37,* 298–303.

Jackson, R. (1975). *Inside hitting with Reggie Jackson.* Chicago: Regnery.

Jacobs, J. E., and Paris, S. G. (1987). Children's metacognition about reading: Issues in definition, measurement, and instruction. Educ. Psychol. 22: 255–278.

James, F. (2004). *Response to intervention in the Individuals with Disabilities Education Act (IDEA) 2004.* Retrieved November 19, 2008, from www .reading.org/downloads/resources/IDEA_RTI/report .pdf.

Jaquith, A., Mindich, D., Wei, R. C., & Darling-Hammond, L. (2010). *Teacher professional learning in the United States: Case studies of state policies and strategies.* Oxford, OH: Learning Forward.

Jasper, K. C. (1995). The limits of technology. *English Journal, 84*(6), 16–17.

Jenkins, S. (2002). *Life on earth: The story of evolution.* Boston: Houghton Mifflin

Jimenez, R., & Gamez, A. (1996). Literature-based cognitive strategy instruction for middle school Latina/o students. *Journal of Adolescent & Adult Literacy, 40*(2), 84–91.

Jimenez, R., Garcia, G., & Pearson, P. D. (1995). Three children, two languages, and strategic reading: Case studies in bilingual/monolingual reading. *American Educational Research Journal, 32,* 67–97.

Jimenez, R., Garcia, G., & Pearson, P. D. (1996). The reading strategies of bilingual Latina/o students who are successful English readers: Opportunities and obstacles. *Reading Research Quarterly, 32*(1), 90–112.

Johnson, A. (2003). *The first part last.* New York: Simon Pulse.

Johnson, D. D., & Pearson, P. D. (1984). *Teaching reading vocabulary* (2nd ed.). Fort Worth, TX: Holt, Rinehart, and Winston.

Johnson, D. W., & Johnson, R. T. (1987). *Learning together and alone: Cooperative, conjunctive, and individualistic learning* (2nd ed.). Englewood Cliffs, NJ: Prentice Hall.

Johnson, D. W., & Johnson, R. T. (1990). *Learning together and alone: Cooperative, conjunctive, and individualistic learning* (3rd ed.). Upper Saddle River, NJ: Prentice Hall.

Johnson, D. W., Johnson, R. T., & Holubec, E. J. (1990). *Circles of learning: Cooperation in the classroom* (3rd ed.). Edina, MN: Interaction Book.

Johnson, D. W., & Steele, V. (1996). So many words, so little time: Helping college ESL learners acquire vocabulary-building strategies. *Journal of Adolescent & Adult Literacy, 39,* 348–357.

Johnson, E., Mellard, D. F., Fuchs, D., & McKnight, M. A. (2006). *Responsiveness to intervention: How to do it.* Lawrence, KS: National Research Center on Learning Disabilities.

Jones, B. F., Pierce, J., & Hunter, B. (1988–1989). Teaching students to construct graphic representations. *Educational Leadership, 46*(4), 20–25.

Kamil, M. (2003). *Adolescents and literacy: Reading for the 21st century.* Washington, DC: Alliance for Excellent Education.

Karchmer-Klein, R., & Shinas, V. (2012). Guiding principles for supporting new literacies in your classroom. *Reading Teacher, 65*(5), 288–293.

Kaplan, L. S., & Owings, W. A. (2003). The politics of teacher quality. *Phi Delta Kappan, 84*(9), 687–692.

Karchmer, R. A., Mallette, M. H., Kara-Soteriou, J., & Leu, D. J. (2005). *Innovative approaches to literacy education: Using the Internet to support new literacies.* Newark, DE: International Reading Association.

Kaywell, J. (1994). Using young adult fiction and nonfiction to produce critical readers. *The ALAN Review, 21,* 1–6.

Keegan, J. (2003). *The first world war.* New York: Random House.

Kieffer, M. J., & Lesaux, N. K. (2007). Breaking down words to build meaning: Morphology, vocabulary, and reading, comprehension in the urban classroom. *The Reading Teacher, 61*(2), 134–144.

Kelly, J. (2009). *The evolution of Calpurnia Tate.* New York: Henry Holt.

Kennedy, B. (1985). Writing letters to learn math. *Learning, 13,* 58–61.

King, C., & Osborne, L. B. (1997). *Oh freedom! Kids talk about the civil rights movement with the people who made it happen.* New York: Knopf.

Kinney, J. (2007). *The diary of a wimpy kid.* New York: Abrams Books.

Kintsch, W. (1977). On comprehending stories. In M. A. Just & P. A. Carpenter (Eds.), *Cognitive processes in comprehension* (pp. 360–401). Mahwah, NJ: Erlbaum.

Kirby, D., Liner, T., & Vinz, M. (1988). *Inside out: Developmental strategies for teaching writing* (2nd ed.). Montclair, NJ: Boynton/Cook.

Kist, W. (2000). Beginning to create the new literacy classroom: What does the new literacy look like? *Journal of Adolescent & Adult Literacy, 43,* 710–718.

Kist, W. (2003). Student achievement in new literacies for the 21st century. *Middle School Journal, 35*(1), 6–13.

Kist, W. (2005). *New literacies in action: Teaching and learning in multiple media.* New York: Teachers College Press.

Kist, W. (2007a). Basement new literacies: Dialogue with a first-year teacher. *English Journal, 97*(1), 43–48.

Kist, W. (2007b). Vocabulary media journals: Finding multimedia to define words. In M. T. Christel & S. Sullivan (Eds.), *Lesson plans for creating media-rich classrooms* (pp. 23–29). Urbana, IL: National Council of Teachers of English.

Kist, W. (2010). *The socially networked classroom: Teaching in the new media age.* Thousand Oaks, CA: Corwin Press.

Kitchen, B. (1993). *And so they build.* New York: Dial.

Klein, N. (2000). *No logo: Taking aim at the brand bullies.* New York: Picador.

Klein, S. P., Hamilton, L. S., McCaffrey, D. F., & Stecher, B. M. (2000). *Issue paper: What do test scores in Texas tell us?* Santa Monica, CA: Rand.

Knickerbocker, J. L., & Rycik, J. (2002). Growing into literature: Adolescents' literary interpretation and appreciation. *Journal of Adolescent & Adult Literacy, 46*(3), 196–208.

Knoeller, C. P. (1994). Negotiating interpretations of text: The role of student-led discussions in understanding literature. *Journal of Reading, 37,* 572–580.

Koretz, D. M. (2008). *Measuring up: What educational testing really tells us.* Cambridge, MA: Harvard University Press.

Koretz, D., & Barron, S. T. (1998). *The validity of gains in scores on the Kentucky Instructional Results Information System.* Santa Monica, CA: Rand.

Kress, G. (2003). *Literacy in the new media age.* London: Routledge.

Krogness, M. (1995). *Just teach me, Mrs. K: Talking, reading, and writing with resistant adolescent learners.* Portsmouth, NH: Heinemann.

Krull, K. (1993). *Lives of the musicians: Good times, bad times (and what the neighbors thought).* Ill. K. Hewitt. San Diego, CA: Harcourt Brace Jovanovich.

Krull, K. (1995). *Lives of the artists: Masterpieces, messes (and what the neighbors thought).* Ill. K. Hewitt. San Diego, CA: Harcourt Brace.

Krull, K. (1997). *Lives of the athletes: Thrills, spills (and what the neighbors thought).* Ill. K. Hewitt. San Diego, CA: Harcourt Brace.

Krull, K. (2000). *Wilma unlimited: How Wilma Rudolph became the world's fastest woman.* Ill. D. Diaz. San Diego, CA: Harcourt Brace.

Krull, K. (2003). *Harvesting hope: The story of Cesar Chavez.* San Diego, CA: Harcourt.

Kubey, R., & Baker, F. (1999, October 27). Has media literacy found a curricular foothold? *Education Week.* Retrieved August 27, 2008, from www.frankwbaker.com/edweek.htm.

Ladson-Billings, G. (1994). *The dreamkeepers: Successful teachers of African American students.* San Francisco: Jossey-Bass.

Ladson-Billings, G. (1995). Toward a theory of culturally relevant pedagogy. *American Educational Research Journal, 32,* 465–491.

Ladson-Billings, G. (1999). Preparing teachers for diverse student populations: A critical race theory perspective. In A. I. Nejad & P. D. Pearson (Eds.), *Review of research in education* (Vol. 24, pp. 211–247). Washington, DC: American Education Research Association.

Lam, R. (2011). The role of self-assessment in students' writing portfolios: A classroom investigation. *TESL Reporter, 43*(2), 16–34.

Lam, R., & Lee, I. (2009). Balancing the dual functions of portfolio assessment. *ELT Journal, 64*(1), 54–64.

Langer, J. A. (1981). From theory to practice: A prereading plan. *Journal of Reading, 25,* 152–156.

Langer, J. A., & Applebee, A. N. (1987). *How writing shapes thinking.* Urbana, IL: National Council of Teachers of English.

Langer, J. A., & Flihan, S. (2000). Writing and reading relationships: Constructive tasks. In R. Indrisano & J. R. Squire (Eds.), *Perspectives on writing: Research, theory, and practice.* Newark, DE: International Reading Association.

Langstaff, J. (1991). *Climbing Jacob's ladder.* New York: Macmillan.

Lankshear, C., & Knobel, M. (2003). *New literacies: Changing knowledge and classroom learning.* Buckingham, UK: Open University Press.

Lapp, D., & Fisher, D. (2009). It's all about the book. Motivating teens to read. *Journal of Adolescent and Adult Literacy, 52*(7), 556–561.

Lapp, D., Fisher, D., Flood, J., & Cabello, A. (2001). An integrated approach to the teaching and assessment of language arts. In S. Hurley & J. V. Tinajero (Eds.), *Literacy assessment of second language learners* (pp. 11–26). Boston: Allyn & Bacon.

Lapp, D., & Flood, J. (1995). Strategies for gaining access to the information superhighway: Off the side street and on to the main road. *Reading Teacher, 48,* 432–436.

Lapp, D., & Moss, B. (2012) *Exemplary Instruction in the Middle Grades.* NY: Guilford Press.

Larson, B. E. (2000). Classroom discussion: A method of instruction and a curriculum outcome. *Teaching and Teacher Education, 16,* 661–677.

Lasky, K. (1994). *The librarian who measured the earth.* Ill. K. Hawkes. New York: Little, Brown.

Lasky, K. (2003). *The man who made time travel.* Ill. K. Hawkes. New York: Farrar, Straus & Giroux.

Lauber, P. (1986). *Volcano: The eruption and healing of Mount St. Helens.* New York: Bradbury Press.

Lauber, P. (1996). *Hurricanes: Earth's mightiest storms.* New York: Scholastic.

Lawrence, L. (1985). *Children of the dust.* New York: HarperCollins.

Lee, C. D. (2004, Winter/Spring). Literacy in the academic disciplines and the needs of adolescent struggling readers. *Voices in Urban Education (VUE),* 14–19.

Lee, J., Grigg, W., & Donahue, P. (2007). The nation's report card: Reading 2007 (NCES 2007-496). Washington, DC: National Center for Education Statistics, Institute of Education Sciences, U.S. Department of Education.

Lee, J. O. (2011). Reach teachers now to ensure common core success. *Phi Delta Kappan, 92*(6), 43–44.

Leffland, E. (1979). *Rumors of peace.* New York: Harper & Row.

Leland, C. H., & Harste, J. C. (1994). Multiple ways of knowing: Curriculum in a new key. *Language Arts, 71,* 337–345.

Lenhart, A., Arafeh, S., Smith, A., & Macgill, A. (2008). *Writing, technology, and teens.* Washington, DC: Pew Internet and American Life Project.

Lenihan, G. (2003). Reading with adolescents: Constructing meaning together. *Journal of Adolescent & Adult Literacy, 47*(1), 8–12.

Lenters, K. (2006). Resistance, struggle, and the adolescent reader. *Journal of Adolescent and Adult Literacy, 50*(2), 136–146.

Lester, J. (1968). *To be a slave.* New York: Dial Press.

Lester, J. D. (1984). *Writing research papers: A complete guide* (4th ed.). Glenview, IL: Scott Foresman.

Lester, J. H. (1998). Reflective interaction in secondary classrooms: An impetus for enhanced learning. *Reading Research and Instruction, 37*(4), 237–251.

Leu, D. J., Jr. (1996). Sarah's secret: Social aspects of literacy and learning in a digital information age. *Reading Teacher, 50,* 162–165.

Leu, D. J., Jr. (2000). Literacy and technology: Deictic consequences for literacy education in an information age. In M. L. Kamil, P. M. Mosenthal, P. D. Pearson, & R. Barr (Eds.), *Handbook of reading research* (Vol. 3, pp. 743–770). Mahwah, NJ: Erlbaum.

Leu, D. J., Jr. (2002). The new literacies: Research on reading instruction with the Internet. In A. E. Farstrup & S. J. Samuels (Eds.), *What research has to say about reading instruction* (pp. 310–336). Newark, DE: International Reading Association.

Leu, D. J., Coiro, J., Castek, J., Hartman, D. K., Henry, L. A., & Reinking, D. (2008). Research on instruction and assessment in the new literacies of online reading comprehension. In C. C. Block, S. Parris, & P. Afflerbach (Eds.), *Comprehension instruction: Research-based best practices.* New York: Guilford Press.

Leu, D. J., Jr., & Leu, D. D. (2000). *Teaching with the Internet: Lessons from the classroom* (3rd ed.). Norwood, MA: Christopher-Gordon.

Leu, D. J., Leu, D. D., & Coiro, J. (2006). *Teaching with the Internet K–12: New literacies for new times* (4th ed.). Norwood, MA: Christopher-Gordon.

Levin, E. (1992). *If you traveled west in a covered wagon.* New York: Scholastic.

Levin, E. (1996). *If your name was changed at Ellis Island.* New York: Scholastic.

Levine, D. S. (1985). The biggest thing I learned but it really doesn't have to do with science. . . . *Language Arts, 62,* 43–47.

Lewin, T. (2008, November 20). Teenagers' internet socializing not a bad thing. *The New York Times.* Retrieved from www.nytimes.com.

Li, G. (2005). *Culturally contested pedagogy: Battles of literacy and schooling between mainstream teachers and Asian immigrant parents.* Albany: SUNY Press.

Li, G. (2009). *Multicultural families, home literacies, and mainstream schooling.* Charlotte, NC: Information Age Publishing.

Lin, G. (2007). *The year of the dog.* Boston: Little, Brown.

Lindbergh, R., & Brown, R. (1992). *A view from the air: Charles Lindbergh's earth and sky.* New York: Viking.

Linek, W. M. (1991). Grading and evaluation techniques for whole language teachers. *Language Arts, 68,* 125–132.

Lipsky, D. K., & Gartner, A. (1997). *Inclusion and school reform: Transforming America's classrooms.* Baltimore: Paul H. Brookes.

Little Soldier, L. (1989). Cooperative learning and the Native American student. *Phi Delta Kappan, 71,* 161–163.

Llewellyn, C. (1991). *Under the sea.* New York: Simon & Schuster.

Loh, V. (2006). Quantity and quality: The need for culturally authentic trade books in Asian American young adult literature. *The ALAN Review, 34*(1), 36–53.

Longo, C. (2010). Fostering creativity or teaching to the test: Implications for state testing on the delivery of science instruction. *The Clearing House, 83*(2), 54–57.

Louie, B. (2006). Guiding principles of teaching multicultural literature. *The Reading Teacher, 59*(5), 438–448.

Loveless, T. (2011). *How well are American students learning?* Washington, DC: Brown Center on Education Policy at Brookings.

Lowe, S. (1990). *Walden.* Ill. R. Sabuda. New York: Philomel.

Lowry, L. (1993). *The giver.* New York: Houghton Mifflin.

Lyga, A. W. (2004). *Graphic novels in your media center.* Colorado Springs, CO: Libraries Unlimited.

Lyon, G. E. (1991). *Cecil's story.* New York: Orchard.

Ma, W. (2004). *Intellectual gazing: Participatory learning in a graduate seminar.* Unpublished doctoral dissertation, University at Buffalo.

Ma, W. (2007). Dialoging internally: Participatory learning in a graduate seminar. In C. C. Park, R. Endo, S. J. Lee, & X. L. Rong (Eds.), *Asian American education: Acculturation, literacy development, and learning* (pp. 167–195). Charlotte, NC: Information Age Publishing.

Ma, W. (2008). Participatory dialogue and participatory learning in a discussion-based graduate seminar. *Journal of Literacy Research, 40*(2), 220–249.

Macaulay, D. (1973). *Cathedral: The story of its construction.* Boston: Houghton Mifflin.

Macaulay, D. (1978). *Castle.* Boston: Houghton Mifflin.

Macaulay, D. (1982). *Pyramid.* Boston: Houghton Mifflin.

Macaulay, D. (1998). *The new way things work.* Boston: Houghton Mifflin.

Macaulay, D. (2008). *The way we work.* Boston: Houghton Mifflin.

MacGinitie, W. H. (1993). Some limits of assessment. *Journal of Reading, 36,* 556–560.

Maguire, K. (2001). *Governors find education bill faults.* Retrieved October 2002 from www.speakout.com/cgi-bin/edt/im.display.printable?client.id=speakout&story.id=10037.

Malinowski, B. (1954). *Magic, science and religion and other essays.* New York: Doubleday.

Manyak, P .C., & Bauer, E. B. (2009). English vocabulary instruction for English learners. *The Reading Teacher, 63*(2), 174–176.

Manzo, A. V. (1975). Guided reading procedure. *Journal of Reading, 18,* 287–291.

Manzo, A., Manzo, U., & Estes, T. (2001). *Content area literacy: Interactive teaching for interactive learning.* New York: Wiley.

Marsalis, W. (1995). *Marsalis on music.* New York: Norton.

Martinez-Roldan, C. & Newcomer, S. (2011). "Reading between the pictures": Immigrant students' interpretation of the arrival. *Language Arts, 88*(3), 188–198.

Martinez, R. (2010). Spanglish as literacy tool: Toward an understanding of the potential role of Spanish-English code-switching in the development of academic literacy. *Teaching of English, 45*(2), 124–149.

Maruki, T. (1980). *Hiroshima no pika.* New York: Lothrop, Lee & Shepard.

Marzano, R. J. (2003). *What works in schools: Translating research into action.* Alexandria, VA: Association for Supervision and Curriculum Development.

Massell, D., Kirst, M., & Hoppe, M. (1997). *Persistence and change: Standards-based reforms in nine states.* Consortium for Policy Research in Education, University of Pennsylvania, Graduate School of Education. Washington, DC: U.S. Department of Education.

Matas, C. (2001). *The war within: A novel of the Civil War.* New York: Simon & Schuster.

Matthew, K. (1996). What do children think of CD-ROM storybooks? *Texas Reading Report, 18,* 6.

McCloud, S. (2006). *Making comics: Storytelling secrets of comics, manga, and graphic novels.* NY: William Morrow.

McColl, A. (2005). Tough call: Is No Child Left Behind constitutional? [Electronic version]. *Phi Delta Kappan, 86*(6), 604–610.

McCullen, C. (1998). The electronic thread: Research and assessment on the Internet. *Middle Ground, 1*(3), 7–9.

McGinley, W. J., & Denner, P. R. (1987). Story impressions: A pre-reading/writing activity. *Journal of Reading, 31,* 248–253.

McIntosh, M. (1991, September). No time for writing in your class? *Mathematics Teacher,* pp. 423–433.

McKenna, M. C., & Robinson, R. D. (2006). *Teaching through text: Reading and writing in the content areas* (4th ed.). Boston: Pearson.

McKeon, C. (2001). E-mail as a motivating literacy event for one student: Donna's case. *Reading Research and Instruction, 40*(3), 185–202.

McKinley, R. (1978). *Beauty: A retelling of the story of Beauty and the Beast.* New York: HarperCollins.

McLaren, P. (1989). *Life in schools: An introduction to critical pedagogy in the foundations of education.* New York: Longman.

McMackin, M., & Witherell, N. (2010). Using leveled graphic organizers to differentiate responses to children's literature. *New England Reading Association Journal, 46*(1), 49–54.

McPherson, J. (2002). *Fields of fury: The American Civil War.* New York: Atheneum.

McTighe, J., & Lyman, F. T. (1988). Cueing thinking in the classroom: The promise of theory-embedded tools. *Educational Leadership, 45*(7), 18–24.

McVerry, J. G. (2007). Forums and functions of threaded discussions: Using new literacies to build traditional comprehension skills. *The New England Reading Association Journal, 43*(1), 17–22.

Merkley, D. M., & Jefferies, D. (2001). Guidelines for implementing a graphic organizer. *Reading Teacher, 54,* 350–357.

MetaMetrics (2008). *The Lexile framework for reading: FAQ.* Retrieved September 19, 2008, from www.lexile.com/DesktopDefault.aspx?view=ed&tabindex=6&tabid=18.

Meyer, B. J. F., & Rice, E. (1984). The structure of text. In P. D. Pearson (Ed.), *Handbook of reading research* (pp. 319–352). New York: Longman.

Miholic, V. (1994). An inventory to pique students' metacognitive awareness. *Journal of Reading, 38*(2), 84–86.

Mike, D. G. (1996). Internet in the schools: A literacy perspective. *Journal of Adolescent and Adult Literacy, 40,* 4–13.

Miller, T. (1998). The place of picture books in middle-level classrooms. *Journal of Adolescent and Adult Literacy, 41*(5), 376–382.

Millman, I. (2005). *Hidden child.* New York: Farrar, Straus & Giroux.

Moje, E. B. (2007). Developing socially just subject-matter instruction: A review of the literature on disciplinary literacy. In N. L. Parker (Ed.), *Review of research in education* (pp. 1–44). Washington, DC: American Educational Research Association.

Moje, E. B. (2008). Responsive literacy teaching in secondary school content areas. In M. W. Conley, J. R. Freidhoff, M. B. Sherry, & S. F. Tuckey (Eds.), *Meeting the challenge of adolescent literacy* (pp. 58–87). New York: Guilford Press.

Moje, E. B., Ciechanowski, K. M., Kramer, K., Ellis, L., Carrillo, R., & Collazo, T. (2004). Working toward third space in content area literacy: An examination of everyday funds of knowledge and discourse. *Reading Research Quarterly, 39*(1), 38–70.

Moje, E., Overby, M., Tysvaer, N., & Morris, K. (2008). The complex world of adolescent literacy: Myths, motivations, and mysteries. *Harvard Educational Review, 78*(1), 107–154.

Moje, E. B., Young, J. P., Readence, J. E., & Moore, D. W. (2000). Reinventing adolescent literacy for new times: Perennial and millennial issues. *Journal of Adolescent & Adult Literacy 43,* 400–410.

Moll, L. (1994). Literacy research in community and classrooms: A sociocultural approach. In R. B. Ruddell & H. Singer (Eds.), *Theoretical models and processes in reading.* Newark, DE: International Reading Association.

Moll, L. C. (1992). Bilingual classroom studies and community analysis: Recent trends. *Educational Researcher, 21*(2), 20–24.

Montelongo, J., Herter, R. J., Ansaldo, R.,, & Hatter, N. (2010). A lesson cycle for teaching expository reading and writing. *Journal of Adolescent & Adult Literacy, 53*(8), 656–666.

Moore, D. W., Bean, T. W., Birdyshaw, D., & Rycik, J. A. (1999). *Adolescent literacy: A position statement for the Commission on Adolescent Literacy of the International Reading Association.* Newark, DE: International Reading Association.

Moore, D., Moore, S., Cunningham, P., & Cunningham, J. (2006). *Developing readers and writers in the content areas K–12.* Boston: Allyn & Bacon.

Moore, J., & Whitfield, V. F. (2008). Musing: A way to inform and inspire pedagogy through self-reflection. *Reading Teacher, 6*(17), 586–588.

Moore, M. T. (2004). Issues and trends in writing instruction. In R. Robinson, M. McKenna, & J. Wedman (Eds.), *Issues and trends in literacy education* (3rd ed.). Boston: Allyn & Bacon.

Morgan, W. (1997). *Critical literacy in the classroom: The art of the possible.* New York: Routledge.

Moss, B. (1995). Using children's nonfiction tradebooks as read-alouds (Teacher's notebook). *Language Arts, 72,* 122–126.

Moss, B. (2003). *Exploring the literature of fact: Children's nonfiction trade books in the elementary classroom.* New York: Guilford Press.

Mraz, M. (2000). The literacy program selection process from the perspective of school district administrators. *Ohio Reading Teacher, 34*(2), 40–48.

Mraz, M. (2002). Factors that influence policy decisions in literacy: Perspectives of key policy informants. Ph.D. dissertation, Kent State University.

Mraz, M., Algozzine, B., & Kissel, B. (2009). *The literacy coach's companion.* Thousand Oaks, CA, and Newark, DE: Corwin Press and the International Reading Association.

Mraz, M., Algozzine, B., & Watson, P. (2008). Perceptions and expectations of roles and responsibilities of literacy coaching. *Literacy Research and Instruction, 47,* 141–157.

Mraz, M., Vacca, J. V., & Vintinner, J. P. (2008). Professional development. In S. Wepner & D. Strickland (Eds.), *The administration and supervision of reading programs*

(4th ed., pp. 133–143). New York: Teachers College Press.

Mühlberger, R. (1993). *What makes a Monet a Monet?* New York: Metropolitan Museum of Art/Viking.

Murphy, J. (1990). *The boys' war: Confederate and Union soldiers talk about the Civil War.* New York: Clarion Books.

Murphy, J. (1992). *The long road to Gettysburg.* New York: Clarion Books.

Murphy, J. (1998). *The great fire.* New York: Clarion.

Murray, D. M. (1980). Writing as process: How writing finds its own meaning. In T. R. Donovan & B. W. McClelland (Eds.), *Eight approaches to teaching composition* (pp. 80–97). Urbana, IL: National Council of Teachers of English.

Myers, W. D. (1991). *Now is your time!: The African-American struggle for freedom.* New York: HarperCollins.

Myers, W. D. (2001). *Monster.* New York: Amistad.

Myers, W. D. (2002). *Patrol: An American soldier in Vietnam.* Ill. A. Grifalconi. New York: HarperCollins.

Nagy, W. E. (1988). *Teaching vocabulary to improve reading comprehension.* Newark, DE: International Reading Association.

National Association of Secondary School Principals (NASSP). (2005). Creating a culture of literacy: A guide for middle and high school principals. Retrieved March 30, 2006, from www.principals.org/s_nassp/sec.asp.

National Center for Educational Statistics. (2007). *The nation's report card: Reading 2007.* Retrieved April 17, 2009, from www.nces.ed.gov/pubSearch/pubinfo.asp?pubid=2007496.

National Commission on Writing. (2003). *The neglected R: The need for a writing revolution.* Retrieved from www.writingcommission.org.

National Council for Accreditation of Teacher Education. (2009). *A continuum of educator preparation and development.* Washington DC: Author.

National Council of Teachers of English (NCTE). (2004). *A call to action: What we know about adolescent literacy and ways to support teachers in meeting students' needs.* Urbana, IL: Author. Retrieved July 7, 2007, from www.ncte.org/about/over/positions/category/literacy/118622.htm.

National Council of Teachers of English (NCTE). (2006). *NCTE principles of adolescent literacy reform: A policy research brief.* Retrieved July 7, 2007, from www.ncte.org/library/NCTEFiles/Resources/PolicyResearch/AdolLitResearchBrief.pdf.

National Council of Teachers of Mathematics (NCTM). (2000). *Principles and standards for school mathematics.* Washington, DC: Author.

National Governors Association Center for Best Practices, Council of Chief State School Officers. (2010). Common Core State Standards English Language Arts. Washington D.C.: National Governors Association Center for Best Practices, Council of Chief State School Officers.

National Institute for Literacy (2007). *What content-area teachers should know about adolescent literacy.* Washington DC: National Institute of Child Health and Human Development (NICHD).

National Middle School Association (NMSA). (2005). *Highly qualified: A balanced approach.* Retrieved September 28, 2006, from www.nmsa.org.

National Middle School Association (NMSA), National Association of Elementary School Principals (NAESP), and the National Association of Secondary School Principals (NASSP). (2004). *Highly qualified: A balanced approach.* Retrieved April 14, 2006, from www.nmsa.org/portals/o/pdf/about/position_statements/EdWeek.pdf.

National Reading Panel. (2000). *Teaching children to read: An evidence-based assessment of the scientific research literature on reading and its implications for reading instruction* (National Institute of Health Pub. No. 00–4769). Washington, DC: National Institute of Child Health and Human Development.

National School Boards Association. (2006). *The next chapter: A school board guide to improving adolescent literacy.* Alexandria, VA: Author. Retrieved May 18, 2008, from www.nsba.org.

Neal, J. C., & Moore, K. (1991). *The Very Hungry Caterpillar* meets *Beowulf* in secondary classrooms. *Journal of Reading, 35,* 290–296.

Neill, M. (2003). Leaving children behind: How No Child Left Behind will fail our children. *Phi Delta Kappan, 85*(3), 225–228.

Neilsen, L. (2006). Playing for real: Performative texts and adolescent identities. In D. Alvermann, K. Hinchman, S. Phelps, & S. Waff (Eds.), *Reconceptualizing the literacies in adolescents' lives* (pp. 5–28). Mahwah, NJ: Erlbaum.

Nelson, B. (2008). *Paranoid park.* New York: Puffin.

Nelson, J. (1978). Readability: Some cautions for the content area teacher. *Journal of Reading, 21,* 620–625.

Nelson, K. (2008). *We are the ship: The story of Negro league baseball.* New York: Hyperion.

Nelson, M. (2005). *A wreath for Emmitt Till.* New York: Houghton Mifflin Harcourt.

Ness, M. K. (2009). Reading comprehension strategies in secondary content area classrooms: Teacher use of attitudes towards reading comprehension instruction. *Reading Horizons, 49*(2), 143–166.

Netiquette Guidelines (retrieved April 26, 2012). Online Student Expectations. Available at http://blogs.lsc.edu/expectations/netiquette-guidelines/.

Neufeld, J. (2010). *New Orleans After the Deluge.* NY: Pantheon.

Neufeld, P. (2005). Comprehension instruction in content area classes. *Reading Teacher, 59*(4), 302–312.

Newcomb, N. (2007). Psychology's role in mathematics and science education. *Research Report.* Washington, DC: American Psychological Association:

Newell, G. (1984). Learning from writing in two content areas: A case study/protocol analysis. *Research in the Teaching of English, 18,* 205–287.

New London Group. (1996). A pedagogy of multiliteracies: Designing social futures. *Harvard Education Review 66*(1), 60–92.

Nichols, S. L., & Berliner, D. C. (2007). *Collateral damage: How high-stakes testing corrupts America's schools.* Cambridge, MA: Harvard Education Press.

Nichols, S. L., & Berliner, D. C. (2008). Testing the joy out of learning. *Educational Leadership, 65*(6), 14–18.

Nichols, W. D., Wood, K. D., & Rickelman, R. (2001). Using technology to engage students in reading and writing. *Middle School Journal, 32*(5), 45–50.

Nieto, S. (2002). *Language, culture, and teaching: Critical perspectives for a new century.* Mahwah, NJ: Erlbaum.

Niles, O. (1965). Organization perceived. In H. L. Herber (Ed.), *Developing study skills in secondary schools* (pp. 36–46). Newark, DE: International Reading Association.

Noden, H. R. (1995). A journey through cyberspace: Reading and writing in a virtual school. *English Journal 84*(6), 19–26.

Noden, H. R., & Vacca, R. T. (1994). *Whole language in middle and secondary classrooms.* New York: HarperCollins.

North Carolina Department of Public Instruction (NCDPI). (2012). *Accountability and curriculum reform effort.* Retrieved from www.ncpublicschools.org/acre.

Noyes, A. (1983). *The highwayman.* Ill. C. Mikolaychak. New York: Lothrop, Lee & Shepard.

Nye, N. S. (2002). *19 varieties of gazelle: Poems of the Middle East.* New York: HarperCollins.

Nye, R. (1968). *Beowulf: A new telling.* New York: Hill.

O'Brien, R. C. (1975). *Z for Zachariah.* New York: Atheneum.

Ogle, D. (1986). KWL: A teaching model that develops active reading of expository text. *Reading Teacher, 39,* 564–570.

Ogle, D. M. (1992). KWL in action: Secondary teachers find applications that work. In E. K. Dishner, T. W. Bean, J. E. Readence, & D. W. Moore (Eds.), *Reading in the content areas: Improving classroom instruction* (3rd ed., pp. 270–281). Dubuque, IA: Kendall-Hunt.

Ohio Department of Education. (2003). *Ohio administrative codes and rules links: Rule 3301-13-01.* Retrieved September 2003 from www.ode.state.oh.us/proficiency/rules.asp?pfv=True.

Oldfather, P., & Dahl, K. (1994). Toward a social constructivist reconceptualization of intrinsic motivation for literacy learning. *Journal of Reading Behavior, 26,* 139–158.

O'Neill, C. (1995). *Drama worlds: A framework for process drama.* Portsmouth, NH: Heinemann.

Osborne, A. B. (1996). Practice into theory into practice: Culturally relevant pedagogy for students we have marginalized and normalized. *Anthropology and Education Quarterly, 27*(3), 285–314.

Palmatier, R. (1973). A notetaking system for learning. *Journal of Reading, 17,* 36–39.

Palmer, R. G., & Stewart, R. A. (1997). Nonfiction trade books in content area instruction: Realities and potential. *Journal of Adolescent and Adult Literacy, 40,* 630–641.

Pang, V. O., & Cheng, L. L. (Eds.). (1998). *Struggling to be heard: The unmet needs of Asian Pacific American children.* Albany: SUNY Press.

Papert, S. (1980). *Mindstorms: Children, computers, and powerful ideas.* New York: Basic Books.

Pappas, T. (1993). *Math talk: Mathematical ideas in poems for two voices.* New York: Wide World.

Paris, S., & Meyers, M. (1981). Comprehension monitoring, memory, and study strategies of good and poor readers. *Journal of Reading Behavior, 13,* 5–22.

Parker, W. C., & Jarolimek, J. (1997). *Social studies in elementary education.* Upper Saddle River, NJ: Prentice Hall.

Parnall, P. (1984). *The daywatchers.* New York: Macmillan.

Parnall, P. (1991). *Marsh cat.* New York: Macmillan.

Parry, K. (1993). Too many words: Learning the vocabulary of an academic subject. In T. Huckin, M. Haynes, & J. Coady (Eds.), *Second language reading and vocabulary learning* (pp. 109–129). Norwood, NJ: Ablex.

Parsons, L. (2001). *Response journals revisted: Maximizing learning through reading, writing, viewing, discussing, and thinking.* Markham, ON: Pembroke.

Partridge, E. (2002). *This land was made for you and me: The life and songs of Woody Guthrie.* New York: Viking.

Partridge, E. (2005). *John Lennon: All I want is the truth.* New York: Viking.

Patterson, N. G. (2000). Hypertext and the changing roles of readers. *English Journal, 90*(2), 74–80.

Pauk, W. (1978). A notetaking format: Magical but not automatic. *Reading World, 16,* 96–97.

Pauk, W., & Ross, J. Q. O. (2007). *How to study in college.* Boston: Houghton Mifflin Harcourt.

Paulsen, G. (1987). *Hatchet.* New York: Viking Penguin.

Paulsen, G. (1989). *The winter room.* New York: Harcourt Brace.

Paulsen, G. (1990). *Woodsong.* New York: Macmillan.

Paulsen, G. (1995). *Nightjohn.* New York: Laurel Leaf Press.

Payne, R. (2003). *Framework for understanding poverty* (3rd ed.). Highlands, TX: Aha! Process.

Payne, R., DeVol, P., & Smith, T. (2005). *Bridges out of poverty: Strategies for professionals and communities.* Highlands, TX: Aha! Process.

Peacock, L. (1998). *Crossing the Delaware: A history in many voices.* Ill. W. L. Krudop. New York: Atheneum.

Pearce, D. L. (1983). Guidelines for the use and evaluation of writing in content classrooms. *Journal of Reading, 27,* 212–218.

Pearson, P. D. (1974–1975). The effects of grammatical complexity on children's comprehension, recall, and conception of certain semantic relations. *Reading Research Quarterly, 10,* 155–192.

Pearson, P. D. (1982). *A context for instructional research and reading comprehension* (Technical Report No. 230). Urbana: University of Illinois Center for the Study of Reading.

Pearson, P. D., & Gallagher, M. C. (1983). The instruction of reading comprehension. *Contemporary Educational Psychology, 8,* 317–344.

Pearson. P. D., Hiebert, E. H., & Kamil, M. (2007). Vocabulary assessment: What we know and what we need to learn. *Reading Research Quarterly, 42*(2), 282–296.

Pearson, P. D., & Hoffman, J. V. (2011). Teaching effective reading instruction. In T. V. Rasinski (Ed.), *Rebuilding the foundation: Effective reading instruction for 21st century literacy* (pp. 3–33). Bloomington, IN: Solution Tree Press.

Pearson, P. D., & Johnson, D. (1978). *Teaching reading comprehension.* Fort Worth, TX: Holt, Rinehart and Winston.

Pearson, P. D., & Spiro, R. (1982). The new buzz word in reading as schema. *Instructor, 89,* 46–48.

Peregoy, S. F., & Boyle, O. F. (2001). *Reading, writing, and learning in ESL: A resource book for K–12 teachers* (3rd ed.). New York: Longman.

Peregoy, S. F., & Boyle, O. F. (2008). *Reading, writing, and learning in ESL: A resource book for teaching K–12 English learners* (5th ed.). Boston: Pearson.

Perie, M., Grigg, W., & Donahue, P. (2005). *The nation's report card: Reading 2005* (NCES 2006-451). Washington, DC: U.S. Department of Education.

Pew Internet and American Life Study (2006). *Internet penetration and access.* Retrieved August 28, 2008, from www.pewinternet.org/topics.asp?page=2&c=3.

Pew Internet and American Life Study (2008). *Home broadband 2008.* Retrieved August 28, 2008, from www.pewinternet.org/topics.asp?page=1&c=3.

Phillips, V., & Wong, C. (2011). Tying together the common core standards, instruction, and assessments. *Phi Delta Kappan, 91*(5), 37–42.

Pichert, J. W., & Anderson, R. C. (1977). Taking different perspectives on a story. *Journal of Educational Psychology, 69,* 309–315.

Pilgreen, J. (2000). *How to organize and manage a sustained silent reading program.* Portsmouth, NH: Heinemann.

Pitcher, S. M., Martinez, G., Dicembre, E. A., Fewster, D., & McCormick, M. K. (2010). Literacy needs of adolescents in their own words. *Journal of Adolescent & Adult Literacy, 53*(8), 636–645.

Plucker, J. A., Spradlin, T. E., Cline, K. P., & Wolf, K. M. (2005). *Education policy brief: No Child Left Behind, Spring 2005 implementation update* [Electronic version]. Bloomington, IN: Center for Evaluation & Education Policy.

Polacco, P. (1994). *Pink and say.* New York: Philomel.

Pradl, G. M., & Mayher, J. S. (1985). Reinvigorating learning through writing. *Educational Leadership, 42,* 4–8.

Preble, L. (2006). *Queen Geek series.* New York: Berkeley.

Pressley, M. (2000). What should comprehension instruction be the instruction of? In M. Kamil, P. Mosenthal, P. D. Pearson, & R. Barr (Eds.), *Handbook of reading research* (Vol. 3, pp. 545–562). Mahwah, NJ: Erlbaum.

Pressley, M. (2002a). Comprehension instruction: What makes sense now, what might make sense soon. *Reading Online, 5*(2). Retrieved October 3, 2005, from www.readingonline.org/articles/art_index.asp?HREF=/articles/handbook/pressley/index.htm.

Pressley, M. (2002b). *Reading instruction that works: The case for balanced reading.* New York: Guilford Press.

Pressley, M. (2006). *Reading instruction that works: The case for balanced instruction.* New York: Guilford Press.

Price, L. (1990). *Aida.* Ill. L. Dillon & D. Dillon. San Diego: Harcourt Brace.

Pruisner, P. (2009). Moving beyond No Child Left Behind with the merged model for reading instruction. *TechTrends, 53*(2)

RAND Reading Study Group. (2002). *Reading for understanding: Toward an R&D program in reading comprehension.* Santa Monica, CA: Science and Technology Policy Institute, Rand Education.

Randall, S. N. (1996). Information charts: A strategy for organizing students' research. *Journal of Adolescent and Adult Literacy, 39,* 536–542.

Ransom, K. A., Santa, C. M., Williams, C. K., Farstrup, A. E., Au, K. H., Baker, B. M., et al. (1999). High-stakes assessments in reading: A position statement of the International Reading Association. *Journal of Adolescent and Adult Literacy, 43*(3), 305–312.

Raphael, T. E. (1982). Question-answering strategies for children. *Reading Teacher, 36,* 186–191.

Raphael, T. E. (1984). Teaching learners about sources of information for answering comprehension questions. *Journal of Reading, 27,* 303–311.

Raphael, T. E. (1986). Teaching question–answer relationships. *Reading Teacher, 39,* 516–520.

Rappaport, D. (2001). *Martin's big words: The life of Dr. Martin Luther King, Jr.* Ill. B. Collier. New York: Hyperion.

Raschka, C. (1997). *Mysterious Thelonious.* New York: Orchard.

Ray, D. (1990). *A nation torn: The story of how the Civil War began.* New York: Scholastic.

Readence, J. E. (2002). Adolescent literacy. In B. J. Guzzetti (Ed.), *Literacy in America: An encyclopedia of history, theory, and practice* (pp. 13–15). Santa Barbara, CA: ABC-CLIO.

Reed, J. H., Schallert, D. L., Beth, A. D., & Woodruff, A. L. (2004). Motivated reader, engaged writer: The role of motivation in the literate acts of adolescents. In T. L. Jetton & J. A. Dole (Eds.), *Adolescent literacy research and practice* (pp. 251–282). New York: Guilford Press.

Reeder, C. (1989). *Shades of gray.* New York: Macmillan.

Reef, C. (2006). *e.e. cummings: A poet's life.* New York: Clarion Books.

Reeves, N. (1992). *Into the mummy's tomb: The real-life discovery of Tutankhamun's treasures.* New York: Scholastic/Madison.

Reinking, D. (1995). Reading and writing with computers: Literacy research in a post-typographic world. In K. A. Hinchman, D. J. Leu, Jr., & C. K. Kinzer (Eds.), *Perspectives on literacy research and practice* (pp. 17–33). Chicago: National Reading Conference.

Reinking, D. (1997). Me and my hypertext: A multiple digression analysis of technology and literacy. *Reading Teacher, 50,* 626–643.

Reinking, D. (1998). Synthesizing technological transformations of literacy in a post-typographic world. In D. Reinking, M. McKenna, L. D. Labbo, & R. Kieffer (Eds.), *Handbook of literacy and technology: Transformations in a post-typographic world* (pp. xi–xxx). Mahwah, NJ: Erlbaum.

Reinking, D. (2003). Multimedia and engaged reading in a digital world. In L. Verhoeven & C. Snow (Eds.), *Creating a world of engaged readers.* Mahwah, NJ: Erlbaum.

Reis, S.M. & Renzulli, J.S. (2005). *Curriculum compacting: An easy start to differentiating for high-potential students.* Waco, TX: Prufrock Press.

Renyi, J. (1998). Building learning into the teaching job. *Educational Leadership, 55*(5), 70–74.

Reyes, M., & Molner, L. (1999). Instruction strategies for second-language learners in the content areas. *Journal of Reading, 35,* 96–103.

Reyhner, J., & Garcia, R. L. (1989). Helping minorities read better: Problems and promises. *Reading Research and Instruction, 28*(3), 84–91.

Richardson, V. (2003). The dilemmas of professional development. *Phi Delta Kappan, 84,* 401–406.

Rico, G. L. (1983). *Writing the natural way: Using right-brain techniques to release your expressive powers.* Los Angeles: Tarcher.

Ride, S., & Okie, S. (1986). *To space and back.* New York: Lothrop, Lee & Shepard.

Roberts, P. (1985). Speech communities. In V. Clark, P. Escholz, & A. Rosa (Eds.), *Language* (4th ed.). New York: St. Martin's Press.

Roberts, T. & Billings, L. (2011). *Teaching critical thinking: Using seminars for 21st century literacy.* Larchmont, NY: Eye On Education.

Robins, J. (2006). Electronic portfolios as a bridge. *Intervention in School and Clinic, 42*(2), 107–113.

Robinson, D. (2006) The Paideia Seminar: Moving Reading Comprehension from Transaction to Transformation, (Unpublished doctoral dissertation). The Faculty of the Department of Language Arts and Literacy of the Graduate School of Education, University of Massachusetts Lowell.

Roby, T. (1987). Commonplaces, questions, and modes of discussion. In J. T. Dillon (Ed.), *Classroom questions and discussion* (pp. 134–169). Norwood, NJ: Ablex.

Rodrigues, R. J. (1983). Tools for developing prewriting skills. *English Journal, 72,* 58–60.

Rodriguez, L. J. (1993). *Always running: La vida loca: Gang days in L.A.* New York: Touchstone.

Rohmer, H. (Ed.). (1997). *Just like me: Stories and self-portraits by fourteen artists.* San Francisco: Children's Book Press.

Rohmer, H. (Ed.). (1999). *Honoring our ancestors: Stories and pictures by fourteen artists.* San Francisco: Children's Book Press.

Rose, B. (1989). Writing and mathematics: Theory and practice. In P. Connolly & T. Vilardi (Eds.), *Writing to learn mathematics and science* (pp. 19–30). New York: Teachers College Press.

Rose, S. A., & Fernlund, P. M. (1997). Using technology for powerful social studies learning. *Social Education, 13*(6), 160–166.

Rosenblatt, L. (1938/1995). *Literature as exploration.* (5th ed.). New York: Modern Language Association.

Rosenblatt, L. M. (1982). The literary transaction: Evocation and response. *Theory into Practice, 21,* 268–277.

Rothenberg, C. (2009). English language learners in the secondary classroom. In S. R. Parris, D. Fisher, & K. Hendley. *Adolescent literacy: Field tested effective solutions for every classroom* (pp. 168–179). Newark, DE: IRA.

Ruddell, M. R., & Shearer, B. A. (2002). "Extraordinary," "tremendous," "exhilarating," "magnificent": Middle school at-risk students become avid word learners with the Vocabulary Self-Collection Strategy (VSS). *Journal of Adolescent and Adult Literacy, 45,* 352–363.

Rumelhart, D. E. (1982). Schemata: The building blocks of cognition. In J. Guthrie (Ed.), *Comprehension and teaching: Research reviews* (pp. 3–26). Newark, DE: International Reading Association.

Rupley, W. H., Blair, T. R., Nichols, W. D. (2009). Effective reading instruction for struggling readers: The role of direct/explicit teaching. *Reading & Writing Quarterly, 25,* 125–138.

Ryan, P. M. (2000). *Esperanza rising.* New York: Scholastic.

Ryan, P. M. (2002). *When Marian sang: The true recital of Marian Anderson.* Ill. B. Selznick. New York: Scholastic.

Rycik, J. A. (1994). *An exploration of student library research projects in seventh grade English and social studies classes.* Unpublished doctoral dissertation, Kent State University.

Rylant, C. (1984). *Waiting to waltz: A childhood.* Ill. S. Gammell. New York: Bradbury.

Sachar, L. (1998). *Holes.* New York: Farrar, Strauss & Giroux

Salisbury, R. (1934). A study of the transfer effects of training in logical organization. *Journal of Educational Research, 28,* 241–254.

Samples, R. (1977). *The whole school book: Teaching and learning late in the 20th century.* Reading, MA: Addison-Wesley.

Sanders, T. (2004). *No time to waste: The vital role of college and university leaders in improving science and mathematics education.* Paper presented at the invitational conference of Teacher Preparation and Institutions of Higher Education: Mathematics and Science Content Knowledge, Washington, DC.

Sansevere-Dreher, D., Dreher, D., & Renfro, E. (1994). *Explorers who got lost.* New York: Tor Books.

Santa, C. M., & Havens, L. T. (1991). Learning through writing. In C. M. Santa & D. E. Alvermann (Eds.), *Science learning: Processes and applications* (pp. 122–133). Newark, DE: International Reading Association.

Say, A. (1990). *El Chino.* Boston: Houghton Mifflin.

Say, A. (2002). *Home of the brave.* Boston: Houghton Mifflin.

Schlitz, L. A. (2007). *Good masters! Sweet ladies!: Voices from a medieval village.* New York: Candlewick.

Schmar-Dobler, E. (2003). Reading on the Internet: The link between literacy and technology. *Journal of Adolescent & Adult Literacy, 47,* 80–85.

Schmidt, P. R. (1998). The ABC's of cultural understanding and communication. *Equity and Excellence in Education, 31*(2), 28–38.

Schmidt, P. R. (1999a). KWLQ: Inquiry and literacy learning in science. *Reading Teacher, 52*(6), 789–792.

Schmidt, P. R. (1999b). Know thyself and understand others. *Language Arts, 76*(4), 332–340.

Schmidt, P. R. (2000). Teachers connecting and communicating with families for literacy development. In T. Shanahan & F. Rodriguez-Brown (Eds.), *National reading conference yearbook* (49th ed., pp. 194–208). Chicago: National Reading Conference.

Schmidt, P. R. (2001). The power to empower. In P. R. Schmidt & P. B. Mosenthal (Eds.), *Reconceptualizing literacy in the new age of multiculturalism and pluralism* (pp. 389–433). Greenwich, CT: Information Age Publishing.

Schmidt, P. R. (2003). *Culturally relevant pedagogy: A study of successful in-service.* Paper presented at the annual meeting of the National Reading Conference, Scottsdale, AZ.

Schmidt, P. R. (2005a). Culturally responsive instruction: Promoting literacy in secondary content areas. *Adolescent Literacy.* Naperville, IL: Learning Point Associates. Retrieved from www.learningpt.org.

Schmidt, P. R. (Ed.). (2005b). *Preparing educators to communicate and connect with families and communities.* Greenwich, CT: Information Age Publishing.

Schmidt, P. R. (2008, December). Secondary pre-service teacher preparation for culturally responsive literacy teaching. Paper presented at the 58th Annual Meeting of the National Reading Conference, Orlando, FL.

Schmidt, P. R., & Finkbeiner, C. (2006). *ABC's of cultural understanding and communication: National and international adaptations*. Greenwich, CT: Information Age Publishing.

Schmidt, P. R., & Lazar, A. M. (Eds.). (2011). *Practicing what we teach: How culturally responsive literacy classrooms make a difference*. New York: Teachers College Press.

Schmidt, P. R., & Ma, W. (2006). *50 literacy strategies for culturally responsive teaching, K–8*. Chicago: Corwin Press.

Schoenbach, R., Greenleaf, C., Cziko, C., & Hurwitz, L. (1999). *Reading for understanding: A guide to improving reading in middle and high school classrooms*. San Francisco: Jossey-Bass.

Scholastic. (2006). *The kids and family reading report*. Retrieved August 30, 2008, from www.scholastic.com/aboutscholastic/news/readingreport.htm.

Scholastic. (2008). *The 2008 kids and family reading report*. Retrieved August 30, 2008, from www.scholastic.com/aboutscholastic/news/readingreport.htm.

Schraw, G. & Moshman, D., (1995). Metacognitive Theories. *Educational Psychology Papers and Publications. Paper 40*. http://digitalcommons.unl.edu/edpsychpapers/40.

Schroeder, M., Mckeough, A., Graham, S., Stocke, H., & Bisanz, G. (2009). The contribution of trade books to early science literacy: In and out of school. *Research in Science Education, 39*(2), 231–250.

Schumm, J. S., & Mangrum, C. T., II. (1991). FLIP: A framework for content area reading. *Journal of Reading, 35,* 120–124.

Schwartz, D. (1998). *G is for Googol*. New York: Tricycle Press.

Schwartz, R. M., & Raphael, T. E. (1985). Concept of definition: A key to improving students' vocabulary. *Reading Teacher, 39,* 198–204.

Sciezka, J. (2005). *Guys write for Guys Read*. New York: Viking.

Scott, E. (2007). *When is a planet not a planet? The story of Pluto*. New York: Clarion Books.

Selznick, B. (2007). *The Invention of Hugo Cabret*. New York: Scholastic Press.

Sender, R. M. (1986). *The cage*. New York: Macmillan.

Service, R. (1986). *The cremation of Sam McGee*. Ill. T. Harrison. New York: Greenwillow.

Seuss, Dr. (1984). *The butter battle book*. New York: Random House.

Shanahan, T. (Ed.). (1990). *Reading and writing together: New perspectives for the classroom*. Norwood, MA: Christopher-Gordon.

Shanahan, T., & Shanahan, C. (2008). Teaching disciplinary literacy to adolescents: Rethinking content-area literacy. *Harvard Educational Review, 78*(1), 40–59.

Shanklin, N. (2006). *What are the characteristics of effective literacy coaching?* Retrieved November 1, 2007, from www.literacycoachingonline.org.

Shanks, A. Z. (1982). *Busted lives: Dialogues with kids in jail*. New York: Delacorte.

Sharan, Y. (2010). Cooperative learning: A divsersified pedagogy for diverse classrooms. *Intercultural Education, 21*(3), 195–203.

Short, K., Harste, J., & Burke, C. (1996). *Creating classrooms for authors and inquirers*. Portsmouth, NH: Heinemann.

Shulman, L. (1987). Learning to teach. *AAHE Bulletin,* 5–6.

Simon, S. (1990). *Oceans*. New York: Morrow.

Singer, H. (1978). Active comprehension: From answering to asking questions. *Reading Teacher, 31,* 901–908.

Sis, P. (2007). *The wall: Growing up behind the iron curtain*. New York: Farrar, Straus & Giroux.

Skinner, R. A., & Staresina, L. N. (2004). State of the states [Electronic version]. *Education Week, 23*(7), 97–99.

Slavin, R. E. (1994). *Using Student Team Learning*. 4th ed. Baltimore: Johns Hopkins University, Center for Social Organization of Schools.

Slavin, R. E. (1987). Synthesis of research on cooperative learning. *Educational Leadership, 48*(5), 72–82.

Slavin, R. E. (1988). Cooperative learning and student achievement. In R. E. Slavin (Ed.), *School and classroom organization*. Hillsdale, NJ: Erlbaum.

Smith, D. B. (1973). *A taste of blackberries*. New York: HarperCollins.

Smith, F. (1988). *Understanding reading* (4th ed.). Hillsdale, NJ: Erlbaum.

Smith, L. (2002). *Unsent letters: Writing as a way to resolve and renew*. San Francisco: Walking Stick Press.

Smith, N. B. (1964). Patterns of writing in different subject areas. *Journal of Reading, 7,* 31–37.

Soto, G. (1997). *Novio boy: A play*. San Diego, CA: Harcourt Brace.

Spellings, M. (2005). *A highly qualified teacher in every classroom: The secretary's annual report on teacher quality, 2005*. Retrieved August 5, 2006, from www.title2.org/secReport05.htm.

Spencer, S. L., & Vavra, S. A. (2009). *The perfect norm*. Charlotte, NC: Information Age Publishing.

Spiegel, D. L. (1998). Reader response approaches and the growth of readers. *Language Arts, 76,* 41–48.

Spiegelman, A. (1986). *Maus: A survivor's tale*. New York: Pantheon.

Spivey, N. M. (1984). *Discourse synthesis: Constructing texts in reading and writing.* Newark, DE: International Reading Association.

St. George, J. (2000). *So you want to be president?* New York: Philomel.

Stanley, D. (1996). *Leonardo da Vinci.* New York: Morrow.

Stanley, D. (2000). *Michelangelo.* New York: HarperCollins.

Stanley, J. (1992). *Children of the dust bowl: The true story of the school at Weedpatch Camp.* New York: Clarion Books.

Staples, S. F. (1991). *Shabanu: Daughter of the wind.* New York: Random House.

Stecker, P. M., Fuchs, D., & Fuchs, L. S. (2008). Progress monitoring as essential practice within Response to Intervention. *Rural Special Education Quarterly, 27,* 10–17.

Stephens, C. (2002). *Magnificent monologues for teens.* New York: Sandcastle.

Stewig, J. W., & Buege, C. (1994). *Dramatizing literature in whole language classrooms.* New York: Teachers College Press.

Street, B. (1995). *Social literacies: Critical approaches to literacy in development, ethnography and education.* New York: Longman.

Sturtevant, E. G. (2003). *The literacy coach: A key to improving teaching and learning in secondary schools.* Washington, DC: Alliance for Excellent Education. Retrieved July 6, 2006, from www.all4ed.org/publica tions/LiteracyCoach.pdf.

Suid, M., & Lincoln, W. (1989). *Recipes for writing: Motivation, skills, and activities.* Menlo Park, CA: Addison-Wesley.

Sutherland, Z., & Arbuthnot, M. H. (1986). *Children and books* (7th ed.). Glenview, IL: Scott Foresman.

Sweeny, S.M. (2010). Writing for the instant messaging and text messaging generation: Using new literacies to support writing instruction. *Journal of Adolescent and Adult Literacy.54*(2), 121–130.

Taba, H. (1967). *Teacher's handbook for elementary social studies.* Reading, MA: Addison-Wesley.

Tan, S. (2007). *The arrival.* New York: Arthur A. Levine.

Tatum, A. (2000). Breaking down barriers that disenfranchise African American adolescent readers in low-level tracks. In P. Mason & J. S. Schumm (Eds.), *Promising practices for urban reading instruction* (pp. 98–118). Newark, DE: International Reading Association

Tatum, A. (2005). *Teaching reading to black adolescent males: Closing the achievement gap.* Portland, ME: Stenhouse.

Taylor, T. (1969). *The cay.* New York: Harcourt.

Tchudi, S., & Yates, J. (1983). *Teaching writing in the content areas: Senior high school.* Washington, DC: National Education Association.

Temple, C., Martinez, M., Yokota, J., & Naylor, A. (2005). *Children's books in children's hands: An introduction to their literature.* Boston: Allyn & Bacon.

Thimmesh, C. (2000). *Girls think of everything: Stories of ingenious inventions by women.* Boston: Houghton Mifflin.

Thimmesh, C. (2006). *Team moon: How 400,000 people landed Apollo 11 on the moon.* New York: Houghton Mifflin.

Thoman, E., & Jolls, T. (2005). *Literacy for the 21st century.* Retrieved February 22, 2013, from www.medialit.org.

Thompson, W. I. (1981). *The time falling bodies take to light: Mythology, sexuality, and the origins of culture.* New York: St. Martin's Press.

Thorndike, E. (1917). Reading and reasoning: A study of mistakes in paragraph reading. *Journal of Educational Psychology, 8,* 323–332.

Tienken, C. H. (2011). Common Core State Standards: An example of data-less decision making. *AASA Journal of Scholarship & Practice, 7*(4), 3–18.

Tierney, R. J. (1998). Literacy assessment reform: Shifting beliefs, principled possibilities, and emerging practices. *Reading Teacher, 51,* 374–390.

Tierney, R. J. (2002). An ethical chasm: Jurisdiction, jurisprudence, and the literacy profession. *Journal of Adolescent and Adult Literacy, 45*(4), 260–276.

Tierney, R. J., Carter, M. A., & Desai, L. E. (1991). *Portfolio assessment in the reading-writing classroom.* Norwood, MA: Christopher-Gordon.

Tierney, R. J., & Pearson, P. D. (1983). Toward a composing model of reading. *Language Arts, 60,* 568–580.

Tierney, R. J., & Pearson, P. D. (1992). A revisionist perspective on "Learning to learn from texts: A framework for improving classroom practice." In E. K. Dishner, T. W. Bean, J. E. Readence, & D. W. Moore (Eds.), *Reading in the content areas: Improving classroom instruction* (3rd ed., pp. 82–86). Dubuque, IA: Kendall/Hunt.

Tierney, R. J., & Shanahan, T. (1991). Research on reading-writing relationships: Interactions, transactions, and outcomes. In P. D. Pearson, R. Barr, M. Kamil, & P. Mosenthal (Eds.), *Handbook of reading research* (2nd ed., pp. 246–280). New York: Longman.

Tobias, S. (1989). Writing to learn science and mathematics. In P. Connolly & T. Vilardi (Eds.), *Writing to learn mathematics and science* (pp. 47–61). New York: Teachers College Press.

Toll, C. A. (2005). *The literacy coach's survival guide: Essential questions and practical answers.* Newark, DE: International Reading Association.

Tomlinson, C. (1995). Deciding to differentiate instruction in middle school: One school's journey. *Gifted Child Quarterly, 39*(2) 77–87.

Tomlinson, C. (1995). *How to differentiate instruction in the mixed ability classroom.* Alexandria, VA: Association for Supervision and Curriculum Development.

Tomlinson, C. (2003). Deciding to teach them all. *Educational Leadership, 61*(2), 5–11.

Tomlinson, C. A., & Strickland, C. A. (2005). *Differentiation in practice: A resource guide for differentiating curriculum, grades 9–12.* Alexandria, VA: Association for Supervision and Curriculum Development.

Topping, D. H., & McManus, R. (2002). *Real reading, real writing: Content area strategies.* Portsmouth, NH: Heinemann.

Toppo, G. (2001). *Education bill could affect funding.* Retrieved from www.speakout.com/cgi-in/udt/im.display.printable?client.id=speakout&story.id=9967.

Torgesen, J. K., Houston, D. D., Rissman, L. M., Decker, S. M., Roberts, G., Vaughn, S., Wexler, J., Francis, D. J., Rivera, M. O., & Lesaux, N. (2007). *Academic literacy instruction for adolescents: A guidance document from the Center on Instruction.* Portsmouth, NH: RMC Research Corporation, Center on Instruction. Retrieved May 19, 2008, from www.centeroninstruction.org.

Trueman, T. (2001). *Stuck in neutral.* New York: HarperTempest.

Tschannen-Moran, M., & Woolfolk Hoy, A. (2011). Teaching efficacy: Capturing an elusive construct. *Teaching and Teachers Education, 17,* 783–805.

Tsuchiya, Y. (1988). *Faithful elephants: A true story of people, animals and war.* Trans. T. Kykes. Ill. T. Lewin. Boston: Houghton Mifflin.

Turner, A. (1987). *Nettie's trip south.* Ill. R. Himler. New York: Macmillan.

Tuttle, H. G. (2007). Digital age assessment. *Technology & Learning. 27*(7), 22–24.

Ung, L. (2000). *First they killed my father: A daughter of Cambodia remembers.* New York: Perennial Press.

U.S. Census Bureau. (2010). 2010 U.S. Census. Retrieved from U.S. Census Bureau website: http://2010.census.gov/2010census/data.

U.S. Department of Education (2001). *The No Child Left Behind Act of 2001.* Retrieved on January 11, 2002, from www.ed.gov/offices/OESE/esea/NCLBexecumm.pdf.

U.S. Department of Education (2009). *Race to the Top Program Executive Summary.* Retrieved at www.ed.gov/programs/racetothetop/executive-summary.pdf.

U.S. Department of Education (2010). *A blueprint for reform: The reauthorization of the elementary and secondary education act.* Washington DC: U.S. Department of Education.

U.S. Department of Education (2010). *Transforming American education learning powered by technology: National Education Technology Plan 2010 executive summary.* Washington, DC: Office of Educational Technology.

Vaca, J., Lapp, D., & Fisher, D. (2011). Real-time teaching. *Journal Of Adolescent & Adult Literacy, 54*(5), 372–375.

Vacca, J. L., Vacca, R. T., Gove, M. K., Burkey, L., Lenhart, L., & McKeon, C. (2002). *Reading and learning to read* (5th ed.). Boston: Allyn & Bacon.

Vacca, R. T. (1975). Development of a functional reading strategy: Implications for content area instruction. *Journal of Educational Research, 69,* 108–112.

Vacca, R. T. (1977). An investigation of a functional reading strategy in seventh-grade social studies. In H. L. Herber & R. T. Vacca (Eds.), *Research in reading in the content areas: Third report* (pp. 101–118). Syracuse, NY: Syracuse University Reading and Language Arts Center.

Vacca, R. T. (1998). Literacy issues in focus: Let's not marginalize adolescent literacy. *Journal of Adolescent and Adult Literacy, 41*(8), 604–610.

Vacca, R. T. (2002a). Content literacy. In B. J. Guzzetti (Ed.), *Literacy in America: An encyclopedia of history, theory, and practice* (pp. 101–104). Santa Barbara, CA: ABC-CLIO.

Vacca, R. T. (2002b). Making a difference in adolescents' school lives: Visible and invisible aspects of content area reading. In A. E. Farstrup & S. J. Samuels (Eds.), *What research has to say about reading instruction* (3rd ed., pp. 184–204). Newark, DE: International Reading Association.

Vacca, R. T., & Alvermann, D. E. (1998, October). The crisis in adolescent literacy: Is it real or imagined? *NASSP Bulletin, 82,* 4–9.

Vacca, R. T., & Padak, N. D. (1990). Who's at risk in reading? *Journal of Reading, 33,* 486–489.

Vacca, R. T., & Vacca, J. L. (2000). Writing across the curriculum. In R. Indrisano & J. R. Squire (Eds.), *Perspectives on writing: Research, theory, and practice* (pp. 214–232). Newark, DE: International Reading Association.

Valdes, G., & Figueroa, R. A. (1994). *Bilingualism and testing: A special case bias.* Norwood, NJ: Ablex.

Valencia, S. (1990). A portfolio approach to classroom reading assessment: The whys, whats, and hows. *Reading Teacher, 43,* 338–340.

Valencia, S., McGinley, W. J., & Pearson, P. D. (1990). *Assessing reading and writing: Building a more complete picture for middle school assessment.* Urbana: University of Illinois, Center for the Study of Reading.

Van Allsburg, C. (1984). *Mysteries of Harris Burdick.* Boston: Houghton Mifflin.

Van Allsburg, C. (1990). *Just a dream.* Boston: Houghton Mifflin.

van der Rol, R., & Verhoeven, R. (1993). *Anne Frank: Beyond the diary.* New York: Viking.

Vardell, S. M., & Copeland, K. A. (1992). Reading aloud and responding to nonfiction: Let's talk about it. In E. B. Freeman & D. G. Person (Eds.), *Using nonfiction trade books in the elementary classroom: From ants to zeppelins* (pp. 76–85). Urbana, IL: National Council of Teachers of English.

Vaughn, S., Cirino, P., Wanzek, J., Wexler, J., Fletcher, J., & Denton, C. (2010). Response to intervention for middle school students with reading difficulties: Effects of a primary and secondary intervention. *School Psychology Review, 39*(1), 3–12.

Vick, H. H. (1998). *Walker of time.* Lanham, MD: Reinhart.

Vintinner, J., Rock, T., Good, A., & Popejob, K. (2011). *Post-survey of teacher candidate's sense of self-efficacy.* Charlotte, NC: UNC Charlotte.

Vogt, M. E., & Echevarria, J. (2008). *99 ideas and activities for teaching English learners with the SIOP model.* Boston: Pearson.

Von Ziegesar, C. (2002). *Gossip girl.* New York: Poppy.

Vygotsky, L. S. (1934/1986). *Thought and language.* Cambridge, MA: MIT Press.

Walker, B. J. (1991, February-March). Convention highlights reading assessment changes. *Reading Today,* 20.

Walls, J. (2006). *The glass castle: A memoir.* New York: Scribner.

Walpole, S., & McKenna, M. (2004). Intervention programs. In *The literacy coach's handbook.* New York: Guilford Press.

Walsh, K., & Snyder, E. (2004). *NCTQ reports: Searching the attic for highly qualified teachers.* National Council on Teacher Quality. Retrieved February 2005, from www.ctredpol.org/pubs/Forum15November2004/WalshPaper.pdf.

Wang, M. C., Reynolds, M. C., & Walberg, H. J. (1994–1995). Serving students at the margins. *Educational Leadership, 52*(4), 12–17.

Waters, J. (2007). Making things easy. *T H E Journal, 34*(4), 26–33.

Waters, K. S. & Kunnmann, T. W. (2009). Metacognition and strategy discovery in early childhood. H.S. Waters,

W. Schneider, & J.G. Borkowski (Eds.). New York, NY: Guilford Press.

Watkins, D. A., & Biggs, J. B. (Eds.). (1996). *The Chinese learner: Cultural, psychological, and contextual influences.* Hong Kong: University of Hong Kong Press.

Webb, S. (2000). *My season with penguins: An Antarctic journal.* Boston: Houghton Mifflin.

Weiss, M. J., & Weiss, H. S. (2002). *Big city cool: Short stories about urban youth.* New York: Persea Books.

Wenglinski, H. (2000). *How teaching matters: Bringing the classroom back into discussions of teacher quality.* Princeton, NJ: Educational Testing Service. Retrieved from www.ets.org/Media/Education_topics/pdf/teamat.pdf.

Whitin, P. (2002). Leading into literature circles through the sketch-to-stretch strategy. *Reading Teacher, 55,* 444–450.

Wiesel, E. (2006). *Night.* New York: Hill and Wang.

Wigfield, A. (2004). Motivation for reading during the early adolescent and adolescent years. In D. S. Strickland & D. E. Alvermann (Eds.). *Bridging the literacy achievement gap, grades 4–12* (pp. 251–282). New York: Teachers College Press.

Wilcox, S. (1997). Using the assessment of students' learning to reshape thinking. *Mathematics Teacher, 90,* 223–229.

Wilen, W., Ishler, L., Hutchison, J., & Kindsvatter, R. (2004). *Dynamics of effective secondary teaching* (5th ed.). Boston: Allyn & Bacon.

Wilkinson, L. E., & Silliman, E. R. (2000). Classroom language and literacy learning. In M. Kamil, P. Mosenthal, P. D. Pearson, & R. Barr (Eds.), *Handbook of reading research* (Vol. 3, pp. 337–360). Mahwah, NJ: Erlbaum.

Williams, B. (1995). *The Internet for teachers.* Foster City, CA: IDG Books Worldwide.

Willinsky, J. (1990). *The new literacy: Redefining reading and writing in the schools.* New York: Routledge.

Wills, J., & Mehan, H. (1996). Recognizing diversity within a common historical narrative: The challenge to teaching history and social studies. *Multicultural Education, 4*(1), 4–11.

Wilson, N. D. (2008). *100 Cupboards.* NY: Bluefire

Wilson, N. S., & Kelley, M. J. (2010). Are avid readers lurking in your language arts classroom? Myths of the avid adolescent reader. *Reading Horizons, 50*(2), 99–112.

Wisconsin Historical Society. (2009). *Thinking like a historian.* Retrieved May 4, 2009, from www.wisconsinhistory.org/ThinkingLikeaHistorian.

Wise, B. (2009, February). Adolescent literacy: The cornerstone of student success. *Journal of Adolescent & Adult Literacy, 52,* 369–375.

Wisniewski, D. (1996). *Golem.* New York: Clarion.

Wolk, S. (2010). What should students read? *Phi Delta Kappan, 91*(7), 8–16.

Wolsey, T.D. (2004). Literature discussion in cyberspace: Young adolescents using threaded discussion groups to talk about books. *Reading Online, 7*(4). Available at www.readingonline.org/articles/art_index.asp?HREF=wolsey/index.html.

Wong, J. L. (2007). *Seeing Emily.* New York: Amulet Books.

Wood, K. D. (1988). Changing perspective to improve comprehension. *Middle School Journal, 22*(3), 52–56.

Wood, K. D. (2001). *Literacy strategies across the subject areas: Process-oriented blackline masters for the K–12 classroom.* Boston: Allyn & Bacon.

Wood, K. D., Lapp, D., Flood, J., & Taylor, D. B. (2008). *Guiding readers through text: Study guides for new times* (2nd ed.). Newark, DE: International Reading Association.

Wood, K. D., & Taylor, D. B. (2005). *Literacy strategies across the subject areas: Process-oriented blackline masters for the K–12 classroom* (2nd ed.). Boston: Allyn & Bacon.

Woodson, J. (2005). *Show way.* New York: Putnam.

Worthy, J., Broaddus, K., & Ivey, G. (2001). *Pathways to independence: Reading, writing, and learning in grades 3–8.* New York: Guilford Press.

Writing in the Disciplines. (2001). *Writing in the disciplines.* Retrieved June 2009 from www.cariboo.bc.ca/disciplines.

Yang, G. L. (2008). *American born Chinese.* New York: Square Fish Press.

Yolen, J. (1992). *Encounter.* Ill. D. Shannon. San Diego, CA: Harcourt Brace Jovanovich.

Yolen, J. (1996). *The pit dragon trilogy.* San Diego, CA: Magic Carpet/Harcourt Brace.

Young, T. A., & Vardell, S. M. (1993). Weaving readers theatre and nonfiction into the curriculum. *Reading Teacher, 46,* 396–406.

Zastrow, C., & Janc, H. (2006). *The condition of liberal arts in America's public schools: A report to the Carnegie Corporation of New York.* Washington, DC: Council for Basic Education.

Zhensun, Z., & Low, A. (1991). *A young painter: The life and paintings of Wang Yani.* New York: Scholastic.

Zipin, L. (2009). Dark funds of knowledge, sleep funds of pedagogy: Exploring boundaries between lifeworlds and schools. *Discourse: Students in the cultural politics of education. 30*(3), 317–331.

Zusack, M. (2007). *The book thief.* New York: Knopf.

Zywica, J., & Gomez, K. (2008). Annotating to support learning in the content areas: Teaching and learning science. *Journal of Adolescent and Adult Literacy, 52*(2), 155–165.

Name Index

Subject Index